vers and commentators from all media and across the political
have acclaimed *Servants of the People* as a landmark in writing
about government and contemporary history.

ngs true. It has the smack of authenticity. People have, it
oken with unusual frankness to the candid friend. The
is enthralling, the story riveting' Allan Massie,
*The Times Literary Supplement*

easure, nothing could quite beat *Servants of the People*'
William Sutcliffe, *Independent on Sunday*

y account, a chronicle rich in revelation . . . [is] the most
ny a year. Its story of the decision to exclude entry into
is particularly significant' Hugo Young, *Guardian*

velation . . . an extraordinary story . . . Rawnsley is
ery well informed' William Rees-Mogg, *The Times*

book has not been written which is worthy of the Blair
ew Rawnsley's book changes that. He has written a
important work which gets to the very heart of this
vernment's difficulties' Iain Martin, *Scotsman*

st talked-about political work for years' David Hughes,
*Daily Mail*

ative and devastating . . . feuds, vendettas, hatreds, loves and
that would have given William Shakespeare the material for a
n plays. Andrew Rawnsley has produced an account of the
cellor's relations with the Prime Minister which literally made
jaw drop on several occasions. I urge anybody with the faintest
st in politics to read Rawnsley's gripping account' Peter Oborne,
*Daily Express*

'The glimpse inside Downing Street's power struggles between Tony Blair and Gordon Brown will ring bells for everyone in Westminster. Author Andrew Rawnsley provides an authentic and scrupulously researched account of what Tony Blair bizarrely describes as a "marriage" between him and his Chancellor' Trevor Kavanagh, *Sun*

'Confirms what Labour has long tried to deny – that the Government is remarkably riven by personality clashes and faction-fighting . . . based on extensive interviews with senior Ministers and advisors who witnessed the controversies which have raged' Michael Prescott, *Sunday Times*

'One of the abiding images of new Labour in power, as described in Andrew Rawnsley's compelling book, is of Gordon Brown being driven away from the Blackpool party conference and heckling Tony Blair's conference speech as it came over the car radio' Stuart Weir, *New Statesman*

'One of the most incendiary and revelatory books ever written about a government in power . . . explores in compelling detail the triumphs and tribulations of Tony Blair's period in office. One of its successes is that it brings to vivid life the Government's leading personalities and the conflicts that have raged between them behind closed doors. This book is worth having just for the sections on Northern Ireland alone as you will see sides of political figures that have not been revealed before' Joanna Braniff, *Irish News*

'Rawnsley's ability to unearth revelation at the highest level of government may leave you suspecting that there are bugs in the vases at Number 10' Owen Parker, *Time Out*

'Andrew Rawnsley interviewed scores of senior Labour figures, from the Prime Minister down. We are treated to the details of what Blair said when alone with his wife on the night that Diana, Princess of Wales, died' Brian Groom, *Financial Times*

'It's all here. Even his two closest aides, Alastair Campbell and Anji Hunter, have clearly decided to give a minute-by-minute account of the chaos behind the scenes at Number 10 when Peter Mandelson was forced to resign' Robert Harris, *Guardian*

'The funniest book I have read this year. His account beggars belief, but the sheer weight of detail is utterly convincing' Chris Woodhead, *Sunday Telegraph*

'As would be expected of Rawnsley, one of the best political columnists, *Servants of the People* is a well-written history of the Blair government . . . laced with dry wit . . . excellent analyses . . . sober, balanced judgements' John Rentoul, *Independent*

'Rawnsley brings out the paradox at the heart of the Blair Government. Its very obsession with presentation – winning the daily, even hourly, battle of spin – has obscured its achievements of substance' Peter Riddell, *The Times*

'Andrew Rawnsley's stunning book . . . has exploded a nuclear weapon in the heart of Downing Street' Stephen Pollard, *Daily Express*

'What *Servants of the People* illustrates about New Labour will deserve to be remembered long after the trivia about who knew what about Bernie Ecclestone's donation to Labour's fighting fund is long forgotten' Roy Hattersley, *Observer*

'What he presents us with is a classic picture of a Shakespearian monarch surrounded by a feudal court. Favourites, flatterers, jesters, even potential rivals for the throne – all take their part in the action. Always vivid narrative . . . Rawnsley has done his eloquent best to offer a candid and dispassionate account of the individual power struggles that have marked the life of this government' Anthony Howard, *Sunday Times*

'Modern politics and its inmates stripped down to their smalls, not least by their ignominious delight in dishing the dirt on each other. The goodies are so plentiful and evenly distributed that much has escaped the chomping jaws of even one of the most fulsome and logistically superior newspaper serialisation exercises in living political memory' George Lucas, *Independent on Sunday*

'Fascinating . . . enthralling . . . reads like a thriller . . . Time will prove this to be the decade's finest political exposé' Paul Dale, *List*

'The rule designed to keep Cabinet secrets from the nation for thirty years has been amended, it seems, to three years. It is extraordinary that the sort of incidents usually reserved for political memoirs long after the event have leaked out so early in the life of an administration' Rachel Sylvester, *Daily Telegraph*

'A thoroughly plausible account' Bagehot, *Economist*

'As vivid and plausible an account of the machinations of contemporary politics as there has been' David Vincent, Amazon

### ABOUT THE AUTHOR

Andrew Rawnsley is associate editor and chief political commentator for the *Observer*. He has made a string of critically acclaimed television programmes and presents BBC Radio 4's *Westminster Hour*. He was named Columnist of the Year 2000 in the prestigious *What the Papers Say* Awards. He lives in London.

# Servants of the People

## The Inside Story of New Labour

### ANDREW RAWNSLEY

PENGUIN BOOKS

PENGUIN BOOKS

Published by the Penguin Group
Penguin Books Ltd, 80 Strand, London WC2R 0RL, England
Penguin Putnam Inc., 375 Hudson Street, New York, New York 10014, USA
Penguin Books Australia Ltd, 250 Camberwell Road, Camberwell, Victoria 3124, Australia
Penguin Books Canada Ltd, 10 Alcorn Avenue, Toronto, Ontario, Canada M4V 3B2
Penguin Books India (P) Ltd, 11 Community Centre, Panchsheel Park, New Delhi – 110 017, India
Penguin Books (NZ) Ltd, Cnr Rosedale and Airborne Roads, Albany, Auckland, New Zealand
Penguin Books (South Africa) (Pty) Ltd, 24 Sturdee Avenue, Rosebank 2196, South Africa

Penguin Books Ltd, Registered Offices: 80 Strand, London WC2R 0RL, England

www.penguin.com

First published by Hamish Hamilton 2000
Revised edition published in Penguin Books 2001

016

Copyright © Andrew Rawnsley, 2000, 2001
All rights reserved

The moral right of the author has been asserted

Set in Monotype Bembo
Typeset by Rowland Phototypesetting Ltd, Bury St Edmunds, Suffolk
Printed in England by Clays Ltd, St Ives plc

www.greenpenguin.co.uk

Penguin Books is committed to a sustainable
future for our business, our readers and our planet.
This book is made from Forest Stewardship
Council™ certified paper.

ALWAYS LEARNING                    **PEARSON**

# Contents

# Preface to the Penguin Edition

At the outset of Tony Blair's campaign to win his second term, I interviewed the Prime Minister in his functional office at party headquarters in the Millbank Tower. Towards the end of the conversation, I offered him the use of a time machine. Imagine he could hurtle back four years to offer some retrospective advice to the untested Blair who had triumphantly brought New Labour to power in May 1997. What was the one thing that Blair wanted to warn his younger self not to do? While the Prime Minister pondered on the question, from the back of the room there came the heckle: 'Not to co-operate with books!' The source of this mischievous interruption was the Prime Minister's press secretary. Alastair Campbell laughed. I laughed. Tony Blair laughed, albeit a touch ruefully.

I embarked on this project – to use one of New Labour's favourite words – to satisfy my own curiosity and in the belief that there was a public thirst for a book which penetrated the façade to explain how its government really worked behind the closed black doors of Downing Street. From the outset I had the suspicion that neither the claims made for itself by New Labour nor the daily headlines were telling the complete story. I was also coming to a view that the image which had for long beguiled the media and the public of a seamlessly united government under the absolute command of the leader was an illusion. More, it was a myth that was actually proving counterproductive for New Labour. I hoped to show that we were governed by human beings, themselves ruled by mortal strengths and weaknesses, men and women driven by ambitions and emotions which entangled with the governing of the country sometimes productively, at other times damagingly.

The book is based on extensive and candid conversations with people at all levels of government, including the Prime Minister. I can spell that out more clearly to readers of this edition because Tony Blair himself subsequently confirmed that he had talked to me. I can now publicly thank the Prime Minister for his time, assistance and frankness. Downing Street has suggested that these interviews concentrated on Northern Ireland, Europe and Kosovo. We certainly talked about those topics. This tells a part of the truth, though not quite the whole truth. To avoid breaking the obligations I entered into in order to write the book, I confine myself to remarking that I appreciate why Number 10 felt it had to be disingenuous about the breadth and depth of the conversations with the Prime Minister.

Andrew Marr, the political editor of the BBC, was one of many who found it 'astonishing' that 'so many of Mr Blair's close aides and colleagues, including the man himself, were prepared to pass on so much'.[1] Rachel Sylvester of the *Daily Telegraph* commented: 'The rule designed to keep Cabinet secrets from the nation for thirty years has been amended, it seems, to three years. It is extraordinary that the sort of incidents usually reserved for political memoirs long after the event have leaked out so early in the life of an administration.'[2]

Why? That is the question I have been most regularly asked. The answer comes in several layers of explanation. Each player in the drama is naturally anxious that his or her point of view should be understood and represented. You interview a great number and variety of actors and observers, often returning to witnesses several times, to establish the chain of events, to grasp the motives of all involved, to build up the full picture. The most fascinating insights are often provided by friends and allies of the protagonists – frequently by the protagonists themselves – as they provide background detail that attempts to explain why they spoke or acted as they did.

On reflection, I sense that something deeper was also at work. In the course of interviewing, I was often struck by how much more frankly and vividly politicians talk in private than they feel they can do in public. I wondered whether they might not be more fondly regarded by the country if they could only translate some of that private passion into their public performances. David Robson, writing in the *Daily Express*, suggested that 'sometimes the compulsion to communicate is more complex and interesting. It's our masters' need for reassurance, not talking spin but the talking cure – journalist as shrink. They just have to tell an outsider because they are so worried about whether it makes sense or, indeed, whether they make sense.'[3]

There may be a lot in that, especially with regard to this government. Of most politicians this is true, and it is truer than most about New Labour. I had the sense that its prominent personalities wanted to have themselves and their achievements and failures interpreted back to them.

The reaction to the book was a tutorial for me about the dynamics of the relationship between politicians and those who write about them. Heisenberg's principle tells us that the very act of observing something changes its nature. The week after the hardcover edition of this book was published, Tony Blair made his set-piece address to the party conference. Afterwards, during a chat with a senior member of the Cabinet, he agreed with me that neuroticism and mistrust lay at the root of many of the government's then troubles, especially the self-inflicted injuries. The minister pointed me towards the passage in Tony Blair's speech where he said: 'All that really stands between us and our destination is confidence. And trust. The confidence that gives us strength to make the choices; the trust that there is a vision, an end to believe in.'[4]

I will suggest that having confidence that he has the capacity to shape our national destiny is the largest test of the next phase of Tony Blair's premiership and the New Labour programme.

This edition contains five new chapters updating the story of New Labour in power up to the June election, through the campaign and on to its immediate aftermath. I have also amplified and adjusted earlier chapters where fresh information has come to my attention. I thank again all the busy people who have made time to help me, as I also thank my agent, Gill Coleridge; Andrew Kidd and the staff at Penguin; my colleagues at the *Observer* and the *Westminster Hour*; and my wife and daughters, the four wonderful women in my life.

I have tried to cast a little more illumination on the hopes, prides, fears, defeats and victories at the heart of New Labour. That is the simple duty of the writer to his readers. While it may at times be awkward for those who rule, I also happen to believe that daylight makes for better government.

Andrew Rawnsley

June 2001

# Introduction: The Few

We are not the masters now. The people are the masters. We are the
servants of the people. We will never forget that.

Delivered at Church House, before the teeming multitude of his
flock of more than 400 MPs, this was the alpha and omega of Tony
Blair sound-bites.

It inverted Old Labour. 'We are the masters now,'[1] Hartley
Shawcross had said half a century previously following the great
Attlee landslide which Blair had surpassed.

It was not true. From the moment Tony Blair became leader of
his party in 1994 and rebranded it as New Labour, he was the
undisputed master of the people. The assumption that he would
win the general election was virtually universal.

Only a small minority did not take that triumph to be inevitable:
Blair and his band of modernisers themselves. Though they invoked
the people, New Labour could not trust them. The people's fluxing
moods were incessantly monitored by opinion poll and focus group,
the better for New Labour to adapt itself to the contours of the
country it aspired to rule. The people's newspapers, especially the
mass market tabloids that had inflicted so much grief on Labour in
the past, were to be ingratiated if they could be turned into allies
and neutralised where they could not.

In pursuit of power, New Labour were supplicants to the people,
but the great design was to use office to master them. The tactics
might be stealthy and cautious, but the strategy was to reinvent
Britain. This country which had delivered power to the Conservatives for most of the twentieth century was to be re-educated into a
nation which would embrace progressive values in the twenty-first.
In an unguarded remark, delivered with an uncharacteristic public

venom that suggested sincere passion, Tony Blair blurted it out: 'I
would prefer to be remembered for having destroyed the Conservative Party.'[2]

That desire for hegemony, to absorb most opposition and crush
the residue, was chillingly suggestive to some of those tyrannical
regimes which call themselves 'People's Democracies' and are
neither. Control-freakism, the charge against New Labour even
before it came to power, was an accusation which would grow
stronger in office. That arrogance was a brittle carapace around a
profound insecurity at the heart of the project and the personalities
who shaped it.

New Labour was the product of traumatic and multiple failures.
Tony Blair's rhetoric might be relentlessly futuristic, but he was
fixated by the past. This was not surprising. Before 1 May 1997,
Labour had not won an election in more than twenty-two years
and had not secured a proper parliamentary majority in over three
decades. The pact between a success-starved party and the power-
hungry group who seized the commanding heights was that the
modernisers would deliver office in exchange for taking control.
In an especially hubristic surge, Blair described New Labour as 'the
political arm of the British people'.[3] Yet the progenitors of this
all-embracing self-styled People's Party were tiny in number. Less
a mass movement, more a junta who had executed a coup, they
were what Harold Wilson once called, in a different context, a
'tightly knit group of politically motivated men'.[4]

The founding axis of New Labour was Tony Blair, whose
Thatcherite father would have become a Tory MP had he not
suffered a stroke, and Gordon Brown, the son of a socialist Church
of Scotland rector. This twinning of opposites was one of the most
talented and tortuous couplings that there has ever been in high
British politics.

By the standards of politicians, Blair came to the profession
exceptionally late. As a schoolboy, he was a conservative rebel,
often stretching the rules, rarely breaking them. Contemporaries
recalled a charismatic teenager with a particular talent for acting
who could nearly always talk his way out of trouble. At university,

he read law but wished it had been history, toyed with becoming a priest, and played at being a rock star. Only after he met a Labour activist called Cherie Booth did his inchoate yearnings to achieve something of substance combine with what one biographer calls his 'appetite for applause' to crystallise into political ambition.

Where Blair was the slow convert, Brown was baptised into the faith. His political memory stretched back to the age of eight when his father let him stay up until one thirty in the morning to hear the results of the 1959 election that Labour lost. Brown was a published political author and an elected student rector when Blair was still fantasising about being Mick Jagger.

When these two bright tyros arrived in parliament together in 1983, their potential was soon spotted as exceptional by the third man, Peter Mandelson. A former Young Communist, trade union researcher and TV producer, Neil Kinnock's director of communications pushed both of them forward. While Mandelson admired Blair, he idolised Brown. Mandelson so pined during separations that he could not bear being on holiday for much more than a day before he started ringing up Brown.

The death of John Smith was the birth of New Labour. The crown of leadership that Brown always assumed would belong to him was taken by the younger Blair. Their relationship survived, but it was ever after strung with tensions which would play out creatively and destructively in government.

The protégé–patron relationship between Blair and Mandelson had been reversed. The bond between Mandelson and Brown turned to hate. Though the truth was not this simple, Brown could never forgive what he saw as Mandelson's vile treachery during the leadership contest when he switched his affections to Blair. Through the election that they were jointly managing and into government, the two men barely exchanged a civil sentence with each other. To further complicate these emotionally racked relationships, though Blair was their chief, he still felt, in crucial respects, subordinate to the other two men, especially Brown.

The triangle became more like a rhomboid with the steady rise in influence of Alastair Campbell. He was already connected with the modernisers before he left his career as a tabloid Labour propagandist to become Blair's press secretary. No group of political animals knew in more intimate detail each other's strengths and vulnerabilities. Campbell was one of the first people to whom Mandelson turned when his father died; when Campbell flirted with death during the alcohol-induced nervous collapse which turned him teetotal, Mandelson was one of the first to come to his side.

To seize control of a party, and then take power over the country, was an immense bonding experience. The ties that both bound and strained this complex cat's cradle of relationships have been decisive in the development of the government. Other characters played large parts in the success of New Labour, and have important roles in this narrative. But it is this quartet who achieved the sensational election victory just as they became the masterminds of the campaign to retain power. They are, in essence, New Labour.

So one of the strands of this book is simply a human story. This small group, each one of them fantastically gifted but also highly peculiar, were brilliant at Opposition – and entirely untested at running anything else. Part of my purpose is to explore what happened to them and the country when they were confronted with the different challenges and choices presented by government.

The idea for this book came early in 1998 when Andrew Kidd, my editor, invited me to lunch to discuss whether I might write for Hamish Hamilton. There were excellent reasons for not embarking on such a project. New Labour's deserved reputation for wanting to control every word written or spoken about it would present formidable obstacles to be overcome to get close to the truth. It would be futile to expect to have the definitive word. Historians, with the benefit of official papers and the long perspective, will still be arguing about New Labour in a hundred years' time when they will know whether Tony Blair's 'radical century' became a reality or transpired to be a mirage.

Historians, on the other hand, will suffer disadvantages. Because of the concentration of power within this government and the personalities involved, many significant exchanges take place without civil servants present to take an official note. When I discussed this with a very senior figure in Whitehall, he encouraged the book by pointing out that many transactions are conducted by ephemeral e-mail and over the phone. Then, there is the tendency of political memoirists to re-write history. There are conversations in this book which participants will not wish to be reminded of, and may conveniently forget when they compose their own chronicles. There was a merit in trying to discover, as contemporaneously to events as possible, what had really occurred.

The tendency of the ravenously competitive media is to 'Avalanche Journalism'. A huge amount of newsprint and airtime comes crashing down on a controversy. Soon the subject is forgotten as everyone moves on to the next event. Revisiting the pivotal junctures in this government's life, I have discovered that journalists, myself included, got some things right, some wrong and were terribly misled about other events.

I have not attempted the impossible task of recording New Labour's every act. What I have endeavoured to do is explore those episodes which I feel to be important and illuminating.

Conversations with hundreds of people, from the bottom of the political pyramid to the absolute apex, have informed this account. I thank all of those who made space in their diaries to help me. I am also grateful to the secretaries and assistants who have been unfailingly patient in chiselling time out of compressed schedules to accommodate my demands.

I had a choice to make about gathering information. I could interview everyone on-the-record and suffer the inevitable penalty in a lack of candour. As Robin Cook is fond of observing: for a politician, the art of the interview is to talk for an hour without saying anything too interesting. In any case, there already exist masses of printed and broadcast material, references to which are given at the back of the book.

I chose to conduct all interviews on a background basis and instead pay the price of frustrating readers who would prefer to have every quote and incident attached to a named source. Where

I quote private dialogue, I have a trustworthy account from one –
and where possible more than one – participant or witness or from
someone reliable to whom the content of the conversation was
subsequently reported. Impertinently, I occasionally describe what
someone is thinking or feeling. I have this either from the individual
concerned or from witnesses to whom they expressed those
thoughts or feelings directly. In the modest expectation that someone may find it of future use, I will make my source material
available when the current Prime Minister is no longer in power.

I apologise in advance to readers who are sensitive to blasphemies
and profanities. In private, politicians and those who work with
them do swear fairly profusely, especially at times of stress.[5]

A note about descriptions. I find it cumbersome to write – and
I am sure it is even more tiresome to read – sentences such as:
'David Bland, MP for Much Wittering, formerly Parliamentary
Under-Secretary for Paving Stones, now Minister of State for
Toxic Waste, later created Lord Bland of Wittering and High
Commissioner to Lilliput'. Unless there is a very good reason not
to, people are given the title they had at the time of the episode
under discussion.

I have drawn insights and stimulation from many colleagues at the
*Observer*, past and present, prominent among them: Roger Alton;
Will Hutton; Bill Keegan, constant friend at times of trial; Andy
McSmith; Paul Webster; and the peerless Patrick Wintour. Peter
Beaumont, Euan Ferguson and Mike Holland, my editors on the
comment pages, have never been less than a pleasure and a satisfaction to work with. Unfailingly helpful have been the superb team
on Radio Four's *Westminster Hour*: Mark D'Arcy, John Evans,
David Jordan, Amanda Lewis and Andrew Rose. David Cowling,
whose knowledge is worth more than his weight in his cigars, has
been of invaluable assistance with polling data.

Andrew Kidd and my agent, Gill Coleridge, have been constant
founts of inspiration and encouragement. The meticulous Bela
Cunha undangled my participles.

Olivia, Jessica and Cordelia tolerated their father's long absences and were always there to uplift him if ever the going got heavy. Nothing, absolutely nothing, would have been possible without Jane, my wife, best friend, researcher, librarian, personal assistant, editor and critic of first resort, rock, guide, comfort and joy. I cannot describe what I owe to her. To define it would be to limit it.

Andrew Rawnsley
July 2000

# 1. Dawn

The sun was setting on eighteen years of Tory rule when Tony Blair received hard, independent information that by the morning he would not only be Prime Minister, he would be enthroned on a majority unprecedented in Labour's history and unequalled by any party for more than half a century. By eight on the evening of May Day, Alastair Campbell, his press secretary, had a leak of the BBC's exit poll indicating a double-digit swing. Even allowing a huge margin of error for the infamous unreliability of such polls, now there was surely no doubt of victory. Campbell found Blair and his wife in the sitting room of Myrobella, the Victorian villa which was their home in Sedgefield. Cherie warned her husband to prepare himself for something astonishing. 'Huh,' Blair responded to this exciting intelligence with a shrug of the shoulders. 'What do they know?'

All day, people had been telling him that he stood on the threshold of a seismic shift in the landscape of British politics. Paddy Ashdown phoned at noon. In contradiction to Blair's public prediction a few days earlier that Britain 'is not a landslide country', the leader of the Liberal Democrats told him he was about to win by a landslide. Blair recoiled at the L-word which he had banned from the vocabulary of the Shadow Cabinet. He assured Ashdown that he was still committed to their secret pre-election pact to form a coalition government in which, so Blair had encouraged the other man to believe, Ashdown would be Foreign Secretary.[1] He had concealed this plan from John Prescott who had been on ebullient form when he came up the dirt track to Myrobella earlier in the day to finalise his remit as Deputy Prime Minister. While Campbell distracted the media throng, Prescott slipped in unnoticed, doing jubilantly vigorous V-signs behind the journalists' backs. Peter Mandelson drove over from his Hartlepool constituency to lobby for the job of Minister for Europe, but had to be content with Blair's insistence that he wanted his human radar close at hand in Downing Street. Even Gordon Brown was buoyant, at least by his congenitally pessimistic standards, when he made the first of several calls to Blair at seven thirty that morning. They had discussed before, but only in general terms, transferring control over interest rates to the Bank of England. In a manoeuvre characteristic of their complex relationship, Brown waited until polling day to spring upon Blair the idea that they should announce Bank independence almost immediately after the election. Blair told Brown he needed time to think about it.

Contacts within the Conservative Party accurately reported that the Tories were anticipating a mammoth defeat. The civil service had long been preparing for a change of governors. A full year before the election, the Blairs had been dinner guests at the south London home of the Cabinet Secretary. Sir Robin Butler showed them a floor plan of Numbers 10 and 11 Downing Street in order to discuss the prosaic − but important − details of their domestic life, such as whether they would want to bring their own furniture. In the dying thrashes of the campaign, the Cabinet Secretary held a briefing for journalists during which he incautiously hinted at these discussions by remarking that it would be 'very difficult to be Prime Minister from Islington'. When the London *Evening Standard* ran hard with the story, Blair had an anxiety attack. This would look as though they were taking power for granted. He told his press secretary to stifle further stories which Campbell did with a counter-briefing that dismissed the Cabinet Secretary as an ignorant official speaking out of turn whose idiocy demonstrated why the Tories were in such a mess. Campbell rang Butler afterwards to apologise for defaming Britain's most senior civil servant. 'I'm sorry I've had to do this to you.' Butler replied, 'I entirely understand.'[2] Their morbid dread of tempting fate was profound. As leader of the Opposition, Blair had refused every invitation to visit Number 10, except for an official dinner for Bill Clinton, and then only because the American President was impossible to refuse.

The people most reluctant to assume the triumph that everyone else took for granted were the tiny group who had conceived and executed it. The atmosphere at Myrobella on polling day was 'Odd, really bizarre. Because we had become so fearsomely anti-complacency, the mindset was as much preparing ourselves for losing as for winning.'[3] Jonathan Powell, the chief of staff, cajoled Blair until he produced a handwritten list of senior ministers. Powell complained to the others that he couldn't get Blair to focus on decisions about more junior appointments, nor about anything much else.

Blair fancied himself to be something of an amateur psephologist. It was his private brag that he had predicted the outcome of the last three elections to within ten seats. By polling day, his guess was a Labour majority of between forty and fifty, which conveniently tallied with the projections of the party's chief pollster, Greg 'Mystic' Cook. 'This was the first election I got wrong,' Blair would later confess among friends. A corner of his mind entertained the possibility that the opinion polls might be right, that a landslide was coming, but this he had deliberately suppressed. The trauma of four successive election defeats was scorched across the soul of the Labour Party, and burnt deep into the small group who had seized its commanding heights in the name of modernisation. With an unswerving dedication to turning it into a vehicle for power, the modernisers had rebranded the image, deconstructed the philosophy, and retooled the policies of their party until its relationship with socialism, as Labour historically understood it, was barely glancing. Power within the party had been concentrated at the top. Discipline was everything. Dissenters were ruthlessly smothered and marginalised. Blair and his band were possessed of little sentiment for much of the history of Labour, especially its tradition of disunity and defeat. This did not mean that Blair and the modernisers were without ideals. By their lights, the acquisition of office was the highest expression of idealism. 'The only purpose of being in politics is to make things happen,' said Blair.[4] His fiercest conviction about his party was that it had been a failure at delivering to the people it claimed to represent. Not just because it had lost four elections in a row. In nearly a century of existence, Labour had held office for the miserably small total of twenty-one years. On those too rare occasions when Labour was in power, Blair believed it had failed again. 'Since the Labour Party was founded in 1900, we have had five Labour governments. All were, in varying degrees, failures. This is our sixth and perhaps last chance. We have got to get it right this time.'[5]

During the campaign, I asked Blair, given his repudiation of so many of the party's past policies and his acceptance of many of the legacies of Thatcherism, whether he was glad that Labour had lost the four previous elections. He evaded the question in a public forum. In private, he wrestled with the conundrum. He concluded that, though gladness was not his emotion, he was intellectually content for that to be the logic of his position.

Blair recognised that much of the Labour Party suffered him only on the basis that he would deliver power. There was one chance to win. Philip Gould, a member of the modernising inner circle, was fond of making black jokes about the grisly fate that awaited Blair if he lost. The day after the election, a vengeful lynch mob of Labour supporters would besiege party headquarters. Blair and his coterie would be helicoptered into exile off the roof of Millbank Tower, like the Americans fleeing Vietnam during the last days of Saigon. Campbell kept a private diary of the campaign, which was a source of acid amusement to Blair, who remarked to another aide: 'When we lose, Alastair can get rich telling everyone precisely how we blew it.'[6]

Throughout the campaign, Blair pressed his ear to the chest of the electorate, nervously monitoring its heartbeat for flutters about New Labour. He wanted constant, sometimes hourly updates on the flux of public opinion. Any politician must be expected to take a close and continuous interest in the popularity of himself and his party, but for no previous British Prime Minister would it be quite such a consuming compulsion. His supremacy in the opinion polls was massive, and had been so from the moment he became Labour leader in 1994. His opponent, John Major, had long since sipped on the hemlock of defeat: 'If I had stood unopposed, I would have come second.'⁷ Yet neither Blair nor those closest to him lost that hard-wired fear of failure.

Tories who knew they could not win fought New Labourites terrified that they would somehow contrive to lose. The walking dead grappled with men scared to breathe. Blair's sharpest anxiety during the campaign was that he had not sufficiently convinced his target audience, the Middle Britons living in the swing seats, that his party was as renewed as he constantly asserted. The three Rs – reassurance, reassurance and reassurance – were the watchwords of New Labour. That fear was overdone. Maurice Saatchi's focus groups for the Tories were telling Major that it was futile to attack New Labour as phoney. The swingers and floaters had been convinced of the authenticity of Blair's changes. He had bomb-proofed himself against the right by investing the greatest weight in what he promised not to do. There would be no increase in income tax. No more spending than the Tories for the first two years. No entry into the European single currency without a referendum. The five laminated cardboard pledges were designed to be symbolic reflections back to the electorate of its concerns. The positives about education, health and employment were framed in cautiously incrementalist language. Blair's refrain was that he would not promise more than he could deliver. 'I feel this very, very deeply. The voters want specified, limited promises made and kept.'⁸ He made a boast of his modesty. The result was an appeal to the country which was safe to the point of constipation, accentuating the negative over the inspirational. The campaign reassured many, but it roused few. Only in the last gasps did Blair speak with conviction about his passion to transform Britain. And then because commentators and focus groups alike were warning that the lingering doubt about New Labour was its absence of passion and conviction.

This 'magisterial vacuity' reminded the American observer, Joe Klein, of another centrist Anglo-Saxon leader who had sold himself on the basis of his newness only to be unwrapped in office as the most tawdry goods.⁹ The apparent similarities with Bill Clinton, from whom New Labour had certainly looted much of its rhetoric, many of its techniques and some of its policies, also struck another American. Maureen Dowd accused Blair of 'cloning himself from a clone'.[10]

Blair implicitly acknowledged that there was something in progressive criticism of the buttoned-up, plastic-wrapped, risk-averse tone of much of his campaign. Three days before polling day, he suggested that he would deliver to left and liberal Britain more than he appeared to promise: 'I am of the centre-left and I want the left to be part of this project. I want the left to realise that, if we win this election, we will have done so without ceding any ground that cannot be recovered. I'm going to be a lot more radical in government than many people think.'[11]

His already developed reputation as a chameleon meant that observers struggled to be sure whether this was not merely another token of reassurance, its noteworthiness being that this was a rare example of throwing something to the left. He spun a gossamer veil of shining ambiguities. Sometimes, he simply shrugged and insisted that an element of mystery about how New Labour would perform in office was inevitable. 'I don't think any project such as this becomes clear to the public until you are in government and you're doing things.'[12] Though he spoke of 'hard choices', even Blair parodied his evasions of the tougher nuts he would crack his teeth on as Prime Minister. Asked during the campaign whether he regarded himself as English or Scottish, Blair grinned: 'We will have to review that very carefully in government.'[13] This was Britain's first postmodern party leader speaking. Here he was making an ironic crack about his device for avoiding choices and in the process swerving away from making one.

Blair's reluctance to give detailed definition to New Labour spread confusion among commentators and critics. Which was, at least in part, his intention. One view from the left – articulated most trenchantly and mournfully by the former deputy Labour leader, Roy Hattersley – was that New Labour would ensure itself 'a permanent House of Commons majority' by neglecting the poor and pandering to the tax-averse 'suburban middle classes'.[14] From a contrary left-wing stance, Ken Livingstone forecast that pressure of events would impel the government leftwards so rapidly that, within a year of the election, taxes would be racked up and Blair toppled in a coup to be replaced by Robin Cook. This entirely wrong-headed prognosis offered a straw of comfort to be grasped at by British Tories. Michael Lewis consoled readers of the *Sunday Telegraph*: 'Six months from the date of his election, Blair will be the most hated man in Britain.'[15] That wasn't the only crystal balls to be printed during the campaign. Six months after his election, Blair would be the most popular Prime Minister since Dr Gallup pioneered the art of polling.

He would take power with the votes of people who had been supporting Labour since its dark ages began in 1979, and people who had never cast for Labour before the renaissance of 1997. The Euro-friendly *Guardian* and the Europhobic *Sun* declared for Blair. The *Financial Times*, self-described as 'a natural supporter' of the Tories, put its cross in the same Labour box as the doggedly faithful *Mirror*. Different brands of centrists willed him to win, prominent among them the apostates who had broken from Labour in the eighties to form the SDP. One of the defunct SDP's former leaders, Roy Jenkins, whose favourite uncle status with Blair had become reasonably well known, saw in him the potential to be a great Prime Minister. Another ex-leader of the SDP, David Owen, whose secret pre-election conversations with Blair would have caused disgruntlement to Jenkins and massive inflammation within Labour's ranks had they been revealed at the time, came close to endorsing New Labour, drawing back only because Owen felt a personal obligation to Major.[16]

Blair had the blessings of Michael Foot, whose Labour Party had planned to nationalise the solar system, as well as the benediction of Margaret Thatcher, who wanted to privatise the cosmos. At a private dinner, Thatcher boomed: 'He won't let Britain down.'[17] The transformation of Labour's policies and presentation, spun around Blair's own winning political charms, sustained an extra-ordinary span of support. At the very outset of the campaign, Blair had said: 'What matters is what works.'[18] Nothing mattered more than winning. For that purpose, New Labour worked.

Just how magnificently became evident to the country when, at ten o'clock, the BBC and ITN broadcast exit polls agreeing that Britain was a landslide country. Blair was still in denial. 'It can't be right,' he muttered. 'It isn't real.' He was alarmed by the television pictures from the Royal Festival Hall, where the Labour victory party was already becoming exuberant. 'They are being too triumphalist,' Blair complained to Campbell. 'Tell them to calm it down.' David Hill, the party's director of communications, came on the line to Sedgefield and not unreasonably pointed out that it was beyond his control: 'When Labour has won every seat so far and the Tories have not won one, it's a bit difficult to convince everyone that it is on a knife edge.'

When Blair emerged from Myrobella around midnight, all he would offer the hungry camera crews was a terse and testy sound-nibble: 'Let's just wait and see, shall we?' His red campaign Jag drove him to the count at Sedgefield, the constituency which had first sent him to parliament in Labour's nadir year of 1983. When the party he led had last won an election, Blair was not even a member of it. He had been at Oxford, wearing loon pants and doing impersonations of Mick Jagger for a student rock group called Ugly Rumours. As they awaited the completion of his personal count, Blair and his intimates gathered on a balcony overlooking the leisure centre. His election-winning coalition was represented within his own family. His father Leo, an admirer of Margaret Thatcher, was one of the many Conservatives who earlier that day had voted Labour for the first time in their lives. Cherie had been joined by members of her extended clan, among them the first Tony in her life, her father, the actor Tony Booth, from whom she had inherited a streak of left-wing Liverpudlian militancy.

The relatives became more excited as the deluge unfolded on a television in the bar area. May 2nd was half an hour old when Labour gained Crosby on Merseyside − Cherie had grown up nearby − with a sensational 18 per cent swing that went off the scale of the BBC's seismograph. The victory − and the scale of it − was no longer deniable. Turning to Campbell, an awed Blair said:

'What on earth have we done here? Have we done something extraordinary here?'

Blair took himself away to a corner of the bar area, and sat at a small table next to a slot machine. He sat there alone, silent, staring into middle space. From a distance, Anji Hunter, his personal assistant through the years of impotent gruel in Opposition, watched him. After a while, she came over, and caught his eye. 'My God,' he said quietly and slowly. 'This is it. This is it.'

Blair's immediate reaction was the opposite of triumphant. He imagined the country to be, as he was, in a state of shock. The voters would be thinking: They've got this landslide. What does it mean? Will the left go out of control? What on earth will happen? It was characteristic that Blair should be seized by apprehension that his victory would alarm the voters of Middle Britain he had so assiduously cultivated. Equally typically, in his first speech of the night, after his constituency result had been declared, he sought to find words to soothe anxiety:

If we have been as successful as the indications are that we have been, and you know me, all the way through I've been against complacency and I'm still against it until those results finally come through. If we have done well, then I know what this is a vote for. It is a vote for the future. It is not a vote for outdated dogma or ideology of any kind.

The ideology-free pragmatist went on:

It is a vote for an end to divisions, an end to looking backwards, a desire to apply the basic, decent British values of commonsense and imagination to the problems we all know we face as a country today.[19]

Blair departed the leisure centre to thank his local supporters at Trimdon Labour club. At around two in the morning John Major phoned – the conversation was a blur to Blair – to concede defeat. This was an unnecessary, but graceful, touch by the rejected Prime Minister. A small, leather-seated, luxury jet flew Blair and his entourage south to London. On the table in front of Campbell was the press secretary's pager, the electronic umbilical cord which was New Labour's essential accessory. It winked with reports of the latest gains. Campbell reported that Hastings had fallen. 'You'll be telling me we've won Hove next,' replied Blair. 'I think we already have,' said Campbell. Brighton's blue-rinsed twin was just one of the many untargeted, undreamt-of constituencies that were returning Labour MPs.

This was one of the few lighter moments aboard the plane. The victory party on London's South Bank now throbbed with raucous intoxication at the violence with which the electorate was purging the Conservatives. They roared when Neil Hamilton, oily symbol of Tory sleaze, was beheaded in Tatton. They greeted the decapitation of Michael Portillo, quiffed embodiment of Tory arrogance and division, and one of seven Cabinet ministers who would be scalped that night, with chants of 'Out! Out! Out!' When Portillo's defeat came up on Campbell's pager just after three in the morning, Blair's first thought was that someone at party headquarters had to be playing a prank.

Absent was any sense of elation. They sipped at cups of tea. Blair would ruefully reflect: 'I was the only member of the Labour Party who was sober that night.' The only passenger who could be described as jolly was the bearded, twinkling figure of John Burton, the constituency agent who had talent-spotted Blair when he was a young London barrister searching for a safe north-eastern seat. Burton had been anticipating the moment all day, repeatedly saying to the others: 'Isn't the plane going to be great?' He wandered the aisle with packets of nibbles, offering drinks, trying to lift the atmosphere. And failing. They felt guilty afterwards that they had let him down.

Blair was sapped by the campaign, and oppressed by what lay ahead. Though his wife told him how 'extremely proud' she was of his achievement, the enormity of what confronted Blair left him humbled, daunted, quite frightened. Cherie talked of his 'great opportunity'. 'But I've never been in government,' he said, plaintively.[20] Blair was never as self-confident as he looked. Cherie, whose rather brittle public persona concealed a steel core, took his hand. 'It's going to be difficult,' she agreed. 'You can only do your best.' As Blair started jotting down notes for the speech he would make at the Royal Festival Hall, Cherie made her regular demand of Campbell: 'When's he going to get some sleep?'

By the time the plane touched down at Stansted, Tony Blair already had far more seats than he needed to form a government. The accretions of power – notably an augmented police escort – waited to speed their convoy into central London. Bill Clinton called with his congratulations. They listened to Radio Five. 'Tony Blair is coming,' announced a breathless reporter from the Royal Festival Hall. 'We're told he's just five minutes away.' He was around the corner, close enough to hear the thrum of the celebrants on the South Bank dancing to D-Ream's campaign tune, 'Things Can Only Get Better'. But he would not arrive for a further twenty minutes. The convoy had driven down a one-way street, found the end of the road blocked, and was reversing out with extreme difficulty. From the inside, the New Labour machine was never as glossily omnipotent as it was imagined to be from the outside. There was a further foul-up when Blair arrived. He dashed out of his car, leaving behind the notes he had prepared for his speech. In his anxiety to keep up, Campbell leapt out of a moving car, catching his ankle under the wheel. He was grateful that no TV camera immortalised the spectacle of a speechless Tony Blair striding ahead into potential catastrophe followed by his hobbling press secretary.

As the pale fingers of the early morning sun reached over the Thames, Blair struggled to be heard over the cacophony of the revelling crowd. Even at this moment, the end of eighteen years of wilderness for his party, the over-sufficient fulfilment of all the modernisers' schemes, the beginning of the age of Blair, there was a pronounced streak of ambiguity. 'A new dawn has broken – has it not?' he asked. 'Isn't it wonderful?'[21] The speech was a medley of his hustings tunes about education and fairness, enterprise and opportunity. It was aimed not so much at the carousers directly in front of him, but at the country beyond, that part of it which was still groggily tuned in to events at five thirty in the morning. Afterwards, Blair and his party went to a waiting room until the

police told them they could leave to grab a little sleep. 'What did
you make of that?' Campbell asked him about the delirium of the
victory party. 'It's weird,' replied Blair. 'I can't get into it at all.'

Had a new dawn broken? On the face of it, the answer had to be
an emphatic yes. Four days short of his forty-fourth birthday, Tony
Blair was about to become the youngest Prime Minister since the
Napoleonic Wars at the apex of a majority which was the biggest
in the history of the Labour Party and the biggest for any party
since the Second World War. The Conservatives, the definers of
an era in which the pendulum of power had for years seemed
permanently rusted on the right, had suffered their worst defeat
since the introduction of universal suffrage. Reckoning the result
even more sensationally, the Tories had not been smashed so
thoroughly since the Great Reform Act of 1832.

Finchley, monument to Margaret Thatcher's triple victories, had
been taken by Labour as had Basildon, totem of John Major's
surprise fourth win in 1992. Places eternally Tory were harvested
by Tony Blair. New towns, Roman towns, cathedral cities and
industrial cities, suburbs and shires, Labour MPs represented them
all. The political map had never been so dramatically recoloured, a
change exaggerated by Britain's winner-takes-all voting system
and further amplified by determined tactical voting to oust the
Conservatives.

'We are elected because we represent the whole of this nation
and we will govern for the whole of this nation, every single day,'
Blair could declare.

We have won support from all walks of life, all classes of people, every
corner of the country. We are now today the people's party, the party of
all the people, the many not the few, the party that belongs to every part
of Britain.[22]

But the conquest of Britain was far from total. The tsunami of
revulsion which engulfed the Tories was not matched by an equal
wave of enthusiasm for New Labour. The heat of the campaign

left much of the electorate cold. Turn-out was the lowest since 1935. 'Things Can Only Get Better' was not, when you considered the lyrics, an enthusing prospectus. The country had responded by restraining its excitement about New Labour. Fewer than one in three of the potential electorate had put a cross by the name of a Labour candidate. As the defeated Major would bitterly remark, Blair had secured his obese parliamentary majority of 179 with half a million fewer votes in ballot boxes than had five years earlier given Major an anorexic majority of twenty-one. Labour's share of the vote was 43.2 per cent.[23] This was a brilliant improvement by the standards of the immediate past, just better than the 1970 election and much better than every election since, but a lot less impressive on a longer historical view. It was lower than Attlee's share in 1945, and Wilson's in 1964 and 1966. It was less even than in the three elections of the fifties that Labour lost.[24] Blair's coalition was wide, and it was shallow.

This twisted a tension around the heart of the new government from its beginning. The scale of his parliamentary majority was bound to arouse great expectations about the rapidity with which Blair could deliver change. The qualified nature of his true support was guaranteed to aggravate New Labour's apprehension about taking any risks with its popularity. The terror of losing would soon morph into an anxiety about the consequences of victory.

Nowhere else in the democratic world is power transferred with such smooth brutality. The moment Tony Blair stopped pinching himself was probably when John Major's bodyguard, Trevor Butler, arrived at the Blairs' home in Richmond Crescent early on the morning of Friday. At a little after eleven thirty, Major took his final ride in the prime ministerial limousine to formally hand his resignation to the Queen, having already declared he was off to watch the cricket at the Oval and would be pulling stumps as leader of the Tory Party. An hour later, Blair had kissed hands at Buckingham Palace and was returning to Downing Street in what was now his limousine. The ejection of the *ancien* Tory *régime* and its replacement with a self-consciously modernising set of rulers, symbolised by the

coming and going of removal lorries outside Number 10, is the closest
a mature Western country gets to a revolutionary event. The media,
for a morning at least, suspended its critical faculties. Commentators
compared the moment to the velvet revolutions that toppled the
one-party states of the defunct Soviet bloc; even to the release of
Nelson Mandela from apartheid's prison.

There was a generational change. The Queen surely noted that
Blair was the first of her Prime Ministers to have been born after
the beginning of her reign. Children would live in Downing Street
for the first time since Asquith was Prime Minister. The average
age of the Cabinet dropped by a decade; the average age of MPs
by twenty years. Departed to the pavilion was Major, the Prime
Minister whose casual wardrobe favoured blazers and cardigans,
and whose rhetoric lingered nostalgically on warm beer, village
greens and bicycle-borne old maids. On to the pitch came a Prime
Minister who would be pictured that weekend strolling the lanes
around Chequers in jeans and open-neck shirt, who offered cold
champagne at Number 10 to current epitomes of pop cool, and
whose oratory relentlessly cast forward into the next millennium.
Whatever the narrowing of ideological space between the parties,
there remained a philosophical chasm between Margaret Thatcher's
declamation that 'there is no such thing as society' and Tony Blair's
declaration that 'we owe a duty to others as well as to ourselves'.

Maybe it was simply a trick of the light – 2 May was brilliantly
sunny – but at that moment Britain suddenly felt like a younger
country. The campaign might have been depressing, but the outcome infected with enthusiasm not just those who had voted for
Blair, but many who had not. The stifling grey cloud that had hung
over Britain was suddenly pierced by light. So, at least, it felt.
The opinion pollsters would soon be reporting a big jump in the
feel-good factor. Millions more people would claim to have voted
for New Labour than had actually done so. Yet it was typical of the
party that Blair had created that they were not prepared to take a
chance on the people's reaction to what the people had just done.
They could not stop themselves injecting a pseudo-element into
this naturally stirring drama. Campbell's diligent deputy, Tim Allan,

had slipped inside Number 10 a few days before the election to choreograph the coronation of the new Prime Minister. He and his wife were greeted in Downing Street by a crowd of exultant citizens, photogenic young children particularly prominent, cheering 'Tonee!' and being gladhanded in return. The superficiality of this contrived spontaneity was instantly obvious. They waved identical plastic Union Jacks. The original idea – which was for them to wave Labour Party banners – had been resisted by officials at Number 10. They wore uniform T-shirts emblazoned 'Britain Just Got Better'. Blair's pageant was composed of party workers from Millbank. Slickness of stage management would in time rebound against the government as it bred the suspicion that nothing done in its name could ever be taken at face value.

The words used by Prime Ministers when they first stand outside Number 10 are often an unreliable indicator of what they will do in office. John Major, who promised 'a nation at ease with itself', presided over a nation mainly united only in its weariness with his viciously quarrelsome government. Margaret Thatcher, who recited the prayer of St Francis of Assisi to preach that she would bring harmony, was one of the most discordant Prime Ministers to hold the office. Blair's doorstep speech was a particular curiosity. 'I say to the people of this country – we ran for office as New Labour, we will govern as New Labour.'[25] This was a strikingly bizarre formulation. In his first remarks to the people of a country which had just elected him, a new leader, especially one who had made a fetish of his pledges, vows and covenants, would be most unlikely to say that he was immediately going to break all the promises on which he had been elected. The point was to combine reassurance to the country with a warning to his party that the size of the majority was not a signal to lurch leftwards off the middle ground. He gave one massive hostage to future fortune with the claim that 'it will be a government that seeks to restore trust in politics'. To Britain, he offered himself as the apostle of togetherness: 'We have secured a mandate to bring the nation together – to unite us – one Britain, one nation in which our ambition for ourselves is matched by our sense of compassion and decency and duty towards others.'

There was only one poetic note in the assertion that his would be 'a government of practical measures in pursuit of noble causes'. The conclusion was prose.

For eighteen years – eighteen long years – my party has been in Opposition. It could only say, it could not do. Today we are charged with the deep responsibility of government. Today, enough of talking. It is time now to do.[26]

After a final photo-call with his family, Blair was ready to enter Number 10. The door was firmly closed to him. The black portal of ultimate power opens only from the inside. Behind it stood a civil servant, Angus Lapsley, who had been in agonies trying to guess when Blair would stop posing for the cameras and make his entrance. Eventually, his rictus by now tiring, Blair heard the door open behind him.

Once over the threshold of power, the first thing a freshly installed Prime Minister sees is the staff at Number 10, lined up in Victorian style to applaud the new lord of the manor. Blair, a man impatient with the flummeries of ceremonial, found the ritual excruciatingly embarrassing, later remarking to one of his intimates: 'Jesus. I didn't need that.' Most of the staff adopted cheerful smiles, but one of the cleaners, who had become extremely attached to John Major, was near to tears. 'I'm sorry,' remarked the new Prime Minister, for want of anything else to say. 'You're not sorry at all,' she retorted. 'You meant this to happen.' Tony Blair had been treated to his first lesson that he would not please – nor fool – everyone all of the time.

# 2. What Do We Do Now?

Among the victory celebrants at the Royal Festival Hall was a ghost of past defeat, the godfather of the modernisers, the former Labour leader, Neil Kinnock. His eyes moist with tears, he clasped the new Prime Minister. In the emotion of the moment, Kinnock's legendary loquacity deserted him. All he could say was: 'Brilliant, kid, bloody brilliant.' Tony Blair, stepping back from the clinch, smiled: 'OK, wiseguy. What do we do now?'

Not for more than a century had a Prime Minister been so new to office in such an absolutely literal sense. Even the first Labour government formed by Ramsay MacDonald in 1924 could draw on more Cabinet-level experience. You had to reach back to the middle of the nineteenth century – to the Derby government of which the aged Duke of Wellington asked 'Who? Who?' as the names of the ministers were read to him – to find a Cabinet of comparable inexperience.[1] They were superlative operators of the politics of Opposition. The obverse was that they were neophytes at government. The Prime Minister had never previously seen the inside of a red box. Neither he, nor any of his key Cabinet ministers, had given instructions to a Permanent Secretary, managed a multi-billion pound budget, or piloted legislation on to the statute book. Only one member of the government had sat at the Cabinet table before.[2]

A Prime Minister less naïve about the pressures and constraints of power might have been more calibrated about what he claimed to be able to achieve with it. Roy Jenkins, to whom Blair turned for tutorials on the performance of past governments, had impressed upon him the idea that every Prime Minister should have what Jenkins liked to style an 'Upper Case' ambition and a 'Lower Case' ambition. For all the pragmatic modesty of specific policies, Blair had set unforgiving tests for his project by articulating goals for his government breathtaking in their vaulting scope. New Labour

would 'save the National Health Service', and provide Britain with
schools and universities that would be 'the envy of the world'. New
Labour would 'end welfare as we know it'. New Labour's New
Britain would have a new constitutional order and be fully engaged
in a Europe which she would lead. Any one of these would have
served as sufficient ambition for many Prime Ministers. At his
most rhetorically excessive, Blair even claimed that his government
would set the pattern of the entire twenty-first century. 'One
thousand days to prepare for one thousand years. A moment of
destiny for us,'[3] he had cried, in a passage which sounded like John
F. Kennedy mistranslated by Adolf Hitler.

The real Upper Case ambition for a unique place in history was
to win two full terms in government, that distinction which had
eluded every previous Labour Prime Minister. When his first international visitor came calling at the end of the month, I asked Bill
Clinton what lessons he might have to offer Tony Blair. Before
Clinton could get in an answer, Blair intervened: 'He got the most
important thing right. He got re-elected.'[4] The pivotal question
about Blair and the government he started forming on 2 May was
how carefully his strategic designs had been thought through, and
how often they would be sacrificed to the tactics deemed necessary
to secure re-election.

Waiting at the end of the welcoming line inside Number 10 was
Sir Robin Butler, the head of the permanent government. Before
the serious business, the Cabinet Secretary gave a brief acclimatisa-
tion tour, noting as he led the Blair family around the house that
the new Prime Minister was much less interested in spending time
in the Cabinet room than in inspecting the garden. In the first-floor
dining room, over a late lunch of quiche, salad and white wine,
Blair and his aides then began organising the appointment of his
government.

The arrival of John Prescott was presentational. The combination
of public school lawyer and secondary modern seaman had proved
to be a surprisingly appetising blend of Islington guacamole and
Hull mushy peas with the electorate. Despite his posture as the
guardian of traditional Labour against the modernisers he privately

scorned as 'nouveau Labour', the deputy leader was a pragmatist. Though Prescott occasionally vented steam at what had been done to the Labour Party, Blair had always relied on the calculation: 'John wants to be in government.' This was borne out by Prescott's attractively child-like thrill when he basked on the steps of Number 10 shouting: 'I've always wanted to do this.' His title of Deputy Prime Minister and the satisfaction of his baronial aspirations with the creation of a sprawling Department of the Environment, Transport and the Regions was settled. Blair insisted on the insertion of one junior minister whom Prescott suspected of being Number 10's mole inside his bailiwick.[5] Prescott's kingdom was otherwise so fashioned to his liking that Blairites took to referring to it as 'The Kremlin' or 'Moscow University'.

The toughest conversation Blair had that first afternoon was with Gordon Brown, joint dynamo of New Labour, closest friend in the Cabinet, rival for power within the government, the source of equal magnitudes of inspiration and exasperation. All politicians are driven animals, but Brown burned with a special intensity. He was the middle son of three, a position in the family hierarchy which often makes for awkward high-achievers. A schoolboy rugby injury had left him blind in his left eye, and half-sighted in his right. The doctor told him that he could not be sure whether or when he might, at some time in the future, go entirely blind. That must have further concentrated Brown's formidable mind. At the knee of his Presbyterian rector father, Brown had learned that the rewards in life are won by virtue and hard work. He had worked hard, and virtuously, for his ideas and his ambitions. The Scot had won his first election, to become student rector of Edinburgh University, when Tony Blair was at Oxford strumming guitar and vaguely thinking he might like to make a difference. Yet Brown's father had been proved wrong. It was Blair, initially the junior in their partnership, who had accelerated past Brown to grasp the most glittering reward. Brown could never be expected to make a complete recovery from his shock and grievance of three years earlier that his assumption that he would be Labour leader had not been shared by Blair.

When he withdrew from the leadership contest, Brown had demanded guarantees that he would have suzerainty over not just economic policy, but the overlordship of social policy as well. From a mixture of obligation, guilt, dependency, fear and sincere admiration for the other man's sacrifice and qualities, Blair had ceded much to Brown, though it would never be quite enough to satisfy the other. They had had serious quarrels since, but it was a tribute to the discipline of both men and their mutual desire for power that they had maintained a public front so united that it seemed to refute Lloyd George's usually reliable rule that 'there can be no friendship at the top'. Blair gave up to Brown the chairman-ship of the economic committee of the Cabinet, the first Prime Minister to grant this to his Chancellor since 1964. Blair wanted to put Peter Mandelson on the crucial committee on public spending. Brown was allowed a veto over his sworn enemy's presence there. His ally and namesake, Nick Brown, held the critical position of chief whip, and in combination they persuaded Blair to insert Brownites into key slots in nearly every ministry.

Whether or not Blair took the same view, Brown conceived of the new government as a dual monarchy, each with its own court. This was a recipe for potential instability at the core of the govern-ment. To resolve the outstanding issues between them on that first Friday after the election, the two men sought the privacy of the garden of Number 10. As they wandered among the flower-beds in the glorious sunshine, they discussed Brown's plan to give independence to the Bank of England and negotiated over some of the junior appointments to the government. It was an indication of the wariness in their relationship, and of New Labour's fixation with image, that a large part, if not the most substantial part, of their forty-five-minute discussion that afternoon revolved around a press officer. Charlie Whelan – the Chancellor's devoted and roguish mouthpiece – was as dedicated to burnishing his master as he was to assassinating the reputation of anyone who might conceivably rival or threaten him. Though not yet enjoying the wide celebrity he would later acquire, Whelan was already the source of great aggravation to Blair. Twenty-four hours earlier, during a lunchtime phone conversation on polling day, Brown had been told by Blair: 'I don't want Charlie in government.' He met blank resistance from Brown.

To accommodate the Blair family, it had been agreed that they would take over the Chancellor's personal quarters at Number 11 and he would have the Prime Minister's flat in Number 10. Cherie encountered Whelan on a reconnoitre of Number 11. 'What are you doing here?' she demanded. 'You haven't got the whole place, you know,' retorted the incorrigible Whelan. Cherie, who cast a jealously protective eye over her husband, was not alone in suspecting that Brown had ambitions to create a government within a government of which Whelan was both symptom and symbol.

Alastair Campbell and Peter Mandelson both urged Blair to deny Brown his independent instrument of propaganda. As Prime Minister toured the garden with Chancellor, Blair tried again to convince him that Whelan should be removed. Many members of the incoming Cabinet nursed bruises inflicted on Brown's behalf by Whelan. The person who would be ultimately most damaged by his activities, Blair argued, was the Chancellor himself. Brown was having none of this. Whelan was loyal. He was excellent at his job. He had worked as energetically as anyone for their election victory. He was Brown's promoter and protector with the media and – though Brown left this thought unspoken – against Blair's entourage. Moreover, for the Chancellor, his own 'credibility', ever a vital concern to him, was at stake. Everyone knew Whelan was his man. If it became known that Blair had forced Brown to dispense with Whelan, it would look like a humiliation at the hands of the Prime Minister on their first day in office. Brown put it to Blair like this: removing Whelan would be 'a blow to my authority as Chancellor'. This would be far from the last time they pursued the dispute, but Brown won this grapple in the garden. Blair refused to sanction Whelan's appointment for twenty-four hours. Then he relented. It was a moment of weakness which the Prime Minister would have months to regret.[6]

Blair's calculations about a coalition having been upset by the size of his majority, Robin Cook became Foreign Secretary. Blair and Cook were not soul-mates, hardly soul distant cousins. Blair rejected all of Cook's nominees for the position of Minister for Europe. The job went to Doug Henderson. With no experience of European issues, his principal qualification for the post was that he was pushed by Gordon Brown. This was an example of Blair's willingness to defer to his Chancellor early in the life of the government.

Jack Straw's appointment was declared before he had even seen the Prime Minister. Straw was deep into a recuperative sleep at his home in south London when he was woken by his political adviser. Ed Owen had just heard the three o'clock radio news report Downing Street's announcement that his chief was Home Secretary. Meeting Campbell in the hallway of Number 10, Straw said: 'Thanks for telling me first, Alastair.' 'Sorry, Jack,' replied Campbell. 'There wasn't much news to release.' Not much news on the first day of the first Labour government in nearly twenty years.

It was a backhanded tribute to the perceived influence of Peter Mandelson that he had accumulated more soubriquets than all of the Cabinet put together. He was 'The Prince of Darkness' to those who saw him as no more than an arch-manipulator and 'Sir Oswald Smish' to his own family. Blair once told Prince Charles that Mandelson was 'my alter ego'.[7] Blair also prized Mandelson, his lightning conductor as well as his antennae, as a personality strong enough to help counterbalance Brown. Mandelson was conflicted. He saw that his power flowed from his proximity to the leader while at the same time harbouring resentments about being a creature of Blair's patronage, 'the person fluttering around at his beck and call'.[8] Denying him the independent ministerial existence he had been privately agitating for and semi-publicly punting for, somewhat to Blair's irritation, the Prime Minister wanted his alter ego to continue to spider at the centre of the New Labour web in the role of Minister Without Portfolio. From there, so Blair believed, his ally and friend could best help fulfil the design to impose Number 10's writ across Whitehall. Mandelson eased his disappointment by taking a Cabinet-level red Rover Sterling rather than the more humble Vauxhall Cavalier usually awarded to ministers of state. The media dubbed him 'Minister For Meddling'. 'Minister Without A Job' was the derisive adhesive applied by Whelan who detested Mandelson with every atom of his body, not just on his boss's account, but on his own.

The consolation for Mandelson was a promise that he would acquire a seat at the top table in the reshuffle that Blair intended to hold within six months. The government that was announced over the weekend was not the one the Prime Minister wanted. Mandelson would count the number of those considered to be true Blairites in the Cabinet and stop before he had used up the fingers of one hand. Clare Short's description of Blair as a half-evil 'Jekyll and Hyde' character, manipulated by 'people who live in the dark',[9] an attack which had inspired the Tories' notorious 'Demon Eyes' campaign, had been neither forgotten nor forgiven. Blair attempted to negotiate her down to a more junior rank outside the Cabinet, but blinked first when she threatened to resign. As late as Friday afternoon, when he gathered aides and officials together for an alfresco meeting on the wicker chairs on the Number 10 patio, Blair was still doing back-of-the-envelope calculations about the government. He could not decide whether to give Cabinet positions to Gavin Strang and David Clark about whom 'there was some awkwardness'.[10] Blair had already decided to deny seats at the top table to Michael Meacher and Tom Clarke. He was convinced not to make a deeper sweep by the argument that the salad days of his government would be soured by a succession of former members of the Shadow Cabinet venting their bitterness. Strang was accommodated in the Cabinet as Prescott's deputy, and Clark at the Cabinet Office as Mandelson's superior in name, but never in power. Both men had dotted lines around their necks from the day they took office, though it would turn out to be more than a year before Blair applied the cut.

With Cabinet-making complete, Blair's new ministers tasted the long-denied fruits of office and found them sweet. Though the Prime Minister instructed his MPs that 'you are not here to enjoy the trappings of power',[11] his colleagues were eager to try them for size. Sir Robin Butler, adopting the role of a high-class estate agent, discussed with members of the Cabinet their claims on Whitehall's grace and favour apartments. Sir Robin offered his apologies to Margaret Beckett – as Trade and Industry Secretary she was not at the top of the pecking order – about the accommodation he had to offer. 'I'm afraid it's only a one-bedroom flat.' When they were taken over to the apartment in Dover House, Beckett and her husband, Leo, appreciated what the Cabinet Secretary meant by a 'one-bedroom flat'. The Becketts, who famously holidayed in a caravan, gawped at its size. 'The hall is bigger than our old flat,' she whispered to Leo.

One woman's idea of a palace is not necessarily another's. Pauline Prescott popped her head around the door of the Becketts' apartment and gave it a once-over: 'So this is the tatty one.' The Prescotts, given the first pick, had chosen the apartment on the top floor previously occupied by Michael Portillo, the ejected Tory Defence Secretary. They arrived to move in only to find that every stick of furniture had been removed on the orders of the Permanent Secretary at Defence, Sir Richard Mottram. It was an early schooling in the proprietorial habits of Whitehall. Prescott later had his opportunity for revenge. When Mottram moved to become Permanent Secretary at Prescott's department, he delighted in greeting the civil servant personally. 'Let me show you to your room,' said Prescott, opening the door to reveal that it had been stripped bare save for a single orange packing crate.

Blair had not troubled to conceal his desire to 'govern from the centre'.[12] To achieve that, he would need to dominate not only the Cabinet. The other estates of the modern political realm are the media, the House of Commons and Whitehall. John Major never mastered any of them. Margaret Thatcher took some years to establish her hegemony and even she did not, as Blair did, issue an edict that all policy and presentational initiatives had to be cleared first through Downing Street. What manifested itself as arrogance was sourced in New Labour's chronic insecurity about itself. Blair hungered to try to control all from the beginning. Into Number 10 he brought an entourage of twenty-two, a number which would swell with time. There was mutual wariness between Blair's young coterie and the civil servants in Downing Street. 'Labour was coming in after eighteen years of Conservative government,' observed a senior civil servant. 'They were suspicious. Politicians think everyone is like them: everyone is ideologically driven. And if not obviously driven on the surface, that is only because they are skilful at concealing it.'[13]

Alastair Campbell, whose formal title of press secretary did no justice to his power, was certainly driven. Officialdom anticipated with trepidation the arrival of the former tabloid journalist, whose pugnacity and contempt for the uselessness of the Conservative government's propaganda skills preceded him. Though born in England, the son of a Hebridean vet had a Celtic temperament. He would never forgive himself for the strange gloom that had overcome him on election night. His politics were not of the philosophical kind, but sprung from a visceral antagonism towards privilege which expressed itself in outbursts against 'public school wankers' whether they were encountered in the media or Whitehall. A tribalist, in his football as in his politics, he placed on the wall of his bow-windowed office overlooking Downing Street a specially printed version of Labour's election poster in the colours of his beloved Burnley. An emotional man, he also decorated it with pictures by his children. He hadn't drunk in over ten years since an alcohol-fuelled breakdown. Those destructive inner urges had since been rechannelled outwards into the pursuit of power. For Campbell, as for Blair, victory was always the first thing. He was over six feet tall and his presence could be used to charm or to bully. The civil servants at Number 10 had laboured over a thick blue folder, grandly entitled 'The Precedent Book', laying out in detail how previous governments had handled major set-piece media events, such as the Queen's Speech and Prime Ministerial statements. Without opening it, he tossed the folder aside, scoffing: 'We won't be needing that.'

In all previous governments, the propagandist would have been outranked by the policy-makers, the mind before the mouth. Not in this one. Campbell, who left Cambridge with an upper Second in modern languages, underlined the subordinate status of the head of the Policy Unit by giving to David Miliband, a First in Philosophy, Politics and Economics from Oxford, the slightly patronising nickname 'Brains'.[14] Miliband's position was insecure until Blair finished a long and fruitless quest to attract a big name from business to be his policy maestro. Miliband was dark-haired and open-faced, an enthuser with a fluid mind. His father was Ralph Miliband, the Marxist historian who predicted failure for the bourgeois reformism of capitalism that the son was now dedicated to proving could work.

Consternation greeted the arrival of Anji Hunter. She had been closer to Blair for longer than anyone but his siblings and parents. Hunter first fixed for him when they were both teen rebels in Edinburgh: the adolescent Blair asked her to act the go-between with a girl he fancied. She had been his Commons assistant for ten years, leaving him only briefly, in the face of Blair's desperate imprecations to stay, to spend time with her children. Living in Sussex with her landscape designer husband, Hunter would read for Blair the pulse of the southern middle classes, relaying back to him the results of the conversations about the government she engineered with shoppers in the supermarket or commuters on the train. A word to her would get through to Blair ten times faster than anything sent by normal channels. Downing Street officials suspected they detected in her the shade of Marcia Williams, Baroness Falkender, Harold Wilson's muse. Officials complained to Hunter that they did not know where to put her. Was she Private Office? Was she Press Office? These conventional civil service distinctions were of no interest to the new governors, but only after some manoeuvring with officialdom did she establish herself as Blair's gatekeeper, taking the American-sounding title of 'Special Assistant'.

Whitehall's profoundest suspicions centred on the person of Jonathan Powell. A curly-headed devotee of soft rock with a taste for public schoolboy jokes, he was another graduate of Oxford. Blair liked to surround himself with people whose curriculum vitae overlapped with his own. 'Chief of Staff' was a White House post

previously alien to Downing Street. Powell had been recruited by
Blair from the diplomatic corps, but to the civil service he was no
longer one of them. Whitehall remembered with a shudder of
distaste the power wielded at the court of Margaret Thatcher by
his elder brother Charles, the Powell who pronounced the surname
to rhyme with 'vole'. For twenty years in British politics, there has
been a Powell behind the throne. The younger Powell had learned
one thing from the older, and attempted to cloak his influence
in anonymity. For several weeks he refused to have an official
photograph taken until Blair suggested he ought to since the newspapers were using a snatched snap which made Powell look like an
escapee from a maximum security prison. Powell was already
famous within the upper echelons of Whitehall having given the
mandarinate an advance storm warning to brace themselves for the
gust which New Labour planned to blow down the corridors of
power. At a pre-election seminar, he told senior civil servants to
anticipate 'a change from a feudal system of barons to a more
Napoleonic system'.[15]

Powell's own placement in this Bonapartist order was the subject
of the first struggle of wills between Blair and Sir Robin Butler.
The silver-haired, sinuous Butler was flexible enough to serve the
contrasting styles of Thatcher and Major, but even his suppleness
was tested by the new regime. It needed a change to the constitutional rule book for political advisers to gain the authority to give
orders to civil servants. Special Orders in Council were issued
granting Campbell and Powell the powers to do just that. This the
Cabinet Secretary could swallow, but he gagged on Blair's desire
to give Powell the critical role of Prime Minister's Principal Private
Secretary, a post which, by long convention, was always occupied
by a career civil servant. 'I'm not making a Sir Humphreyish point,'
Butler tried to assure Blair that he was not being difficult for the
sake of it. There was a real problem with violating the distinction
between political partisan and neutral official. The Private Secretary
dealt with the honours system, as well as relations with Buckingham
Palace, the security services and the leader of the Opposition, all
aspects of government which shouldn't have 'political fingerprints'

on them. Surely, Butler contended, Blair didn't want to send a
signal that he was politicising Whitehall. Blair did not, probably
could not, see the objection. It was not that he had a low regard
for the civil service. He had no plans for a cull, he told Butler.
What he was insistent about was Powell. 'I want to have people
close to me who I have complete confidence in, who I can always
trust.'[16] The Prime Minister and Cabinet Secretary agreed to disagree. A final decision about Powell's precise status would be
delayed until the retirement of the Principal Private Secretary, Alex
Allan, in the summer. Butler resisted Blair again in June: setting
out his arguments in a strongly worded memo and making a public
admission, highly unusual for the Cabinet Secretary, that he was
'seriously unrelaxed' about the Prime Minister's plans. The
compromise was that John Holmes, the Private Secretary for
Foreign Affairs, would formally succeed to the title. This preserved
the dignity of the civil service, but Butler lost the essence of the
argument. Powell worked from the same office, possessed the
commanding desk within it, had access to the same papers, wielded
virtually all the powers traditionally belonging to the Principal
Private Secretary, and then some more. New Labour had an early
and significant victory over Old Whitehall. Left and liberal critics
who accused Blair of behaving like a Leninist – in his methods of
control, obviously not in his politics – shared that analysis with
those in the inner sanctums of the Establishment. After a few days
observing them, a senior civil servant came to this conclusion:

Within New Labour, they were a revolutionary cell within the party.
Tony Blair and Gordon Brown had a project which they imposed from
the centre. They and their small group were used to working intimately
together with as few people as possible privy to their secrets. They wanted
to carry on like that in government.[17]

Bliss was it to be New Labour in that dawn – but who the hell
were these 419 MPs? All those unknowns who would be flooding
into the Commons, washed up on Tony Blair's unexpectedly high
tide, were a cause of instant anxiety. As light broke on 2 May, Peter

Mandelson had ordered staff at Millbank to make an immediate trawl of their personal and political particulars. The resources which had been used to such spectacular effect against the Tories would now be turned against the new government's own representatives. A list of forty potentially off-message deviants from Blairite ortho-doxy – described with such unflattering labels as 'mentally unstable' – had been drawn up within days. This would not help New Labour's burgeoning reputation for control-freakery.

The truth about these parliamentary virgins was that they were far too stunned to think anything mutinous, and then far too preoccupied organising themselves offices and staff. 'It was euphoric. It was blissful,' one of their number reflected later. 'We all sat on the park benches in St James's Park with the bags of congratulations . . . rows of us, with wonderful, wonderful weather, watching the pelicans and dictating our mail. They were very good days.'[18] Catching sight of Chris Leslie, the twenty-four-year-old who had unseated the chairman of the Tory 1922 committee at Shipley, Blair thought the face was familiar: 'You know, he looks just like that guy who used to do Gordon's photocopying.' His diary secretary, Kate Garvey, replied: 'Tony, that *is* the guy who used to do Gordon's photocopying.'

New Labour regarded its MPs not as its conscience, but as its cheerleaders. The record number of women MPs obliged by being photographed around Tony Blair, like pilot fish swimming in the wake of a great shark. They attracted the patronising appellation 'Blair's Babes' and their slavish obedience would subsequently earn the even more demeaning label of 'Stepford Wives', the male equivalent of which was 'Tone's Clones'.

There was a universal standing ovation for the Prime Minister when he addressed them in the chamber of the General Synod at Church House on the Wednesday after the election. Almost universal: Dennis Skinner, the doyen of delinquency from Bol-sover, would not give a standing ovation to Jesus Christ.

'Be under no illusion. It was New Labour wot won it,' Blair told them, lapsing into tabloid argot to drive home his point that they owed their victory to him. After the doors had been closed on the television cameras, he spelt out more precisely which people – or rather which person – he expected them to serve. 'It's not your job to tell us what to do,' he instructed his MPs.[19] They were to be 'ambassadors for the government'. His massive majority was apparently not only willing, but for the most part eager to be enslaved to its pagers. Skinner, having cast a sour eye over his new colleagues, told a fellow left-winger: 'That lot are not going to cause any trouble.'

Nor, in these roseate early days, was the media. Blair's assiduous wooing of newspapers which had historically been Labour's enemies did not cease with his election. He was already casting forward to the next one. He found time, that first busy weekend, to write letters of appreciation to journalists who had supported him. One recipient of a thank you note was Stuart Higgins, the editor of the *Sun*. The 'magnificent support' of the tabloid, Blair wrote, 'really did make the difference'. This was nonsense. The *Sun* had clambered aboard the New Labour bandwagon only when it was clearly motoring into office. Still, Blair felt it cost him nothing to suck up to a newspaper which his wife had once declared she would never have in the house. His efforts were amply reciprocated with a flattering early press. Temporarily bored with reporting government as a failure, the media narrative of the Major years switched overnight to projecting the new government as a dynamic success.

Tony Blair had a Cabinet which, if not as entirely in his image as he desired, could be expected to be compliant. He was enthroned on a massive and obedient parliamentary majority. Whitehall, professionally frustrated by the paralysis of the death rattling Tories, was eager to please its new master. Foreign leaders regarded the Blair phenomenon with some amazement. The domestic media was uncharacteristically unjaundiced, even willing to be impressed. Tony Blair had set large ambitions for his government. He had not left himself with any obvious alibis for failure.

# 3. Bank of Brown

Late on the Sunday afternoon after the election, Gordon Brown left his new domain at the Treasury to be driven to the Blairs' home in Richmond Crescent. Stepping through the clutter of cases, crates and boxes of a family preparing to move, they talked together in the front room, the location of so many of their internal debates in Opposition. The difference now was that their words could be made into the flesh of change. They were the two most powerful men in Britain. From the street outside came the chatter of police radios.

The Chancellor had come to get a decision from the Prime Minister about handing control over interest rates to the Bank of England. This audacious stroke had been the subject of conversations between the two men for some time before the election. Brown had decided that he wanted to announce Bank independence immediately they came to power, but he had deliberately waited until polling day to bounce that element of the plan on Blair.[1] This was partly tactics: it would give Blair little time to consult others who might be cool about the idea. It was partly temperament. Brown dealt with issues by brooding, alone or within his tight ring of trustees, before crashing his decision on colleagues. Blair circled and circled around subjects, like a plane endlessly orbiting a runway, more often casting widely for advice, before descending on a conclusion. While warm to the boldness of the Bank plan in principle, and enthused by the political dividend of winning the instant approval of the City, Blair had mildly irritated Brown by not going snap immediately. He asked one of his own advisers, Roger Liddle, to write a memo detailing the case for and against, and used Peter Mandelson as another sounding-board. Both were positive.

To Brown, the plan meshed with his conception of what his

Chancellorship was going to be about. He was less interested in operating the levers of macro-economic management than any previous incumbent at the Treasury, and independence for the Bank would be both a confidence-building marker with the markets and offer more freedom to devote himself to the structural, social and employment reform that really engaged the new Chancellor.

With him to Richmond Crescent, Brown brought his economics adviser, Ed Balls, who first germinated the Bank plan in the Chancellor's mind. From Number 10, there was Moira Wallace, Private Secretary for Economic Affairs. The civil servant, unschooled in New Labour's ways of transacting major decisions, asked the Prime Minister: 'Would you like a detailed strategy paper?' Shrugging and turning to Brown, Blair asked: 'This is the right thing to do, isn't it?' Brown replied emphatically: 'Yes, it's the right thing to do.' The arguments were compelling. Here would be an early and large demonstration that Labour was serious about economic stability. It was also clever politically. A pre-election conversation with the Governor of America's independent bank, Alan Greenspan, had left Brown impressed that interest rates in the United States were not a source of political controversy. This led to another, highly tactical motive for giving Britain an independent central bank. The Bank would take responsibility for the increase in interest rates, probably a sharp series of them, which would be needed after the election. Also on Brown's mind was the thought that interest rate decisions had historically been the cause of conflict between inflation-wary Chancellors and popularity-bothered Prime Ministers.

Making the move quickly was essential, urged Brown: 'If we're going to do it, we've got to do it immediately.' To postpone would leave them in 'a position of weakness'. Delaying until later in the life of the government – Treasury civil servants had initially reacted by saying they needed a month to prepare – would expose them to the accusation that they had been forced into it because they weren't competent to run the economy. Brown showed Blair the letter he proposed to give to the Bank's Governor, the product of a frenzied weekend of work at the Treasury. To the credit of both the politicians and the officials involved, not a murmur of it leaked. When Blair agreed to Brown's plan to make the announcement that Tuesday, the Chancellor departed a satisfied man.

On Monday, however, a dispute blew up between them. Fearing that the Tories had relaxed the grip on inflation, as his last act in charge of interest rates, Brown wanted to accompany his Bank announcement with an increase of a half per cent. Blair – whose adviser on economics, Derek Scott, was worried that it would drive up the pound – was leery.[2] Was that really necessary? Why not – so Blair argued with Brown – leave the decision to the Bank once it had got its independence? It was also at the back of the Prime Minister's mind that putting up the mortgages of Middle Britain less than a week after he had been elected was not a strikingly popular curtain-raiser for his new government.

The plan had also brought Blair into another collision with the Cabinet Secretary about the centralist style of governing. Handing over control of monetary policy was, by any standards, a sensational step, and the more so because it had not been advertised in advance either to the electorate or anyone else in the Cabinet. When the Prime Minister allowed him into the secret, Sir Robin Butler was astounded to learn that Blair and Brown were planning to act without consulting any other ministers. The Cabinet would not meet until two days after the announcement. Butler suggested to Blair that his senior colleagues should surely be involved in such a momentous change. The Prime Minister was not interested in giving the Cabinet a vote. 'I'm sure they'll agree,' responded Blair. The Cabinet Secretary persisted: shouldn't the Cabinet at least be informed? 'They'll all agree,' repeated Blair, more emphatically. Butler made a final attempt to convince Blair to follow what Britain's most senior civil servant regarded as the constitutional proprieties. 'How do you know that the Cabinet will agree with the decision when it's still a secret?' Blair replied very simply: 'They will.'[3]

Blair knew his Cabinet better than Butler. Whatever doubts they had – and some harboured quite grave misgivings – no minister would dissent from the announcement. To semi-assuage Butler and to satisfy the *amour propre* of the Deputy Prime Minister and the Foreign Secretary, Blair told Brown that he should inform – not, mind you, consult – John Prescott and Robin Cook. The pattern of big decision-making in the Blair government – a duopoly, albeit an often volatile one, between Prime Minister and Chancellor – was set at the start.

Into the Treasury, Gordon Brown had imported his praetorian guard. Charlie Whelan was a beast apart from other merchants of spin. The teetotal Campbell ran on tea, and Mandelson irrigated himself with glasses of hot water and sliced lemon. Whelan liked a serious drink. He was more complicated than he looked. Though Whelan adopted an aggressively proletarian manner, his civil servant father had sent him to a Surrey boarding school and his mother was a Tory. He was, like Mandelson and a considerable number of the New Labourites, an ex-communist. Unlike most, Whelan had framed portraits of Marx and Lenin on the walls of his home, and a bookshelf lined with the collected speeches of Stalin. Whelan's iron hero now was Gordon Brown. The shy, socially awkward, disciplined Chancellor and his extrovert and indiscreet ruffian of propaganda were, in many ways, at the opposite ends of the poles of personality. That is why the relationship worked. Whelan filled a gap in Brown.

The Chancellor rarely took a decision without consulting Ed Balls. Behind the economics adviser's bland steel spectacles was an intellectually dextrous brain. Just in his thirties, Balls, who read PPE at Oxford and was a Kennedy scholar at Harvard, was impatient with the routines of meetings and minute-taking. Like Brown, he did not suffer fools, or anyone he took to be less clever than himself, gladly. Like Brown, he did not enjoy being disagreed with. Civil servants muttered that he was 'the deputy Chancellor'. The most mischievous officials regarded him as 'the real Chancellor'.

The third Brown musketeer, who exuded an air of gentle discretion which set him apart from the rest, was Ed Miliband, younger brother of David, the head of Blair's Policy Unit. The Brownites worked and played together, drank and ate together, often at the expense of the sugar-daddy of the Brown court, Geoffrey Robinson, the Paymaster-General. Genial and portly, Robinson had a guileless demeanour for a multi-millionaire. Worldly as he was in business, he gave the impression of being an innocent abroad in politics. He would draw a triangular diagram with himself as the connector between Blair and Brown. Such delusion of grandeur, which would be pompous in many other men, seemed to testify in this case to a simple naivety. He had buttered his generosity widely across the Labour Party, funding both research and recreation for its leaders and footsoldiers. Robinson's parties were famously lavish. New Labour; vintage champagne. The Paymaster's favours had been bestowed on Blair, who would spend part of that summer holiday at Robinson's villa set in a forty-five-acre estate in Tuscany. But he was now predominantly associated with the Chancellor. It was to Robinson's penthouse suite in the Grosvenor Park Hotel, overlooking Hyde Park, that Brown and his entourage would retreat. Steaks and pizzas, wine and beer from room service fuelled their plotting and scheming away from the ears of civil servants. It was there that Balls with Robinson had drawn up the first draft of the letter to the Governor of the Bank of England.

It was a beaming Eddie George who emerged from his audience at the Treasury with Gordon Brown on Bank Holiday Monday. He told Brown that he was 'delighted' with this 'wonderful news'. This was a 'historic moment' for the Bank to which George had been devoted all his working life. But his joy was not unconfined. The Chancellor had also revealed to George an intention to examine the Bank's powers of supervision over financial institutions and the management of government debt. George sought from Brown a promise that he would have the opportunity 'to argue the Bank's case' before a decision was made. The Governor left the meeting with a second letter, not to be published on Bank independence day, containing guarantees from Brown of consultation. Anxious to make sense of this extraordinary event, the Governor sought out his old friend at the Treasury, the Permanent Secretary, Sir Terry Burns. Burns reassured him that nothing was likely to happen about the Bank's other powers in the near future. It wasn't even clear whether there would be room for the legislation in New Labour's crowded programme.

Both men were seriously misreading the nature of the new Chancellor, and neither had grasped Brown's hidden agenda concerning them both. 'Gordon wanted an independent Bank of England,' says another senior minister. 'But he didn't want a Governor independent of Gordon Brown and Ed Balls.'[4]

The Chancellor, possessed of an almost pathological urge to be in control of everything and everyone around him, had long before determined to be rid of Eddie George, the stout, chain-smoking incumbent at Threadneedle Street. Balls had been present at a pre-election lunch in the House of Commons at which George had been fiercely critical of Kenneth Clarke's reluctance to raise interest rates. When this was reported back to him, Brown hardened in his conviction against George. 'If he attacks a Tory Chancellor like that, what's he going to do to us?'[5]

Tony Blair was aware of Brown's animosity, though not attuned to the scale and determination of it. When the Governor again angered Brown by criticising aspects of his policies in a pre-election interview, Blair dispatched Mandelson to give George a private friendly warning about the perils of provoking the wrath of Brown.[6]

'Eddie has to go,' Brown would fume in the intimacy of Robinson's penthouse, and he wanted Burns gone with him. A monetarist appointee of Thatcherite vintage, Burns was politically, economically and temperamentally uncongenial to Brown. The Chancellor and his acolytes would refer to the Governor and Permanent Secretary as 'The Manchester Mafia'.[7] A third man in their sights was an alumnus of Manchester Grammar School, the deputy at the Bank, Howard Davies. In his previous incarnation as Director-General of the CBI, Davies had sharply attacked some of Brown's policies, criticism which had never been forgotten by the new Chancellor, a man with an elephantine capacity for remembering slights. From their first day in office, the Hotel Group had marked the Manchester Mafia with the Brown spot.

The moment of combustion was delayed while the covert preparations for the Bank announcement were completed. On Tuesday, 6 May, speaking at a press conference the like of which had never before been organised at the Treasury, Gordon Brown revealed what he called his 'revolution at the Bank'. It was a demonstration, he declared, that this Labour government would not 'shrink from the tough decisions needed to deliver stability for long-term growth'.[8] The Prime Minister was not over-guilty of hyperbole when he described it as 'the biggest step in economic policy-making since World War Two'. Interest rates went up – Brown and Blair compromised over this – by a quarter of a per cent.

The City celebrated with spree-buying of shares, gilts and sterling. The FT-SE 100 soared to a new record, and the pound reached its highest level against the Deutschmark since sterling's ejection from the Exchange Rate Mechanism. Brown had sought the endorsement of every living predecessor as Chancellor, except one. He forgot John Major. For the most part, previous Chancellors hailed his decision. Expert and inexpert opinion agreed that Brown had pulled off an astonishing *coup de théâtre* and a strategic masterstroke. Praise flowed from the *Sun* – which reckoned it a 'brilliant bid to defy Lefties' – to the *Economist* – which accounted it 'an astonishingly bold start'. There were critics, of whom Ken Livingstone was the hardest, from the ranks of the left. The harshest commentator, Anatole Kaletsky, despaired to readers of *The Times* that Brown was 'locking the pound in a golden casket and throwing away the key'. Like Ramsay MacDonald's metallic Chancellor, Philip Snowden, Iron Gordon would be 'tested to destruction'.[9] It was a compliment to Brown – and graceful of Kaletsky – that two years later he would concede that 'opponents of bank independence, myself included, must feast on humble pie'.[10] Brown had been right.

The Chancellor might be releasing his control over interest rates, but he was also forcing Eddie George to share that power with a new Monetary Policy Committee of nine. The Chancellor rejected a proposal that membership of the MPC should be subject to confirmation by the House of Commons select committee on the Treasury. He was not relinquishing his power to select who did the setting. Though few remarked upon it at the time, he was also ominously silent about whether Eddie George would be reappointed as Governor when his term expired in 1998. As for the plan to strip the Bank of its supervisory powers, that remained a secret to a tiny number within Whitehall.

Two days later, the first Labour Cabinet in eighteen years met at Number 10. Photographs were taken; anecdotes swapped. Harriet Harman moaned about her civil servants. George Robertson entertained with a tale about getting lost in the corridors of the Ministry of Defence where he was challenged about his identity by a cleaner. Once his ministers had settled around the coffin-shaped table, Tony Blair let some of the air out of the self-congratulation. Of all the failings of past Labour governments, of all the reasons that not one had won two full terms in office, he and Brown were most haunted by being swamped by an economic calamity. This was the Banquo at their feast. Each previous Labour government had indulged in a spending splurge early in its life, lost the confidence of the markets, and then been impelled to slash and burn, greatly at the expense of their natural supporters, in the run-up to the next election. It was bad economics; it was atrocious politics. The 'prudence' which was Brown's favoured rhetorical squeeze ever had an electoral purpose.

Avoiding the fate suffered by past Labour governments formed the core of the lecture the Prime Minister delivered to this first Cabinet. If anyone around the table harboured any expectations that the size of their majority was a licence for a binge, the Prime Minister was going to disabuse them. They were going to strap themselves into the corset of the spending limits they had inherited from the Conservatives, even though the outgoing Chancellor, Kenneth Clarke, described them as 'eye-wateringly tight'. Jack Straw bumped into John Major in a Commons corridor a few weeks later. 'Why on earth are you sticking to our spending plans?' asked the former Tory Prime Minister. 'We would never have.' Straw replied: 'Yes, but you have more latitude than us.'

Proving their competence as governors was at a premium in their first months in office. It was vital not to do anything to scare the markets. That was the thrust of what Blair said at that first Cabinet. Ministers were to co-operate with the Chancellor. 'If anyone comes complaining to me about what Gordon is asking them to do in terms of their budgets, well you can just forget it.'[11]

How painful this was going to be was already troubling some ministers around the table. David Blunkett, the Education Secretary, told Brown – and the Chancellor did not warm to either message or messenger – that his department had to have more resources. The Health Secretary couldn't believe his luck, nor that it could last. Frank Dobson joked to colleagues: 'I went to talk to the nurses, said there was no money and everybody cheered.'[12] While they waited at Buckingham Palace to be sworn in as Privy Counsellors by the Queen, Brown had been buttonholed by George Robertson. Within two hours of his arrival at the department, the head of defence procurement, Sir Robert Walmsley, had come to his new secretary of state apologetically begging for an immediate cheque for £201 million to pay for the refit of the nuclear submarine HMS *Sceptre*. The Tories had put off a decision. It could no longer wait. Penalty payments would be incurred. Robertson told Brown of the request. 'Stop it,' rumbled the Chancellor. 'You should know where it's being refitted,' said Robertson. 'Where?' asked Brown. 'It's Rosyth, Gordon,' replied Robertson, not needing to explain that the naval base was in the Chancellor's own constituency. 'Oh,' Brown paused. 'All right, then.'[13]

The early challenge for the new rulers was to show that things could get better without spending more money. It was met by moving resources around, such as injecting cash from the scrapped assisted places' scheme into the drive to bring down primary school class sizes. There was a frenetic wave of announcements, high on symbolism and low on cost, from the restoration of trade union rights at GCHQ to the banning of handguns. As reviews and initiatives spewed forth from the machine, the cliché of the moment was that New Labour had 'hit the ground running'. It was a compliment to these novices to government that they started out with such a convincing display of energy and grip. An admiring Roy Jenkins observed: 'For the first three months, they took to the

ice and skimmed over it like highly skilled skaters.'[14] Only those
privy to the government's inner machinations could know how
thin that ice really was. 'There was really no proper co-ordination
of announcements,' one of the government's senior spinmeisters
confessed. 'I was amazed it didn't all fall apart on the first day.'[15]

A fortnight after the election, the Queen delivered Tony Blair's
speech from the throne in the House of Lords, her cut glass intoning
New Labourese: 'My government will govern for the whole
nation.'

What did the nation think of their government? The emperors
of Rome employed soothsayers to read the future from the guts of
chickens. The new master of Britain relied on the polling and focus
groups conducted by Philip Gould to dissect the mood of his
kingdom. Gould had worked in advertising before introducing
himself into New Labour's inner circle more than ten years previously. He wore his frizzy hair unfashionably long and could be
engagingly shambolic. On the day the election was called, he left
Labour's campaign plan at a Burger King in Euston station. The
son of a teacher, he had been brought up in the suburbs of Woking
and believed that Labour could be successful only by creating a
'middle-down coalition' which represented 'ordinary people with
suburban dreams'.[16] Gould's palmistry of public opinion tended to
be infected by his pessimism. Despite New Labour's smashing
victory, he believed, as did many of those close to Blair, that Britain
was basically a conservative country.

He reported to Blair a few days after the Queen's speech. Lurking
under the surface of a 'breathtaking' mood of public 'optimism',
Gould accurately detected New Labour's 'large strategic dilemma'.
They had been elected on 'a cautious programme but the size of
the mandate leads people to want bigger and bolder change. They
expect that a majority of 179 at the end of four years will mean the
education system, the NHS, crime and the state of society will
have radically improved.' Worse, a worrying proportion of his
samples had been led to believe that they could have all this for
nothing. 'Some people think that we pledged that we will not
touch any form of personal taxation.'[17]

The shadow between dreams of New Labour and the reality of government had been further darkened by a depressing prognosis from Brown once he and Balls had had a week to analyse Treasury papers. Brown told Blair that their first year in office was likely to be fine. After that, the economy would become 'difficult'. While the country was warming in the rays of its new government, the governors were already anxiously scanning the horizon for dark clouds. The first clap of thunder and crackle of lightning would hit Blair even earlier than anticipated. It came out of a Brown sky.

A fortnight after his first meeting with the Governor of the Bank, Gordon Brown summoned Eddie George for another audience. The surprise he now sprang on the Governor was an entirely unwelcome one. As they sat facing each other in his study at Number 11, Brown told a pole-axed George that the following day he would be announcing to MPs his plan to transfer the Bank's supervisory powers over financial institutions to a Securities and Investment Board. Legislative time had become available. The Chancellor had already settled on a chief for this 'super-SIB', as it would become known. The job had already been offered and accepted, once the Treasury had managed to track him down in Argentina, to Howard Davies. As a former head of the Audit Commission, among other qualifications, he had the right pedigree. His CV wasn't Brown's paramount consideration. By appointing Davies to the job, Brown would remove one of the Manchester Mafia from the Bank, and George would be deprived of an ally in resisting the Chancellor.

Brown had good cause. A series of scandals – from corruption at the Bank of Credit and Commerce International to the Maxwell pensions saga to the destruction of Barings Bank by a single rogue trader – had undermined confidence in the Bank's regulatory abilities. His presentation of this to George as a *fait accompli* was, however, brusque to the point of brutality. The Governor listened with reddening rage. George, a bridge-player, felt that Brown had been dealing from the bottom of the deck. The promises of consultation had been broken. He had been deceived. This, he told Brown, was 'a betrayal, an intolerable betrayal'.[18]

That anger was sharpened by humiliation. The Governor had given assurances to senior colleagues at the Bank about its future which Brown had now rendered worthless. It would look as though he had misled his own staff, five hundred of whose jobs were at stake.

As he was driven back to the City, George concluded that his position was untenable. He rang his private office back at the Bank. Between lungfuls of Rothmans cigarettes, he began to dictate a letter of resignation.[19] By the time his car had returned him to Threadneedle Street, George was still boiling, but the temperature of his anger had dropped sufficiently for him to first discuss what he should do with senior colleagues at the Bank, who were divided about whether he should resign, and his ally at the Treasury, Sir Terry Burns. The Permanent Secretary urged George not to take a knife to his veins until he had raised the alarm with Sir Robin Butler at Number 10. The news that Eddie George had been driven to the brink of resignation was rapidly conveyed to the Prime Minister. 'Jesus,' gasped Blair. 'What has Gordon done?' The resignation of the Governor of the Bank of England, barely a fortnight into the government's life, would ignite precisely the crisis with the City that he and Brown were supposed to be dedicated to avoiding at any cost. This would be catastrophic, thought Blair.[20]

He got hold of the Chancellor. The Prime Minister did not argue with the plan to remove the supervisory powers of the Bank, but the resignation of the Governor was far too high a price to pay for it. Blair told Brown: 'There will have to be a negotiation, Gordon.' The Prime Minister also made a personal call to George and – as one witness to this episode puts it – 'poured some balm on his wounds'.[21]

Brown never reacted well to being thwarted. This displeasure he expressed by delegating the task of the detailed bargaining with George to his deputy, the Chief Treasury Secretary, Alistair Darling. With Burns acting as the go-between, a concordat would eventually be negotiated which left the Bank with sufficient responsibilities for the overall stability of the financial system to satisfy Eddie George's honour and save his face at the Bank.[22]

Into Brown's statement to the Commons was inserted an unremarked upon – but to George, crucial – line making a public pledge of consultation with Threadneedle Street. Kenneth Clarke attacked the hastiness of the new order at the Treasury, likening them to 'eighteen-year-olds in the saloon bar trying every bottle on the shelves'.[23] George expressed some mild public criticism of the new mega-regulator, but attempted to play down rumours circulating in the City that he had been close to resignation. 'All sorts of things go through your mind,' he replied to a question about it, but the thought of resigning 'went away very quickly'.[24] For 'Steady Eddie' even to hint that he had been wobbling was enough to send a tremor through the markets.

Was this simply an exhibition of Brown's habitually insensitive approach to relationships? Or had the Chancellor deliberately set out to provoke into resignation a Governor he wanted to be rid of? There is no question, according to one confidant of Brown, that had George gone through with his resignation 'Gordon would have jumped at it'.[25] At the time, one anonymous ministerial associate gloated that the Governor had 'played into our hands'.[26]

When Darling presented the agreement he had come to with George for Brown's inspection, the Chancellor indicated his continuing fury by approving it with little more than a grunt. He was redoubled in his determination to prise out both the Governor and the Permanent Secretary. A campaign of destabilisation was under way against Eddie George. Candidates to replace him were regularly floated in the newspapers. The press speculation, often inspired and never discouraged by Brown's aides, centred on Gavyn Davies. He was a highly respected economist, a multi-millionaire and a partner of Goldman Sachs. More importantly, he was also the partner of Sue Nye, Brown's political secretary. At Whelan's instigation – he made exhaustive efforts to humanise the dour public image of his boss – Brown would even borrow their children to play Uncle Gordon at one of his Budget photo-opportunities. Such an intimate connection made appointing Gavyn Davies impossible without fatally compromising the Bank's independence in the eyes of the City. Brown and his closest aides were aware of that, though it is doubtful that they were frank with Sue Nye that her husband was simply being used. Davies was a useful stick with which to rattle the Governor. After several representations were made to the Prime Minister, Tony Blair finally confronted his Chancellor about the briefings against Eddie George and told him to put a stop to the campaign of poisoned whispers.[27]

He had just one problem with his next door neighbour – so ran Gordon Brown's party joke – and that was the nightly visits from David Blunkett and Jack Straw to make sure that the Blair kids were doing the compulsory homework ordered by the Education Secretary and obeying the Home Secretary's child curfew. This crack was based on a harmless fib. Brown rarely spent the night in Downing Street, preferring to sleep at his own small flat elsewhere in Westminster in Great Peter Street. Other legends that soon began to attach to the Chancellor were more than the confections of Charlie Whelan. His vast appetite for work was confirmed by a senior Conservative MP who, very early one morning, registered the astonishing sight, at least to this Tory, of Brown shambling from his flat to the Treasury in a baggy sweater with his papers bulging out of a plastic shopping bag.

Dressing down became a Brown trait. He delivered his speech to the Mansion House, spangled date in the City's calendar, wearing not the customary stiff collar and white tie, but a lounge suit. It personified a paradoxical truth about this government. The dress might break conventions; the speech contained all the orthodoxies that the City wanted to hear. Pledging the government to a stable economic framework, Brown said that the Governor would have to write him a letter explaining himself if the inflation target of 2.5 per cent was exceeded by 1 per cent, and further announced that he would enshrine in law the so-called 'golden rules' to chain down borrowing. Far from trying to wriggle free of the straitjacket, New Labour was binding itself in more tightly.

The idea of which Brown was deservedly most proud and

planned as the centrepiece of his first Budget was the New Deal, a brilliantly conceived device for demonstrating that New Labour could make a difference to the country without taxing the pocket of the voters. Before the cream could be skimmed off the utilities' profits, it was essential to ensure that the windfall levy was financially sound and immune from legal action, which was being openly threatened by British Telecom. Geoffrey Robinson organised the City accountants, Arthur Andersen, to crunch the numbers. Sympathetic City lawyers worked at making the levy legally fire-proof. 'Operation Autumn', as it was code-named, was the best example of the seriousness with which New Labour had worked through some of its plans for government.[28] When they were finally allowed to see the details, officials at the Treasury expressed themselves impressed. Here was New Labour's pre-election planning at its most productive. The windfall levy on the privatised utilities was that rare creature: a popular tax for a worthy aim. It would initially finance schemes to bring 250,000 of the young and long-term unemployed back into the economy. To Brown, the son of Kirkcaldy, work was duty, opportunity and fulfilment. As it should be, so he believed, for everyone else. Ever steeper penalties would be imposed on those who refused to participate in his schemes or take up his incentives to find employment.

The Chancellor's personal working habits were causing consternation within the Treasury. Paperwork is crucial in Whitehall; paperwork is power. The flow had dried up. Civil servants began to complain that, when it came to big decisions, they were being excluded: 'Brown plays his cards so close, they are stitched to his chest. The first thing he gives us is the press release.'[29]

Low intensity warfare between Brown's aides and Sir Terry Burns, an expression of the Chancellor's dislike of his Permanent Secretary, broke out. Burns raised a complaint about the size of the aides' salaries which went across to the Cabinet Office for resolution. A week after the election, Burns summoned Whelan to question him about the security form he had submitted. 'You've ticked the box saying that you haven't been involved in any subversive activities. Weren't you a member of the Communist Party?' Whelan retorted: 'Denis Healey was a member of the Communist Party, and he was Chancellor of the Exchequer, wasn't he?'[30]

The softly spoken, steel-haired Burns found it difficult to be treated as less than an equal to Ed Balls, someone nearly half his age. Balls struggled to mask his disdain for the Permanent Secretary.

Reports of the Chancellor's worsening relations with the official Treasury troubled Blair. The Prime Minister's greater complaint was that the newspapers seemed to know more about what would be in the Budget than he did. Blair's irritation spiked when the *Financial Times* carried a remarkably prescient report that the Chancellor was planning to abolish tax credits on dividends for pension funds and companies.[31]

'What the hell is going on? Where are these stories coming from?' Blair would demand in front of officials and aides with increasing regularity. 'Who is leaking all this stuff?'[32] Blair was surely protesting too much. He knew who guided the flow of information into the newspapers. The flying of kites, the softening up of victims, the bouncing of colleagues, the massaging of expectations, these were black arts that New Labour honed into a form of perfection. Apart from Blair's own team of Campbell and Mandelson, no one was more accomplished at media manipulation than Brown's outriders, Charlie Whelan and Ed Balls. Whelan, no expert in economics, painted with a broad bristle, dipped in highly coloured expletives. Journalists who needed bullying heard from him. Balls, a former leader writer on the *Financial Times*, was the man for the details. He guided the more cerebral end of journalism through more complicated issues. What is leaked by parties in Opposition rarely matters. A headline today, it is gone tomorrow. Government – and especially the Treasury – was a much more perilous environment in which to spin highly sensitive information on which fortunes might be made or lost. The postwar Labour Chancellor, Hugh Dalton, had been obliged to resign when he – quite inadvertently – revealed a relatively trivial Budget detail just an hour too early. Here was a growing cascade of leaks, weeks before the event, and going to the core of the Budget.

The Monday morning presentation meetings at Number 10 between the Prime Minister's men and the Chancellor's descended into acrimony. In one particularly ugly scene, Mandelson and Whelan slung accusations at each other about who had spun most of the Budget. Abrasion between Prime Minister and Chancellor increased. When Blair told Brown the leaks were coming out of the Treasury, Brown in turn labelled the leakers as Campbell and Mandelson. Neither would acknowledge to the other any responsibility by their own intimates. Between Prime Minister and Chancellor: deadlock. 'There was a complete impasse between Tony and Gordon.'[33]

Following another well-informed report in the *Financial Times* on the day of the Budget itself, Blair asked the Cabinet Secretary to conduct an unpublicised leak inquiry. Sir Robin Butler's first point of reference was naturally Sir Terry Burns. He and his officials, schooled in elaborate protocols to preserve Budget secrecy, were equally appalled. The Permanent Secretary reported his suspicions that the source was the Chancellor's own advisers. There was 'a good deal of circumstantial evidence' that the dividends story had come from Ed Balls.[34] When Butler brought this intelligence back to Blair, he used it to challenge Brown. If Blair calculated that this was killer ammunition against Brown's aides, the Prime Minister misfired.

Brown called Burns into his cavernous office at the Treasury. These leaks were 'terrible', he agreed. He, the Chancellor, had no idea who was responsible. If the Permanent Secretary could produce hard proof which would identify the culprits as Balls and Whelan, then he should bring it to him, and they would be sacked. Brown smiled. Circumstantial evidence was not enough. He could say this confident that Burns would find it impossible to gather conclusive proof that the source of the leaks was the Chancellor's own aides.

The relationship between the Chancellor and his highest official was becoming progressively more Antarctic. Brown saw him as a fifth columnist in his camp, and not just because of his friendship with Eddie George. According to another very senior official: 'Brown trusted Burns even less now because he thought that anything he told him would go straight back, through Butler, to Blair.'[35] This is an illuminating commentary on how very rapidly and how very early in the life of the government it was that the relationship between Number 10 and the Treasury deteriorated.

Fearful of that 'difficult' second year he had predicted to Blair, Brown wanted to use his Budget to raise additional revenue. The Chancellor's urge to gather cash in hand conflicted with the Prime Minister's reluctance to hazard the government's popularity. The married couples' allowance, a tax break for which the bachelor Brown could see no useful purpose, was in his crosshairs. So was mortgage tax relief. The value of the latter had been shaved down by the Conservatives, and there had long been a strong argument for abolishing it altogether. Blair told Brown he was nervous. He had just won an election during which he had said, offering an inadvertent hostage to fortune which annoyed Brown, that there would be no increases at all in personal taxation. He was also being told by Gould that abolition of mortgage tax relief played particularly unpopularly with his focus groups. Blair hesitated to offend the swing suburbanites of Middle Britain whom he had courted.

The married couples' allowance and mortgage tax relief would both be erased three years later, but the argument on this occasion concluded in Blair's favour. So the Prime Minister thought. Then, just as the Budget was due to go to the printers, Brown told Blair that a reduction in the value of mortgage tax relief by five pence in the pound was essential to the Budget arithmetic. 'They were always doing this to each other,' according to a well-placed civil servant. 'Always bouncing each other at the very last moment.'[36]

The July Budget gave expression to the emerging personality of New Labour as a government. The welfare-to-work programme had its critics, but no one argued that raising the skills and improving the prospects of the unemployed wasn't an important ambition. VAT on fuel was cut to 5 per cent, as promised. The pension funds squealed at the £5 billion a year milched by Brown, but he had been cunning in making revenue-raising changes in complex tax areas which the majority of voters would not, at least not immediately, comprehend. A 2 per cent cut in corporation tax – taking it down to the lowest ever rate – produced headlines designed to be friendly to enterprise. The International Monetary Fund, not an admirer of previous Labour governments, praised 'an excellent start . . . aiming to maintain stability and foster long-term growth while seeking fairness and developing human potential'.[37]

The cream topping to the Budget was unexpected additional cash for the most crucial public services. With surplus funds from the windfall levy, and by releasing money in the contingency reserve, Brown could announce an additional £1.2 billion for the health service and £2.3 billion for education. This surprise had been long planned. Brown and Blair had been told by Treasury officials before the election that extra money was available from the reserve. What they had not done was tell anyone else, not even the Shadow Cabinet, for fear that the Tories would use it to portray them as a party of big spenders. It is a commentary on the electoral restraints facing New Labour – or what they perceived them to be – that they hadn't dared tell the voters that they would be able to spend additional sums on hospitals and schools. The money was, in truth, a very modest increment for two public services which would demand much more in resources if New Labour was to fulfil the expectations of radical improvement in health and education. It was nevertheless a source of relief to Labour MPs that the corset of restraint had apparently been loosened, albeit only by a notch. Their order papers flapped with more than ritual enthusiasm as a grinning Prime Minister patted his Chancellor's arm with congratulations.

This breathless first three months of New Labour as a government had proved a lot to the country. It had also been instructive to Tony Blair. Gordon Brown was both his most creative – and potentially most destructive – partner in power.

# 4. Hail to the Chief

That beautiful spring day, the two men stood at the window, looking out on the small lawn at the back of Number 10. Sunglassed British and American journalists waited in ranks of chairs for the leaders to occupy twinned lecterns. The Union Jack and the Stars and Stripes rippled in a pleasant breeze. Tony Blair apologised to his guest that this was not quite the White House's rose garden, the flowery stage from which American Presidents are accustomed to performing alfresco.

Bill Clinton was glad of that. He had come, at the end of May, to escape a hostile Congress pursuing his lies about Monica Lewinsky by bathing in the warmth of his British younger cousin's election victory. For his part, Blair was happy to pay homage to the man who tutored New Labour in the acquisition of power. Blair and those around him had a fascination shading on the obsessional with the White House. Told by Clinton that there were more than a hundred interns at the disposal of the occupant of the Oval Office, Blair expressed open envy, though his interest was not of Clinton's carnal variety.

At a photo-opportunity with the Cabinet, Clinton expressed a reciprocating lust for Blair's majority of 179. He might be the leader of the world's only remaining superpower, but there are checks and restraints on an American President which are wholly absent in Britain. Within his own universe, no democratic leader is potentially more powerful than a British Prime Minister with a reliable parliamentary majority and an obedient Cabinet. In Britain's unwritten constitution a Prime Minister is *primus inter pares*, first among equals. Tony Blair recognised no equal in his Cabinet, and only his Chancellor was sufficiently strong to challenge that supremacy. This Prime Minister planned to be *primus*. From the beginning, it was designed to be a presidential premiership.

This caused an early ruction with the titular head of state. Buckingham Palace was angered that no one at Number 10 had seen fit to ask whether the American President might like to see the Queen, and court officials took the unusual step of ventilating their agitation through the newspapers.[1] There was no malevolence intended by Blair and his court: the Queen just hadn't occurred to them.

This was not the first occasion on which the monarch had been upstaged by the Prime Minister. On the day of the Queen's Speech, she and Prince Philip clattered up the Mall in the traditional gilded isolation of the Irish State Coach, escorted by the Household Cavalry. The media was much more seized by a wheeze dreamt up by the Keeper of the Premier Image, Alastair Campbell. He got Blair and Cherie to stroll round to parliament from Downing Street on foot, shaking hands with the crowds, symbolically contrasting the fustian monarchy with the thrusting new regime. It went unremarked that they took the car back. The stunt worked magnificently. In the afterglow of his election victory, Blair could win a eulogising media simply by demonstrating that he had the use of his legs.

This outward informality was intended to be taken only so far. Though he usually bowed to Campbell's advice about the media, the Prime Minister rebuked his press secretary for telling reporters that titles had been dispensed with around the Cabinet table and everyone was on Christian name terms. It was true, and Campbell had assumed that 'Call me Tony' struck an appropriately breezy note. For Blair, it was a diminishing act of *lèse majesté*.

The media was a willing accomplice to the weaving of a presidential aura. When it emerged that the Prime Minister desired more comfortable arrangements when flying abroad, this was reported as a plan to launch 'Blair Force One'. This was not an expression of personal vanity – Blair was almost wholly impregnable to flattery – but a deliberate political strategy. It sprang from a determination to repeat neither Labour's previous past indiscipline in government, nor the more recent history of the disintegration of John Major. 'There is one big difference,' he had taunted Major. 'I lead my

party. He follows his.'[2] What Blair had learned best from Margaret
Thatcher was the need for leaders to articulate to the country a
crystal sense of purpose and direction. Being seen to be dominant
was as important, perhaps more vital, than actually being in charge.
Blair's first call on Thatcher's private advice, when he invited her
round to Number 10 to talk man to man a month after his election,
would be far from the last. One of the pearls of Thatcherite wisdom
that Blair would often repeat to his aides was the dictum: 'Always
leave yourself a way out.'[3] As her own record had displayed, leaders
do not remain strong for long unless they are sane and shrewd
enough to appreciate when to flex.

She had warned him – as had Jim Callaghan – about the amount
of time consumed by Prime Minister's Question Time. The twice-
weekly quarter of an hour sessions were condensed into one half
hour session on a Wednesday. When this provoked an uproar about
Blair's contempt for parliament, Number 10 responded by hurriedly
launching a nationwide tour of monthly 'People's Question Times'.
These were abandoned and forgotten just as soon as the controversy
they were designed to douse had fizzled out.

Political opponents admitted to being impressed by his skills.
Michael Portillo, eyes emerald with envy, observed:

He's a consummate politician, brilliant at presentation, he has a wonderful
style. He has a real knack for putting his finger on what people are
thinking about and what they want to hear. He has gained control of his
party and offered leadership.[4]

Blair was openly contemptuous of the idea that the Cabinet was
an appropriate forum in which to make decisions. He derided 'the
old days of Labour governments where meetings occasionally went
on for two days and you had a show of hands at the end'.[5]

The Cabinet had already been given a preliminary lesson in its
marginality by being excluded from the Bank of England decision.
A joke became popular among ministers. Why does the tea trolley
serve only half the Cabinet? Because the meetings are over before
it can reach the other side. Cabinet meetings rarely lasted more than

forty-five minutes. That time was largely occupied with ministers reporting and the Prime Minister or the Chancellor pronouncing. The presence of Alastair Campbell, the first press secretary ever to be in regular attendance at Cabinet discussions, acted as both a restraint on debate and a deterrent against leaks. The emasculation of Cabinet government also flowed from Blair's nature. He was a man more interested in moods than in structures, preferring to settle business bilaterally with the relevant minister or in small, informal groups, rather than governing by committee. Senior civil servants recoiled at what they saw as a trampling on the time-tested conventions. Sir Robin Butler gently chided the Prime Minister about his habit of holding meetings without civil servants present to take a note, especially the bilaterals with Brown. 'That's the way Gordon likes to operate,' Blair told Butler with a shrug. It was also the way Blair liked to operate.

Two attempted Cabinet mutinies in the early life of the government were put down. One was about their own pay. Gordon Brown told his colleagues that, as an example to the country, they would not be getting the £16,000 a year pay increase proposed by the salaries review body. After all, reasoned Brown, they'd already had a large pay rise simply by becoming ministers. The hairshirt fitted the Son of the Manse. For the Prime Minister, with rent-free homes in London and the country and his wife's earnings as a Q C to draw on, this did not represent great hardship. 'It's all right for Tony, he hasn't got a fucking overdraft,' complained one of his Cabinet.[6] Around the Cabinet table, things were getting bitter. That aggravation increased in the autumn when Derry Irvine, the Lord Chancellor with already legendary tastes for luxury, declared that he would be taking his salary increase in full. Blair asked John Prescott to calm ministers down only to find his deputy returning to him in the role of the Cabinet's shop steward, a task the former seamen's leader threw himself into with characteristic bluntness. Ministers should be paid 'the rate for the job'. The pay freeze was 'gesture politics', Prescott told Blair, a remark calculated to hurt. It was one day's headlines, which would be forgotten tomorrow. When

Cabinet pay was capped again the following year, Prescott got personal: 'Look, Tony. You've got a wife who earns a quarter of a million a year. I've got a wife who spends a quarter of a million a year.'[7] Blair, while making sympathetic noises about his colleagues, told Prescott that he was between 'a rock and a hard place'. He could not countermand the Chancellor: an illustration of how Blair sometimes hid behind Brown. The Cabinet – realising that their own remuneration was unlikely to be a cause to inspire a popular uprising against Blair and Brown – grudgingly swallowed the salary freeze.

The other, equally abortive Cabinet revolt was against the Millennium Dome. Blair was in a state of procrastination for weeks about whether to continue with the mammoth plastic marquee in Greenwich inherited from the Conservative government. One of the advantages of a presidential seal is that it can serve to conceal the fact that the Prime Minister is actually in a terrible pother. Though he was instinctively warm to the idea of making a big statement to mark the year 2000, all the information he had to work on suggested to Blair that the Dome threatened to be a flop. Peter Mandelson was the lonely but influential proselytiser for the Dome. For the grandson of Herbert Morrison, who had organised the 1951 Festival of Britain, there was an ancestral impulse for the project. It would also give Mandelson the opportunity to come out of the dark and play the impresario; to add substance to his reputation for shadowiness. Gordon Brown was as passionately opposed, and not just because the Dome was being promoted by Mandelson. Scornful of the entire phenomenon known as 'Cool Britannia', the Chancellor envisaged an expensive folly. Should it fulfil his expectations of failure, he worried that the Treasury would pick up the bill.

With less than a week to go before the deadline for commencement of building, Blair had yet to make a decision. Early on the morning of Thursday 19 June he asked Mandelson up to his Downing Street flat to take another tour around the arguments. As the Prime Minister finished dressing, he totted up his anxieties. The costings were dubious; the sponsorship was absent; the contents were vague when not non-existent. The newspapers – from the

*Sun* to the *Financial Times* – were hostile. Downstairs, Blair and Mandelson were joined by Jonathan Powell, Alastair Campbell and members of the Policy Unit. Mandelson, as he had done before, played to the side of Blair he knew to be attracted by the potential glamour and modernity of the Dome. It would be the largest and most impressive celebration in the world, symbolising the rebirth of a creative and dynamic Britain under New Labour. But what – the Prime Minister kept nagging – if it were a costly failure? They could not be sure what the mood of the country might be like in January 2000. People might ask: 'Why are they spending all this money on that Dome instead of schools and hospitals?' Mandelson had not succeeded in quelling these anxieties by the time Blair was overdue for his weekly pre-Cabinet meeting with John Prescott.

'Bring him in,' said Blair. 'Let's see what Presco says.' Prescott now played the doubly unlikely role of friend to a quintessentially New Labour project and ally of Peter Mandelson. Though initially a sceptic about the Dome, he had been converted to the notion that the revival of a disused gas site on the Greenwich peninsula would be a large statement of his own beliefs in regeneration. Prescott had an under appreciated liking for the *grand projet*.

'I don't know what to do about this Dome,' Blair told his deputy. 'Throw in the towel?' replied Prescott. 'You think we should go ahead?' asked Blair, slightly taken aback by his deputy's reaction. Prescott: 'I do. If we can't make this work, what will people say? They'll say we're not much of a government.' 'OK,' said Blair to the relief of Mandelson. 'That's that, then.'

Not quite it wasn't. Chris Smith, the Culture Secretary and a Dome-sceptic, joined them, along with the Dome-phobe Chancellor. Gordon Brown wouldn't break openly with Blair in front of the Cabinet, but the price of his acquiescence was an absolute guarantee that it cost the Treasury nothing. When the Cabinet gathered at ten thirty that morning, Blair presented the case for committing to the Dome to his colleagues. His own anxieties not entirely conquered, Blair said to Mandelson afterwards that he did not think he made a convincing evangelist for the Dome. When he left Cabinet early, for a memorial service at St Margaret's in

Westminster, Prescott chaired the ensuing discussion. This was a new experience for everyone around the Cabinet table and, for Prescott, a bruising one. Of the senior figures present, only Jack Straw, the Home Secretary, was greatly warm to the Dome on the basis that he had fond memories of his pride at being British when his parents had taken him to the 1951 Festival. Vehemently antagonistic were Frank Dobson and David Blunkett who asked why a cash-tight government was spending towards £1 billion on this giant tent instead of public services. The Dome should be 'fired into outer space', said Dobson. Clare Short, a Birmingham MP, articulated the views of a sizeable faction of the Cabinet which did not want the celebrations so centred on London. As other hostile voices piled in, Prescott was reduced to pleading 'Tony wants it'. He dared not risk taking it to a vote. Had he done so, it would certainly have been lost. The Deputy Prime Minister concluded this unusually vigorous outbreak of Cabinet debate by telling them: 'I will have to talk to Tony.'[8]

When the news was conveyed to Blair that a large majority of his Cabinet were fiercely against the Dome, his response was to ignore them. That afternoon, Blair, urged on by Mandelson, summoned Prescott and Smith to join him on the Greenwich construction site where he announced that work would begin with the declaration: 'These plans require a leap of faith.' It was a leap that he had dithered over, but once he had made it he would throw himself behind the project with Messianic enthusiasm. The agnostics and doubters were overridden, even though they formed the majority of his Cabinet, the media and the public. The Dome was commissioned without any further discussion among his ministers who believed to complain about it would succeed in doing nothing except aggravate the Prime Minister.

The personal frailties of his colleagues worked to Blair's advantage in fashioning a presidential premiership. As much as he had admired Robin Cook's ferocious destruction of the Tories in Opposition, so Blair feared his capacity to make waves as the spokesman for a more radically leftist approach to government. When turbulence did begin to swirl around Cook it was not political, it was personal. On the morning of Friday 1 August Alastair Campbell was contacted by the *News of the World* to be told that the newspaper which had debagged a sequence of Tories was planning to expose the Foreign Secretary's affair with his assistant, Gaynor Regan. This was not an exclusive to Campbell, nor to Blair. They both knew about the affair well before the election, and had been relieved that it had been kept quiet until after they had won. To compound the hideousness of the situation, Cook was at Heathrow airport with his wife, en route to a riding holiday in Colorado, when Campbell phoned to warn him of the impending story. 'You're in the shit,' the Foreign Secretary was told by Campbell. 'But I can buy you a few hours.' Only, however, as long as he fell in with the deal Number 10 had struck with the newspaper. The tabloid would not pursue Cook, his wife or Regan in return for a statement. The way to close down the story rapidly, Campbell continued, would be for Cook to speak with 'clarity' about his intentions towards the two women in his life. 'We need a decision,' said Campbell. 'I understand,' Cook replied into his car phone, the usually eloquent Foreign Secretary virtually dried up by his situation. Campbell had not been so crude as to issue him with an explicit ultimatum to choose between his wife and his mistress. He did not need to do so. Cook was a clever man, and it hardly required the skills of GCHQ to decode what the press secretary was telling him to do. Though Campbell would take fierce criticism for presuming to advise a Cabinet minister to dump his wife, Cook privately expressed himself grateful that he had been forced to make a decision over which he had prevaricated for too long. He took Margaret into the VIP lounge at Terminal Four to tell her that the holiday was terminating there. So was their marriage.

Then Cook took a call from Blair. At the end of it, Margaret asked: 'He wants you to resign?' 'No,' the Foreign Secretary replied. 'I shan't lose my job.'[9] Cook returned to London and, on Saturday night, made a brief statement, taking upon himself the blame for the break-up and announcing that he was leaving his wife for his secretary. Sunday's *News of the World*, followed by the rest of the media, salivated over the first sex story to engulf the new government. That a political marriage had broken down was neither novel nor necessarily damaging. Cook, who had no record as a moralist on family values, could not fairly be accused of hypocrisy. Nor did it come as a blinding revelation that politicians have affairs with their secretaries, even if the physiognomically challenged Foreign Secretary had not been on many people's A list of New Labour Lotharios. The undressing of a public figure's private life is inevitably diminishing. Cook was made to look particularly ridiculous by the photographs of the elaborate routines he had employed, involving moving rubbish sacks and feeding parking meters, in his futile attempt to keep the affair secret.

This was a sweet-and-sour episode for Downing Street. The new government had proved no more immune than the old one to the ravenous media interest in the sex lives of politicians. An attempt by Blair to placate the embittered Margaret Cook went wrong when she reacted badly to a handwritten note from him which she read as being more concerned with the media frenzy than the collapse of her marriage. Within forty-eight hours, Peter Mandelson had been dispatched to Edinburgh to deploy his feline charms to persuade her not to hiss-and-tell. His considerable efforts were unrewarded by success, and the discarded Margaret would inflict upon Cook months of damaging publicity. The upside for Blair was that the stature of Cook was diminished, and with it any capacity to cause trouble. A potential focus of opposition within the Cabinet became so dependent on the goodwill of the Prime Minister that he would soon be delivering a speech written by Number 10 in slavish adherence to Blair's Third Way.

Just as their weaknesses tended to serve the establishment of Blair's dominance, so too did the hatreds between his colleagues. However much they might privately seethe about the power of Downing Street, the Prime Minister could be reasonably confident that his colleagues loathed each other more than they ever would him. During his August holiday in Tuscany and south-west France, the public faces of the government were the always potentially explosive combination of Mandelson and Prescott. The alliance over the Dome was fleeting. In the absence of the emperor, and with vague instructions from him about their division of responsibilities, the two satraps squabbled over which of them was in charge. Prescott got the better of it. Visiting Greenwich to survey plans for flood defences to protect the Dome site, the Deputy Prime Minister chanced upon a specimen jar containing a Chinese mitten crab. Christening the crab Peter, he proceeded to strike up a surreal conversation with the bottled crustacean. 'Me and my mate Peter. Do you think you will get on the executive, Peter?' Afterwards, Prescott rang Mandelson to semi-apologise that his little joke might get bigger headlines than he had intended. The truth was he knew exactly what he was doing. Prescott was angered by newspaper reports suggesting that he was supporting Mandelson's bid for election to the National Executive Committee, stories which Prescott not unreasonably assumed were planted by Mandelson himself. Prescott wounded with intent.

The Prime Minister returned home from his summer holiday to headlines about 'Labour's Awful August'. Conceding that the government had taken a 'mild kicking' and urging everyone to concentrate on the 'big picture', that last weekend of August he took his family up to Sedgefield. These squalls irritated Blair, but they also flattered him. It was widely remarked how rapidly things fell apart in his absence. His aides told him that the worse the rest of the Cabinet did, the better he looked. What no one could anticipate was the event which would be the most transforming moment in the making of the Blair presidency.

The lights had been switched off early at Myrobella on the night of Saturday 30 August. The Prime Minister and his wife both felt the need of a good sleep. He went to his bed not knowing that he would spend barely two hours in it. Shortly after one in the morning, Blair was woken by the bedside phone. Angus Lapsley, the Downing Street official on call over the weekend, briskly reported a communication from the British embassy in Paris via the Number 10 duty clerk. There had been a car crash involving the Princess of Wales. Details were sketchy at this stage, but it was

believed that her summer lover, Dodi Al-Fayed, was dead. Diana
was thought to be seriously injured.

Blair woke his wife: 'There's been a car crash. Diana's been
hurt.' There is nothing that prepares a Prime Minister for an event
like this. 'God. How could this happen?' He would repeat the same
or similar phrases again and again in the small hours. As Blair hauled
on tracksuit bottoms and a T-shirt, he began to engage his mind
with this completely unanticipated emergency. The phones were
patched together so that he could take a conference call with
Lapsley and Alastair Campbell. Blair was beginning to grasp what
he was likely to be dealing with. He said to Cherie and to his aides:
'If Dodi is dead, then Diana is dead.'[10]

Blair received confirmation that his expectation was correct at
around two in the morning. Diana had been killed. By now,
Campbell's home phones were ringing so dementedly that he had
dashed round his house in North London unplugging them all. He
used a mobile whose number was known to very few people to
communicate with Blair in Sedgefield. Both men, who had come
to know Diana reasonably well, were shell-shocked by the enormity
of this event. As they talked, there were long stunned silences,
punctuated by expletives of incredulity. Blair said: 'God. This is
unbelievable.' Campbell: 'Fuckin' hell. Just unbelievable.' Silence.
Campbell: 'Fuckin' hell. What do we do with this?' Blair: 'God.
This is big.' Campbell: 'It's too big. It's just too big a story.' Blair:
'This will produce grief on a scale that is hard to imagine, that
we've never seen.' With the rest of the government machine
dormant, only their own creative resources to draw on, the two
men worked on a response to the death. Blair intuitively sensed
that, despite some of the less savoury publicity that had accompanied
Diana's cavortings across the Mediterranean with Dodi, a massive
wave of emotion was about to break over Britain. He paced round
his study in Myrobella, sipping from a mug of tea, scribbling down
thoughts, and phrases that might express them, on bits of paper.

A legend would grow that Blair spent the entire night rehearsing
the script that he would deliver the next morning. In fact, he only
finished writing down his tribute to Diana twenty minutes before

he uttered the words. In the early hours, he was in considerable anguish about what to say, how to say it, and undecided at this point whether he should even say anything at all. 'Is it appropriate? Is it my place to say anything?' he asked Cherie and Campbell.

As light broke over Myrobella, Blair was arriving at an answer. 'I've got to say something. People are going to have to make sense of this. I've got to try and articulate what people will be thinking and feeling.' What finally convinced him was a breakfast conversation with the Queen who told the Prime Minister that none of the royals was planning to say anything at all. Campbell, the man with the tabloid touch, supplied the phrase 'People's Princess'. Blair was still composing the rest of his thoughts as he watched some television where the schedules had been cleared for continuous news. A rotating cast of politicians issuing mechanical tributes, historians groping for precedents and commentators delivering foggy predictions of the consequences were already exhausting their capacity to find something novel to say by the time the Blairs set off for Trimdon parish church.

Just after ten, all the television channels switched to the outside broadcast cameras that had been scrambled to Sedgefield to record the Blair family arriving in their people carrier. Wearing a dark suit along with a black tie and cufflinks that he'd borrowed in a hurry from local party activists, Blair stood before St Mary Magdalene and delivered his encomium to the dead Princess.

I feel, like everyone else in this country today, utterly devastated. Our thoughts and prayers are with Princess Diana's family – in particular, her two sons, her two boys – our hearts go out to them. We are today a nation in a state of shock, in mourning, in grief that is so deeply painful for us.[11]

It is the outstanding example of Blair's ability to entwine emotional vernacular ('utterly devastated', 'our hearts go out to them') with formal, ceremonial expressions of regret ('we are today a nation in mourning'). He imported his reaction as a normal person – 'like everyone else' as he put it – into his role as Prime Minister.[12] It

made him sound both less of a politician, and more of a politician.
He went on:

She was a wonderful and a warm human being, although her own life
was often sadly touched by tragedy. She touched the lives of so many
others in Britain and throughout the world with joy and with comfort.

The American networks and satellite channels had joined the coverage to broadcast Blair around the globe.

How many times shall we remember her in how many different ways,
with the sick, the dying, with children, with the needy? With just a look
or a gesture that spoke so much more than words, she would reveal to all
of us the depth of her compassion and her humanity.

Lips pursed, fingers arching together into a cathedral roof, his voice
apparently on the edge of breaking, the performance worked up
to the climax by which it would be most remembered. 'People
everywhere, not just here in Britain, kept faith with Princess Diana.
They liked her, they loved her, they regarded her as one of the
people. She was . . .' – here a swallowing pause for effect – '. . . the
People's Princess and that is how she will stay, how she will remain
in our hearts and our memories for ever.'

    The moment confirmed Tony Blair as the consummate political
actor of his age. Those who criticised it for being an act missed the
point. All successful modern politicians have – or acquire – thespian
talent. Blair instantly and accurately divined what the country – or
at least a large proportion of its people – needed to hear. It proved
that his own instincts were often his most reliable focus group. He
defined public sentiment and by doing so surfed and channelled
the emotion that was washing across much of Britain.

    There were those who thought the performance merely
exhibited Blair's genius for goo. It was the sort of 'touchy-feely
stuff' that Gordon Brown groaned: 'I can't bear.'[13] One of Blair's
closest aides was queasy. Tim Allan, the deputy press secretary, was
spending the weekend playing golf in Scotland. He went into a

newsagent to buy the papers and found himself watching Blair on the shopkeeper's television. Allan thought his master had gone several degrees too far over the top. He adjusted that opinion when he turned to the shopkeeper to find she was crying.

'The People's Princess' rapidly eclipsed 'The Queen of Hearts' as the newspapers' favoured epitaph and the dedication of choice among the mourners mounding cards and flowers at the gates of Buckingham and Kensington Palaces. There was an inescapable irony in posthumously rebranding the daughter of an earl who was divorced from a Prince as a Princess of the People. Yet when the Tories muttered that it was a brazen attempt to hijack her memory for the self-styled 'People's Prime Minister', it was they who were accused of tastelessness. Blair, with the assistance of Campbell, had reached, in an emergency, for formulations that served them well in the past. The calculated politics would come later, in his party conference speech in the autumn when, to significantly much less effect, Blair would claim Diana as the patron saint of a 'Giving Age', a phrase that shrivelled into nothing after a day.

On that Sunday morning, he distilled the feelings of a large part of the nation in a way achieved by no one else. The anger of Tories was an expression of how remote and alien they felt in Blair's Britain. One former member of John Major's Cabinet confided: 'I walked through the crowds in St James's and realised that this was no longer a country I truly understand.'[14] Another Tory floundering in the sea of emoting was William Hague. The Conservatives' new leader spoke of Diana as 'a unique and very lively and attractive individual'.[15] He made Diana's death sound like the loss of a fondly regarded envelope-licker in his constituency association. The starkest contrast was with the House of Windsor, summering in the tweedy, salmon-fishing isolation of Balmoral. When a frozen-faced royal family were driven to their local church that Sunday morning, the prelate was instructed to make no mention of Diana. Even in the face of tragedy, it was royal business as usual. At Buckingham Palace, the Changing of the Guard carried on. At noon the Royal Regiment of Wales marched out of the gates, followed by their regimental goat.[16] On her death, the House of Windsor seemed to be making no concessions to the woman whom, in life, they had stripped of the title Royal Highness.

Blair was flown south to RAF Northolt that afternoon to join the party that would receive Diana's body back from France. He was ushered into the airfield's VIP suite where there were already gathered court officials headed by the Earl of Airlie, old Etonian, merchant banker, Scottish grandee and, for fifteen years, Lord Chamberlain. Casting his eye over Airlie and the rest of the royal panjandrums, Blair were suddenly struck by the thought: 'In this room are all the people who hated her.'[17] They were also the people who were supposed to be in charge of producing a funeral which would rise to the expectations of the people. 'This is going to be a very, very difficult funeral,' Airlie said to Blair. If the Queen or the Queen Mother had died 'then we would know what to do'.[18] As it was, they evidently didn't have much of a clue. Blair joined the line of dignitaries on the flat, grey tarmac as Diana's coffin, draped in the Royal Standard, was carried off the RAF plane by the Queen's Colour Squadron and placed in a hearse. Exchanging a few words with Prince Charles, he grasped both royal hands in a double handshake. By now, Blair was trying to plot how he would cross the minefield of public emotion and royal protocol. Manoeuvring the royals towards Downing Street's conception of how the mourning should be conducted, by Sunday evening Campbell was telling the media that Blair wanted a funeral that allowed 'the people to show the nation's gratitude to Princess Diana'.

He and his aides had to manage the politics of the royal family, an area in which their collective experience was indistinguishable from zero. As Diana's coffin was placed in the Chapel Royal at St James's Palace, Downing Street attempted to navigate the differences between the estranged royal houses over the funeral arrangements. Blair determined that these highly sensitive negotiations should be entrusted not to civil servants, but to his intimates at Number 10. Alastair Campbell and Anji Hunter were appointed his representatives along with Hilary Coffman, who had been involved in organising John Smith's funeral. At nine o'clock on Monday morning, they went to their first meeting with royal officials, chaired by the Earl of Airlie in a first-floor room at the Palace overlooking the gates and fountain. It soon became apparent to the Downing Street contingent that they were dealing with a factionalised royal family. Three agendas were represented around the table: 'There was BP, JP and KP.'[19] The Buckingham Palace agenda was to protect the monarchy as an institution. The St James's Palace agenda was to bodyguard the reputation of Prince Charles. The Kensington Palace agenda was to burnish the memory of Diana. The Queen's officials made it evident that Her Majesty would not countenance a full state funeral for her deceased former daughter-in-law. This honour had only previously been afforded to three people who had not been members of the royal family, and Diana had divorced herself from it. This was not a particular concern for Downing Street, which was much more interested in its concept of a 'people's funeral'. When the Blair team suggested that it would be sensible media politics to include newspaper editors among those invited to the funeral, one of the royal officials erupted. 'Why?' she heaved with disgust. 'We don't want bloody journalists.'

Cowed only briefly by accusations that their intrusive methods had been accessories to the death, the tabloids were now howling for the Windsors to show themselves. The press was both following the crowd and rousing the mob. The Palace switchboard became jammed with members of the public shouting obscenities at whichever hapless official happened to be on the receiving end. The walk along the Mall from Downing Street to Buckingham Palace took Campbell and Hunter past the mounds of flowers, cards and soft toys, and the tumultous crowds of mourners and gawpers. By midweek, they could taste the bitterness in the air about the House of Windsor. 'It's getting nasty,' Hunter reported to Blair. Campbell, typically, adopted a soccer metaphor: 'You know how it is when you're coming out of a football match and your side has lost. There's an ugly mood about the place.' Blair agreed: 'It's out of control. It's going to go horribly wrong.' This threatened, he feared, to turn into something the country would be ashamed of afterwards. Blair's phone calls to Balmoral attempting to gently persuade the royal family to make themselves more visible had so far failed. A siege mentality enveloped the Windsors. Prince Charles, the focus of most of the public anger, was concerned that the mood would turn even more hostile if the royals suddenly made a show of emotion about Diana. Wouldn't he – Charles worried to Blair – then be attacked as a hypocrite?[20] The House of Windsor appeared to be staying put in Scotland.

Blair concluded: 'If they won't take a grip on it, we'll have to.' Campbell suggested: 'You'd better do a clip.' On Wednesday, Blair came out on to Downing Street to plead for understanding for the royals' wish to grieve in privacy before substituting himself for them with a walkabout among some grievers who had gathered at the gates of Number 10.

That evening, Blair went into his study to communicate again with Balmoral. The conversations between Prime Minister and Queen were awkward and not especially productive. 'Is there anything we can do?' he asked, reluctant to spell out directly what he and his aides believed had to be done. There was not much natural empathy between them. A gulf of attitudes and generations divided monarch and Prime Minister. His populist, classless style had few touching points with the world of the Windsors. Cherie, a quite passionate republican, had complained to her husband that she knew exactly how Diana must have felt after being treated coldly when they had visited Balmoral earlier in August. Even if the Queen was open to being advised directly by the Prime Minister, Blair was not as robust with her as he would have been with anyone else.

Blair's conversations with Charles were easier and more direct. Labelled the murderer who had martyred her by the more hysterical Dianists, the heir to the throne felt in mounting jeopardy. Blair found he was winning the argument when he urged the Prince that the royal family had to come out of seclusion.

When Campbell displayed for Blair the Thursday morning headlines, it confirmed both men in the view that the clamour had to be answered. 'SHOW US YOU CARE', demanded the *Express*. 'YOUR PEOPLE ARE SUFFERING – SPEAK TO US MA'AM', screamed the *Mirror*. 'WHERE IS OUR QUEEN? WHERE IS HER

FLAG?', bellowed the *Sun*. 'LET THE FLAG FLY AT HALF-MAST',
thundered the *Daily Mail* with inside features asking 'Has the House
of Windsor got a heart?'

The flag caught even the impresarios of symbolism at Number
10 by surprise. Across the country, from government buildings to
scout huts, Union Jacks flew at half-mast to salute Diana. Everywhere, that was, except over Buckingham Palace. The Queen's
flagpole was bare. Blair and his aides were initially oblivious to how
this would swell the growing hate of the Windsors. They accepted
the arguments of Sir Robin Fellowes, the Queen's Principal Private
Secretary, that the Royal Standard flew over the Palace only when
Her Majesty was in residence. Fellowes was indignant at the idea
of the royal family being bullied into submission, but he was also
alive to the twin dangers of public revulsion against the House of
Windsor and of a visible gap opening between a popular government and an unpopular monarchy.

On Thursday morning, Fellowes rang Blair with the result of
the Windsors' own debates at Balmoral. They were ending their
internal exile. As one mark of this abrupt change, the Union Jack
would fly at half-mast from Buckingham Palace. Princes Andrew
and Edward would walk down the Mall to test the reaction of the
crowd. That going well, Charles and his sons would meet those
paying homage outside Kensington Palace. The Queen, Blair was
told, 'is thinking of doing a broadcast'.

This news was greeted with relief in Downing Street mixed with
a fresh anxiety. A great deal of concern centred around what the
Queen would say and how she would say it. Impromptu broadcasts
were not familiar territory for a monarch who was accustomed to
the security of recording her Christmas addresses to the nation
some weeks in advance. The Queen was originally to record
the broadcast at 4 p.m. for later transmission. When Blair's aides
suggested that, for maximum effectiveness, the broadcast should be
live into the six o'clock news bulletins, they were first told 'the
Queen does not do live'. Number 10 won that argument with the
Palace only to be dismayed again when, on Friday morning, court
officials sent over a copy of the proposed text. The accusation

against the Windsors, and it was not an entirely unfounded one, was that what feelings they had for Diana were venomous. It was widely suggested that they were even secretly pleased that the turbulent Princess was dead. The chilly, impersonal tone of much of the initial draft of the Queen's broadcast threatened to reinforce that charge. Campbell went to work on her words. It would not be possible to cajole the Queen into expressing her 'love' for Diana. But several humanising phrases coined by Campbell – including 'speaking as a grandmother' – were successfully inserted by the Press Secretary.[21]

On Friday evening, speaking from the room where the funeral negotiations had taken place, with the crowds visible behind her through the window, the Queen delivered the script to camera. It was a broadcasting first: the monarch live on every TV and radio channel. There was a humbled tone to the address. She dropped the royal we. 'I for one believe that there are lessons to be drawn from Diana's life and from the extraordinary and moving reaction to her death.'[22]

The trick of injecting the Queen live into the top of the six o'clock news bulletins worked as it was intended to do. Jennie Bond, the BBC's court correspondent, instantly pronounced on its success, a view which became the accepted wisdom. In truth, and perhaps to her credit, the Queen would never get an Equity card. She gave little impression of being grief-stricken by the loss of Diana, and offered a truer measure of her feelings in her next Christmas broadcast when she dwelt longer on her sorrow at the decommissioning of the royal yacht than she did on the loss of the mother of her grandchildren. What was achieved by the Queen's broadcast on that critical Friday was a dissipation of the hostility to the Winsdors.

It might be an exaggeration to say that Number 10 had coaxed and coached the monarchy to save itself. What, in a Disraelian manner, Blair and his aides had done was guide the royals to safety at what looked like a highly perilous hour for them. The mass of flowers gave bloom to many varieties of theories about the meaning of the moment. Martin Jacques hailed 'the Floral Revolution' as a triumph for 'modern values . . . honesty, informality, humour, meritocracy, the personal . . . vulnerability, the casual, the female'.[23] Others quailed before what they saw as floral fascism and an explosion of almost medieval irrationality. As Ian Jack put it in *Granta*: 'September was not a good month for those who imagined that human society is . . . governed by reason.' The sociology of it did not much interest Blair. He held to a thoroughly managerial view. It was a crisis which had to be moved to a consensually safe outcome.

The paradox was that he headed the most anti-monarchical government Britain has ever had. John Prescott, on a visit to Chequers, took huge delight in swinging the sword of Oliver Cromwell, a warts-and-all republican like himself. The majority of the Cabinet were republicans, albeit most of them closet ones. Campbell, a republican also, would laugh out loud listening to Blair trying to reconcile his dynamic, meritocratic New Britain with a hereditary monarchy of Old Hanoverian extraction.

Some of this contradiction was expressed in the funeral on the Saturday. The great of the Establishment and celebrity, salted with a selection of good 'ordinary people', gathered in Westminster Abbey to hear Elton John recompose a song originally memorialising a dead American film star and the Earl of Spencer offer himself as the voice of the people.

Many of the claims made for this event would, with hindsight, come to look grossly overblown. Aspects of those days touched upon insanity when some grievers claimed to have seen visions of Diana the Martyr. But the hysteria proved to be a passing spasm. Not all of the nation mourned and many of the tears dried with startling rapidity. Television executives and newspaper editors would be surprised a year later by the low level of public interest in the programmes and supplements prepared for the anniversary. Republicans were disappointed in their hopes that this tolled the bell on the monarchy. Nor were the royals conspicuously modernised in the aftermath of the death; their public relations simply became a little more adept. The Queen visited a pub and Prince Charles posed with the Spice Girls. Buckingham Palace was acquiring some of the spin-doctoring skills of New Labour.

Blair supported the continued existence of the monarchy, not because he had any sentimental attachment to it, but for reasons which were entirely pragmatic. He could think of nothing better to put in its place. The crown provided a cover of stability when so much of the rest of the constitution was in upheaval.

Moreover, the monarchy might be exploited to the advantage of New Labour. At a risibly entitled 'People's Lunch' in November to mark Elizabeth and Philip's golden wedding anniversary, John Prescott was drolly seated beside the Queen Mother. The Queen presented herself as a student, albeit a reluctant one, of New Labour populism. The royal family, she said, could not ignore public opinion any longer: 'Read it we must.' Blair, taking a higher profile in the proceedings than desired by some court officials, used his speech to ladle flattery on the Queen, not so much with a trowel as a dumper truck. 'I am as proud as proud can be to be your Prime Minister today, offering this tribute on behalf of the country. You are our Queen. We respect and cherish you. You are simply the best of British.'[24] Drowning her in this treacle, Blair had studiedly ignored an imprecation from the Queen not to be 'too effusive'. If her advisers feared that Blair's eager and lavish demonstrations of support were diminishing of the monarchy's independence, they were right. The prime ministerial endorsement insinuated that, since the death of Diana, the monarchy endured on his terms. They were being enveloped into his project.

The tragedy in Paris had, for Blair at least, a happy outcome. The week of eruptive emotion had been framed by his two performances, first outside Trimdon parish church on the morning after her death, then the reading from Corinthians at the funeral in the Abbey. It transfigured Blair from a popular but partisan political leader into a spokesman for the nation. Philip Gould, having examined his focus groups, reported to Blair that he had 'connected' with the people. The role of uniter and healer that had traditionally belonged to the monarch had been seized, part by design, part from necessity, by Tony Blair, sovereign of national sentiment. Popularity ratings historically enjoyed by the monarch now belonged to the Prime Minister. That title seemed too modest to describe the position he had acquired in the short time since the election. Britain appeared to have the constitutionally novel arrangement of possessing both a Queen and a President.

On the eve of the Labour Party conference at the end of the month, his pollsters reported to Blair that his score had soared to stratospheric levels never previously touched by any British leader. His approval rating stood at 93 per cent, a level usually only manufactured in the realms of totalitarian dictatorships. To his friend Gould, Stan Greenberg, an American pollster who worked for New Labour, remarked: 'Even Saddam doesn't get that.'

# 5. Dragons and Lions

Tony Blair was in the top-floor flat of Number 11 when the phone began to ring, irritatingly. That evening, Thursday 16 October, the Prime Minister had given instructions that he was not to be interrupted except in an emergency. A small nightmare already sat in front of him. Clare Short had embarrassed herself at the party conference in Brighton a fortnight earlier. Returning to the secure cordon around the conference area after an evening on the party circuit, the International Development Secretary had objected to being searched and had become involved in an emotional altercation with the security staff and the police. Had she been arrested, it would have been terrible for her and the government. The worst had been averted: party officials intervened. The 'men in the dark' she once savaged were conducting an operation to keep this damaging story out of the newspapers. Blair was discussing with Short how she would handle herself if it did become public.

Then, the phone rang. At the other end of the line was Gordon Brown, anxious to resume with the Prime Minister an argument that had been flaring between them for much of the week. With fatiguing intensity, the Chancellor was pressing to make a statement clarifying the government's attitude towards the European single currency. Since the beginning of autumn, there had been mounting media speculation about a split between the Prime Minister and the Chancellor. All of their argument was not re-rehearsed in this brief phone conversation. Distracted by Short and bludgeoned by Brown, Blair now agreed to the Chancellor's plan to give a newspaper interview. 'But talk to Alastair first,' said Blair before putting down the phone.[1] This five-minute call had consequences for Britain that would last for years.

★

Of all Blair's strategic objectives, few were as central to his project as the European Question. 'Under my leadership,' he declared before the election, 'I will never allow this country to be isolated or left behind in Europe.'[2] For Britain to remain at the edge of Europe, rather than take up a leading role at the centre of Europe, would be 'to deny our historical role in the world'.[3]

On no other territory did his principles conflict more sharply with his populism. He had surrendered conviction to expediency during the election campaign in which New Labour deployed slogans and symbols which pandered to anti-European prejudice. At Peter Mandelson's instigation, the party adopted as its campaign mascot a bulldog, the symbol not only of the right, but of the tattooed forearm, crop-headed right. It was an illustration of New Labour's neurosis about being painted as soft on Europe that there had been a frisson of panic when a rumour spread that the dog's name was not Fitz, but the Germanic Fritz. As part of his Faustian bargain with the *Sun*, Blair had put his name to opinions which might have been penned by one of the tabloid's most jingoistic writers. Under the heading 'We'll See Off Euro Dragons', Blair allowed this rant to appear alongside his face:

Tomorrow is St George's Day, the day when the English celebrate the pride we have in our nation. On the day we remember the legend that St George slayed a dragon to protect England, some will argue that there is another dragon to be slayed: Europe.[4]

He told *Sun* readers about 'my love for the pound' to which 'there's a very strong emotional tie . . . which I fully understand'. Abandoning sterling was 'not just a question of economics. It's about the sovereignty of Britain and constitutional issues, too.'[5]

Pro-Europeans who recoiled at language that could have come from the lips of a Michael Portillo or a John Redwood were privately reassured by Blair. He might be talking the language of Europhobia to win an election, but nothing had been surrendered in policy. On the pivotal issue, the single currency, there was formally little difference between the parties. Where John Major wanted to wait-and-see, Tony Blair would see-and-wait. There was nevertheless little doubt that New Labour's approach would be much more positive than that of a Tory Party in which Europhobic forces were ever more ascendant. By conviction and personal taste, Blair was pro-European. He spoke French more fluently than any Prime Minister since Anthony Eden. When, in March 1998, he addressed the French National Assembly in its native tongue, he managed to get his audience to laugh at his jokes, a rare feat for an Englishman. He holidayed in Tuscany, the favoured summertime retreat of the European progressive élite. To sympathetic private audiences he would describe it as his historic mission to drain the poison of Europhobia from the bloodstream of the British body politic. Gordon Brown, though culturally more at home in America, was intellectually signed-up to the idea of Europe. In fact, there was an assumption at this time, as universal as it was rather misleading, that he was more Euro-enthusiastic than Blair. As for the third man of the modernising triumvirate, Peter Mandelson was – for all that bulldogging – the most ardent in the belief that Britain's manifest destiny was as a fully engaged player in Europe.

A decision was due in early 1998 about which countries would join the single currency on its launch date on New Year's day 1999. About the euro as an economic device, Blair came to office an agnostic. He had institutionalised his own indecision by appointing as his personal guides on the issue two men with diametrically opposed views. His adviser on Europe, Roger Liddle, a former Social Democrat of the Jenkinsite persuasion, was as passionately for the single currency as his adviser on economics, Derek Scott, another refugee from the SDP but of an Owenite inclination, was against the euro. Blair would take exhaustive circuits around the arguments with them. What about the peripheral economies? Could one exchange rate and one interest rate really fit the whole of Europe? On the other hand, if Britain stayed out, would not foreign companies gradually withdraw investment? One of Blair's first acts as Prime Minister was to dispatch Margaret Beckett, the Trade and Industry Secretary, to Tokyo to reassure Japanese companies of Britain's intention to join. When Liddle and Scott compared notes of their discussions with Blair, on one thing they agreed. Neither of them could be sure whose side he was really on.

Then there was the politics, for this Prime Minister always more important than the economics. He wanted, so he declared, to be 'a leader in Europe'. David Owen, reporting to friends on his conversations with the Prime Minister, said Blair was 'obsessed' about having a seat at the captain's table. Owen was correct. 'So long as we're out, there will be a ceiling on our influence,' Blair would say to colleagues. 'That's a fact.'[6]

The politics of Europe collided with the politics of the domestic audience. Alastair Campbell, instinctively a Eurosceptic, did not relish an early war with the right-wing papers he had worked so energetically to neutralise. Philip Gould's focus groups showed deep hostility to the euro.

If the dilemma could not be resolved, might it be avoided? One idea, advocated to Blair by Gordon Brown, was to evade the moment of decision by persuading the rest of Europe to delay the launch of the euro. This was a sign of the new government's innocence. New Labour was enjoying a honeymoon in Europe as it was at home. Blair had ended the Tory opt-out from the Social Chapter. The Amsterdam Treaty negotiations were concluded harmoniously. Other leaders marvelled and envied the size of his victory. They also smarted at the new kid on the Euro-bloc's injunctions to embrace the Anglo-Saxon approach to free markets. Blair startled an audience of European socialists by exporting to them one of his favourite domestic sound-bites. 'Modernise or die,' he lectured them.[7] The Dutch Foreign Minister was heard to remark sardonically that some things never changed: yet another British leader was telling the Europeans where they were going wrong.[8] Jacques Chirac, the President of France, teasingly asked Blair whether he, the Gaullist, was right-wing enough to be 'an honorary member of New Labour'. From other European capitals came the warning that there was no question of postponing the launch of the single currency at London's behest. Britain's ambassadors in Bonn and Paris reported back that to pursue this idea would court a diplomatic disaster. It would make Albion look perfidious in the eyes of the continent. Should the single currency be delayed for other reasons, then Britain would be cast as the scapegoat.

In the spring and early summer of the new government's life, an alternative, much bolder course was pressed on the Prime Minister, especially by his friends in the Liberal Democrats. Roy Jenkins, passionate Europeanist and a regular dining companion at Number 10 and Chequers, counselled Blair to 'take it at a run' by exploiting his popularity to call an early referendum on the single currency. Paddy Ashdown alike urged Blair to 'seize the day'. Peter Mandelson also leant towards an early referendum, though his enthusiasm markedly cooled after the narrowness of the result for the Welsh Assembly. Blair replied to those arguing the case for swift entry into the euro that he had a more modest conception of his ability to beguile the electorate. 'Look, the British like me, they like what they've seen of New Labour so far. But if I suddenly turn round and say: "Hey, I know what, let's get rid of the pound," they'll say: "Hold on a minute, mate, you've only been there six months, now you want to scrap the pound. Don't try to run before you can walk." '[9]

This chimed with the thinking of Gordon Brown who believed to call a referendum without a date for entry would be simply 'mad'.

As heated as they were inconclusive, by the end of the summer of 1997 these arguments within New Labour's high command had still not produced an actual policy. The Cabinet, a forum in which the issue had not once been discussed since New Labour came to power, was excluded from the great debate raging within small circles. When one of his officials asked the Foreign Secretary about rumours of a development, Robin Cook replied: 'That's the first I've heard of it.'[10]

Clarification was promised early in the New Year of 1998. 'I don't think we'll get to the end of the year,' Mandelson warned Blair, a forecast truer than he knew. In early September, Ed Balls, the Chancellor's economics adviser, and Jonathan Powell, the Prime Minister's chief of staff, met and agreed that they needed to persuade their masters to co-ordinate a settled position. That the government's mind was divided was not going to deter newspapers – indeed it was most likely to encourage them – from speculating about the direction in which it might shift. Nor was it going to prevent members of the government using journalists to try to push the policy towards their favoured course. On the Friday before the party conference, the *Financial Times* reported that the government 'is on the point of adopting a much more positive approach to the European economic and monetary union, with a statement shortly that sterling is likely to join at an early opportunity after the 1999 launch'. Political editor Robert Peston quoted an unnamed minister as saying 'we must indicate our willingness to be in there'.[11] He suggested entry might even come 'possibly before the next election'. The confidence and the prominence of this report in the City's house journal gave it market-moving impact. Sterling fell in value. Shares and gilts rose, as the markets began to anticipate early entry.

This was the cause of consternation within Number 10 and high alarm at the Treasury. 'Kill it,' Gordon Brown told Charlie Whelan, which the Chancellor's press secretary attempted to do by rubbishing the report as 'pure speculation' and, employing the wonderful Whelanism, 'a package of bollocks'. Such vehement denials might have killed the controversy were it not for the government's already burgeoning reputation for being loose with the truth, a characteristic that was particularly attached to Whelan. That autumn he was seen in a television documentary making the professionally hazardous confession that he told lies. 'You just have to be economical with the truth . . . you should never lie, but it's very difficult. But they understand: they'll all understand tomorrow and forgive me.'[12] Magicians – if they are to keep the disbelief suspended – should not share their tricks with the audience. Over a drink in his hostelry of choice, the Red Lion pub opposite the Treasury, Whelan decoded his denials for one political correspondent: 'Telling a journalist a story was "bollocks" meant it was true. "Total bollocks" meant something similar. "Speculation" meant get on and write it.'[13]

The documentary, in which Brown's team portrayed themselves

as swaggerers, intoxicated with their new power, trampling on civil servants and intimidating journalists, had enraged Campbell. He complained to Blair and others at Number 10 that Whelan was on 'a total ego trip'. He was 'a fucking menace'. Relations between the Prime Minister's chief propagandist and the Chancellor's mouthpiece had begun a descent into the same seething mistrust as that between Whelan and Mandelson. Only in a government as media driven as New Labour would this matter so much.

When Whelan denied the *FT* story, bollocks had actually meant bollocks. The trouble was that he was widely disbelieved, not least at Number 10. Campbell's suspicion that the Treasury was the hidden hand behind this speculation hardened in mid-October when the *Daily Mail* reported that the government was poised to announce that Britain would enter the single currency shortly after its launch. That didn't bother him half as much as the depiction of this as 'a victory for Gordon Brown . . . who had put enormous pressure on the Prime Minister'.[14] An enraged Campbell tracked down the Brown entourage to a meeting of European finance ministers in Luxemburg. He might have believed Ed Balls, but not Charlie Whelan, when they denied being the source of the story. The following morning, the *Independent* stirred into the plot an anti-Brown twist. That paper's political editor, Anthony Bevins, whom Campbell described as his favourite journalist in the lobby, reported that 'a damaging rift' had been caused by attempts by Brown 'to bounce Blair into a decision which could lead to the early death of the pound'.[15] These were silly games. They were also highly dangerous ones. Someone would get hurt.

This report did not move the markets. It did move Brown: to fury. Brown went to Blair complaining that he was being 'slaughtered' in the press. 'A wedge' was being driven between them. It was destabilising the government and – most importantly in Brown's mind – it was undermining him. He wanted Blair's agreement to a newspaper interview which he said he would use to bury suggestions of a rift between them. Blair was more sanguine. 'Do we want to look as if we are making policy in reaction to one newspaper story?' he asked Brown. 'Won't that look like panic?'

Blair urged Brown to 'relax'.[16] That was the last time in a fortnight that anyone in New Labour's innermost circles would talk about relaxing.

The Chancellor had got his way by the end of that brief phone conversation on Thursday night. Blair wearily turned back to the problem of Clare Short thinking that, between them, Brown and Campbell would construct a line blandly asserting the government's unity on the subject of the single currency. Brown kept his promise to ring Campbell and told him that he would calm the speculation by fulfilling a long-standing request for an interview from Philip Webster, the political editor of *The Times*. Campbell, who had himself been arguing that clarity needed to be brought to the government's intentions, was content. On the assumption that Blair and Brown had reached an agreed position, and wrung out at the end of an exhausting week, Campbell agreed a text with Ed Balls. Campbell, who does not appear to have discussed it further with the Prime Minister, would later confess that this was the scene of one of his greatest mistakes.

The media, in common with most of the Cabinet, had presumed that this was a repeat of the drama, familiar from the Conservative years, of a Euro-enthusiastic Chancellor trying to drive a Euro-cautious Prime Minister towards the single currency. After all, had not Blair imposed upon a reluctant Brown the pledge to hold a referendum? What this obscured was the role reversal between the two men. Blair, always temperamentally inclined to leave every option open, wanted to keep alive the possibility of entering the single currency before the election, at the very least as a signal to the rest of Europe of his good intent. But treating the euro as a political gesture was regarded as a nonsense by Brown who saw it as an issue of economics. A man compulsively inclined to close down debates he did not want to have, Brown wanted to shut off the option altogether. Not the least of the many extraordinary features of this episode is that the two most powerful men in government had not settled such a critical difference. Had they done so, they might have avoided days of calamitous confusion.

Brown had been moving towards a view that the economies of Britain and the continent were not sufficiently synchronised to make early entry desirable or practical. He and Balls were horrified to discover how little preparatory work had been done at the Treasury. Brown brooded over the problem with Balls. If Britain could never be ready to join before the next election, the government should say so clearly. Constant speculation about their intentions would be damaging, not least to Brown himself. Hypersensitive about his personal status, he feared that his Chancellorship would be undermined by conjecture about the government's intentions just as the Thatcher government had been bedevilled over the Exchange Rate Mechanism. A fixation with leading members of the Blair government was the fear of being stranded on the wrong side of an argument. Brown was not going to charge the guns of the Europhobic press while Blair observed the battle from a safe distance behind the lines. Personal and economic calculation combined in the Chancellor's mind to produce the conclusion that he should unequivocally declare that Britain would not join the single currency before the next election.

It was against this background that Webster of *The Times* was rung to be told that he had got his interview and was about 'to make history'. This was not an interview in the sense that an innocent newspaper reader might imagine, but a device that had become common practice between politicians with a message to get out and lobby correspondents eager for a story. The crucial passage about the single currency was provided to Webster by fax. It restated the government's position with a sceptical flavour:

We said in our manifesto, and it remains true today, that it is highly unlikely that Britain can join in the first wave. If we do not join in 1999, our task will be to deliver a period of sustainable growth, tackle the long-term weaknesses of the UK economy and to continue to press for reform in Europe.

This rather Delphic statement was a wink to the wise. The sensation was the headline that *The Times* printed over it: 'Brown rules out single currency for lifetime of this Parliament'.[17] Though this was probably a little harder than had been intended by the Chancellor, it was the interpretation that Webster had been guided to put on his story during phone conversations with Brown, Balls and, most of all, Campbell who gave the journalist a very strong steer that the government was ruling out the euro. This was also the line that Whelan spun out to other journalists. Brown wanted his change in policy trumpeted in a Europhobic tabloid. 'I'll get on to Higgy,' said Whelan. He suggested to the editor of the *Sun* that he should headline his version of the story: 'Brown Saves Pound'.[18] Higgins would run a variation of that tune: 'Brown Says No to the Euro.'[19]

To spin such bold headlines over an ambiguous text on an issue of massive consequence was living dangerously. Not quite riskily enough, though, for Whelan. By the time other journalists were alert to the U-turn being announced in *The Times*, Whelan had repaired to the Red Lion pub to celebrate what he regarded as a great coup. He confirmed the story to BBC *Newsnight* and ITN. Two Liberal Democrat press officers observed Whelan repeatedly leaving the bar and shouting into his mobile phone: 'Yes, Gordon is ruling out British membership . . . No, it doesn't say it in the interview, but Gordon is effectively ruling out joining in this parliament.'[20] Rapidly the word spread that not only was the government executing a massive change in policy, briefings on what Gordon Brown called 'the most important question the country is likely to face in a generation'[21] were being conducted down a mobile phone from the pavement outside a pub.

Someone had been sliced out of the loop: Peter Mandelson. Knowing that he would fight the shift, Gordon Brown had left the self-styled 'Minister for Looking Ahead' blindsided. The first Mandelson knew about it was when the Media Monitoring Unit at Millbank faxed a copy of the front page of *The Times* to him at home in Hartlepool. A little after ten o'clock, a palpitating Mandelson rang Chequers. Someone even more important had been left in the dark: Tony Blair. The Prime Minister had retired to his Buckinghamshire retreat on Friday evening, entirely oblivious to what was being perpetrated back in London. 'Did you authorise this?' asked Mandelson. 'I don't know,' replied Blair. 'What's going on?'[22] Mandelson read from his faxed copy of *The Times*. What Brown had done was disastrous, he argued with Blair. Unequivocally ruling out entry would cause untold damage to Britain's relations with Europe and the government's reputation among pro-European businesses. Now Blair began to fathom the magnitude of what was happening. He ended the call by telling Mandelson that he would immediately speak to the Chancellor. But Brown, who had disappeared to his Scottish constituency for the weekend, was incommunicado. Even the operators of SWITCH, the Downing Street switchboard fabled for its ability to connect the Prime Minister to anyone in the world at any time of day or night, couldn't reach the Chancellor. Nor, even more remarkably, could Blair get hold of Campbell. He had all of his press secretary's phone numbers wired in his head. As he punched the phone, from none of them could the Prime Minister raise an answer. Campbell had gone missing just when Blair vitally needed him.[23] Isolated at Chequers, marooned in the Chilterns, cut off from both Chancellor and press secretary, Tony Blair had one last desperate option. He phoned Charlie Whelan. The Prime Minister had been reduced to asking the man he never wanted in government what government policy was supposed to be tonight. When Blair came on the line, Whelan dived out of the bar of the Red Lion to find a discreet corner.

'What the hell is all this stuff in *The Times*?' Blair demanded. 'It's our policy,' replied an insouciant Whelan, still revelling in what he took to be a magnificent triumph. 'What's the problem? It's in *The Times* because it's our policy.' 'Who says it's our policy?' inquired a stunned Prime Minister. He had never authorised this. 'The headline – it's far too hard. You've got to row back.' 'Sorry, Tony,' replied Whelan. 'It's too late.'[24]

Had Blair turned on *Newsnight*, he would have seen the presenter also demanding to know what the hell was government policy on the single currency? Was it, as the official spokesmen for the Treasury were still insisting because Brown had left them entirely in the dark as well, to keep the option open? Was it, as both Campbell and Whelan had been spinning, to rule out entry?

The confusion extended to Britain's two most senior civil servants. On Saturday morning, the Cabinet Secretary rang the Treasury's Permanent Secretary. 'What on earth is going on, Terry?' asked Sir Robin Butler. 'I've no more idea than you, Robin,' Burns had to admit. The officials could take the grim, but arid, satisfaction of seeing all their private warnings to the Prime Minister about New Labour's way of governing being vindicated in grisly technicolour.

This was turning into an exhibition of New Labour's worst traits. Manoeuvring between its two leading men, exacerbated by the mutual loathing and paranoia of their entourages, and further aggravated by the government's haphazard forms of decision-making, was creating mayhem in the most fundamental area of foreign and economic affairs.

By Saturday morning, the Conservatives were baying for the recall of parliament, and the media was savagely questioning the competence of the government. 'That's done it,' Brown told Whelan. 'They'll crucify us for this.' Whelan offered to resign 'if it will help'. Brown instantly dismissed the idea: it would make him look weak.[25]

The spinners went into damage-limitation mode, and not entirely unsuccessfully. Some of the Sunday newspapers carried apparently authoritative reports that the new policy had been meticulously agreed by Blair and Brown the previous week when, in fact, the farrago had flowed from a five-minute phone call. This fiction had been manufactured by Whelan for the consumption of the media to try to dress up the chaos as a well-ordered decision. Campbell and Mandelson both knew this to be mendacious, but felt compelled to fall in with the deception. To do otherwise would be to expose the rupture between Prime Minister and Chancellor.[26]

Members of the Cabinet, left in unblissful ignorance of what was going on, stumbled about in no man's land. The Health Secretary, appearing on breakfast television that Sunday morning, doggedly stuck to the line that the government was not ruling out euro entry, but sticking to its original policy of wait-and-see. Frank Dobson could not be blamed. He did well to sound coherent at all given that there was no policy.

There was a brittle conference call between Blair, Brown, Mandelson, Campbell, Balls and Whelan. Mandelson made plain that he thought they had blundered because they had failed to consult him. But there was not time for involved recriminations. Those would have to wait. It was agreed that the Chancellor would give radio and television interviews sticking to the opaque line that he would say no more than that the government would be making a statement in due course. This was an attempt to put a straight face on this twisted farce.

Monday's press was the worst for New Labour since it had come to office, and the theme of the papers, whether of right or left, was the same. 'Labour spins into a crisis' from the *Guardian*[27] was echoed back by the *Daily Telegraph*'s 'Brown in a spin over euro policy'.[28] The media tempest was accompanied by turbulent markets when the City opened for the new working week. By excruciatingly unfortunate timing, Brown was due to inaugurate the new electronic trading system at the Stock Exchange. As the Chancellor's gnawed finger activated the system, the screens behind him began to glow red. In twenty minutes £20 billion was wiped off share values. This would prove to be a blip in the great bull run of the nineties, but 'Brown Monday', as it was inevitably dubbed, was a humiliation. Television pictures of Brown drowning in a wash of red were simply awful for a Chancellor dedicated to maintaining the confidence of the markets and for a government that had persuaded itself and the rest of the world that they were the masters of discipline, competence and presentation.

Blair called the principal players together in Number 10 on Tuesday for a post-mortem. The two tribes lined up, Brown, Balls and Whelan on one side of the table; Blair, Mandelson, Campbell and Jonathan Powell on the other. Blair delivered an acidic commentary on the débâcle of the previous ninety-six hours, finding it convenient to assign most culpability to the frictions between his entourage and the Chancellor's retinue. 'The feuding must end,' the Prime Minister declared. Though he rarely ventured even implicit criticism of his Chancellor in the presence of large numbers of witnesses, at one point Blair looked directly across at Brown: 'Everyone is to blame, Gordon, but you have chief responsibility for making sure that something like this never happens again. Our credibility is at stake.'[29]

Campbell, as complicit in the disaster as Whelan, was hardly in a position to demand, much as he might have liked to, that the other man be sacrificed. Mandelson was not so constrained. In the absence of the Brown team, Mandelson urged Blair to seize this opportunity to get the head of Whelan. 'We are all to blame,' sighed the Prime Minister. 'It wouldn't be fair.' 'Life's not fair,' snapped back Mandelson. 'Look,' said Blair. 'I'll get rid of him by Christmas.' Whelan had cast himself into the role of villain of this piece. The image of him – fag in mouth, drink in hand, mobile wedged into his neck, spinning economic policy from a pub – was indelibly burned into the episode. But Blair was right: to heap all the blame on a press officer would not be fair. Whelan was the Chancellor's creature following Brown's instructions. Whelan's methods were an application, albeit a crude one, from the New Labour textbook of spin. His most heinous sin against the New Labour commandments was to get caught. Campbell had been an accomplice to the briefings, and then went AWOL at exactly the moment when Blair needed him. Brown was guilty of attempting a clumsily executed bounce on Blair who had failed to keep control of an area of policy so important to him.

That Wednesday, 22 October, it was the Prime Minister's turn to feel some of the heat. As he toured the trading floor of LIFFE, some of the dealers greeted him with joshing and scattered jeering, which the *Daily Mail* amplified into the headline 'Blair Rocked By City Boos'.[30]

When he flew to Scotland for the Commonwealth Summit at the end of the week, still there was no policy. Mandelson was fighting to reverse Brown. Though unwilling to go that far, Blair was not ready to agree to closing off entry altogether. The Chancellor wanted the door slammed; the Prime Minister wanted it left ajar. Drafts of the statement banged back and forth between London and Edinburgh. Down from Scotland from the Prime Minister came his desired text which left the option of joining semi-open by qualifying Brown's policy of closing it off with the phrase 'barring a change in economic circumstances'. Back to Edinburgh went the Brownian version with that phrase removed. They played ping-pong. Each time Blair put the words in, Brown struck them out.[31]

Campbell, thinking an apology might draw some of the sting of the criticism, wrote an opening paragraph for Brown's speech expressing regret about the shambles. That Brown also flatly rejected. He was not going to admit failure. He declared he would use his statement to take 'the high ground'. Nor had they settled the substance of the dispute between Blair and Brown. Though civil servants were now being employed to help craft the statement of the new policy, Blair and Brown had still not agreed it. With the negotiations between Prime Minister and Chancellor deadlocked, Blair issued a nuclear threat. He told Brown that he would make the statement to the Commons himself. Brown was fissile with fury, raging that this would undermine his authority as Chancellor and expose the division between them to the world. Brown did not know it, but he had an unfamiliar ally in Mandelson who was not convinced about the wisdom of this idea. 'It would be better,' he separately told Blair, 'to get Gordon to announce your policy.'[32] There was some foundation to Brown's suspicions about being used by Blair.

Eventually they ground out a compromise. Britain would not join the single currency before the next election 'barring some fundamental and unforeseen change in economic circumstances'. The door had been left open but only by a crack which time would turn into a victory for the Chancellor. Five 'tests' of economic convergence were refined to determine entry. There was nothing especially scientific about these tests, nor the number of them. It could have been three; it might have been seven. The number five – whether it be attached to pledges or tests – always seemed to have a mystical attraction for New Labour. The tests, originally taken to be conveniently elastic, would ironically come to be seen as serious hurdles.

Late on Friday afternoon, it was finally announced from the Treasury that the Chancellor would be making a statement to the Commons on the Monday. It was a tribute to the parliamentary skills of Gordon Brown – as well as a commentary on the complete absence of them displayed by his Tory opposite number, Peter Lilley – that his statement was a theatrical triumph for the Chancellor. From the nettle, Brown plucked a bloom. He framed his new policy within an overall intent to join the single currency at some point. 'We are the first British government to declare for the principle of monetary union, the first to state that there is no overriding constitutional bar to membership.'[33] If the tests were met and the single currency proved 'successful' then 'Britain should be part of it'. Blair, sitting beside him, had been particularly insistent on this gloss. The new policy was announced as 'prepare and decide', a formulation originally fathered by the pro-European Tory, Michael Heseltine.

Euro-enthusiasts believed an opportunity had been missed. Roy Jenkins rang the Prime Minister that evening to tell him that he had made 'a grave mistake'. Blair replied: 'Well, maybe.' Eurosceptics interpreted it as the death knell for sterling.

When Blair and Brown healed their breach, they found grounds for mutual satisfaction. The Conservatives had hardened their opposition to the single currency, which both men believed to be to New Labour's advantage. Brown had stifled speculation about the government's immediate intentions. The moment of confrontation with the forces of Europhobia at home had been delayed. Blair ordered a concerted effort by British ambassadors to do some diplomatic spinning in European capitals to the effect that the statement should be regarded as another British step towards the heart of Europe. Blair gave Mandelson the reassurance: 'They still think we are going to join.' Sir Robin Butler offered a cliché of congratulation to the Prime Minister: 'With one bound you are free.'

Free of making an immediate choice, this was true, but there was a cost to that influence in Europe which Blair regarded as so precious, and it would be swiftly apparent. The crisis had passed;

the dilemma remained. Hard on this decision, other European finance ministers declared they would not have Gordon Brown at their meetings to shape the currency. Adding insult to this injury, they refused to let him join their family photograph and sent him away without an invitation to dinner. At the end of the year, Blair launched the six-month British presidency of Europe at Waterloo station, claiming it as 'an opportunity to demonstrate that Britain now has a strong voice in Europe, that the indecision, vacillation and anti-Europeanism of the past have gone'.[34] There was praise from other European ministers for the manner in which their British counterparts, especially Robin Cook, processed the business of Europe. But from its most momentous enterprise, Britain was now self-excluded. Despite the vast presentational energies devoted to selling a 'People's Europe' to the sceptical British, the presidency ended with public opposition to the single currency as strong as ever. Blair chaired the final session in May 1998 at which eleven countries committed themselves to the single currency. He stood as a man on the quayside waving others off on their great voyage.

His predicament over Europe, the conflict between strategy and tactics, the vacillation and indecision, that was not over. The reckoning had only been delayed.

# 6. They'll Get Me for This

The Prime Minister was in a panic. 'Find Gordon,' Tony Blair urged his assistant, Anji Hunter. For all the tensions between them, Gordon Brown was still one of his first ports of call in a crisis.

On that November Friday in 1997, Prime Minister and Chancellor had been playing host to Jacques Chirac, the President of France, in the glass and steel citadel of Canary Wharf. The Anglo–French summit was designed as a showcase for the New Britain born under New Labour. The summiteers sat on Conran furniture and consumed the finest cuisine that Britain could offer to demanding French palates. Yet the topic Blair urgently wanted to address with Brown was neither relations with France nor the business of Britain, but New Labour's financial entanglement with one particular tycoon which, if exposed, could be hugely damaging to his claim to represent an aerosol-fresh era of hygienic integrity in public life.

As the prime ministerial limousine nosed its way out of the Isle of Dogs and back towards central London, Blair and Brown sat together on the leather back seat, discussing what to do about Bernie Ecclestone. Should they confess that the party had received £1 million from the motor-racing tycoon? Should they cover it up? Both Alastair Campbell and the press secretary's deputy, Tim Allan, had been arguing all morning for admitting to the donation. Blair wasn't yet convinced. Neither was he, said Brown.

Labour had long courted endorsements from business, and they were the more welcome if they came attached to cash. There was a crucial distinction between Blair and his immediate predecessors as leader of the party. Neil Kinnock, who would rather spend his time in the company of actors, had regarded the task of schmoozing the corporate world as a bore. John Smith, who had an abiding distaste for anything suggestive of the spivvy, had regarded it as a chore. For Blair, winning the endorsement of business was more than a way of imprinting free market credentials on New Labour. As he remarked to one corporate mogul, he enjoyed the company of entrepreneurs because 'you make things happen'. Blair's belief in what dynamic individuals could achieve by solo and risky endeavour was reinforced every time he looked in his shaving mirror. The portals of Downing Street were thrown open to business as widely as they had been during the Tory years. When one of the residual representatives of Bearded Labour in the Cabinet was invited to one of these affairs, he returned from partying at Number 10 to remark that: 'The publican may have changed, but the same people are jostling at the bar.'[1]

Corporate cheerleaders for New Labour ranged from the long committed to the recently converted, from Chris Haskins of Northern Foods to Gerry Robinson of Granada. These were useful men to have around for New Labour. They were an entrée into the commercial experience which was lacking in the lawyers, journalists, TV producers and lecturers who actually ran the government. David Simon, the chairman of BP, was elevated to a peerage and parachuted into the DTI to become Minister of European Trade. Gus Macdonald, who travelled a personal and ideological odyssey from Trotskyite fitter on Red Clydeside to media millionaire to Blairite minister, was another example of the Prime Minister's preference for promoting outsiders with ability over the talent available among his own MPs. David Sainsbury, who contributed some of his many grocery millions to party funds, became Minister of Science.

Blair was not being quite as modern as he assumed. He was in the tradition of David Lloyd George and Winston Churchill, two other Prime Ministers who reckoned to be larger than their parties and who were more impressed by the qualities of tycoons than the talents of many of their colleagues. Just as with Lloyd George and Churchill, Blair was to discover that businessmen also brought something else to government. There had already been an early warning about the dangers of conflicts of interests, whether real or simply perceived, when the otherwise enfeebled Conservative Opposition managed to harry Lord Simon until he disposed of his shares in BP.

Moneymen brought another essential commodity to the party: hard cash. Blair had told Tom Sawyer, the party's general secretary, that they needed to raise £25 million for the 1997 election campaign to be able to spend on something like even terms with the Tories. The leaking to the media of some of the corporation donations had not been a source of shame, but a cause of satisfaction. It demonstrated to the country that companies were betting on Tony Blair. There was the niggling question about the implications of the goldrush for the pious incorruptibility of the Prime Minister who had pledged to 'restore faith in public life'. The phrase 'Tony's cronies' had first caught fire with the publication of the August honours list. The imaginative selection from the New Labour Establishment included Ruth Rendell, the crime novelist; David Puttnam, the film producer; and Michael Levy, tennis partner and fund-raiser of the Prime Minister. Many of the New Labour aristocrats had donated substantially to the party. Though they might have as good a claim on membership of the House of Lords as anyone else, the presence of money in the equation inevitably introduced a taint to it. The Tories started talking about hypocrisy.

Had Bernie Ecclestone been hoping for a peerage the affair that now unfolded would not have been so dire. The £1 million that he had given the party in January had been banked with the personal approval of Blair. Even then, there seemed to be some awareness of its enormous potential for embarrassment. Ecclestone and Labour had a mutual pact to keep silent about the donation. On his account, he told them: 'If someone puts me up against the wall with a machine gun, I will not confirm or deny anything about the donation. They said, 'OK, OK, we will do the same.'[2] The money was due to turn up in the party's accounts in October 1998, but only under the anodyne heading 'more than £5,000', a category which hardly did justice to the magnitude of this generosity. Explaining his largesse, Ecclestone would say he'd been impressed by the New Labour leader as a man who would keep the unions down and taxes low. 'I thought Blair had the same ideas as me, that he was anti-European and anti-Common Market.'[3] The motor-racing boss could not easily be confused with a political scientist or a starry-eyed idealist. Senior Tories told the media he had previously been a big investor in the Conservative Party. Ecclestone had made his donation to New Labour at a time when it was evident to a one-eyed inner Mongolian that the Tories were about to lose power.

There was 'no question', he would later insist, that his money was intended to persuade Labour to exempt Formula One from a ban on tobacco advertising. He obviously had a problem neverthe-less if their manifesto pledge to stop tobacco advertising meant the end of cigarette money for the sponsorship of motor-racing. The impression that Labour's ban would indeed be that comprehensive had been reinforced since the election by aggressive declarations from the Health Secretary, Frank Dobson, and the Minister for Public Health, Tessa Jowell. This pair was one of the government's odder couples. Dobson, with facial hair as unmodernised as his jokes were filthy, was a self-confessedly unfashionable figure. The pastel-hued Jowell was a quintessential moderniser. Yet they had an amicable relationship, developed during their days as councillors in Camden. In their determination to take on the tobacco baronies, they were as one. Addressing the annual conference of the Royal College of Nursing a couple of weeks after the election, Dobson had been warmly applauded for the promise that the government would shortly legislate to ban 'all forms of tobacco advertising, including sponsorship'.[4] Sports like Formula One which drew heavily on tobacco money would have to recognise that by helping to promote the sale of cigarettes they were 'harming the health of many of their own spectators and viewers'.[5] Jowell had taken a similarly uncompromising message to a meeting of the European Union's Health Council in June where she had positioned Britain in support of a pan-European ban.

This was unwelcome news to the men who ran British motor-racing. It would strike not only at their biggest source of funding, but threatened to have a direct bearing on Ecclestone's personal wealth. He was planning to float Formula One on the Stock Exchange which, it was estimated, would net his family £1 billion. Getting insufficient satisfaction from lobbying the fiercely anti-tobacco Jowell, at the end of September he appealed over her head, asking Jonathan Powell to arrange an audience with the Prime Minister. The chief of staff obliged. When the tycoon was ushered into Downing Street on 16 October, he needed no introducing. As leader of the Opposition, Blair had accepted an invitation to the British Grand Prix. He was treated to the intoxicating experience of being driven around the Silverstone circuit while the crowd waved Union Jacks at him. With Ecclestone was another donor to the Labour Party, Max Mosley, the head of the Fédération Internationale de l'Automobile, and son of Oswald, the leader of Britain's pre-war fascists. Also present was David Ward, a former adviser to John Smith, whose enthusiasm for motor-racing had translated into lobbying for the industry. The racing tycoon and the scion of Britain's would-be führer rolled out their case to the Prime Minister and his chief of staff, deploying arguments designed to seduce Blair. Motor-racing was a world class industry which put Britain at the hi-tech edge. Deprived of tobacco money, Formula One would move abroad at the loss of 50,000 jobs, 150,000 part-time jobs and £900 million of exports. Blair's first error was to have granted a privileged audience to a man who had given £1 million to his party and at a time, it would subsequently emerge, when the party was soliciting for more. The second mistake was to keep no formal minute of the meeting. What is clear from the note that was eventually published was that he was ready, even eager to be persuaded that day.

The racing tycoon seemed to have a sharper nose for the potential danger to Blair than the Prime Minister himself. As Ecclestone left the meeting at Number 10, his parting words to Blair were: 'Don't hang yourself on this.' Blair's next mistake was not to subject the highly arguable case presented by Ecclestone to any sort of searching examination. Not an expert on motor-racing himself, he appears to have consulted no one with knowledge of the industry. Nor did he invite representations from other sports which might be affected by the ban. It did not occur to him that a special exemption for motor-racing would seem grossly unfair to more Old Labour pursuits such as darts, snooker and greyhound racing. If this inequity did strike him, he did not care. Nor did he seek to hear the other side of the argument from health groups. Very shortly afterwards, Blair told Dobson that they should find a compromise to exempt Formula One from the advertising and sponsorship ban.

The smell of burning rubber began to come off the government on 4 November when it emerged from Brussels that Jowell was now arguing for an exemption for Formula One, instead proposing to operate a voluntary code of restraint of the type which had been ridiculed as ineffective when Labour was in Opposition. There was soon a media hue and cry about New Labour bending its principles for the convenience of a glamour sport. The initial prey was Jowell, whose husband, David Mills, had been involved with the Benetton racing team, a connection he had severed the day after Dobson's speech to the RCN. This was a false trail.

A few journalists had a sniff of the big scent. On the afternoon of Thursday 6 November, Tom Baldwin of the *Sunday Telegraph*, Jon Hibbs of its daily sister, and Nick Wood of *The Times* started asking the Labour Party whether it had received any money from the racing tycoon. These inquiries sent a ripple of fear through Number 10. Blair discussed with his inner circle what should be done about Downing Street's dirty big secret. It would have to be shared with the health ministers, a task which was deputed to Tim Allan. When he telephoned Frank Dobson, the Health Secretary greeted this sensational news very simply. 'Fuckin' hell,' whistled Dobson.[6] At first angered, Dobson swiftly realised that his ignorance was also an alibi. No one could say he had been influenced by Ecclestone's secret million. Tessa Jowell took a precise note of the time of day when the news was broken to her. She, too, could swear her innocence. The Health Ministers had no difficulty grasping how appalling this would look. In Opposition, they had savaged the Tories for refusing to ban tobacco advertising, a failure which they attributed to the generosity with which the baccy barons had funded the Conservative Party.

The worst of Tory sleaze was Mohammed Al-Fayed's claims to have bribed Conservative MPs to promote his cause in the Commons. This was not backbenchers. Here was the Prime Minister himself ordering a policy change after being privately lobbied by a man who had donated a huge sum to his party.

The atmosphere inside Downing Street was frantic. On their return from Canary Wharf, Blair and Brown went into Number 10 together where they were joined by his key advisers. Campbell had already designed a strategy to contain the damage. He argued with Blair that they should confess to the donation. This was not because Campbell was a passionate advocate of honesty and openness by government. The former journalist was simply calculating that this was a story that the press would pursue until they had an answer. On the Friday morning, as Blair and Chirac conducted their cordial entente, the press secretary dashed off a memo. They should admit that a donation had been received from Ecclestone. They would not be returning the money because they would deny that it had any influence on the decision to exempt Formula One. It would be stressed that Dobson and Jowell had not known of the donation when they reversed on the tobacco ban. All this the press secretary proposed to say at his briefing of political correspondents at four on Friday afternoon. Campbell distributed this memo to other players who needed to know the line he was proposing to take, among them Charlie Whelan, the Chancellor's press secretary.

Campbell was not proposing to be entirely candid. He was not planning to admit that, at the time Ecclestone lobbied Blair, the Labour Party had been interested in a further donation. But even Campbell's half-honest approach was squashed. Peter Mandelson and Jonathan Powell didn't see the sense of helping the media to damage the government. Blair consulted his old pupil master, Derry Irvine, who was strongly and loudly of the opinion that a confession, even on the limited grounds proposed, would be 'utterly absurd'. The Lord Chancellor told Blair that 'to give the money back would make it look as though you had done something wrong'.[7] This goes to prove that expensive lawyers can give costly advice. The lawyers' view was that anything the Prime Minister said would be taken down and used in evidence against him. This prevailed over the journalists' view, taken by Campbell and Allan, that this was a story that would not lie down until the truth was out.

During that limousine ride with the Chancellor, Blair developed with Brown an alternative ruse. What they would do was send a confidential letter seeking the advice of Sir Patrick Neill, the newly appointed chairman of the commission on standards in public life. Should Ecclestone's donation be uncovered, the letter could then be produced as evidence of the government's propriety. The letter, drafted by Powell and approved by Blair, was crafted to conceal, beginning with the fact that it was sent under the name of someone else, Tom Sawyer, the party's general secretary. In Sawyer's name, Sir Patrick was told:

After discussion with the Prime Minister, I am writing to seek your urgent advice on a matter of interest to us, and we believe, the public interest. The Labour Party accepted a substantial donation in January this year from Bernie Ecclestone for the general election campaign.[8]

The letter then went on to explain – using Ecclestone's arguments – why the government had sought the exemption for Formula One.

These decisions were not, of course, in any way influenced by Mr Ecclestone's contribution some months before . . . Mr Ecclestone has, since the election, offered a further donation. The Prime Minister has decided that in the light of our approach to the directive and to avoid any possible appearance of a conflict of interest we should consult you on whether it may be properly accepted. The position which we have adopted thus far has been to refuse this further donation, but we wish to be advised whether this is a position we need to maintain.[9]

There was a striking omission from the letter: the actual size of Ecclestone's donation. When he received the letter, Sir Patrick would wrongly assume that the donation was of the order of £100,000.

Other decoys were deployed in an attempt to conceal the cen-
trality of Number 10's role in the affair. The spokesman chosen to
handle the media that weekend was David Hill, Labour's director
of communications, a moustachioed veteran of the party with a
wearily frank air about him, who was well liked by journalists. In
the trade of spin-doctory, a profession notorious for its flexible
interpretation of the truth, Hill enjoyed a reputation among political
correspondents as a practitioner of unusual integrity. He was therefore ideally cast as the bodyguard of the truth about Ecclestone's
donation. Hill subsequently denied that he told any outright lies
that weekend, but he was quite candid about the evasions and
menaces he deployed in order to deflect journalists from the truth.

My job that Saturday night, when we knew the Sunday papers were on
to the story, was to try to throw everyone off the scent, but I failed. I did
say Ecclestone was litigious. I know I was turning somersaults. I did not
say to journalists that Ecclestone had not given us any money although I
know I did say everything but that.[10]

Hill, who would later describe this as his worst week in more
than ten years of working for the Labour Party, did not entirely fail.
The *Sunday Telegraph*, ignoring ferocious denials from Ecclestone's
solicitors, reported that the motor-racing tycoon had donated a
substantial sum, but could not put a precise figure on it. The whole
of the media was ravenous for that information by the Monday
morning. Gordon Brown, due for an interview on the *Today*
programme about economic policy, was ambushed with a question
about the developing furore. Asked directly whether Bernie Ecclestone had given money to the Labour Party, Brown replied: 'You'll
have to wait and see, like I'll have to wait and see when the list is
published. I've not been told and I certainly don't know what the
true position is.'[11]

The Chancellor did know the truth and he had not told it. He
departed from the interview that morning in a red mist which
staggered even those who had long endured his titanic tempers.
'Gordon went mental,' says one witness. Brown raged at his staff:

'I lied. I lied. My credibility will be in shreds. I lied. If this gets out, I'll be destroyed.'[12] Charlie Whelan endeavoured to douse down his troubled master. As Brown and his entourage travelled by train up to Birmingham for the CBI conference, Whelan got staff at the Treasury to play a recording of the interview over the phone, hoping that this would show that the Chancellor had been evasive rather than mendacious. He could not really do that: Brown had denied what he had known. To his credit, it can be said that the Chancellor evidently hated being trapped in a lie.

The cover-up began to unravel at two o'clock on Monday afternoon when Sir Patrick sent his response to the 'Sawyer' letter. Neill was not playing the role of dupe into which they had tried to cast him. He had consulted the 'Code of Conduct and Guidance on Procedure for Ministers', which had been published by the Cabinet Office that July. 'One principle which emerges clearly is that the conduct of those in public positions must be judged not only by the reality but also by the appearance.'[13] This was the principle which the Prime Minister and everyone around him had forgotten. Even if the £1 million had not made a scintilla of difference to the policy change, what was it going to look like? Neill recommended that Blair should not accept any further money from Ecclestone. His really unwelcome instruction was that the first donation, about which they had not invited him to rule, should be returned in order to avoid 'even the appearance of undue influence on policy'.[14]

Blair called together his key aides: Sally Morgan, the political secretary, joined Campbell and Powell. David Hill – who had been at home with the flu – was dragged out of bed. After discussing their narrowing options, Blair conceded they would have to tell some of the truth, even if there was still resistance to telling the whole truth. Desperate to try to maintain distance between himself and the donation, Blair told this meeting: 'It must continue to be treated as a *party* matter.' So it was Hill who was instructed to hurriedly arrange a briefing at the Commons late that afternoon where he gave a partial account of the two as yet unpublished letters. He announced that, gladly and rapidly accepting Sir Patrick's ruling, the party would be handing the money back to Ecclestone. This was a heroic attempt to win plaudits for the government's probity against an accumulation of evidence to the contrary. That night, at the Lord Mayor's Banquet, Tony Blair amplified on his theme that his Britain would be 'a beacon to the world'.

When *The Times* speculated that the donation was £1.5 million, it was dismissed as a 'wild guess'. Challenged later, Hill threw up his arms: 'What was I supposed to do?' He was only following orders; orders which had come down from the Prime Minister.

Not the least of the risks involved in attempting to hide Ecclestone's donation was that Number 10 had no control over the donor. After five days of stonewalling by the government, it was the Formula One tycoon himself who, cornered by sports reporters, finally coughed that the sum involved was £1 million.

Labour MPs caustically referred to Number 10 as 'Bernie Inn'. John Major, relishing the opportunity to attack Blair as Blair had attacked him, talked of 'hypocrisy on a very grand scale'. Newspapers began to count the lies. 'Why did Downing Street deceive us for days?' demanded the *Sun*,[15] the tabloid barometer most closely monitored at Number 10.

Tony Blair felt the world he had constructed beginning to collapse on him. The man who had mercilessly prosecuted Conservative scandals, who had pledged to be 'tough on sleaze and tough on the causes of sleaze', was mired in the slurry himself. Blair could not believe that he had done anything venal, but the cover-up had allowed that complexion to be put on his behaviour. He went through a very bleak period. His nerve was shredded; his confidence profoundly shaken. At one point he indicated to those closest to him that he believed that it could even cost him the premiership. After just six months as Prime Minister, he would be forced to resign. 'This is the end,' Blair despaired to one of his most long-standing intimates. 'They'll get me for this.'[16]

Who did he mean by 'they'? The Labour left? The Conservatives? The Cabinet? The media? Blair meant everyone would get him.

Given how besieged and vulnerable he inwardly felt, it was a bravura outward display which Blair produced at Question Time on the Wednesday. The Prime Minister adopted attack as the best form of defence. He gloated at the expense of William Hague when the leader of the Opposition failed to nail him. 'We were told at lunchtime that the Right Honourable Gentleman had some killer points; that it was an open goal and he was going to put the ball in the net. He has walked up to the penalty spot and booted it over the bar,' shouted Blair. He was roaring – with relief. Other Tory barbs were easily shrugged off: 'I have fought elections with the Labour Party being outspent by the Tory Party £4 or £5 to £1, because they never disclose the source of their donations at all.'[17] This was fair comment. It was also true that he had asked the Neill Committee to examine the whole issue of party funding, a subject that had been forbidden to it by the Conservatives because their sources of income were such a crippling embarrassment. It was nevertheless a mark of desperation that Blair's best plea in mitigation was to ask for his clean-limbed, fresh-faced government to be judged against the debauched standards of the Tory regime he had so relentlessly portrayed as poxed with corruption. Less casually swept aside was Martin Bell, the former BBC correspondent, now an Independent MP, whose decapitation of Neil Hamilton at Tatton had given him a special authority to pronounce on sleaze. In his trademark white suit, Bell booked himself a prominent place on the evening news bulletins by inquiring of the Prime Minister whether he agreed 'that the perception of wrong-doing can be as damaging as wrong-doing itself? Have we slain one dragon only to have another take its place, with a red rose in its mouth?'[18] Some months later Bell would endure a bout of unpleasant publicity about his election expenses which he was not alone in believing was New Labour's revenge for slighting the Prime Minister.

Though he had promised MPs that he would give a full statement with 'enthusiasm and relish', Blair still neglected to tell the House of Commons that his party had been interested in the possibility of a second donation from Ecclestone. This was disclosed only when, in the next of the daily instalments by which the truth was extracted like a rotten tooth, Sir Patrick Neill's letter leaked.

Jack Straw was in the middle of a radio interview when he

learned about the size of the donation from a message on his pager. That was not an experience the Home Secretary was ready to repeat. Straw withdrew from an interview with *Channel Four News* on Thursday evening, offering the excuse that he was 'too tired'. Other ministers did not see why they should be spattered by association with decisions which they had never been party to. John Prescott flatly refused requests from Downing Street to put himself up to defend the Prime Minister. The Cabinet ran for cover, literally so in the case of the Health Secretary. Frank Dobson fled up a staircase followed by a pursuing pack of reporters. On Thursday night, *Newsnight* displayed an empty chair in the studio. Presenter Jeremy Paxman sighed that 'no ministerial bottom' could be found to fill it. By Friday night, a bottom had been found. Its owner was Peter Mandelson. Those willing to defend Blair had been reduced to the hardcore of his closest and oldest allies. It was this sort of guts and loyalty that esteemed Mandelson in the eyes of Blair. When everyone else was taking cover, he put himself up before a studio audience to make the point that no one could prove that the donation had influenced the decision. The difficulty for the Minister Without Portfolio was that it was impossible to prove the reverse either. 'There was no wrong-doing,' he insisted, when he could be heard over the audience's mocking laughter.[19]

Blair's aides complained that the media was treating the affair as if it were the equivalent of Watergate. It wasn't, of course. The misjudgement of the Prime Minister was to have behaved as if it were Watergate. If there was no crime, why the cover-up? It was the smoke that they had manufactured to screen the truth about Ecclestone that was choking them.

At the end of an appalling week, and anticipating a further mauling in the Sunday press, the challenge for Number 10 was to terminate interest in Ecclestone. What they needed, Campbell and Allan argued with Blair, was 'closure'. They had to put 'a full stop' on interest in the affair. His media advisers believed this could be achieved by the Prime Minister subjecting himself to a television interview and offering an apology. For Blair, however, sorry was a hard word. 'I've nothing to apologise for,' he stropped. His mood, despairing earlier in the week, had swung into defiance. According to someone involved in these internal debates who knows Blair very well: 'Tony is stubborn. He believed he'd done nothing wrong. If he'd done nothing wrong, why should he come clean? He couldn't see it at all. He was very stubborn.'[20] Philip Gould weighed in to the effort to cajole Blair. They had sold him to the electorate as a young and fresh leader of integrity. That hugely advantageous image was at risk. By the end of a telephone conversation on Friday, Gould was screaming and swearing down the line at the Prime Minister that he had to do something before the damage to his reputation became irreparable.[21]

On Saturday morning, Blair finally agreed to put himself on television and give what would be his first live interview since the election. Deploying Blair on the soft sofa of Sir David Frost's Sunday breakfast show was not an option. If this exercise was to have credibility, the Prime Minister would have to subject himself to a more rigorous interrogator. Campbell suggested that Blair 'take a kicking' from John Humphrys of *On the Record*.

That Sunday's papers led with headlines, fed to them by Campbell, that Blair would use the interview at Chequers to say sorry. In a typical negotiation with the programme team, he demanded that the opening part of the interview be devoted to the prospect of a military intervention against Iraq, this being a device to present Blair as a statesman concerned with momentous matters of war and peace alongside which a fuss about a tobacco ban was trivial froth. The interview did not go entirely to plan. Understandably anxious that his behaviour looked shifty enough without breaking out into a Nixonesque sweat on camera, Blair demanded an extra thick coating of slap from the make-up artist. The unfortunate effect was to make him look like a rouged-up waxwork. The apology was oversold. Blair, who had not wanted to apologise at all, said he was 'sorry' only for the manner of presentation.

It hasn't been handled well and for that I take full responsibility and I apologise for that. I suppose what I would say to you is that perhaps I didn't focus on this and the seriousness of it in the way that I should as I was focusing on other issues.[22]

He maintained that he was neither wrong to meet Ecclestone, nor to order the exemption for Formula One, making the reasonable point that the Germans were also against a ban. What had not been 'satisfactory or right' was 'the way that this was sort of dribbled out'. The suggestion that his mind had been elsewhere was disingenuous. He had been intensively and frantically focused on how to contain the truth about the Ecclestone donation for the ten days since that car ride from Canary Wharf with Gordon Brown. It had 'dribbled out' as a result of their decision to opt for concealment over candour.

Blair was being his own spin doctor. Peter Mandelson had unwisely revealed earlier in the year that the purpose of spin-doctoring was 'to create the truth'.[23] Here Blair was being creative with the veracity. Humphrys pressed him on to the dangerous territory of why it was only a fortnight after the meeting with Ecclestone that the letter had been written to Sir Patrick Neill, and only after the media had started taking an interest in the relationship. Blair insisted:

Before any journalist had been in touch, anything to do with donations and Mr Ecclestone, we had informed his people that we couldn't accept further donations. The question then arose which was uppermost in my mind, what about the original donation? We decided to seek the advice of Sir Patrick Neill. We did so on Friday.[24]

It was fortunate that the Prime Minister did not have his hand on a bible. As Campbell and others monitoring Blair's performance knew, this was not true. They had not sought Sir Patrick's advice about the original £1 million donation. What the letter asked for was his advice about the second donation, which also made a nonsense of the Prime Minister's claim that as soon as they started to seek an exemption for Formula One 'I said we can't accept any

further donations from Mr Ecclestone'. Why then ask Neill if they
could?

Aficionados of the affair would detect that Blair had slid into
mendacity, which made it all the more important that he should
attempt to radiate integrity. The lawyer Blair was not convincing
on the details. The actor Blair was summoned on stage. He made
a risky — but it turned out effective — appeal for the public's
continued trust. Expressing his 'hurt' that anyone should think he
would change a policy for money, he shifted into the gear of
super-sincerity:

I hope that people know me well enough and realise the type of person
I am to realise that I would never do anything to harm the country or
anything improper. I never have. I think most people who have dealt
with me think that I am a pretty straight sort of guy.[25]

Always his habit to want notes on his performances, Blair afterwards asked his familiars: 'How did I do?' Campbell's verdict was
clinical: 'It did the job.' His cynical view of the media's attention
span was borne out by most of the newspaper coverage on Monday
morning. The headlines concentrated on the Prime Minister's
semi-apology. Only on the inside pages were some of the inconsist-
encies of his account explored. Though Blair had originally resisted
it, the 'closure' tactic had proved effective. Gould later reported to
Blair that his reputation for trustworthiness had been dented, but
the continuing goodwill towards the government had carried him
through. There was some damage, but not much.

Campbell personally prospered, enhancing his position in the
inner circle at the expense of those who had urged a cover-up.
What Peter Mandelson initially dismissed as a 'bushfire' had become
a firestorm. He sought to explain why in a speech three days
later which offered itself as the definitive judgement on what the
government had learned from the most wretched episode of its
young life.

'My verdict on the week is very simple,' Mandelson said.

The government acted out of character. We acted against our own principles – that honesty is the first principle of good communications; that quick communications are essential to good government; and that the purpose of communicating is not to stall or hide but to put in context and explain.[26]

This was the most outrageous spin. New Labour had been acting true to the dark side of its character: first, the denials and the aggressive counterblast of rebuttals; followed by the partial retreat under pressure of revelations. And only when the truth had been agonisingly tweezered out of them bit by bit, only then the expressions of half-regret.

There was a worthwhile lesson to be learned about the perils of believing that New Labour could spin its way out of anything. Ecclestone had demonstrated that those who weave webs of deception tend to get trapped in them. But was it obvious to Blair and his circle that this was the lesson at all? Emerging from the affair with the opinion polls still generally glowing, the *pretty* straight kind of guy and his truth doctors could convince themselves that they had got away with it.

Yet it was inevitably corrosive. The most ugly complexion that could be put on this episode – the one that provoked Blair to expressions of pain and anger that anyone might suggest such a thing – was that his government had price-tagged its principles at £1 million. Even if the charge was false, he had exposed himself to it. The more generous interpretation was that he had been foolish to take Ecclestone's donation in the first place, naïve to have swallowed a self-serving argument from a former car dealer, and then been unscrupulous with the truth in the organisation of the cover story. The money returned to Ecclestone was replaced.[27] Something more priceless had been tarnished. Tony Blair had not proved himself any worse than other occupants of his office. The point was that he claimed to be so much better. The Prime Minister was still smiling, but with a tobacco stain on his teeth.

# 7. Department of Social Insecurity

Of all his appointments, none gave the Prime Minister more pleasure, none was more essential to the fulfilment of his Big Idea. So Tony Blair told Frank Field when he welcomed him into government in the ground-floor study at Number 10 after the election. As they rose from their seats, Blair clasped Field by the upper arms. 'Frank,' beamed the Prime Minister, lasering a shining gaze into the other man's eyes, 'we're going to reform welfare!'

If Field's taut smile did not radiate so much satisfaction in return, this was because he was already a disappointed and suspicious man. The pale, thin and neat MP for Birkenhead carried himself with the air of a medieval monk awaiting martyrdom. But he was also a man possessed of a lively ambition both for his ideas and for himself. He had departed from his last substantial conversation with Blair, in the leader's hotel suite at the party conference before the election, with the impression that Blair had promised him he would be Secretary of State for Social Security. That had been Blair's intention until Gordon Brown and Peter Mandelson, neither of whom shared Blair's great regard for Field, prevailed upon him to award the Cabinet seat to Harriet Harman instead.

The Prime Minister deployed all his considerable charms on Field that first weekend after the election to persuade him to work in harness. 'You and Peter have a special place with me,' he told Field. That privileged status aroused a great deal of jealousy among other, less blessed Labour MPs. Both he and Mandelson needed to demonstrate, so Blair smoothed the ruffled ego of Field, that 'you can be team-players'. Both needed to prove themselves in government before they could be elevated to the Cabinet. Since everyone assumed that Mandelson would join the top table in the first reshuffle, Blair was leading Field to believe that it was only a matter of time, a short time at that, before he would join him there.

Field played hard to get. On the Saturday morning after the election, an official at Downing Street called to ask at what time the minister would like his government car to collect him from home. Field replied, awkwardly, that he did not yet know whether he would be joining the government. He was still bargaining for status and power. Blair gave him membership of the Privy Council, a special privilege for a minister not of Cabinet rank, and a place on the committee on public expenditure. His dignity satisfied, Field's appointment as Minister for Welfare Reform was proclaimed along with the Cabinet. Alastair Campbell bugled that this should be read as an emphatic statement of the Prime Minister's determination to deliver on his grand yet opaque vision of reforming the welfare state. When Number 10 released an early list of the government's achievements, headed 'It's Time To Do', the only item listed for 3 May was the appointment of Field.

Blair's admiration for a fellow High Anglican who had battled with the hard left was genuine. What he had not grasped was the implications of the man's ideas. When he said to Field 'I agree with everything you say, Frank', the man on the receiving end correctly concluded that Blair was hearing him, but not listening to him. Field's principal attraction to the Prime Minister was that he talked robustly about ending the 'dependency culture' and made scourging sounds about welfare fraud. He answered to Blair's weakness for totemic figures who seemed to symbolise bracing and radical reform.

In Blair's eyes, the combination of Field with Harman was a potential dream team. The daughter of a Harley Street doctor, she was a moderniser when they were a small and vulnerable group. Harman was detested by John Prescott who could barely mention her name without associating it with an expletive. Campbell never forgave her decision to send a son to a selective school. To the Prime Minister, she was loyal, pliable and unswervingly on-message. Her Dutch doll looks seemed to have media appeal, especially to women. Field would prescribe the medicine for the welfare state. Harman would be the sugar to make it go down.

For a man who prided himself on his judgement of the character of colleagues, and his ability to use them to advantage, Blair could not have made a worse misjudgement. Between Field and Harman, it was hate at first sight. Both were warned by friends that the other would be a horror to work with. Within a week of being thrown together, both were working to make that horror come true. She saw him as a threat; he regarded her as a liability.

Field, though technically her inferior, was regarded, not least by himself, as Harman's intellectual superior. He relished, if he did not invent, the joke that she believed Beveridge was a hot drink. Their mutual suspicion was fed by the civil servants at the Department of Social Security. The hierarchy-minded officials were confused about the precise status of the odd couple they had been sent by Blair. If Harman was in charge – so her civil servants asked the secretary of state – why was Field sitting on the Cabinet committee?

Turf wars broke out across Whitehall as new ministers grappled to establish ascendancy in the new regime, but none of these struggles was as bitter as that between these two contestants. The pattern of their relationship was established by a wrangle over personnel. Field wanted to have his own political advisers. Harman attempted to frustrate him by stopping them working from within the department. She refused to sanction giving his advisers security clearance to enter its headquarters at Richmond House. This preliminary skirmish was eventually resolved only by calling on the Prime Minister himself to arbitrate. The fact that he was being asked to settle disputes over junior personnel should have served as an early warning to Blair about how rancorous the atmosphere was at social security.

Their offices were only fifteen yards apart. The mental corridor between them was fifty thousand miles. Whenever humanly possible, Field and Harman avoided meeting one-to-one. On the rare occasions that they were unavoidably forced into each other's company, the result was explosive. As is frequently the case between warring couples, their most incandescent confrontation turned on something relatively footling. Field wanted to appoint Kate Hoey, the MP for Vauxhall, as his parliamentary private secretary. Part-

confidant, part-gofer, part-spy, part-propagandist for his or her
ministerial master, the PPS is the lowest form of government pond
life. Such appointments can, however, be symbolic. Hoey, like
Field, did not swim in the Labour mainstream. Her causes included
support for fox-hunting, an eccentric enthusiasm for a Labour MP.
She had been with the majority of her party – indeed she was one
of the sharpest critics – in attacking Harman's decision to send her
son to a grammar school. Harman had ample motive to block Hoey
becoming Field's PPS. When he repeatedly failed to gain approval
for the appointment, Field had every reason to suppose that he was
being stymied by Harman.

In the summer, they confronted each other across the meeting
table in her ministerial suite. The suppurating mistrust and resentment between the two burst out. Challenged about Hoey, Harman
denied that she was blocking the appointment, telling Field that
the problem was with the whips. 'I don't believe that,' replied
Field. Fists pressing down on the table, their voices grew louder. 'I
can't work with someone who thinks I'm a liar,' Harman told him,
pinking with anger. White with fury, Field shouted back: 'And I
can't work with someone who *is* a fucking liar.'[1]

The Golden Girl of New Labour and the Saint of Birkenhead
had reduced themselves to this. Blair was at a loss how to drain the
poison infecting this crucial department. Both ministers would
come to him complaining about the other. Field said Harman was
instructing officials not to send him vital papers. Harman said Field
was not taking his share of ministerial responsibilities. He refused
to take charge of the programme to computerise the benefits
agency, seeing in it a plot by Harman to bury him in administrative
work. Harman moaned to Blair that Field locked himself in his
room 'to think'. Field composed sulphuric personal notes about
Harman groaning to Blair that 'you have chained me to a maniac'.
Field would handwrite his acrimonious missives, too sensitive and
too personal to be delivered through official Whitehall channels.
Then he would walk out of the department, slip across the road to
Downing Street, and hand the letter to the policeman at the door
of Number 10 to pass on to an increasingly anxious Blair.[2]

The Prime Minister was most prepossessed by the embarrasssment that Field might cause by leaving the government. Extraordinarily, it was to Harman that Blair turned for help, telling her that at all costs this had to be prevented. He shared with her his fear that Field was seeking an excuse to quit. 'You've got to stop Frank resigning,' Blair implored her. The Prime Minister had evidently not plumbed the depths of the ocean of bad blood between them.

This Whitehall mud-wrestling would simply have been a grisly entertainment were Harman and Field not jointly charged with realising what was supposed to be one of New Labour's great designs. Welfare reform, Blair declared, was 'one of the fundamental objectives' of his government.[3] In a pre-election conversation with Viscount Rothermere, the owner of the *Daily Mail*, Blair used a metaphor designed to appeal both to that paper's right-wing prejudices and to its Francophone owner. It had taken De Gaulle, the great nationalist, to extract France from Algeria; so it would take a Labour Prime Minister to radically reshape the welfare state. This played its part in the Tory press baron's conversion to New Labour on the grounds that the party was the 'New Conservatives'. At the same time as Blair was wooing Tory press lords, Labour spokespeople were indicating to those drawing benefits, and groups that represented them, that no one could possibly be worse off under a Labour government than they had been under the Conservatives.

That contradiction of messages was compounded by a conflict of aims. Field conceived a welfare system rebuilt on the principles of universal benefits provided by contributions. His contention was that reinventing the idea of national insurance would produce long-term savings for the government. What was about to come as a shock to Blair was the initial price of Field's schemes. He was invited into Downing Street to expand on his ideas for reforming pensions to Blair and the head of his Policy Unit, David Miliband. The Prime Minister was anxious to learn what cost Field put on it. He was open-jawed at the answer to his inquiry. 'Only eight billion pounds, Frank?' gasped Blair. He wanted Field to think the unthinkable, not spend the unspendable.

That horror was more than shared by Gordon Brown, who regarded himself as the overlord of welfare reform, and social security as the first department ripe for colonisation into the Brown Empire. The Chancellor's idea of welfare reform was more targeting: means-testing by any other name. The Treasury was looking for large savings from the welfare budget. Harman, whose lack of her own powerbase left her reliant on the patronage of Blair and Brown, made herself the instrument of the Chancellor.

The decision to strap themselves into the corset of the Conservatives' spending limits would cause breathing difficulties at all departments, but the price of doing this was going to be most painfully and quickly apparent at social security if it meant that Labour would implement benefit-cutting legislation planned by the Tories. Brown told Harman that, to remain within her budget limits, she would have to choose between two Tory cuts, both of which Labour had bitterly attacked when in Opposition. It was her choice, Brown told her. One cut was to the housing allowance paid to under twenty-five-year-olds living alone. The other removed the extra payment to single parents, predominantly lone mothers. A more alert or secure politician than Harman might have resisted making this choice at all. 'The lesson,' according to another member of the Cabinet, 'is that a secretary of state should tell the Chancellor when he is wrong.'⁴ Between strychnine – making youngsters homeless – and cyanide – eating her pre-election pledges about maintaining the support given to single mothers – Harman chose to find the money from the lone parent premium.

It was a decision with which, for once, her deputy agreed. Field had an ungenerous view of single mothers, an opinion formed, he would explain to friends, by his experience in his constituency. 'There are no single mums in Birkenhead,' he liked to claim. 'They all have a boyfriend somewhere.'

A cut of £6 a week was a large bite out of the income of some of the poorest people in the country. So those involved in the decision were pleasantly surprised to find that the early stages of the legislation passed through parliament without generating much heat among Labour MPs. There were rumblings against the single parent benefit cut at the party conference, but they were too low level to sound a cautionary klaxon to Blair and Brown.

It was with the return of parliament in October that Labour MPs began to question openly why they were inflicting this cut on some of the neediest and most vulnerable people in society. The left had also been emboldened thanks to, of all people, Peter Mandelson. His run for a place on the party's National Executive had been defeated by Ken Livingstone who thus acquired a more elevated platform for his criticism of the cut. In an attempt to quell the increasingly restive backbenches, Gordon Brown turned his November financial statement into a mini-Budget. Announced as 'the biggest ever investment in childcare,'[5] £300 million was earmarked to put nearly a million children in out-of-school childcare clubs so that their parents could work. Four hundred million pounds was spent on extra grants to help pensioners with their winter fuel bills. Brown could disclose that, thanks to falling claims for unemployment benefit, social security spending was undershooting. Though something for the government to boast about, this blew away the cost argument for terminating the premium to lone parents. Rather than suppress the rebellion, Brown had further agitated it. If he could spend all this money on childcare and pensioners, Labour MPs asked, why couldn't he find the relatively small sum of £60 million to avoid the cut to lone parent benefit? Deprived of the argument that they were forced to make the cut, ministers could not muster a coherent case that it was a principled act. Even in New Labour's own terms of luring and cajoling the unemployed back to work, this made no sense. Anyone who took a job, and then lost it, would return to benefit on the lower rate. That was no incentive to seek work.

More than one hundred Labour MPs, among them six chairs of select committees, signed a letter to the Chancellor urging him to delay the cut at least until the compensating measures helping mothers into work had come on stream. Nick Brown, the chief whip, warned Prime Minister and Chancellor that they were confronted with the first serious mutiny of the government's life. The pager-slaves were in revolt.

A fortnight before the crucial vote in the Commons, Blair called a meeting at Number 10. Along with Harman, there was Alastair Campbell, Peter Mandelson and Philip Gould, and Gordon Brown and Charlie Whelan. The Prime Minister was whirling. 'What do we do?' he asked the others. 'What do we do?' Blair toyed with the possibility of a compromise. Campbell declared against. They would be 'crucified' by the right-wing tabloids as 'feeble'. The *Sun* and *Daily Mail* were bound to depict it as a defeat for the government by the left if they were seen to be buckling to the back-benchers. Campbell found himself in rare agreement with Whelan who afterwards muttered to one of the others: 'Pippa [his wife] would murder me if she heard what I said in there.' Gould had been focus-grouping. After the government's autumn of con-fusions, Gould reported that the voters were beginning to attach worrying descriptions to the Prime Minister. Blair was being called 'vacillating' and 'aimless'. Retreat would look 'weak', said Gould. It would make things 'ten time worse'. They had to 'tough it out'.[6]

For those in the highest commands of New Labour, what was at stake was not principle, nor the small amount of money involved. This had turned into a virility test. The most powerful voice at the discussion, as so often, belonged to Gordon Brown. Retreat was unthinkable, he declared. The credibility of his spending controls, his authority as Chancellor, and the reputation of the government would be wrecked if they gave way to this first challenge from the backbenches.

Blair came to a similar view, with a slightly different nuance. 'We can't be blown around like Major,' he told the others.[7] Scanning the list of rebels drawn up by the whips, Blair complained: 'This is the same bunch who opposed everything I've done to reform the party.' The mutineers did have a core of left-wingers, but the opposition to the cut went much wider both within the party and out in the country. Opinion polling suggested that a majority of the public were against cutting benefits to single mothers.

Blair would rather ignore that evidence than flunk what he regarded as a challenge to his toughness. Better to demonstrate the machismo of the Prime Minister even at the price of placing him on the unpopular side of a poor argument. If the choice was between being seen as weak and dithering or harsh and unbending, then he would choose to be seen as Margaret Thatcher rather than John Major. The cut was going to proceed.

As she made her way into the House of Commons on 10 December, Harman sighed: 'It's time to take the shit.' She took it alone. The government frontbench was a lonely place that night. Only one Cabinet colleague turned out to lend her support. Harman, who had a formidable talent for losing friends and alienating people, was the mistress of much of her own misfortune. Eyebrows had jumped around the Cabinet table when she criticised the Agriculture Minister's controversial ban on beef-on-the-bone. Even those who agreed it could have been better handled were astonished to hear Harriet Harman offering lessons on the arts of presentation.

The most conspicuous absentees from the debate were the true authors of the cut. While their handmaiden was chewed up by Labour backbenchers, Chancellor and Prime Minister deserted her. Blair was hosting a party at Number 10 for media celebs, among them the disc jockeys Chris Evans and Zoe Ball. For a government so fixed on image projection, this created a dreadful conjunction. The enduring negative burned into memories of the night was the spectacle of the Prime Minister pouring champagne down the throats of wealthy media stars while he took money from the pockets of the poor.

Forty-seven Labour MPs voted against the government. A junior minister and four parliamentary aides resigned. Others registered their opposition by staying in their seats during the division, hiding in their offices, or keeping away from the House of Commons altogether. Gordon Brown stalked the swarming division lobby in a high dudgeon about the rebellion. Searching for an outlet for his anger, he caught sight of Clive Soley, MP for Hammersmith, and chairman of the Parliamentary Labour Party. Soley had delivered a subtly crafted speech in which he appealed to Labour MPs to bury their misgivings and support the government on this occasion, reassuring them that the lesson had been so well learned that the leadership would never stretch their loyalty so painfully in the future. As the vote progressed, Soley suddenly found himself grabbed by Brown. Stabbing his finger in the direction of the Labour MPs voting against the government, Brown raged: 'We'll deal with them. We'll get these bastards.' Soley was momentarily winded by the ferocity of the blast. Recovering, he replied: 'They're not the ones you should be worrying about, Gordon. It's them you should be worrying about.' Soley motioned at the miserable faces of the Labour MPs who were supporting the government.[8] A few cried. One MP confessed he had not been able to sleep the night before, 'I was so ashamed'.[9]

Soley was right. Those who rebelled could at least present their consciences as clean to the angry Labour activists back in their constituencies. Those voting with the government did so from a mixture of loyalty, ambition and fear. Few Labour MPs supported the cut with any conviction that it could be justified.

This marked a loss of innocence for the many parliamentary virgins swept into the Commons seven months earlier, and they could not have been deflowered more rudely. It is one of those quaint parliamentary conventions that a secretary of state stands in the division lobby to thank MPs for supporting his or her legislation. Harriet Harman disappeared as soon as she could. Her Conservative predecessor at Social Security, Peter Lilley, whose legislation Labour was enacting, stood in the lobby, crying 'This way for the cuts', rubbing vinegar into their wounded consciences. John Redwood proferred his sardonic congratulations to Margaret Beckett. 'Piss off,' she spat back.

The morning after, Number 10 woke up in a mood to flex the Prime Minister's biceps again. The media was briefed that the rebels should anticipate severe punishment for their defiance. This alarmed the chief whip. Nick Brown argued with the Prime Minister that this could create a permanently disaffected faction. The mutineers were too numerous, and enjoyed too much sympathy among the rest of the party. The rebels went unscathed, much to their gloating satisfaction.

Welfare reform had been launched in the most counterproductive manner conceivable. As one of the participants in the decision subsequently conceded: 'We should never have impaled ourselves on this.'[10]

That weekend, the Prime Minister sounded implacable. 'It's the Big Idea,' he insisted. 'We mustn't get deflected.'[11]

This was the mask on backstage panic. Harman was in a bad way at next week's Cabinet. Ivor Richard, the leader of the Lords, was warning that the cut would meet fierce opposition in the Upper House. On Blair's instructions, Jonathan Powell told Richard not to bring up the prospect of a defeat in the Lords at Cabinet. The chief whip flagged the danger anyway. If the cut was blocked in the Lords, said Nick Brown, it would have to come back to the Commons, threatening a repeated, even greater revolt. 'Don't mention it! Don't tell anyone!' urged Blair. It was hardly a secret, pointed out the chief whip. Everyone could work it out.[12]

There was the sound of clattering chairs at the top of the government as the participants in the decision scrambled to dump responsibility for the débâcle on each other. Number 10 put it out that it was Brown's fault for misreading the situation. Brown blamed Harman for not finding money for lone mothers from elsewhere in her budget. Harman claimed that she had been opposed to the cut all along. Labour MPs and welfare groups were now super-sensitive to the government's intentions. There was a lot, more than they actually knew, to be suspicious about. Brown had told Harman that he wanted her to find more than £1 billion of savings from disability benefits.

David Blunkett, the Education Secretary, had personal experience of both disability and the deprivations that could afflict single mothers. When he was twelve, his father suffered an agonising month-long death. As a result of a workmate's negligence, Arthur Blunkett fell into a vat of boiling water. Blunkett still remembered the smell of burnt flesh when he visited his dying father in hospital. His mother lived in bread-and-dripping poverty while she fought for compensation from the Gas Board. At the age of four, Blunkett was sent to blind school where the highest ambition his teachers had for him was to turn him into a piano tuner. He composed a stream of letters to both Harman and the Chancellor protesting about the Treasury's drive to cut benefits for the sick, the disabled and those suffering industrial injuries.

'Dear Gordon,' Blunkett wrote, the day before the benefits revolt.

While we would welcome humane and sensitively judged reforms to support disabled people to work . . . deep cuts in support for disabled people who either cannot work or can only find very modestly paid work would make a mockery of our professions on social exclusion and the construction of a more just society.[13]

This letter leaked. Amidst the ensuing uproar, a militant disabled group took direct action to the suicide bomber gates of Downing Street, which they sprayed with red paint. Blair, feeling the lash of what he had unleashed, was deeply shaken. He told Brown: 'We can't have the disabled chaining themselves to the gates.'

The government had put itself in the worst possible of political worlds. It was under attack not just for what it had done, but for things it had not yet done. John Prescott, who had been at the global warming summit in Japan during the benefits revolt, returned from Kyoto to complain to Blair that 'it's out of bloody control'. People saw Prescott as the ambassador from Old Labour to New at the top of the government. His postbag groaned with livid letters from Labour supporters, some of whom were tearing up their party cards.

In an attempt to soothe the party, and quell the Cabinet uprising against the Treasury, the Prime Minister declared he would take personal control of welfare reform: 'making sure the changes are consistent with social justice'.[14] In the New Year, he launched a series of public meetings – 'welfare roadshows' – styled on those which had sold the reform of Clause Four to the Labour Party. Eggs were thrown at Brown during an appearance in North London, but the meetings served the purpose of relieving some of the anger by allowing it expression. What they did not do was provide the government with a plan for welfare reform. Public relations was being substituted for policy; the roadshow was coming before the strategy.

Blair admitted: 'I am beginning to see why most politicians tend to steer clear of welfare'[15] – a confession of how naively he had approached reform. The welfare committee of the Cabinet, over which the Prime Minister had taken personal charge, was regarded, by the non-combatants among its number, as a waste of valuable ministerial time. Frank Field used the occasions to attack Gordon Brown with a nakedness which suggested that he did not expect to be in the government for much longer. Brown withdrew into whispering conclave with his advisers. When Harman spoke, other ministers who caught Blair's gaze were rewarded with the sight of the Prime Minister rolling his eyes to the ceiling.

In an attempt to save her neck, Harman started briefing the press that she was winning from the Treasury massive sums for childcare provision. Gordon Brown's annoyance that someone else was spinning his Budget was matched by anger from Blair when Harman's office briefed Patrick Wintour, the political editor of the *Observer*, that the government would introduce 'affluence-testing' to claw benefits back from the better-off.[16] This was the drift of their thinking – it subsequently proved to be exactly what happened – but it served to inflame a controversy that Blair was presently anxious to put back to sleep.

He had come to see that the Harman–Field dream team of his original imagining was a nightmare ticket. Exasperated by the two ministers' relentless sniping against each other, Campbell instructed Field and Harman that they were to do no further press briefing without clearance from Downing Street: 'No matter how much we urge silence, congenital briefing goes on about who is responsible for what.'[17] Six weeks later, their fax machines were burning with a further rebuke from the Prime Minister's press secretary: 'Given the speculation on welfare changes in the Budget in recent days . . . it is important you both enter a period of pre-Budget purdah.'[18] In other words: shut up. Campbell sarcastically told Harman that he would be 'grateful for an explanation' for why she had given newspaper and radio interviews which had not been 'cleared through this office'.

After she had been chastised by the Prime Minister, Harman was not so clueless that she could not guess what would happen next. She pleaded to Campbell: 'Don't set the dogs on me.'

The pack began to circle. The press predicted, with increasing regularity and certainty, that she would be fired in the reshuffle. When Harman challenged him, Campbell denied any responsibility for spreading these stories. When she took her complaint directly to Blair, he shrugged: 'You know Alastair.' There was an even more significant signpost that Harman was being embalmed prior to burial. Gordon Brown, a man ruthless at severing damaged limbs that had become a liability, got Charlie Whelan to indicate to selected journalists that the Chancellor was looking for a new Social Security Secretary.

Just as Harman was being starved of support by her erstwhile patron, so Field's star had crashed in the eyes of Tony Blair. Field's Green Paper on welfare reform, first due in October and trailed as one of the agenda-setting blockbusters of the first term, had still not appeared by the New Year. Drafts bounced back and forth between Field and David Miliband at Number 10 at least a dozen times. The Green Paper that was eventually published just before Easter was reduced down to a list of general principles rather than an agenda for action.

The futility of provoking the revolt was underlined when the cut to lone parent benefit was effectively reversed in the March Budget. The rebellion had a lasting consequence. Blair's inchoate desire for a large bang of welfare reform, a perilous approach in such an inflammatory, sensitive and hideously complex area, was abandoned. As were the ill-starred, mismatched couple at Social Security. Having swung in the wind for months, they were finally put out of their misery in the Cabinet reshuffle in July 1998.

Field chose to jump, Harman was given the push. Blair, a nervous and fretful butcher, spent weeks toying with all sorts of options to retain her in the government in a different role. The view of his aides, notably Alastair Campbell, that this would look weak prevailed over the Prime Minister's hesitancy. Harman was sensible enough to her likely fate – the early hour at which she had been summoned to see Blair should have been a sufficiently large clue –

to have already booked airline tickets for a holiday in France. 'I'm sorry. It just hasn't worked out,' said Blair. He wrapped the blade in cottonwool, telling her that 'she needed a rest'. After shedding tears on the sisterly shoulder of Tessa Jowell, Harman said farewell to the department. The civil servants in her private office, among whom there were clearly black humorists, presented her with a large bunch of white lilies, the bouquet of death.

Blair, still worrying that the departure of Field would damage the government's prestige, tried to make it a soft landing. He asked the new Cabinet Secretary, Sir Richard Wilson, to see if he could negotiate Field into a role as 'fraud czar'. Field would settle only for the Cabinet seat he believed Blair had promised him. At their last interview at Number 10, there was none of the clasped arms and beaming smiles of the first encounter. Field wondered of Blair why, if he wouldn't put him in the Cabinet, he still wanted him in the government at all. 'Well, it's about your ideas and so on,' replied Blair, foggily. 'You can have my ideas from the back-benches,' retorted Field, and walked out on to Downing Street to declare that he would fight on from outside the government.

With Frank Field's ministerial career died whatever prospect there was of New Labour reinventing the welfare system on the basis of universality. Insightful though he could be, he proved an inept Whitehall operator, incapable of turning his ideas into policy which could command the support of colleagues. He was always going to be the casualty in a full-frontal war against Gordon Brown, as Field would belatedly acknowledge by wryly suggesting to Blair that the Department of Social Security might just as well be folded into the Treasury. Harriet Harman was an object lesson in the perils of patronage and the dependency culture of New Labour. The over-obedient servant to the wishes of Blair and Brown, she was sacrificed by them when the consequences exploded in the government's face.

The new hand at Social Security, the former Treasury man Alistair Darling, was the type of managerial technocrat increasingly preferred by Blair. Darling anticipated a massive amount of home-work to get up to speed at his new department. After being shown his ministerial suite, he asked whether he could have all the briefing material on the work in progress on welfare reform. 'Oh,' replied the Permanent Secretary, Dame Ann Bowtell. 'That shouldn't take you long.'[19]

This was the moral for Tony Blair. Announcing a Big Idea was not the same as having one.

# 8. Long Good Friday

The black anti-terrorist gates at the mouth of Downing Street were drawn open to admit Gerry Adams and Martin McGuinness. On the other side of the street, a thick blue line of police separated protestors yelling 'Murderers!' and supporters cheering them in. The two men walked up Downing Street past the crash barriers behind which were corralled representatives of the world's media assembled to record a moment which few, if any, of them ever expected to witness. Posing with the rest of the Sinn Fein delegation by the Number 10 Christmas tree, Gerry Adams, who first grew his beard when he was a fugitive from arrest and internment, described it as 'a good moment in history'. The day for historians to mark was 11 December 1997. Martin McGuinness, the former chief of staff of the IRA and commander of its Derry brigade through some of the bloodiest years of the Troubles, stood stone-faced. Behind them, the door to Number 10 was opening; the door that had shuddered with the force of the blast six years previously when the IRA had come in uninvited through the back way with bombs that almost murdered the Prime Minister.

Tony Blair did not come out to greet them but lingered down the corridor, outside the Cabinet room. The handshakes inside were not to be recorded for the cameras. The day was already heaving with enough controversial symbolism.

The Prime Minister and his colleagues faced the Sinn Feiners across the coffin-shaped Cabinet table. Adams wondered out loud: 'Is this where Michael Collins met Lloyd George in 1921?' Collins was the last Sinn Fein leader to visit Number 10, and it was not an auspicious precedent for either side. The founder of the IRA returned from making peace with the British to denunciation, civil war, and the deaths of thousands, including his own.

'Yes, I think so,' replied Blair. The Northern Ireland Secretary couldn't restrain her wonderfully wicked humour. Pointing to the window looking out on to the back garden of Number 10, Mo Mowlam said: 'And that's the window the mortars came through.' There was brittle laughter around the table. Even the hard features of McGuinness softened into a smile and a little warmth sparkled in his ice-blue eyes.

Neither Mowlam nor Blair had any doubt that when they parleyed with Adams and McGuinness, they were talking, through them, to the IRA. They could never be certain of their sincerity. But, as Mowlam always said to Blair, the only way to know that they wanted to end the violence was to put them to the test. What was sure was that without Sinn Fein and the IRA there could be no lasting settlement to the Troubles that since 1969 had claimed more than 3,000 lives and maimed so many more. There is no greater challenge for a politician than to guide the terrorist into the ways of democracy. There were also large risks, as many commentators predicted when the Sinn Feiners were ushered into Number 10, that Blair would look like the naïve dupe of terrorists. On one occasion, Adams and McGuinness were told by Blair that he would do everything he could to find an agreement. Then, he gave them a hard stare: 'But if you ever do a Canary Wharf [bomb] on me, I will never talk to you again.'[1]

The intensity of New Labour's engagement with Northern Ireland had surprised the province's politicians. Before the election, John Hume, the veteran Nationalist and midwife of the peace process, told friends that he did not expect Tony Blair, a new Prime Minister with so many other agendas, to devote much energy to the six counties. Blair was taken aback to learn how much of John Major's time had been consumed by Ulster, only to find himself being drawn in as deeply. Northern Ireland was the one subject most likely to keep the Prime Minister awake at night.

For Blair – an Anglican married to a Catholic and an anti-sectarian of any sort – a bloody quarrel over borders was an offence to his view of how the world should be. This presented the greatest opportunity to demonstrate that his consensual politics could yield a result in the most tribally antagonistic of territories. It was the hardest test of Blair's belief in his own abilities to charm the apparently irreconcilable into transcending their differences.

'I know I'm insanely optimistic,' Blair would say to staff at Number 10. 'But it's really very simple.' This innocence was a form of strength. A more world-wearied politician, a more experience-worn Prime Minister would have been much more cautious about challenging the odds that said he would fail.

He came to office with some advantages over John Major. By May 1997, the IRA had returned to what the terrorists called 'war', but there were signals from Sinn Fein that they saw a change of government as an opportunity to resume talking about peace. Faced with a Prime Minister in possession of a parliamentary majority of 179 who was universally assumed to be assured of re-election, intelligent Unionists recognised that they would have to find a more creative approach than the ancient bellowing negative of 'No Surrender'. The commitment to devolution provided a more promising context for fashioning new self-governing institutions for Northern Ireland. New Labour's very newness was itself a rebuke to the perma-frosted politics of Ulster; a challenge to its cold warriors to find a better way.

Blair initially concentrated on winning the confidence of the Unionists. He flew to Belfast a fortnight after the election to tell the Protestant community that they had 'nothing to fear' from his government. Their status within the United Kingdom could be changed only by consent. 'A political settlement is not a slippery slope to a united Ireland', which he did not expect to happen 'within my lifetime'.[2] In the Unionists' leader, David Trimble, Blair identified a man with whom business could be done. The bespectacled, buttoned-down, prickly and precise Trimble was a very different political animal from Blair. But there were touching points of which the most obvious was that both were lawyers. Though elected as the most hardline of the candidates to lead his party, Trimble was, by the standards of Unionism, a moderniser. Blair had been investing in this relationship since he was his party's Shadow Home Secretary. 'David, I'm a Unionist actually,' Blair told him, not insincerely. Trimble was susceptible to being flattered by the attention of the new Prime Minister; Blair was an expert charmer. When he was in Tokyo in January 1998, he made time to ring Trimble no fewer than six times. Over frequent tête-à-têtes in Number 10 or at Chequers, Blair used the intimacy of the occasions to build a bond of trust with the Unionist leader. These reassurances to the Unionists smoothed the path to re-opening a dialogue with Sinn Fein.

Mo Mowlam concentrated her different, but formidable charms on the Nationalist community. 'Get me a chopper,' she demanded of startled officials on her first day in post, and was duly helicoptered to Belfast that weekend where she plunged among startled and impressed crowds. They had never encountered a secretary of state like this. Neither had the officials at the Northern Ireland Office. Behind Mowlam's desk in her London office, she hung a particularly excremental example of modern art. A splodge of dirty white, the painting was entitled *Discipline Over Desire*.[3] Mowlam called it her 'bullshit detector'. She would ask visitors for an opinion of the painting. Anyone who claimed to like it was not to be trusted.

Mowlam put her popularity down to 'the hair'. By that she meant the lack of it after the treatment for a brain tumour. She used 'the bloody wig' as a theatrical prop: throwing it around the room, hurling it at people. This vulnerable, gritty, bloody-minded woman's unconventionality – she swore, she held conversations with aides while seated on the loo with the door ajar, she told filthy jokes – was shock therapy to Northern Ireland's atrophied system. She did what so many predecessors had yearned to do, but never dared, and told Ian Paisley to 'fuck off'. The blood Orangeman called her 'the sinner'. Unionists, a breed whose sexual attitudes were roughly twenty years behind the rest of Britain's, recoiled from her touch. Ken Maginnis was one of the most liberal of Unionists, but he could not cope with the tactile Mowlam. Trying to explain why, he waved his arms in a circle and shivered: 'She was . . . like an octopus.'[4]

The Catholic community, however, warmed to the first Northern Ireland Secretary not to appear to them like a remote and

patrician British viceroy. Mowlam's immediate Tory predecessor
in Belfast, Sir Patrick Mayhew, generously accounted it a 'splendid'
thing if the contrast between 'stuffy old Mayhew' and the unstiff
style of Mo had transformed the atmosphere.[5]

The joint endeavours of Blair and Mowlam began to melt the
ice. Following the IRA's return to a ceasefire in July 1997, by
October all the important parties except Ian Paisley's rejectionists
were in talks under the chairmanship of the former American
Senator, George Mitchell. But they were still posturing more than
they were negotiating. They had not even reached agreement on a
detailed agenda. It is an illustration of the scale of the mountain that
even Mitchell's legendary patience was being mined to exhaustion.

For hundreds and hundreds of hours I had listened to the same arguments
over and over again. Very little had been accomplished. We were about
to adjourn for the Christmas break. Failure would be crushing. Yet here
the delegates were, furiously debating what had or had not been agreed
to in an earlier meeting about whether we should or should not move
the whole process to London and Dublin, and who had said what to
which newspaper.[6]

Making peace in Ireland was like digging a trench through
a minefield: numbingly slow and tedious work punctuated by
life-taking explosions. Barely more than a fortnight after Adams
and McGuinness visited Number 10, the entire process was suddenly and violently at risk. At ten thirty on the morning of Saturday
December 27, Billy 'King Rat' Wright, a loyalist terrorist, was
murdered inside the Maze prison by members of the republican
sect, the INLA. Loyalists retaliated. The same day, a hotel in a
Catholic area was riddled with gunfire, killing one man and wound-
ing four others. On New Year's eve, a man was gunned down in a
bar. The following day, a Protestant home was attacked. A descent
back into the grisly vortex of tit-for-tat sectarian killings threatened
everything. Four of Trimble's ten Westminster MPs demanded
that he pull out of the talks.

The loyalist terrorists in the Maze voted to withdraw their

support for the talks. If the loyalist ceasefire broke down, then it was not likely to be long before the IRA resumed its terror campaign. The prisoners were bargaining chips: the republican and loyalist parties wanted the terrorists associated with their causes released. The prisoners, heroic freedom fighters in the theology of sections of their traditions, were also actors of influence with a near-decisive say over some of the parties.

On Wednesday 7 January, Gary McMichael, the leader of the Ulster Democratic Party, one of the parties associated with the loyalist prisoners, took a delegation to see Mowlam. Despairingly, McMichael told her that they could not change the prisoners' minds. They did not know what else to do. The only thing that might break the impasse was some sort of 'big gesture'. Everything seemed imperilled. 'Right,' declared Mowlam, with typical impulsiveness. 'I'll go there myself.'

She walked straight out and into the nearby office of the Permanent Secretary at the Northern Ireland Office. 'I'm going into the Maze,' she announced to him. 'Oh,' he replied. 'Right.' When other officials got to hear of the idea, they were less polite. 'No one's done that before, secretary of state,' they said, Whitehall's way of telling a minister that she should be measured for a padded cell. Mowlam did not bother to inform Number 10, and she did not need to. Civil servants at the Northern Ireland Office were rapidly on the phone to Downing Street. Appalled and terrified by her idea, they lobbied Number 10 to veto their own secretary of state.[7]

Tony Blair was startled when he was first told. He called together the aides who helped him navigate the treacherous bogs of Northern Ireland. Jonathan Powell was the linkman to the Unionists; so much so that Blair had awarded his chief of staff with a nickname, 'The Unionist'. John Holmes, a civil servant inherited from John Major, was treasured for his encyclopedic knowledge of previous agreements and the bargaining positions of Ulster's protagonists. Alastair Campbell joined them. They could instantly produce all the arguments for why the Northern Ireland Secretary should not go into the high-security H-Blocks to talk to the prisoners. It would be attacked by Unionists as appeasement of terrorism, said Powell. And by a lot of the British press, added Campbell. Mowlam was risking her stature and the government's authority without any certainty that the gesture would work. Yet, the more they talked, the more it intuitively felt like a gamble worth taking. Despite all the self-evident hazards, Blair concluded that the impulsive Mowlam was right. After all, the progress they had made so far had come by repeatedly breaking the old rules in Northern Ireland.

The size of the risk Mo Mowlam took when she went into the Maze on the Friday can be appreciated from the nature of the men she met in the prison's tatty gymnasium. She talked to five members of the Ulster Defence Association, including Michael Stone, the gruesomely tatooed multiple killer responsible for one of Northern Ireland's most horrific atrocities in 1988 when he used guns and grenades on mourners at the Milltown cemetery. Mowlam also met the Maze's IRA prisoners, among them a man serving life for the murder of two soldiers. The visit attracted exactly the criticism that was anticipated. John Alderdice, leader of the non-sectarian Alliance Party, complained that the Northern Ireland Secretary had made the terrorist prisoners 'important arbiters of our future'.[8] Nicholas Winterton, Tory backbench foghorn, described it as 'One of the most diabolical instances of pandering to terrorists I can think of.'[9] Ian Paisley junior, chip off the reverend block, lambasted an 'ego trip' which ransomed Northern Ireland to 'the gangsters'.[10]

This illustrated how disastrous it would have been for the government had Mowlam failed. The critics were rapidly deflated. The prisoners were persuaded by her unpatronising frankness and treated her with almost gentlemanly courtesy. 'It was one of my most civilised meetings,' she joked to an aide afterwards. Within hours of her visit, she had a success when the prisoners reversed position and announced their continued support for negotiations. Her daring and gutsy risk had paid off.

The talks were saved, but there was still a wall of pain and mistrust to climb to get even within sight of agreement. The Unionists would not talk directly to Sinn Fein. During discussions in London at Lancaster House in late January, Gerry Adams made an overture to Ken Maginnis. According to Adams, Maginnis walked away, spitting: 'I don't talk to fucking murderers.'[11]

When Tony Blair met the Irish Taoiseach, Bertie Ahern, at Number 10 in late February, the two Prime Ministers were encouraged that the parties had started negotiating issues of substance. But in virtually all the areas vital to a settlement they remained leagues away from agreement. They might have got them into roughly the same solar system, but the protagonists were living on different planets. The ever-present danger, highlighted by the wave of sectarian violence sparked by the Maze killing of Billy Wright, was that atrocities by extremists would blow the talks apart. That peril had been emphasised again when Sinn Fein was temporarily suspended from the talks after evidence of IRA complicity in this spiral of killings.

Rather than permit further drift, the psychological pressure of the deadline was employed. On 25 March, Senator Mitchell announced that he had signed up all the parties to a mind-concentrating fifteen-day programme to get agreement. They would succeed – or fail – by midnight on Thursday 9 April, the day before Good Friday. The Holy Week had been chosen for its symbolic importance in a religious society. And because, without an agreement at Easter, it would not be possible to conduct a referendum and elect an assembly before the sectarian heat of Northern Ireland's July marching season. It is worth taking a measure of the awesome scale of the challenge. Vast differences on key issues – from the powers of the proposed assembly to the timing of the release of terrorist prisoners – would have to be bridged in an exceedingly short span of time. Parties whose first presumption about each other was complete bad faith had to be won over to common agreement.

On the evening of Monday 6 April, George Mitchell completed a sixty-nine-page draft agreement which he distributed just after midnight to the delegations gathered at Stormont. Optimistically, Mitchell declared: 'I believe we are close to bringing this to a successful conclusion.' Mowlam confidently forecast that they would reach final agreement by the midnight Thursday deadline.

Back in London, when Blair started reading the document, he

reacted with alarmed consternation. A crucial section – 'Strand Two' – covered the creation of cross-border institutions covering Northern Ireland and the Republic. This was the 'Irish dimension' eagerly desired by the Nationalists, and feared with an equal passion by the Unionists who saw it as a device for reunification by stealth. The tightrope of tension that had to be walked to get to agreement was one side's need to see each step taking them towards Irish unity, and the other side's need to see each step locking them into the United Kingdom. Blair had been in discussion about Strand Two with Bertie Ahern over the weekend. The two Prime Ministers talked generalities, but left the details to the civil servants, and the Irish officials appear to have got the upper hand over their British counterparts. The document was not what the Prime Minister had anticipated. 'They've screwed it up,' he complained to his aides. The document had a Nationalist flavour which would be much too strong for the Unionists. 'They've blown it. This is much too green,' he steamed.[12]

His fears about the Unionist reaction were quickly realised on Tuesday morning when Blair took a telephone call from Trimble. The Unionist, who burnt on a short fuse, was explosive. Talking of betrayal, he told Blair that his party would never agree to this 'bad' document. Unless there were fundamental changes, then 'that's it', there was no point in talking at all.[13] Blair was accustomed to the use of the temper tantrum and the threatened walk-out by all the parties as a bargaining device. But Trimble sounded genuine. He had been so aghast at the document that at first he refused even to show it to other members of his delegation. Trimble's deputy, John Taylor, rejected it out of hand. 'I'm away,' he declared to the media encamped outside the talks venue, Castle Buildings in Belfast. 'I wouldn't touch this thing with a forty-foot pole.'

The entire process was threatening to implode before the negotiations had even begun. Blair threw aside his original intention to travel to Belfast at the end of the talks to put the prime ministerial stamp on an agreement. Abandoning plans for a Cabinet reshuffle that week, he hurled his own prestige at the disintegrating talks. Mitchell was in no doubt about the importance of Blair's decision.

'He was making a total commitment, personal and political, to this negotiation. That didn't guarantee success, but without it there was no chance.'[14] The riskless option for Blair would have been to maintain a safe distance, especially when the chances of success seemed so remote. His own aides were divided. Holmes and Powell believed that an agreement could yet be possible. Campbell was hugely pessimistic, saying to the others: 'I just can't see how we get through this.'[15] Nine out of ten people in Northern Ireland, according to polls, believed that an agreement was impossible. Blair took off for Belfast in such a depressed state of mind that he shed his usual practice of sounding upbeat in every circumstance. 'I am very pessimistic,' he said before he left. 'There is only a slim chance we can recover from this.'[16]

At shortly before six that evening, the Prime Minister arrived at Hillsborough Castle, the Northern Ireland Secretary's seat near Belfast. A jeering mob of Paisley supporters waving Union Jacks wished failure upon him and the talks.

'Now is not the time for sound-bites, we can leave those at home,' remarked Blair, before delivering one of his most celebrated sound-bites. 'I feel the hand of history upon our shoulders.'[17]

He was begging to be mocked, not least by history, which warned politicians with ambitions to solve the Northern Ireland Question that their pretensions would be smashed by the fist of fate.

Blair's first priority, to which he devoted an evening meeting, was massaging Trimble by assuring him that the Mitchell document was only a basis for negotiation. On Wednesday morning, Bertie Ahern flew into Belfast for a seven o'clock breakfast with Blair. The Irish Prime Minister and leader of Fianna Fail, Ireland's most avowedly green party, had political, familial and sentimental attachments to republicanism. On the wall of his Dublin office was a portrait of Patrick Pearse, who led the rebels against British rule in the 1916 Easter Rising. Ahern's father was a member of the 3rd Cork brigade of the IRA. When he left Belfast after breakfast to return to Dublin for the funeral of his mother, Ahern buried her in a republican plot in Glasnevin cemetery, close to the graves of

Michael Collins, Eamon de Valera and Charles Stewart Parnell. For all that, Ahern, a hospital accountant by pre-political trade, was a modern man, a pragmatic and non-ideological politician as desirous for an end to the bloodshed in Northern Ireland as was Blair. Without the trust they had established in each other, there was no chance of success.

The two Prime Ministers went out for a walk in the grounds of Hillsborough Castle. 'David is serious. It's too much. He can't accept this,' Blair warned Ahern that Trimble was not bluffing. Ahern could have insisted on sticking to the agreement about cross-border institutions. Instead, he said that the north–south issues could be put back into the melting pot to accommodate the Unionists. It was an act of selflessness without which the negotiations would have been aborted.

Blair then met Trimble and his deputy. The ruggedly featured and gruffly spoken John Taylor had had his jaw shot off by an IRA gunman. A mercurial man, capable of changing his opinions by the hour, he was the weather-vane of the Unionists. Trimble would never carry his party unless he had Taylor pointing in a supportive direction. The Prime Minister was sitting on the table when the two Unionists came in. 'John, what is this forty-foot thing people keep talking about?' Blair asked, deftly lifting the atmosphere with a joke.[18]

The talks were saved, but they marked time until Ahern returned from his mother's funeral that evening. At the end of a formal meeting with officials, the two Prime Ministers spent some time alone together to choreograph a routine to deal with the Unionists. At 7.15 that evening, Blair and Ahern met Trimble and Taylor. Seeking to assuage their neuralgia about unification-by-stealth, Blair urged the Unionists to hang on to the principle of consent. There could be no change of Northern Ireland's status against the wishes of the majority. Crucially, he had prearranged with Ahern that the Irish leader would underline the point as emphatically. The personal chemistry, so vital to a successful outcome, gelled. Trimble told Ahern how much he appreciated his rapid return to Belfast after the funeral of his mother. Taylor was gyrating positively by the end of the encounter, telling Trimble that he had been convinced of the Irish premier's sincerity.

At breakfast time on Thursday, Blair told a stock-taking session of officials and ministers that he was optimistic after the encounter between Ahern and the Unionists the previous night. A neat formula was located to suppress the mistrust between the two sides. The Northern Ireland Assembly, which the Unionists wanted, and the cross-border bodies, desired by the Nationalists, were made dependent on each other. Both would function together, or neither would operate. What Blair called 'a mutual destruction' provision was a cunningly designed fail-safe for both sides.

Putting together an agreement between eight competing and volatile parties was like standing on a heaving ship's deck trying to succeed at that executive puzzle in which you have to manoeuvre steel balls through a maze until they all rest in holes. Tilting to move one ball into place risked displacing another. Reacting negatively to the concessions to the Unionists, Gerry Adams and Martin McGuinness, declaring 'there can be no agreement which will work without Sinn Fein', now threatened to walk out. At a ninety-minute meeting with the Prime Minister, they produced a long list of demands which would be utterly unacceptable to the Unionists. Blair knew that Sinn Fein's primary goal was the early release of terrorist prisoners. Movement on that could induce them to swallow a lot of other things. The crucial concession made by Blair was to reduce the release timetable for the prisoners from three years to two.

As the Thursday midnight deadline approached and then passed without an agreement, Campbell and Powell badgered Blair to play 'the Clinton card'. The American President's telephone seduction techniques had acquired global notoriety from the tapes of his heavy breathers with Monica Lewinsky. When applied to politics, Clinton's telephone diplomacy could be highly effective, and had several times before helped in Northern Ireland. Blair rejected his aides' advice. 'We can't use Clinton to push the pieces into place,' he told them. 'We have to use him when the pieces are in place.'[19]

Outside, Ian Paisley led several hundred rejectionists in an attempted march on Castle Buildings. They were halted by the police at the statue of Carson, the founding father of Unionism. Paisley found himself on the wrong side of history as Protestants from the smaller parties connected to the loyalist paramilitaries started barracking: 'You didn't have to fight the war.'

What Paisley thirsted for – the collapse of the negotiations – seemed alarmingly probable. The design of Castle Buildings, a particularly brutalist example of sixties architecture, did not inspire hope. All the corridors looked identical, as if the participants were trapped in a Kafkaesque maze from which there would never be an escape. Blair and his team were installed in the third floor office of a junior Northern Ireland minister. Enormous energy had already been expended meeting the protagonists, separately or together, to try to hammer through to an agreement. A shoeless Mo Mowlam wandered the corridors, popping into delegations to pick up intelligence, reassuring other parties that their interests were not being neglected as the greatest effort went in to spanning the most yawning divide, that between the Unionists and Sinn Fein. She squeezed. She threatened. Cornering a recalcitrant Gerry Adams in a corridor, Mowlam growled at him: 'You fuckin' well get your act together.' Adams came over affronted: 'That's no way to speak to me.' So she swore at him in Irish. He couldn't help himself laughing.

The structure of the assembly was the subject of grinding negotiation between the Unionists and the largest Nationalist party, the SDLP, led by John Hume and his deputy, Seamus Mallon. In the early hours of Friday morning, this vital dimension of the talks was deadlocked. Even Mowlam, the incorrigible optimist, became so disheartened that she told her officials: 'We may as well go home.'[20] Blair had swung back towards pessimism: 'It was about four o'clock on Friday morning that I thought we were going to lose it.'[21]

Many of the participants were manic depressive, swinging between elation when a deal seemed tantalising near, and deflation when agreement appeared to be slipping through their fingers. It infected Blair as well. He told his party conference later in the year that, in the small hours of the morning, he stood with his back to the door yelling at one delegation: 'You're not going till we've sorted this.'[22] Another participant in the talks recalls a despondent and drained Blair. Limply sprawled over a sofa, when they turned to him for his help, the Prime Minister groaned: 'Oh, for God's sake, deal with it yourselves.'[23]

Gloom was punctuated with flashes of dark humour. Gusty Spence was a former leader of the Ulster Volunteer Force who had renounced a previous life of vicious loyalist terrorism and was negotiating on behalf of one of the smaller paramilitary-linked parties. Seeing Blair's frustration with Trimble's party, Spence asked him: 'If I shoot them, will I get out in two years?'

At five o'clock on Friday morning, there was a major advance, and a potentially fatal setback. Trimble's Unionists and the SDLP of Hume and Mallon had come to an agreement about the structure of the assembly. It would be headed by a First Minister and run by a power-sharing executive – a form of cabinet – on which all parties would have representation. Afterwards, in the basement canteen, a bleary Trimble left his own table to wander over to a gaunt Mallon. Trimble had some suggestions about how the SDLP might present the deal to its supporters. As the Unionist turned to go, his Nationalist adversary touched his hand to his forehead in half-salute, crinkled his face, and said: 'Yes, First Minister.' Such a scene would have been unbelievable but a few months previously.

Adams and McGuinness were again talking of a walk-out. Up on the third floor, Blair strode around his temporary office, munching on a bacon sandwich, and snapping fingers at the two clerks he had brought over from London. 'Get Clinton,' he said. Now was the moment to play in the American President. At ten to six in Belfast – ten to one in the morning in Washington – Clinton began a twenty-five-minute phone conversation to urge Adams to sign the agreement. At six thirty, Blair met Adams and McGuinness. With the Unionists and Nationalists agreed, the British and Irish governments working together, and the American President applying additional leverage, Sinn Fein would be isolated and blamed if they wrecked everything at the last gasp. Mixing threat with blandishment, Blair reminded them of the deal they had secured on prisoners, and the commission to consider reform of the Royal Ulster Constabulary. Always conscious that every actor in this drama had an audience outside to satisfy, Blair suggested to Adams and McGuinness that, with a 'positive spin', they could sell this agreement to their supporters.

A weak sun rose over Stormont on Good Friday morning. Blair, fuzzy from sleep deprivation and existing on a diet mainly composed of butties and bananas, Twix and Mars bars, asked: 'Where can I get some air?' He wanted a walk, but away from the gaze of the TV cameras and reporters besieging the building. The only location that answered his desire for privacy was a thin strip of grass behind a wall topped with razor wire. Taking Campbell for company, the Prime Minister paced the tiny enclosure under a lowering Belfast sky. They joked that they were like two prisoners allowed out for recreation.

Release seemed in sight. At half past noon on Good Friday, George Mitchell circulated copies of the agreement. John Hume wandered outside the building doing the thumbs-up and shaking hands. The lunchtime news bulletins reported it as a done deal. Blair phoned Cherie, who had already taken their children to Spain to begin an Easter holiday. 'We're there,' Blair sighed to his wife. He told her he would be with her by the evening.[24] Campbell and Powell helped Blair to begin writing a speech hailing a historic moment.

This was premature elation. When David Trimble presented the deal to his thirty-strong delegation, the Unionist leader encountered fierce internal dissent. John Taylor, the weathercock, swung into opposition, announcing to the meeting that he had sixteen objections to the agreement. Jeffrey Donaldson, the MP for Lagan Valley, a protégé of Trimble in the process of becoming a rival and opponent, weighed in. He had spotted what he saw as a fatal flaw to the bargain made with the SDLP in the early hours. Members of Sinn Fein could become ministers before the IRA had disposed of any of its weapons. Nor was there any explicit linkage between decommissioning of the terrorist arsenal and the release of prisoners.

Snow and hail began to fall, as if the weather was pronouncing the negotiations doomed. At twenty past three, Trimble and Taylor came up to Blair's office, the tables and carpet strewn with drafts and redrafts, the room littered with exhausted cups of black coffee. Blair told the Unionists that it was impossible to start unpicking one corner of the agreement without unravelling the whole tapestry. The Irish government would not stand for it, nor the Nationalists. 'If we renegotiate on one front, they will renegotiate on another.'[25] Campbell pleaded with Trimble to contemplate the consequences if the agreement collapsed: 'We will all be crucified. People won't understand.' The Unionist leader did not want to shoulder the blame for failure, but he told them he had to have something extra to sell the deal to his party.

While Trimble went back to his delegation, Powell drafted a side-letter in Blair's name which was constructed to help the Unionist leader. The letter in hand, Powell went down to the Unionists' delegation room. When he tried the door, Powell found it locked, and his knocks unanswered. When his increasingly urgent banging on the door finally gained the attention of those within, the missive from the Prime Minister was handed over. Trimble absorbed it, then handed it on to Taylor. The crucial passages assured the Unionists that, if the mechanism for excluding politicians connected with terrorist groups did not work, Blair would 'support changes to these provisions to enable them to be made properly effective'. It also said that, in the view of the British government, 'the process of decommissioning should begin straight away' after the elections to the assembly in June. Trimble was asked to keep the letter confidential lest its publication destabilise the support of other parties for the agreement.

This artfully worded letter was a fudge, if not a contradiction of the Good Friday document. But those who subsequently attacked the device on those grounds were blinding themselves to the alternative. Without the letter, there would have been no deal at all. Everything would almost certainly have collapsed. Sinn Fein, for whom the agreement effectively meant repudiating the central tenet of their ideology by accepting the partition of Ireland, seem to have been assuming that they would be let off the hook by the Unionists. Adams and McGuinness were expecting Trimble's party to reject the agreement, leaving the Unionists to take the blame for destroying peace. According to Reg Empey, one of Trimble's closest confidants, the Unionist delegation had been five minutes away from walking out before the delivery of the letter.[26]

It was enough to swing the pivotal John Taylor back in favour of the agreement. Ken Maginnis, who would describe these hours as 'the most traumatic event of my political life', made an impassioned appeal to the assembled Unionists to support the deal.[27] 'I'm going for it,' declared Trimble. 'Anyone who is with me, come now.' At quarter to five, the Unionist leader told Mitchell and Blair that he would 'do the business'. It was a brave decision by Trimble, and he would not have been so emboldened had he not had so much faith invested in the British Prime Minister.

The eight parties to the talks emerged for the final ceremony rubbing their eyes with a mixture of exhaustion and astonishment. They sat around the same table, signifying their agreement, Unionists and Nationalists, extremes of loyalism and violent republicanism together, a tableau no one who knew anything of the history of Northern Ireland thought they had a right to expect to see. David Trimble would not clasp the palm of Gerry Adams, but they had put their hands up to the same agreement. It had been written so that each protagonist could interpret it as a victory for his tradition. Trimble hailed the Union: 'We in the Ulster Unionist Party rise knowing that the Union is stronger than it was when we sat down.' Adams conversely promised republicans that it marked a 'phase in our struggle' towards a united Ireland. Only because both men could claim a triumph was agreement possible at all.

At the end of the longest, most sleepless, most intense three days of his premiership, Tony Blair echoed the words with which he had arrived:

Today I hope that the burden of history can at long last start to be lifted from our shoulders. Even now this will not work unless in your will and in your mind you make it work; unless you extend the hand of friendship to those who were once your foes.

He was frank: 'Today is only the beginning. It is not the end. Today we have just the sense of the prize before us. The work to win that prize goes on.'[28]

There was another sudden shower of snow. Northern Ireland would not easily escape the long shadow of its dark past, but this was a momentous step towards a lighter future. Both sides had made compromises long thought unthinkable. Republicans effectively recognised the legitimacy of Northern Ireland, a creation of partition that for generations they had been dedicated to destroying. Unionists agreed to share power with Nationalists and conceded a say in the affairs of Ulster by the Republic. Dublin would renounce from its constitution the territorial claim on the North.

In the surveys of opinion, north and south of the border, taken in the immediate aftermath, more than half of those polled gave the agreement a strong chance of establishing a lasting peace, and most credit was awarded to Tony Blair.[29]

William Hague, on behalf of the Conservative Party, hailed 'an historic moment'.[30] John Major spoke of 'a great step forward'.[31] Sir Patrick Mayhew praised Blair for taking 'risks with his own reputation' to secure the agreement. 'It could, right up to the last minute, have ended in failure in which case he would have been tainted with it,' said the former Conservative Northern Ireland Secretary. 'He went for it. It was real leadership.'[32]

This was generous, and it was deserved. These negotiations displayed the best qualities of Tony Blair to shining advantage. He kept a grip on the detail without losing sight of the big picture. The connections of trust he had established with the key actors paid dividends. With creativity and persistence, they had been induced to an agreement few thought possible.

As Blair and his party departed Belfast by Sea King helicopter on Friday evening, Jonathan Powell's mobile phone rang with a communication from Buckingham Palace. The Queen wished to convey her congratulations to the Prime Minister for getting closer to an end to the Troubles than five previous occupants of Number 10. Before she could speak to Blair, an RAF crewman intervened, barking at Powell to switch off the phone at once. The royal congratulatory call would have to wait until they landed at Northolt.

What had not been resolved, because it could not have been cracked that Easter, was the disagreements about the decommissioning of terrorist weapons. That this would bedevil further progress was apparent as the campaign began to win endorsement for the agreement in the referendums on both sides of the border. On the core issue that mattered most to them, the security of Northern Ireland within the United Kingdom, the Unionists had won. But many of them were too slow and too trapped in the past to grasp the fact. A large section of Old Unionism was in revolt. The Orange Order rejected the agreement. More than half of David Trimble's own MPs opposed their leader.

Protestant support was further undermined by a sequence of poor judgements and bad timing. The Irish government released the four Balcombe Street IRA bombers to parade with Gerry Adams at the Sinn Fein annual conference in early May. The pictures of unrepentant terrorists being fêted as heroes sharpened Unionist revulsion at the prospect of the release of the prisoners. Blair, in an effort to salve their fears, pronounced himself equally revolted by that spectacle and made a speech taking a hard line on decommissioning. To the intense frustration of Downing Street, he was knocked down the news bulletins by a disastrously counter-productive appearance at a Yes rally by a paroled Michael Stone. With a week before polling, 43 per cent of Protestants, woefully short of half of the community, were saying they would vote for the agreement. A vital 27 per cent were undecided.[33]

Bill Clinton was asked to cancel a planned visit; Mo Mowlam's profile was lowered. It was the Unionists who needed most reassurance, and research suggested that the politician they most trusted and were most likely to listen to was Tony Blair. He had demonstrated his skills as a negotiator at Stormont, now Northern Ireland needed his virtuosities as an electioneer. His advisers were divided about how to conduct the campaign. John Holmes cautioned Blair and Campbell that they were dealing with a different type of electorate in Northern Ireland. The slickeries of New Labour might turn off old-fashioned Protestants. Blair decided to gamble that what had worked on the mainland could also win over Ulster. In the last week of the referendum campaign, he threw himself on to a carousel of interviews, phone-ins and street walks as if he were fighting for his own re-election. His most significant visit was his last, on the eve of poll. He descended by RAF Wessex helicopter on a hotel on the outskirts of Belfast to project the final images of the campaign. Blair posed for a unity photo-call with David Trimble and John Hume. Then, on a mobile hoarding, Blair unveiled five pledges, New Labour's talismanic number, in his own handwriting. This was the technique to authenticate his sincerity which had worked well at the general election a year earlier. The pledges were principally designed to bring over doubting Unionists. The actual text of the Good Friday Agreement was stretched as far as it could go, and perhaps a little beyond, with the pledge: 'Prisoners kept in unless violence is given up for good.' This would be used against Blair in the future.

At that moment, trust-in-Tony proved effective in Northern Ireland as it had in Britain. The period during which he was most active in the campaign saw a marked shift among Protestants towards supporting the agreement.

On Friday 22 May 1998, the people voted to grasp the hand of history. In Northern Ireland, 71.2 per cent supported the agreement; 28.8 per cent were against. With a turnout of 81 per cent, more than half of the total potential electorate had said Yes. An overwhelming majority of Catholics voted for the agreement. Exit surveys suggested that Protestant voters were either evenly balanced,[34] or there was a small majority in favour.[35] In the Republic, there was a 94.4 per cent Yes vote, on a turnout of 55.6 per cent. The votes were counted 200 years to the day that Irish republicans first took up arms against British rule. Seamus Heaney's line – 'The moment when hope and history rhyme' – was much quoted.

Mo Mowlam declared, with understandable joy, that 'they have voted to take the gun out of politics'. It was never going to be that simple. Decommissioning was finessed, not resolved. But to acknowledge the imperfections in the agreement does not diminish the enormity of the achievement. Republicans had, for the first time, recognised the principle of consent. Northern Ireland's status within the United Kingdom would not be changed against the will of the majority of its inhabitants. Unionists had accepted that they shared that space with a different tradition which deserved representation in power and an equality of respect.

On offer was the best ever chance of founding a lasting settlement. The Omagh bomb in mid-August, which killed twenty-nine men, women and children, was a spasm of the violent past which even so signalled the possibility of a better future. Amidst cross-community revulsion at that horror, splinter terrorist organisations, which had been previously opposed to the agreement, announced a cessation of violence. For the first time in three decades, every terrorist group in Northern Ireland was on ceasefire.

The hand of history proved slippery. Over the following two years, there were ugly acts of community violence by both the IRA and loyalists. The protracted dance between the protagonists was fitful and agonisingly slow. Tony Blair was impelled to dedicate continuing and enormous amounts of time to keeping the process breathing. Yet the general peace held. That brought gains in investment and jobs, and great strides towards normal, civic life in Northern Ireland. Put at its very simplest, at its most human, there are fathers and mothers, brothers and sisters, sons and daughters alive today because of the agreement. It was a long Friday. It was a Good Friday.

# 9. Psychological Flaws

The drink and the conversation were flowing at Number 12 Downing Street. Nick Brown – such a dedicated ally of Gordon Brown that they even shared the same surname – was delighted to let the Chancellor use the chief whip's official residence for entertaining. Gordon Brown was on excellent form, holding the audience of Labour MPs who clustered around him in his powerful thrall. One of the guests that night in Christmas 1997 was Bob Marshall-Andrews, the Labour MP for Medway. A persistent backbench scourge of the government, a witty satirist of the folly of Peter Mandelson's Dome, the MP for Medway was *persona non grata* among loyal Blairites. As he collected his coat, Marshall-Andrews effused to his host. 'That was a great party, Gordon.' The Chancellor responded with a dark smile. 'The Labour Party? It *was* a great party, wasn't it?' Even cloaked in a joke, the suggestion was unmistakable. The man who was supposed to be the joint strategist of New Labour was implying that he was also the greatest dissident about its direction.

The Chancellor's parties – and the complexion of some of his guests – caused teeth-grinding at Number 10. Suspicious eyes around the Prime Minister counted them in, and counted them out: the party activists, union leaders and MPs welcomed to the Chancellor's parlours. In the wary view of those protective of the Prime Minister, the Chancellor was establishing a rival powerbase. They smelt a threat.

It had become a persistent theme of media commentary that, in New Labour plc, Blair was the chairman and Brown the chief executive. The Prime Minister giddied around the globe from summit to summit; the Chancellor was the colossus who bestrode the peaks at home. The implication was that while the Prime Minister was the grinning, travelling salesman of the government, the man of substance and action was the Chancellor.

Tony Blair was initially sanguine about all this. To one aide who worried that the Chancellor was becoming over-mighty, Blair expressed himself unbothered: 'When I sit in the garden of Chequers, and the sun is on my face, I *know* who is the Prime Minister.' Others around him nagged about the markedly more comradely noises in Brown's speeches which seemed designed to pitch himself to Labour MPs as a more radical substitute for Blair. The Prime Minister again appeared unfazed. 'If Gordon uses a bit of left-wing rhetoric, so what? It keeps the party happy.'[1]

Blair believed he knew all there was to know about Gordon Brown. They shared an office as parliamentary new boys back in 1983 and rose as the golden twins of the Kinnock era. No two politicians had spent more hours in each other's most intimate company. According to Brown: 'There's no closer relationship in the world.'[2] That had to be a slight exaggeration – unless he believed that he was more intimate with Tony than Cherie – but it is true that no other Prime Minister and Chancellor had been so close for so long. A civil servant remarked to Blair that when Margaret Thatcher and Nigel Lawson were together it was like 'watching two strangers talking'. Blair replied that his relationship with his Chancellor was like 'a marriage'.[3]

Blair was the junior of the partnership when he and Brown came into parliament together. The *ingénu* Blair had a lot to learn; the older and much more politically grizzled Brown had much to teach. According to one of his oldest and closest friends, Blair was 'mammothly dazzled' by the cleverness and energy of Brown.[4] Blair caught up with, and then eclipsed, Brown to become leader in 1994. But he remained, to an extent, bedazzled. 'Gordon has a much more developed political philosophy than me,' he explained to one confidant. Blair told a civil servant: 'For all his faults, Gordon is crucial to me.'[5]

Lurking in the recesses of any argument between Prime Minister and Chancellor was Brown's belief that he had been the making of Blair. The Prime Minister couldn't entirely subscribe to that, but he did acknowledge his debts to Brown. 'It's always there when

Gordon is arguing with Tony – "you owe me" – even if it's not very often expressed,' says a Cabinet minister.[6]

The marriage survived Blair's assumption to the leadership, but it was also hugely complicated by it. A friend of Blair puts it like this: 'The pleasure and thrill at the beginning, the magic of discovering each other, making progress together, that's gone. They are never going to be as good as that again. I think it's still strong, but it's much harder.'[7]

The itch that Brown couldn't stop himself scratching was the smouldering resentment that Blair had taken the first prize of politics. History might judge that time and chance dealt them roles best suited to their respective abilities. Brown, whose grasp of the economic rigging was much firmer and whose ideas about social reform were much profounder, was turning into a stunningly better Chancellor than Blair was ever likely to have been. Blair, whose inter-personal skills were the more accomplished and who had a broader vision about transforming Britain, was the better equipped for the role of Prime Minister. That was how most of the Cabinet would view it, and most of those who had known both men for a long time. Gordon Brown would not be human – he certainly would not be Gordon Brown – if he could not see it that way.

Officials marvelled as they were also shocked at the open disdain with which Brown would sometimes treat Blair. Aides and colleagues remarked upon the extraordinary efforts Blair devoted to managing Brown. 'He mediates, he negotiates, he defuses, he cajoles, he rails, he shouts, he hugs, he flatters,' according to a close observer of the relationship.[8]

'I keep telling you Gordon, you will be my Lloyd George' was a stroke which Blair used during this period in an effort to make Brown feel confident and content with his position. Did the dark thought cross either man's mind that the great Celtic radical Chancellor eventually supplanted the more conservative English Prime Minister Asquith? Blair's smoothing techniques did not work so well on Brown. He had known Blair far too long.

The most obvious public contrast sprang from their private lives. With the bachelor Brown 'it was politics, politics, politics and I needed nurturing', complained one of his former lovers, Margarita, the 'Red Princess' of Romania.[9] Blair was durably, contentedly and fecundly married. Though he and Cherie were intensely protective of the privacy of their children, Blair regularly used 'the kids' as props. Shortly after the election, he went to New York to tell a United Nations summit: 'I speak to you not just as the new British Prime Minister, but as a father.' The Millennium Dome was set the 'Euan Test'. Blair said – and much regretted it later – that the arbitrator of the Dome's success would be his then thirteen-year-old son. He exploited the image advantages of being seen as a regular kind of family guy. Blair sat on the soft sofa of Richard and Judy and presented himself for the less than scouring interrogation of Des O'Connor, dropping into the accent of estuarial English which he was never taught at public school.

Despite heroic efforts by Charlie Whelan to soften his master's severe outlook, Brown's attempts to look relaxed came over as forced and uncomfortable when he ventured into TV soap.

The 'normality' of Blair was an act, but it was more than a performance. It was his self-conceit that 'I do not think of myself as a politician.' Of course, he was a politician, a most extraordinary politician. What he meant was that he had not been born and bred by the machine; his every breath was not politics. There were other things, so Blair liked to believe anyway, he could be content doing. The same was not true of Brown, a man consumed by the political since an early age. 'Gordon's problem is that he hasn't got a family,' Blair told one confidant, which he also believed to be the central explanation for what was wrong with Peter Mandelson.[10]

Blair thought that he had a unique capacity for dealing with his turbulent and talented friends. Ministers, aides and civil servants who brought him complaints about the Chancellor's uncollegiate behaviour were told by Blair: 'I can handle Gordon,' in the manner of a psychotherapist talking about a brilliant but temperamental child.

Gordon went through 'uncooperative' stretches, the Prime Minister explained to one close friend, but 'he always comes back in the end'.[11]

A senior civil servant who has observed them at close quarters confirms: 'It *is* like a marriage, a tempestuous marriage. The rows can be terrible. But if you're on the outside and you interfere, you won't be thanked for it afterwards. You come between them at your peril. When it comes to make-up time, everyone else is to blame, rather than they themselves.'[12]

By the New Year of 1998, the marriage was increasingly strained by stretches of crockery-throwing. Blair's ambition to turn Number 10 into the corporate headquarters of his government had been frustrated. While his energies were dissipated, the design to turn the Cabinet Office into a Department of the Prime Minister, imposing his writ across Whitehall, was not realised. Brown saw the vacuum and rushed to impose himself in it. The Chancellor's comprehensive spending review was an opportunity to delve deep into every department which he further exploited by binding ministers to his will through 'public service agreements' with the Treasury. The good reason for this – ensuring that money was efficiently spent – was allied to a manipulative motive. It was an attempt to make the rest of the Cabinet agree to serve the Treasury.

Brown's power-hugging caused rebarbative relations with Cabinet colleagues. Regular, and from a variety of ministers, were the protests to Blair that Brown's idea of consultation was to pick up the phone and bark his decisions at them. David Blunkett complained that Brown would block his ideas and then repackage them as the Chancellor's own under the New Deal label. Brown was aggravated by Blunkett's use of the Department for Education and Employment to fashion an alternative, more expansionary economic strategy. This relationship was bad in Opposition, improved later, but at this time was dire. 'Blunkett would go bananas,' says a civil servant.[13] So provoked was Blunkett by Brown on one occasion that the Education Secretary stormed from his ministerial suite shouting 'the mendacious sod', demanded his car, and told the driver to take him straight round to Blair. His alarmed officials rang Number 10 to warn them of the imminent arrival of an incendiary secretary of state.

Blair began to tire of dousing colleagues inflamed by Brown.

Expressions of his exasperation with the Chancellor became more
frequent. 'Jesus,' Blair despaired to officials and aides. 'What has
Gordon done *now*?'[14]

Brown's relationship with Whitehall was also abrasive. Some civil
servants did find favour at the court of the Chancellor. Gus O'Don-
nell, John Major's former press secretary, and Steve Robson, who
headed Nigel Lawson's privatisation unit, were preferred. Sir Terry
Burns, however, was cast further into the darkness. Blair tried to
find a role at Number 10 as a lifeboat for the Treasury's Permanent
Secretary whom Brown finally succeeded in gouging out in the
spring of 1998. His capital offence – at least in the eyes of the
Chancellor and his men – was to refuse to help them extract
Geoffrey Robinson from the quicksand of allegations about his
financial affairs. In November 1997, it was revealed that the Paymaster-General was the beneficiary of a bequest from a Belgian
widow, the exquisitely named Madam Bourgeois. Millions of
pounds were parked offshore in a Channel Island tax haven. As
politicians often do when they need a heat shield, Robinson sought
exculpation from the civil service. A statement from the Permanent
Secretary saying that he had been informed, and by implication
approved, Robinson's financial arrangements might sanitise them.
Gordon Brown sat at his word processor in the Treasury on a
Friday night, crafting a press statement defending Robinson which
they wanted the Permanent Secretary to put his name to. Burns,
who believed he had been told by Robinson only that he had a
'family trust', not that it was in a tax haven, refused. The embarrassment for a party which had attacked tax avoidance with the fervour
of evangelical preachers was compounded a few days later when
Robinson launched Individual Savings Accounts, schemes which
would offer less generous tax breaks to 750,000 savers than those
they replaced.

The Tories taunted Blair at Question Time. The Prime Minister
talked about trust; the Paymaster-General kept his trust offshore.
The Prime Minister did not enjoy that. The view from Number
10 – clearly a self-serving perspective – was that all the troubles

descending on the government were pouring out of the Treasury. Blair had gradually moved from sanguinity about Brown, to perplexion, to increasing outbursts of frustration. At moments of extreme exasperation, Blair would cry: 'God! Gordon can be impossible.'[15]

The surface tension of the relationship manifested itself in increasingly demented infighting between the rival entourages at Downing Street and the Treasury. Alastair Campbell made time in his frantic schedule to compile a bulging file of cuttings of newspaper stories inspired, or so he believed, by Charlie Whelan to promote the Chancellor at the expense of the rest of the Cabinet and the Prime Minister.[16] The relationship was so fissiparous that something as apparently innocuous as a friendly biography of Brown provoked mounting agitation at Number 10. In early January, Campbell demanded of Whelan that he let him have a prepublication copy of Paul Routledge's life of Gordon Brown. Campbell called him a liar and smashed down the phone when Whelan replied that he couldn't, because he had lent the only copy in his possession to John Brown, the Chancellor's older brother. It was long beyond the point of mattering whether or not Whelan was telling the truth: he probably was in this case. The relationship between him and Campbell had collapsed.

This grudge match between the spinners was amplification and aggravation of the stress lines between Prime Minister and Chancellor. It also served as a proxy for the battle for ascendancy between them. It suited both Blair and Brown to pretend to each other, even to themselves, that vicious briefing by their rival coteries was not of their making. Whelan's excesses occasionally made Brown wince; some of Campbell's activities caused Blair to flinch. Yet both gun dogs were broadly following their masters' wishes. Otherwise, they would have been muzzled or put down. On one of the many occasions when Peter Mandelson demanded of the Prime Minister that he force the Chancellor to dispose of Whelan, Blair replied: 'How can I sack Charlie when he's only doing what Gordon's telling him to do?'[17]

The biography of Brown – written with 'his full co-operation' –

was an admiring account of a man about whom there was much to admire. Routledge revealed that Nick Brown had 'spilled the beans' about the Brownite version of the leadership contest and accurately depicted the Chancellor as a man scarred by the way in which he had been denied the crown by Blair. Picking the scab off this old wound presented Brown, a picture that was not as kindly as the biographer intended, as a man eaten by past wrongs. Calculated to infuriate Blair was the book's tendentious suggestion that he was a cheat and a charlatan who broke a blood promise to his oldest political ally and robbed of his birthright the man who was supposed to be his closest friend.

The anger this stirred inside Number 10 did not abate as the immediate furore detonated by the book began to subside. The nature of the Blair–Brown relationship was a subject I thought worth exploring in my column for the *Observer*. Of many conversations I had with people that week, the most significant was with a person I described at the time as 'someone who has an extremely good claim to know the mind of the Prime Minister'. I would describe them that way today.

For the first five minutes of a long conversation with this person, I was spun the familiar party line that no political coupling was more blissful than that between Tony Blair and Gordon Brown. The Prime Minister esteemed the Chancellor as 'a great talent' and 'a great force'. But, after a little prodding, an entirely different account began to tumble out. Brown's self-promoting biography was 'a classic piece of misjudgement'. The government could not afford 'any more lapses into this sort of nonsense'. Why, I wondered, did Brown behave like this? 'You know Gordon, he feels so vulnerable and so insecure. He has these psychological flaws.' Warming to the theme, the other person poured out a litany of complaint about how all the government's afflictions had been caused by the Treasury. 'If you go through the real disasters of our time in government – EMU, the Geoffrey Robinson affair, ISAs, single parents – I'm afraid there is a common thread to them all. They are coming out of the Treasury.' This was not entirely just: chief responsibility for the Ecclestone Affair lay at the door of

Number 10. The complaint continued: 'What Gordon has done is cut out the civil service, and that just leads to trouble.' Blair was obliged to take control of the committee on welfare because other members of the Cabinet 'just don't trust Gordon. There's so much venom against him.'[18]

The highlights of the insight this offered into the nature of the relationship between Prime Minister and Chancellor formed the basis of the column I wrote that weekend. The vivid phrase 'psychological flaws' was projected on to the front page of the *Observer*. There was a media excitement.

Peter Mandelson spoke truthfully when he denied authorship of 'psychological flaws'. Many, though, thought they heard the voice of Mandelson, who had been depicted as a treacherous Iago in the Brown biography, speaking later that Sunday. It was reported by a BBC political correspondent on Radio Four's main evening news that 'close allies of the Prime Minister are furious at the Chancellor for, as they see it, reopening old wounds'. The reporter continued that 'some have warned' that while the Chancellor is in a very strong position 'that may not last for ever, and nobody is indispensable'.[19] The reporter was Lance Price, known to be close to Mandelson, who would a little later succeed Tim Allan as a press spokesman at Number 10.

Monday's newspapers seized on this startling evidence that the friction between the Treasury and Downing Street was much more inflamed than had hitherto been appreciated. The *Mirror* had 'Britain's two most powerful men at war'. Labour MPs, the more innocent of whom had swallowed the line that it was always harmony and sweetness between the neighbours of Downing Street, reacted with shock. The drone-like discipline that they were expected to obey was not being matched by those at the very top.

In an attempt to smother the flames, an over-protesting Alastair Campbell declared on the Prime Minister's behalf that he regarded Brown as 'an extremely excellent Chancellor'. Brown, who happened to be in Brussels, made a professional job of publicly shrugging it all off as 'essentially rumour, gossip and tittle-tattle'. He was masking a profound hurt. He smarted at the attack, partly perhaps because this complex man could recognise some of himself in the description of his vulnerabilities and insecurities even as he was understandably insulted that they were labelled 'psychological flaws'. On Brown's return to London, there was a clench-jawed confrontation with the Prime Minister. Brown dressed his anger in a concern for the standing of the government. It was 'destabilising', Brown complained to Blair, as well as being 'unfair' to him person-ally. 'This damages me and you,' Brown thundered at Blair. 'Why are you letting this go unpunished?' Brown's desire for retribution was thwarted because Blair could not – or would not – tell him who was responsible. 'I can't believe it was anyone here,' responded Blair. Brown thought Blair was lying to him. Blair was apologetic that things had got so out of hand, but he had his own grievances. He told Brown that he had brought this on himself with 'that bloody stupid book'. How long had he been warning him that Brown would be the one damaged by 'the Whelan operation'?[20] Brown came to the opposite conclusion. This episode confirmed to him how important it was to retain the services of Whelan as the bodyguard of his reputation against Number 10, and as the instrument of the Chancellor's retaliation.

There were those around both men who believed that the episode served a purpose. Brown's aides thought the ferocity of the counter-reaction had got them 'off the hook'. Around Blair, it was felt that a timely warning flare had been fired at Brown.

In the wake of this eruption between Prime Minister and Chan-cellor, Brown tried rebuilding bridges with other members of the Cabinet. Robin Cook, whose attempt to employ Gaynor Regan at the Foreign Office had been exposed, was suffering a diabolical press at the end of January. As they left Cabinet, the Foreign Secretary was the surprised recipient of an invitation from Brown to have a chat. Over a bottle of malt in Cook's Commons office, they agreed a truce. Brown also started talking to Peter Mandelson again. A burning resentment about 'the marriage' with Blair was that there were three people in it. Brown could not abide Mandelson's access to and influence over Blair, not least because Brown believed Mandelson was trying to drive wedges between him and the Prime Minister. He had not held a proper conversation with the other man since 1994. Blair, who believed it was the poison between Brown and Mandelson which was the cancer gnawing at the guts of his government, was eager for a reconciliation between them. He urged both men to meet and expressed himself delighted when they had an apparently amicable exchange in late January. Brown and Mandelson had more encounters, meeting again, at Easter, in Brown's room at the Commons and at the Treasury. The first reshuffle was widely anticipated, though it would actually be delayed by the negotiations in Northern Ireland. Brown, knowing how Mandelson thirsted for a seat in the Cabinet, was offering himself as a lobbyist with Blair to win for Mandelson the post of Culture Secretary. The Chancellor's undisguised agenda was to prevent Mandelson taking on the bruited role of 'Cabinet Enforcer', at the centre of a new strategic unit at Number 10 proposed by the Cabinet Secretary as the latest mechanism for Blair to impose his will on the government. The Treasury even tried to slice away 30 per cent of the funding of the Cabinet Office. Not only was Brown determined to wreck the Prime Minister's idea, he was proposing to set up his own rival unit at the Treasury. Anything Blair had, Brown had to have, and bigger and better.

In an aside, the Chancellor suggested to Mandelson that they were both exploited by Blair. 'When one of us gets too strong,' said Brown, 'Tony builds up the other.'[21] This flattered Mandelson by treating him as an equal when, in the balance of power, the heavier man was clearly the Chancellor. It also illustrated how Brown, for all his ability and all his power, felt he was being jerked on strings held by the puppetmaster Prime Minister.

The other way to look at Blair and Brown was not as a marriage but as contrasting twins. The Old Testament tells us that the Lord said to the pregnant Rebecca:

There are two nations in thy womb; in thy body the separation of two peoples has begun; here is victory for people over people, and it is the elder that shall be subject to the younger . . . The first to come was of a red complexion, and hairy all over as if he had worn a coat of skin; this one was called Esau. Then the second came, with his hand clutching his brother's heel, and she called him, for that reason Jacob, the Supplanter ... When the twins grew up, Esau turned into a skilful hunter; Jacob was a tent-dweller.[22]

Blair was younger and the more fervent Brownites would regard him as 'The Supplanter'. An aspect of Esau and Jacob did come into it. Brown had a more reddish political complexion and he was a temperamentally hairy man. Anyone who was not entirely with him was absolutely against him. If you were not his friend, you were his enemy. Blair was a smooth man. He would try to charm into support anyone who might be susceptible. So long as you were not his enemy, you could be his friend. In political struggle, Blair would rather take a prisoner. Brown would leave a corpse.

It is hard to imagine the son of Kirkcaldy inviting to come dine at Chequers, as Blair did, Michael Winner, director of the *Death Wish* films, and Joan Collins, most famous for her parts in *The Stud* and *Dynasty*. Blair was wider but shallower. Brown was deeper but narrower. The Chancellor was much more steeped in Labour tradition, and sceptical about Blair's attempt to gather a multi-coloured consensus inside one 'Big Tent'. When Robin Cook delivered a speech, much of it written in Downing Street, extolling the tent-dweller's Third Way, the hunter Brown privately scorned it as 'vacuous'.

The elections to the party's National Executive, a once-strong body stripped of power but retaining symbolic significance, was a trial of strength between loyalists to the government and a 'Grassroots Alliance' of left-wing opponents of New Labour. Gordon Brown supported one of the dissidents – or so, at least, Charlie Whelan put it about – by voting for Mark Seddon, the editor of *Tribune*, the left-wing newspaper which relentlessly and often viciously attacked the government.[23]

Much of this was simply gamesmanship on Brown's part: an attempt to carve for himself an alternative profile to Blair. Though the Chancellor signalled leftwards in front of suitable audiences, he was not a reliable friend to left-wing causes. It was he who steamrollered over Margaret Beckett and forced upon the Trade and Industry Secretary a 20p cut in the minimum wage for young workers. Union leaders tried to recruit him as an ally in their struggle with Blair over the legislation enhancing employees' rights. The Prime Minister leant so heavily in the direction of the employers that their representatives found him raising objections to the unions' case they hadn't been intending to press. Adair Turner, the Director-General of the CBI, expressed to colleagues his amazement that the government was 'so craven' towards business.[24]

The unions looked for allies in the Cabinet. They got help from John Prescott, but not from Gordon Brown. John Monks, the TUC General Secretary, sought a meeting at the Treasury to lobby for support from the Chancellor. Brown listened with great interest as Monks railed against Blair. But when Monks had expended himself, Brown told him: 'I won't side against Tony on this one.'[25]

Within the Chancellor, two impulses warred with each other. One half of him recognised that the Prime Minister was his only friend in the Cabinet. Without him, Brown would be isolated and exposed. He blocked Sir Terry Burns' scheme to renovate the Treasury, which would have involved temporarily relocating outside central London. The reason offered to Burns by Geoffrey Robinson was that 'Gordon needs to be near Tony.' The other half of Brown chafed against his ultimate subordination to Blair, and detested it on the, actually quite rare, occasions when he was overruled.

'When he's with anybody but Tony, Gordon is the complete adult, dominating everyone in the room,' explains another member of New Labour's inner circle. 'With Tony, he feels constrained. When he doesn't get his own way, he goes into child mode, angry child mode.'[26]

Brown possessed a valuable weapon – information – which he used to disadvantage Blair. The Chancellor was always confident of winning an argument about economics with the Prime Minister, much the less confident in this area of the pair, so long as Blair did not have independent sources of advice. Brown decreed to the

Treasury that the Number 10 Policy Unit, including Blair's personal adviser on economics, was not to be supplied with information about the March Budget.

This, the first full Labour Budget in twenty years, exhibited both the combative and the constructive sides of the partnership. Some abrasion was the natural product of different roles and contrasting temperaments. The Presbyterian Scot was inclined to hoard cash for a rainy day, and the Chancellor who enjoyed his reputation as Iron Brown wanted to maintain his good notices in the City. Blair, the maestro of Middle Britain, was most concerned with the government's popularity and always kept his ear to the heartbeat of the swing voter.

Brown was again keen to sweep away tax breaks that he regarded as illogical and redundant such as mortgage tax relief. 'Is this wise, Gordon?' Blair would ask, a favoured formulation for framing his worries about something proposed by Brown. Among his own intimates, Brown took to saying: 'Tony is the master of wise politics' in a voice that hovered over being a compliment before descending into sarcasm.[27]

Yet it was the combination of Blair's 'wise politics' with Brown's sound economics that was the government's fundamental strength and the principal reason for its continuing and massive popularity. On this occasion, Blair preserved for the suburban middle classes most of their tax perks. Mortgage tax relief was spared; married couples allowance was shaved down to 10 per cent. Taxation of child benefit did not happen. At Blair's insistence, the rules for tax-free savings in Individual Savings Accounts were made more generous, a bequest of the embarrassments of Geoffrey Robinson.

Raising income tax was forbidden to New Labour by their pledges. Brown found a way round this restraint by making a big adjustment to national insurance to create a tax cut for the working poor paid at the expense of the better-off. He raised the threshold at which employers and employees started paying national insurance while raising the rate of employer contributions on higher-paid staff. Audible sighs of relief could be heard around the Treasury after the Budget that this large shift aroused so little media attention.

Blair had put a pre-election block on Brown's desire for a new 50 per cent top rate of tax. He found an alternative revenue stream from a series of increases on the stamp duty paid on expensive homes which actually came to raise substantially more money than a new top rate.

The centrepiece of this Budget was what Brown presented as a 'once-in-a-generation'[28] change to taxes and benefits to help the less well-off. The working families' tax credit would 'make work pay' by ensuring that it was always more rewarding to have a job than to stay on benefit. The Budget, with its emphasis on providing a platform for anyone with aspiration and ambition to fulfil their potential, conveyed the themes that had animated Brown since he was a student. It confirmed him as a large, serious and, in many ways, old-fashioned politician who believed that the state could be a force to change for the better people's behaviour and lives. The friendly tone towards Middle Britain displayed the touch of Blair. The two men worked together on Brown's Budget speech at Chequers the weekend before. They batted back and forth ideas and phrases. It was almost like the good times again.

The result was a large success. Right-wing newspapers praised it for not being an Old Labour Budget by helping enterprise and keeping taxes down. Leftish papers praised it for not being a Tory Budget by concentrating help on the working poor. 'Brown spares middle class,' the *Daily Telegraph* wheezed with gratitude, describing it as 'better than anything Labour has ever offered us before'. Yet the Budget had also managed to please the very different audience of the *Guardian* which reported that Brown 'offers relief to working poor without punishing Middle England'. 'A prudent hand to those in need,' judged the *Financial Times*. The *Evening Standard* thought it 'A victimless Budget'. An equally wonder-eyed *Times* declared: 'It all adds up: everyone's a winner.'

The experts at the Institute for Fiscal Studies calculated that the cumulative effect of the two Budgets since the election had actually been the biggest redistribution from rich to poor for decades. The skill was to locate an answer to the dilemma that had so long afflicted the left: how to assist the disadvantaged without alienating the better-off. The marriage of Brown and Blair, when functioning creatively, could be one of the most productive partnerships British politics is ever likely to see.

The Budget also gave cash increases of £220 million to education and £500 million to the health service, evidence that the supposedly iron rules about spending could be bent by popular pressure. Blair was brought polling evidence that spring revealing the public to be increasingly restive that they were not seeing palpable improvements to schools and hospitals. Reducing hospital waiting lists by 100,000 and guaranteeing that no five-, six- or seven-year-old was in a class of more than thirty had been two of the famous five pledges on which they had won the election. Pledges that could be condensed on to laminated cardboard the size of a credit card were much mocked for their modesty, but achieving these targets had David Blunkett and Frank Dobson tearing their beards out. Blunkett was at least grateful that he had managed to persuade Blair away from an idea that the classroom pledge should have been made starker by setting it at twenty-five. As he remarked to a colleague: 'Then we really would have been screwed.' As it was, though he was making progress, what had been described as an 'early' pledge had already been reinterpreted as a promise that would be fulfilled by the time New Labour next presented itself to the voters. Dobson was in serious trouble meeting the waiting lists pledge, which he privately regarded as 'bloody crazy'. At the time he expressed that opinion to a colleague, before the election, he did not know that he would be made Health Secretary charged with making good on the Prime Minister's word. By the April of 1998, the waiting list in England had risen to a record 1,312,618, not down on May 1997, but up by more than 150,000.[29] The public was already tiring of hearing Dobson express himself 'embarrassed'.[30] At a meeting at Number 10 in advance of the publication of another sickly set of figures, it was suggested to Blair that they should gently drop the waiting list target and emphasise instead the more flattering fact that the number of patients being treated was rising. Blair toyed with the notion, finally to dismiss it. It reminded him too much of a Tory politician who had discredited herself by Panglossian massaging of statistics. 'Oh God,' he groaned. 'I can hear myself sounding like Virginia Bottomley.'[31]

Blair began to agitate with Brown to award a generous spending settlement to health and education. The Chancellor was resistant to simply satisfying the hazily detailed large cash bids put in by Dobson and Blunkett. The Chancellor did not want his carefully harvested revenues sucked away without guarantees that the money would be spent on modernising projects that he approved of. And he scathingly told Blair that he could have more for education and health 'if you didn't want to waste so much on defence'. In Treasury tradition, Brown saw the Ministry of Defence as a profligate squanderer of money. George Robertson, the Defence Secretary, had craftily pre-empted the spending negotiations by conducting a needs-led strategic defence review which was acclaimed by the military as much superior to the Tory approach of cutting first and thinking later. Brown attempted to unravel the outcome of the defence review with an eleventh hour demand for swingeing cuts to Robertson's budget. Believing that he could usually grind Blair into submission as long as he had him alone, Brown refused to attend meetings with the Chief of the Defence Staff, Sir Charles Guthrie. On a rare occasion when they did meet, it was not a meeting of minds. 'You don't think I understand defence, do you?' challenged Brown. 'No, I bloody well don't,' replied the general.[32]

Guthrie and Robertson, with the important ally of Peter Mandelson, skilfully played to Blair's anxiety to look strong on defence, as did John Reid, the Minister of the Armed Forces, who implanted fears in the Prime Minister of the future consequences of diminishing Britain's capability. 'I am not going to be the first Prime Minister in a hundred years to lose a war,' Blair told Brown, who would return to the Treasury complaining that Blair had been taken captive by the military.[33]

In this argument, Brown was outgunned. In most of the disputes with the Prime Minister about spending, the Chancellor prevailed. This was not least because Blair was never entirely sure of his own mind. There was a lot of truth in Brown's dry observation to close allies: 'Tony wants to tax less, spend more, and borrow less. Our job is to make it add up for him.'[34] Calls from the left and the Liberal Democrats for the release of the Treasury's burgeoning surpluses tended to make Blair more inclined to agree with Brown that they should resist the pressure. For all the antagonisms between them, Blair would nearly always rate Brown's judgement higher than competing advice. The Health and Education Secretaries enjoyed mixed fortunes trying to use the Prime Minister as a higher court of appeal against the Chancellor. David Blunkett thought he had arranged a private tête-à-tête with the Prime Minister at Number 10 only to arrive in his study to be greeted by a familiar, unexpected and wholly unwelcome Scottish accent.

The Chancellor kept his corset tight, though this was not how it initially appeared. The outcome of the CSR, setting spending for the next three financial years, was announced on 14 July. That morning Blair told Peter Mandelson that Brown would produce a sensational-sounding £40 billion extra for education and health. 'Isn't that good news?' bubbled Blair. Mandelson choked. 'People will either think it's a revolution,' he replied. 'Or they will say it has to be shit.'

Jubilant Labour MPs thought it was a revolution as Brown made it sound as though he was showering manna from heaven. 'A total £40 billion will be invested in the nation's priorities – health and education,' the Chancellor told the Commons, appearing to rip off the spending straitjacket. 'On the fiftieth anniversary of the NHS this government will now make the biggest ever investment in its future, giving the NHS for the first time for decades the long-term resources it needs.'[35] The delirious backbenchers were not the only ones to fall for the Chancellor's conjuring trick. 'Massive boost for health, education,' reported the *Guardian*, inviting its readers to hail 'Brown's blockbuster'. Credulous television and radio coverage repeated the figure of £40 billion. The *Daily Mail* hit the jackpot: 'SPEND! SPEND! SPEND!'

The Prime Minister behaved like a lottery winner. With an infants school as symbolic scenery for his speech, Blair described it as a turning point. 'Millions of people have waited for this moment since they elected a New Labour government. This is the time when we deliver on the people's priorities. This is the biggest ever increase in resources for education and health: £40 billion over three years.'[36]

The people would actually wait longer for delivery. These increases were nothing like as significant as they had been made to sound, and in as much as there was extra money, it would not begin to kick in until nearly a year later. Blunkett and Dobson, who had both argued with Blair against presenting the spending figures as a bonanza, received roughly three quarters of what they bid for. The notion of hyping the settlement as £40 billion was Brown's brainstorm. After days of studying the tables of annual increases, he suddenly wondered aloud why he couldn't just accumulate them. None of his aides raised an objection. But the £40 billion was funny money. This phoney total had been manufactured by rolling up the increases so that the first year rise was counted three times and the second year's twice.[37] Strip out this creative accountancy and account for inflation, then the actual sum was much smaller. Allowing for the two-year freeze, by some measures real spending would barely compare with the Conservatives' in the previous parliament. As this reality gradually became evident, it fed suspicion and cynicism about all government announcements, genuine or not. The upshot of trying to reconcile Blair's restlessness to meet public demand for improvements to health and education with Brown's determination to hold down spending was that the two of them turned their own rules inside out. Careful in the past not to over-excite expectations, Blair and Brown had suddenly pumped them up without providing the resources to turn rhetoric into reality.

One thing was tangible from the Chancellor's performance that afternoon. He had wrapped his tentacles even more firmly around the Cabinet. 'Each department has reached agreement with the Treasury, effectively a contract with the Treasury for the renewal of public services. Money will be released only if departments keep to their plans,' he declared,[38] prompting complaints afterwards to Blair from ministers that they thought they were supposed to be accountable to the Prime Minister.

Brown motioned at his colleagues and magisterially declared that Prescott, Dobson, Blunkett, Straw and the rest of them would be dealing with the details later, as if they were his parliamentary under-secretaries. A never stronger Gordon Brown bestrode the political world, casting a chilly shadow over the rest of the Cabinet, including the Prime Minister. The prevailing mood was captured by the *Observer*'s cartoonist, Chris Riddell, who depicted Blair as the monkey to Brown's organ-grinder. The monkey was about to bite back.

By four o'clock on the last Sunday in July, all of the Prime Minister's key aides were safely and secretly gathered inside Number 10. There were no cameras to watch them arrive: Alastair Campbell had artfully misled the media that Tony Blair was spending the entire weekend up at Chequers. Gathered around the Prime Minister were Campbell, Jonathan Powell, Anji Hunter, Bruce Grocott, his parliamentary private secretary, and Sally Morgan, the head of his Political Office. Morgan had a little list: ministers who were camp followers of the Chancellor. They were marked for execution.

'How will he take it?' Blair worried out loud. No one expected the Chancellor to take it well; all agreed that it nevertheless had to be done. So did the Cabinet ministers – David Blunkett and Mo Mowlam had made the point to Blair with particular force – who were pressing Blair to assert himself over the Chancellor. According to one of the aides in the room that afternoon: 'It was Blair versus Brown. Blair had to win.'[39] At any rate, he had to be seen to win. No Prime Minister can afford for it to be believed that someone else is the source of patronage and preferment. In the kingdom of the Sun King, there could be only one radiant of power.

Brown had a premonition of what to expect because he had been shut out from the debates within Number 10 about the reshuffle. When Blair finally showed some of his hand, ringing Brown at eight on Sunday night, it was with unpalatable news. Blair told Brown that he was satisfying Mandelson's long ache for a seat in Cabinet by making him Secretary of State for Trade and Industry, a position within the economic empire that the Chancellor regarded as his exclusive hemisphere. Blair seems to have believed that by throwing Brown and Mandelson together he might force them to re-establish working relations. The Prime Minister was testing the theory of creative tension to destruction. Blair suggested that Brown should be the one to tell Mandelson of his great promotion. Then Blair phoned Mandelson, himself in a frantic state about the reshuffle discussions from which he had been excluded, to tell him to present himself at ten that night at the Chancellor's flat in Great Peter Street.

Brown was capable of considerable charm, when he wanted to find the on-switch. He welcomed Mandelson with apparently sincere congratulations and real surprise that the other man was still in the dark about his fabulous elevation. Had Tony really not told him? It was 'one of the top jobs': the DTI. Brown fetched out a bottle of champagne. 'I've always wanted you to be in the Cabinet,' he told Mandelson. 'I want you to know that.' 'Even if not actually in this job,' Mandelson replied, pleasantly surprised by Brown's generosity of spirit, but not so overwhelmed that he forgot this was a conversation between two highly calculating animals. For nearly an hour they discussed how to make their relationship less dysfunctional before Mandelson departed, talking afterwards about how 'genuinely nice' the Chancellor had been and convincing himself that he was on better terms with Brown than he had been for more than four years.[40]

The casualties of the reshuffle – this was Campbell's idea – were spared the ritual humiliation of walking up to Number 10, past the ghoulish gaze of the media which always assembles on Downing Street like a crowd at a hanging. Instead the victims were invited to attend on the Prime Minister in his oak-pannelled room at the House of Commons, behind the Speaker's chair. Campbell and Powell sat outside, looking rather sheepish, avoiding eye contact with the ministers shuffling through to see Blair. Anji Hunter parked early arrivals in a side room until it was time to see the Prime Minister. He brought along Sir Richard Wilson, the Cabinet Secretary: an insurance against any unpleasantness.

As the reshuffle was announced, it became evident that Blair was carpet-bombing the network of supporters Brown had placed in the government. The smoothly thuggish Jack Cunningham, not a friend of the Chancellor, was made Cabinet 'Enforcer'. The Blairite Stephen Byers was sent into the Treasury as Brown's number two, in the hope, rather a vain one as it transpired, that the supply of intelligence from the Treasury to Number 10 would improve. Some of the Brownites departed quietly, some tearfully, some angrily. Nigel Griffiths, who had been a campaign manager of Gordon Brown's aborted leadership bid, was sacked from the Department of Trade & Industry. Unusually, Griffiths would be restored as a Minister at the DTI after the next election. Tom Clarke, the Films Minister, was another Brownite ejected. Doug Henderson was shifted from Minister for Europe to the Ministry of Defence and would be out of the government altogether a year later. Nick Brown was removed as chief whip, the job he loved, and sent to the Siberian pastures of Agriculture. 'You can tell how powerful Gordon Brown is,' he ruefully remarked. 'Look at the job he got me.' There were objectively sound reasons for all these moves. The partisan purpose of the exercise was underlined by Blair's refusal to give any balancing jobs to MPs, even of promotion-worthy ability, associated with Brown.

As the scale of the purge became apparent, on Monday evening the Chancellor locked the civil servants out of his room at the Treasury and gathered together his intimates to curse Blair. The Prime Minister was trying to get rid of Geoffrey Robinson, the cause of another rash of unpleasant headlines in February about the enmeshment of his affairs with the late and unlamented villain, Robert Maxwell. In mid-July, Robinson was ticked off by MPs on the Standards and Privileges Committee for failing to register some of his directorships.

The Lord Chancellor had that lunchtime called in his deputy, Geoff Hoon, to tell him that he was being promoted to Paymaster-General. The Cabinet Secretary had minuted Blair that Robinson had to go. Personally, as well as politically, this was acutely uncomfortable for the Prime Minister when he and his family had been the recipients of Robinson's favours. Blair tried to get others to do the deed for him. In the afternoon, Sir Richard Wilson was sent over to the Treasury to tell Brown that the Prime Minister wanted him to deliver Robinson's resignation. When the Chancellor refused, Wilson then went to Robinson, telling him 'it's rather more dignified to resign than to be sacked'. Brown demanded a meeting with Blair at Number 10 to plead Robinson's defence. He was a good and creative minister, Brown argued with Blair. The government benefited from his knowledge of the world of business and his contacts in the City. 'I need him,' said Brown. He then fixed for Robinson to go over to Blair's Downing Street flat to plead his own case. Blair, unconvinced that he should keep a minister whose embarrassments had rendered him incapable of speaking from the dispatch box, said he would sleep on it.

The headlines on Tuesday morning were as Downing Street ordered. The *Daily Mail*: 'Blair's Scalpel Shows Brown Who Is The Boss'. The *Express*: 'Blair Shows His Steel'. The *Sun*: 'Blair Shuffle Is Put-Down For Brown'. One of the tabloids, the *Mirror*, had a novel take: 'Brown told Mandelson he'd got top job'.

Charlie Whelan, the inspiration of this account, was endeavouring to save some face for the Chancellor. The paper reported that, during their Sunday-night *rapprochement*, Brown and Mandelson drank white wine – presumably it was thought that champagne did not strike quite the right note for *Mirror* readers – as 'Peter listened carefully' to Brown. A 'source' told the *Mirror*: 'Peter knows that Gordon's the boss and he will defer to him. He wants to learn from him.'[41] The canvas this painted – an ignorant pupil Mandelson prostrate at the feet of the master professor Brown – provoked Mandelson to spit with rage. Their armistice had lasted just thirty-six hours.

Gordon Brown returned to Number 10 on Tuesday morning to plead again with Blair for Robinson to be spared. On top of all the other changes, Brown contended, this would undermine 'my authority' as Chancellor, always Brown's argument when he wanted to get his own way. Blair havered, then relented. His press secretary twisted the knife. Campbell let it be known that only

Brown's intervention had saved Robinson, the intention being to suggest that any further embarrassment caused by the Paymaster-General's interesting finances should be laid at the door of the Chancellor.

This was a rite of passage for the Prime Minister and for New Labour. The reshuffle was designed to establish who wore the trousers in Tony Blair's 'marriage' to Gordon Brown. There was talk from Number 10 of a more 'formal' style of decision-making. The bumpy transition from party of opposition to party of government was complete. So it was, to a point. The Cabinet looked more Blairised. The Budget put substantial flesh on the claim that New Labour could be both radical and credible. But the bogus hyping of the money assigned to health and education betrayed a continuing weakness for governing by headline without a care for the long-term consequences of swelling unrealisable expectations. The tensions twisted around the heart of the government had not been loosened, but further tautened.

Chairing his first co-ordination meeting at Number 10, Jack Cunningham looked around at Campbell and Whelan. He was never going to challenge the power of the Prime Minister's press secretary, nor was there a realistic hope of controlling the Chancellor's propagandist. Still, Cunningham made a display of taking charge. In future, he demanded, everyone would 'sing from the same sheet'. He thumped the table: 'The feuding must stop!' The feuding would last much longer than Doctor Jack.[42]

# 10. The Ethical Dimension

The pretty, dark-eyed, olive-skinned young girl – she was about nine years of age – lay on Robin Cook's desk and gazed into the Foreign Secretary's eyes. She looked out of the front cover of the shiny brochure produced by the Foreign Office to mark his first year in power.

Few thought there was much to celebrate. Labour MPs and the liberal media were outraged that, after his lofty promises that human rights would be the lodestar of foreign policy, arms were still being shipped to the Indonesian dictatorship of President Suharto, who was using British-supplied water cannon and tear gas to put down pro-democracy protesters on the streets of Jakarta in spring 1998. The Tories and the right-wing newspapers meanwhile pilloried Cook's personal morality.

If the Foreign Secretary could not get a good press from anyone else, he could at least print his own. He began to flick through the satisfyingly thick and glossy Annual Report on Human Rights. He noted the pictures of the Prime Minister and himself in dynamic poses in capitals across the world, and the happy snaps of children from around the globe smiling gratitude at Britain's benign concern for their well-being. Then, he reached page thirteen of his advertising brochure, captioned 'Building Partnerships'. The Foreign Secretary's eyes froze on the illustrative picture in the bottom right-hand corner. Cook's forensic brain went into overdrive. Was this a horrendous mistake? Was it a deliberate act of sabotage by one of the civil servants who hated him? Was there a conspiracy within his department to shame him?

He buzzed through to the Private Office and summoned officials. The Foreign Secretary jabbed a finger at the picture of himself and Suharto, shaking hands and exchanging pally smiles, as if they were two traders who had just clapped flesh on a weapons deal.

Cold and white with fury, Cook demanded: 'Who the hell is responsible for this?'[1] He never did find out.

Robin Cook had swept into the Foreign Office with such swagger. He had been fêted in Opposition as one of Labour's sharpest minds, the custodian of the party's conscience from the Blairites, and the best parliamentary orator of his generation. Like Gordon Brown, his great antagonist, Cook was a man whom colleagues found easy to admire, but hard to like. He was the only child of a teacher, and his innate shyness and awkwardness translated into an aloof and spiky manner. He was baffled that he so often left a first impression of being conceited. He had never troubled to make many friends, but then he felt no need of a coterie of hangers-on when he was such a success. Though the Foreign Office was not his original ambition, he arrived there determined to make as large a splash as any other senior minister. He would bring radical change to how the world was dealt with by King Charles Street and how that marvellous address was seen by the planet.

He announced himself portentously by ordering that the grand iron gates opening on to Downing Street, which had not been used for years, should be unlocked in order to provide an imposing entrance for his arrival. Once established in the finest ministerial quarters in Whitehall, he would show off the 'black box' which was the hot-line he had had installed to his American counterpart. Once visitors registered a suitable amount of respect for this gadgetry, Cook would then reveal that it had not rung for a fortnight, and when it did, the first caller was not the US Secretary of State but a man wanting to order a takeaway pizza.

This attractively self-deprecating note was not characteristic of the beginning of his reign. The rivalry for attention between senior figures in the Cabinet tempted them to out-boast each other to long-term dangerous effect. After Brown's great triumph announcing independence for the Bank of England, Cook was fired with desire for a place in the sun. His contribution to the hyperbolic whirl of launches and pronouncements in New Labour's narcotic early days in office was to summon the media, academic experts and diplomats to the ornate splendour of the Locarno Room to proclaim an overturning of the cynical Conservative approach to foreign policy. The man of the left adopted the corporate language of New Labour to give the Foreign Office a revitalising 'mission statement'. Henceforth 'the national interest cannot be defined by narrow realpolitik', he declared, stitching his morals on his sleeve. Britain would 'once again be a force for good in the world'. Human rights would be placed 'at the heart' of everything he did. When this subsequently became the rod with which he was thrashed, Cook would claim that he had never used the phrase 'ethical foreign policy'. But he certainly talked of an 'ethical content'. Indeed he used the 'e-word' more than once. 'Our foreign policy must have an ethical dimension and must support the demands of other people for the democratic rights on which we insist for ourselves.'[2]

Human rights campaigners were delighted. David Puttnam, New Labour's favourite film director, was asked to make a video to proselytise Cook's missionary position to all British embassies. *Cook: The Movie* was left on the cutting room floor as the Foreign Secretary's hubris began to unravel with a startling rapidity.

As is not untypical of politicians, his compulsion for vainglory was married to an idealistic belief that he would genuinely be a force for improvement. It was a good but inexpensive gesture to support a world ban on anti-personnel landmines, a cause that had been popularised and glamorised by Princess Diana. The hard test of his pieties was whether they would prevail against the British arms industry which made annual sales abroad worth an estimated £5 billion, and whose share of the global weapons market was second only to the United States.

Cook had been cavalier about the delicacy of dealing with 19,000 licences to export arms inherited from the Conservatives. He was also foolish to underestimate the resistance he was bound to confront from the Ministry of Defence and the Department of Trade and Industry, the friends of the arms industry in Whitehall. Most crucially, Cook was regarded cooly in Downing Street. His mission statement was not popular at Number 10. Jonathan Powell, the most influential voice on foreign affairs at the Blair court, was infuriated by what the former diplomat saw as Cook's naïve and simplistic approach. For days afterwards, Powell could be heard wandering Number 10 spitting scorn about the Foreign Secretary. It was Powell and those who took his view, not Cook, who possessed the ear of the Prime Minister. The pragmatic and inexperienced Tony Blair was easy prey for the 'realist' school of diplomacy, which argued that the way to deal with big powers who abused human rights was to speak softly and carry not a large stick, but a carrot. When the Chinese premier, Zhu Rongji, visited Britain for the Euro-Asian Summit in April 1998, Blair praised this autocrat as 'a fellow moderniser'. He would also bestow that supreme benediction on Vladimir Putin, the former KGB operative who waged a vicious war in Chechnya. This flowed as much from temperament as from judgement. The Prime Minister believed that he could conquer the world with his charm. He was the first Western leader to call on Moscow when Putin became President of Russia. Blair returned to Number 10 fizzing: 'I have really made a connection.'

The Foreign Secretary's notions about restricting weapons exports also collided with the Prime Minister's domestic priority to look strong on defence and protect the half million jobs of British workers in the arms industry.

The first hot crucible of New Labour's ethics was the 125 licences for exporting arms to Indonesia. Suharto's kleptocracy had been a *cause célèbre* on the left since the slaughter of 200,000 people in East Timor, and no one had been more excoriating about the West's collusion with the dictator than Robin Cook. In the summer of 1997, human rights groups pressed the Foreign Office to stop the next arms shipment to Indonesia which included sixteen Hawk jets, armoured cars and water cannon. The defence industry concentrated its lobbying at the top of government. British Aerospace, manufacturers of the Hawks, were the most skilled persuaders in the business and had excellent connections. Cook would privately blame his defeat on the influence of Clive Hollick, Labour lord, media proprietor, adviser to the DTI and a former director of British Aerospace. It was the contention that jobs would be at risk if Britain sent a signal that it was an unreliable supplier which captured the Prime Minister. Amidst conflicting advice from government lawyers about whether it would be legal to revoke the licences, Number 10 ruled that the arms package was to be sent to Indonesia.

Few were angrier about this than Cook's own parliamentary private secretary, Ken Purchase. A bluff and plain-spoken MP from the Black Country, Purchase had idolised the Foreign Secretary as the great ginger hope of the left. He felt bitterly let down by his hero. 'We've done all this parroting and spouting, and we're just backing off,' Purchase laid into Cook. 'There's no morality to letting these contracts go ahead.' Cook replied that there was 'no evidence' that the planes were being used for 'internal repression', an argument which he had previously ridiculed when it was deployed by the Conservatives. 'That's not a Labour argument,' shouted Purchase. 'We're supplying lethal weapons to a dictator we've damned to eternity.'

On 17 July, Cook made another preachy speech. Attached to it was a twelve-point plan, including a ban on the export of weapons 'with which regimes deny the demands of their people for human rights'.[3] Just eleven days later, slipping the announcement out as parliament was about to go on holiday and while Cook was out of the country, the Foreign Office confirmed that the arms would be allowed to go to Indonesia. The sneakiness did nothing to defuse the fury of those who had taken his promises at face value. One hundred and thirty-six MPs, most of them Labour, signed a motion attacking the decision. Demonstrators outside Downing Street unfurled a banner: 'Ethical Foreign Policy RIP'. Cook tried to recover some ground with his erstwhile supporters on the left just before the party conference by leaking to the *Guardian* that he had blocked two arms contracts to Indonesia. An annoyed Blair called in Cook to dress him down for indulging in 'gesture' politics.[4]

On the wider issue of future export licences, the Foreign Secretary made modest progress in his disputes with the Prime Minister. The criterion for rejecting licences was hardened from 'likely to be used' for internal repression to 'might be used'. But that was watered down by Number 10's insistence that arms could still be sold for the 'protection of members of security forces from violence'. Though the new guidelines were issued by the Foreign Office, the stamp of the Prime Minister was all over them, with the preamble emphasising 'the maintenance of a strong defence industry'.[5]

Cook then fell out with the one member of the Cabinet who should have been his natural ally in changing the priorities of foreign policy. Clare Short, the International Development Secretary, was ending suspect trade-for-aid deals where she could, and trying to place less emphasis on emergency relief to developing countries and more on long-term development. But Short frequently undermined herself by opening her mouth to change feet. When the British dependency of Montserrat was consumed by volcanic eruptions in August 1997, Short scorned the islanders' demands for more British aid, scoffing in the manner of a colonial governor: 'They'll be wanting golden elephants next.'[6]

As Short was lampooned by the media, Cook's efforts to soothe the ensuing furore by establishing an action group led by the Foreign Office earned him not her gratitude, but her enmity. She complained of being used as a 'whipping girl', oblivious to the fact that at least some of her lacerations were self-inflicted, and took to disparaging him as 'Robin Redbox'. She ostentatiously aligned herself with Gordon Brown by lavishly praising the Chancellor's contribution to reducing Third World debt. She and Brown had their own falling-out in November 1998 when, in an echo of golden elephants, she dismissed calls to write off the debts of hurricane-torn Honduras and Nicaragua as 'an irrelevance'. Overruled by the Chancellor, she was obliged to stand mutely by his side as he announced emergency debt relief for central America. Such were the unstable alliances of convenience between the Cabinet's febrile personalities.

Cook, with few close supporters at the high table, was constantly defeated. A much-vaunted element of his cleaner-handed foreign policy was a diversification programme to encourage arms manufacturers to switch to non-lethal products. After three years in power, it emerged that the programme's budget was forty times smaller than the amount spent on promoting arms exports.[7] British arms continued to flow to Saudi Arabia, China, Kenya, Zimbabwe and many other unsavoury regimes.[8] Britain belatedly joined a temporary European Union embargo of Indonesia when Hawk jets were used during the ugly repression of East Timor in the autumn of 1999. It was too late. The next delivery of Hawks had already flown.

After just six months in office, Cook was already rationalising the evaporation of his fine sentiments. 'Inconsistency is inevitable to compromise, and compromise is inevitable to foreign policy. That is real life.'[9] Ethics man had joined the realpolitikers.

A strong and well-allied Foreign Secretary might have won more of his internal struggles. The stature of the largely friendless Cook was remorselessly weakened by the scrutiny of his personal ethics. He had set himself up for this fall with the language he used in the Locarno Room. The higher the moral rhetoric, the greater the plunge when the moralist is found wanting. There is nothing more enjoyable to the crowd, and nothing more humiliating for the victim, than the preacher whose trousers are torn down.

For the first few months after their brutal break-up in the VIP lounge at Heathrow airport, Cook's estranged wife had largely kept silent. But he was petrified of what the ditched Margaret might do to him. On her account, he mixed appeals for mercy with financial menaces, telling her: 'If you talk, I'll lose my job and go bankrupt and you'll lose the house.'[10]

From the New Year of 1998, she began to feed the media's appetite for anti-Cook copy with a series of progressively more savage commentaries about his failings as a human being. For twelve months she stripped him bare, culminating in the publication of a book which depicted him as an emotionally stunted serial adulterer who hit the bottle at times of stress and had destroyed his personality by 'selling his soul to the devil' of New Labour.[11] Only with this attack, so venomous that Cook became the object of some pity, did his ex-wife exhaust her capacity to damage him. By then, the dismembering of his character was immense.

It became open season on Cook. Anything he did or said was given the most negative interpretation. As a token of his determination to purge King Charles Street of the vestiges of imperial attitudes, he announced he would be updating the décor in his office. He wanted rid of the picture of a potentate over the fireplace, a massive portrait of the Maharajah of Nepal. It was subsequently reported that the picture had been replaced with an enormous mirror, the better for the Foreign Secretary to preen before his reflection. That this was not actually true was less to the point than that many people found it easy to believe.

His successes – such as persuading the Iranians to lift the *fatwa* against Salman Rushdie and helping to establish an international war crimes tribunal at the Hague – went largely ignored. His failures were projected in technicolour. An accident-strewn royal tour of India and Pakistan was symbolised by a photograph of Cook looking ridiculous in overlarge gold-rimmed sunglasses and a white panama hat borrowed from the Old Etonian High Commissioner. In the middle of the tour, Cook made an 8,000-mile round trip back to Britain which the press immortalised as 'the lost weekend'. Though the Queen was said to be quite content to be deprived of the company of the Foreign Secretary, the media seized on the fact that he had spent time with Gaynor Regan. The charge was that he had deserted his sovereign to be with his mistress.

Much worse for Cook, it emerged that, shortly after he became Foreign Secretary, he attempted to have Regan appointed as his diary secretary. This must have struck Cook as a conveniently cosy continuation of their arrangement in Opposition. What did not cross his mind – or was conceitedly dismissed from it – was how this would look if it ever got out. It was going to be construed as having his lover at the taxpayers' expense. High intelligence is no prophylactic against behaving stupidly.

When this misjudgement was revealed in the New Year of 1998, Cook first claimed that he had dismissed the idea of employing Regan at the Foreign Office 'very quickly', then admitted that he had toyed with it 'for about a week'.[12] One theory which circulated within the Foreign Office was that the Permanent Secretary, Sir

John Coles, deploying the mandarin talents which had taken him to the top of the diplomatic corps, requested a private interview with the Foreign Secretary after civil servants noticed that Regan had given Cook's address on her application form. Coles told Cook that, regretfully, it had come to officials' attention that Gaynor Regan would fail security screening because she was involved in a relationship with a senior member of the Foreign Office. Cook told friends that this was not true. It was Gaynor herself who had decided to withdraw her application when she realised it would mean they would be parted for long periods while he was abroad.

This episode featured another woman scorned. Anne Bullen had been removed as the diary secretary. She was not a career civil servant, but the personal choice of a Tory predecessor. Cook was within his rights to find himself a more congenial member of personal staff, but that point was lost in the impression that he had fired Bullen to create a vacancy on the Foreign Office payroll for his lover. A ferocious barrage of negative publicity pounded him from the New Year of 1998. Cook had made himself the target of choice for Conservatives and the media who wanted to portray the government as profligate, hypocritical and cronyistic.

A press conference with the Russian Foreign Minister was entirely consumed by questions about his private life. At another press conference, this time with the bemused-looking Foreign Minister of Albania sitting by his side, the tormented Cook described Bullen as 'impossible to work with'. Instead of smothering the flames, he had poured on more fuel. A typical tabloid headline bellowed: 'COOK THE CAD'S SLUR ON WOMAN HE SACKED'.[13] He even contrived to make his behaviour sound worse than it actually was by comparing his position to the impeachment-ensnared Bill Clinton. 'It is important that he continues with his duties, as I do myself,' said Cook, his pomposity expanding as his credibility shrank.

One broadsheet asked: 'Could he cope in a real crisis?'[14] Another queried: 'Can he still do his job?'[15] The same questions were being asked at Number 10. The endless and increasingly grotesque Cook soap opera caused mounting frustration to Tony Blair. On three successive days in January, tales of Cook, his wife and his lover stole headlines from a prime ministerial tour of Japan. Blair defended the minister in distress, telling one interviewer: 'On the international stage, he has made a huge reputation for himself. That guy is doing a tremendous job.'[16] Off-camera, Blair despaired to his aides about Cook's inability to 'sort it out'.

Not even his worst enemies would have predicted that this once bright star could have so swiftly imploded into a black hole. This serious and ambitious man was now assigned the status of the Cabinet's figure of folly. In early April, he secretly married Gaynor, even giving his Special Branch detectives the slip for paranoid fear that it might leak out to the media. They plighted their troth on a rain-soaked day in the Tunbridge Wells register office, sandwiched between a fire station and a funeral parlour, a setting which provided a perfect metaphor for what had happened to Cook's once great reputation.

After the short ceremony, Cook came out punching the air, not in celebration of his marriage, but because he had succeeded in keeping it secret from the hated media. When the papers still managed to have the last giggle by ridiculing him for what he wore, Cook mourned: 'It's now one of the things I shall probably go to my grave with: married in a green anorak.'[17]

His reputation for integrity, competence and judgement had been shredded. He confided to friends his fears that he was so weakened that Tony Blair would shortly sack him. This was not a man in a frame of mind to cope calmly with the sand storm that was about to blow in from Africa.

Sierra Leone was a faraway country in the armpit of West Africa about which most Britons knew little and cared less. The nation's mineral wealth was also its curse. Struggle for control of the diamond fields had plunged it into years of civil war. In May 1997, Ahmed Tejan Kabbah, the elected president, was overthrown by Johnny Paul Koroma, a Sandhurst-trained army officer, who unleashed a wave of violence atrocious even by the brutal standards of African coups. The revolting specialities of the cannibalistic

Revolutionary United Front included macheting legs and arms off men, women and children.

Britain was committed to restoring Kabbah to power. So much so that he was the Prime Minister's personal guest at the Commonwealth summit in Edinburgh. But in this blood-drenched corner of Africa, ethical choices were presented not in black and white, but in dirty shades of grey. The only regional power capable of restoring Kabbah was Nigeria, itself an international pariah which had been expelled from the Commonwealth for extreme violations of human rights. In the attempt to equip himself with a fighting force, Kabbah was trading arms for mining concessions through one Rakesh Sakena, whom Cook would memorably describe as 'an Indian businessman, travelling on the passport of a dead Serb, awaiting extradition from Canada for alleged embezzlement from a bank in Thailand'.[18] The arms to Kabbah were supplied by Sandline International, a company of British mercenaries.

This murk was thickened by farcical confusion about the means and ends of British policy. As Sir John Kerr, the Foreign Office's Permanent Secretary, would eventually concede: 'It's not a pretty story.'[19] If the tragedy of Sierra Leone recalled Joseph Conrad's *Heart of Darkness*, then the Foreign Office's role could have been scripted by Evelyn Waugh. A sloppily worded United Nations resolution, principally drafted by British officials, could be read as imposing an arms embargo on not just the junta, but also the ousted democrats that Britain supported. It was then translated into British law as a blanket ban. Even though ministers understood that, Foreign Office briefings to MPs, the media and their own diplomatic staff gave the impression that the embargo applied only to Koroma's regime. After Kabbah was returned to power in a counter-coup in March 1998, Tony Lloyd, the Minister for Africa, told the Commons that the resolution 'imposed sanctions on the junta'.[20]

This was the interpretation being followed by the FO's man in West Africa, Peter Penfold. The British High Commissioner to Sierra Leone was a local hero for his strong support for Kabbah. Penfold holed up at a hotel in Conakry, the capital of neighbouring

Guinea. His communications with London were worse than pigeon post. Crucial documents went astray or were destroyed. His satellite phone didn't work. He had been sent a coded fax machine, security cabinet and deciphering material, but left them at the airport because he judged them too large to fit through the hotel bedroom door.[21]

Penfold had on several occasions discussed the mercenaries' plan to arm Kabbah with Tim Spicer, the former Guards officer who ran Sandline. Though the civil servants hotly disputed this, Spicer maintained that he also told officials on the Africa desk in London of his intention to run guns to Kabbah.

The Foreign Office was formally committed to an arms embargo while its man on the spot was, if not actively encouraging, apparently not discouraging armed intervention to get the result Britain wanted. This was – as the report by MPs would conclude – the result of 'dealing in half-truths – a dangerous commodity'.[22]

That his own department was running two policies towards Sierra Leone was something about which Cook would thereafter maintain he was in blissful – but hugely perilous – ignorance. On the evening of 28 April, the Foreign Secretary returned to his official London residence at Carlton Gardens looking forward to a relaxing evening with his new wife. He found two of his aides waiting for him in a state of great agitation. One of them, Andrew Hood, had discovered a ticking fax buried in Cook's in-tray back at the Foreign Office. It was a letter from solicitors acting on behalf of Sandline, saying that the company was under investigation by Customs and Excise for sanctions-busting. The company said it was guiltless because its activities were known to officials on the Africa desk and encouraged by Penfold. Attached to the fax was a note from officials, saying that, after a tip-off about the allegations of sanctions-busting, they had referred the case to Customs in March. In fact, Customs had already raided the Foreign Office. According to Sir John Kerr's subsequent account, the Permanent Secretary did not pass this sensational information to the Foreign Secretary for three weeks.

What his aides told him that evening left Cook aghast. The

combination of mercenaries and arms-running sounded deadly. It could smash the remaining brick of what was left of his crumbling reputation. His greatest achievement in Opposition had been his merciless prosecution of the Conservative government's secret connivance in the supply of arms to Iraq. An arms scandal would surely be the final, mortal blow. When the story began to break publicly on Sunday, it was with precisely the interpretation feared most by Cook. One headline announced: 'Cook snared in arms for coup inquiry'.[23] In a mounting panic, Cook rang Blair to assure him that he would get to the bottom of it.

What 'put the story on stilts', as Cook would subsequently lament, was a woeful performance by Tony Lloyd when he was ambushed with questions about gun-running by the foreign affairs select committee on Tuesday. As they pressed him to explain who knew what and when, Lloyd floundered like a sprat in a net. In the wake of that débâcle, Cook called together an emergency meeting of senior officials and ministers in his high-ceilinged office overlooking Horseguards. Denis MacShane, one of the parliamentary private secretaries, reported that there was restlessness on the backbenches and the press was likely to be dreadful. 'Thank you, Denis,' snapped a nervy Cook. 'I think we fucking well know that.'

The Blairite minister at the Foreign Office was Liz Symons, the former General Secretary of the First Division Association of Civil Servants. She was reflecting both a desire to protect those whom she used to represent, and Number 10's general view, when she questioned whether announcing an inquiry was really necessary. Penfold, she said, should be 'treated properly'.

Ken Purchase, in his blunt Black Country way, turned on Lady Symons. He reckoned that was the sort of argument which he used to hear when he was a local councillor and there were allegations of abuse in children's homes. 'You're talking like a bloody NALGO official.' Symons flushed up: 'Well, thank you very much.'

Cook felt acutely vulnerable to the accusation that he had been involved in deception. 'No one must be able to suggest a cover-up,' he told the meeting. On Wednesday afternoon, he promised the Commons that: 'There will be no whitewash.' If there had been a breach of the arms embargo 'that is a very serious matter which must be fully and openly investigated'.[24] He implied – much to the fury of civil servants at the Foreign Office – that officials had left ministers in the dark and suggested there was a case to answer by offering them the services of criminal lawyers.

Fearing that he would be accused of prejudicing the Customs investigation, Cook was opaque about many details of the affair. While this may have been technically proper, it added to the impression that there was a scandal which was being covered up. 'Coup plot Cook never noticed,' chortled the *Independent*. 'We are invited to believe that, to adapt an old joke, Mr Cook has been treated by his staff as a sort of political mushroom – kept in the dark only to find himself now covered in the rich manure of political embarrassment.'[25] The *Sun*, a newspaper not previously distinguished for interest in West African affairs except of the sexual variety, devoted four pages to what was now known as 'Arms-to-Africa'.

Number 10 watched with mounting infuriation. This was yet another case of the Foreign Secretary getting himself into a mess. To his aides, Blair vented his exasperation: 'For God's sake, the good guys won.' The Prime Minister discussed it with Alastair Campbell, Peter Mandelson and Jonathan Powell; they were agreed that Cook had lost the plot.

On Monday 11 May, doing a media 'doorstep' at a London college, Blair delivered an apparently extempore, but actually carefully rehearsed, interpretation of what had happened. Britain had been helping democrats back into power against a military junta. 'Don't let us forget,' said the Prime Minister, 'that the UN and the UK were both trying to help the democratic regime restore its position from an illegal military coup. They were quite right in trying to do it.' Penfold had done 'a superb job'. Blair repeated the message in the Commons two days later, dismissing the furore as 'a lot of hype in the media and on the Opposition benches . . . I described it as overblown hoo-hah and that is what it is.'[26]

On the large fact – that Britain had taken the side of the democrats – the Prime Minister was perfectly correct. President Kabbah wrote an open letter expressing his profound thanks for the 'principled and ethical position' of Britain.

What Blair dismissed as a 'hoo-ha' on Wednesday blew up again the following morning courtesy of the Permanent Secretary himself when he appeared before the foreign affairs select committee. Sir John Kerr, though more modern-minded than his predecessor, had a traditional view of the loyalties he believed civil servants and politicians owed to each other. Kerr was angered that Cook had dumped the blame on officials. Now the Foreign Office's senior civil servant dropped the politicians in it. The usually smooth mandarin cut up rough in an acrimonious 100-minute confrontation with the MPs. Asked how far up warnings of illegal arms shipments had gone, he replied: 'I don't know.' Disastrously for the government, he told the MPs that ministers had been told about the Customs investigations in March, contradicting the categorical and repeated assertions by Cook and Lloyd that there had been no briefing about the allegations of sanctions-busting until much later.

When news of Kerr's performance was conveyed to him, the Foreign Secretary was furious. After a seething exchange in Cook's office at lunchtime, Kerr sent a letter of clarification to the MPs. 'I have checked my memory,' read his recantation. The 'briefing pack' prepared for Lloyd when he spoke to MPs on 12 March 'does not mention arms shipments', though it had reported a possible deal between Kabbah and Sandline.

Briefing packs were at the centre of the controversy, which was particularly unfortunate for Cook. He was once again hoist by the braggadocio of his early days in office. Finding a bust of Ernie Bevin hidden behind a pot plant at Carlton Gardens, Cook had it dusted off and given it a proud place. That January, he had been seen on television comparing himself with the great post-war Labour Foreign Secretary:

The story goes that Ernest Bevin, on his first weekend, was left with five red boxes and a note saying: 'Foreign Secretary we thought you would like to do these five red boxes over the weekend.' And on Monday, when the staff came in the private office, they found the five red boxes in the same place with a note in his handwriting: 'A kind thought, but sadly erroneous.' I'm happy to say that nobody's ever tried to present me with five red boxes, but ever since I heard that story I have recognised that you can be a successful Foreign Secretary if you focus on the big questions, not necessarily if you finish the paperwork.[27]

His own suggestion that he did not finish his paperwork reverberated back at Cook to add weight to the charge that he was incompetent. The accusation of idleness was unfair, but his conceit had handed this hurtful weapon to his critics.

On 18 May, there were two announcements designed to draw a line in the sand under Sandline. The Attorney-General said that there would be no prosecution of the company. Cook simultaneously set up an inquiry by Sir Thomas Legg, a retired civil servant, who savaged 'systematic failures of communication' within the Foreign Office, but cleared ministers of deceit. Blair had already pre-empted the verdict by declaring: 'When people say they run an ethical foreign policy, I say Sierra Leone was an example of that.'[28]

The foreign affairs select committee continued to dissect the Foreign Secretary, his ministers and officials. The MPs' report was scheduled to be published on Tuesday 9 February 1999. The Friday before, the committee's chairman, Donald Anderson, bumped into Cook in the House of Commons. 'Don't rubbish our report, Robin,' said Anderson, suggesting it could even be quite helpful. Cook said nothing in reply. What Anderson did not know was that the Foreign Office, in breach of parliamentary rules, already had possession of his committee's report.

Contrary to Cook's subsequent explanations of the leak, it was not faxed to the Foreign Office out of the blue. Ernie Ross, an MP on the committee, had approached Ken Purchase in a Commons tearoom and asked him whether he wanted an advance copy. Ross had it faxed to himself, which is why his name was later discovered on the document, then passed it over to Purchase, who walked around clutching the brown envelope for two hours until he met Cook and handed it over. The Foreign Secretary then dropped it

– whether he opened it or not is unknown – into the in-tray of his political adviser, Andrew Hood.[29]

When Ross was revealed as the leaker and forced to resign from the committee, Cook said he had 'nothing to apologise for'. He was rebuked after admitting that his office had received not just that report, but two others leaked from select committees. Cook claimed: 'Any use of that knowledge would have been an offence, but I made no use of it.'[30]

Yet the Foreign Office was giving to the media a detailed rebuttal of the report before it was officially released. The morning of its publication, Tony Blair was extraordinarily well acquainted with the contents of a report he could not have had time to study when he attacked the MPs' findings on the Jimmy Young programme. This was a typical display of New Labour's manic combination of arrogance and insecurity. For it was all rather unnecessary. The inquiry had actually cleared ministers of the killer charge that they had been complicit in the breach of an arms embargo.

The excoriating findings were about the mismanagement of the Foreign Office. Sir John Kerr had 'failed in his duty to Ministers': just about the gravest charge that can be levelled at a Permanent Secretary. Officials were accused of 'at best political naivety, and at worst a Yes–Minister like contempt'. Yet Kerr remained in post. The officials accused by the committee of treating policy on the arms embargo 'in a disgracefully casual manner' and 'making serious errors of judgement' were promoted.[31] The whitewash that Cook had forsworn was thrown over the Foreign Office by the bucketload.

As the furore dissipated, it left behind confusion in New Labour's collective head about what was an ethical foreign policy. The murderous gangsters of the RUF, now led by Foday Sankoh, continued to destabilise President Kabbah. With encouragement from Britain, Kabbah signed a peace deal which brought them into the government of Sierra Leone. 'The good guys', as Blair had called them, were sharing power with the vile guys. Sometimes in foreign policy there are no clearly moral options, just choices between evils. This did not prove to be the right choice. Sankoh was soon back on a murderous rampage. In the spring of 2000,

British troops were sent to rescue a hopelessly inadequate United Nations force. Rather than boast of protecting the democrats, ministers pretended that the mission was confined to securing the safety of British citizens. Even when they were operating something that might resemble an ethical foreign policy, they were either too muddled or embarrassed to say so.

When the jowly generalissimo landed at Heathrow and was smoothed through the VIP lounge, he received the five-star treatment that he took for granted on his trips to Britain. So regular were his visits to what he called this 'ideal' country that General Augusto Pinochet, the retired dictator of Chile, had established routines. He dined in clubland at White's, lunched at Fortnum & Mason, went shopping at Harrods and Burberrys, and took in Madame Tussauds to examine the waxworks of fellow tyrants. This visit, in September 1998, was his second since New Labour had come to power. Leading lights of the Cabinet had been student campaigners against the murderous regime he had established after toppling the elected Marxist government of Salvador Allende in 1973. But the ideals of these ministers' youth seemed to have been forgotten. Unlike the socialist government of France, which made it clear Pinochet was no longer welcome on their soil, no one raised an objection when he informed the British embassy in Santiago of his travel plans. As the red carpet rolled under the octogenarian general's gait, just as it had always done during the Tory years, he could be forgiven for concluding that nothing had changed his status as an honoured guest of the British. It was still like the old times as he took tea with his great friend Margaret Thatcher at her home in Belgravia before being admitted to the London Clinic in Harley Street for a minor operation on his back.

This time, though, there was a snag in the red carpet. The general was recuperating from the operation when, shortly before midnight on Friday 16 October, he was arrested by Scotland Yard detectives acting on a request from a Spanish prosecutor for Pinochet's detention pending extradition on charges of murder, torture and terrorism.

The world was stunned and divided; no one more so than the British government. This ethical test for New Labour was not one it had wished upon itself. The Foreign Office had facilitated Pinochet's arrival. The Home Secretary didn't even know he was coming. Jack Straw was only alerted when, during a flight to address a conference on crime in Marseilles, one of his civil servants showed him an item in the *Guardian* about the Spanish prosecutor's surprise for the general. A startled Straw responded: 'This is going to be one helluva of a story.'

By Sunday morning, armed police were guarding the clinic as Pinochet's opponents, who had forlornly dreamt for years of seeing the grisly brute brought to justice for his regime's murder of more than 3,000 people, demonstrated in delight. The general's outraged right-wing supporters and the Chilean government meanwhile contended that, as a retired head of state who had been made a senator for life, international law immunised him from prosecution.

Hatred of Pinochet was burnt deeply into the collective consciousness of the left. A sign that the radical flames that had fired their youthful protests against his regime were not entirely smothered by middle age came from a most unexpected quarter. Peter Mandelson, appearing on breakfast television, declared with a passion that suggested sincerity: 'The idea that such a brutal dictator as Pinochet should claim immunity; I think for most people in this country would be pretty gut-wrenching stuff.'[32] Mandelson's gut had never before wrenched so eloquently for the vast majority of left and liberal opinion.

But he had annoyed Number 10. As Mandelson got up from the studio sofa to make his way to the hospitality room, his pager was vibrating with a warning signal from the Prime Minister's press secretary. 'I agree with everything you say,' read the message from Alastair Campbell. 'But that is not the line.'[33]

Mandelson paid for his transgression of the line, as he had so often penalised others guilty of veering off-message, by reading in the newspapers that government sources were calling him 'unhelpful and emotional'.[34]

The line which Mandelson had crossed was that Pinochet was a matter for the courts. The government did not wish to get embroiled. Downing Street regarded the general's arrest not as an opportunity to amplify the ethical dimension, but as a nuisance. Juanita melodies might still sing softly in New Labour's hearts. In their heads – those worldlier and wearier organs in which everything was subjected to a cost–benefit analysis – they were for disposing of the controversy as quickly as possible. When the Prime Minister discussed it with his aides, principally Jonathan Powell and Alastair Campbell, the view was that this was – in Campbell's words – a 'no win'. The Chilean government was angry. The United States, fearing exposure of its role in the coup that had brought Pinochet to power, was unhappy. There would be weeks of raging controversy at the end of which either Pinochet would be released, which would inflame the left, or he would be sent for trial in Spain, which would infuriate the right. Margaret Thatcher was booming for her ally in the Falklands War to be released immediately, a demand which was hollered across the pages of the Conservative press. The initial prognosis inside Number 10 was that it would be better to face a short-term fury from the left by releasing him than let the case wind through the courts and endure a long-term controversy with no votes at the end of it.

Tony Blair, though he followed the legal proprieties in public, offered a glimpse into his mind when he addressed a private meeting of Labour MPs that week. He apologised for the absence of Peter Mandelson. 'Unfortunately, Peter could not be with us because he is at a meeting of the Socialist Workers' Party.'[35] The MPs roared at the notion of 'Red Pete'. The Prime Minister's joke was illuminating of his attitude. To Blair, bringing Pinochet to trial was a cause fit only for Trots.

He was wrong. Even some Tories, John Major most prominently, did not believe Pinochet's help in the Falklands War effaced the crimes of his regime. It was characteristic of New Labour's neurotic fear of being associated with anything about the party's past that Blair seemed to feel vulnerable to the right-wing accusation that his government was playing 'student politics'.

At Thursday's Cabinet, Blair instructed ministers not to say anything about Pinochet. That same day, however, there was another indication of his desire for a quick resolution when out came a welter of statements about the Home Office's role in the case. Alastair Campbell highlighted for the media's attention the discretionary powers enjoyed by the Home Secretary to free Pinochet to Chile on 'compassionate grounds'.[36]

There had been general relief in Number 10 that this dynamite was being handled not by the cack-handed Robin Cook, but by sure-fingered Jack Straw. During his first eighteen months as Home Secretary, he had enjoyed a reputation as an expert in political bomb disposal. Straw had even managed to alchemise a potentially awful embarrassment into an enhancement of his reputation when he persuaded his son, Billy, to turn himself in at the local nick after a newspaper had enticed him into dealing cannabis.

The Home Secretary's real name was John Straw. As an adolescent he renamed himself Jack after one of the leaders of the Peasants' Revolt in 1381. There was more directly inherited radicalism in his ancestry. His great-grandfather fought the landowners over enclosure, his grandfather was a Labour activist during the party's early years, and his father was a wartime conscientious objector.

At school, Straw suffered from the bigotry of other boys who would insert an E into his initials of JWS. He had an abiding loathing of prejudice. Straw established an inquiry, which the Conservatives had refused to do, into the murder of the black south London teenager, Stephen Lawrence. The findings of the Macpherson inquiry, which described the Metropolitan Police as 'institutionally racist', created the context for subjecting the police to race relations legislation. Straw attracted the compliment of being attacked by the *Daily Telegraph* for championing the equalisation of the age of homosexual consent. In a speech, he remembered how a gay schoolmate had gassed himself in desperation.

This face of Straw was classically liberal, but his was not a heart that bled. With his curfews, banning orders and zero tolerance, the other aspect that he presented to the world was authoritarian. As if determined to cultivate the image, 'Hard Jack' confessed to having been a bully at school, though contemporaries remembered a bespectacled, uncoordinated and asthmatic boy who was more set upon by others. His deaf ear seemed permanently turned to civil libertarians and human rights groups, who were repelled when he introduced a vouchers' scheme for asylum-seekers which, when it was previously proposed by the Tories, he had condemned as 'inhumane'. The side of his personality that craved order tempted him into rhetoric about asylum-seekers that risked inflaming the very racism that he so clearly abhorred.

Straw was not a man for the 'vision thing'. His time as president of the National Union of Students was less remembered for rousing speeches, and more for the efficient process of business. He regarded his metier as being 'a good administrative politician'.[37] Number 10 could not have asked for a sounder fellow to sort out the Pinochet affair without prolonged fuss.

Yet they had not quite understood their man. Even within the tough guy of the Home Office there still flickered some of the spirit of the student who had marched against Pinochet.

When Downing Street continued to emit signals that it wanted the general sent on his way, Straw went to the Prime Minister. 'This is my decision,' the Home Secretary told Blair. 'I'll tell you when I've decided.'

This was the Home Secretary being legally proper. The law required him to adopt a 'quasi-judicial' role. The partisan politico was expected to set aside his own opinions and adopt the Olympian detachment of a judge coolly reviewing argument and fact. But dressing a politician in a wig makes him no less a politician, and the law gave him quite a lot of latitude. Straw's two most recent Tory predecessors at the Home Office, Michael Howard and Kenneth Clarke, though from different wings of their party, declared that they would have released Pinochet. Had the Conservatives still been in power, there would have been no possibility whatsoever of bringing him to justice.

One minister, with a good claim to be able to read Straw's mind, told me at the time: 'Jack thinks Pinochet is a murdering old bastard who deserves to be thrown into prison.'[38] That may have over-coloured his view, but it was Straw's gut instinct.

By Wednesday 25 November, Pinochet's claims for immunity from prosecution had reached final adjudication in the House of Lords. Straw slipped past the crowds of pro- and anti-Pinochet demonstrators trying to drown each other out in Parliament Square, and went into his room in the Commons to watch five lords of appeal deliver their verdict live on television. The grey heads of the judiciary contrived to invest the event with the drama of a football penalty shoot-out. Lord Slynn and Lord Lloyd ruled that Pinochet did have immunity. 2–0 to the general. Lord Nicholls and Lord Steyn judged that he did not. 2–2. The score would be settled by Lord Justice Hoffmann. With a glance up to the terraces of the public gallery, he made it 3–2 against the general. The final decision now fell to the Home Secretary. The voice of ethics – and the majority of Labour MPs – urged him to send Pinochet towards trial. The rumble of the realpolitikers of Whitehall counselled sending him home. *The Times* pronounced that the decision facing Straw was 'the biggest dilemma of his career'.[39] The *Guardian* agreed that it was 'the most uncomfortable fortnight of his political life'.[40] The *Independent* concurred that this was 'the most agonising decision of his career'.[41]

Straw, who had a cheerfully cynical view of the political game, was amused that everyone assumed he must be in agonies. 'It's not difficult,' he would say. 'There's no Third Way. I either say Yes or No.'

On Monday 7 December, he sat at his desk in the Home Office, considering the representations winnowed down by officials from the hundreds submitted from around the world. Some contained evidence of the horrors of Pinochet's regime: the corpses dumped from helicopters with their bellies slit open, and 'the grill' on which victims would be stretched out naked and given electric shocks. Against that were the drier submissions from the Ministry of Defence and the Foreign Office fretting about the disruption caused by the arrest to trading and diplomatic relations.

On Thursday, the Home Secretary announced that he would allow extradition proceedings to continue. When the news was relayed on their pagers, Labour MPs erupted in spontaneous cheers. There was a roar for Straw when, later in the day, he turned up on the government frontbench.

But after it emerged that Lord Hoffmann had failed to reveal a connection with Amnesty International, a protagonist in the proceedings, the case was referred back to a different panel of law lords. In March 1999, following their 6—1 ruling that Pinochet could still be tried, albeit on more limited grounds, Straw again decided there were no compassionate grounds for the general's release.

Pinochet – 'desperately humiliated', according to his wife – remained under house arrest in Surrey for more than a year. This was the mildest of punishments compared with the atrocities inflicted on the victims of his regime, but it served a purpose. The patina of respectability acquired by the old tyrant was stripped away before the world as his dictatorship's crimes were heard in the British courts.

There had been a change of attitude in Downing Street, at least for party political purposes. By the autumn of 1999, Blair was using what he now called the 'unspeakable' Pinochet to attack the Tories as the torturers' friend.

Behind the rhetoric, there was diplomatic manoeuvring. That June, Robin Cook privately met the Spanish Foreign Minister, Abel Matutes, during a summit in Rio de Janeiro, where they discussed rumours that Pinochet's health was failing. Neither wanted a corpse on his government's hands. Cook reportedly said: 'I will not let him die in Britain,' to which his Spanish counterpart replied: 'I will not let him come to Spain.' Chile's centre-left government feared that the general's death on British soil carried the large risk that his right-wing supporters would embalm the monster with the wrappings of martyrdom. By the end of November, the Home Office, working with the Chilean embassy, had the agreement of Pinochet's lawyers to independent medical tests.

Straw read the doctors' reports sitting at the kitchen table of his town house in Kennington, south London. He had been anxious that an ambiguous medical verdict would make a decision open to challenge. So what he read was, in a way, a pleasure and a relief. According to the doctors, Pinochet was so brain-damaged by a series of strokes that he was no longer fit to stand trial. Those who advocated human rights could not argue for the denial of them even to a man as wicked as the general.

After further legal wrangling, on 3 March 2000 Pinochet was taken to RAF Waddington, where he boarded a Chilean air force jet. There was no red carpet for his exit. He was returning home a humiliated figure who would almost certainly never again dare to leave his country's borders. Spared by his senility, he flew home to the freedom the victims of his torture squads never enjoyed.

There were cries of 'Shame!' from the Labour benches when the Home Secretary informed the Commons that Pinochet was gone. Straw concluded the affair by telling MPs that the case had 'a world-wide impact'. Was he also right to claim that it did 'lasting' good? Though human rights groups criticised the disappointing denouement, they declared that the Pinochet case was the most important precedent for international justice since the Nuremberg trials of Nazi war criminals. Amnesty International, which had been at the centre of the case, said: 'The fact that Augusto Pinochet was arrested – almost unthinkable seventeen months ago – has sent a powerful message: no one is above international law.'[42]

Democracy in Chile, far from being weakened as the apologists for the general had claimed, gave every appearance of having been strengthened. The idea that a former head of state could somehow claim immunity from prosecution for atrocities committed by his regime had been squashed. Not long after his return to Santiago, proceedings began there to bring Pinochet to trial in Chile: an unthinkable development before his arrest in London. It was established in British law and a message was sent around the planet that dictators could not always and everywhere expect to retire to a life of leisurely, respectable globe-trotting and never be made to answer for their crimes. In a way that it neither anticipated nor wished for, New Labour had nevertheless managed to set an ethical example to the world.

# 11. Operation Hoover

Tony Blair couldn't sleep. He was restless, buzzing as the plane carrying him back from the handover of Hong Kong to China streaked to Britain in the summer of 1997. Word was sent down the VC-10 for Paddy Ashdown to come join the Prime Minister in his private quarters. The two men, leaders of rival parties though they were, supposedly fierce competitors in the gladiatorial arena, chatted and laughed as intimate friends until they became so noisy that they disturbed a pyjama-clad Cherie. The ceremonialising and speechifying in the Far East had been long and draining. The Prime Minister's wife *did* want to get some sleep. Couldn't the two of them find somewhere else to do their business?

At a refuelling stop in Siberia, Blair and Ashdown got out to continue their conversation on the tarmac. They were challenged by a Russian official who did not recognise the man wearing tracksuit bottoms and a Denver Fire Service sweatshirt, a souvenir of the G7 Summit, as the Prime Minister of the United Kingdom. Once that little local difficulty was resolved, the two men walked and talked in the Siberian dawn, carrying on with their tryst of Novosibirsk.

They were taking up where they had left off before the election. A clandestine understanding had been struck that there would be a coalition government between the two parties, with at least two Liberal Democrats in the Cabinet, if Tony Blair didn't have a majority significantly better than John Major's. It was third party insurance for Blair against a hung parliament or a majority vulnerable to left-wing rebellion. The landslide upset the coalition calculations of both men when they spoke on the Friday after the election, just as Blair was about to go to Buckingham Palace. Ashdown was in his Commons office, accompanied by two trusted Liberal Democrat Lords, Richard Holme and Roy Jenkins. There

was not time for a long conversation. It is one of the weaknesses of
the British way of changing governments that on their first day in
office, at a moment when they are utterly exhausted, new Prime
Ministers have to make snap judgements with enormous long-term
consequences. Blair had a thousand decisions to make that day. It
became evident to Ashdown that negotiating all the twists and turns
involved in forming a coalition with the Liberal Democrats was
not something that was going to happen the morning after the
landslide. Though he would later rue an opportunity lost, at the
time Ashdown himself was very uncertain about whether a coalition
was now feasible. He was worried how he would explain to his
contingent of forty-six MPs that they would not be swallowed up
by a government with such a huge majority. Blair did not pop the
question. 'It was like an old-fashioned romance between two
would-be lovers,' says one of those involved. 'It was up to Blair to
propose. He didn't.'[1]

Ashdown did not press his suit. Watching television that afternoon, the Liberal Democrat leader saw Robin Cook come on the
screen captioned as Foreign Secretary. Ashdown asked himself
whether he minded. He decided he was relieved.[2]

His conversation with Blair had, however, ended on a collaborative note. Ashdown was told by Blair: 'I still want to do things
with you, Paddy.'

The first product of that desire 'to do things', a bargain sealed
during the return from Hong Kong, was the formation in July 1997
of a joint committee of the Cabinet on constitutional reform. Some
of Ashdown's colleagues revelled in being the first Liberals for
decades to stretch their legs under the Cabinet table. Others could
detect a disturbing irony about their situation. Alan Beith, Ashdown's deputy and a sceptic about the sincerity of Blair's intentions,
said: 'This is the first time I've had to sign the Official Secrets Act
to get a Freedom of Information Bill.'[3]

No secrets of any substance were ever going to be shared around
the Cabinet table – a fairly redundant item of furniture in the Blair
government. The joint committee was a decorative addition, a
presentational token of his often voiced desire to embrace a more

inclusive, more pluralistic style of politics. The much deeper plot between Blair and Ashdown was being negotiated away from the ears of their colleagues. The two had been talking about co-operation for years. A warm mutual regard had grown between them, developed during dinners at each other's houses with their wives. Both men were impatient with the artificial walls dividing British politics. Both disdained what they viewed as the conservatives within their own parties. Each estimated the other much more highly than they did many of their own colleagues.

Blair had also forged a strong attachment with Roy Jenkins, the grand old duke of social democracy. He found Jenkins easier company than other representatives of his Labour vintage. Jim Callaghan and Denis Healey were too avuncularly patronising; Jenkins was wise and amusing company. Over the after-dinner coffees and spirits at Chequers, Blair would invite the great historian to expatiate to the assembled company about the lessons of previous progressive governments. Jenkins could not help but be a little seduced that the first Labour Prime Minister in nearly two decades was eager to hear the counsel of a man who had broken from it. When he split from the Labour Party in 1981 to form the SDP, it had been Jenkins's mission to 'break the mould of British politics'. The party he invented proved unequal to the task, but the same end might be achieved through the different means of New Labour.

Blair was a keen – and apparently convinced – student of Jenkins's thesis that it was the division between Labour and the Liberals at the beginning of the twentieth century which had been fatal to the progressive cause. The result was a century dominated by the Conservatives. Blair's belief that this was largely Labour's fault is made explicit by one of his closest advisers, Philip Gould:

In establishing itself as a socialist party immutably linked to trade unionism, Labour broke with Liberalism and cut itself off from the other great radical movement in British politics. The separation of Labourism and Liberalism stopped dead the possibility of building one united progressive party, similar to the broader coalitions in the United States and Scandinavia. The division of the left gave the Conservatives a dominance in government which their electoral support rarely justified.[4]

Blair and Jenkins would have good-natured arguments about who first minted the phrase, but 'the radical century' became a common currency of Blair's speeches. 'The radical century' is what 'I want the twenty-first century to be', he told his first party conference as Prime Minister. Even in this tribalistic gathering, he declared: 'My heroes aren't just Ernie Bevin, Nye Bevan and Attlee. They are also Keynes, Beveridge, Lloyd George.'[5]

Ashdown and Blair would talk on the phone nearly every week and meet face to face, usually with a note-taker each, at least once a month. When the Liberal Democrat leader slipped into dinner at Number 10, which he did regularly in the early months, he would use the back routes through anonymous entrances in Whitehall. The cloak-and-dagger aspect to this subterfuge was calculated to appeal to Ashdown, the former Special Boat Squadron commando. Blair gave the other man plenty of reason to believe that he was as deeply committed to their conspiracy. They would joke together about how they were 'comprehensively deceiving' both their own parties. They would share frank confidences about the strengths and weaknesses of colleagues. 'Charles Kennedy, all that talent,' Blair remarked on one occasion. 'Why is he so idle?'[6]

Blair was reasonably open with Ashdown and Jenkins about the obstacles that lay in the way of ever-closer union between Labour and the Liberal Democrats. His essential difficulty was convincing his party. 'I have taken from my party everything they thought they believed in, I have stripped them of their core beliefs,' Blair confided. 'What keeps it together is success and power.'[7] How would he explain to his colleagues that they should share the long hungered-for spoils of office with the Liberal Democrats?

In July, there was a dinner in the Prime Minister's small upstairs dining room at Number 11. Blair, with Cherie, Ashdown, Jenkins and Peter Mandelson, the main link man to the Liberal Democrats, discussed how to proceed with Labour's promise to hold a referendum on electoral reform. Who should chair the commission to recommend a new voting system? Mandelson suddenly said: 'I know, why doesn't Roy do it? There's no one better qualified.' This could well have been a staged intervention pre-agreed with Blair to flatter Jenkins into ready acceptance of the task. Jenkins was indeed keen, but did not want to be seen with his tongue hanging out. At a subsequent meeting with Blair and Pat McFadden, his constitutional adviser within the Policy Unit, Jenkins sought assurances that if it was 'a serious report' – there was actually little question of Lord Jenkins of Hillhead not producing a tremendously serious report – the Prime Minister would be 'predisposed to support it'. Blair responded positively.

By October 1997, the two Liberal Democrats believed they were on the verge of taking their party into power. As they worked their way through another dinner at Number 10 of chops in breadcrumbs and bottles of Macon Villages, Blair pricked Ashdown's appetite for office. After eating they moved to the intimacy of the Prime Minister's sitting room where Blair indicated he could sacrifice 'two easy people'[8] from his Cabinet to bring in two Liberal Democrats, Alan Beith and Menzies Campbell. Ashdown, desperate as he was to rekindle the coalition moment that had passed by on election day, said that he would not hold a position in the government to begin with. He wanted to avoid the appearance of a 'grubby deal' so 'an old man can get his foot into the Cabinet'.

Ashdown departed from that dinner believing he was within an ace of leading the third party into government for the first time in peacetime in nearly a century. He was keeping a diary. 'Paddy's pension plan', it was called by one colleague who knew about it. Ashdown confided to his diary his belief that OMF (Our Mutual Friend was his codename for Blair) was poised to go for TFM (The Full Monty was his cipher for coalition).[9] 'It's going to happen,' an ebullient Ashdown told one Liberal Democrat MP whom he trusted with the secrets of his plotting. 'It's all in train.'

Had he been fooled by Blair – or was Ashdown fooling himself? There was an element of both at work. Blair possessed the great political gift of leaving most people who met him feeling warmer about themselves – and therefore about him. Jenkins, drawing from his well-stocked mental cellar of historical references, called it Blair's 'Rooseveltian quality'. Jenkins could recognise it as a technique and nevertheless admire it and to an extent be drawn in by it. Blair never said never to Ashdown. Nor did he ever absolutely say now. When Ashdown agitated that the longer he waited to bring in the Liberal Democrats, the harder it would get, Blair responded that he needed time to prepare his party for what would be a hugely controversial development. Ashdown wanted a coalition that November; Blair said he could not move until the following May.

One of Ashdown's shrewdest advisers, Richard Holme, warned him not to think of it as 'a film script'. This was not the Kipling poem in which 'when two strong men stand face to face' they can conquer the world. 'It's not going to be that easy,' cautioned Holme.

The deal was not as clinched in Blair's mind as it was in Ashdown's. For one thing, it would have been impossible to sell to the Liberal Democrats without a clear commitment from Blair in favour of changing the voting system for Westminster. The Prime Minister's official position was that he was 'unpersuaded', which was widely taken to be a mask for his real view. Robin Cook, one of the minority of electoral reformers in the Cabinet, could come away from conversations with Blair believing that he was ready to be persuaded. Jack Straw, champion of sticking with first-past-the-post, could be equally convinced that Blair was of a like mind, and this was all a great game to neutralise the Liberal Democrats as a force of opposition to the government. The likeliest truth was that Blair's two faces were actually the fronts on two minds, though the stronger side of his brain was the one sceptical about PR. One of the agnostic members of his Cabinet once remarked to him:

Whenever I hear one of those buggers speaking in favour of proportional representation, I'm convinced we should stick with first-past-the-post. Whenever I hear one of those buggers arguing for first-past-the-post, I think maybe we should look at PR.

To this, Blair smiled and replied: 'You know, that describes my position exactly.'[10]

It was not just Blair's indecision that stood in the way of a coalition deal. So did the resistance it would encounter from within the party and Cabinet, most robustly embodied by John Prescott. His hatred of electoral reform was as abiding as his loathing of Ashdown's party. Prescott would not spit on a Liberal Democrat who was on fire. Prescott saw politics as warfare by other means, and the 'liberals' – he never deigned to use their full title – were an enemy. In the hope of convincing his deputy of the Liberal Democrat leader's qualities, Blair engineered a meeting between Ashdown and Prescott. The encounter, over a cup of tea in Prescott's room at the Commons, was reasonably civil. But Ashdown left with Prescott telling him: 'You've got to understand, we'll always be on opposite sides of the fence.'

Prescott suspected that in the Blairite scheme, whose innermost plots he knew were concealed from him, coalition was a device which would complete a progression from Labour to New Labour to No Labour. Blair had kept his dealings with Ashdown entirely secret from the Deputy Prime Minister, as he had kept them hidden from the rest of the Cabinet. But Prescott could read the runes in the media. He knew how to interpret Blair's refusal to publicly rule out coalition.

Prescott discussed what to do with his close ministerial allies, Richard Caborn and Ian McCartney, who had their own weekly plotting dinners in his government apartments on the top floor of Dover House. Prescott's metaphor of choice for his relationship with Blair was drawn from the railways in which his father worked. 'There is no doubt who is the train driver. I have got a little handbrake. It's about giving a red light.'[11] After talking it over with his friends, Prescott determined to yank the brake with a violence designed to derail any coalition with the Liberal Democrats. When Prescott's red light started flashing, Blair's smoothing techniques were usually sufficient to defuse his deputy. He would assure him that reaching out beyond the Labour Party was really nothing more than a tactic. 'It's one of the things people like about me,' Blair would tell Prescott. 'The fact that I appear, even if I don't, to put the interests of the country before those of the Labour Party.'

This would usually satisfy Prescott, but this time he was not to be blanded into submission by Blair. Any coalition deal with Ashdown would have to be agreed by the whole Cabinet, Prescott told Blair. He would demand that it be put to a vote. And, whatever the outcome, Blair would face his deputy's implacable opposition to bringing in Ashdown. Prescott was menacing: 'The day that man walks through the door is the day that I walk out of it.'[12]

Prescott's resignation threat effectively torpedoed whatever prospect there was of Blair inviting the Liberal Democrats into government in the autumn of 1997. It also provided Blair with an excuse for not making up his own mind, an alibi to offer the crestfallen Ashdown. The Liberal Democrat leader would pass it on to colleagues who feared that he was being taken for a sucker. Blair himself would like to go faster, so Ashdown would reassure them. They had to sympathise with the Prime Minister's difficulties. If Blair wasn't careful, 'Prescott will be storming round his study shouting that he will chuffin' resign.'

The Liberal Democrats were only a piece in a wider game. Tony Blair's 'Big Tent' was growing capacious enough to accommodate willing Conservatives. In many ways, he found Tories easier to deal with than those independent-minded, querulous, unpredictable Liberals. Being men of power like himself, Conservatives would cut a deal. Blair paid particular attention to Tories with large reputations that resonated in the country. So long as Michael Heseltine, a quite frequent secret visitor to Number 10, was such a prominent supporter of the Millennium Dome, it made it difficult for the Opposition to attack. Another respected former Tory Cabinet minister, Chris Patten, found employment from Blair as the chairman of the commission of inquiry into the Royal Ulster Constabulary.

Blair's willingness to exploit talents from any party or none was a refreshing change from the 'One of Us' culture created by Margaret Thatcher. As ever with Blair, a decent principle conveniently married with low politics. By drawing moderate Tories into his orbit, it was easier to paint the Conservative frontbench as an isolated rump of extremists. John Major – who understood Blair's game – pleaded at length, but in vain, with his old friend Patten not to take up Blair's offer to become a European Commissioner. Blair managed to be on reasonably benign terms with Major himself, and also with Margaret Thatcher, a feat hardly any member of the Tory Party could achieve. He made a point of going over to Thatcher at the memorial service for Viscount Rothermere in January 1999 and gracefully let her do most of the talking, like a young prince humouring an aged dowager queen. She might sometimes claim, as she did at a Buckingham Palace banquet, to worry that 'he's getting awfully bossy', but this surely had to be taken as a compliment from the epitome of bossdom. She let it be known, through her office, that 'The Prime Minister is always very courteous to her, he carries himself impressively, and they get on well.'[13]

Peter Mandelson described the process as 'Operation Hoover'. Alastair Campbell had a characteristically more vulgar description. He called it 'Operation Gobble', which he reputedly illustrated by making extravagantly salivatory slurping noises. A dispassionate observer – a senior civil servant – entertained no doubt that the purpose of the exercise was 'to suck them in'.[14]

Blair was even willing to sugar left-wingers who could be usefully charmed into submission. Special attention was paid to that icon of rebellion, Dennis Skinner. Blair and Skinner went back years. Shortly after the 1983 defeat, the MP for Bolsover humiliatingly monstered the newly elected MP for Sedgefield at a public meeting. A Blair asset was his ability to bury old grudges to serve a present-day purpose. Keeping Skinner sweet helped keep the left down. When Skinner, after a year's absence, was re-elected to Labour's National Executive Committee, Blair made an extravagant fuss of heralding the return of the prodigal left-winger. He welcomed him at the door, poured him a cup of tea, told him how greatly they'd missed him, and how 'simply brilliant' it was to have him back. Blair himself, who had long harnessed his natural friendliness to political effect, was the virtuoso of sucking. His rule was to kill enemies with cream.

★

One Conservative the Prime Minister badly wanted to hoover up in 1998 was the Tory leader in the House of Lords, Viscount Cranborne. The expulsion of the hereditary peers from the Upper House was a cause which united both the meritocrats of New Labour and the class warriors of Old Labour. Blair's reiterated pledge at the party conference to finally put them to the sword won the throatiest, most guttural cheer from his audience. The problem was that the hereditaries had the potential capacity to wreck a year of the government's legislation. 'He doesn't want a row,' his first leader in the Lords, Ivor Richard, correctly concluded from his discussions with Blair. The challenge was to persuade the hereditaries to climb into the tumbrel without too much fuss.

For this purpose, Derry Irvine made advances to Viscount Cranborne to explore whether, in return for sparing a few of their number, the rest of the hereditaries would go quietly. The Lord Chancellor and the Conservative leader in the Lords both conceived of themselves as outstanding schemers. Cranborne's ancestors in the House of Cecil had been intriguing at the highest levels of British politics since Elizabeth I was on the throne. Irvine, the son of a roof slater and a waitress, had much more modest antecedents, but had so swollen with office that he suggested himself to be a reincarnation of the great Tudor Chancellor, Cardinal Wolsey.[15] The High Lord of New Labour and the High Tory Viscount were, at least in their own estimation, peerless negotiators.

'I'd like to talk,' the Cardinal told the Viscount when he rang him in the summer of 1998. Negotiations got underway in the Lord Chancellor's apartments, the Pugin *folie de grandeur*, notorious for its lavish redecoration at the taxpayers' expense. Irvine fetched a fine white burgundy, the greater part of which – or so Cranborne archly told friends afterwards – the Lord Chancellor consumed. They settled in the sitting room. Under the gaze of the nudes hanging on the £300-an-inch orangey wallpaper, the two began to sound out each other's bottom line.

'It would be good if we could avoid a row,' suggested the ruddy-faced Irvine. The sallow Cranborne concurred: 'I think it would be good, too.' Irvine went on: 'I'm not in the business

of bargaining.' Then he made his opening offer. 'What about
ten hereditaries?' 'Not enough,' responded Cranborne. He had
discussed what they should aim for with the Tory whip in the
Lords, Thomas Strathclyde. They had concluded that Conservative
peers could not be persuaded to accept many fewer than one
hundred survivors. Cranborne made an opening bid of 150. Irvine
dismissed it with a light chuckle. 'I'm not in the business of bargaining. What about fifteen?' 'No deal,' replied Cranborne. 'I'm
not bargaining,' replied Irvine. 'Right then,' said Cranborne. 'Then
it's the battle of the Somme and Passchendaele. It's the complete
buggerisation of your legislative programme.'[16]

Negotiations resumed in October by which time the government
was more anxious about the havoc to its legislation threatened by
guerrillas in ermine. Irvine was sanctioned to up his offer to the
survival of seventy-five of the hereditary peers pending the second
stage of Lords' reform. 'We really do want a deal.' Cranborne had
come down to 100. To bridge the gap between them, the Viscount
wondered if the government would throw in the fifteen hereditaries
who held offices. 'I'll talk to young Blair,' replied Irvine. The next
day, Cranborne heard from Irvine: 'Done.' Cranborne asked: 'Will
you give me the Earl Marshall and the Lord Great Chamberlain?'
Irvine: 'Done.'[17] The Viscount and the Cardinal, these peers of the
realm, bargained about the future composition of one half of
parliament with the sophistication of a couple of used-car dealers.
Thus was British constitutional history made.

To seal the bargain, on Thursday 26 November, Cranborne was
smuggled into Downing Street and up to the Prime Minister's flat.
He was given a large malt to nurse until Blair came in with Irvine
and Jonathan Powell. Blair frowned at him: 'But will Hague back
this?' Cranborne was operating behind enemy lines: William Hague
and his fellow Tories in the Shadow Cabinet had told him they
didn't want a deal with the government. Cranborne expressed
himself relaxed. He had already 'rolled the pitch' with key Tory
peers. He expected Hague to come round. 'If he has any sense he
will,' said the Viscount. 'And have some fun at your expense on
the grounds that the government has done a huge U-turn.'

The following Monday, Cranborne slipped into Number 10 again, this time to agree with Alastair Campbell a press release announcing the fix. The idea was for it to be presented by a neutral, Lord Weatherill, the convenor of the independent cross-bench peers. The question arose as to who should propose it to Weatherill. 'What about Margaret?' said Cranborne, suggesting Baroness Jay, the Labour leader in the Lords. 'Margaret,' Campbell had to admit, 'doesn't know about any of this.' Campbell was concerned. Wouldn't Hague go 'ballistic' when he found out that Cranborne had been double-dealing behind his back? 'I'll take the risk,' said the Viscount, smugly assuming that he could present it to his leader as a *fait accompli*.

The Tory leader did go ballistic. When the deal was revealed, Hague renounced it and sacked Cranborne. Then, confronted with a rebellion by Conservative peers, Hague was abjectly forced to swallow the fix done with the government. The furore among the Tories, playing brilliantly for Tony Blair, distracted attention from the fact that he had bent his manifesto promise to remove all the hereditary peers with one swing of the axe. A year later, 650 of the hereditaries were gone from the Lords with much less sound and fury than originally anticipated.

If Blair could suck in characters as diverse as the haughtily aristo-cratic Cranborne and the proudly proletarian Skinner, it was unsur-prising that his charms worked on a man much closer to being a soul-mate, Paddy Ashdown. Despite his earlier disappointments at the hands of Blair, the Liberal Democrat leader was still understand-ably tantalised by the idea of coalition. He could rationalise to himself why it had not yet happened. He talked about 'Zen Blair-ism'. Blair was waiting for the right alignment of stars and tide before beginning their great voyage together. The task Ashdown and Jenkins set themselves was to ripen the Prime Minister to their way of thinking.

The title of the Independent Commission on Electoral Reform chaired by Jenkins was a joke to be enjoyed by those who knew the truth. Both the Liberal Democrats were secretly talking to Blair about its recommendations. By the summer of 1998, Jenkins was ready to present a voting scheme which introduced more fairness while accommodating Blair's anxiety that the link between MPs and constituencies be retained and any new system produce 'strong government'.

Blair always stressed with Jenkins that he liked the purgative 'kick the rascals out' effect of first-past-the-post which had worked with such memorable effect against the Tories. For Blair, it was principally a question of power. Jenkins explained that, under his proposed reform, Blair would still have won a majority in 1997, albeit a reduced one, as would Thatcher in 1983 and 1987. 'What about 1979?' Blair wanted to know. 'There would have been a hung parliament,' estimated Jenkins. 'That's a pity,' replied Blair, not a sentiment which would be widely shared in his party. 'The country wanted a change.'

Jenkins and Ashdown had by now come to believe that they had led Blair across the emotional and intellectual Rubicon and won him as a convert to the cause of electoral reform. He certainly encouraged them in that belief, not least with wistful expressions of regret that he had not formed a coalition the day after the election. 'The right moment would have been the moment that I missed,' Blair said more than once to both men. Jenkins had been especially encouraged when Blair began to repeat back to him one of Jenkins's own arguments that the current electoral system created 'wastelands' in which large numbers of people were never represented by the party they voted for. The challenge was to persuade Blair to go public with the private promises they thought they were hearing from him. After eighteen months of 'constructive Opposition', Ashdown's party was becoming increasingly restless that they were being neutered by his strategy of co-operation with Blair.

At his party conference in September, Ashdown sought to quieten the dissidents by listing the gains he'd made from co-operation, but he won his largest applause for playing to the gallery. He had, he said, a personal question to ask Tony Blair. 'Are you a pluralist or are you a control freak? Your language tells me you're the first, but too many of your government's actions tell me you're the second. Your decision on fair votes will tell us which.'[18] Ashdown had actually answered that question to his private satisfaction. He believed Blair was essentially a pluralist struggling to get out of a control freak. To those who understood the code, the Liberal Democrat hinted at his belief that a coalition was again possible, telling his party that if it 'kept its nerve' then they would be 'at the centre of one of the greatest periods of reform our nation has ever seen'.[19] Beneath the grandstanding, Ashdown was anxious to prove to Blair that his party was worth sharing power with. 'He hasn't reformed his own party just to bring in another rabble,' Ashdown would tell colleagues in his officer-commanding voice. They had to demonstrate they were 'disciplined'. In his understandable hunger to fulfil his strategy, dependency crept into Ashdown's relationship with Blair. Like all party leaders, the keen commando himself had a tendency to be a control freak. When he suffered an embarrassing defeat by his party over education policy, Ashdown panicked that it might wreck his relationship with Blair. The first thing he did afterwards was phone to apologise for the behaviour of his own conference. 'Don't worry,' Blair reassured him. 'These things happen, even to me.' Ashdown exhaled with relief, his mood instantly relaxing.[20]

He believed that that autumn, as the year before, he was on the cusp of getting into government with Blair. Once the party conferences had been put safely behind them, Blair would use the publication of the Jenkins report to finally declare himself persuaded of the case for electoral reform as a first step towards bringing Liberal Democrats into the Cabinet. This would prove to be the third, and terminal, disappointment of Ashdown's ambitions. He and Jenkins were always surer of the Prime Minister's mind than Blair was himself.

The project to build a progressive coalition had also become a victim of its author's success. With Labour still registering stratospheric poll ratings, and the Conservatives at subterranean levels, how could he convince his party that there was any pressing need to deal with the Liberal Democrats? Why risk an incendiary row and a massive split when he was not even properly persuaded himself? At Labour's conference in Blackpool, hostility to electoral reform hardened, and John Prescott led a gang of Cabinet ministers openly suggesting that the promised referendum would not happen before the next election.

Jenkins unveiled the findings of his commission in late October 1998. Many previous reports on electoral reform 'lie mouldering on the shelves', noted Jenkins. 'We hope to do better than that.'[21] He explained that most MPs would continue to be elected by constituencies, but overall representation in the Commons would be made more proportional by 'top-up' MPs. 'AV Plus', as it became known, was widely praised for its elegance by those who had taken an interest in electoral reform. Its clever complexity was also its handicap. Jack Straw could not conceal his pleasure that the scheme, which he ridiculed as 'ingenious' and 'complex', could not possibly be implemented before the next election. The fundamental disappointment for the Liberal Democrats was the coolness of Blair's official response: 'The report makes a well-argued and powerful case for the system it recommends.'[22] Ashdown sounded upbeat, declaring himself 'happy and elated. This is a day I have looked forward to for half a century . . . I am quite convinced that Mr Blair has made his mind up. He has made the decision for PR both intellectually and emotionally.'[23] Once again, he was reading into Blair's mind what he wished was there, rather than what he could be sure was there. Privately, Ashdown was cast down by Blair's response. What the Prime Minister had not said was that he was persuaded, raising the prospect that Jenkins' report was also going to moulder on the shelf. Blair had not come off the fence. He had shuffled along it.

Three times now, Ashdown's desire for a coalition had been unrequited. The marine was nearing the end of the rope. He had banked his political credibility on Blair. 'Paddy refuses to recognise that he has been betrayed,' commented one senior Liberal Democrat. 'He is in too deep.'[24] Ashdown continued to believe that the more the fortunes of the two parties were entwined, the more inevitable electoral reform and coalition would become. He urged

Blair to show that there was still momentum in the project. On 11 November, having waited until John Prescott was safely out of the country in Latin America, the two leaders put their names to a joint declaration, widening the areas of co-operation on the Cabinet committee and declaring this to be an 'important step' away from the 'destructive tribalism' of British politics.[25] The tribalists in both parties thumped their clubs in anger. The Liberal Democrats, increasingly suspicious that the Tories might be right when they described Ashdown as 'Mr Blair's poodle', were inflamed. The more so because of crude briefing from Campbell to the effect that they had just been signed up to government policies on everything from health to welfare. One obvious sign of Ashdown's increasing isolation within his own party was that the two MPs most obviously positioning to supplant him – Simon Hughes and Charles Kennedy – had both been signalling opposition to his collaborative strategy. Ashdown came away bruised and battered from a three and a half hour meeting with his hostile MPs. As politicians ever do, he wore a brave face in public, warning off any colleague who thought there might soon be a vacancy for leader. 'My advice to those who are overeager to try on the crown is very simple – don't hold your breath.'[26]

Under the defiant mask, this attractively energetic and creative politician was feeling weary and disillusioned. Not, at least not yet, with the Prime Minister. When friends asked him whether Blair had not played him for a fool, Ashdown would sigh: 'He was sincere at the time.'

It is nearly always the case that leaders come to resent their own parties much more than they ever do their opponents. Ashdown felt that he had achieved much for his party, not just at the election but since. It was a creditable claim. Home Rule and proportional representation for Scotland and Wales, and the incorporation of the European Convention of Human Rights into British law. These causes, long cherished by liberals, had come to fruition. Ashdown had a good case to make that such reforms might well not have happened, certainly not all of them, without his strategy of engagement with Blair. When the legislation became blocked in the Lords, and the government seemed happy for it to fall, Ashdown's last service to his party was to threaten Blair with the collapse of the joint Cabinet committee unless the government delivered proportional representation for the elections to the European Parliament.

Yet the thanks he got from his party was open rebellion. And his foot was hurting like hell: a gym injury was being slow to heal. The famously hyperactive and super-fit marine was battered and drained. He had had enough.

Roy Jenkins comported himself like a politician from the Gladstonian or Asquithian ages he wrote about with such grace and distinction. His home at East Hendred in Oxfordshire was nevertheless equipped with the modern gadgets of communication. Late in November, the fax machine began to churn out a startling missive. It was a letter from Ashdown telling his fellow partner in their great project that he was quitting as Liberal Democrat leader. Jenkins shared the contents of the fax – and his shock – with others close to Ashdown. His confidants pressed him to reconsider. He replied: 'I've gone as far as I can go.' He did agree to delay his resignation until the New Year when he put a cheerful disguise on it, saying it was always best to retire when people were asking 'Why is he going?' rather than 'Why hasn't he gone?'

The publicly stated reason for his going was that he wanted to spend more time with his wife and watch his grandchildren grow up. He had promised Jane that he would not lead the party into another election, and had told Blair the same. He also resigned as a man wearied of waiting for fulfilment from the Prime Minister. 'This government will do anything in order to do nothing. Almost everything has been kicked into the long grass,' Ashdown would complain two months later, as some bitterness began to eat into his soul. 'New Labour boasts that it roars like a lion, but far too frequently it squeaks like a mouse.'[27]

The sunset of Paddy Ashdown was a loss to Tony Blair as well as a warning that there were limits to his seduction techniques. He had flirted with Ashdown without making an honest man of him. He would not find anyone among the Liberal Democrats more personally easy or politically co-operative. Chances to turn the talk of the radical century into something more solid had passed by. As the sand dribbled through the glass, it was not certain that the opportunity would present itself again.

Ashdown resigned with a sigh. Someone even closer to the Prime Minister departed with a bang that shuddered the foundations of New Labour.

# 12. Black Christmas

Gordon Brown left Blackpool early after delivering a speech which was not among his best. Usually the most reliably effective of party conference orators, the Chancellor possessed an ability lacking in Tony Blair to translate the New Labour message into language which appealed to party activists. The autumn of 1998 did not, however, find Brown on peak form. He was oppressed by the precariousness of global markets, nervous of recession, and still stinging from Blair's July purge of Brownites from the government. The Chancellor felt his political stock weakening. 'Ours is a journey with a purpose,' he boomed from the platform, but the most widely reported line of his speech was Brown's suggestion that he had reached his last destination. 'These are my political ambitions, not the ambitions of office, but in the office I hold, to help fulfil our shared ambitions for our country,'[1] said Brown, a sentence which the media was encouraged to interpret as a disavowal of any ambition to replace Tony Blair.

One minister said to another: 'There goes a man who has finally realised he will never be Prime Minister.' The other minister replied: 'Gordon will never give up.' The latter was right.

The following day, he departed Blackpool for a meeting of the IMF in Washington. The Chancellor, and his advisers, Ed Balls and Charlie Whelan, were driven to Manchester airport by a local party activist. As they sat in his people carrier that Tuesday afternoon, the car radio broadcast Tony Blair's speech. 'Yes, we are New Labour. But don't give me this nonsense that we're just a more moderate or competent Tory government,' said the Prime Minister, listing New Labour's achievements.[2] As Blair orated, Brown began a muttering heckle of the voice coming out of the radio. 'The New Deal is up and running,' cried Blair. 'He didn't want that,' grunted Brown. 'What Tory Government would have introduced the first statutory minimum wage,' boasted Blair. 'He opposed that,' rumbled Brown. 'The working families tax credit,' soared Blair. 'He fought that,' growled Brown.[3] The Chancellor's mood blackened as Blair sucked in applause for successes Brown regarded as his own.

More hatefully for the Chancellor, Peter Mandelson was in the first flush of a honeymoon as Trade and Industry Secretary. Civil servants reported how much they enjoyed working for one of the big hitters of New Labour. Mandelson was making an effort to woo the trade unions. Even his old foe, Clare Short, paid a half-compliment when she thanked Mandelson for his party conference address with the remark: 'Peter, you're much better out of the dark.'

Tony Blair had been casual of the risks involved in putting Mandelson in charge of the DTI. Questions were immediately asked about potential conflicts of interest between his responsibilities for regulating companies and the pursuit of corporate sponsorship for the Millennium Dome. He had already been embroiled, before the reshuffle, in an affair which cast ugly illumination on the underbelly of New Labour. In early July, an investigative sting by the *Observer* revealed how some of New Labour's children were feeding on their connections with the government. Reporters posing as representatives of an American energy company seeking 'an influential presence in Britain' lured a variety of young New Labourites making money from lobbying to boast about their ability to extract confidential information from inside government and influence policy. The most self-damnatory quotes were elicited from Derek Draper, a former assistant to Mandelson. The sorcerer's apprentice was quoted as saying 'I just want to stuff my bank account at £250 an hour' and 'Your Mayor Daley has nothing on me.' He boasted of providing 'inside information' to a client, and 'if they had acted on it they'd have made a fortune'.[4] At a lavish lobbying company reception in Whitehall's Banqueting Hall, Draper introduced Roger Liddle, another of Peter's friends as well as being an adviser to the Prime Minister. Liddle was quoted as giving Draper a character reference highly embarrassing to New

Labour: 'There is a Circle and Derek is part of the Circle. Derek knows all the right people.' Liddle gave the 'businessmen' his card with home and Number 10 phone numbers. He would later admit to having invited them to 'give me a call', but couldn't 'remember any more than that', excusing himself on the grounds that 'I had several glasses of champagne'.[5]

The government's initial defence was to say that nothing improper was proven against Liddle and that Draper was a boy braggart of no consequence. As the controversy grew, Mandelson pressed Blair to unleash the full power of New Labour's black propaganda machine in an attempt to discredit the newspaper, a strategy which served only to further magnify 'Lobbygate', as it inevitably – if somewhat unoriginally – became known. Alastair Campbell was active in attacking the *Observer*, and the Prime Minister blustered defiantly from the dispatch box that the government had nothing to apologise for. But, as the week wore on, Blair began to appreciate that this was a useful warning to New Labour about the dangers of conflicts of interest. Influence-peddling and cronyism were particularly corrosive to a Prime Minister whose special selling proposition was supposed to be trust. He asked the Cabinet Secretary to draw up some rules about how the government should relate to lobbyists. Blair made a rather reckless comparison with Caesar's wife when he declared: 'We are on the side of ordinary people against privilege. We must be purer than pure.' The Prime Minister swore: 'People need to understand we will not have any truck with anything that is improper in any shape or form.'

The most damagingly resonant of Draper's brags was his claim that 'there are seventeen people who count'. This was only inaccurate in as much as it exaggerated the number of people who made the essential decisions in the government. From someone with intimate knowledge of New Labour's modes of operation, here was testimony that the self-styled government of 'The Many' was actually a tight clique of 'The Few'.

Peter Mandelson's misfortune, albeit one to which he made the greatest contribution, was to personify the least attractive aspects of

New Labour's personality to its critics. He was a gift to satirists, Rory Bremner portraying him as a malevolent, swivel-headed android who 'knows where you live'. *Private Eye* cast him as the Reverend Blair's devilish churchwarden in the parish of St Albion. Even his own aide, Ben Wegg-Prosser, referred to his boss as 'the sinister minister'. Many of the legends about Mandelson were journalistic or self-invention. The pale intriguer was the most overblown myth of all. Mandelson was capable of intestinal deviousness, that was true. What he was not was cool. Contrary to his public image, this highly emotional man was as changeable as the British weather. Depending on his state of mind and the company, Mandelson might be charming, kind, witty, unswervingly loyal and utterly reliable; or petulant, bullying, vain, aloof and manipulative. The Machiavellian mantle cloaked profound insecurity. Mandelson was the Wizard of Oz.[6] Behind the front of omnipotence trembled a man frantically pulling levers to keep the disbelief of the audience suspended and terrified that someone would tear aside the curtain.

He claimed to be 'tribally, habitually, congenitally Labour'.[7] There was more Labour in the genes of the grandson of Herbert Morrison than there was in the marrow of Tony Blair. Yet Blair did not insult the tribe as gratuitously as Mandelson whose professed love for his party was unrequited. Addressing an audience of executives in Silicon Valley in October, he told them that New Labour 'is intensely relaxed about people getting filthy rich'. It was one thing to have ended Labour's past visceral aversion to wealth creation. It was quite another – and here was a lesson to be learned by everyone in the high commands of New Labour – to replace it with a dumb adoration of riches and a contempt for more humbly endowed folk. In the same month, at the party conference of all places, he disdained 'blue-collar, working-class, northern, horny-handed, dirty-overalled people'.[8] Mandelson was speaking ironically. A more disciplined politician – such as Blair – would have appreciated that many delegates and much of the media would be tone deaf to irony.

'Peter was on this extraordinary, violent rollercoaster,' says one of his friends. 'In the space of eighteen months, he had gone from a well-known figure in London to one of the most famous politicians in Europe.'[9]

Mandelson swanked around the salons of the wealthy, the powerful and the right-wing. His friend and, for a time, upmarket landlady, the Tory hostess Carla Powell, called him 'a groupie for greatness'.[10] To Rupert Murdoch was attributed the observation that Mandelson was 'easy' because he was 'a star-fucker'. He was teased by Tony Blair: 'Whenever I call you, I can hear the tinkle of glasses in the background.' Mandelson would subsequently have a flash of self-recognition: 'I came over a bit grand. I was trophy-like. I was caught up in a bit of a whirl.' In pride of place on the mantelpiece of his, soon to be infamous, house in Notting Hill, he displayed his invitation to Prince Charles's fiftieth-birthday party. He was the only member of the Cabinet to go. His friends feared that Mandelson was falling into the Ramsay MacDonald syndrome of being beguiled by the company of the rich, the glamorous and the titled. This was a source of some amusement in Downing Street. Tony Blair particularly savoured the joke when, at Tim Allan's leaving party at Number 10, the aide expressed himself privileged to be one of Peter's friends 'when I am not, so far as I am aware, a member of the royal family'.

His stay with Prince Charles and his mistress, Camilla Parker-Bowles, at Sandringham, a visit which inevitably became publicised, angered those friends who tried to protect Mandelson from himself. 'It was an idiot thing to do,' according to someone very close to him who appreciated how this behaviour fed the resentment against Mandelson.[11]

His style of life caused increasing aggravation within Number 10. Alastair Campbell mocked Mandelson's love of the 'fancy dinner party' circuit. Anji Hunter told Mandelson: 'You've got to stop walking around with your nose in the air.' She worried to Blair that 'Peter is riding for a fall.' Blair gave Mandelson more than one private warning to mind the more exotic company he was keeping.[12]

Another swirl of personal publicity gusted around him in the autumn. Ron Davies's nocturnal safari on Clapham Common – the 'moment of madness' which cost him his job as Welsh Secretary —[13] sparked a media hunt to drag homosexual members of the Cabinet out of the closet. Matthew Parris, the former Tory MP and openly gay *Times* columnist, told an uncharacteristically discombobulated Jeremy Paxman and viewers of *Newsnight* what many of them already knew: 'Peter Mandelson is certainly gay.'[14] Mandelson might have calmed the ensuing frenzy by saying in public what he said privately: 'I will not apologise for what I am.' He instead leant on the BBC. He rang, though he denied it, to protest to both the corporation's chairman and director-general. He was effectively seeking a blackout of further mention of what he regarded as his private life. Whereas he might have been seen as the victim of a rather noxious hounding — especially after the *Sun* ridiculously suggested that the government was run by 'a gay Mafia' — this heavy-handed intervention turned him from the persecuted into the aggressor by transforming the story into one about New Labour gagging the BBC. Nick Brown, who was profoundly embarrassed that his homosexuality was revealed by the *News of the World* when he had not told his mother, reacted to his outing with a short and dignified statement. Interest in the Agriculture Minister soon dried up. The Mandelson tale ran for weeks. The acumen so valued by Blair when it was employed for the government deserted Mandelson in almost any situation involving himself. Blair frequently sighed to his aides: 'I wish Peter would listen to my advice the way I listen to his.'[15] One of the friends who rallied to Mandelson during the outing episode was Philip Gould. As they sat together in Mandelson's Notting Hill house, staked out by reporters and photographers, Gould scented the fear on his friend. He worried that Mandelson would soon be plunged into something ten times worse.

This autumn of tribulations for the Trade and Industry Secretary was relished by no one more than his enemies in the Treasury, not least because the Brown camp believed that Mandelson, during the campaign to win the leadership for Blair in 1994, was responsible for spreading dirty rumours about the Chancellor's sexuality.

The war of manoeuvre between Brown/Whelan and Blair/

Mandelson did not end with the July reshuffle. One piece of
territory to be struggled over – a salient on this battlefield of ego,
mistrust and ambition – was the *New Statesman*. Geoffrey Robinson
had rescued the ailing magazine before the election. Subsidised
with his money, and edited by talented journalists who recruited
excellent writers, the *New Statesman* was restored to its former glory
as a news-breaking forum for debate on the left. The magazine had
become essential reading for anyone interested in understanding
the government. Yet its number of readers barely matched the
population of a small town. It was an illustration of the sharp
rivalry between the camps that this low-circulation magazine was
nevertheless considered a prize worth grappling over.

In early November, Robinson was summoned to Number 10 to
see the Prime Minister. Brown hastily convened his cabal in the
Chancellor's cavernous quarters at the Treasury to wish good luck
to Robinson. They all assumed that Blair, having been persuaded
by Brown not to dispose of the Paymaster-General in the summer,
was now about to ditch him out of the government. Arriving at
Number 10, Robinson was surprised to be greeted by a smiling
Prime Minister. There was something else on the agenda. Blair
wondered whether he would consider selling the *New Statesman*.
Robert Harris, the millionaire author so close to Peter Mandelson
that he was a godfather to one of the Harris children, wanted to
buy it. Why not – Blair suggested to Robinson – give up the
magazine to Harris? Though Blair was much too subtle to make
this explicit, Robinson took the implication to be that this could
be a quid pro quo for remaining in the government. Having told
Blair he would 'talk to Harris', Robinson returned to the Treasury
to share this conversation with the rest of the Chancellor's gang.
Brown and company expressed their disgust at the schemes of
Mandelson and Blair's willingness to be a frontman for the plot.

What Robinson was not to know was that Brown, the man he
took to be his friend and protector, was behaving most deviously
towards him. That same month the invigilators of MPs' behaviour,
the Commons Committee on Standards and Privileges, ordered
Robinson to apologise to the House of Commons for failing to

declare all of his financial interests. He made the apology notable
by its fifty-four-second brevity. Since September, the DTI had
been investigating Robinson. By November, the inquiry was
examining thirteen possible breaches of company law. As all this
produced a cascade of black headlines, Brown felt threatened by
association. The Chancellor went to the Prime Minister to discuss
the Paymaster-General. Blair listened with growing astonishment
as Brown told him that Robinson had become an 'embarrassment'
to the government and to him as Chancellor. Fending off the
deluge of damaging publicity was a 'distraction' which was
undermining his work and his position. Brown said: 'You should
have got rid of Geoffrey in the summer.' Blair could not believe
what he was hearing. He erupted: 'For fuck's sake, Gordon, I
wanted to sack him. It was you who made me keep him on.'[16]

Robinson was, of course, entirely unaware that Brown, whom
he took to be his guardian against Blair, had conspired behind his
back to have him sacked.

The site of an acrimonious three-way struggle that autumn between
Blair, Brown and Mandelson was the Post Office, the future of
which was a litmus test of New Labour's attitude towards the
public sector. Blair was eager for the Post Office to be privatised.
Mandelson, who suffered a rough ride from the trade unions and
the party over the issue, finally nudged the Prime Minister away
from the idea of selling off the Post Office. It would be hard to
reconcile with their manifesto pledge to keep it in state hands, and
Mandelson believed he had hit upon a 'Third Way' compromise.
He proposed giving the Post Office more commercial freedom to
break into new markets and raise investment. This satisfied Blair,
but it attracted the contempt of Brown. The Chancellor regarded
Mandelson's plan as intellectually feeble and a costly fudge. The
Treasury would lose part of its revenue stream from the Post Office
without gaining any of the proceeds of a privatisation. When the
Chancellor did all he could to wreck the proposal, Mandelson
appealed to Number 10, asking Blair to throw his weight into the
wrestling match with Brown. Prime Minister and Chancellor had

one of their most murderous arguments on the subject of the Post
Office. A witness describes it as 'a foetus-position row', meaning
that everyone else present hunched themselves into a ball until
the storm blew over.[17] Blair's decision was doubly aggravating to
Brown. Not only did the Chancellor resent being overruled by the
Prime Minister, he acted even more the wounded bull-elephant
because Blair had taken Mandelson's side.

There is no politician who enjoys losing an argument. Few react
to being frustrated with such dark wrath as Gordon Brown. When
the Post Office scheme was announced, Charlie Whelan gave a
brutal and barely disguised briefing against Mandelson. He had
'bottled out' of making a tough decision and come up with a 'dog's
breakfast'. *Ad hominem* abuse against senior members of the Cabinet
was far from without precedent from the Chancellor's megaphone,
but Whelan was setting a new standard of brazenness. Mandelson,
supported by Alastair Campbell, pressed Blair to finally deliver on
his promises to them. They urged him to seize this opportunity to
force Brown to sack Whelan.

'I'll get rid of him by the end of the year,' Blair replied, a pledge
to which they reacted with knowing laughter. They had heard this
sort of declaration from the Prime Minister so frequently since the
election that they no longer placed any faith in it. Blair's repeated
failures to make Brown dispense with the vexatious Whelan had
turned the Prime Minister into a butt of ridicule among his own
intimates. Jonathan Powell, Anji Hunter and Alastair Campbell
would mock Blair to his face about it. 'He'll be gone by Easter.
He'll be gone by the summer. He'll be gone by Christmas,' they
would torment Blair, taunting the Prime Minister with reminders
of how often he had assured them that he would deal with Whelan
and how he had as frequently failed. Blair responded with a pained
frown and the feeble insistence: 'I could get rid of him. I just
don't work like that.'[18] This was, on the face of it, a most remarkable
situation. Here was Tony Blair, reputedly equal in power to Margaret Thatcher in her pomp. This titan of Number 10 could not
remove a mere press officer. That makes it sound more straightforward than it was. For Blair to insist would mean full-frontal combat

with Brown, an incendiary conflict that he was shy of risking. The Prime Minister was scared of provoking the Chancellor.

They were not to be aware of this in Downing Street, but Whelan himself was arriving at the conclusion that his days were numbered. He shared with friends ideas about quitting the Treasury of his own volition to pursue a new career as a journalist, which is exactly what he would do after he left the government's employment. But it would be utterly out of character for Whelan to depart gently into the night. If he was going, he had the means to take Mandelson with him. It was Whelan's boast – which he indiscreetly shared with several people – that there was a bomb which would annihilate the hate object of the Brownites. He confided to one journalist that there was a 'thermonuclear device under Peter and it's primed to go off in January'. This was the £373,000 soft loan that Geoffrey Robinson had given to Mandelson, before the election and before they moved into warring camps, to purchase his £475,000 house in west London. Whelan had the means of detonating this sensational information into the public domain. A biography of Mandelson, due for publication in the New Year, was being written by Paul Routledge, the close comrade who shared both Whelan's dedication to Gordon Brown and the intensity of his hatred for Peter Mandelson.

Mandelson was not oblivious to the danger posed by the biography. He even asked Blair to intercede with Brown to prevent publication. 'I can do nothing about it,' Brown replied to Blair,[19] and it is highly unlikely that the Chancellor could have done, even if he had wanted to.

With or without the book, Geoffrey's largesse to Peter was a story begging to see the light of day. Mandelson's secret loan from Robinson was hugely threatening to him, not least because it was not a secret to several of his enemies. Apart from Charlie Whelan, Ed Balls knew. Gordon Brown had known about it for a long time. The exchange of letters fixing the loan had been faxed over to Robinson's suite at the Grosvenor Park Hotel when Brown and his coterie were present. The existence of the loan became known to the Chancellor's closest friend in the Cabinet, Nick Brown, who shared his animus towards Mandelson. An embittered Robinson was telling friends that he was fed up to the point of resignation after being hounded by the media. He was also sour that the ungrateful Mandelson hadn't even invited him to the house-warming party.

The secret loan was becoming increasingly less secret, at least within the inner, incestuous circles of New Labour. Michael Wills, the MP for Swindon North, knew. Though a Brownite, he managed to be on amicable terms with a man very close to the Prime Minister. Wills was an old university chum of Charlie Falconer. Falconer and Blair shared a flat together in Wandsworth, south London, when they were both young lawyers carving out the beginnings of their careers. Blair, having tried and failed to secure a seat in the Commons for Falconer, had placed him in the Lords, first as Solicitor-General, and then as number two at the Cabinet Office, in the centre of government. A sharp mind in a bluffly genial wrapping, Falconer answered to the need in Blair, common among Prime Ministers, for lieutenants and confidants who could be entirely trusted because they would never turn into competitors. That August, Michael Wills and Charlie Falconer, finding themselves holidaying near to each other in Malaga, southern Spain, got together. Wills passed on word of Mandelson's loan to Falconer.[20] Sworn to a confidence, and not thinking it his place to raise it with Tony Blair, Falconer kept the secret to himself. So Falconer, that best of chums, knew. Brown long knew. Extraordinarily, the one person who had been kept in a state of complete ignorance was the Prime Minister.

The most culpable failure to confide in Blair was clearly Mandelson's. He should have told the Prime Minister when Blair made him Secretary of State for the department investigating the allegations into Robinson's financial affairs. When, in conversation, Blair made references to 'your flat', Mandelson huffily replied, 'It's a house actually.' Recklessly, he encouraged media interest in 9 Northumberland Place. *Vogue* was invited *chez* Mandelson, where Lord Snowdon photographed him posing in the £1,800 tanned leather Balzac chair. The house was given a self-consciously chic

£50,000 make-over by a top-of-the-range interior designer. Original features were stripped out to turn it into a shrine of soulless minimalism. It was as if he couldn't stop himself providing the critics with metaphors for what he had helped do to the Labour Party. Campbell occasionally ragged Mandelson about how exactly he had afforded a house worth ten times an MP's salary. 'Where did you get the money then, Peter?' Campbell baited him. Mandelson never gave a straight answer, but implied to Campbell, as he did to others, that the money had come from his mother. Various explanations were later advanced for why the great strategist had placed himself in the perilous position of concealing this lethal loan from his friends when it was known to his enemies. Was he socially embarrassed? Did he genuinely think it was not anyone else's business? Could he believe that his secret would remain for ever safe with Gordon Brown and his acolytes? Sometimes the simple explanation is the correct answer. According to one of his closest friends, Mandelson concealed the loan because 'Peter knew what he had done was wrong.'[21] Another person who has known Mandelson for many years says: 'He was ashamed to admit it to Tony.'[22]

Public shame loomed by early December. The proof copy of Routledge's book was inadvertently sent to the wrong office at the House of Commons, where it was opened and read by another journalist. There was a tip-off to Mandelson's aide, Ben Wegg-Prosser, young, gently spoken, bespectacled, and sometimes known as Oofy, after the Wodehouse character. By Tuesday 15 December, Wegg-Prosser was aware that exposure was imminent. Not wanting to destabilise his boss until he had finished presenting a White Paper on competition, designed to be an early crowning glory of his work as Trade and Industry Secretary, the aide left it until Wednesday evening to tell Mandelson. He had no choice now but to confess the secret to his Permanent Secretary, Sir Michael Scholar, and Number 10. Unable to face telling Blair, Mandelson got Wegg-Prosser to ring Alastair Campbell to tell Downing Street about the loan and that it would shortly become public.

Tony Blair was in his study that Thursday lunchtime working

on the statement he would give to the Commons in the afternoon about military action against Iraq. He had less than two hours to find the appropriate words to announce his first act of war as Prime Minister. Campbell knew that Blair did not want to be interrupted. But what he had just learned from Wegg-Prosser was dynamite which would produce far more explosive headlines than the munitions raining on Saddam Hussein. The press secretary rushed to the Prime Minister to give him the bones of what Campbell would later characterise as this 'big, bad story'. At first, Blair struggled to muster coherent sentences to express his shock. Then, anger at Mandelson's stupidity transferred itself to fury with the messenger.

'Why the fuck are you landing this on me now?' he demanded of Campbell. 'Because it can't fucking wait,' retorted his press secretary. 'We have to decide what we are going to do, how we are going to handle it.' As the awfulness of the implications began to sink in, Blair turned to wondering who else had been concealing this timebomb at the heart of New Labour.

Did Anji Hunter know? His personal assistant was on friendly terms with Robinson. She was also a pal of Wegg-Prosser. Blair called her in. She could immediately tell something was badly wrong. Blair looked terrible. 'Did you know?' he demanded aggressively. 'What?' said Hunter. 'That Peter took a loan from Geoffrey for his house.' She felt faint and sat down. 'No, honestly, Tony. Christ! If I'd known, I would have told you.' How big, she asked, was the loan? 'Oh, God,' Blair shook his head in despair. 'Hundreds of thousands of pounds.' Hunter phoned Wegg-Prosser to berate him for not confiding in her about the loan. 'Why did you never tell us?' she shouted. 'I couldn't. He swore me to secrecy. I kept telling Peter,' replied a tremulous Wegg-Prosser. 'I kept telling him he couldn't keep it secret. He wouldn't listen.'[23]

The Cabinet Secretary would have to be involved. Blair broke off from speech-writing to phone Sir Richard Wilson to ask him to initiate inquiries into whether the loan and the DTI's investigation into Robinson meant Mandelson had broken the rules about conflicts of interest.

It is a tribute to Blair's ability to mentally compartmentalise that he could confidently pronounce on Iraq in the Commons that afternoon while the loan crisis was consuming his mind. It was an illustration of how angry, aghast and anxious he was that, even while heavily engaged in presenting and presiding over the action against Iraq, he devoted attention to Mandelson.

He slipped into Number 10 under darkness at the end of the week to face a bleakly furious Blair. 'Jesus Christ, Peter! What a misjudgement,' Blair raged at the ally and confidant he had so esteemed. The man who was supposed to be so well equipped with political savvy had shown a catastrophic lack of it. Worse, complained Blair, Mandelson had treated him, his friend and Prime Minister as a dupe. Mandelson pleaded that he did not believe he had done anything 'fundamentally wrong'. This was not Blair's angriest grievance. Mandelson's selfishness and vanity had betrayed him and their project.[24] Everything they had worked for was imperilled. For not only was Blair shocked, he was also fearful. He and those closest to him were already mentally writing the headlines which would be used against New Labour by its enemies within and without.

The Prime Minister's press secretary vented his personal rage at Mandelson even more fiercely. The full heat of Campbell's flame-thrower temper was turned on him. To his face, Campbell told Mandelson that he had been a 'stupid cunt'.[25] The violence of these reactions is understandable. Everyone feels it most acutely when they are let down by their friends.

Blair talked to Mandelson again on Saturday, by which time the Prime Minister's mind was turning to what might be done to contain the damage. He told Mandelson to get rid of the Robinson loan as rapidly as possible. Paying it off before it became public knowledge might improve the chances of constructing some sort of defence for him. But Blair was already sceptical that Mandelson could be saved.

Routledge was to be denied his exclusive, a scoop which he subsequently insisted he was going to excise from his book anyway in an attempt to protect his friend Whelan from being fingered as

the source. The mysterious financing of Mandelson's mansion
had attracted the interest of several journalists, among them the
*Guardian*'s David Hencke, an award-winning investigator of political scandal. After months of truffling, Hencke's assiduity had not
been rewarded with the story. Then he got what must have looked,
to this reporter, like an amazing break. In early December, Hencke
received a call from a source he had dealt with before on anti-
Mandelson stories. The reporter met this informant on Tuesday 8
December. Information is often traded between journalists and
politicians over good lunches and dinners at fine restaurants. This
transaction, however, took place at a most unusual location where
both Hencke and his source could be certain they would not be
seen by other journalists or politicians. They met at a greasy spoon
in the West End. The source did not have the precise figure, but
revealed to the reporter the Mandelson home loan from Robinson.
They met again at the same greasy spoon six days later, on 14
December, this time with another *Guardian* reporter present, when
the source added the fascinating detail that the solicitor who handled
the purchasing of the house was Wegg-Prosser's father. Hencke's
source was a senior politician closely associated with Gordon
Brown.[26] The motive for priming Hencke was twofold: using
another conduit might shield Whelan; and the Brown camp, suspecting that Mandelson knew that exposure was imminent, may
have feared that he would find some way of suppressing or minimis-
ing the impact of the story.

How complicit was Gordon Brown in the immolation of his
fellow Cabinet minister and founder of New Labour? The Chancellor had multiple motives for bringing down the man who rivalled
him for influence over the Prime Minister, whom he had never
forgiven for switching affections from Brown to Blair in the leadership contest, and with whom he had since pursued a fratricidal
feud. Another member of New Labour's innermost circle, who has
known Brown for more than a decade, says: 'Gordon is absolutely
capable of it.'[27] Even if the Chancellor did not pull the trigger, he
knew it was being squeezed. Whether or not he gave the precise
instruction to strike against Mandelson, Brown willed the act.

Wearing a public mien of calm, on Monday 21 December, Peter Mandelson went down to Greenwich for an inspection tour of the Millennium Dome, which was soon interrupted by urgent instructions to talk to Downing Street. Back at Number 10, Derry Irvine and Charlie Falconer, the lawyers of the Blair court, were brought into the discussions with Campbell about how to try to control the loan story. At this meeting, Jonathan Powell produced a note from Sir Richard Wilson. After talking to Sir Michael Scholar, the Cabinet Secretary confirmed that Mandelson had been properly insulated from the DTI inquiries into Robinson. But both the civil servants also took the view – which Wilson conveyed to Blair – that for Mandelson to be so hugely and secretly indebted to the Paymaster-General was nevertheless 'a very big problem'.

On Monday afternoon, the *Guardian* formally approached Mandelson and Robinson for confirmation of the details of the loan. Blair, mindful of how the Ecclestone cover-up exploded in his face, saw nothing to be gained from attempting to stall or lie. Into the placidity of the Christmas recess, a period usually devoid of big political events, the bomb detonated.

A strangely unperturbed Mandelson convinced himself that he could walk through the fire. Blair was instinctively and immediately doubtful that he could possibly survive what he and Campbell both knew would be an inferno. The press secretary briefed political correspondents that the Prime Minister did not regard it as 'a hanging offence', which fell far short of a ringing statement of confidence in Mandelson's ministerial life expectancy. All requests for interviews with Blair himself were turned down.

For the next twenty-four hours, beginning with Monday's *Newsnight*, on which he declared 'There is no conflict of interest so the question of resignation does not arise',[28] Mandelson toured the TV and radio studios, determined to tough it out. As he told one friend: 'I've learned from my personal life that you have to stand up to these fuckers. If they scent blood, they will come for the kill.'

But the more Mandelson talked, the more questions were raised. Should he have declared the loan in the Register of Members' Interests? In the summer, Elizabeth Filkin, the commissioner of parliamentary standards, ruled that he should have done. Had he revealed the loan to the Britannia Building Society when he applied to them for a mortgage? After a period of equivocation, Mandelson confessed that he had not. Wegg-Prosser was alerted to this deadly question on Monday night during a conversation with Piers Morgan, the editor of the *Mirror*. Mandelson's own aide concluded then that his master could not survive as Trade and Industry Secretary against the allegation that he had misled a financial institution. 'Peter's finished,' Wegg-Prosser told one of Blair's aides. In January, the Britannia said that they would not be pursuing Mandelson about his mortgage application. It can only be speculated whether they would have reacted differently had he remained in office.

There was nothing to suggest that Mandelson acted corruptly, but it was far short of honouring Blair's description of a government that was 'purer than pure'. It grated terribly with the Prime Minister's claim that New Labour was on the side of 'ordinary people against privilege'. The kingpin of spin, the Merlin of image, this master of perception had behaved as though he were blind to how this would look printed in the largest type on the front page of every newspaper.

In a breakfast-time interview on Tuesday morning, Mandelson illustrated why he was his own worst advocate by describing himself and Robinson as 'fairly exotic personalities'.[29] This was the peacockery that had made enemies and alienated so many people in his own party. 'It's the size of it,' was Blair's private verdict to aides and officials about why the loan was so devastating. For the price of Mandelson's house in an élite enclave of west London could be bought a street of homes in his constituency of Hartlepool.

Blair's initial prognosis that Mandelson was not to be saved was hardening by Tuesday morning into a certainty that he had to be severed. This was a cancerous growth, eating into New Labour's integrity, that could only be stopped from spreading by the rapid amputation of Mandelson from the government. Alastair Campbell, thinking that the media would never let go until Mandelson resigned, and Anji Hunter, protective of Blair's reputation, were both urging the Prime Minister to dispatch the Trade and Industry

Secretary.[30] Blair turned to another close confidant for advice. He rang Philip Gould, who was spending Christmas in Jamaica. As warm as the weather was in the Caribbean, the chilly fury of the Prime Minister transmitted itself down the line. 'Why aren't you here when I need you?' Blair snapped. Gould, while registering Blair's shock and anger with Mandelson, attempted to offer pleas in mitigation. After everything Mandelson had done to create New Labour, should he have his five-month career in the Cabinet terminated? 'You should hold on to Peter. You shouldn't give in to our enemies,' Gould argued with Blair. 'If you let Peter go, you'll be weakened.' Blair perceived that, but he saw himself and the government being much more damaged by letting Mandelson hang on. In response to Gould's entreaties to save Mandelson, Blair was stony: 'Look. Read the papers, Philip. Think again.'[31] The phone went down.

The Prime Minister had retired to Chequers when, at ten on the night of Tuesday 22 December, he talked again to the man whose skills once so mesmerised him. Blair was not good at breaking bad news. He particularly did not relish telling a friend as old and as close as Mandelson that he wanted him gone. He allowed the other man to lead the conversation, asking for his own assessment. Mandelson still believed himself to be the victim of a 'stitch-up' by the Brownites. The press were 'completely hysterical' and 'out of control'.[32] He had made a mistake, he was prepared to admit that now. Yet he clung to the belief that he could and must remain in the Cabinet. This was an unsurprising attitude. Many of his friends thought resignation would be the end of his career. He could not know whether he would ever return.

Mandelson did float the idea that he might have to resign. By describing this as 'very painful', he evidently hoped that Blair would respond by dismissing the idea. The words that would have been music for him were the Prime Minister saying that he wasn't going to sacrifice him under pressure from the media, and that the Number 10 propaganda organ would be pumped to save him. How Blair replied was therefore a crushing disappointment. He told Mandelson that they should 'sleep on it'. Such an expert reader of the codes of political conversation grasped what Blair was semaphoring. The Prime Minister and those advising him wanted to see the following morning's newspapers before they made a final decision.

The press was savage, though not unanimously so. The *Guardian*, the paper that broke the story, pronounced him guilty of 'more vanity than venality' and judged that resignation would be a sentence out of proportion to the crime. The *Sun*, which Mandelson once so assiduously courted, had gone down on him. The tabloid shrieked: 'So How The Hell Can Mandy Stay?' The *Daily Mail* branded him 'The Master of Deception'. *The Times* likened Mandelson to *Vanity Fair*'s Becky Sharp, who had tried to live a high life on low means and was brought down by social climbing. There were ironies to be savoured. Among the people whom Mandelson had cultivated was Elizabeth Murdoch, daughter of the man who owned *The Times* and the *Sun*. Even now, a large percentage of Mandelson believed he could yet save his place in the Cabinet. At seven on Wednesday morning he phoned Wegg-Prosser to tell him to organise a 'fight-back' meeting at the DTI with Campbell, his deputy, Lance Price, and Jonathan Powell. Mandelson also talked twice to Gordon Brown. It is an example of the weird convolutions of their relationship that, at his hour of extreme personal crisis, Mandelson turned to the man whom he suspected to have played a large role in precipitating the most traumatic moment of his career. In their first conversation, Brown expressed the view that he should apologise but not resign. Guilt may have been speaking. Mandelson would later come to the conclusion that, while Brown intended to damage, the Chancellor did not expect to destroy him. Anxiety was also informing Brown's reaction. He had reason to fear that, if Mandelson went, all the heat would concentrate on whether he and his coterie had connived to demolish a fellow Cabinet minister to the detriment of the government. An exiled Mandelson would thirst for revenge. When he spoke to Brown for a second time that morning, the Chancellor sombrely rated Mandelson's survival prospects to be much more occluded. By now, Brown had spoken to Blair and discovered how conclusively determined the Prime Minister was to sack Mandelson.

The fight-back meeting never happened. At shortly after ten, Campbell and the others from Number 10 arrived in Mandelson's ministerial suite on the seventh floor of the DTI tower in Victoria Street with its panoramic view of Westminster Abbey. Almost immediately, Campbell ordered everyone else out of the room and into the next door Private Office so that Mandelson could be put through to Blair.

The Prime Minister effectively decided the day before that Mandelson had to go. Any remaining doubt about that was settled by the ferocity of the media that morning. Blair was now explicit. The longer Mandelson tried to cling on, the more Mandelson and the government would be damaged. Mandelson repeatedly asked Blair if that was really his opinion, in an effort to seek out a chink of weakness. That was his view, Blair flatly confirmed, offering the consolation that the quicker he left the Cabinet, the better chance there would be of a reasonably rapid return. By the end of the conversation, tears were trickling down Mandelson's sepulchral white cheeks. A dark-eyed Campbell, himself blubbing, gave Mandelson a hug.

Recovering from this lachrymose moment with professional speed, Campbell then wrote a resignation letter for Mandelson and a reply for Blair. Campbell took his compositions out to the Private Office, and handed them to Wegg-Prosser to type up. The wretched Mandelson signed Campbell's draft virtually unaltered, though he first faxed it over to Gordon Brown for him to see. He wanted the Chancellor to taste some of the grief that had been inflicted on him. Blair faxed back Campbell's draft of the Prime Minister's reply with some added personal touches.

The Chancellor spread the word among his entourage that their enemy had fallen. Ed Balls and his wife, Yvette Cooper, were on the road, driving to spend Christmas with parents. At precisely the moment that Gordon Brown rang his mobile, Ed and Yvette realised they had forgotten the turkey they were providing for the family Christmas. 'He's gone,' announced Brown. 'We've got to turn back,' Balls said to his wife. 'No, you don't understand. There's no turning back,' said Brown. 'He's resigning at eleven o'clock.'[33]

The announcement actually came slightly later, just before the lunchtime news bulletins. Soon after, Robinson was gone as well. Mandelson's resignation missive began: 'I can scarcely believe I am writing this letter . . .', which was scarcely surprising to those who knew that it had been composed by Alastair Campbell. In the reply from Blair was inserted a phrase Mandelson had supposedly used in their Tuesday evening conversation. This government could not afford to be seen to behave 'like the last lot'. Generously and accurately, Blair wrote: 'It is no exaggeration to say that without your support and advice we would never have built New Labour.' The softening of this devastating blow was the prospect of a royal pardon: 'In future, you will achieve much, much more with us.'

'Goodbye . . . For Now' was the Guardian's prophetic interpretation the next morning. The roasting Christmas Eve front page of the Sun pictured Mandelson's head coming out of a turkey with the single word headline: 'STUFFED'. Few members of the Labour Party wore black, but even his many enemies did not dance a great jig on Mandelson's warm grave. The swiftness of his departure, and the manner in which it had been dressed up in the resignation letter ghosted by Campbell, succeeded in creating the impression that he had honourably withdrawn to spare the government prolonged torture at the hands of its opponents. Denis MacShane, the Labour MP for Rotherham, voiced a widely believed platitude: 'Nothing became Peter's holding of high office as the manner of his leaving.'[34] The notion that this was a graceful, selfless sacrifice was deceptive. Peter Mandelson did not fall on his sword. Tony Blair gently, firmly, ruthlessly and necessarily thrust Mandelson on to the blade.

Succour for the former Cabinet minister came from unlikely quarters. John Prescott – at the prompting of his ministerial lieutenant, Richard Caborn – suggested to Blair that Mandelson might begin his rehabilitation by going out to South Africa to help the ANC election campaign. When the trip was all fixed up, Prescott could nevertheless not resist saying: 'Good. Just make sure it's a one-way ticket.'[35]

Mandelson's more reliable friend, Roy Jenkins, drew from his rich stock of historical examples to construct an apologia for the fallen minister. Lord Jenkins pronounced that Disraeli, Gladstone and Churchill had placed themselves under much more compromising financial obligations and no one dreamt of demanding that any of them should resign.[36]

Blair's fury with Mandelson was accompanied by a sense of loss. He saw the gaping tear left in the Cabinet. Mandelson had been a Blairite before Blair. He was one of the few who could be called believers in New Labour from more than convenience or sycophancy. There was also the worry for Blair of what a wretchedly depressed Mandelson might do.

At around noon on the day of the resignation, the Prime Minister asked Mandelson to Chequers, a characteristically kindly, but also calculating, gesture. It is a sign of the *froideur* between them that Cherie initiated the call. 'You will always be part of the family,' she told Mandelson. Only when his wife had broken the ice did Blair himself come on the line to say: 'We want you to be with us.'[37] Mandelson and his partner, Reinaldo Avila da Silva, joined the Blairs' family supper and spent the night. Mandelson was now contrite. 'I know I've done a terrible thing,' he confessed to Blair. 'I've hurt you and I've hurt the government.'[38] Blair had written out some advice about how to work his passage back: sell the house, get around the constituencies, be a team player. 'For God's sake,' he said directly to Mandelson. 'Make some friends in the Labour Party.'

An ocean of bad blood had been spilt. To the poisonous feud between Brown and Mandelson, and the destabilising rivalry between Blair and Brown, there had now been added a twist to the relationship between Blair and Mandelson. Blair could never again invest quite the same level of trust in Mandelson's judgement.

The Prime Minister soon became irritated when, contrary to his advice to adopt a humble profile, Mandelson's name began to surface in the newspapers connected with various new jobs from prime ministerial emissary in Europe to – this a most improbable idea – candidate for mayor of London. Campbell stamped on this savagely. During Blair's New Year trip to South Africa, travelling journalists were briefed that 'the Prime Minister has moved on'. Mandelson was now 'out of the loop'. He had 'disappeared from the Prime Minister's orbit'.[39] This casting into outer space reflected Campbell's own anger that Mandelson was not keeping his head down.

Mandelson was confused and conflicted. Looked at impassively, he would have advised Blair to excise with extreme prejudice any member of the Cabinet who had wreaked so much damage on the government. On the day of his resignation, he sent a second, private handwritten note to Blair, praising him as a strong and decisive leader. Dwelling upon the wreckage of his Cabinet career, as time passed Mandelson became quite recriminatory towards Blair. Six months later, he would be talking of his resignation as if it were a bereavement, telling an audience of trade unionists: 'I have only just got out of the habit of jumping into the back of cars and wondering why they don't move off.'[40]

He confided to a senior peer close to both the Prime Minister and the fallen minister that he, Mandelson, felt 'cross and bitter with Tony'. The Prime Minister should and could – so reckoned Mandelson in more self-pitying moods – have fought to save him.[41]

From a delayed winter sojourn in the Seychelles, Tony Blair reconstructed his government after the most searing five days of his premiership. To have cancelled the holiday would stink of panic, but this presented some difficulties with communications. Blair could get a reliable link back to London only by having his bodyguard row him out to sea. Perched aboard a rubber dinghy undulating in the Indian Ocean, the Prime Minister had some unfinished business with Gordon Brown. Charlie Whelan had gone walkabout in the Scottish Highlands, but the Chancellor's hit-man was still at large in the government. A final line could not be drawn under this episode until the 'little oik' – Campbell's description – had been removed. Brown was torn. It would be taken as an admission of guilt that the Chancellor's tool had been responsible for Mandelson's assassination. But Brown could at last see that Whelan had outlived his usefulness. There are two kinds of poisoners: successful ones and famous ones. Whelan had become far too notorious for his own or his master's good. Eighteen months after Blair had first told Brown he did not want Whelan in the government, the Chancellor was finally persuaded that he would have to go. He was nevertheless insistent that Whelan's resignation be presented as a voluntary departure.

Brown's compensation was to secure a ministerial position at the DTI for his ally, Michael Wills. Into the position of secretary of state, the Prime Minister plugged another Blairite, Stephen Byers. One aspect of his promotion troubled the new DTI Secretary. On the spur of the moment, but very presciently, Byers blurted to Blair: 'I don't want the Dome.' From his rubber dinghy, Blair also called his friend, Charlie Falconer, to transfer to him Mandelson's responsibility for the Dome. 'Hold on,' Blair suddenly said midway through their conversation. 'There's someone waving at me.' This was a Danish tourist. In a highly embellished account Campbell later fed to the press, it would be claimed that the man had been 'saved' from drowning by the Prime Minister.

The promotions won by Byers, Falconer and Wills demonstrate that there is always a sliver of silver for someone in every political thunderstorm. Two of the men who had harboured Mandelson's secret profited from its exposure. Gordon Brown was also arguably a winner by getting Peter Mandelson out of the Cabinet. These were the only people for whom this brought any benefit. As in the last scene of a Jacobean play, by the end of this revenge drama at the warring heart of New Labour, the stage was littered with corpses: Mandelson gone, Robinson gone, Whelan gone.[42] Those who had so relentlessly impressed discipline and unity on their party had been possessed by the most demonic infighting which had brought obloquy down on the government.

Downing Street waited with trepidation for the first opinion polls of the New Year. They registered a turning point. The reputation for trustworthiness was soiled. By their viciously inter-necine quarrelling, leading personalities of New Labour had exposed the small and mutilating aspects of their characters to the country. The worst of three post-apocalypse polls showed a drop in the government's rating of 7 per cent. Yet that still left the government standing at a remarkable 48 per cent[43] which, translated into a general election result, would mean an increased parliamentary majority of 250. The carnage was also catharsis. To the surprise of no one more than its creators, New Labour proved to be larger, stronger and more durable than the sum of its feuding parts.

# 13. New Britain

Tony Blair and Gordon Brown were having one of their quieter, more sinuous arguments. 'Shouldn't you do it?' wheedled Blair as they debated in his study that day. 'No, I think you should do it,' refused Brown.

As part of the New Year relaunch of his government, the Prime Minister wanted to make a major event of the announcement of a National Changeover Plan to prepare for the European single currency. Ever since the decision to rule out the euro until the next election, he had been searching for other tokens of engagement with the European Union. Just before Christmas, he signed a joint defence initiative with the French at St Malo. Now that the single currency was a fact, Blair was under pressure to send a positive signal to restive pro-Europeans in Britain. But – and this was rather typical – he hesitated to lead a cavalry charge against the artillery of the Europhobic press which would risk a repeat of the *Sun* headline describing him as 'The Most Dangerous Man In Britain'.

'It's important,' said Prime Minister. 'It's important,' nodded Chancellor. Brown, hardening in his belief that they should suffocate all argument about the euro, was determined not to let Blair persuade him to make the speech about the changeover plan. Brown had already decided with his aides – though he hadn't told Blair this – that if Number 10 insisted that the Treasury make the announcement, then they would slip it out as a written parliamentary answer. 'If it's so important, Gordon, perhaps you should do it,' said Blair, trying to flatter Brown into the task. 'If it's that important, you should do it,' stonewalled Brown. The watching aides exchanged smirks at their masters' manoeuvres.[1]

It was Blair who made the speech to the House of Commons, announcing 'a change of gear' towards the single currency while Brown sat silently by his side devoting great attention to his fingernails.[2] The pro-European Tories, Michael Heseltine and Kenneth Clarke, whose responses were secretly co-ordinated with Number 10, warmly welcomed what Heseltine hailed as a 'step forward'. Giles Radice, the Euro-enthusiastic Labour chairman of the Treasury select committee, cried with delight: 'This is it!' The anti-euro forces were equally convinced of the significance of the occasion. The *Sun*'s black frontpage tolled: 'Blair Prepares To Scrap The £'.[3] There was talk, on both sides of the passionate argument, that the Prime Minister was crossing the Rubicon. And both sides were wrong. He had kept his feet dry. What momentum was created by the speech was not followed through and soon petered out. This was not least because, by early 1999, both Prime Minister and Chancellor were increasingly distracted by the state of the union of Britain.

Early in February, Tony Blair headed west across Offa's Dyke for his third visit to Wales in less than three months. Before the election, Blair devoted little more attention to the affairs of Wales than he did to those of Ruritania. But now, the Celtic fastness, rock solidly loyal to the party for decades, was in revolt against New Labour and against its leader. Addressing party activists, the Prime Minister begged them: 'Don't think: "Wouldn't it be nice to give Tony Blair a bloody nose?"'[4] Many in the audience mentally clenched their fists.

The threat to years of Labour rule in Scotland had become so serious that Gordon Brown was taking time off from running the economy to take charge of the campaign against the Nationalists north of the border. Devolution, one of the government's largest claims to be radical and modernising, had caused months of grief. When the Prime Minister discussed what to do with his advisers, hanging in the air was the thought that it had been a monumental mistake. Blair would shrug and say: 'I had to do it.'

He had made enthusiastic noises about the dispersal of power before he came to office, telling one pre-election audience:

The era of big, centralised government is over. Ordinary people have lost confidence in the ability of a distant central government to offer solutions to their problems. They have become unprecedentedly cynical about politics and politicians.

He spoke eloquently, and with every appearance of sincerity, about his support for devolution:

We need to move decision-making closer to the people. I know it is easy to talk about pluralism in opposition but much harder to give up power when in government. I am determined that we should do so.[5]

That indeed proved to be easy, Opposition talk. Blair found it very hard to surrender power once he had acquired it. His personality was split. As one hand kept the promise to give up power, the other hand reached out to grab back control.

That he wanted to have devolution only on his own, tightly managed terms was evident from the beginning. In the chair of the Cabinet committee which developed the policy was Derry Irvine. The Lord Chancellor liked to run committees as though he were the prosecuting counsel and whichever unfortunate found himself up for cross-examination was a serial killer. Irvine was capable of interrupting a minister before he was halfway through his opening sentence. In this case, his victim was Donald Dewar, the Secretary of State for Scotland, and a Labour politician with the rare distinction of having been committed to devolution for the whole of his career. Dewar had lost his wife Alison to Irvine. That was not the only reason relations between the two men were never warmer than frigid. Irvine, a bully of a man swollen with his importance in the government, enjoyed the finest things in life, whether they be wines or paintings. The pessimistic Dewar was the acme of frugality. It was said, and it was quite believable, that in the fridge of his Glasgow flat he kept nothing more than a packet of frozen fish fingers.

After his trials at the hands of Irvine's committee, Dewar would hunch back to the Scottish Office enveloped in clouds of gloom about the prospects for devolution. The first draft of his White Paper for the Scottish Parliament was thrown out for being overly nationalist in tone. It was 'too Braveheartish' for Tony Blair who wanted to emphasise the Union and the supremacy of the House of Commons.

On the details, however, Dewar proved to be a tenacious negotiator who won most of his important battles. The over-representation of Scottish MPs in the Commons and Scotland's relatively generous financial settlement, both of which were challenged by the English ministers on the committee, were kicked into touch, to be reviewed at some indefinite point beyond the next election. The blueprint for the parliament that the Scottish Secretary unveiled in the summer of 1997 was so well received that it attained the unusual accolade for a government publication of being a bestseller north of the border.

Wales was treated as Scotland's small and ugly sister. Interest in the less powerful assembly proposed for Cardiff was confined to the Welsh, and the idea did not enthuse many of them. Wales had rejected devolution by a margin of four to one on the last occasion it had been offered. His colleagues' indifference was exploited by the Secretary of State for Wales, Ron Davies. A barrel-shaped man with a face which appeared to have just emerged from a rugby scrum, Davies was more devious than he looked. He would wait for the other ministers on the committee to exhaust themselves disputing Scotland and then get his proposals through on the tired nod.

Tony Blair's singular and controversial contribution to devolution had been to insist – in the teeth of opposition from nearly all his senior colleagues – that the transfer of powers to Edinburgh and Cardiff had to be approved by referendums. Labour and the Scottish Nationalists temporarily laid aside their bitter animosity to work together for the parliament. Dewar and Gordon Brown campaigned alongside the Nationalist leader, Alex Salmond, and Sean Connery, the greatest living Scotsman, briefly interrupting his tax-avoiding exile abroad to campaign for a Yes vote. There was never any doubt about the result in Scotland when all the non-Tory parties and every civic organisation of importance were united in support of the parliament. The Conservatives, who had lost every MP north of the border in May 1997, were enfeebled. Two days before the poll, they sent northwards Margaret Thatcher, a woman remembered less affectionately by Scots than the Duke of Cumberland. The referendum result in September 1997 (74.3 per cent in favour to 25.7 per cent against) was a thumping, nearly three-to-one endorsement of the parliament. On the second question, whether it should have tax-raising powers, the answer was Yes by 63.5 per cent to 36.5 per cent. This vindicated Blair's insistence on a plebiscite. If devolution was founded in the popular will, a future Conservative government could not dismantle the Scottish Parliament. The Tories quickly reversed their opposition. What Blair had not foreseen here, or elsewhere, was that the new institutions would also acquire the legitimacy and the authority to defy him.

The poll in Wales was set a week later in the hope that Scottish zeal for devolution might rub off on the more sceptical Welsh. The Cardiff Assembly, with neither the tax nor the legislative powers enjoyed by the Scots, risked being too weak to enthuse home-rulers, while being too much for those who saw it as an expensive job-creation scheme for yet more blathering politicians. The Welsh Office spent nearly £1 million promoting the assembly,[6] while the No campaign was an amateur, virtually penniless outfit. Despite this imbalance of forces, Blair discovered that there were limits to what could be achieved even by an extremely popular Prime Minister in the early flush of his honeymoon. The referendum in Wales was won by the wafer margin of 0.6 per cent on a turn-out of less than half of the potential electorate. The voters shared Blair's own lack of enthusiasm. He dutifully went to Cardiff to appear alongside a relieved Ron Davies. But afterwards, Blair said to him: 'This is a fine mess you've got us into.' Blair's tone did not suggest that he was entirely humorous. Those close to the Prime Minister were convinced that, rather than giving life to the assembly by such a tentative margin, he would rather that the Welsh had throttled it at birth.

Donald Dewar unveiled the legislation for the Scottish Parliament in December 1997 to a largely laudatory reception. The principal merit of his Scotland Bill, in comparison with the failed

effort by the last Labour government in the late seventies, was that
it delineated the powers of the new parliament. Health, education,
justice, law and order, housing, local government and transport
were devolved to the Scots; economic policy, social security, space
exploration, foreign affairs and defence remained in the control of
the Commons. As did some sensitive subjects, such as abortion.
And some curiosities, such as the regulation of hypnotists. The
attractiveness of defining the separation of powers was that it
appeared to reduce the potential for later dispute. Launching his
bill, the Scottish Secretary could justly claim that the moment
was both 'historic' and 'radical'. The usually dour Donald Dewar
permitted himself a moment of excitement: 'In well under 300 days
we have set in train the biggest change in 300 years of Scottish
history.'[7]

But the delivery of long hungered-for Home Rule was not
having the effect that had been expected of it by New Labour. The
law of unanticipated consequences began to operate on Tony Blair.
Rather than kill nationalism 'stone dead', as George Robertson had
once predicted, devolution injected more vigorous life into the
Scottish National Party. By early 1998, the opinion polls suggested
a steady rise in support for the SNP at the expense of the government. A series of controversies grated on Scottish sensitivities. Sean
Connery was denied the knighthood which many Scots felt was
due to the former 007. The decision, it emerged, had been made
just at the time when Connery was being recruited to the Yes
campaign. The shipment of nuclear waste from Georgia to Doun-
reay – after Blair struck a deal with Bill Clinton over the head of
the Scottish Office – was politically radioactive. These were the
symptoms of a profounder problem. To England, New Labour
might look like a fresh and dynamic government. In Scotland, long
years of Labour rule in town and city halls made it the establishment.
Complacent, frequently factional and sometimes corrupt, several
Labour councils were mired in allegations of sleaze, as were some
Labour MPs. Mohammed Sarwar, the Labour MP for Glasgow
Govan, was charged with electoral fraud. Though he was eventually
acquitted, that episode couldn't help but be tarnishing. The suicide

of the MP, Gordon McMaster, who left a note saying he had been hounded into taking his own life by malicious gossip that he had Aids, lifted the lid on the slimy side of Labour politics in the west of Scotland. Tommy Graham, the multiple-chinned MP for West Renfrewshire, was expelled from the party. There was too much bad Old Labour in Scotland, but that didn't mean Scots instinctively warmed to New Labour either. Student tuition fees and the private finance initiative to build hospitals, heresies against socialism which had largely been swallowed in England, were inflammatory in Scotland. All of which was gleefully exploited by the Nationalists. By March 1998, one opinion poll showed a surging SNP just a point behind Labour in voting intentions for the Edinburgh Parliament.[8] Tony Blair and Gordon Brown assumed that the Nationalist bubble, and the SNP claim that New Labour was just Tory Lite, would be pricked by the Budget. They were wrong. At the beginning of May, one poll gave the Nationalists a 5 per cent lead.[9] Salmond announced that if they became the largest party, they would call a referendum on independence. This was a strategic mistake – making it impossible for any other party to work with them – but it increased the perplexity in Downing Street. Consternation deepened into angst in June when a poll put the Nationalists on an unprecedented 44 per cent, nine clear points ahead of a crumbling Labour vote.[10] For the first time, polls suggested that a majority of Scots would vote for independence. What was particularly damaging was the widespread feeling north of the border that the Nationalists 'stood up' for Scotland, and New Labour didn't.[11]

Tony Blair had limited empathy with Scotland, and the Scots felt cool towards him. He had been educated in Edinburgh, but Fettes College – 'Eton with a kilt' – was an atypical school. Hostility to the Prime Minister was fed by an aggressive media north of the border that portrayed him as an Islingtonite, obsessed only with looking after the interests of Middle England, who had no care for the more collectivist minded people of Scotland. He and his press secretary returned the insults. Alastair Campbell ridiculed the Scottish press as 'anally retentive'; Blair called them 'unreconstructed wankers.' On flights from London to Edinburgh, the two of them

would often draw bitter amusement from recalling previous disastrous forays north of the border, most notably when Blair had made
a clumping comparison between the Scottish Parliament and a
parish council.

Blair turned to Gordon Brown, a good example of his dependency on his Chancellor, asking him to 'sort out' Scotland. This
meant trying to sort out Donald Dewar. As the architect of the
parliament, the Scottish Secretary had been the uncontested candidate to be First Minister – equivalent to Prime Minister – of the
parliament. Dyspeptic, cautious and angular, Dewar was not New
Labour, not new anything. An aversion to fashion was an abiding
characteristic of this stooped and bespectacled man, famous for his
propensity to mislay raincoats, uninterested in the politics of image.
Dewar had few great enemies. Nor did he possess many great
friends. One of the few was the Liberal Democrat, Menzies Campbell. He and his wife, Elspeth, shared their family Christmas with
Dewar until he made it evident that he would really much rather
spend the festivities by himself. He was a loner in a profession
which prizes gregariousness, or at least the ability to fake it. He was
a melancholic in a job which demanded optimism, or at least the
talent to pretend it. He was incapable of delivering a sound-bite,
punctuating his sentences with 'erms'. His waspishly incisive wit
could be a delight, but the amusement he caused was not always
intentional. At one of his own drinks receptions, Dewar was introduced to the Grand Prix champion, Jacques Villeneuve. Dewar
asked what he did for a living. Told by his guest that he was a
'driver', Dewar followed up: 'What sort of driver? A bus driver? A
taxi driver? A lorry driver?'

Blair was fond of Dewar, but increasingly bracketed his name
with sighs. Brown was irritated that Dewar would not take his
advice to put together a proper media operation. The Scottish
Secretary's fastidious distaste for the black magic of spin-doctoring
was naïve and arrogant in the view of Blair and Brown. The
Chancellor believed that Dewar was making a mistake when he
attacked the idea of 'independence'. The Scots found the sound of
independence appealing. What New Labour should be doing was

portraying the Nationalists as 'wreckers' and 'separatists' bent on 'divorce'. Brown's analysis made sense to Blair. They also agreed that, since decent Donald was incapable of biting legs himself, they should equip him with a Rottweiler to do the job. In July, Helen Liddell was detached from Brown's Treasury team to the Scottish Office and announced herself at her first press conference as the 'Hammer of the Nats'. All Liddell hammered was nails into her own coffin. She fell out with officials at Labour's headquarters in Scotland, and revealed herself to be inept at modern campaign tactics. The Nationalists continued to wax stronger.

To Brown, Blair groaned: 'This wasn't my idea.' But by the autumn of 1998, there was no joking about the way things were turning out. Blair – telling Brown that he despaired of Scotland – asked the Chancellor to take personal charge north of the border.

While Scotland forced its way to the front of New Labour's mind, Wales was put right out of it. In the eighteen months that Ron Davies had been Secretary of State for Wales, the longest conversation he had had with the Prime Minister lasted little more than fifteen minutes. Only in the context of Wales might Davies be regarded as a moderniser. But he had earned himself the title 'Father of Devolution' by securing, albeit very narrowly, the vote in favour of the Cardiff Assembly. In September 1998, Davies was chosen as Labour's prospective First Secretary – putative premier of Wales – over his rival for the job, Rhodri Morgan, the Labour MP for Cardiff West. Blair's limited interest in the affairs of the Welsh evaporated. In as much as the country was thought about at all, Number 10 shared the universal belief that Labour would process, as it had always done before, to a crushing victory in Wales at the elections for the Cardiff Assembly.

That assumption – and with it much else – was blown asunder on 27 October 1998. Early that morning, his Private Secretary came into Jack Straw's ministerial suite with news that is the staple of a Home Secretary's worst nightmares. John Stevens, the Deputy Commissioner of the Metropolitan Police, was on the phone to report that a member of the Cabinet had been involved in a serious crime. Straw was a reformed smoker who satisfied his craving using a plastic substitute nicotine tube. This was a moment for some hard sucking. Straw's mind reeled through which of his colleagues this might be, what they might have done, and how he was going to handle it. The Home Secretary was initially relieved when Stevens was put through to explain that the Welsh Secretary had been the victim of a robbery. Straw's anxiety heightened again as Stevens told him that the police officers who had interviewed Davies did not believe that he was telling the truth about what had happened to him the previous night. Straw raised the alarm with Number 10. By the time he had made phone contact with Jonathan Powell, Stevens had walked across from Scotland Yard and put his head round Straw's door. Straw passed the phone over to Stevens so that he could brief the Prime Minister's chief of staff. To Powell's growing astonishment, Stevens explained why the police were having difficulty believing Davies's account of how he had ended up in an area of Brixton known as 'crack alley' where, at knifepoint, he was robbed of his wallet and his car.

Alastair Campbell would suggest to the media that Downing Street was in the dark about Davies's nocturnal activities. But not only did Stevens talk to Powell, a fact which would embarrassingly emerge a few days later, Blair himself was directly briefed by the Deputy Commissioner.[12]

As soon as they were alerted to it, the Davies emergency threw Number 10 into a frantic flap. The Cabinet Secretary was dragged out of a meeting. At Blair's request, Sir Richard Wilson scurried mole-like around Whitehall trying to do his own detective work about what had really happened, an investigation which included a visit to Scotland Yard to get a detailed police account about Davies.

After being interviewed by his Permanent Secretary at the Welsh Office, at eleven o'clock Davies was summoned to see the Prime Minister. Alongside Blair in his study were Powell and Alastair Campbell, and they were soon joined by Sir Richard. They were by now in possession of enough information about Davies's walk round the wild side of south London to have come to a conclusion about his fate. Before he came in, Blair had already said: 'He's got to go.'[13]

Davies was red-eyed, dishevelled and manic. Crouched on the Prime Minister's sofa, he told his story. He'd gone out for an evening stroll around Clapham Common, fallen into conversation with a stranger and agreed to the man's suggestion that they meet up with two of his friends for a drink and a meal. Then he had been jumped and robbed.

Blair's eyebrows formed into arcs of incredulity. 'You went off with a Rastafarian you'd never met before? I mean, Ron. For God's sake, why?'[14]

Davies, a man in a state of some derangement, did not offer an explanation that made any sense. He hadn't slept for three nights. His wife was unwell, he said. There had been floods in his constituency. He felt under pressure. 'I needed some space.' His account of his nocturnal safari was garbled and inconsistent.

Five times they asked him what he had really been doing the previous night. After about three quarters of an hour of this, Blair told Davies that he would clearly have to resign, but they would endeavour to make it as painless as possible. Campbell suggested that the best way to explain away his behaviour was as 'a serious lapse of judgement'.

Shortly afterwards, Campbell made the short walk across Whitehall to the Welsh Office to supervise Davies's removal. The press secretary went into the Private Office to dictate Davies's resignation letter, including the phrase – 'a serious lapse of judgement' – of his own invention. The letter was shoved under Davies's eyes in the middle of another police interview. He scanned its contents, and signed. Remarkable as this may seem, Davies would tell friends that he did not read his resignation letter until three weeks later.[15] He claimed to be horrified to discover what he had put his name to.

At four o'clock that afternoon the resignation became public with the exchange of letters, containing the customary phoney declarations of mutual sorrow and admiration between a departing minister and the Prime Minister. With Campbell minding him, Davies did one pooled interview for television and radio in which he maintained: 'I was the innocent victim of a crime.'[16] Then the former Welsh Secretary disappeared.

The media was understandably tantalised by the mystery of why Davies had been obliged to quit if he was the innocent party. Was this a bizarre case of the government being tough on the victim of a crime? The following morning the press provided their own explanation. 'Cabinet Minister Quits In Gay Sex Scandal' was the *Sun* headline,[17] with which the *Mirror* agreed: 'Shame of Gay Sex Cabinet Minister'.[18] The area of the common where Davies had gone for his ramble was, according to police officers quoted, so notorious as a gay pick-up that it was known as 'Gobblers' Gulch'.

At his lobby briefing for political correspondents, Campbell repeated the denials which Davies had offered to Blair that gay sex or drugs were involved. The press secretary appealed for sympathy for the Prime Minister's predicament. 'You think there are elements to the story that have not been fully explained. Maybe we feel the same way too.'[19]

Campbell was being economic with the truth. Number 10 had known more and known about it much earlier than he implied. One of the several people rung for emergency consultations on the day of Davies's resignation was told by Anji Hunter: 'Ron Davies is resigning. It's about male prostitutes.'[20] It was also not true, as the press secretary initially claimed, that 'to his credit' Davies had come to the Prime Minister of his own volition. Campbell's motives for attempting to mislead were not entirely discreditable. He was trying to put a tourniquet on the severed stump of a Cabinet minister whose crazed behaviour had brought humiliation on himself, distress to his family and havoc for the government. As was often the case with New Labour, an attempt to spin the media produced even worse publicity. Acres of print were devoted to untangling what the Prime Minister and his aides had really known about Davies and – as he called it when he emerged from hiding at the end of the week – his 'moment of madness'.

The desire to bring the affair to a rapid and neat ending was to have a much more significant long-term consequence. Blair wanted to have ready a replacement for Davies as Welsh Secretary before they announced his resignation. That decision was therefore made in extreme haste. At lunchtime Blair called together Campbell, Powell, Anji Hunter, and Sally Morgan, the Prime Minister's political secretary. They were joined by Peter Hain, a junior minister at the Welsh Office. Curly headed and perma-tanned, the former anti-apartheid activist was a member of the soft left trusted by Number 10. Various options were floated as replacements for Davies – Hain himself among them – but the choice soon narrowed down to two men.

Blair would not have Rhodri Morgan, the runner-up to Davies in the first Welsh leadership contest, at any price. Morgan was an unbiddable maverick with Bardic hair and a colourful turn of phrase which gave him the air of an eccentric professor. Years previously, in Opposition, he had worked under Blair, and memories of Morgan's disorganised style lingered with the Prime Minister. He also brought out the snob in Blair who had been repelled by the domestic chaos he encountered during an overnight stay at Morgan's home in Michaelston-le-Pit. One legend had it that Blair was revolted to see the family dogs licking the breakfast plates. It probably did not help that Morgan's elderly mother-in-law greeted the future Prime Minister: 'I know who you are. You're that Lionel Blair.'[21]

Since the election Morgan had aroused the enmity of influential members of the Downing Street court. As chairman of the Public Accounts Committee, he summoned Alastair Campbell to account for his activities during which the press secretary had been obliged to swear himself innocent of ever briefing against Cabinet ministers. The same committee had been the arena in which Derry Irvine had made an Olympian ass of himself by defending the fabulous sums spent on the refurbishment of the Lord Chancellor's apartments by drawing a scornful contrast with the DIY practised by humbler Britons. The animus against Morgan was not confined to Blair.

The alternative candidate, Alun Michael, the MP for Cardiff South and Penarth, and a junior Home Office minister, had also

worked under Blair in Opposition. The Prime Minister did not
have a vaulting regard for Michael either. His inability to do
anything without the boss's approval was something of a weary
joke in Blair's office at the time. In the context of this emergency,
the dutiful, swottish and loyal Michael recommended himself.

'But will he want to do it?' asked Campbell. This was a smart
question. It would have been an even sharper question had anyone
in Blair's study that lunchtime taken a breath and wondered
whether the majority of members of the Welsh Labour Party, or
the Welsh electorate, would want Alun Michael. He had made it
evident that he saw his career not in Wales, but shinning up
Westminster's greasy pole. That day, he was lunching with a journalist at Christopher's restaurant off the Strand. Michael had just
finished his red onion salad starter when his face paled at a message
telling him to go to Number 10 at once. There he accepted the
job of Secretary of State for Wales, allowing Downing Street to
announce his appointment simultaneously with Davies's resignation.

The attempt to parcel the affair up neatly continued to unravel
over the next few days. Campbell made his own contribution to
the lurid headlines about Davies when he lost his rag at a briefing
with Sunday lobby journalists. 'You lot just want his agony to
continue,' Campbell flailed. 'You would probably not care –
because it would be a good story – if he topped himself.'[22] The
suggestion that Davies was suicidal duly splashed all over the front
pages that weekend.

Blair had three sets of arms to twist. Incredibly, Davies initially
clung to the idea that he could still be the leader of the Cardiff
Assembly and, equally remarkably, the Prime Minister had not
made it clear, at their first interview, that this was inconceivable. It
took several phone calls from Number 10 to cajole Davies to
step down. Michael, who had not even been a candidate for the
assembly, had to be encouraged to declare that he would now seek
to be Labour's leader in Cardiff, which he finally did nearly a week
after his appointment as Welsh Secretary. 'I have always wanted to
see an elected assembly bring democratic accountability to the

people of Wales. As a Welshman, I cannot think of a greater privilege than to help bring that dream to a reality,' said Michael, to a great deal of disbelieving mockery.[23] The impression that he was a most reluctant candidate was reinforced when he muddled the title of the job he claimed to regard as so privileged.

The final arm that Blair set out to bend into submission belonged to Rhodri Morgan. Asked whether he would again be a candidate for the leadership in Cardiff, Morgan had answered in typically idiosyncratic fashion: 'Do one-legged ducks swim in a circle?'[24] The Prime Minister wanted this duck sunk. He planned to crown Michael as his Prince of Wales without further argument. Such was Blair's determination to prevent a contest that he invited Morgan into Number 10 on no fewer than three occasions to attempt to persuade him to step aside.[25] Blair tried a mixture of appeals to ambition and loyalty. Why not be Michael's deputy? Do you want to divide the party? The meetings were civil, but Morgan proved impervious to the Prime Minister's entreaties. So anxious was Blair to induce the Welshman to leave the contest that he even made an hour in his schedule to see Morgan during Gerhard Schröder's first official visit to Britain as Chancellor of Germany. Sally Morgan (no relation) took a note as they argued in the Prime Minister's study. In exasperation that he was not wearing down the Welshman's resistance, Blair finally told him that it would be 'inappropriate', no it would be 'impossible' for Morgan to be First Secretary because 'you have no experience of government'. Morgan riposted that this was because Blair had not given him a job, a passing over which had both baffled and hurt the MP. Morgan replied: 'You can't have experience when you haven't been a minister.' Come to think of it, if inexperience counted so much, then Blair would not be where he was. 'We should all have voted for Margaret Beckett in 1994 and she would now be in your chair, Tony.' At this outburst of *lèse majesté*, Blair's jaw froze. Sally Morgan dropped her pencil.[26]

Blair's preference for his own man in Wales was understandable. His desire not to have a contest was comprehensible. But why go to such strenuous – and ultimately counter-productive lengths – to block Rhodri Morgan? New Labour's insecurity was manifesting itself again in this urge to control. Scarred by the party's history of division and indiscipline, Tony Blair was terrified to let go.

What was a crime, and a terrible mistake, was to fix the fight. In a clean contest, it was apparent from the outset that Rhodri Morgan would beat Alun Michael, tagged already as the creature of Number 10. Michael's own campaign manager, Peter Hain, was staggered by the hostility that his candidate aroused among traditionally loyal Welsh Labour activists. 'He's not even Welsh, is he?' they would tell Hain. When he truthfully protested that not only was his man Welsh, but he spoke the language fluently, people simply refused to believe it. Rhodri Morgan cut the much more attractive figure. Despite Hain's desperate pleas, his own constituency party nominated Morgan.

John Prescott, alert to the damage that was being done to the party, tried to persuade Blair to drop his compulsion to block Morgan. Blair responded: 'What do I do if he wins?', to which Prescott countered: 'Say it's democracy, for Christ's sake. That it's a triumph for democracy!' This argument, excellent though it was, could not budge the Prime Minister.

Tony Blair's desire to stop the Welshman – an obsession out of all proportion to any conceivable threat he might pose to New Labour – impelled the Prime Minister to make a massive misjudgement. 'One Member One Vote' had been an article of faith in his modernising gospel, and one of the most appealing contrasts with the discreditable deals and fixes of Old Labour. The Prime Minister claimed that the electoral college used to decide the Welsh contest was 'precisely the same' as the system that had elected him and John Prescott as leader and deputy leader. This was stretching the truth until the elastic snapped. In his own election, unions were obliged to ballot their members. In the Welsh contest, a barony of old-style union bosses wielded the block vote that Blair had condemned until he needed a fix himself. The archetype union boss was George Wright, the General Secretary of the Welsh Transport and General Workers Union, and a throwback to Labour's Jurassic era. An independent survey showed that the vast majority of his members wanted Morgan, but all of the union's votes were cast for Michael.[27]

At the end of a rancorous campaign, which besmirched New Labour's democratic credentials and scarred the party in Wales, on 21 February 1999 Alun Michael emerged the hollow victor. Party members voted for Rhodri Morgan by nearly two to one. It was the undemocratic block votes of the unions and the whipped votes of MPs, MEPs and assembly candidates which tipped the result. Even then, the deals and the personal pleas of the Prime Minister could still deliver the Welsh leadership to his candidate only by the anorexic margin of 5 per cent.

New Labour shamefully employed the worst of Old Labour machine politics to bend democracy to suit the Prime Minister. The charge that Tony Blair was a control-freak took root and it would have cumulatively corrosive consequences for the government. By stooping to conquer in Wales, Blair made it much harder for himself to make a case that would be listened to when confronted in London by Ken Livingstone, a man much more potentially menacing to the government.

When Ron Davies's nocturnal peregrinations around south London were yellowing cuttings, Tony Blair's own moment of madness in Wales would continue to reverberate against the Prime Minister. He had simultaneously given away powers, while attracting to himself the charge that he behaved like a dictator. It was a damaging paradox of his own making.

In Scotland, the weather began to get less heavy for the government. A poll published in February 1999 put Labour firmly in the lead over the Nationalists.[28] Gordon Brown was throwing his political weight around to impose some organisation and focus on the faction-ridden Scottish Labour Party. He seized on the opportunity to demonstrate why his strategic and cerebral talents were so vital to the government, and to establish Scotland as his fiefdom. He put in charge of the campaign Douglas Alexander, the Paisley MP and a former speech-writer to the Chancellor. Dark, intelligent and square-jawed, Alexander reflected Brown's preference for protégés who were pocket versions of himself.

The annihilation of the Conservatives in Scotland was the cause of a strange and unanticipated mutation to Labour. With a vacuum where the Tories used to be, Labour was becoming the Unionist Party. Brown, demonstrating how he did a lot of the government's intellectual heavy-lifting, addressed himself to the challenge of remaking the case for the Union in New Labour's terms. 'The British question, in the run up to May's Scottish and Welsh elections, is whether what binds our different nations together will triumph over a nationalism which would break us apart,' he wrote. Once the Union was held together by flag, army and monarchy. Brown sought to redefine it around the 'shared values' of the components of the kingdom.

I understand Britishness as being outward-looking, open and internationalist, a commitment to democracy and tolerance, to creativity and enterprise and to public service, and to justice or, as we often put it, to fair play.

He went on: 'The case for Britain is straightforward – that we achieve more working together than working apart.' His 'vision of Britain' was one 'where unity comes not from uniformity, but from celebrating diversity'.[29]

The slogan 'strength through diversity' was a nice encapsulation of the idea of devolution, but New Labour was schizophrenic in Scotland, just as it was in Wales, when it came to applying the theory to itself. The exclusion from the list of Labour candidates of the left-winger Dennis Canavan became another *cause célèbre* of control-freakism. Canavan wondered, and it was hard for ministers to give a logical answer, how he could be fit to be a Labour MP at Westminster, but not a Labour MP in the Scottish Parliament. He left the party to run as an independent.

The Nationalists were not to be beaten back just by Brown's intellectual creativity. Cruder tools were also to hand. Some were gifted to Labour by the SNP. The party's leader, Alex Salmond, declared the NATO action in Kosovo to be an 'unpardonable folly'. That was a point of view, but even some who agreed with it were repelled by his comparison of the bombing of Belgrade with Hitler's blitzes of London and Clydebank. This at last presented Labour with the opportunity to turn the 'patriotic card' against the Nationalists. Salmond was pilloried by Robin Cook, who dubbed him 'the toast of Belgrade'. The Saturday before polling, the Foreign Secretary posed with a group of Kosovan refugees. The message was unsophisticated: vote against rape and murder, vote Labour.

It had not entered into Brown's calculations when he announced a penny cut in income tax in his Budget that the Nationalists would pledge to reverse it in Scotland and spend the additional revenues on public services. Handed this ammunition, Brown pounded away with it, bargaining that the Scots were actually just as averse to tax increases as the English. The campaign Labour fought against the SNP in 1999 was lifted from the Tories. It was, in many essential respects, a reprise of the slogans and scares the Conservatives had used to defeat Labour in the British general election of 1992. Salmond and his party were presented as a threat to the integrity of the United Kingdom, not to be trusted on defence, and reckless taxers and spenders. Apocalyptic Labour broadcasts pictured the United Kingdom breaking apart. The most effective billboard campaign yelled 'MORE TAX', the X of TAX growing out of the SNP's thistle symbol.

Donald Dewar was detached from the bruising side of election-eering which he found so distasteful by dispatching him on a bus tour of Scotland. He had finally conceded to the advice to acquire spin doctors who would send him into interviews pleading: 'Remember, be happy. Try to smile, Donald.' Occasionally something passing for sunshine would briefly break across his face. His wardrobe was given a make-over, but the executive ties soon became unknotted, the suits rumpled, and observers were often rewarded with the sight of the tail of his shirt hanging out. 'They are supposed to re-create me, but actually they simply try to tidy me up,' said Dewar. 'And even that defies them.'[30]

The unflashy decency of the sixty-one-year-old Dewar was an asset. Labour presented him as the wise and moderate father of the nation to be contrasted favourably with smart-Alex Salmond, who diminished himself with a display of juvenilia during a speech by the Prime Minister. Polls indicated that a majority, extending beyond Labour supporters, felt that Dewar would make by far the best First Minister of Scotland.[31] Salmond complained of 'a London-controlled campaign, based on a deeply negative agenda'.[32] His real grievance was that it was working.

The same could not be said of the Labour campaign in Wales. Ten days before polling there, Greg Cook, the party's pollster, showed Peter Hain the results of his private surveys. Labour was on 31 per cent, the Nationalists on 28 per cent, and the Don't Knows were 30 per cent. 'Is this number of Don't Knows usual?' asked Hain. 'No,' replied Cook. 'It's normally about 10 per cent.' Hain had a premonition: 'I don't like the feel of this.'

The leader of the Welsh Nationalists, Dafydd Wigley, astutely softened his party's commitment to independence and instead presented Plaid Cymru as truer heirs to the socialist tradition of Nye Bevan than New Labour. Plaid, whose posters invited a vote for Wigley because he was 'no one's poodle', exploited the massive resentment against Alun Michael, the Prime Minister's pet. On the eve of the poll, Anita Gale, Labour's general secretary in Wales, was discussing their prospects with Hain. 'We are heading for a disaster, Peter,' she told him. The tan drained from Hain's face.

Britain woke up a changed country on 7 May 1999. Labour was the largest party in Scotland and in Wales, but was denied absolute power in both capitals, a predictable outcome in Edinburgh, a seismic shock in Cardiff. Proportional representation in Scotland delivered 56 of the 129 seats in the Edinburgh Parliament to Labour, more than comfortably ahead of the Nationalist tally of 35. In one of the night's rebukes to Downing Street, Dennis Canavan won a crushing victory as an independent over his Labour opponent.

It had long been envisaged that Labour would form a coalition government in Edinburgh with the Liberal Democrats. Tony Blair's central and characteristic concern was that the new constitutional settlement should look strong and stable. He pressed Dewar to conclude swiftly his coalition negotiations with the leader of the Liberal Democrats in Scotland, Jim Wallace. The Prime Minister

also made calls to Paddy Ashdown and Roy Jenkins urging them
to impress on Wallace the necessity to strike a rapid deal. Ashdown,
more attuned to the sensitivities than Blair, warned him that neither
of them should look as if they were 'meddling' by dictating terms
from London. The main obstacle to a bargain was overcome when
Wallace, who had previously named the abolition of student tuition
fees as the price of a deal, abandoned this pledge for a review of
student support.

There was trauma in Wales. Ron Davies saw his majority savaged
in Caerphilly. This began to look like a great success as other
results came in. The heartlands of the Rhondda, Llanelli and Neil
Kinnock's Islwyn, constituencies where Labour had historically
mined votes by the ton, were won by the Nationalists. The single
Labour candidate to stand proud against the anti-Labour swing was
Rhodri Morgan, who saw his personal vote increase. The only
consolation for Downing Street was that Alun Michael was elected
to the assembly for the perverse reason that Labour could get him
in as a top-up candidate because it had done so badly in the directly
contested seats. Labour, with twenty-eight of the sixty seats in the
assembly, was deprived of a majority. The Nationalists, scoring
their best ever result, had seventeen.

Devolution delivered something to everyone. Thanks to a proportional voting system which they condemned, the Tories were
restored to representation in Scotland and Wales. In Edinburgh,
Liberal Democrats were enjoying a first taste of power for decades.
The Scottish and Welsh Nationalists had established themselves as
the principal parties of opposition. Labour was in government in
both Edinburgh and Cardiff.

Tony Blair could hail this as a triumph. More than a hundred
years after William Gladstone first attempted to introduce Home
Rule, New Labour succeeded where all other progressive governments had failed. Scotland had its first parliament since the reign of
Queen Anne, and its first elected parliament ever. Wales had its
first representative body since Owain Glyndwr, and its first elected
assembly ever. A new politics was springing to life, changing for
good and for ever the political landscape of Britain.

Yet a proud sense of achievement did not exude from the Prime Minister. The man conflicted about this modernised, more loose-limbed kingdom was its author. Speaking in Downing Street after the election results, the Prime Minister chose to derive most satisfaction not from the success of devolution, but the survival of the Union. 'The vast majority of people voted for parties opposed to the nationalist agenda of independence.'[33]

The celebrations in Edinburgh and Cardiff did not surge through Tony Blair. As the New Britain was born, no one looked more anxious about how it might grow up than the midwife.

# 14. On a Wing and a Prayer

Downing Street was very quiet that afternoon. The chatter of what John Prescott called the 'teeny boppers' in the Policy Unit dropped to a nervous murmur. The buzz of officials fell to a whisper. Inside the Prime Minister's study, he was making the decision to take Britain to war in Europe for the first time since 1945.

At two o'clock, in strode General Sir Charles Guthrie, the Chief of the Defence Staff, his chest a polychromatic display of ribbonry. Though he commonly wore a pinstripe suit at his desk in the Ministry of Defence, Britain's most senior military officer invariably donned an intimidatingly resplendent uniform when he went over to Number 10. Encountering him in a lift, a Defence Minister inquired of the general why he was in full fig. 'I'm going to see the Prime Minister,' smiled Guthrie.

They were joined by George Robertson, the Defence Secretary. The son of a policeman, he had spent his youth protesting against American submarine bases in Scotland. Brisk, paunchy and genial, Robertson had won the respect of the military, but he had never fired a shot in anger. Robin Cook, the Foreign Secretary, had been a left-wing rebel against the nuclear bomb and NATO. He had no doubts about 'fighting a war against fascism'. He had no experience either. Tony Blair had worn uniform only under duress as a member of his school cadet force. He opted out to do community service as soon as he was able. These were the men about to go to war.

Slobodan Milošević had rejected the last of a series of ultimatums to cease his murderous campaign in Kosovo. Intelligence had warned for months that Operation Horseshoe, Milošević's spring offensive, would be an expanded and more brutal version of his operations against the Kosovo Liberation Army and the ethnic Albanians of the region. Spring came early. In January, fifty-four

Kosovars were massacred in the village of Račak. The terror intensi-
fied following the Serbs' refusal to sign an agreement at Rambouillet
and the withdrawal of international observers.

When the prospect of taking military action against the Serbian
dictator had been discussed over the preceding weeks, Blair told
his colleagues that Milošević had to be 'shown some steel' to
convince him that NATO wasn't bluffing. At the moment of
truth, bellicosity melted into apprehension. Blair confided to one
close ministerial friend: 'This is not a war I wanted.'[1] Even at this
last hour, he thought that Milošević would surely see the folly of
confronting the world's most powerful military alliance. When he
asked the professionals what the Serbian dictator would do, none
of them could give Blair a definite answer. Cook's Foreign Office
leant towards the view of the American State Department that
Milošević would crack after a few nights of what the Americans
termed 'representational' bombing. When Blair turned to Guthrie
for advice, the broad and smooth soldier–politician was much too
foxy to pin himself to any guarantees. He told the Prime Minister
that, whatever assumptions they started with, 'warfare has a dynamic
of its own'. They could hope that 'he will buckle quickly' but Blair
should be prepared for a 'long haul'. The final Cabinet Office
paper, drawing together the confused and conflicting advice from
the Foreign Office and the Ministry of Defence, listed a variety
of scenarios, from a short bombing campaign to an engagement
enduring many months. The paper avoided coming to a conclusion
about which outcome was the most likely. 'What's the end-state?'
Cook asked Guthrie at one point. 'The end-state? I don't bloody
know,' replied the general.[2] They were flying blind.

Going to war for Kosovo breached the cardinal principles of
New Labour. The Americans were providing the vast majority of
the firepower, and many of the European allies were queasy about
the enterprise. Blair was taking an uncalibrated gamble using uncertain means over which he had limited control for an imprecisely
defined end. The stakes were high; the rewards unguaranteed.

When he spoke to the Commons on the afternoon of Tuesday,
23 March, he swallowed his own anxieties to trumpet a clear note:

We have made a very plain promise to the Kosovar people. To walk away now would not merely destroy NATO's credibility. More importantly, it would be a breach of faith to thousands of innocent civilians whose only desire is to live in peace and took us at our word: to protect them from military suppression.

Reciting the agreements betrayed by the Serbs, the 2,000 Kosovars already killed, and the many more driven from their homes by Milošević's latest offensive, Blair went on: 'We must act to save thousands of innocent men, women and children from humanitarian catastrophe, from death, barbarism and ethnic cleansing by a brutal dictatorship. We have no alternative to act and act we will.'[3]

NATO's initial plan was for three nights' bombing of ninety-one targets. In his statement, Blair made what was, as he would realise within less than a month, a major mistake. He rejected the use of the threat most likely to convince Milošević that the intent of the West was serious. Echoing Bill Clinton's broadcast to America, Blair set his face against using ground forces to expel the Serbs. 'We do not plan to use ground troops in order to fight our way into Kosovo,' he told MPs. 'No one should underestimate the sheer scale of what is involved in that action. We would be talking about 100,000 ground troops, and possibly even more.'[4] Under subsequent questioning, he lifted the figure upwards to '200,000 ground forces', making the idea of mustering such an army sound lunatic. Ground troops did not feature in the calculations as the 'action' – at its outset they refused to describe it as a war – began. Robertson had a map of Kosovo on the wall behind his desk at the Ministry of Defence. He would point to the three, narrow entry points into this region the size of south Yorkshire, and observe that the last time it had been successfully invaded by land was in the fourteenth century. Robertson dismissed the idea of trying again: 'It would be fine if someone had built a motorway into Kosovo, but no one has.'[5]

The first of NATO's bombs shook Kosovo's capital, Priština, at just after eight in the evening on Wednesday 24 March. When the Cabinet met the next morning, there was 'a sense of guilt'[6] around

the table that the West's previous inaction in Bosnia had contributed
to the deaths of 200,000 people and the displacement of millions.
Critics were already loudly questioning the air strategy. In the
course of a half-hour discussion, some ministers articulated their
own nervousness that the objectives were not entirely precise, nor
was it clear what would be achieved by bombing. Blair's insistence
that it would work was hope speaking louder than experience. On
the first night of the raids, and in contradiction to the public claims
that the operation was 'running on rails', the RAF failed to hit a
single one of its targets.

Early indications from telephone polls and radio phone-ins suggested – misleadingly, as it turned out – that there was no public
enthusiasm for the air strikes against the Serbs. His other engage-
ments were rapidly unscrambled. On Friday afternoon, Blair
recorded a television address for transmission that evening. 'I may
have to send our forces into action again. And when I do, I want
them to go with the whole country united behind them.' He
dressed himself in patriotic colours, changing his tie to a striped
red, white and blue number, weaving a pseudo-regimental pattern.
Poppies were suggestively arranged in a vase behind Blair. It was
'simply the right thing to do' to 'defend our fellow human beings'.
His insistence that bombing was 'for the sake of humanity' sounded
clichéd, but it was true. There was no strategic imperative to defend
Albanian Muslims in one of the poorest corners of Europe. From
right-wing isolationists in the Conservative Party, the absence of
any selfish British interest was precisely the charge levelled against
Blair. Nor was there any electoral advantage for an already popular
Prime Minister. The potent criticism – the charge that stung because
he possessed no good answer to it – was that bombing was a crude
and probably useless instrument of coercion, like trying to hit a
wasp with a shotgun. 'To those who say the aim of military strikes
is not clear, I say it is crystal clear,' insisted Blair. 'It is to curb
Milošević's ability to wage war on an innocent civilian population.'[7]

As he said it, he knew this was not being achieved by the air
campaign. At eight each morning, Robertson, accompanied by
Guthrie and often by Cook, would take a lift descending them

sixty feet underground below the Ministry of Defence. They would walk along narrow air-pressurised tunnels, pass through two sets of red, steel blast doors, and take their seats around the table in the dimly lit Crisis Management Centre. 'The Bunker', designed to withstand nuclear or biological attack, was a relic of the Cold War. Blair did not bother with it. The only time he was seen in the Bunker was for a photo-opportunity designed by Alastair Campbell to spin a war leader's halo around Blair.[8] The Bunker's video screens connected the politicians and military to all key points from NATO HQ in Belgium to RAF strike command at High Wycombe. Information about the previous night's raids and strike plans for the twenty-four hours ahead would be brought back from the MoD to Blair in his study at Number 10. After three days of the campaign, the message from the Bunker was that the bombing was a failure. It had been so telegraphed in advance that the targets NATO struck had largely been emptied by the Serbs. Worse, pictures from reconnaissance planes and satellites revealed that Milošević was intensifying his 'final solution' in Kosovo. By the first weekend, the roads were rivers of desperate humanity. More than half a million Kosovars were already fleeing from the killing grounds and torched villages for the borders. At a conference call between Blair, Cook, Robertson and Guthrie it was agreed that they should try to persuade the Macedonian government to accept the refugees on to their soil.

When Blair and Clinton spoke that weekend, another assumption, that of effortlessly invulnerable Western technological superiority, was shattered. The global television village watched pictures of an old Serb peasant woman dancing on the broken wing of a dismembered US stealth fighter-bomber. Public opinion in America was flaky about the conflict and mistrustful of its President, who demonstrated his lack of engagement with what he had unleashed by spending much of Saturday playing golf. Clinton told Blair that he needed political cover from Europe, especially Britain, if they were to augment the air campaign. Mike Short, the American general in charge of the bombing, was of the 'fastest with the mostest' school of combat. Short agitated to 'go for the jugular' with an aerial blitzkrieg of Belgrade which would 'make Milošević's eyes water'. There was little enthusiasm for this among the Britons. Guthrie referred to Short as 'Doctor Strangelove'. The Prime Minister agreed with Clinton that the RAF would commit more planes. But Blair, in common with other European leaders, was not ready to countenance saturation bombing of Belgrade. 'What if we cut off the power to a hospital?' he worried. 'Then we'll be accused of killing babies.'

Blair and Clinton were equally frantic to counter the increasingly vocal criticism that the air campaign was serving only to worsen the plight of the Kosovars. What they wanted was television pictures of NATO planes destroying the Serb soldiers and paramilitary police committing the killings in Kosovo. This was a media-driven decision by the politicians taken against the advice of the soldiers. Klaus Naumann, the German general who chaired NATO's military committee, complained that it was asking the impossible:

They want us to stop the individual murderer going with his knife from village to village and carving up some Kosovars. That you cannot do from the air. You cannot hit this guy. You have to be in there to stop it.[9]

On the night of 3 April, orange flames ballooned over Belgrade as cruise missiles hit the Interior Ministry and the police headquarters: just 600 metres from a hospital. The citizens of Belgrade responded by presenting themselves with targets around their necks, defying NATO to do its worst. The allies weren't winning, and everything the Serb regime was hearing from the West emboldened it to believe that, for all the belligerence of British rhetoric, even they were not prepared for a real fight. Robin Cook declared again that there were 'no plans for an invasion or to fight our way in. Nor could we claim to have such a capability.'[10]

By the first week of April, virtually the whole of Kosovo's Albanian population was in hiding or in flight. In the face of the biggest humanitarian disaster in Europe since the Second World

War, the allies were already falling out in public. The American military claimed to have warned the politicians that this would happen. 'We were not surprised by what Milošević has done,' maintained the Pentagon's spokesman. 'I think there is historical amnesia here if anyone says they are surprised by this campaign.'[11] A British official more candidly confessed: 'We did not expect Milošević to move the levels of population that he is moving: perhaps that was a failure of imagination.'

This was an important moment. The packing of Kosovars into trucks and trains, scenes which Blair now took to likening to the Nazi holocaust, was the point when he began to invest an emotional commitment demonstrated by none of the other NATO leaders. 'This is no longer just a military conflict,' he declared that weekend, framing the war as a religious struggle. 'It is a battle between good and evil; between civilisation and barbarity.'[12] Promising that air strikes would continue with 'iron resolve', Blair nailed himself to a pledge to the Kosovars that Clinton had studiously avoided. 'We will not let you down. We will make sure that you are able to return to your homes, and live in peace.'[13]

There was chaos in the Western capitals about how the biblical flood of humanity should be helped. On Sunday morning Blair insisted that it would be 'a policy of despair' to give haven to the refugees elsewhere in Europe. 'Our goal must be to ensure that those people can return to their homes. We cannot and must not accept Milošević's ethnic cleansing. That means we must try, if possible, to avoid dispersing these people around Europe.'[14] By Sunday evening, after the Germans revealed a European Union plan to offer sanctuary to at least 100,000 of the refugees, Blair's policy had already been semi-reversed with a promise from Britain of some temporary accommodation.

Clare Short, the International Development Secretary, flew out to the frontline that Easter weekend. The transformation in the volatile, dark, Irish Catholic atheist personified the shift in the British left's attitude towards making war on dictators. Short had resigned from the Labour frontbench in protest about the Gulf War against Saddam Hussein. She was now one of the most sharp-beaked hawks. When British soldiers shot a war criminal in Bosnia, Short planted a kiss on the cheek of a startled General Guthrie.

On her tour of the borderlands, she successfully pressed the Macedonian government to allow more refugees across their border. She also visited K-For, the international force established to police a settlement. In the disused shoe factory that served as K-For's headquarters, Short was briefed by Sir Mike Jackson, the British lieutenant-general in command of the force. Jackson wore the face of a wise bloodhound and spoke in a voice sieved through gravel. His military career had been devoted to operational soldiering. 'Milošević and NATO are in a race,' Jackson told Short at a meeting with his senior officers. 'Milošević is winning the first lap.' Short, whose passion to assist the Kosovars was stronger than her comprehension of military logistics or chains of command, demanded: 'Why aren't you in there already?' Intentionally or not, she seemed to imply that Jackson and his men were cowards. The soldiers bit their lips. The general explained that he had neither the orders to invade Kosovo, nor the strength. He could call upon just 12,000 troops, fifteen tanks, and eight mobile artillery guns. 'That's bugger all. That's no invasion force by any stretch of the imagination.'[15] This difficult exchange served a purpose. Clare Short returned to London as a vigorous lobbyist for increasing forces on the ground.

NATO was still committed to winning from the air. Bad weather and failing technology – none of the British planes could drop their laser-guided weapons through the clouds – were the alibis offered for the failure to hit Serb forces in Kosovo. Bombing from a great height satisfied a political desire to minimise the risk of allied pilots returning home in coffins at the cost of greatly increasing the hazard that they would inflict accidental casualties on civilians. Pilots were being asked to pick out Serb units from an altitude of 15,000 feet. On 14 April American F-16s, flying over the Prizren–Djakovica road, spotted what they took to be a column of military trucks. Video from the pilots' six-inch gunsight monitors later revealed that this is what the vehicles could easily be mistaken for from a jet flying at screaming speed at a height of three miles. The fighters attacked. What they destroyed was a convoy of tractors pulling trailers packed with Kosovar refugees. When the onslaught was over, at least seventy innocents were dead, the first, grave allied blunder of the conflict.

The carnage on the ground was awful and made worse by five days of chaotic and apparently dissembling explanations from NATO headquarters and Western capitals. NATO's supreme commander in Europe, Wesley Clark, initially maintained that 'we struck a Serb convoy' until the story collapsed when it was incontrovertibly demonstrated otherwise. When they talked that Wednesday night, Blair told Clinton that they were 'losing it' in that crucial arena of the conflict which shaped public attitudes: television. The allies' mistakes were propaganda victories quickly exploited by the Serbs. A long stretch of a heavy conversation dwelt on how to improve the presentation of their war. Clinton readily agreed to Blair's suggestion that he dispatch Downing Street's élite company of para-spinners to Brussels. Jamie Shea, the NATO spokesman, who had been floundering trying to reconcile the contradictory information about the refugee bombing, received a warning call from a friend in Washington to brace himself for an imminent appearance by Alastair Campbell. When he got to NATO headquarters on Thursday, the press secretary was horrified. NATO, never before having fought a war, was hopelessly inadequate to a propaganda battle. Shea was under-resourced and rather naïve. He was allowing journalists to wander freely around his office, the same journalists who were dicing him at his press conferences. Campbell's arrival at first aroused fears in Shea that he was going to be sacked as NATO spokesman. Instead he became the grateful recipient of a detailed tutorial in New Labour's arts of media manipulation.

That night Campbell had dinner with Wesley Clark at the American commander's château in the Belgian countryside. Clark greeted the British spin-merchant with considerable suspicion, but he was won over to Campbell's argument that the military had to start providing reliable information of quality to the propagandists. He offered Campbell a bed for the night. A ground invasion began, not of Kosovo, but of the converted maternity hospital in the suburbs of Brussels which was NATO headquarters. Campbell summoned Anji Hunter. He wanted her organisational energies. Such was their collective ignorance of the military that when he told her to pack for a trip to SACEUR she wrote it down in her notepad as SACKER. Javier Solana, the NATO Secretary-General, told them: 'You can have anything you want.'

For New Labour, war was politics by other means. Campbell wrote a six-page guide to information warfare, detailing the deployment of 'talking heads', the spinning of 'lines', the uses of 'monitoring' and the techniques of aggressive 'rebuttal'. He also diagrammed a chain of propaganda command with himself second only to the NATO Secretary-General. On Campbell's instruction, information from Shea, especially about bad news, suddenly became much more restricted. The advice extended to the sartorial. Shea was told by Campbell: 'Get yourself a darker suit.'

A clone of the Millbank election machine was created by knocking through the wall between two rooms. It would be staffed by dozens of spinners from America and Europe. The biggest contingent was British. Civil servants were drafted in from Number 10, the Foreign Office, the Ministry of Defence, even the Scottish Office. Campbell would not quite take possession of everything he wanted. Believing that they were under-exploiting the propaganda asset of having a British general in charge of the frontline troops, he complained to General Jackson about the way K-For was promoting itself. Campbell backed off when the soldier diplomatically reminded the press secretary that, as the leader of a multi-national force answering to NATO, 'I can't be partisan.'

Propaganda was no substitute for victory. As April grew older, there was no sign that NATO was getting nearer to winning. Tony Blair was increasingly dissatisfied with the quality of the information and advice he was getting. That he chose to employ Paddy Ashdown as his personal envoy and intelligence-gatherer on the Kosovo borders was a demonstration in itself of the way the Prime Minister's mind was moving. The former marine commando was an expert on the region and long an advocate of robust action against the Serbs. Having rejected his calls for intervention the previous autumn, now Blair wanted to draw upon Ashdown's contacts and experience. Ashdown's four-day tour encompassed a long session with General Jackson where they considered NATO's diminishing options into the night over glasses of Bell's whisky. The confidential note that Ashdown wrote for Blair began starkly: 'You think you are winning this war. I think you are losing it.' Ashdown reflected Jackson's concerns:

There is uncertainty on the ground among the military about what they are being asked to do and what happens next . . . they know that an opposed ground operation in one form or another is increasingly likely. They are not, however, equipped for this, have not been asked to plan for it, and do not know what their aim is likely to be. NATO has at most a month to make up its mind what it wants to do.

The urgency of Ashdown's note was reinforced by warnings from Cook that, if Kosovo was not liberated before the winter, then it was unlikely the refugees would ever return. Ashdown summarised it neatly in his note: 'This is the first war in history that is being fought for refugees. And we have set ourselves an unforgiving measure for its success. If they don't go back, we have lost.'[16]

No one would lose more starkly than Blair. By mid-April he had grasped what a fundamental error it was to rule out the use of troops. It broke the first rule of warfare: keep the enemy guessing. Milošević had been allowed to calculate that he only had to endure the air campaign until the nineteen uneasy allies of NATO lost heart or fell apart. On 20 April Blair flew out to NATO head-quarters to deliver even more uncompromising rhetoric:

To see people herded on to trains and taken away from their homes and to hear the stories that those refugees have come back from Kosovo with – and heaven only knows what we will find when we get into Kosovo – to hear those is either to awaken our conscience and make us act or is to say we have no conscience and no will to act in the face of something which is appalling and wrong . . . a whole people, displaced and dispossessed simply because of their ethnic identity. My generation never

thought we'd see these scenes in Europe again. Our task is very simple.
Our will in seeing it through is total.[17]

As for Milošević: 'It is very simple, we carry on until he steps
down.' This was a Freudian slip by Blair: the removal of Milošević
had never been among NATO's stated objectives. Campbell subsequently explained that the Prime Minister had mis-spoken. He
meant to say 'backs down'.

The visit had much more than a rhetorical purpose. Blair needed
to have two significant conversations at NATO headquarters. One
was with the Supreme Allied Commander in Europe, Wesley
Clark. Silver-haired, wiry-framed and tautly strung, Clark had
fought in Vietnam, though only briefly. As they talked in Clark's
wood-panelled office at SHAPE in Mons, Blair asked him: 'You
realise how much is at stake? You are in this thing to win?' Clark
replied: 'Are you?' He knew this was 'do or die' for NATO, and
for his own military reputation. It was already being whispered that
he was losing the confidence of the White House. Part of Blair's
purpose was to bolster the commander. He told Clark: 'We are
backing you all the way.' Part of Clark's purpose was to recruit
Blair as an ally for ratcheting up the war. The air campaign was not
working: there were now more Serbs in Kosovo than when the
bombing began. Clark was wrestling against the restraints imposed
by the politicians. Bombing missions were being aborted in flight
when national representatives ran in to stop them. President Chirac
had demanded that a French general be put into Clark's office with
a veto over targets. Blair was horrified to learn that targets had to
be approved by a committee of the nineteen. 'You can't run a war
like this,' he complained to one aide afterwards.

Clark wanted Blair to push for an intensification of the air
campaign and join him in trying to open the White House's mind
to planning for troops. That had become Blair's view. It was shared
by Javier Solana, NATO's Secretary-General. The Spaniard had
almost as much invested in a successful outcome as the British
Prime Minister. It was Solana's idea – the previous autumn – that
NATO should be the instrument of chastisement against the Serbs.

Yet the political obstacles to introducing ground forces into the equation were as formidable as ever. Italy and Germany were against even talking about troops. Solana told Blair that he feared that the NATO summit in Washington at the end of the month would be wrecked by public arguments between Blair and Gerhard Schröder, the German Chancellor.

An idea developed that they would creep towards troops by blurring the difference between soldiers as peace-keepers and as war-makers. It would be suggested that ground forces could be deployed into 'a semi-permissive environment'.

At Question Time in the Commons the following day, Blair gave a public hint of how dramatically he had changed his mind in less than a month. He told MPs: 'The difficulties of a land force invasion of Kosovo against an undegraded Serb military machine are formidable,' but he was no longer ruling out the use of troops. Several times, Blair said: 'Milošević does not have a veto on NATO action. All options are always kept under review.'[18] Robin Cook was adjusting the Foreign Office's line. He now said it was 'possible to conceive of circumstances in which it may be feasible to commit ground troops'.[19]

Nothing was possible without the Americans. Tony Blair thought, as have so many British Prime Ministers before him, that he enjoyed a special relationship with the President of the United States. There was a personally easy chemistry and a similar outlook. To Blair and those around him, Clinton had been an example and an inspiration. Campbell, watching Clinton perform alongside Blair on one occasion, turned to a journalist and said: 'I wish I could get my guy to do that.' Blair's very private tribute to Clinton's political guiles was to joke: 'Bill gives great blow.'[20] Since the election, Blair had handsomely paid off any debts he might owe to Clinton by offering himself as a supportive figleaf for the morally denuded American President. Blair was virtually alone in defending Clinton when the American President bombed Sudan at a time when his action was widely seen as an attempted distraction from the Lewinsky impeachment. When the total and tawdry seediness of his mendacities was finally exposed, and even Hillary Clinton was attacking her husband, Blair flew to the side of 'my friend' in the Oval Office. Though he offered himself as a body shield to Clinton in public, Blair now appreciated the character flaws in the man he had regarded as a mentor in power.

Clinton was politically and emotionally desiccated by the Lewinsky saga. Deferential to the American President at the outset of the conflict, Blair had found him frustratingly unfocused, frequently confused, and fixated with American public opinion. When Blair tried to get Clinton to think about what they would do if the air campaign failed, Clinton kept replying: 'We keep on bombing. We can bomb for ever.'[21]

As a Boeing 747 flew Prime Minister, Foreign Secretary and Defence Secretary across the Atlantic for the NATO summit, Blair knew two things from his previous conversations with Clinton. It was going to be a struggle to get 'my buddy Bill', as he had sardonically taken to calling him, to engage on the subject of ground troops. He nevertheless had to try.

The moment they touched down at Andrews air force base on the evening of Wednesday 21 April, Blair and British officials were whisked in a convoy of limousines to two hours of talks at the White House. Clinton invited Blair to begin by sharing with them an outline of the speech on international ethics he would later deliver in Chicago.

Madeleine Albright, the US Secretary of State, nodded vigorously at Blair's arguments for intervening when human rights were grossly violated. Her family had fled Czechoslovakia from the Nazis. This self-described 'child of Munich' was the administration's hawk. But Albright did not reflect the majority view within the White House. William Cohen, the Defense Secretary, believed that the use of US troops was 'an almost impossible sell' to an American public still haunted by its bloody embroilment in Vietnam. Blair recognised that 'Kosovo is a long way from Kansas.' Nevertheless they needed to start thinking about troops. He tried to persuade the sceptical Americans by pitching it positively. Troops would be needed to police a settlement. They should be readying themselves for that. They needed 'to start planning for success'.

Listening, but not agreeing, was Sandy Berger, Clinton's national security adviser. He was hardest with Blair. Talk of committing troops would be read as a sign that the air campaign had failed, countered Berger. The Pentagon view was that it could still work. As for this British notion of a 'semi-permissive' battlefield, Berger did not recognise the concept. There was no such thing as a 'half-fight'. 'I'm worried about the Russians,' said Clinton. Talk of troops would inflame Moscow. They needed Boris Yeltsin to broker a deal with the Serbs. This was a genuine concern, but Clinton's greatest fright was risking the lives of American soldiers. 'You've got to understand my difficulties, Tony,' he said. Torn between his advisers, muddled within himself, Clinton gave little hope to the British Prime Minister.

Blair came away depressed by the encounter at the White House. There was more discouraging news from Guthrie, who had gone to the Pentagon to try to open minds there. He had been rebuffed, politely but firmly.

The following night, the American President hosted a banquet for NATO, originally intended as a fiftieth birthday celebration, now a sombre feast of war. The dinner was mainly memorable because the drinking water tasted as if it had been drained from a swimming pool. The banqueters finished at eleven, and Clinton and Blair, Hillary and Cherie, retreated to the Clintons' private quarters to talk into the early hours of the morning. On his visits to the White House, Blair was always surprised by how much time Clinton could find just to sit around watching videos, drinking beer and shooting the breeze. Alone with Blair, away from the company of his advisers, Clinton emitted more encouraging signals. 'What's the bottom line?' asked Blair. 'The bottom line is this. We have to see this thing through. Milošević has to know that we will do whatever it takes to win.' Clinton replied: 'Whatever it takes, whatever it takes. We will not lose.'

Could Blair be sure that the American meant this? Was it merely a demonstration of Clinton's talent for giving 'great blow'? Blair afterwards confessed to one aide that he still had 'no idea' whether Clinton would really commit to ground troops.

Blair's growing frustration with the vacillating American was reciprocated by Clinton's mounting irritation with the adulatory media Blair received in the United States, much of it at the President's expense. The morning after their talks at the White House, the conservative *Wall Street Journal* acclaimed Blair for pressing firmness on 'a reluctant White House'.[22] The liberal *New York Times* dubbed him 'King Tony'. The *Los Angeles Times* reported that 'Britain's Prime Minister is emerging as the alliance's most outspoken hawk.'[23] Blair's appearances on *Larry King Live*, *Meet The Press* and other prestigious current affairs TV shows won the glowing approbation of Republicans, including the presidential-aspirant John McCain. Clinton's political opponents relished making a contrast between the waffling prevarications of the American President and the vigour of the purposeful-sounding British leader.

The White House was annoyed. Clinton's aides mocked Blair's 'Churchillian tone'. The Winstonesque pose played well with Blair's audience back in Britain, which was the principal concern of his press secretary. But Blair was beginning to worry about the consequences of shaming Clinton. On the flight to Chicago, Blair and Campbell squabbled. An interview had been arranged with the BBC's Jon Sopel. Campbell suggested to the reporter that he should ask about troops. Blair, anxious not to further aggravate Clinton, interjected: 'Do we have to?' Campbell argued that it was 'the only issue in town', adding: 'You don't have to answer it, but the question has to be asked.' The question was asked; Blair didn't answer it.

At Chicago's Hilton Hotel, Blair laid out his new 'doctrine of the international community', his most serious effort in the course of the conflict to provide the moral reasoning behind the NATO action. 'This is a just war, based not on any territorial ambitions but on values,' said Blair. The practical arguments were threefold. In an interdependent world, we could not afford to 'turn our backs on conflicts and violations of human rights' with consequences which would spill across borders. In the specific case of Milošević, not acting now would only mean spending 'infinitely more blood and treasure to stop him later'. Thirdly, there was the deterrent effect. Were NATO to fail, other dictators would be encouraged to doubt 'our resolve'. These were essentially contentions of enlightened self-interest. He turned to the ethical foundation for the action. The international community could not regard 'acts of genocide' as a 'purely internal matter'.[24] The inviolability of national sovereignty, the doctrine of the United Nations since its creation, was overturned by this new Blair doctrine that, in extreme cases of the violation of human rights, there was both an obligation and a right to intervene. No other leader in the alliance delivered such a clear and cogent justification for NATO's action.

The fine phraseology of the theory couldn't but jar with the increasingly crude conduct of the war. To coincide with the summit, Wesley Clark arranged a display of fireworks in Belgrade, including the headline-grabbing but militarily valueless destruction of Milošević's party headquarters and one of his homes. In the early hours of the following day, the headquarters of Serbian television was bombed. Sixteen Yugoslavs died. Blair, on the advice of government lawyers that this could be considered a breach of the Geneva Conventions, had not allowed the participation of British aircraft. But for some weeks beforehand he had been arguing within NATO for attacks on what he called the Serb 'propaganda machine'. The morality of killing young technicians and a female make-up artist was hard to locate. The just cause was looking dirty. And incompetent: Serb TV was back on the air in an hour.

For a nineteen-country alliance, prosecuting a conflict for which its members had wildly varying degrees of enthusiasm, the summiteers achieved a creditable semblance of unity in public. Their closed sessions exposed the divisions and indecision. General Naumman briefed Blair and the other leaders about the time-scale involved and the numbers required if troops were to be deployed. Wesley Clark undermined the case by putting a bullish gloss on the air campaign. At his briefing for the leaders, Clark gave the impression that the air strikes were being hugely successful. The Danube was choked with wrecked bridges. Belgrade was being bombed into rubble. Clark painted a picture of Serb forces in

Kosovo that were cut off from supplies, throttled of fuel, and incapable of moving about in daylight. This was eagerly seized upon by the Americans, who wanted to give the air campaign more time to work, and by those European countries hoping to extricate themselves through a compromise with Milošević mediated by the Russians.

Blair made little progress pushing for troops. Gerhard Schröder was flatly opposed, not least because of the risk of collapsing his Social Democrat–Green coalition government. Schröder told Blair that the British 'liked fighting' but since 1945 the Germans had become 'fundamentally pacifist'. As far as Schröder was concerned, troops were 'not on the table'. Blair was refused by the Americans and rejected by the Germans. His isolation was confirmed by NATO officials: 'There is only one person arguing for ground troops and that is Tony Blair.'[25]

The Washington summit was a failure for the British. The best that Solana could broker was a 'review' of all military options. Worse, the end-of-summit statement offered to stop bombing once Belgrade had 'begun to withdraw its troops': a defeat for Blair who had argued that the condition should be total retreat by the Serbs. Clinton flaked under pressure. Stung by questioning at the final press conference about what would happen if Milošević was not broken by air strikes, Clinton fled back to the White House at such furious speed that he left behind the military officer who is always supposed to be at an American President's side with the 'football' to launch a nuclear strike.

Tony Blair returned from the NATO summit feeling bleak. 'Nothing has been resolved,' he despaired to one aide.[26] He was fearful that he had strutted too hawkishly in Washington. 'I've gone at it too hard,' he confided to a close friend back in London. By 'upstaging' Clinton, he had made the President look 'weak' and the situation 'worse'. Clinton would be 'even more reluctant' to make a commitment to troops because it would look as if he had been 'bounced by me'.[27]

Confirming Blair's anxieties about him, the President began grasping after anything that might provide a fire escape from the conflict. In early May he commended 'Mr Milošević' – unlike Blair, he gave the Serb dictator the honorific – for freeing three US servicemen who had been snatched a month earlier. Clinton suggested that the Serbs had only to begin withdrawing for there to be 'a pause' in the bombing, a rupture with the British line which provoked heated traffic between Downing Street and the White House. An increasingly fraught Blair worried that these signals of appeasement would only encourage Milošević to believe that NATO's resolve was weakening.

The Serbian dictator was calculating that Western public opinion, consuming the conflict through television, would not long tolerate a blundering war inflicting casualties upon civilians. In an attempt to re-dramatise the suffering of the refugees, on the first Monday in May, the 3rd, Blair became the first Western leader to fly out to the Kosovo borders. Anji Hunter had preceded him on a preparatory mission ten days beforehand.[28] The Prime Minister's special assistant told General Jackson and his officers that Downing Street needed pictures of Blair with the British soldiers and the refugees. They wanted to emphasise both the martial and the humanitarian aspects of the Christian soldier of Number 10. 'We want the Prime Minister as close to the border as possible,' Hunter informed Jackson's staff. She prepared the ground well. For its propaganda value, the visit could not have paid a larger dividend. The Prime Minister and his wife were greeted with chants of 'To-nee! To-nee!' Then the enormity of the human catastrophe hit Blair and Cherie. More than 1,000 tents were spread out before them on a disused aerodrome. Each tent was emergency shelter for up to 100 Kosovars, living on bread, tinned fish and fruit. Twenty-eight thousand victims of Milošević's ethnic cleansing were here, and more were coming over the border at the rate of 5,000 a day.

The Blairs were shown to Tent 230B to meet the family of Susana Nazifi, a twenty-two-year-old English student from Priština, who gave them an eye-witness account of a man being shot by the Serb police. She had, of course, been selected because she had a harrowing story to tell and could do so in good English. Her mother, Fahrie, explained that they had been driven from their home by the Serb paramilitary police. As the woman described how Milošević's thugs stabbed her son in the stomach, Cherie put an arm around her shoulders. The quotes the two women offered to British reporters were more affecting than anything manufactured by spin doctors. 'They were upset,' said Susana. 'I saw it in their eyes. Cherie took my hand and said: "I hope everything is fine for you." '[29] Fahrie added: 'I think Tony Blair is the best. He is going to help us. He cares about the refugees.'[30] On emerging from the tent, Cherie shed genuine tears. They would weep across the news bulletins and the front pages.

'This is not a battle for NATO. This is not a battle for territory. It is a battle for humanity,' Blair declared. 'It is a just cause.'[31]

The visit indelibly marked how Blair had been changed by the course of the war. The reluctant, apprehensive warrior when the conflict began was now the most coldly determined and passionately expressed of the allied leaders to prosecute it to success, even in the face of colossal military and political risks. Blair travelled ideologically light, but certain convictions went very deep. His Christianity was an important driver. He often carried a Bible with him on trips abroad, though he never read it in front of Campbell who derived a strange pleasure from privately mocking Blair about the Prime Minister's faith. So was his profound and genuine detestation for the barbarity Milošević was inflicting on the Kosovars. Whatever residual doubts Blair might have had were erased from his mind by what he saw at Bradze on the Kosovo–Macedonia border. Out in no man's land, there were 10,000 people who had arrived overnight. The very old, the sick and disabled, newborns in their mothers' arms, all cowered in the blistering heat. Wiping angry sweat from his brow and lip, Blair was steaming: 'This is obscene. It's criminal. Just criminal. How can anyone think we shouldn't be stopping this?'

The justice of the cause was not being matched by the means to guarantee its success. Blair needed to hear, at first hand, from the commander on the ground. The Prime Minister, General Guthrie and General Mike Jackson met to talk about the war. They shaded themselves from the heat – and hid from the probing eyes of reporters and lenses – under camouflage netting on the military training ground. Jackson opened the hour-long discussion by addressing the problem of the refugees. Aid workers had already warned Blair that the lack of sanitation threatened an outbreak of cholera. That, said Jackson, was nothing compared with 'the nightmare' that would confront them if the refugees were still encamped on the border by winter. Winter in the Balkans 'came early', around mid-October. He and Guthrie worked backwards from there. Assume it would take a month to get the refugees back into their homes. Then, optimistically, estimate that it would take another month to clear Kosovo of Serb forces. Add in the six, probably eight weeks required to assemble sufficient allied troops to defeat Milošević's army. That led to the conclusion that the very latest time to make a decision to commit ground troops was mid-June, barely more than a month away. The soldiers were asked by Blair: 'What about casualties?' How many British troops might die? The wily Guthrie wasn't prepared, or thought it unwise, to offer a prediction. He and Jackson were both alarmed by the talk of a 'semi-permissive' environment. The soldiers feared it meant that the politicians would send too small a force for the task. The larger the number of men, said Guthrie, the lesser the risk. Jackson was more explicit about the casualties: 'You are probably looking at somewhere in the order of the Falklands.' Blair nodded, and fell pensively silent as the soldiers watched him absorb the enormity and the hazards of his situation. Casting the two generals a rueful look, Blair eventually said: 'I never thought I'd be in this position.'[32]

The real victor of the NATO summit was the American air force. Wesley Clark and Mike Short had finally won their argument that success was being limited by the shackles imposed upon them by political nervousness of casualties, a contention General Short had reinforced with several threats to resign. Whether this was true or not – it served as a useful excuse for the military's own failings – the politicians were now groping for anything which might offer a breakthrough. They conceded to the military's urge to 'go down-town' and blitz Belgrade. Dr Strangelove was given his head. He was allowed to target power supplies and other civilian structures which Blair had initially recoiled from attacking for fear of 'killing babies'. At the outset of the war, Blair wanted to know where each individual Harrier and Tornado was going. He insisted on personally vetting any targets that might risk civilian casualties. According to RAF officers, when the daily plans came in, they were immediately taken round to Number 10 for Blair's 'blessing'. As the conflict endured, this task had been delegated to the Defence Secretary who had, in turn, passed it further down the chain. By early May, George Robertson was asking to see only highly sensitive targets. The British politicians had surrendered virtually all control over the air campaign. Not that, since it was so predominantly waged by the Americans, they ever had that much command over the bombing. Clark circumvented NATO's systems of restraint by excluding other nations from decisions about sorties involving only American planes. The Americans had their own targeting team, separate from the NATO operation. Even the British – in theory Washington's most trusted and reliable ally – were not being given comprehensive information about US plans. The conflict had switched to American auto-pilot. This was about to prove an extremely unreliable mechanism.

On 7 May, a B2 'Spirit' stealth bomber, the most expensive war machine on the planet, took off from its base in Missouri to make the fifteen-hour flight to Belgrade. As the American aircraft ploughed above the clouds, George Robertson was not at Winston Churchill's desk in the Ministry of Defence. In the middle of the war, the British Defence Secretary had found time to join the election campaign for the Scottish Parliament. As Robertson pressed the flesh, the B2 opened its black belly over the Adriatic to disgorge the Joint Defence Air Munition, the most sophisticated flying bomb possessed by the American air force. A few minutes before midnight in Belgrade, the bomb struck Number 3 Cherry Blossom Street and demolished the southern wing of the embassy of the People's Republic of China.

The first Robertson heard about this catastrophe was on his car radio. 'Oh shit,' he shouted to himself. Once Robertson had got on to a secure line to Washington, the American Defense Secretary gave him the official explanation. Robertson was told by William Cohen that they had planned to hit the Hotel Yugoslavia, a base for the war criminal, Arkan. That had been achieved, though they had missed Arkan himself, who would soon turn up on Serb TV gloating at NATO. The Americans also targeted the Federal Palace being used as the headquarters of the Serbian arms agency. The CIA, using out-of-date maps, had instead directed bombs at one of the most sensitive buildings in Belgrade: the embassy of a member of the UN Security Council and a nuclear power. It was incredible, Cohen confessed to Robertson, but true. Another theory would surface later. The Americans, far from making a mistake, had deliberately struck the embassy because it was being used by the Serbs to communicate with their death squads in Kosovo.[33]

Mistake or deliberate, hitting the Chinese embassy was a diplomatic disaster. Robin Cook was in Edinburgh. The Foreign Secretary's war had been a rehabilitation for his mauled reputation. The daily 'Quint' calls between Cook and his American, French, German and Italian counterparts were instrumental in maintaining a face of unity for NATO. The day before, Cook had been buoyant after helping to secure the Russians behind terms which included the withdrawal of Serb forces. Now, he was preparing for a visit from the Russian Foreign Minister, Igor Ivanov. Cook planned to take him to the opera to see *Aida* and – Igor liked a drink – lubricate the diplomacy with a call on the Scotch Whisky Association. This was part of a charm offensive to induce Russian and Chinese support for a UN Security Council resolution authorising an international force into Kosovo. All that diplomacy was derailed in the rubble of the embassy.

At seven that morning, as he showered in his Edinburgh flat, Cook was called from his ablutions by the phone. 'Ivanov has cancelled,' his Private Secretary, Tim Barrow, informed the Foreign Secretary. 'Why?' asked Cook. Barrow: 'Because we've bombed the Chinese embassy.' Remarking that 'this is not the best start to the day of my life', Cook consoled himself that 'at least I won't have to appear on *Today* any more'. He was wrong. 'Number 10 is keen for you to do *Today*,' replied Barrow, 'and explain how it happened.' Given that he had not a clue how it happened, Cook did a manful job defending NATO that morning.

From Chequers, down a secure line to the British ambassador in Beijing, Blair dictated an apology to the Chinese premier. NATO's mistakes were multiplying alarmingly. The same day, an American cluster bomb, supposed to hit an airfield, instead exploded over a crowded outdoor market in the southern Serbian city of Niš, killing at least sixty people.

Bill Clinton was aboard Air Force One that weekend when he was connected with the British Prime Minister. Blair told his irresolute partner that the Chinese embassy bombing had re-emphasised the dangers of the air war. The media was overcome with 'refugee fatigue' – a criticism Blair would make public in a speech to the Newspaper Society – while forensically dissecting NATO's mistakes. Blair worried that the more errors there were, the more likely NATO's fragile coalition was to fracture. He again pressed Clinton to start preparing for a ground war.

During their conversations, Blair tried a variety of levers on the American President. Knowing Clinton to be obsessed with his place in history, he pressed him to think of his 'legacy', the unspoken implication being that the stains of Lewinsky might be erased if Clinton did the honourable thing in Kosovo. He attempted to get the American engaged by urging that their 'focus' had to be on winning. Could not Clinton at least order the Pentagon, as Blair had already authorised the Ministry of Defence, to do some secret planning for ground troops? Clinton was frightened: 'It will leak.' Then what would happen? The less committed Europeans might pull out. He'd be toast in Congress.

Blair's exasperation with Clinton was the more intense because it was accompanied by disillusionment. 'The scales fell from Blair's eyes about Clinton,' according to a senior military officer.[34] That is confirmed by one of Blair's oldest friends: 'Tony thought Clinton was clever. Always before, he seemed so analytical and logical when addressing problems. Tony despaired at Clinton's failure to get focused. Tony was deeply frustrated.'[35]

The heart of the problem was that Clinton was terrified of American public opinion, which the White House was polling daily. There was a blackly comic side to this. At Clinton's feet had New Labour been tutored in the use of polling to give the people what pleased them. His ability to flex to the public mood had been as admired by New Labour as it had been aped. Now, Tony Blair was confronted with the limits of governing by opinion poll. He was doing some polling himself. Philip Gould was sampling public opinion to divine how the conflict was playing with the British electorate. But even the focus group guru regarded his results as of dubious value. 'Ignore it,' Gould advised Blair. 'The only important thing is to win.' The British public would tolerate anything except a defeat.

As May ground on, victory remained elusive. Those who had opposed the war from the outset combined with those who had always maintained it could never be won from the air to declare their opinions vindicated by NATO's manifest failings. The Conservatives, whose attitude was opportunistic and animated by a craving to see Blair humiliated, were emboldened to become openly critical. 'The action is being made up as we go along,' mocked the Shadow Foreign Secretary, Michael Howard.[36] Martin Bell, the BBC war correspondent turned MP, scornfully observed that 'the greatest military alliance in the world is becoming the gang that cannot shoot straight'.[37] As if to prove him right, NATO bombs killed more than eighty Kosovars in the village of Korisa. A steelier carapace had grown around Blair. The man initially terrified of civilian casualties began to sound dismissive of NATO's errors, saying: 'Mistakes will happen from time to time.'[38]

Blair had never been so isolated and exposed. At one meeting, Sir Richard Wilson felt it necessary to caution the Prime Minister that the conflict could go 'badly wrong' and Blair had placed himself in 'a very dangerous' position.[39] The Cabinet Secretary was correct. NATO was being used for a purpose for which it had never been designed, and the war was turning into a catalogue of terrible errors. Blair had completely identified himself in the media and the public mind with the successful prosecution of the cause. He would pay a vast penalty for failure. Wilson intimated to another senior official that he feared it might even destroy Blair's premiership.[40] Blair thought so himself, telling his confidants: 'This could be the end of me.'

Something approaching terror gripped Number 10. Blair's aides discussed among themselves whether the enterprise was a huge miscalculation by the Prime Minister. David Miliband 'never took a vote', according to members of the Policy Unit, but when they talked about it, a majority of Blair's personal staff feared that he was plunging headlong over a cliff. The Cabinet, which was being informed about the conflict only on an irregular and unspecific basis, kept their heads below the parapet. Apart from Cook and Robertson – whose own reputations were invested in a successful outcome – other senior ministers were conspicuously mute. John Prescott's contribution was to stand in for Blair at Question Time and reduce the Commons to laughter with his excruciating inability to pronounce 'Milošević' correctly. Gordon Brown disappeared below sea level. When asked, in private, what he thought, the Chancellor confined himself to saying: 'We must assume Tony knows what he is doing.' It was an illustration of the thinness of ministerial solidarity that Clare Short, previously held in low regard, was now accorded war heroine status at Number 10. 'She's being fantastic,' Blair told aides after her belligerent comparisons of opponents of the war with the appeasers of Adolf Hitler.[41]

A siege mentality seized Blair's immediate entourage. Alastair Campbell kept bulging files of press cuttings from which he calculated that eight out of ten newspaper commentaries were hostile to the war. The press secretary briefed against John Simpson, the highly regarded BBC correspondent, for accurately reporting from Belgrade that the bombing had solidified support for the Milošević regime. Under duress, Campbell wrote a letter of semi-regret. It was entirely insincere. He continued to fulminate against the media. Anji Hunter would seek out journalists who had written critically and shout at them to 'show some patriotism'. Had Hunter possessed a stock of white feathers, she would undoubtedly have handed them out to these faint-hearts. The right-wing press was erratic, while left and liberal newspapers were broadly supportive. This railing against the media spoke to the emotional wroughtness inside Number 10.

Blair himself 'never wavered once', according to someone very close to him.[42] Officials and aides pressed him to prepare exit strategies, to give himself enough room in his statements to leave a way out. To their high alarm, he refused. 'This is shit or bust,' replied Blair.

The spectrum of critics of the war ranged from Tony Benn, the veteran peacenik of the left, to Denis Healey, grand old man of the Labour right and former Labour Defence Secretary, to General Sir Peter de la Billière, the former commander in the Gulf, to General Sir Michael Rose, the former commander in Bosnia, to Peter Carrington, the former NATO Secretary-General. The opposition of Benn was expected and dismissed. Blair stopped talking to Roy Jenkins. He knew his favourite uncle was cool about the war. What most angered him was the rising rumble from the ranks of the military, political, diplomatic and civil servant elders, active and retired, that he was a reckless amateur who had blundered into a suicidal adventure. Around Whitehall and Westminster, there was talk of Kosovo being his Suez. Blair blew up with one confidant: 'The Establishment! The bloody Establishment! What would they have done?'[43]

Stranded on a limb, he went out further still. In too far to retreat, he advanced deeper. To the heaps of uncompromising rhetoric, he piled on more. 'There are no half-measures to Milošević's brutality. There can be no half-measures about how we deal with it. No compromise, no fudge, no half-baked deals,' he declared during a trip to Germany in mid-May.

We are not talking here about some faraway place of which we know little. We are talking about the doorstep of the European Union, our own backyard. Women raped. Children seeing their fathers dragged away to be shot. Thousands executed, tens of thousands beaten, 100,000 men missing. One and a half million people driven from their homes . . . A just war against the most evil form of genocide since my father's generation defeated the Nazis.[44]

A few days later, in Henry V mode, he dropped his heaviest hint that he was prepared to commit troops to expel the Serbs from Kosovo: 'Whatever it takes, we must succeed.'[45] Visiting a refugee camp Blair offered himself as an incarnation of Moses: 'Our promise to all of you is that you shall return in peace to the land that is yours.'[46]

Delivery of that promise — a promise none of NATO's other leaders was willing to make — appeared to be as distant as ever. The claims made for the bombing campaign were increasingly threadbare when even General Short was forced to admit that Serb air defences had not been 'properly suppressed'.[47] The Apache ground-attack helicopters, introduced with great theatricality at the time of the NATO summit, proved to be an empty gesture. When not crashing during training flights, they fired nothing more lethal at the Serbs than leaflets. General Guthrie's view — which he made plain to Blair — was that the Serbs were overrated as soldiers and could be beaten in a summer campaign. Only, however, as long as they mustered sufficient forces. 'You can't have a semi-invasion,' Guthrie cautioned Blair. Admiral Sir Ian Garnett, the Chief of Joint Operations, was another warning voice to Blair about the hazards of delay. They had to be in there before the winter. 'You don't want to be wading through snowdrifts if you are into street fighting.'[48] General Jackson went public about the urgency of the crisis: 'We haven't got long.'[49]

On 17 May, Robin Cook flew to Brussels to press the British argument that soldiers could be put into Kosovo without a peace agreement if the Serbian forces were sufficiently shattered. He encountered instant resistance from the Italian Prime Minister, Massimo D'Alema, who was again talking up the possibility of pausing the bombing, and from the German Chancellor, Gerhard Schröder. After a meeting with the Italian the next day, Schröder publicly declared, to British consternation, that any talk of ground troops was 'unthinkable'. The American polls which so mesmerised the White House were showing shrivelling support for the air campaign, a majority against the use of troops and a majority in favour of negotiating a deal with the Serbs. Clinton, desperate for an easy exit, was thrashing around for precisely the half-baked fudge that had been inveighed against so passionately by Blair.

It was likely that a hint, if not the full measure, of the British Prime Minister's angst about the American President would eventually surface in the media. On the morning of 18 May, Clinton was shown a *New York Times* report about Downing Street's pressure for troop deployment. Clinton exploded into one of his legendary temper tantrums. Early in the afternoon – evening in London – he rang Blair to berate him. 'Get your people under control,' Clinton bellowed across the Atlantic. 'This briefing has got to stop.' He told Blair they could have their private debates but 'it isn't doing anybody any good' for their arguments to emerge in the media. This just played into the hands of Milošević. In public, they should be presenting 'a united face', said Clinton. 'I promise you,' replied Blair, 'there isn't any briefing by us.' This was true: Blair had always taken the view that, much though he despaired of the pusillanimous Clinton, it was counter-productive to expose the division between Downing Street and Oval Office. The American's temper subsided. The remainder of a ninety minute conversation was more measured and productive. 'We've got to get this sorted,' Blair contended, as he had argued so many times before. 'We can't let it drag on.' They had to 'focus' on bringing it to a successful conclusion. Blair, the flexi-pragmatist, had discovered his moral bottom line in the Balkans. What he could not be sure of by the end of this conversation was whether he had yet fathomed Clinton's. Blair did manage to get a promise that in a speech that evening the American President would say that 'no options' – code for troops – 'were off the table'.

But were they *on* the table? Clinton had finally allowed Wesley Clark to present his case for a ground invasion at the Pentagon, but the NATO commander came away without authorisation. In an attempt to mask the Anglo–American fracture, Robin Cook aborted a trip to Moscow and flew by Concorde to America. Over a crab-cake dinner in a Washington restaurant, Cook and Madeleine Albright constructed a unity line which they presented during a tour of American TV studios. This plastered over the split between London and Washington without resolving it. European leaders were becoming more vociferous in their hostility to using troops. The Italian Prime Minister was openly decrying planning for a ground invasion as 'a totally useless exercise'.[50]

In this context, Tony Blair took a neck-prickling gamble. Among the military options drawn up, there was 'Operation Bravo', the full-scale invasion of Serbia itself, and 'Bravo Minus', a ground offensive to expel Milošević's troops from Kosovo. In late May, Blair ordered the activation of 'B-Minus'. Guthrie and Robertson were working to assemble a 'coalition of the willing': NATO countries that would be prepared to join a land invasion. The largest element offered was from Britain. 'B-Minus' called for 50,000 British troops, the largest force assembled by Britain since 1945, effectively the entire combat army. So stretched was the army that the plan required 14,000 part-time reservists to be called up, the first compulsory mobilisation since the Second World War.[51] On 26 May, George Robertson revealed the first instalment by announcing to the Commons that an additional 12,000 personnel would be joining General Jackson's force, bringing the British contingent up to more than twice the level that had previously been described as the cap. That they included troops from the Parachute Regiment, the Gurkhas, the Royal Marine commandos and the Royal Irish Rangers, supported by helicopters and armour, was freighted with a significance no one could miss. Just in case anyone did, Blair indicated that these did not have to be peace-keepers. They could fight their way in. The announcement was designed to send messages east and west. To Milošević: one NATO country was serious about expelling him from Kosovo. To the Europeans and to Clinton: Britain was putting its men where its leader's mouth was.

The Prime Minister convinced himself that it had the desired effect. At the end of May, Clinton told him, with more conviction than before, that if a ground invasion was necessary 'it will be done'. Was Clinton serious? Was he yet again 'giving blow'? A large element of Blair's risk was that he still could not be really sure of Clinton. Cowed as ever by public opinion in the United States, the President had even refused to discuss the war with his own chiefs of staff. He didn't agree to a meeting until less than a fortnight before the deadline for a decision about a ground invasion. Clinton had written Blair a cheque. He still hadn't signed it.

Tony Blair had been at a summit in Berlin on the night that the 'three-day war' began. Seventy-two days later, on Wednesday 2 June, he was in Germany again, for a meeting of European leaders in Cologne. The Renaissance Hotel, the venue for their dinner, seemed particularly inaptly named. The guerrillas of the Kosovo Liberation Army were harrying Serb units. Anti-war protesters had appeared on the streets in Serbia, and the bombing was hurting the assets of cronies of Milošević's regime. Viktor Chernomyrdin, Moscow's envoy, and President Martii Ahtisaari of Finland were on a mission to Belgrade with a joint demand from NATO and Russia for Milošević to withdraw all his troops from Kosovo. But there was no one at that dinner of European leaders who expected Milošević to crumble immediately. 'It was like an avalanche,' according to Cook. 'The snow was on the edge of the precipice. It was a question of whether it would be a matter of two months or two days before it fell.'[52] NATO did not have two months. It had a week to decide about a ground invasion, and the divisions within the alliance were as great as they were becoming more public.

Blair packed the quasi-regimental tie he wore for his television broadcast in the first week of the conflict. It was around his neck at lunchtime the following day as he posed for a strained family photograph with his European counterparts on the steps of Cologne's Festival Hall. As the group broke up, Blair was intercepted by Alastair Campbell. His mobile had just rung with information that was as sensational as it was unanticipated. Reuters was reporting that the Serbian Parliament had that morning accepted NATO's demands. Cook's avalanche appeared to have crashed, just in time. Or had it? Blair was wary that this was another in a long line of feints by Milošević — the Serbian dictator's latest ruse to split Nato. He went into a quick huddle with the Foreign Secretary. Before the Italians and the Germans could seize on this to argue for a stop to the bombing, Robin Cook was on the airwaves demanding that they first receive verification of Miloševi-ić's intentions. When the German Foreign Minister, Joschka Fischer, produced champagne for his colleagues, Cook diluted his fizz with orange juice, declaring that he would only quaff champagne neat when the first Kosovar refugee crossed back over the border.

That caution was merited. One and a half days of negotiations between General Jackson and Milošević's commanders broke up over the Serbs' insistence on keeping troops in Kosovo. Only after forty-eight hours of further bombing did Milošević send his generals back to sign an agreement on Wednesday 9 June. News of the treaty signed in Jackson's tent reached the Prime Minister as he was having dinner at Number 10 with David Blunkett. Blair's first call was to Campbell. 'I shouldn't do a Thatcher,' said Blair. The country was not in a mood to hear the Prime Minister proclaiming: 'Rejoice! Rejoice!' Then Blair talked to Robertson about the late-night statement the Defence Secretary would deliver to the Commons.

The war was hell; the peace was remote from paradise. 'I feel no sense of triumph. We end it with no sense of rejoicing,' said Blair outside Number 10 the following morning.

Nothing we say or do can compensate for the loss of loved ones killed in this conflict. But we can say they did not die in vain. War is never civilised. The innocent die as well as the guilty. But war can be necessary to uphold civilisation. Good has triumphed over evil. Justice has overcome barbarism. And the values of civilisation have prevailed.[53]

The Kosovo conflict was a perilously close run thing. The war that was supposed to last seventy-two hours had taken seventy-eight days, not least because of military errors and political miscalculations by NATO. Around five hundred Serb soldiers had been killed for the accidental loss of just two allied pilots. That was a soldier-pleasing statistic. None of the other numbers could comfort anyone. Thousands of civilians were dead. One and a half million Kosovars had been driven from their homes. The cost of reconstructing the Balkans was put at over £20 billion.[54] Kosovo would effectively be a NATO protectorate into foreseeable time.

To all that tragedy was added an epilogue that teetered between the farcical and the dangerous. General Jackson now had nine battalions under his command, four of them from Britain, a demonstration of the size of the British commitment compared with any of the other allies'. He was ready to begin 'Operation Agricola', the liberation of Kosovo, at dawn on 11 June. Then, Jackson received an order from Wesley Clark to delay for twenty-four hours. The ineffable Clinton wanted US marines, at that moment sunning themselves on a tourist beach in Greece, in the vanguard of the liberation forces. Into this vacuum, the Russians swooped. Three hundred of their troops in Bosnia motored south to snatch Priština airport. Clark was now on to Jackson with a 'warning order' to send airborne troops to seize control of the airport from the Russians. The American four-star general out-ranked the three-star Brit. But the proposition that he should confront – even fight – the Russians struck Jackson as madness. He got on his satellite phone to London to talk to Guthrie. Sharing Jackson's extreme nervousness at the prospect of hostilities with Russia, Guthrie raised the alarm with Blair who agreed they were 'not about to start World War Three'. Cook and Robertson concurred that they needed to undramatise the situation. Five hours later, Jackson told his men to stand down. Clark was prevented from giving the 'executive order' that would have implemented his hazardous plan. George Robertson rang the American commander to tell him that if he issued the order, the British would veto it.[55] Blair had been as solid in restraining American rashness at the end of the conflict as he had been firm in buttressing NATO's resolve during the war.

As they began rolling into Kosovo on Saturday 12 June, British troops uncovered the failure of the bombing to destroy Milošević's forces on the ground. According to a British senior officer: 'When we got into the place, it was not littered with knackered T-55s.'[56] That was also obvious from the columns of withdrawing Serb tanks carrying sunglassed soldiers giving the finger to Western TV crews.

Then the liberating forces began to unearth evidence to support the refugees' stories of the multiple and horrifying atrocities perpetrated by Milošević's killers.

Would Milošević have completed his 'final solution' for Kosovo without the role played by the British Prime Minister? While other Western leaders spoke with weaselly equivocation, Blair clearly articulated the ethical basis for NATO's action, and was the least flinching in pressing it to victory. When other members of the alliance scrambled to find escapes from the commitment to the Kosovars, Blair sought to deliver the West's pledges. He had been as wrong as the rest of NATO's leaders to rule out ground troops at the beginning, but takes credit for being the first of them to recognise the gravity of that mistake. The threat of a ground invasion – a menace made most real by Britain and by Blair – was surely crucial in forcing Milošević to surrender.

This was a 'tempering experience' for Tony Blair.[57] He learned that the judgement of mentors in the White House and professionals in Whitehall was not to be relied on. He had to make his own decisions. Blair invested great emotional and political capital in the enterprise and would have paid massively in both for failure. A man most often portrayed as a skilful opportunist exposed the moral, stubborn, zealous dimensions of his character. He took a stance and, as others scurried for cover, he held to it.

That was most recognised by the Kosovars themselves. There was a tumultuous welcome for the British Prime Minister when he visited the liberated Priština at the end of July. It was a British Christian whom Albanian Muslims thanked for their salvation.

# 15. Scars on My Back

Shattered by the war, Tony Blair saw no reason to stay up for the results of an election he could no longer influence. He went to bed at ten thirty on the night of Sunday 13 June. The Prime Minister woke up to the worst performance by the party since it was led by Michael Foot, the donkey jacketed embodiment of Old Labour's electoral disasters. The official reaction from the government to its defeat in the 1999 election to the European Parliament, and the setbacks of May's elections, was to blame the pitiful turn-out. John Prescott claimed it reflected 'a culture of contentment'. This suggestion that the electorate was so paralysed by delight with its rulers that voters could not summon up the energy to get to a polling station was unconvincing. The Deputy Prime Minister didn't really believe that was the explanation. Tony Blair knew it wasn't.

There were no victory laurels for Kosovo from the voters. During the war, Philip Gould reported to Blair that the conflict was hurting him on the home front. There was 'no public acclaim' for Blair's steadfastness. The reverse was the case. People 'saw in you a passion for the war' which they didn't see demonstrated for their domestic concerns, Gould told Blair. The voters were complaining that they were 'neglected' by the Prime Minister. The verve and dedication he displayed in the Balkans actually annoyed them. People didn't want Kosovo sorted; they wanted 'their country fixed'.[1] The post-mortem into the election reverses by Greg Cook, the in-house pollster at Millbank, added weight to this thesis. He concluded that there was 'alarming' evidence of 'discernible disappointment amongst sections of Labour voters at what they see as the slow pace of change'.[2]

This was ironic. By the summer of 1999, there was no one in the country more exasperated by the government's lack of progress, and his own inability to hasten the pace, than Tony Blair. Since

January he had been obsessing to officials and aides about making 1999 'the year of delivery'.

He entered Number 10 believing that the command and control systems which he imposed on his party in Opposition were the model for governing the country. Blair was now making the rude discovery that there were limits to prime ministerial power. It was not for want of trying to extend it. Units, task forces and review groups, commissars of modernisation on every subject from silicon breast implants to social exclusion, proliferated.[3] To tackle what the Cabinet Secretary liked to call 'wicked issues', such as drugs and cancer, Blair was crowning more 'Tsars' than all the Russias. The government had more targets – over 6,000 on one count – than Stalin. In March, Blair dedicated himself to a twenty-year plan to abolish child poverty. At a less sublime level, councils were instructed on the annual gross weight of dog turds they were expected to scoop. 'It's just not technically feasible, never mind desirable, to have that much centralisation,' noted Tony Wright, the impeccably New Labourite chairman of the Public Administration Committee. 'If everything is a target, nothing is a target.'[4]

The government would come to acknowledge that by slimming the number and sharpening the focus of targets. There was some merit in concentrating minds on objectives. David Blunkett was making progress in improving literacy and numeracy, and fulfilling the pledges on class sizes and nursery places. At health, however, targeting perverted priorities as easy operations – 'zits' – were undertaken at the expense of more serious cases in an effort to ease the political panic about waiting lists. The waiting list to get on to the waiting list meanwhile grew longer.

Each Monday morning, the Prime Minister convened his advisers – the most regular attenders being Alastair Campbell, Philip Gould, Anji Hunter, David Miliband and Jonathan Powell – for a 'strategy' session. The night before, their home fax machines chuntered out rolls of handwritten notes from Blair expressing the ideas and anxieties clattering around the boss's mind. Hunter would be alerted to the arrival of the fax by her husband shouting: 'Here comes your Sunday-night stream of consciousness.'[5]

The outside perception of a turbo-charged machine in the masterful control of the driver was a cleverly spun illusion. The man at the wheel privately complained that when he pressed the pedal it was an agonising wait before he got movement, if anything happened at all. According to one of Blair's closest advisers: 'It is the defining image of the government. Tony sits there at the Monday morning strategy meetings screaming: "What are we doing about health? What are we doing about crime? What are we doing about transport?" And nothing happening.'⁶ Senior civil servants noted the frustration of the Prime Minister's ambitions to govern from the centre. In the spring of 1999, one official commented: 'Blair is still trying to run the operation from Number 10, but is gradually realising its impossibility.'⁷

It was also wearing him out as his energy was stretched too thin. Blair's bad humour expressed itself in snappy outbursts at his staff and increasingly regular displays of irritation about the performance of the civil service and the Cabinet. 'Why can't they get a grip?' had become a regular moan to his aides. Even Jack Straw, usually prized by the Prime Minister as one of his safest pairs of hands, felt the rough end of Blair's tongue over the summer passports fiasco.

Civil servants pointed out, though it was a brave official who did so to the Prime Minister's face, that some of the problems were of his own creation. As a political type, Blair was an artist, not an engineer. His strengths lay in reading political moods, not reconfiguring structures. He wanted product, but he was not interested in the nuts and bolts of the machine.

'When he came in, he assumed that government was a bit like a barristers' chambers,' says one very highly placed official. 'The senior partner indicates what he wants, and it magically happens. He had to learn that government does not work like that.'⁸

The conundrum was that the top-down, finger-clicking, checklist approach to government could actually be counter-productive in getting results. Blair's irritation with his ministers was answered by them with complaints that they were the victims of a governing hierarchy which didn't encourage independent initiative or the collective ownership of responsibility. Blair could be hands-off if it suited him. When Stephen Byers, the Trade and Industry Secretary, had to rule on Rupert Murdoch's bid for Manchester United, a call which would either inflame the party or anger the media tycoon, the minister received a communication from a senior aide at Number 10 telling him that the Prime Minister hoped he was clear that it was 'your decision'.[9]

Subjects which did not attract Blair's sustained interest, or the sponsorship of Gordon Brown, languished in the Prime Minister's in-tray or became gridlocked as departments quarrelled with advisers in the Number 10 Policy Unit.

By the sultry summer of 1999, there was a culture of discontent in the government – and no member of the cabinet was more disgruntled than John Prescott. His pugnacious and occasionally clownish exterior was the front for a sensitive man who feared that the New Labour order permitted him a limited shelf-life to fulfil his ambitions. Prescott was the self-bettered son of a railwayman and grandson of a miner. One of his tutors at Ruskin, the trade union college, likened him to Jude the Obscure. He had a large appetite for knowledge, fiercely independent opinions, and a pride which was easily wounded.

Prescott enjoyed some early successes, notably using his trade union bargaining skills to negotiate a bond deal, at little cost to the taxpayer, to save the rail link to the Channel Tunnel. Prescott was a details man – to a fault. One visitor to his ministerial suite was rewarded with the spectacle of the Deputy Prime Minister deciding on a planning application for a supermarket by spreading a large map of Manchester over the floor and crawling across it on his hands and knees.

By 1999 his stock was sliding. Understudying for Blair at Question Time, the Deputy Prime Minister mispronounced the names of foreign leaders, and got his brief in a twist, giving the right answers, but to the wrong questions. Leaving the dispatch box with mocking jeers ringing in his ears, Prescott regarded it as the most shattering experience of his political life. He told friends that he would rather leave politics than suffer such humiliation again.

Though he was built like a rhino, Prescott's skin was tissue-thin. He could be thrown into paroxysms of private rage against 'the snobs' who patronised his daily struggle to conquer the English language, and the mockers who dubbed him 'Two Jags'. Among friends, Prescott fulminated: 'No one ever attacked fucking Heseltine because he drove a Jag.' The *Guardian* cartoonist, Steve Bell, drew him as a zipped and castrated bulldog, a portrayal which Prescott loathed with such intensity it suggested that he feared there was a kernel of truth in the caricature.

Some of the ridicule he invited. At the party conference that autumn, he used two cars to make the 300-yard journey from his hotel to the platform to deliver a speech urging less car use. Prescott then made it worse for himself by implausibly suggesting that it was 'for security reasons'. Other ministers managed the walk. The human and rather touching truth was that Pauline Prescott, a woman proud of her husband, wanted to be seen arriving as a couple at the conference centre and looking her best, especially for her mum who liked to see Pauline's picture in the newspapers. But John Prescott exposed himself to further media torment by making himself sound ungallant about Pauline. He had taken the car because 'my wife doesn't like having her hair blown about'.[10]

Prescott himself was feeling blown out. In the summer of 1998, he unveiled the White Paper containing his great plan to make good on his promises to cut congestion and pollution by taxing drivers off the road and reinvesting the proceeds in public transport. 'This is the day transport policy bursts into the light of a new day,' he claimed, using the macho hyperbole so beloved of this government. 'There is a clear mood for change and I am in a position to deliver it.'[11] A year on, that bombast was an empty echo. A scathing report by the Labour-dominated Select Committee on Transport concluded that his 'department's achievements have been largely confined to the publication of documents and policy statements and the establishment of task forces. As yet, there have been few tangible improvements.'[12] Prescott admitted that he was 'treading water'.

Deputy Prime Minister was a grand title, but it did not come with commensurate power. He was squeezed between the immovable object of the Treasury and the irresistible force of Number 10. Gordon Brown treated Prescott as a useful idiot. The Chancellor was interested in transport principally as a source of revenue, and what money for investment he did release to Prescott came with a punishing price. The Cabinet's supposed conscience of the left was obliged to front an unpopular private finance scheme for the London Underground and privatisation of Air Traffic Control, which Labour had bitterly attacked as 'selling the nation's air' when it was proposed by the Tories.

Blair had sent three different Transport Ministers to the Department in less than as many years. Prescott had not wanted any of them. He complained that Gavin Strang couldn't make a decision, John Reid plotted against him, and Helen Liddell was not up to it. When they discussed replacing her, Prescott said to Blair: 'You've sent me three fucking Scots – can I have an English next time?'

Prescott was also a victim of New Labour's abiding tendency not to think further than the next headline, an approach especially ill-suited to transport, which suffered from years of neglect that demanded a long-term remedial strategy. In this government, a day was a long time in politics. Blair tried to counter the voters' complaint of neglect by throwing himself into a frenzy of domestic activity. If it was Tuesday, it was a health speech. If it was Wednesday, it was a television question and answer about education. If it was Thursday, it was a rail summit. Whether this whirlygig achieved anything apart from making him even more ragged was questionable. That July, he tried to quieten discontent on the left by saying that he very much hoped to bring forward legislation to ban fox-hunting, but there was no such legislation in the Queen's Speech three months later. The habitual weakness was to make a gesture, rather than to take action. This was an ecology of government unfriendly to policies which might make a difference in the long term but which carried the risk of immediate-term controversy.

Tony Blair was initially content to leave Prescott alone because transport and green issues were simply not subjects which engaged the Prime Minister. In the election manifesto they were bundled together with second-order policies under the headline 'We will help you get more out of life' illustrated with saccharine pictures of a mother and child on a fairground carousel. At the very first Cabinet meeting of the Government's life, Blair dismissed the subject by saying: 'Railways are not a top priority.' When Number 10 did take an interest, it was to veto those of Prescott's policies which might cause discontent among motorists. Implementation of congestion charging and taxes on out-of-town shopping were first diluted, and then delayed. Prescott would return from discussions with Downing Street complaining: 'They keep throwing the fuckin' focus groups at me. They're attacking me for what we were elected to do.' His relationship with the Prime Minister's transport adviser, Geoff Norris, became so appalling that eventually Blair had to accede to Prescott's demands that Norris be moved off the brief.

By the sticky summer of 1999, the public was noticing that Britain's railways were no more reliable, and its roads were no less congested, than when New Labour came to power promising that things could only get better. Few voters thought that train services had improved, and a large majority believed that traffic was more jammed.[13] Railtrack announced record profits while failing to meet its regulator's targets for investment and reducing delays. The closure of a small part of the London Underground reduced large sections of the network to chaos. This was not the ideal week to announce that Railtrack was to be given a leading role in running the Underground. As transport hurtled up Philip Gould's polling as a source of electoral angst, the issue finally began to blip on the Prime Minister's radar.

At a meeting at Number 10 in mid-June, Blair told Prescott that they had to 'get ahead of the game'. It wasn't that 'your policy is wrong, John' but they had to be careful that 'the press can't attack it' as hostile to motorists. Where was the master plan? Where were the improvements with which the public could identify? Prescott replied, with some feeling, that he had had a plan, but it had been stymied. To his great distress, the legislation to create a strategic rail authority was squeezed out of the parliamentary programme because Downing Street did not treat it as a priority. Blair did concede to him: 'We should have let you have your bill.'[14]

A few days after this abrasion, a report surfaced that the Prime Minister himself endured personal experience of what the Tories were dubbing 'Standstill Britain'. Trapped in a tailback on the M4 near Heathrow airport, the Prime Minister's driver swung into a new bus-only lane to escape the jam. The story was leaked with an interpretation designed to discredit Prescott. Sources at Number 10 were quoted saying that Blair was ordering no more of these bus lanes and felt embarrassed because 'he could see thousands of voters fuming as he drove past'.[15]

Fuming did not do justice to the volcanic reaction from Prescott when he saw this story. Convinced that Number 10 was running an operation to destabilise him, Prescott instructed his staff to go through Alastair Campbell's briefings to look for evidence that the press secretary, the one person at Number 10 with whom he thought he had a good relationship, was now blow-piping poison darts into his prickly hide. This combination of an unbalanced Prescott and a maddened Blair was dry tinder waiting to be lit.

It was the Prime Minister who struck the spark. In early July, making some off-the-cuff remarks to an audience of entrepreneurs, Blair let rip with his aggravations.

One of the things I would like to do, as well as stimulating more entrepreneurship in the private sector, is get a bit of it into the public sector as well. I mean, people in the public sector are more rooted in the concept that 'if it's always been done this way, it must always be done this way' than any other group of people I've come across.

'You try getting change in the public sector and public services' – Blair gave them a theatrical grimace – 'I bear the scars on my back after two years in government. Heaven knows what it will be like after a bit longer.'[16]

His immediate audience, a group of venture capitalists, clapped with delight at Blair's contrast of their can-do spirit with the hidebound public sector. But it was clumsy to launch what sounded like a sweeping attack on five million public sector workers. Peter Hain, whose loyal service in Wales had given him some licence to go off-message, blamed the alienation in Labour's heartlands on the government's 'dangerous' habit of 'being gratuitously offensive to its own natural supporters'.[17] The Prime Minister had done just that. Labour MPs and trade unionists reacted with hot indignation. Rodney Bickerstaffe, the General Secretary of Unison, representing the worst-paid public sector workers, complained that the real scars were borne by his members as a result of the government's failure to remunerate them properly. Bickerstaffe got on the phone to his old friend, John Prescott. He urged a counter-blast.

Prescott's boiler really did not require much stoking. The following day, he was addressing a local government audience in Harrogate. Minutes before he was due to speak, Prescott furiously scribbled insertions into the prepared text. He defended the victims of Blair's speech by heaping praise on the public sector. 'Since the nineteenth century it has been local councillors and the public sector who have forged a modern society. When the private sector failed, the public sector stepped in,' he said, listing universal education, public transport, clean water, libraries and council housing. 'Indeed the contribution of the local authorities and the public sector did much to civilise this century.'[18]

Making no attempt to disguise his remarks as anything other than a calculated rebuke to Blair, Prescott finished by hawking: 'Now, I've got that off my chest.' On the train back to London, he gave an interview to the transport correspondent of *The Times* in which he attacked the 'faceless wonders' at Number 10 who briefed against him and blocked his policies.[19]

Futile attempts by Alastair Campbell to pretend that Prime Minister and Deputy were as one could not prevent the following morning's headlines shouting the split. Before Thursday's Cabinet, Blair adopted his usual technique of hosing down Prescott with honey. Their wires had got crossed, said a conciliatory Prime Minister. His own outburst about 'scars on my back' was provoked by the doctors' trade union, the British Medical Association, and its self-interested obstruction of NHS Direct, the telephone diagnosis service, and walk-in treatment centres. When the Cabinet assembled, Prescott purged his residual anger by delivering a pointed little speech about the Labour Party being a coalition of new and traditional supporters. None of them should forget it. The following weekend, there was a concerted attempt to suggest that Prime Minister and Deputy were back in harmony. Striking a 'One Nation' note, Prescott declared that the government was 'not just for the council estate or the man in the Volvo estate. It's not just for *Mirror* readers or *Daily Mail* readers. It's for the whole country.'[20] Yet the venues for their speeches told its own story. The Prime Minister spoke to 'Labour Future', the Blairista youth wing, whom he addressed in the language of modernisation without mention of council estates. Prescott spoke to the Durham Miners' Gala, festival of Old Labour.

Blair maintained that he and Prescott were members of the same broad church who simply happened to sit on different sides of the aisle. 'Even though I am from the modernising wing of the party and John is from the traditional wing, we believe the same things.'[21] This was true, but in the sense that Protestants and Catholics both believe in God. Prescott did not much conceal his contempt for the whole concept of New Labour. 'Not a term I use myself,' he told one interviewer. He exploited the fall of Mandelson and Blair's absence in the Seychelles at the turn of the year to call for more 'substance' and 'interventionism' in a 'Keynesian way'.[22] This roughly translated into meaning that he wanted an increase in spending. Blair was not threatened by anything from Prescott which amounted to a sustained challenge or a coherent alternative to New Labour. What Prescott's eruptions reflected was the hunger among a large section of the party for a more avowedly socialist government which paid more respect to Labour's history and devoted less attention to sweetening Middle Britain.

Prescott aligned himself with the increasingly vocal complaints that Blair did not just neglect the party's traditional supporters, he treated them with unconcealed distaste. John Monks, the leader of the TUC, was distressed: 'It often seems as if those of us who voted Labour before the 1990s are being accused of poor judgement, or seen as embarrassing elderly relatives.'[23] Monks actually enjoyed as much access to ministers as his counterparts from business. What this moderate union leader articulated was the burgeoning disgruntlement that Blair promoted the 'modernising wing' at the expense of the 'traditional wing'. Before the election, he had used Old Labour as the foil with which to enhance the electoral attractiveness of New Labour to middle-ground voters. Traditionalists had endured this as the necessary price to attain power. Two years into office, they were no longer prepared to suffer in silence.

The leader's instinctive reflex was to reject the critique. At a conference on the New Deal, Blair struck an implacable note:

While I am leader of my party and Prime Minister of this country, I will never again have Britain forced to choose between a Labour Party that ignored the importance of business and ambition and a right-wing Conservative Party which ignored the need for justice and compassion. That is the New Labour message and it will remain 100 per cent proof.[24]

Blair insisted: 'We have done more as a Labour government for, if you like, traditional Labour supporters than any Labour government there has ever been. But we don't do it by alienating new support, middle-class support.'[25] The predilection for keeping 'new support' content had encouraged reform-by-stealth. Even where policies were being delivered to traditional supporters, there was a hesitancy to boast about it. A first draft of the manifesto for the European elections heralded the introduction of the maximum working week. That and other achievements that might appeal to Labour activists and core voters were deleted on the instructions of Number 10, nervous of attracting attention to policies that might annoy companies.

Blair often repeated Bill Clinton's axiom: 'Never forget your new voters.' The final proofs that this was not a Labour government like any previous Labour government were delivered in the 1999 Budget. It was a glum occasion for Tory MPs as they sat watching

Gordon Brown raid the Conservative wardrobe. New Labour laid claim to be the party of business with tax breaks to promote enterprise. Brown had finally won his argument with Blair to abolish the married couples allowance and mortgage tax relief, but he was able to blunt Tory opposition by reminding them that he was only finishing what they had started. His last and wholly unanticipated flourish was plucked from the tricks book of Tory Chancellors. The headline-winning tax changes were a new 10p band and a cut in the basic rate of income tax to 22p, taking it to its lowest level in seventy years. Blair was seized with delight when Brown came up with this idea, though the Chancellor himself was slightly apprehensive about how it would be received by the party. As it turned out, only one member of the Cabinet – Brown's old antagonist, David Blunkett – questioned the income tax cut. Most Labour MPs cheered themselves delirious. At the Eddisbury by-election in late July, Labour ran the Tories a close second in one of the truest of blue constituencies.

What Blair was much less well equipped to do was galvanise the traditional wing of his coalition for which he had neither feel nor sentiment: it was impossible to imagine him at the Durham Miners' Gala. His basic assumption, which he made explicit in an interview with me that autumn, was that they had nowhere else to go.

As we move into the election, people will see the alternative. The choice is not between the Labour government you have and Utopia. The choice is between the Labour government you have and a Conservative government that is more extreme than ever before. You wait till people see that – and they'll be out there.[26]

This was getting close to telling Labour's traditional supporters that they could like it or lump it. He had yet to see the risk, though it was indicated by the low turn-out in Labour's heartland areas in the elections that spring and summer, that they might decide to lump him. They could defect to the Nationalists, or the Liberal Democrats, and they could protest by staying at home.

★

The Prescott rebellion was also fired by a struggle over territory. It was as much about power within the Cabinet as it was about the government's direction. Speculation about a Cabinet reshuffle, which Downing Street did nothing to quell, swelled to a feverish pitch that July. Prescott had been wound up to fear Blair's intentions by a warning from Gordon Brown: 'They went for my people last year. This time they will go for yours.'[27] The Deputy Prime Minister worried to his friends that Blair planned to break up his bailiwick. He feared walking into Cabinet one day and finding himself surrounded by 'Blairite kids'.

Frank Dobson suffered endless rumour-mongering that he was to be ejected from the Department of Health and forced to run for mayor of London. A typical headline that febrile summer claimed: 'Dobson told to run for mayor or face oblivion.'[28] The truth was that Blair had not and never did ask Dobson to run for mayor of London.[29] He was coming to a conclusion that he wanted a more zealously modernising agenda for the health service, but he simply could not make his mind up what to do with Dobson. The speculation that he had a short life left in the government provoked an understandably aggrieved reaction from the Health Secretary. Like a bear that has been prodded with sticks, Dobson lashed out at the 'fancy Nancies' and 'anonymous liars' predicting he was for 'the chop' and growled: 'I intend remaining the Secretary of State for Health.'[30] This broke the convention that ministers do not make public comment about reshuffles.

Dobson's mutiny was followed by that of another victim of reshuffle fever, Mo Mowlam. She declared: 'I haven't had my fill of Northern Ireland' and that she wanted to stay 'long enough' to see the peace process to final fruition.[31] Less than a year previously, at the 1998 conference, she was the star of the Prime Minister's speech. When he referred to 'our one and only Mo', the entire conference sprang cheering to its feet, conferring on Mowlam the unique distinction of winning a standing ovation in the middle of the leader's address. As is often the case in politics, the moment of public glory concealed private decline. The Unionists – and crucially their leader, David Trimble – had never taken to her. By now, relations between the spontaneous Mowlam and the rigid Trimble had collapsed to the point where he would not deal with her. During the abortive attempt to implement the Good Friday Agreement at Hillsborough Castle in June, Mowlam sat doing letters from her red box while Blair conducted the negotiations with Trimble. The Unionist leader was lobbying Blair to send Peter Mandelson to Belfast. That idea appealed to Blair's aides who felt that too much of his energy was sapped because of the breakdown between Mowlam and Trimble. Jonathan Powell was particularly vehement in arguing that the Prime Minister could not afford to be spending a large part of nearly every day on Northern Ireland. Earlier in the year, Blair had told Mandelson that 'if things go really well for you' he would bring him back into the government in the summer of 2000. Now he was toying with an earlier recall of Mandelson, an impulse quickened by the feeling that the strategist was missed during the Euro-elections. Blair floated with Mowlam the idea of sending Mandelson to Belfast. Misunderstanding him, at first she reacted quite positively, saying 'it will do Peter good' to begin his rehabilitation as a minister of state in the province. With horror, she learned that Blair was actually thinking about giving her job to Mandelson.[32] The heat was further turned up on her pressure-cooker temper by incessant media chatter that Mandelson was bound for Belfast. He phoned Mowlam to deny all responsibility for planting these stories, telling her: 'I'm not angling for your job.' She answered his protestations of innocence with a hail of scornful expletives, and slammed down the phone.[33] That evening, Mandelson rang Blair. 'I told her it wasn't me. She wouldn't believe me.' Blair replied: 'Well, she wouldn't. Would you?'[34]

The knifing of Cabinet members by shadowy briefers in corners, the Chinese water torture of rumours dripping through the media on to individual ministers: this all served to turn government into a convention of paranoiacs. The result was entirely counter-productive for Blair. The Prime Minister was in an agonising quandary about Mowlam. He did not desire to humiliate the most popular member of the Cabinet; he would much rather exploit her public appeal. After more than two years in Belfast, Mowlam was actually ready to leave Northern Ireland. But all the speculation that she was to be dragged away contrived to make her more determined to dig in her heels when she discussed her prospects with Blair at Number 10 in mid-July. She bluntly spurned his entreaties to become the anti-Livingstone candidate for London.[35] Mowlam believed that, after her punishing service in Northern Ireland, she deserved better. She wanted to be Foreign Secretary. 'My strength is people,' she put it to Blair. The Foreign Office was 'the best chance' for her to use that skill. Blair reckoned there was rather more to being Foreign Secretary than that, though he tried to rebuff her tactfully. He responded: 'You're not ready.'[36] This unhappy argument concluded without agreement about her future. She departed for a holiday abroad in a visible huff, telling the world that the Prime Minister knew where to find her if he needed to.

Mowlam's bid for the Foreign Office was not a shot in the dark. There was the possibility of a vacancy that July. NATO needed a new Secretary-General, and Blair was desperate for the post to be filled by a British candidate as a demonstration of his influence in Europe. NATO was first offered to Robin Cook. He did not turn it down instantly. The invitation carried an implication about Blair's low enthusiasm for retaining him at the Foreign Office in the long term. After considering it for a few days, Cook eventually told Blair he wanted to stay put. The Prime Minister then passed the NATO offer on to George Robertson. The Defence Secretary also turned it down.[37] His wife didn't want to move to Brussels, it was essentially a bureaucratic job, and Robertson believed he could climb higher in British politics. He, too, had set his sights on the Foreign Office. Robertson tried to sit tight at the Ministry of Defence. Twice or more daily, for a fortnight, Blair, Alastair Campbell and Jonathan Powell shelled the Defence Secretary with phone calls cajoling him to go to Brussels. At Blair's behest, Campbell asked the Chief of the Defence Staff to join their press-gang.[38] Sir Charles Guthrie refused, partly because he liked Robertson too much to want to lose him, and partly because he feared they would replace him with

Mowlam. Blair finally wore Robertson into submission. His move
to NATO was announced in August whereupon the reluctant
candidate pronounced himself 'privileged' by such an honour. By
then, with everyone on holiday, it was too late to conduct a Cabinet
reshuffle.

The resistance of Dobson, Mowlam and Robertson resulted in
a botch. When the long anticipated reshuffle got underway on 28
July, there was no change to the Cabinet. There were some strikingly wide moves at a junior level, including the promotion of a
record number of women, and the positioning of upwardly mobile
talents to create a second XI of ministers of state to keep the
Cabinet on its toes.

At noon that Wednesday, midway through the shuffling, John
Prescott charged round to Number 10. Blair was bringing in the
businessman and peer, Gus Macdonald, to take charge of transport,
which initially aroused Prescott's suspicions. 'Another Scot,' he
groaned. He was sore that there was no promotion for his ally, Ian
McCartney. And he was angry about what Blair was doing to his
ministerial friends by sacking Alan Meale and moving Richard
Caborn. This was 'vindictive', Prescott complained. Though Blair
denied it, Prescott believed that this was a punishment for his
rebellion of a few weeks earlier. Later, licking his wounds among
his intimates, Prescott told them: 'The message is: Number 10 is in
charge. And don't you ever fucking forget it.'

The paradox was that Tony Blair did not feel in charge, nor did
he look in command. The *tricoteuses* of the newspapers, denied the
guillotining of Cabinet heads that the press had been predicting for
so many weeks, lampooned Blair's 'Night of the Short Knives'.
The frequent bouts of chaos and indecision at the centre of government had been skilfully concealed by the spin of the strong leader.
The mask slipped a bit. Blair seemed incapable of imposing his
authority on the Cabinet, a display of weakness which broke the
first of the Number 10 commandments.

The *élan* and vigour of election day seemed long in the past.
Before and after pictures contrasted the fresh-faced, adrenalin-
charged Blair of May 1997 with the office-engraved, shop-worn

visage he displayed in July 1999. A frustrated Prime Minister departed Britain to try to heal the scars on his back in the restorative rays of the Tuscan sun.

# 16. Making Enemies

He was sitting at the small, leather-topped desk by the window when she came in to the study. 'I've got some interesting news for you,' said Cherie. 'It's going to be rather shocking. It's about the children.' Her husband asked: 'Is there something wrong with one of them?' 'There's nothing wrong with the kids we *have*,' she said. 'I think we're going to have another.' He was pole-axed: 'You're joking.' She said: 'No, Tony. I'm not.' When he recovered, Cherie laughed that now she understood what people meant when they said: 'His jaw hit the floor.'

The surprise for Cherie, albeit a milder one than the shock she had just dropped on him, was to find her husband writing at the desk. He was not usually a desk man: his preferred working posture was to sit on the sofa of his small den, legs up on the coffee table, papers spread around him. He had been at the desk that day in September because he felt pregnant with an idea, conceived during their holiday in Italy. The Prime Minister was labouring over his speech to the party conference later in the month in which he planned to give birth to his latest attempt to define the government.

This quest to explain New Labour was a feature of his premiership as never-ending as the hunt for the snark. Blair was nearly thirty months into power, and he still didn't feel he had conveyed his purpose to the country. Why did he even feel it necessary? The country did not appear to need an explanation. The government continued to enjoy an unprecedented opinion poll lead over the Tories. The Prime Minister was more than four times as personally popular as the widely derided leader of the Opposition. The disorientated Conservatives struggled to attack Blair precisely because of his lack of bold definition. He had abandoned the old trenches of class struggle to adopt a war of mobility. The intelligentsia might complain, but he proclaimed his lightness of ideological being as a virtue. 'There is a greater understanding of this position among non-political people than the political cognoscenti,' he wrote after a little more than a year in office. 'They distrust heavy ideology, right or left.'[1]

Questioners who sought precise detail about the project frequently found themselves pelted with cliché and platitude. He was constructing 'a new and better Britain' and 'a new national moral purpose'. He startled a meeting of European socialists by bursting at them: 'New, new, new. Everything is new.'[2]

As a political tactic, substituting conflict and choice for this rhetoric of change and momentum had obvious advantages. A lesson the Blairites learned from the Thatcherites was that, in order to control the debate, you must command the language in which it is conducted. By casting himself as modern, moderate and dynamic, he painted his opponents, whether they be to the left or the right, as antiquated, extreme and obsolete. New Labour, he told a business dinner, rejected alike 'the outdated ideology of state control of the Old Left and the laissez-faire of the New Right'.[3]

In the Blairites' lexicon there was nothing more disdained than 'dogma'. Yet they were simultaneously gnawed by a contradictory hunger to possess an ideology. The easiest way to sting Blair – itself a demonstration of New Labour's lack of intellectual self-confidence – was to attack his government as unprincipled.

His longest effort to refute the proposition that he was no more than a populist pragmatist was provided in a pamphlet for the Fabian Society. 'I have always believed that politics is first and foremost about ideas,' he began what was his most considered attempt to compose a personal manifesto.

Without a powerful commitment to goals and values, governments are rudderless and ineffective, however large their majorities.

Ideas need labels if they are to become widely and popularly understood. The 'Third Way' is to my mind the best label for the new politics which the progressive centre-left is forging in Britain and beyond.[4]

The 'Third Way' was actually a label of last resort. Like a man searching for an off-the-peg suit, but not finding anything he likes the look of in the mirror, Blair toyed with and discarded a succession of garbs. 'Stakeholding' and 'Communitarianism' came into his vocabulary and as rapidly dropped out. The baggy cloth of the 'Third Way' was a term open to such a variety of interpretation that it had been employed by characters as various as Colonel Gaddafi, Benito Mussolini and Sir Oswald Mosley, and adopted by creeds as diverse as fascism, anarchism, Trotskyism, anabaptism, Euro-Communism, non-alignism and, occasionally, even socialism. As early as the thirteenth century, St Thomas Aquinas mused on the Third Way: 'A thing that need not be, once was not, and if everything need not be, once upon a time there was nothing.'

John Prescott derisively told the party conference that he had gone looking for a book on the Third Way and found it in 'the mystery section'. Privately, Prescott pleaded with Blair to drop it because the phrase meant nothing to voters and raised the hackles of Labour activists. Lionel Jospin, the socialist Prime Minister of France, refused to use the term. The German social democrats rebelled against their leader's attempt to adopt it. Even the head of Blair's own Policy Unit who helped compose the pamphlet, David Miliband, told colleagues that the Third Way was something they ended up with for want of a better idea.

Blair wrote:

The Third Way stands for modernised social democracy, passionate in its commitment to social justice and the goals of the centre-left, but flexible, innovative and forward-looking in the means to achieve them. It is founded on the values which have guided progressive politics for more than a century – democracy, liberty, justice, mutual obligation and internationalism. But it is a third way because it moves decisively beyond an Old Left preoccupied by state control, high taxation and producer interests; and a New Right treating public investment, and often the very notions of 'society' and collective endeavour, as evils to be undone.[5]

The claim for the Third Way was that it could combine the best of other political traditions. New Labour brought together the economic reforms of Margaret Thatcher – 'necessary acts of modernisation', according to Blair – and combined them with values of social solidarity.

Liberals assert the primacy of the individual liberty in the market; social democrats promoted social justice with the state as its main agent. There is no necessary conflict between the two, accepting as we now do that state power is one means to achieve our goals, but not the only one and emphatically not an end in itself.[6]

The double advantage was that he believed this to be true and that it put him in the middle ground where he thought elections were won. This was not socialism, a word that rarely passed his lips, but nor was it Thatcherism. The meritocrats of New Labour believed in individual achievement, but not that the merciless free market alone should be left to reward talent and discard chaff. The state's role was to invest in people's potential, especially through education and training, with a special obligation to the disadvantaged. By extending opportunities, both individual life chances and national competitiveness were enhanced. Blair's basic belief could be simply put: healthy economies made for strong societies, healthy societies made for strong economies.

'This is the Third Way,' Blair declared in the back garden of Number 10, launching one of his annual reports on the performance of the government. 'A belief in social justice and economic dynamism, ambition and compassion, fairness and enterprise going together.'[7]

Where the Third Way took a wrong turning and became a barrier to understanding was when Blair tried to use it to claim that all other political beliefs could be synthesised into redundancy.

My vision for the twenty-first century is of a popular politics reconciling themes which in the past have wrongly been regarded as antagonistic –

patriotism and internationalism; rights and responsibilities; the promotion of enterprise and the attack on poverty and discrimination . . .[8]

This was the Third Way as a food-mixer. It churned together social democracy with global capitalism and added, in the claim that it was the only scientific way, a dash of Marxist inevitability. The attempt at a united field theory of politics pretended that there were never any choices to be made between competing interests and contradictory values. But to govern is always to choose. The interests of business and the requirements of social justice were sometimes reconcilable, but they could also be mutually incompatible. It was a useless compass when confronted with a decision which did not permit of compromise. One of the most acute of liberal critics, the philosopher Ralf Dahrendorf, identified the Third Way as a politics that speaks of the need for hard choices but avoids them by trying to please everyone. Roy Hattersley, enjoying an Indian summer as a lancing critic of New Labour from a more egalitarian stand point, deplored 'the idea of producing an appeal which is so amorphous that it can embrace virtually everyone'. It was 'little more than a benign version of the one-party state. Taking the politics out of politics is not only absurd, it is democratically dangerous.'[9] The historian David Marquand, writing from the perspective of a social democrat, suggested that the Third Way was wallpaper over the unresolved contradictions within New Labour.[10]

This criticism was not so much answered by Blair as deflected. He insisted it was only natural that much of his project should appear vague. This was 'work in progress' which was at 'an early stage'. He dealt with the attack on himself as a managerial compromiser by asserting it was principled to be pragmatic. 'Our approach is "permanent revisionism", a continual search for better means to meet our goals.'[11] This took the Third Way back up its own fundament. The ideology was not to have an ideology. It was notable that his 'philosophical' speeches contained long lists of current government policies. Blairology was whatever the government happened to be doing at the time.

Blairism was not a philosophy which he was trying to put into practice, but a practice in search of a philosophy. The guru of the Third Way was the Director of the London School of Economics, Professor Anthony Giddens, who wrote the quintessentially Blairite text, *Beyond Left And Right*. Giddens confessed: 'Theoretical flesh needs to be put on the skeleton of their policy-making.'[12]

In April 1999, Blair and other leaders of Western progressive governments met in Washington for the global leaders' equivalent of group therapy. These summit-seminars were a roughly biannual event, and it was tempting to observe that they had to meet so often to talk about the Third Way because they had yet to discover what it was. Among themselves, they could acknowledge the joke. Blair prompted laughter from his fellow leaders by reporting on a conversation with the Chancellor of Germany. 'As Ger Schröder was saying to me on the way in, I haven't found the first two ways yet, so you tell me where the third one is.'[13] Attempting to answer Schröder's question, Blair asked: 'What is it that we're really, really about? I believe that what we are really, really about is community, opportunity and responsibility.' No one could be against that blessed trinity. This was the appeal, but it was also the problem. For a philosophy to be meaningful, it must be open to challenge and argument.

Responding to a contribution by Bill Clinton, the Prime Minister of Holland, Wim Kok, provoked more merriment: 'I have the impression that the Third Way is a very broad Third Avenue, but anyhow it is symbolic of renewal.' The Italian Prime Minister, Massimo D'Alema, asked:

Is it possible to have a dynamic economics and the society based on solidarity? I think it is. But this is the challenge. There is no prescription that you can write down for this. It is an effort pursued day after day. The Third Way is not an ideology. The answers are to be found day after day.

This was effectively saying that they were making it up as they went along. Blair himself admitted as much: 'I think that our whole process really is a voyage of discovery.'[14]

If the voyager searched the heavens for a guiding star, it was unsurprising that there was bafflement among the public and mockery from the media. By his own gauge of success – that political ideas need labels which are popular and widely understood – the Third Way was a failure. Blair could get quite petulant about this. It was his regular complaint that they paid more respect to the Third Way in South Korea than in Britain. At another leaders' talk-shop in Florence in November 1999, he was cross that the prophet of the Third Way was so little honoured in his own homeland. 'In the rest of Europe, I get a lot more publicity for the ideas of New Labour and the new government than I do in Britain, which I think says something unfortunate about the state of the debate about ideas in our media.'[15]

Complicated ideas – most notoriously Gordon Brown's 'neoclassical endogenous growth theory' – did not have the headline simplicity of socialism or Thatcherism. The complexities of some of the concepts did not fit into the sound-bite culture which New Labour had itself done so much to create.

Blair even blamed the weakness of the Conservatives for the fuzziness of New Labour's definition. 'When our opponents finally come up with a clear position and fight for it, then the political battle can really begin.'[16]

But no one more than Blair had endeavoured to take the battle out of politics. There were one or two striking exceptions to the rule, but his natural mode was as a conciliator, not a warrior. His 'Big Tent' was erected to spread out from the centre bivouacking all men and women of goodwill in a consensus of reason. This politics without frontiers excluded only the extremities of left and right. He was for boardroom and shopfloor, suburb and shire, young and old, rich man in the castle and poor man at the gate, lion and lamb. This meant practising not the politics of conflict, but of equilibrium. He was persuaded to introduce a statutory 'right to roam' opening up private acres to public access. But he overruled the relevant ministers to insist on making a balancing gesture by putting the new Countryside Commission in the charge of a former chairman of the Country Landowners' Association. He told a

Labour Party magazine that his favourite food was fish and chips; in an Islington cookbook, his top dish was 'Fresh fettuccine garnished with an exotic sauce of olive oil, sun-dried tomatoes and capers'. In that November's Queen's Speech, he put the words 'modernising' for 'the new Millennium' in Her Majesty's mouth, but he vetoed any updating of the Gilbert and Sullivan rigmarole of the flummery in the House of Lords. A speech hailing the introduction of the minimum wage would be invariably balanced by a celebration that they had also cut business taxes. His first instinct when confronted with most choices was to blur them. Blair was a sandpaper politician. Sharp edges were to be smoothed.

Yet there was a contradiction in the leader's head, which meant it split the personality of his government. The consensual pragmatist made noises of crusading certainty. In the early autumn of 1999, before his Tuscan tan had begun to fade, Blair launched himself into a series of interviews in which he announced that 'the modernising revolution has only just begun. I can really only be Prime Minister of a transforming, radical government.'[17] 'Revolution' was the flavour of that month's Blair-speak. He used it more than a dozen times in an interview with me that autumn. 'When you say: when does the revolution ever stop? I'm not sure the revolution ever stops.'[18]

This Maoist talk of permanent revolution came oddly from the head of an administration of incremental, evolutionary reform. As if embarrassed by the managerial gradualism of the government's actions, he talked as if he was a Robespierre. The anti-ideologist was possessed by a contrary craving to be a barricade-storming controversialist.

At the end of the summer holidays, a memo was circulated by Alastair Campbell saying that the government lacked definition. They needed to find a way of dramatising themselves. At a think-in with the Cabinet at Chequers towards the end of September, Blair told the ministerial gathering that there was a feeling in the country that things were just coasting along. David Miliband believed that Margaret Thatcher had been 'defined by her enemies'. What they lacked were dragons – their equivalents of Arthur Scargill and General Galtieri – to slay.

Most governments would be glad of a lack of serious challenge. Bizarre though this may seem, the Blairites lusted for some foes. The logic of their internal discussions went like this. The absence of tough opposition meant there was no sense of struggle. The lack of the din of battle meant that the way they were changing Britain was being under-appreciated. So Tony Blair, the master consensualist, set out to make himself some enemies.

'The forces of conservatism' was a phrase of his own invention. He had returned with it from his holiday. The venue for these forces' first appearance in his political discourse was the seaside resort of conservatism, Bournemouth. As Blair's party assembled on the Dorset coastline for its 1999 conference, where they would hear him assail the old Establishment, there was – another paradox – confirmation of the extent to which the government had become the new Establishment. The conference area heaved with stands expensively hired by corporations; events were sponsored by slicks of the City. The Saatchi brothers, ad men to the Conservatives at the high noon of Thatcherism, threw the most extravagant party of the week. After his speech assaulting the élite and the privileged, that evening Blair would take dinner with an élite of businessmen and women who had paid £350 a plate for the privilege of eating with the Prime Minister. At Bournemouth, the party conference looked like a trade fair crossed with an American convention. Howling from the wrong side of the police lines were those marginalised by New Labour's apparent hegemony. A group of Greens with a pantomime Frankenstein cow protested against genetically modified foods. The following day, the Countryside Alliance, looking out of time and out of place with their bucolic faces, amateurishly scribbled placards and tweedy caps, marched past in defence of fox-hunting. 'Tally-ho!' Blair mocked them from the conference platform.

It was a further indication of how permanent the New Labour order seemed to be, the extent to which it was almost universally taken for granted that Blair would cruise to re-election, that the main media interest that weekend revolved around how long he intended to remain Prime Minister. The Sunday newspaper lobby correspondents trapped his press secretary into saying that Blair would serve at least two full terms as Prime Minister, which the journalists mischievously construed into stories that Blair was deliberately snubbing the leadership ambitions of Gordon Brown.

Longevity was not the distinguishing mark of Blair's previous conference speeches as leader. The only truly resonant address was his first in 1994 which climaxed with the *coup de grâce* on the old Clause Four. The rest of the Blair conference canon had what George Orwell called the solidity of wind. 'A Young Country' (1995); 'A New Age Of Achievement' (1996); 'The Model 21st Century Nation' (1997); 'The Year Of Challenge' (1998). These sound-banquets were the rhetorical equivalents of a Chinese takeaway. A few hours later, the consumer felt empty again. The 1999 speech was intended to be different.

In the weeks working up to the conference, David Miliband had bent his brain to the task of reinterpreting equality for New Labour's meritocratic purposes. He came up with the phrase 'equality of worth'. Campbell was, as usual, responsible for crafting the jokes and the phrases designed to be catapulted on to the front pages. He also tried to give more solid form to Blair's 'forces of conservatism'. Brainstorming with Peter Hyman, a full-time speech-writer for Blair at Number 10, they came up with the idea of linking them with 'the allied forces of racism' as the jailers of Nelson Mandela, the assassins of Martin Luther King and the murderers of the black south London teenager, Stephen Lawrence. Crucial contributors to the mood of the speech were the party's pollsters. A confidential report, prepared by Greg Cook for the pre-conference Cabinet gathering at Chequers, and entitled 'The Electorate At Mid-Term', warned that the headline poll lead concealed a 'cooling of support' for the government. 'There is a drift downwards in many of the image ratings, notably arrogance, being in touch and keeping promises.'[19] Image, always so central to New Labour's calculations, was also on the mind of Philip Gould. He presented to Blair worrying findings that Labour supporters thought he 'did not care' about either them or their values. One respondent complained: 'He spends all his time on planes going abroad'.[20]

In an attempted answer to these criticisms, passages were written into the speech designed to display the Prime Minister as a man of humility. 'You'll see me on the TV, getting on and off planes, meeting Presidents and Prime Ministers, Kings and Queens' but what mattered to him was 'getting my sleeves rolled up and pushing through the changes to our country that will give to others by right, what I achieved by good fortune'. An especially blokeish, *faux* modest passage ended: 'If anything happened to me, you'd soon find a new leader. But my kids wouldn't find a new dad.'[21]

At eleven thirty on the Sunday night of the conference, the speech-writing team gathered in Blair's suite at the Highcliff Hotel to examine the slabs of text. Peter Mandelson joined them. 'I don't think it's quite you, Tony,' said Mandelson. Anji Hunter also worried to Blair that the assault on the 'forces of conservatism' would be interpreted as an attack on Margaret Thatcher. 'A lot of people still have a lot of time for her,' said Hunter. Alastair Campbell, by nature a tribalist with more Old Labour in his marrow than the other two, liked and defended the partisanship of the speech. 'You've got to say and do tough things. If you don't stoke up opposition, you don't rouse people,' he contended. 'We need dividing lines.' Blair concluded this discussion by saying that he didn't know whether he liked the speech either.[22] He ordered a redraft.

The high point of the conference Monday was Gordon Brown's speech, which was widely judged to be a personal career best. The Chancellor stood before them as the master of his economic universe, and much else besides. Citing mortgage rates at their lowest in twenty years, inflation at its lowest in thirty years, and more people in work than ever in history, the Chancellor invited his audience to celebrate economic responsibility. Then he lifted his prudently Victorian skirt to give them a flash of socialist stocking top. 'Our values, our history, our movement teach us that we are in politics not just to serve an electoral purpose but to serve and realise a greater public purpose.'[23] Brown did not once use the term

'New Labour'. He spoke instead of 'this Labour Party' and 'the Labour government' and 'Labour values'. He revived full employment as an ambition. He talked of his pride in organising debt relief for the world's poorest countries and the war against child poverty at home. His speech contained an overture of Blair's theme of the following day when Brown attacked 'the forces of reaction and privilege'. He also made one mention of 'the forces of conservatism', but it went unremarked upon. The Chancellor sat down to a thunderous ovation before magisterially sweeping off to the IMF which had just accoladed him with the chairmanship of its most important committee. Brown's conference triumph increased the pressure on Blair to match it.

By Monday teatime, when he gathered together his writing team, Blair was agitating for more material that could be guaranteed to get his audience on their feet, and keep them there. He had already had a notion of a morality tale based on the life chances of two babies. Peter Hyman had put emotional words round the idea. After some re-working by Blair himself, it would emerge like this:

There is no more powerful symbol of our politics than the experience of being on a maternity ward. Seeing two babies side by side. Delivered by the same doctors and midwives. Yet two totally different lives ahead of them. One returns with his mother to a bed and breakfast that is cold, cramped. A mother who has no job, no family to support her, sadder still – no one to share the joy and triumph of the new baby. A father nowhere to be seen. That mother loves her child and her baby's life is a long, hard struggle. For this child, individual potential hangs by a thread. The second child returns to a prosperous home, grandparents desperate to share the caring, and a father with a decent income and an even larger sense of pride. They're already thinking about schools, friends she can make, new toys they can buy. Expectations are high, opportunities truly limitless . . . If we are in politics for one thing – it is to make sure that all children are given the best chance in life. That the moment they are born, their potential and individuality can sparkle . . . That is our national moral purpose.

This passage would prove to be one of the most unintendedly controversial of the speech. It divided the world into those who found it an affecting expression of the wellspring of Blair's beliefs and those who gagged on it as hammy schmaltz. Though it would be universally assumed that the tale of two babies was prompted by Cherie's pregnancy, in fact the idea had come to Blair before he knew. After she told him she was pregnant, he almost removed the passage from the speech.

Blair was still not happy when he had another conference with his speech-writers at midnight on Monday. 'The tone, the tone, is the tone right?' was his repeated refrain. They went back to work again, hammering away until three in the morning of Tuesday. After breakfast, an autocue was wheeled into Blair's suite so that he could spend the morning rehearsing his delivery. He was still filleting, inserting and fiddling about with the words at lunchtime. By then, it was too late to change anything else.

When he rose in the conference centre that afternoon, the familiar medley made its obligatory appearance. 'The Third Way is not a new way between progressive and conservative politics,' declared Blair. 'It is progressive politics distinguishing itself from conservatism of left or right.'[24] Dividing the world between the new (good) and old (bad) was a cover version of previous tunes. What distinguished the Bournemouth speech was its targets. Previous conference speeches had been used to challenge his party as much as to rouse it. This time, most of the fire was concentrated on the right. The Tories were damned as 'the party of fox-hunting, Pinochet and hereditary peers: the uneatable, the unspeakable and the unelectable'. The activists roared with Pavlovian applause at this trio of easy hate objects. William Hague was ridiculed as 'weird, weird, weird. Far right, far out.' Blair was emboldened to talk about 'the struggle for true equality', a word he would never have said before the election. He essayed a variation on Rousseau: 'People are born with talent and everywhere it is in chains.' New Labour represented 'the forces of modernity who have the courage to change' against 'the old élites, establishments that have run our professions and our country too long . . . the old order . . . held people back. They kept people down . . . the forces of conservatism, the cynics, the élites, the Establishment. Those who will live with decline.'[25]

'The forces of conservatism', a trope which put in seventeen appearances, were blamed for everything from stopping women rising in the workplace to keeping bright children out of university. The rhetorical savagery of the speech was the more searing because of the contrast with Blair's usual emollience. The healer had become a warrior who seemed to be declaring war on large swathes of the population. It was not just Tories, but Scottish Nationalists, civil libertarians, Irish terrorists and environmentalists who were lumped together as 'forces of conservatism'. It sounded as if damnation awaited anyone who happened to disagree about anything with Tony Blair.

His audience of activists inside the conference hall rewarded the fifty-five-minute speech with the most rapturous ovation he had received as leader. The speech drew a dividing line through the media. For the first time, the reaction to a Blair conference performance split the press along left–right lines. There was lavish praise from the *Mirror*, the *Express* and the *Guardian*, which reckoned the speech to be his 'best yet as leader'. The right-wing press was hostile. Blair's proclamation that 'our destiny is with Europe' was interpreted by the *Sun* as a plot to 'dump the Pound'. The *Daily Telegraph* – headlining its report: 'Blair Moves In For The Kill' – saw a dictator-bidding conspiracy to destroy all opposition.

The most allergic reaction from the right came from those whom Blair had previously snake-charmed into believing that he was an ersatz Tory. The super-reactionary, Paul Johnson, who once boasted of private prayer sessions with the young Christian hero, exploded in ginger-haired apoplexy. 'Like a large number of people, I believed Tony Blair was special . . . The Blair who stepped forward yesterday was a low-grade party political orator, feeding cheap jokes and old-style demagoguery to a partisan audience,' Johnson burst his spleen in the *Daily Mail*.[26] Johnson had not complained when the same sort of stuff was doled out year after year by his old heroine, Margaret Thatcher. His bile exploded with such screaming pain because he had been made to look a fool.

Cherie, who had been forced to gag on her own distaste for Johnson and his right-wing ilk in pursuit of her husband's ambitions, expressed herself overjoyed that she would not be dragooned into his company again. She privately declared: 'I'll be delighted if I never have to see that man again.'[27]

Cherie was made of sterner material than her husband and his aides. The enfeebled Tories were a soft target. The 'forces of conservatism' that Blair had not planned to arouse to battle, though they really would have provided him with opponents of a power equivalent to a Scargill or a Galtieri, were the Europhobic right-wing newspapers. 'The speech has gone wrong,' jittered Philip Gould. Invited to comment on television about Blair's performance, Peter Mandelson declared that it was 'smashing' while letting it be known off-camera that he regarded it as a terrible error to have attacked the right with such ferocity. On Tuesday night, when he first heard about the *Sun*'s front page, Alastair Campbell went to the News International drinks party and angrily upbraided the paper's editor, David Yelland. 'You've gone mad!' Campbell told him. 'Editors always go bonkers, but we didn't think you'd go mad this quickly.' But the following morning Yelland was invited to meet Blair at his room in the conference centre. When the Prime Minister complained that the *Sun* had been 'unfair', Yelland replied: 'We are a conservative paper – you were attacking us.'

An attempt was also made to mollify the editor of the *Daily Mail*, Paul Dacre. The *Mail*, against usual type, had run a vigorous campaign to bring the racist killers of Stephen Lawrence to justice. Dacre told Blair that he regarded the speech as a personal insult and they would have little further to say to each other until he received an apology.

This marked the close of that unnatural period when Blair stretched out his embrace so expansively that he seemed to think it could accommodate nearly every shade of opinion in the nation. William Hague, while complaining about the speech in public, privately told colleagues he was delighted: 'At last he's given us something to attack.'[28] The right-wing newspapers, whom Blair had managed to beguile for so long, fell out of love with New

Labour. Though Blair would continue to cultivate them, he would not again attract the adulatory press enjoyed before. Their sensation that they had been suckered injected additional virulence into the attacks they would launch on the government. Tony Blair wanted the 'forces of conservatism' to be a defining moment which drew some battle lines. So it was, but not quite in the way that its author intended.

## 17. Dome's Day

As Tony Blair looked back from the boat, cruising up the Thames in the early hours of the twenty-first century, the translucent giant breast of the Millennium Dome gradually shrank in size. At the stern of the cruiser, Peter Mandelson, the daddy of the Dome, who boasted that it 'is going to knock your socks off,'[1] celebrated with his Brazilian partner, Reinaldo Avila da Silva. Amidships sat John Prescott, the Dome's godfather, who said they 'would not be much of a government' if they could not make this a success. The Deputy Prime Minister had been wearing his scowling bulldog face all night.

At the prow was Tony Blair, the arch-patriarch of the Dome, who promised it would be 'the best day out on earth'. His wife had thrown herself into the New Year's Eve celebrations in Greenwich with a much remarked gusto which was the more creditable because Cherie was not only five months pregnant, but also afflicted with the flu. Cherie wondered of a steward whether it might be possible to have a glass of hot water. The steward apologised that there was no drinking water. Cherie sniffled a sigh and got stuck into the champagne like everyone else. They were not even able to supply the Prime Minister's wife with something as undemanding as a glass of water – the opening night of New Labour's monument was a fiasco.

A special, sealed tube service – it was dubbed 'the nomenklatura express' – had whisked the Blairs to the celebrations. Less privileged members of the élite endured hours of chaotic queuing at a freezing station in east London. Those suffering this indignity included the Hinduja brothers, controversial millionaire sponsors of the Faith Zone, and James Blyth, the chairman of Boots, sponsors of the Body Zone. When he finally gained admittance, only to find that the Tesco house champagne in naff self-assembly plastic flutes had run out, an infuriated Lord Blyth exploded: 'New Labour can bloody well wait for their £12 million.' Among the panjandrums of the media scrumming in the mayhem were the Director-General of the BBC, who spent the night tearing into Mandelson and any other minister he could lay his angry hands on, and seven editors of national newspapers, which guaranteed vilification of the Dome in the press. One of New Labour's favoured sons, the candidate for deputy mayor of London, Trevor Phillips, was incandescent. 'The New Millennium Experience Company has been give a billion pounds for this! After one billion pounds there can be no excuses for this!', he raged to Dominic Lawson, the editor of the *Sunday Telegraph*. 'That should be your front-page headline this Sunday! After a billion pounds, no excuses!'

The comedian Stephen Fry won the biggest cheer from the crowd of 10,500 inside the Dome when he joked that the Queen had not yet arrived because she was 'still queuing for her ticket'. The Queen was actually conveyed to the celebrations over water, though this did not improve her temper at being dragged into the occasion which her eldest son boycotted. Her Majesty was not amused. On the boat to the Dome, she spent the entire trip huddled with Prince Philip and Princess Anne, the regal back turned against everyone else on board.[2] Michael Heseltine, the Tory grandfather of the Dome, who had bragged that it would be a 'triumph', tried to attract the Queen's attention. Even this great flaunter was snubbed with a magisterial ignoral.

The opening celebrations tried to be all things to everyone with a result that was not quite right for anyone. Rock was mixed with classic. The Archbishop of Canterbury's prayers were dropped into the programme between Jools Holland and the Corrs. An ethereal new millennium anthem by John Tavener was followed by the ancient dirge of 'Auld Lang Syne'. The Queen, somewhat bewildered, did not cross her arms in front of her in the traditional manner, but held out a hand to the Prime Minister who jogged her up and down with an enthusiasm which was evidently not mutual. Legions of near-naked dancers with tinselled buttocks then shimmered across the stage to a jungle throb. One dancer flaunted a mock, rainbow-coloured, spiky three foot penis at the audience.

The Queen, drawing on her long experience of native displays during tours of Pacific islands, stared implacably ahead. John Prescott did not know where to look. Peter Mandelson did at least manage to knock his own socks off, especially during the erotic aerial ballet. Even the Dome's biographer and enthusiast, Adam Nicolson, admitted: 'I loved the carnival myself but I am not sure that most of the audience did.'[3]

The Prime Minister sounded intoxicated by the event, gushing that he wished 'I could bottle the atmosphere'. But the morning after the night before, his government woke up with an appalling hangover which would last for months. The press reported the incompetent running of the Dome with increasing savagery. Peter Stothard of *The Times*, one of the queuing editors, filled four consecutive front pages with stories hostile to the Dome. Blair bitterly remarked to his aides: 'We should have let the editors bring their bloody limousines.' Mandelson wailed about a media 'vendetta'. The unremittingly negative coverage was surely tainted by the souring personal experiences of the aristocracy of the press. But no one had less grounds for complaint than New Labour, the supreme specialists in the media pitch and image manipulation. No government had devoted so much money and energy to public relations. If there was one product launch that should have been perfect, it was this one.

The Dome was intended to be New Labour's Xanadu and Tony Blair its Kubla Khan. Imperially imposing yet inclusively embracing, this cathedral of modernity built on poisoned land on the Greenwich peninsula was supposed to symbolise the regeneration of the creativity and genius of Cool Britannia. The Prime Minister rashly told friends that it would be 'the first paragraph of my next election manifesto'. This was Tony Blair's Big Tent made Teflon by his closest allies. It was designed by Richard Rogers, New Labour's architect of choice; the company was chaired by Bob Ayling, New Labour's favourite businessman; and its impresarios were the Prime Minister's friends, Peter Mandelson and then Charlie Falconer.

Lord Falconer apologised for the opening night 'inconveniences' inflicted on what he maladroitly called 'VIPs and ordinary people' but attempted to burble away the criticism by describing everything as 'amazing, fantastic, brilliant'. This served only to make more jarring the disconnection between the inflated promises and the deflating disappointment of the reality.

Not in the way that was ever intended, the Dome did symbolise Britain at the turn of the century. The Great Exhibition of 1851 was a celebration of the industrial and trading prowess of mid-Victorian Britain. The 1951 Festival of Britain was an uplifting tonic after wartime adversity and austerity. The Greenwich blancmange also distilled the spirit of its era, but the least attractive aspects of the time. It embodied the most meretricious features of the consumer age which New Labour had absorbed too well. The Dome was the vapid glorification of marketing over content, fashion over creation, ephemera over achievement.

It was a Frenchman who asked the pertinent question. Shown a scale model, Jacques Chirac asked: 'What's it for?'[4] Years of ministerial time and nearly £1 billion of public wealth were expended without ever producing an answer to that most important question. Jennie Page, the project's chief executive, was a feisty bureaucrat with no experience of the creative or leisure industries. It was said that she had taken only one holiday in eight years, and didn't much like children. Peter Mandelson's most imaginative contribution was to invent features – a game called Surf Ball and a Baby Dome – that existed only in his fantasies. The most experience Charlie Falconer had of organising entertainment was as a member of his Cambridge college May Ball committee. That they made so much of their one undeniable achievement – getting the Dome completed to time – revealed a mindset that viewed it as a building project.

Lord Rogers accurately identified the fundamental flaw when he said that there had never been a creative thread or a resonant theme to the Dome content. 'It dumbed down and simply tried to go for numbers,' he said. 'It was like an orchestra without a conductor.'[5]

The politicians who lusted to make a giant noise had confused a bellowing note with an attractive sound. The corporate sponsors treated it as a gigantic commercial hoarding.

Visitors complained that the Talk Zone was like being enclosed in a BT advert. The Journey Zone was plastered with Ford logos. Even Heseltine lamented that the companies had turned it into a 'trade show' as if a man with his business smarts could not have anticipated that.

Finding the exhibits trite and tacky, the press gave the Dome scourging reviews. They lambasted it as naff, tat, joyless, ugly, ghastly, chaotic, an upturned porridge bowl, an inverted wok, a decomposing beetle, and a scandalous waste of money. Many had gone determined to loathe it, but that could not be said of Polly Toynbee of the *Guardian* who had been a lonely supporter of the Dome. She mourned: 'I hate to join the chortling ranks of Dome rubbishers in the right-wing press . . . but, alas, I have to admit the Dome is a lemon.'[6]

The government's response was to resort to more boosterism. 'I defy anyone who sets foot in the Dome not to be awed by its sheer scale, variety or range of attractions,' said Tony Blair, desperately trying to puff up his torn balloon. The Dome would 'see off the cynics', and 'once people see it they will flood to visit it and be part of a great British achievement'.

The test that New Labour's populists set themselves was not aesthetics, but what Falconer called 'numbers who come' and Michael Grade 'bums on seats'. But by their chosen measure, the Dome was also a failure. Visitor numbers in the first few weeks were half what was projected. It had not been open a month when the Dome needed to be rescued with a further £60 million of lottery money.

By early February, the government was in the panic zone. Jennie Page – whom the Prime Minister had declared was doing a 'brilliant job' just a month earlier – was forced out after Ayling gave her an ultimatum to resign or be sacked. Her replacement, Pierre-Yves Gerbeau, was recruited from Eurodisney in Paris. After barely more than a month of operations, New Labour's 'great British achievement' was being run by a Frenchman parachuted in from an American company.

The first priority for the man from Paris was to deal with the extraordinary state of disrepair. Even as a fairground, it wasn't functioning. Half the lightbulbs in the Work Zone went out. A sculpture in the Self Portrait Zone blew up.[7] On one day in February, sixteen of the computers had crashed in the Learning Zone's Classroom Of The Future, nine games were broken in the Living Island Zone, and the robots in the Mind Zone were inactive. Most metaphorically of the sickness of the Dome, the heart in the much vaunted Body Zone had developed an irregular beat and its brain was broken.[8]

In May, Ayling joined Page in the sacrifice zone when his scalp was demanded as the price of a further injection of lottery money without which the Dome company would have gone bankrupt. More than sixty Labour MPs, among them three select committee chairs, signed a motion demanding a judicial inquiry, and the National Audit Office launched an investigation. What was supposed to be a celebration of British genius had required two crisis cash calls amounting to £1 million for each day it had been open. Though ministers could claim that the Dome was the biggest attraction of the year, after five months of operation the company admitted that it was never going to reach the break-even figure of 12 million visitors, a number which transpired to have been plucked out of an opinion poll. The target was slashed in half. Each visitor was being subsidised to the tune of £90, four times the support received by art galleries and museums. That it need not have been like this was illustrated by the contrastingly great success of the Tate Modern. Radical, imaginative and popular, everything the Dome was not, the new gallery opened in the spring to rave reviews and clamorous queues.

As Blair, Mandelson and Heseltine put increasing distance between themselves and their bastard creation, the lonely task of defending the Dome was left to Lord Falconer. He had to make his face braver by the month, but his words grew thinner until he was eventually reduced to pleading that 'whatever anyone may say, it's a very successful building'. Thus came the final admission from its own ringmaster that the Dome was a magnificent shell enclosing a vacuum of banality.

Repercussing back at Tony Blair was the hubristic hyperbole which he poured out when the super-structure was completed in June 1998. The Dome would be 'so bold, so beautiful, so inspiring that it embodies at once the spirit of confidence and adventure in Britain and the spirit of the future of the world'. What it actually embodied was the sterility of spin. It was an echoing oratorium; an edifice of hype; a *folie de* bombast. New Labour was being taught a painful lesson. Grand delusions create great disillusion.

The Prime Minister had half a premonition that it might turn out like this. When he was wrestling with his own anxieties about the project, back in the summer of 1997, Blair had told David Puttnam, the film producer and New Labour peer, that a successful Dome would be 'a huge mood statement and a fantastic run-in to an election'. But what if it went wrong? Then, people would be saying: 'Ah ha, fifteen hospitals please.'[9]

He was right the second time. What the people wanted was not a vacuous temple to political vanity but a health service that worked.

David Miliband had a theory, which he popularised among colleagues at Number 10, that governing was about managing the gap between expectations and reality. When the gap grew too wide, governments fell down it. For New Labour, the condition of the National Health Service was opening the most alarming chasm between hopes and experience.

The NHS was in crisis, or on the edge of it, from the moment they came to power. The inheritance from the Tories was a demoralised and eviscerated service which was constantly pleading with Gordon Brown for emergency cash infusions which were never large enough to make a significant difference. In the summer of 1999, just three months into the new financial year, Frank Dobson sought an additional emergency injection of £2 billion.[10] He was rebuffed.

The government had made it worse for themselves with the phoney '£21 billion' which was supposed to come on stream from April 1999. When Dobson departed as Health Secretary in the autumn, his final shot to Blair was that this deceptive inflation of what they were actually spending was 'a strategic mistake'. They had raised expectations 'sky high' while not providing the money to deliver.

His successor at health, Alan Milburn, was the very model of a New Labour moderniser. He was tough and intelligent with a hip-rolling swagger and a soft Geordie accent which made him sound less of an automaton than many of the Blairites. His mother was a secretary in the NHS; he never knew his father. Like Tony Blair, he got into politics only after university. Unlike Tony Blair, he became a Trotskyite. A cloud of cannabis smoke hung over his time running a radical bookshop in Newcastle called Days of Hope and also known as Haze of Dope. He was not a shank head himself; he was keeping his mind clear for the revolution. A background in hard left politics, far from being unusual, was one of the distinguishing features of many of the Blairites. Milburn shared the pedigree with Stephen Byers, the Trade and Industry Secretary, and Alastair Darling, the Social Security Secretary. Having been what they would now denounce as extremists, they grew up into the middle-managers of Blair's modernising 'revolution'.

Milburn had been a junior minister at the Department of Health before spending a brief period at the Treasury. When he returned as Health Secretary in October 1999, it was to discover that the NHS was in an even more critical condition than he had feared. Outpatients waiting lists were soaring. He was forced to take a gamble on future revenues from tobacco taxes to keep health authorities afloat. To meet the ballooning price of generic drugs £150 million was begged from the Treasury reserve. In a brutal slash-and-burn exercise, officials were ordered to cancel other programmes to concentrate on the priority delivery areas of cancer, coronary heart disease, waiting lists, and the recruitment of doctors and nurses.

Milburn wanted to confront what he saw as the privileges and outdated practices of consultants and GPs. His animus towards them was fired by the views of his partner, Ruth, a psychiatrist. But he had come to the conclusion that, as long as the debate about the health service revolved around its funding, the government would never get through that noise to sell reform either to the professionals or the public.

When Milburn made this argument to the Prime Minister, he found a persuadable audience. Blair had belatedly realised that the health service required a large investment of serious money. There was a moment of personal revelation in September 1999 when Blair and his personal adviser on health, Robert Hill, toured a new elective surgery unit at the Central Middlesex hospital. Having goggled at the state-of-the-art facilities, he returned to Number 10 waxing lyrically to his staff about how this 'revolutionary' facility attended to everything patients needed on the one site. 'This is what we must drive right through the health service,' he told them. 'Why can't everywhere be like this?' The question revealed the Prime Minister's frequent and surprising innocence. The answer was money.

That autumn, Blair began to agitate with Gordon Brown about the funding of the health service. The Prime Minister had been convinced by Milburn that they could not afford to wait until the outcome of the next spending review in July 2000. Blair argued with the Chancellor that they should bring forward a programme of increased health spending in the next Budget. Brown had heard these arguments before from Milburn and had not been convinced by them.

Blair's usual desire to spend met the familiar resistance from Brown for what seemed like compelling reasons to the Chancellor. He had given emergency cash injections to the NHS in each of his Budgets, as well as every previous November. That November he refused to do it again. It would, he argued, make a mockery of his supposedly immutable three-year spending rules. Brown also complained to Blair that the money would simply disappear into 'the bottomless pit' of the NHS. The Chancellor believed – and he had a large point – that they had 'wasted' their first two years by not producing a modernising strategy for the health service.[11]

As this argument rumbled between Number 10 and the Treasury, the immediate challenge was to get through the winter. The Prime Minister's wife was not the only Briton afflicted with the flu. No data was more anxiously awaited at the Department of Health than the weekly chart of influenza cases. Alan Milburn was feeling pretty relaxed until New Year's Eve. Then, in the first week of the new century, the flu graph suddenly jumped higher. The dispute about whether it amounted to an epidemic became beside the political point as the crisis pitifully exposed the inadequacies of the health service that Blair had promised would be 'saved' by his government.

Every day in the first fortnight of January, the media ran horror stories of overcrowded hospitals, cancelled operations, patients rattled hundreds of miles around the country in frantic searches for treatment, and corpses stored in refrigerator lorries.

The sky was thickening with New Labour's sound-bites and slogans coming home to roost. They had promised to be tough on crime; recorded violent offences rose for the first time in six years amidst a fall in police numbers. They pledged an ethical foreign policy; British arms were shipped to Zimbabwe, Robert Mugabe's bankrupt autocracy. General Pinochet was released back to Chile just when Mike Tyson, the convicted rapist, was let into Britain for a boxing match.

'The Week That It All Went Belly-up For New Labour' from the *Sun* was matched by the *Guardian* devoting an entire front page to New Labour's multiple troubles. The press was unanimously and vitriolically battering the government. 'It's a nightmare,' Alastair Campbell despaired to Tony Blair. Nothing they had faced from the press before 'has anything on this'.

Nothing was as damaging as the headlines about the health service. Two particular cases were seen as emblematic of the dire condition of the NHS. The Prime Minister received a letter from the daughter of Mavis Skeet, a seventy-three-year-old whose throat cancer had become inoperable after operations were cancelled four times in five weeks because of bed shortages.

When the crisis seemed to be abating in mid-January, a relieved Milburn told his aides: 'I think we're through the worst of it.'[12] He discovered that the worst was to come on the evening of Thursday 13 January. Milburn was in his London flat. Having finished his red boxes early, he switched on the BBC's *Nine O'Clock News*. The lead item was devastating criticism of the government's stewardship of the health service from Britain's most famous doctor.

For this critic, the ailing condition of the NHS was encapsulated by the plight of a second elderly woman. Eighty-seven-year-old Ruth Winston-Fox suffered a thirteen-hour wait in a casualty department. When a bed was eventually found, it was in a mixed-sex ward, an indignity to the elderly which Labour had pledged, but so far failed, to end. Drugs were not dispensed when they should have been. She missed meals. She fell out of bed one night and was found on the floor the next morning. Catching an infection, she developed a leg ulcer.

This might have been another sad and unreported story from an under-funded and over-stretched hospital were it not for the identity of her son. Professor Robert Winston, eminent fertility expert, television celebrity and peer of the New Labour realm, had the means to make his angry voice heard. The NHS was 'gradually deteriorating', he told the *New Statesman* in an interview which received saturation media coverage. Britain's health service was 'much the worst in Europe', worse even than Poland's. He suggested that the government – 'which contained very few original thinkers' – was not making it any better. 'We've been quite deceitful about it . . . our reorganisation of the health service was very bad.' As a result 'we have made medical care deeply unsatisfactory for many people'. The Lord Professor excused Tony Blair of malignancy. He suggested – which was barely less damning – that the Prime Minister was simply ignorant. 'I don't think he knows this. I don't think he would allow this. I think he is a good man. I don't think he realises.'[13]

Winston's remarks had to be set in the context of a dreadful personal experience, and his disappointment that more money had not been put into his speciality. This was nevertheless a searing commentary on the government. After three years of 'modernising' New Labour, this doctor of great celebrity and distinction was saying that the NHS was more decrepit than the health service in Poland, an ex-Communist basket case.

At breakfast time on Friday morning, Milburn defended the

government with the standard line that the NHS had already received 'the biggest cash injection in its history'.[14] But the Health Secretary indicated that he didn't believe that to be true when he added that he saw it as his task 'to get more resources for the health service', a remark that caused annoyance at the Treasury.

As soon as Number 10 got wind of the Winston interview, there was frantic activity. Attacks from the Conservatives could be deflected as opportunist and media coverage as alarmist. This was lacerating and informed criticism from a medical eminence whose *This Is Your Life* had featured a guest of honour appearance by Tony Blair.

Number 10's instant and characteristic reflex was to attempt to anaesthetise Winston. On Friday morning, the professor received a heated phone call from Alastair Campbell's partner, Fiona Millar. In a convenient paired arrangement, she was personal assistant to Cherie Blair. Winston had foolishly discussed with his interviewer how and where the Prime Minister's wife was going to have her baby. Millar conveyed to the professor how 'very upset' Cherie was that he had talked about such intimate and confidential details. The purpose of the call was not just to communicate Cherie's anger. It was to discomfort the professor in order to soften him up for his next caller from Number 10. They were doing a one–two routine on him. Next on the line came Alastair Campbell to cajole the professor into a retraction of his criticisms of the government. Following this operation by the double-edged scalpel of Doctor Campbell and Nurse Millar, at mid-morning a statement was put out in Winston's name. He had adjusted his view, now saying: 'The basic direction of NHS policy is right.' But the recantation was by no means total. Winston maintained that 'Successive governments – and this one included – have not yet paid sufficient attention to the needs for funding that are going to be required in the future.'[15]

The operation did not work. Other medical eminences piled in. The President of the Royal College of Surgeons, Barry Jackson, disputed the government's claim that the number of doctors was rising. The President of the Royal College of Physicians, Sir George Alberti, said: 'The government has shot itself in its collective feet by not increasing resources sufficiently.'[16]

Tony Blair was the more scalded because he knew that most of this criticism was both deadly accurate and chimed with a wider disenchantment. Two thirds of the public didn't believe the government's claims that waiting lists were falling, and only a third expected the NHS to improve over the next three to four years.[17] Philip Gould, reporting to Blair with the findings of his polling, told the Prime Minister that the public mood towards the government had turned 'negative', 'sour', even 'vicious'. People felt they had been 'conned' by the regurgitation of spending announcements, the recycling of old money as new, and the promises of vast-sounding resources for the NHS which had never materialised.[18]

When Milburn and Blair talked that Friday, it was common ground between them that this was deep trouble. Of all the emergencies faced by the government, none had struck it so squarely in the solar plexus. As tax was for the Conservatives, so the health service which it had founded was the fundamental trust issue for Labour. The crisis could be defused, thought Milburn, only by talking about hard cash, real money. Blair agreed.

On Saturday, the Prime Minister had a long and fractious phone conversation with Gordon Brown. The Chancellor thought they should be toughing it out. Fearing that Blair and Milburn were trying to ramp him into a spending commitment he did not yet want to make, Brown remained resistant to making any promises about future spending on the NHS. He had a good reason for taking this view: the Chancellor had not yet determined how much money he thought it prudent to allocate. He also had a selfish motivation. Brown was coming round to the view that an announcement of extra money for the NHS should be made in the March Budget. Indeed he was now thinking that it would make a splendid centrepiece for the biggest occasion of a Chancellor's year. Brown wanted to make the announcement and take the credit himself.

Blair, much less prepared to defer to his Chancellor than earlier in the life of the government, was insistent that he would have to talk money when he appeared on television on Sunday. The Prime

Minister would describe the case of Mrs Skeet as 'deeply distressing' and 'accept personal responsibility to make sure the situation does not recur'. But he knew that expressions of sympathy for victims of the crisis would be ridiculed as empty words if they were not accompanied by an indication of how the government was going to keep his promise that it would never happen again. The Prime Minister's approval ratings in the polls were plummeting. His personal prestige was on the line. According to one Cabinet minister: 'The Budget was written by Mavis Skeet and Robert Winston.'[19]

At the end of two hours of argument, Brown eventually agreed a form of words which would allow the Prime Minister to give a 'signal' about future spending, but the Chancellor was adamant that Blair make it clear this was dependent on economic growth and reform.

From Sir David Frost's sofa that Sunday morning, Blair put aside the unbelieved claim that the health service had already had the biggest cash injection in its history. 'We've had two years in the health service of pretty tight funding, we've put in slightly more than the Conservatives, but only slightly more because we had to sort out the borrowing we inherited.' Blair now admitted: 'There is no easy way of rebuilding the health service other than more money.'

He said there would be above-inflation pay awards for doctors and nurses, particularly aimed at addressing the large number of vacancies for middle-grade nurses which had contributed to waiting lists. His boldest and most unanticipated pledge was to bring health spending in Britain up to the average of the European Union over five years. 'If we run the economy properly, I am entirely confident we will get those 5 per cent real term rises.'[20]

Gordon Brown, watching the interview from his home in Scotland, was not pleased. Matching the EU average could be taken to imply additional spending of as much as £16 billion, more than a third again of the NHS allocation. The moment the interview was over, Brown rang his advisers, Ed Balls and Ed Miliband. Blair's breakfast interview had been watched by Balls in bed alongside his wife, the Public Health Minister Yvette Cooper and their young baby. He was still in bed when Brown rang. 'Tony was a bit strong,' the Chancellor grumbled to his aides, but he was not that angry yet.

Other members of the Cabinet, alarmed that committing the cake to the health service would leave crumbs for their departments, were jumpy. David Blunkett was soon on the phone to Blair that Sunday. The Education Secretary believed that the NHS was a black hole which was permanently in crisis. Health was capable of sucking away every coin in the Treasury at the expense of education. In response to the complaints of Blunkett, Blair soothed that he had not forgotten saying that education, education, education were supposed to be his government's three greatest priorities.

It was the coverage of Blair's interview by Monday morning's newspapers that threw Gordon Brown into one of his great tempers. He was livid to find the press universally reporting this as a massive new pledge to the NHS, an interpretation which had been encouraged by Robert Hill at Number 10 and by the Department of Health.

When the Chancellor confronted the Prime Minister, Brown accused Blair of breaking their Saturday agreement. There were three dimensions to Brown's fury, in ascending order of heat. He protested – and this was a legitimate complaint – that Blair had not put enough emphasis on additional resources being tied to modernisation. He was angrier still that by plucking at European averages as the goal, a target had been set that was huge, imprecise and moving. Brown was most incandescent that Blair had robbed the Chancellor of his glory. 'You've stolen my fucking Budget!' raged Brown at a sheepish Blair.[21] The running sore of their relationship – who was in control and who gained the credit – was weeping again.

The Prime Minister endeavoured to assuage Brown and placate Blunkett. Alastair Campbell briefed the media that 'we always said education is our number one priority'. Future health spending, he added, would be dependent on growth.[22] The Chancellor's aides, effectively rebuking the Prime Minister on behalf of Brown, let it be known that what Blair had said was 'not a commitment, but an aspiration'.[23]

In the space of twenty-four hours, the Prime Minister's great pledge had apparently shrivelled into a wispily unbankable aspiration. At Question Time that Wednesday, William Hague was at his most mocking. 'So far we've had Frost on Sunday, panic on Monday, U-turn on Tuesday and waffle on Wednesday.'[24] Tory MPs jeered.

Stung and cornered, Blair responded by re-hardening the commitment, expressing himself 'entirely confident' that the government would achieve the pledge to get up to the EU average.

This was a turning point for New Labour. Blair had thought that the way to stay abreast of public opinion was to ape the Tory policy of income tax cuts. Just over a year earlier, he had said: 'My own gut feeling is that there is a long-term trend away from higher personal tax rates . . . that is definitely the way the world is going.'[25] Only six months earlier, he had put his name to a pamphlet saying that 'Public expenditure as a proportion of national income has more or less reached the limits of acceptability.'[26]

Now Blair found himself behind public opinion. His assumptions were revised when confronted with this immediate crisis, popular pressure and polling majorities telling the government that voters would rather have more spending on public services than tax cuts. Even discounting for the propensity of people to lie about their willingness to pay tax, 83 per cent in favour of spending over tax cuts was an unprecedentedly large total. The trade unions, the CBI and the City were also as one in cautioning against tax cuts. The penny off the basic rate that Brown had announced in his last Budget was not dropped, but the idea of spending his surpluses on any further tax cuts was put aside in favour of public spending.

Throughout February and into early March there was what those close to the bargaining describe as 'hard tussling' between Prime Minister and Chancellor about precisely how large a sum could be committed to the health service. Blair was anxious that, as well as the long-term investment programme, the Budget should contain an upfront cash salve for the NHS. Brown was playing his usual game of concealing his hand from the Prime Minister until the very last moment. They finally settled on the sum of £2 billion just before the Budget was due to go to the printers. When he returned to the Treasury to announce the outcome of his arguments with Blair to aides and senior officials, Brown smiled and said: 'That should keep Tony off my back until the election.'[27]

In his Budget speech, the Chancellor made no mention of European averages, and he had persuaded Blair to drop it from the statement by the Prime Minister the following day. That target for success was quietly cast aside. But the future investment pledged to the health service was nevertheless unprecedented. 'In the years from now until 2004, NHS spending will grow by 6.1 per cent a year over and above inflation, by far the largest sustained increase in NHS funding in any period in its fifty-year history,' declared Brown. 'Last year the equivalent of just over £1,850 per household was spent on the NHS. By the year 2004 more than £2,800 will be spent on the NHS. Half as much again for health care for every family in our country.'[28]

He abandoned the phoney cumulative totals which had engendered so much cynicism about spending announcements. David Blunkett, who had been intensively lobbying that they had to be seen rewarding success as well as failure, received an additional £1 billion for education. It was accompanied by a broad hint of more to come later in the summer spending announcements in order to meet Blair's pledge to increase the proportion of national wealth spent on education.

On the morning of the Budget, Milburn phoned the most elevated representatives of the medical profession, the heads of the royal colleges, to invite them to watch the Budget at the Department of Health. At the sound of the sums being announced, Sir George Alberti banged the table with astonished delight. Dr Ian Bogle of the British Medical Association had declined Milburn's invitation, thinking his afternoon would be better spent writing a press release expressing the BMA's bitter disappointment with the government. Amazed and enthused by the Budget, he ripped up his first draft, and began again with the words: 'We are delighted.'[29]

On behalf of the TUC, John Monks called it a 'real Labour Budget'. Another unremitting critic, Roy Hattersley, was warm to the government. Even Ken Livingstone described it as 'a big step in the right direction'.

The most telling reaction came from the Conservatives. William Hague felt compelled to 'unambiguously' welcome the increases for health and education. Michael Portillo, whose return to the Commons at the Kensington and Chelsea by-election was swiftly followed by his appointment as Shadow Chancellor, bound the Conservatives to match New Labour's spending increases for the NHS.

This was a paradigm shift in the argument between left and right. At the election, Tony Blair and Gordon Brown felt constrained to bind themselves to tight Tory spending plans. Three years on, the Conservatives were forced by the electoral realities to sign up to expansionary New Labour spending plans for health.

Portillo also reversed Tory opposition to the independence of the Bank of England and accepted the minimum wage which he had once predicted would cause massive unemployment. These were important shifts in the terms of political trade between right and left. After nearly two decades which Labour spent ceding intellectual ground to the Tories, now the Conservatives were surrendering territory to Labour.

The investment programme was only the foundation stone of the ambition, but it had the potential to be as significant, popular and durable as the benighted Dome was not. A properly funded and modernised National Health Service would be a worthy monument and a lasting legacy.

# 18. Control Failure

At the strategy meeting in Number 10, some of his aides nagged the Prime Minister to focus on the threat. 'Can't we leave London?' sighed Tony Blair, his mind busy with Northern Ireland, Kosovo, a thousand and one things that seemed to be more pressing that Monday morning early in 1999. 'Ken will burn himself out, won't he?'[1]

The idea that Ken Livingstone – personification of everything that Blair reviled about the schismatic, self-destructive, unelectable Labour Party of the past – could possibly become mayor of London was not just repugnant, it was inconceivable. Blair was convinced that his party and the voters would see, as he saw with such clarity, that Livingstone was a lethal menace. There was an additional reason to go into denial. New Labour was built on the grave of leftists like Livingstone. It was against logic that Blair, the architect of New Labour, could possibly be responsible for resurrecting a politician he detested as profoundly as this *bête rouge*.

The introduction of American-style directly elected city mayors was Blair's personal enthusiasm in the programme of constitutional reform. He insisted on the innovation in the face of resistance from virtually all of the relevant senior colleagues. He envisaged mayors revitalising moribund local government as city halls were shaken by their arthritic necks by dynamic, reforming pragmatists possessed of star quality. Local models of himself, sons and daughters springing from the ear of Blair, would arise to modernise civic government as he was modernising the country.

They would look like anything but Ken Livingstone, a man accorded special prominence in New Labour's demons' gallery. A product of sixties bedsit activism, in 1981 the thirty-five-year-old councillor executed an internal putsch to take control of the Greater London Council which he turned into a laboratory and a playground for the left. His equality agenda was ahead of its time. But he set back the cause with indulgences which handed ammunition to a Thatcher government branding Labour as 'loony' and looking for excuses to justify the abolition of the GLC in 1986. Livingstone's GLC postured its own nuclear-free foreign policy, and used ratepayers' money to fund Babies Against The Bomb, Lesbian Left and Revolutionary Feminists. He invited IRA-supporters to County Hall when the terrorists were bombing the heart out of the capital. On his own account, Livingstone became the most hated leader and his regime the most unpopular administration in the history of the GLC.[2] He epitomised the alienating, election-losing extremism of Labour in the eighties to the young, moderate barrister from a northern seat who came into parliament in the suicide election of 1983. Burnt into the memory of Tony Blair's formative political years was the near-implosion of his party when Livingstone and his like had the run of the asylum.

That red mist clouded the view of Blair and everyone around him to the way perceptions of Livingstone had since changed among the public. The wise-cracking individualist who performed on chat shows and panel games, kept amphibians as pets and advertised Red Leicester cheese on the telly, did not look as though he had cloven-feet. Folk memory of his rule in London more benignly recalled an urban hero who tried to make travel cheap and so defied Margaret Thatcher in her autocratic pomp that she had to abolish him because she could not beat him. The politician formerly known as Red Ken had skilfully reinvented himself as Charming Ken.

Unlike his fellow-travellers from the eighties London Left – Tony Banks, Paul Boateng, Margaret Hodge – he did not accommodate himself to New Labour. A solitarian, he acted the witty dissident in the New Labour gulag. This was a mischief-making and well remunerated existence, but it was politically impotent. He was a pygmy heckling the juggernaut. That he would have remained – had not Tony Blair created the one job perfectly designed for Ken Livingstone and his style of political showmanship.

Following the affirmative referendum in May 1998, he made no secret of his ambition. He discarded his previous view that the idea of a mayor was 'absolutely barmy' with a characteristic shamelessness. Livingstone declared his intentions during the passage of the legislation through the Commons by expressing the hope that 'the voice for London has a pronounced nasal quality'. By February 1999, he was running an advertising campaign: 'Let Ken Stand'.

Among those becoming increasingly agitated about the spectre of Mayor Livingstone was Clive Soley, the senior London MP and chairman of the Parliamentary Labour Party. In March, at one of his regular meetings with the Prime Minister, he tried to concentrate Blair's mind. Soley fretted: 'Unless we get someone in place soon, it's going to be impossible to stop him.' Blair agreed that it was important, but he did not think it that urgent. 'We're working on it,' he responded. In the light of events, Soley would kick himself for not being more forthright. He should have refused to leave the Prime Minister's study until he had got an answer.

Other competitors were beginning to warm up for the race. Peter Mandelson promoted his friend and former colleague at London Weekend Television, the broadcaster Trevor Phillips. Alastair Campbell pushed Tony Banks, the jesting Sports Minister, as an acceptable retread from the old GLC. The cook Delia Smith, the football manager Alex Ferguson and the actress Joanna Lumley were names tossed about in New Labour circles. Blair originally invested his hopes in Glenda Jackson, on the grounds, as he put it to several people, that 'she's a famous name'. This betrayed his weakness for being seduced by the superficial. The Oscar-winning actress was a brittle personality with much less spangled political skills. She was approached by one of Blair's aides at the end of 1997, but the suggestion that she should run was not accompanied by a solid promise of endorsement from the Prime Minister. The failure to give a clear signal where his favours lay encouraged this proliferation of candidates. All of them struggled to be heard against continuous background noise from Downing Street that the Prime Minister was scouring the land for a heavier hitter. This handed a double boon to Livingstone. It declared him as the man that Tony Blair was desperate to kill long before the Prime Minister had arrived at a decision about what weapon to use. Livingstone meanwhile cavorted down the track unconfronted by serious challenge. He cheerfully acknowledged the debt he owed to Number 10, saying: 'It's only because they keep doing everything they can to stop me that I'm getting all this support and publicity.'[3]

The lack of urgency in Downing Street flowed in large part from the belief that the easy solution was to break his legs. Gordon Brown, Peter Mandelson, Alastair Campbell, Philip Gould, everyone of account around Tony Blair, believed they could simply prevent Livingstone being a candidate. It was unthinkable to allow him anywhere near an office with the largest personal mandate in Europe apart from the President of France: a brilliant platform from which to grandstand against the government. The same view was taken by Margaret McDonagh, the party's general secretary, known to some of her staff as 'the iron lady'. Officials at Millbank had already drawn up a charge sheet of heresies and disloyalties to use to exclude Livingstone. Campbell, an especially aggressive proponent of blocking Livingstone, contended that whatever short-term controversy this caused would be much less damaging than the years of mayhem he would create as mayor.

It was events in Wales, a country with an influence on the development of New Labour that no one ever anticipated, which began to change the nature of that debate. The high command of New Labour were deeply taken aback by the electoral backlash in the May 1999 elections which followed Blair's imposition of Alun Michael over the much more popular Rhodri Morgan. The veto remained a live option for dealing with Livingstone, but belatedly the Prime Minister began to trawl for a candidate capable of beating him.

No one wanted to do it. The Home Office Minister, Paul Boateng, responded to an approach by saying he would not be the leadership's candidate 'come hell or high water'. Mo Mowlam publicly advertised a lack of interest by turning up at the launch of a biography of Livingstone and giving him one of her famous hugs in front of journalists. In fact, though Mowlam was very reluctant, she was not completely ruling it out. She was in a strop with the

Prime Minister and his acolytes because she was fed up with reading about her future in the papers. When Soley talked to her at Easter, she told him that if Blair wanted her to do it, 'Tony should ask me himself.'[4]

There were several qualities to apparently recommend Frank Dobson. Though he was born in Yorkshire, his political career had been built in the capital. The former leader of Camden council, and a London MP since 1979, he was believed to be well liked by London party members. Dobson was a team player, but his grizzled beard and a filthy sense of humour in the tradition of northern night clubs declared him not to be a smoothly cloned Blairite.

The Prime Minister was unconvinced that the job he created for a New Labour dynamo should go to the Old Labourish Dobson. He did discuss London with Dobson. 'Ken must be stopped,' said Blair with a vehemence that suggested he would rather have hot needles stuck under his fingernails than see Livingstone become mayor of London. Dobson expressed his agreement and waited to hear more from the Prime Minister. Blair smiled: 'Of course, you would be mad to give up such a great job as Health Secretary.' There was a pregnant pause while Dobson waited for the inevitable 'but' to fall from Blair's lips. It didn't. Blair never explicitly invited Dobson to run for mayor.[5]

His hesitancy about Dobson was increased in May 1999 when Philip Gould brought worrying news from his market-testing of opinion. Gould told the Prime Minister that Livingstone was ahead of the hirsute Yorkshireman by what he calculated to be an unbridgeable margin. 'Mo is the only person who can beat him.' Livingstone himself thought the same. She 'could definitely beat me'.[6] Mowlam was by far the most popular member of the Cabinet. Whenever she appeared on party political broadcasts, there was a surge in membership applications. And the added attraction to Blair of getting her to run for London was that it would solve his difficulty getting her out of Belfast.[7]

He had his favourite, but she refused the starting gate. When he broached the idea with Mowlam in the spring, Blair pitched it to her as a 'stepping stone' to higher things. But his appeals met resistance from Mowlam, not least because her relationship with Blair had been progressively soured by the constant speculation about his intentions feeding out of Number 10 to the media. She was not a Londoner, she told him. And it was 'a shitty job' sandwiched between central and local government.[8] The absence of substantial powers was a problem constantly encountered by Blair in his efforts to persuade any high-profile candidate to take it on. Richard Branson of Virgin and Bob Ayling of British Airways, New Labour-friendly business figures who were Blair's initial notion of ideal candidates, had not been interested. Downing Street approached Michael Cassidy, a businessman and leading figure in the City of London corporation. More clear-sighted than those canvassing him, Cassidy concluded that an outsider could never beat a candidate from within the Labour tribe. The flailing around for a candidate led to feelers being put out even to Martin Bell, the Independent MP for Tatton. Blair came to see it very slowly, but he had created a job fashioned to serve no one's ambitions more perfectly than those of that superbly accomplished practitioner of personality politics, Ken Livingstone.

The Prime Minister made his strongest entreaties to Mowlam when they talked in mid July. She was even more disgruntled with Blair by then, especially because he was not offering the reward for her gruelling service in Northern Ireland that she thought she deserved, which was the Foreign Office.[9] Mowlam rebuffed him with a definitive no.

Livingstone naturally relished the Prime Minister's evident failure to find someone of stellar quality to take him on. 'I think they will let me run,' he said. 'Once Tony Blair comes back from Tuscany after a nice margarita by the swimming pool, he will say to me: "You stand, sunshine, be my candidate." '[10] Blair would rather quaff neat nitric acid.

By the time of the party conference in late September, the Prime Minister was getting into a ludicrous position. After months of Micawberishly hoping for something to turn up, nothing had. For a highly significant office of his personal creation he lacked a candidate. Mowlam would not do it. Dobson, needled by the constant speculation that he was on an exit trajectory from the Cabinet, could scarcely have been more emphatic that he was not interested. He belligerently declared that 'I love' being Health Secretary. This was the 'only job I ever wanted' and he hoped to stay there 'for a very long time'.[11] His disavowals of London were so strident that a reverse would look as incredible as it would suspicious. At the Bournemouth conference, Dobson went out of his way to suggest that the last thing on earth he wanted to be was mayor of London. He crossed the road to wish good luck to Glenda Jackson. He also cleared the path for a run by Nick Raynsford, the Minister for London. Highly able, popular among Labour councillors in the capital and intelligently loyal, the bald and bespectacled Raynsford did want to be mayor. His disadvantage was an under-endowment of charisma. Knowing that he could not compete with Dobson to be the approved candidate, over a lunch that summer Raynsford ascertained that he would not be standing. To be absolutely certain, the day before he launched his own candidacy at the party conference, Raynsford again checked with Dobson that he was not going to run. Dobson replied that he was not interested and swiftly moved on to regale the other man with his latest dirty joke about a pill which was a cross between Viagra and Prozac: 'So you don't give a fuck when you don't get a fuck.' Raynsford's laugh was not in appreciation of the awfulness of the joke, but an expression of relief that he was free to stand. When he sought the Prime Minister's blessing, Raynsford received the clear impression from Blair that he entertained no hope of Dobson. The machine began to groom Nick Raynsford.

In the twenty-four hours after Raynsford's launch at Bournemouth, something strange came over Frank Dobson. By Friday, he was secretly briefing that he was suddenly in the running. When an understandably furious Raynsford rang him later to demand an explanation for this extraordinary volte-face, Dobson claimed to have been 'mugged' in the gardens outside the conference centre by two members of the engineering union who bullied him into standing. This was more of an excuse than an explanation for Dobson's double backwards somersault. Several things seem to have sparked together in his head to cause this mental flip. Margaret McDonagh viewed Raynsford as a nice but grey man who could not possibly beat the cunning but colourful Livingstone. She browbeat Dobson to save London. Neil Kinnock, a vehement detester of Livingstone, had for weeks been trying to persuade Dobson to run. The Health Secretary couldn't be deaf to the persistent buzz that he did not have a long-term future in the Cabinet. Dobson's relationship with Downing Street was so wary that he did not inform Blair of his abrupt change of mind. Had he done so, the launch of his candidacy might not have been such a disaster.

The weekend after the conference, employing the bizarre conduit of the Conservative *Sunday Telegraph* to indicate his intentions, Dobson revealed that he now did want to be mayor of London. Blair, caught as much by surprise as everyone else, rang round Alastair Campbell, Anji Hunter, and Sally Morgan, his political secretary. 'Is this true?' Blair asked his aides. 'Find out if it's true.'[12] On Sunday afternoon, Dobson phoned Blair to confirm that he was in the contest.

The Prime Minister at last had a candidate of weight, but one who was saddled with a handicap so heavy that it would crush his credibility. Everything Dobson had said before, and the manner in which he sprang his candidacy, couldn't help but make him look like a pressed man. He was instantly on the defensive against the accusation that Blair had twisted his beard. 'It's a lie,' Dobson angrily rejected the charge of being a puppet. 'He never even asked me to do this job.'[13] This was absolutely true, as were Blair's protestations to the same effect.

The paradox about the opening act of the mayor saga is that it was characterised, not least on Blair's part, by prevarication and muddle. But the image of iron control that New Labour had done so much to cultivate in the mind of the media and the public – though laughably remote from the truth – rebounded on those who had created it. The penalty for control-freakery and the punishment for spin was that, even when they weren't meddling and fixing, the denials were greeted with incredulity.

Dobson's departure from the Cabinet meant that Blair could

return to the business left unfinished by the abortive reshuffle of July. On Monday 11 October, Peter Mandelson was summoned from the flat he was now renting in Notting Hill – 'the House of Death', as he called it, had been sold – to be re-elevated to the Cabinet as Northern Ireland Secretary. It was the fastest rehabilitation from disgrace in modern political history. To Mo Mowlam, Blair offered Health Secretary. To his surprise, she turned him down. Her career aim, as it had been when they talked in the summer, was to be Foreign Secretary. When they resumed argument about her future in the autumn, she said to him: 'I know you won't give me the Foreign Office now because you think I'm not ready.' As a step towards her goal, how about giving her the departing George Robertson's job at Defence?[14] Blair refused. He was putting Geoff Hoon into Defence. A lawyer, capable, personable, recently shorn of his moustache and completely unknown to the public, Hoon was an impeccably qualified Blairite. All the Prime Minister had left for Mowlam was a scraping from the bottom of the barrel: Minister at the Cabinet Office. The fate of the outgoing 'Enforcer', Jack Cunningham, who lasted there barely more than a year, was a warning not to sup at that poisoned chalice. Mowlam didn't want to be 'Minister for the *Today* programme'. 'She's been put in the parking lot,' derisively commented a senior member of the Cabinet.[15] Miserable and miscast at the Cabinet Office, within a few weeks of the reshuffle, she let Blair know that she would now run for London, after all.[16] What she wouldn't do was compete against Frank Dobson. He would have to be persuaded to step aside. Blair tried and failed. Margaret McDonagh approached Dobson and suggested he should pull out. Dobson, who regarded that as a humiliating request which would make him look completely ridiculous, was now as determined to stay in the race as he had previously been adamantine that he wouldn't enter it. If Dobson had not mind-flipped at the conference, and if Mowlam had decided she wanted London just a few weeks earlier, the entire outcome could have been so much happier for New Labour. On such accidents of timing and clashes of character does the river of events turn.

Mowlam would have been an unquestionably popular candidate with both the public and Labour members. Dobson's prospects of beating Livingstone were much more doubtful if the candidate was chosen by a simple ballot of the 68,000 Labour members in the capital. Margaret McDonagh was particularly influential in persuading Blair that the way to fix Livingstone was to use an electoral college, despite the certain controversy that this would cause. Nick Raynsford, speaking in his capacity as Minister for London, had told the Commons in May that the election would be conducted by One Member, One Vote. That was still the plan in a July note issued by the National Executive Committee:

It is proposed that the Labour mayoral candidate should be selected by one-member, one-vote of all the relevant party membership, to reflect the fact that he or she will have a higher profile and a wider electoral mandate.

These promises were cast aside on 12 October when the National Executive Committee instead voted to employ the electoral college, the distortion of democracy which had already caused such discontent and brought such discredit upon New Labour in Wales. This was not just a product of Number 10's desire to tilt the playing field against Livingstone. Old Labourite forces, anxious to preserve the link between the party and the unions from the Blairites, exploited the leader's vulnerability. At the NEC meeting, it was Margaret Prosser, deputy General Secretary of the Transport and General Workers' Union, who proposed using the electoral college. Ian McCartney, a close ally of John Prescott, was most vociferous in arguing that a third of the votes should be given to the trade unions. Another third was set aside for London MPs and MEPs, and candidates for the London Assembly. A fortnight after a conference speech in which Tony Blair dedicated himself to 'equality of worth', an unequal system was adopted which gave to an MP a vote worth the equivalent of those of a thousand party members. It stank.

This 'stitch-up', as Glenda Jackson called it, was denounced by constituency parties, the media and, of course, by Livingstone.

Even Dobson, the candidate the system was designed to favour, complained about this 'stupid decision' with a bitterness that suggested sincerity. Downing Street and Millbank were proving to be the best campaign managers that Ken Livingstone could have asked for. Just as Margaret Thatcher had done before, Tony Blair was creating exactly the environment in which Livingstone could thrive as the plucky David against the autocratic Goliath of the machine. It was a pose. Livingstone had no history as a champion of One Member, One Vote. The last time he was near power, he operated by deal and cabal himself. The people's champion was a costume of convenience. New Labour's disastrous misjudgement was to have tailored it for him.

A massive barrage, from backbench popguns to the heavy artillery of the Cabinet, was unleashed to pound Livingstone. David Blunkett scorned him as frivolous. Gordon Brown and John Prescott assailed him as dangerous. Neil Kinnock denounced him as an opportunist. This served to betray their own confusion about how to tackle the infuriatingly popular Livingstone. They could not make up their minds whether he was a chancer, a clown or the devil incarnate. The MP for Tottenham, Bernie Grant, described Livingstone as a 'dodgy politician'.[17] Brian Sedgemore, another left-winger who could not be remotely described as a Blairite toady, was blistering: 'Ken is a sad and lonely figure. He continually portrays himself as a victim when he is a destructive manipulator.'[18]

All that could be true, and none of it had any traction on Livingstone, because New Labour's own manipulations allowed him to brilliantly play the role of victim. The onslaught actually fed his popularity. Livingstone was a mutant politician. Like the coprophagous beetle, the more dirt they hurled at him, the stronger he became. Essential to his anti-political appeal was his unpopularity among other politicians.

By mid-October, an opinion poll placed him as the overwhelmingly popular choice to be Labour's candidate. With 63 per cent of the vote, he thrashed the then Tory contender, Jeffrey Archer, by a margin of almost three to one. Even more disturbingly for Downing Street, if Livingstone stood as an independent he was still an easy winner with 43 per cent of the vote to Archer's 25 per cent. In this scenario, Dobson came a disastrous third on 23 per cent.[19]

This prompted frenzied and bitter argument in the high commands of New Labour. As Livingstone waited to be called before the candidate vetting panel, Blair cast around his intimates for advice. Alastair Campbell was still for blocking him as was Peter Mandelson: 'Don't let him through.' Blair muttered back: 'But then I'll be called a control-freak.'[20] Most trenchantly against Livingstone being allowed to become a candidate was Gordon Brown. The Chancellor's detestation was not just fired by the fact that Livingstone had – ludicrously – called for Brown to be sacked. Brown argued with Blair that to let Livingstone be the candidate would compromise the authenticity of the government. They had to keep New Labour 'pure'. When Blair replied that he had become queasy about using the veto, he and Brown got into one of their shouting matches. Brown railed at the Prime Minister that 'at any cost' Livingstone had to be stopped 'whatever it takes'. He told Blair to show some spine.[21] The Prime Minister was being pulled in two as other influential voices implored him to let Livingstone run. Philip Gould, originally a blocker, had turned 180 degrees. He lamented to Blair that they should have had a strategy either to 'incorporate' Livingstone or to 'destroy him'. But it was too late for that now. Blocking him would divide the party with 'terrible' electoral consequences. Margaret McDonagh had also stood on her head. She told Blair that the party might haemorrhage ten thousand or more members in London. Dobson also warned Blair against giving Livingstone the martyrdom he was seeking as a springboard to run as an independent.

Signals came out of Number 10 that the Prime Minister wanted the MP for Brent East to be permitted to run to avoid a cataclysmic split in the party. On Tuesday 16 November, Livingstone was summoned to the party's headquarters in Millbank Tower to be interviewed by a twelve-member vetting panel. Concealing his nerves with a display of flippancy, he arrived saying that he would happily swear an oath of loyalty on the bones of a saint or pull a sword from a stone if that was required to get on the short-list of candidates. The panel confronted him with a much more stretching test. The manifesto for London was bound to include the government's policy to invest in the Underground through a public–private partnership. Opposition to what he excoriated as privatisation was the centrepiece of Livingstone's populist campaign. When the interview began, in a first floor room overlooking the Thames, he soon clashed with his principal inquisitors. They were Ian McCartney, a Glaswegian former seaman who packed gallons of aggression into a pint-sized body, and Clive Soley, a former probation officer who wanted some guarantees of good behaviour from a man he regarded as a serial recidivist. McCartney asked Livingstone whether he would abide by the manifesto. Emboldened perhaps by the prior briefing that Blair now feared the consequences of blocking him, Livingstone repeatedly refused. 'If I couldn't accept the manifesto, I would stand down as a candidate,' he replied. McCartney, whose temper was as short as his stature, turned on him: 'You are putting the party in an intolerable situation.' Soley, usually the mildest of men, was scandalised. When he angrily pursued the point, Livingstone replied casually: 'You would have to get yourself another candidate.' What made this impasse particularly difficult was that there was right on both sides. A party cannot have a candidate who reserves the right to abandon them if he does not like the manifesto. But it was not in the spirit of devolution to bind the most popular choice for mayor of London to a policy he had so vigorously opposed.

Livingstone was sent away, leaving the panel to spend hours arguing about what to do. Soley wanted to exclude him there and then on the grounds that: 'Any other candidate who behaved like that would be shown the door.' But this was not any other candidate. To veto him now, after so much previous chicanery, would cause uproar. McCartney, though he shared the fear and loathing of Livingstone, was more scared by the consequences of excluding him. 'People will not understand,' he said to the others. 'The party will never get over it.' Jim Fitzpatrick, the chairman of the London Labour Party, had no love for Livingstone, but forecast a 'meltdown' if they struck him off. As the panel debated, it grew dark. The waiting media reported the proceedings as farce. From Number 10 came increasingly frantic phone calls. On the assumption that Livingstone would go through, television crews had been summoned to Downing Street in order for Blair to launch into a series of interviews denouncing Livingstone on the teatime news bulletins, *Channel Four News* and *Newsnight*. When Soley eventually surfaced, four hours later than scheduled, it was to announce that they would be calling Livingstone back for a further inquisition in two days' time. The interviews with the Prime Minister were cancelled. This pantomime of interminably inconclusive meetings while the Prime Minister dangled at Downing Street recalled the most shambolic days of Old Labour.

On Thursday, after a further four-hour session with the panel, Livingstone was put on the candidates' list even though he had still offered only very conditional promises about the manifesto. That evening, Blair went on the offensive. Fear of Livingstone and the resurgence of the left that he might represent reduced the Prime Minister to angry cliché. 'While there is a breath left in my body', he would fight a return to the extremism of the eighties.

My problem with him is that while I was growing up in the Labour Party, he and Arthur Scargill and Tony Benn were in control of the Labour Party. They almost knocked it over the edge of the cliff into extinction. It became unelectable. If that is the politics he still represents, then I am going to have to go out and fight for the party I believe in.[22]

It is understandable why the civil war that almost destroyed the party during his political adolescence still raged so vividly in Blair's head. Later, reflecting back, he conceded: 'Sometimes I think the experiences in the early eighties almost scarred me too much, in terms of the Labour Party and how it had to be.'[23] Paradoxically, it was Blair, rather than Livingstone, who was refighting the battles of the eighties. Blair's fixation with not repeating Labour's past mistakes drew him into making a catalogue of disastrous blunders of his own. Livingstone was much more cleverly adapting himself to the climate of the moment. He sought to please whichever audience he happened to be addressing, and cheerfully ditched any commitments that might stand between him and election. To the Prime Minister's bemusement, the man he had mistaken as an unreconstructed old leftist could be as skilled a political chameleon as Blair himself.

The disgrace of Lord Archer of Lies and the low comedy which attended his replacement as Tory candidate by Steve Norris provided some temporary relief from the government's torments. So did the revelation that Cherie was expecting a fourth child. But it was an indication of the cynicism with which New Labour was now viewed that some people could not be budged from the belief that what was so obviously an accidental pregnancy had been deliberately timed to boost the Prime Minister's flagging virility with the electorate. On that cynicism, Livingstone played, cynically. He could be as slippery and cold-blooded as his amphibian pets. In early December, stories began to surface that Dobson was so dejected about his prospects that he was on the verge of quitting the contest. It was true that Dobson, a man previously noted for his *bonhomie*, was in an increasingly bad humour. He lashed out at the 'cretinous journalists'[24] who portrayed him as Blair's hairy booby and the apparatchiks at Millbank who had made it look as though that was precisely what he was. They had, he complained, 'messed things up from start to finish'.[25]

It was put about that Dobson was 'clinically depressed'. Though Livingstone denied authorship of this smear on his opponent, the distinguished journalist, John Lloyd, said Livingstone used the phrase in conversation with him. Livingstone referred to Dobson in the same terms during an off-the-record session with a roomful of writers and editors from the *Guardian*. Dobson was inevitably undermined by this picture of him as a dribbling, hopeless wreck only certification away from the funny farm. He was more damaged by the dirty tricks that were employed on his behalf. Party membership lists were of crucial help with canvassing. The release of them from Millbank to the Dobson campaign, but not to the other candidates, made the contest look even more rigged. Glenda Jackson, a natural loyalist converted into a disillusioned dissident by all the machinations, was infuriated by continual briefing that she would withdraw, the effect of which was to entrench her determination to carry on. She made common cause with Livingstone to lodge complaints about the conduct of the election.

Party members were febrile and disaffected. When Tony Blair and Gordon Brown arrived to address 1,400 activists at the Institute of Education in mid-January, the entrance of Prime Minister and Chancellor was greeted with slow handclapping by sections of the audience. Booing and hissing followed. Before the meeting, Downing Street pre-released a text in which the Prime Minister savaged Livingstone. He delivered some of it, urging them to 'get serious' and not indulge in Livingstone who would be 'a disaster for London'. But, as barracking erupted from the audience, Blair moderated his tone. Brown, adding his *basso profundo* to the prime ministerial tenor, warned against a return to the 'divisive, sterile, self-defeating policies of the 1980s'.

Blair's greatest ire was provoked by an intervention from a woman in the audience who concluded a long litany of complaint by accusing him of spending 'the whole social services budget per night on Kosovo'. There was nothing synthetic about the fury of Blair's response. 'Let me deal with that. You were saying effectively we've done nothing for anybody,' he started hotly.

When we introduced the national minimum wage, that was the first time that had been done in one hundred years by a Labour government. When you say that one hundred pounds is not enough for the winter allowance for pensioners – well we'd like to do more, but it's one hundred pounds that the Tories never gave people. And when you say that we've done nothing for families . . .

Blair motioned at Gordon Brown. 'He's put in the largest increase in child benefit this country has ever seen. It's money that would never have gone in under the Conservative Party.' His voice was rising:

And you say we've done nothing for inequality and poverty. Ask the one and a half million beneficiaries of the working families tax credit that has put twenty or thirty pounds into the pockets of families, hundreds of thousands of them.

Then his questioner felt the full heat of Blair's scorching scorn. 'And what do people like you say? Because it's not perfect, you've done nothing and therefore I'm walking away. It's pathetic.' Large parts of the audience were roused to cheering approval as he reached his crescendo:

As for this rubbish, this *rubbish* that we took the whole of the social security budget and blew it on Kosovo. First of all, the figures are nonsense. And, secondly, I want to tell you this. The day this movement, when we could do something about it, would walk away from the worst case of racial genocide since World War Two, then we'd have something to be ashamed of.

There was a magnificence to Blair's anger. But it could not conceal the fact that the misjudgements of the preceding months had incited large parts of his party to a passion to punish its leader. Blair begged them to learn from the past.

We've never had two full terms. What has always caused problems are the economy and fighting in the party. Going back to those divisions, those ghastly things that destroyed the last Labour government completely: the result isn't a left-wing Labour government, it's a Tory government.[26]

The terror of that history drove him to try to impose rigid control on the party. Discipline was the forging of New Labour. And yet it was obsessive control which was now responsible for igniting rebellion against the controller and creating those very 'ghastly divisions' which made him tremble.

★

The mutiny against autocratic leadership which fuelled Livingstone was not confined to London. Since becoming leader in Wales, Alun Michael had not made either himself or the devolved administration in Cardiff more popular. Michael had taken the template of Blairite command politics and exaggerated it into a parody of control-freakism. His ministers were not even allowed to write their own replies to letters from MPs. Everything had to go across Michael's desk for approval. This did not live up to the promise of a more consensual style of politics. Michael was running the Welsh Assembly as though he had an impregnable majority, when he possessed no majority at all. The Nationalists, looking for a device to use against Labour, located an issue in the question of whether the Treasury would provide the matching funds necessary to attract aid to deprived areas of Wales from the European Union. Gordon Brown could have helped Michael by indicating that the money would be made available. The Chancellor refused. Though Brown would break his spending rules in the Budget little more than a month later, he would not do so to rescue a colleague. A no-confidence motion was tabled against the Welsh First Secretary for 9 February.

In an attempt to throw the drowning Welshman a rubber ring, Blair sought the assistance of the Liberal Democrats, who held the balance of power in Cardiff. In the days leading up to the vote, the leader of the Liberal Democrats, Charles Kennedy, was called by the Prime Minister no less than three times, on each occasion with a different appeal to save Michael.[27] But the role of auxiliary to New Labour held no attraction for Kennedy. He believed his predecessor, Paddy Ashdown, had been exploited and gulled by Blair. The lesson Kennedy drew from this was to reassert his party's independence. Before his first meeting with the Prime Minister, the previous autumn in his study at Number 10, Kennedy pondered what gambit might prove to Blair that this Liberal Democrat leader was not a patsy. He opened his conversation with Blair by asking: 'Do you mind if I smoke?' On Cherie's instructions – she made Tony quit before they married – Downing Street was a no-smoking zone. But Blair accommodated Kennedy who enjoyed the satisfaction of watching the Prime Minister scurry out of the study to ask one of the staff to search for an ashtray.[28]

Kennedy was in self-assertive mood when Blair pleaded for help in saving Alun Michael. The last of their three conversations was on the night before the no-confidence vote in Cardiff. Blair was sounding desperate, not least because of the prospect that his man would be replaced by Rhodri Morgan whom he had strained so many sinews and rules to stop. 'We simply can't have Rhodri,' Blair told Kennedy. 'He'll be a disaster.'[29] The pleas fell on deaf ears.

At Question Time in the Commons the following day, Blair mounted a stout defence of Alun Michael, saying: 'I believe the Welsh First Secretary is doing an excellent job.'[30] The Conservatives, whose pagers were pulsating with a news flash that Michael had decided to jump before he was pushed, roared with delight: 'He's resigned!' A floundering Blair endured his most humiliating moment at the dispatch box since becoming Prime Minister. That evening, he accepted the inevitable by offering a glowing endorsement to the 'total loyalty' of the 'highly effective' Morgan, the man he was privately describing as 'a disaster' just twenty-four hours earlier.

Blair would have found it much easier to present a case against Ken Livingstone had the Prime Minister not attracted the label of control-freak by imposing his placeman on Wales. Now, Alun Michael was gone anyway, and the leadership had been taken by Rhodri Morgan. Another bitter irony was added to the Prime Minister's groaning collection.

The collapse of the fix in Wales left his face egged with embarrassment, but New Labour clung to the hope that it would still turn the trick in London. At around five thirty on the afternoon of Wednesday 16 February, four days before the scheduled public announcement of the result, Ken Livingstone received a leak of the outcome of the electoral college from a sympathiser working at Millbank. His informant reported that Dobson was the winner by three percentage points. It was time for Livingstone to feel depressed.

His disappointment was lifted on Friday evening when he

received an unexpected invitation, through a chain of intermediaries. It originated with the Prime Minister, of all unlikely people. Blair would like Livingstone to come and talk at Chequers on Saturday morning. Though Livingstone was both astonished and encouraged by this invitation, with his customary chutzpah, he at first replied that he was not sure he could fit in the Prime Minister because he had promised that he would take his nephew and niece sightseeing in London. That was not a difficulty, the answer came back. The Prime Minister would be entirely happy if he brought them up to Buckinghamshire.

At ten o'clock on Saturday morning, Livingstone arrived at the prime ministerial mansion in the Chilterns for an encounter neither ever imagined happening. Blair was parleying with a man whom he detested in every fibre of his being. It was all pleasantries to begin with. Blair chatted to Livingstone's nephew and niece about their GCSEs, and then they wandered the grounds of the Tudor house – 'doing a bit of vandalism', Livingstone later joked – while the two men moved to the drawing room. Livingstone sat at one end of a sofa. Sally Morgan, Blair's political secretary, at the other. Blair motioned Livingstone's aide, Simon Fletcher, to an armchair, and then took one himself. They sat in a circle. Coffee was served in china cups. Both were dressed in trainers, jeans and open-necked shirts, but the superficially informal air was entirely false. These two consummate operators, both highly accomplished at camouflaging their game with charm, started to play verbal poker. Each wanted to test the other man's intentions without revealing his own hand.

'I don't know the result,' said Blair. Livingstone reckoned he was probably telling the truth, though if it was not a bluff he thought it an astonishing example of New Labour's incompetence that he was better informed about the result than the Prime Minister. Blair made a friendly gesture, saying he would campaign for Livingstone if he won. But his main purpose was to find out what Livingstone would do if he lost. 'You will stay in the party, won't you?' Livingstone winked towards his intentions. Apart from mayor, he could think of only two more exciting jobs in politics. 'But I don't think you'd give me the same leeway as Gordon, would you?' They wrangled inconclusively about the financing of the Underground. The masks of cordiality began to slip. Livingstone said that Dobson was already terminally damaged. If he was Labour's candidate 'there's no way we'll win London'. Blair would have to tell Dobson to step aside. 'I can't tell him what to do,' retorted Blair. Livingstone became a little menacing: 'It's going to be very bloody.' At the end of fifty minutes of shadow boxing, they shook hands. Through a gritted smile, Blair said: 'We will have to get together again very quickly.'

Livingstone's mole in Millbank was proved correct when the result of the electoral college was announced at party headquarters on Sunday afternoon. Once the votes of the third-placed Glenda Jackson were redistributed, Frank Dobson beat Livingstone by 51.53 per cent to 48.47 per cent.

Members had voted for Livingstone over Dobson by a margin of three to two. The unions had voted for him by a margin of nearly three to one. Dobson owed his whiskery victory to the overwhelming support among MPs, MEPs and assembly candidates, whose ballot was not secret and some of whom were allegedly leant on. The absence of a members' ballot by the engineering union and other dubious aspects of the process were seized upon by Livingstone to make plausible his claim that Dobson had won with 'stolen votes'.

That this was the most pyrrhic of victories was immediately apparent when Dobson and his running mate, Trevor Phillips, appeared before the media. As they vainly tried to talk up their policies, virtually every question from journalists was about the manipulation of the contest. Livingstone appeared outside his home in Cricklewood to declare the result 'tainted'. Eighty thousand people had voted for him; just 25,000 for Dobson. Beginning a strip-tease about his intentions, he said he would spend some time 'listening to Londoners' before announcing what he would do next. For all his denials, Livingstone had been exploring the option of running as an independent for many months. Approaches were made to people outside the Labour Party about being members of an independent administration. Before Christmas, he printed light blue and green pledge cards, an imitation of those which Blair had used at the general election. They were emblazoned: 'Vote London' and 'KEN LIVINGSTONE'. Nowhere on them was printed the word 'Labour'. Though he gained mileage from satirising New Labour's spin doctors and pollsters, since the beginning of the month Livingstone had been using focus groups to test whether he could win as an independent. The media provided the answer. London's paper, the *Evening Standard*, reported that 61 per cent of the capital's voters wanted Livingstone to run as an independent and predicted that he would enjoy an overwhelming victory over all other candidates.[31]

On the last Sunday of February, the Labour Party marked its hundredth anniversary. The occasion at the Old Vic theatre in south London was a festival of ambiguities. Traditional music-hall acts, of which John Prescott was only one, were introduced in the format of a modern television show. A video celebrated a century of Labour achievement and Blair dutifully name-checked all his predecessors, but the burden of his speech was that the Labour Party was a failure. 'Throughout our history, radicalism has too often been followed by long periods of Conservative rule,' he said. 'We have great achievements to our credit. But we have been out of power more often than in power, and won more arguments than elections.'[32] One of the lessons of this history of defeat was the need for unity and leadership, said Blair, moving into the lecturing mode that antagonised many in his party. 'Remember, there's only one thing the public dislike more than a leader in control of his party, and that is a leader not in control of his party.' Yet he couldn't entirely control even this birthday party. When he referred to receiving a message from one of the world's greatest men, by which he meant Nelson Mandela, a heckler shouted from the Upper Circle: 'Ken!' The curtain fell to the strains of a gospel choir and steel band rendering 'Swing Low Sweet Chariot.' Tony and Cherie left with a haste which suggested immense relief to be getting away. In their absence, the audience broke out in 'The Red Flag'.

\*

One tradition which had continued from Old Labour into New Labour was hatred of the sneering traitor. Every loyal Labour larynx stretched in unison to condemn him as a liar and charlatan when, on Monday 6 March, Livingstone declared that he would run as an independent. His pledges not to break from Labour had been repeated and unequivocal. As recently as January, he had said: 'I will not stand against the party I have spent my whole adult working life serving.'[33] Standing as an independent was 'an option I rule out one hundred per cent'.[34]

Launching his campaign at BAFTA, he swallowed his heap of pledges in one gulp: 'I'm not hiding the fact that I am backing out of commitments I made.'[35] He was saying: at least I honestly admit to lying. This could have been extremely damaging in other circumstances, but not in the ones created by New Labour. Livingstone excused himself: 'I do not intend to take any lectures from those who have set new standards in ballot rigging.'[36] His opponents' behaviour had been so bent that it furnished Livingstone with the alibi for his own mendacity. And the ferocity of the attacks on him served only to make him look even more like the lovable maverick – 'upholding the democratic rights of Londoners', as he put it – victimised by humourless robots.

'Unlike other candidates I will not have a slick party machine or spin doctors,' said Livingstone, portraying as a weakness what was actually his great advantage. Like a talented artist of judo, he had turned the blundering weight of New Labour against itself. He was also being extremely disingenuous. New Labour was consistently out-slicked and out-spun by Newt Labour. Livingstone was as brilliant at media manipulation as anyone in the government, which was one of the things they found so bewildering. Crowds of reporters, photographers and TV crews tracked him across central London, obligingly picturing him posing in front of Eros, and on the top deck of a bus. He had the media beguiled. Faced with a taunt from Dobson that 'the ego has landed', Livingstone replied with his salamander smile: 'I'm almost at that Buddhist level where there is no ego any more.' It had been 'beaten out of me by the ruthless media'. His audience of journalists dissolved into laughter.

The polling in the immediate aftermath of his declaration suggested it would not be a contest, but a coronation. He scored a staggering 68 per cent to Dobson's 13 per cent.[37] Not only did Livingstone possess three quarters of the vote of Labour supporters, he also commanded the affections of a majority of Liberal Democrats and Tories. He beat his rivals in every social group.

This was utterly confounding for Tony Blair who had claimed that Livingstone's support was confined to 'a ragbag of Trotskyists and Tory papers'. How could he be so incredibly popular? The answer stared back at the Prime Minister from the mirror. It was New Labour which had helped Livingstone create his rainbow coalition. It spanned hard leftists looking to him to be a focus of opposition to the government; punters who reckoned he was a bit of a card who would provide London with a distinctive voice; everyone in the Labour Party and outside it provoked to give a poke in the eye to an over-domineering Prime Minister; and Tories seizing on any available instrument to hurt the government.

At the Drapers' Livery Hall, hard by the Stock Exchange, in the heart of the City that New Labour claimed would be ruined by Livingstone, he turned up for a speaking engagement in his trademark amphibian-green suit. Disarming the City swells with the remark 'there must be some bugger out there who supports me', he had fun at Blair's expense, recalling that he had wanted a business figure as mayor. 'But they're not paying enough for you to take that sort of cut in your income. So you're left with the same old clapped-out party hacks.'[38] Livingstone's ability not to sound like a party hack, however misleading that was, was a key to his popularity just as it had been for Blair at the last general election. Afterwards, I fell into conversation with some of his audience. 'My taxi driver is voting for him, and so am I,' said an insolvency accountant. 'He's of the far left. So what? We could do with a bit of variety. I quite like Blair, but he can't have it all his own way.' His friend in pensions agreed: 'If he goes too far, the government will rein him in. He's a character. It'll be fun. Why not?'

When the candidates appeared together at the London School of Economics, students mobbed Livingstone like a pop star. Plastered body parts were proffered for his signature. Dobson was introduced to a pitying 'Aaaah'. He accurately said of Livingstone: 'Those who know him best, trust him least.' But no one wanted to hear that. Dobson was answered with barking noises, and cries of 'Poodle!'

Nothing Dobson could do or say would shift the indelible label of stooge which was so fatal to his ponderous campaign. The effort to prove his independence drove the machine to the risible lengths of leaking against one of its own. Philip Gould, the focus group guru, was reported to have told Dobson to make himself more voter-attractive by shaving off his beard. Dobson purportedly told Gould where he could stuff this suggestion.[39] This was the apotheosis of spin. In an attempt to prove that Dobson was wholesomely unspun, the spin machine span against itself. Even the reporter who broke the beard story – Patrick Wintour, political editor of the *Observer* – gave it a sceptical treatment.

The *Mirror*, announcing to its many Labour readers that he was 'Dead As A Dobbo', campaigned to dump him as the Labour candidate and draft in Mo Mowlam. Though this idea was ridiculed as simply too incredible, this last resort was not only being canvassed inside Number 10, but a frantic Tony Blair actually tried to execute the option.[40] Mowlam, still out of sorts at the Cabinet Office, indicated a willingness to be catapulted into the contest. The Prime Minister personally and directly asked Frank Dobson to withdraw. 'We can't do it for you, Frank,' he said to Dobson. 'I'm sorry, but you're not going to win.' If he pulled out, then emergency procedures could be used to replace him with Mowlam. Dobson, though he too knew he was doomed, had become stoically resigned to his fate and almost masochistically determined to see it to the death. 'No one else will do any better. No one can beat Ken now,' he told Blair. 'Someone's got to lose. It might as well be me.'[41]

Would parachuting Mo Mowlam into the contest have worked anyway? Had she offered herself as a candidate when Blair first pressed her, the previous summer, Livingstone and everyone else believed she would have beaten him in a membership ballot. In those circumstances, he could never have successfully run as an independent. Labour would have won London. Livingstone would have returned to his well-paid, but politically marginalised, life of restaurant-reviewing, after-dinner speaking and chat-show appearances. For Blair, it was a great 'if only' to be sighed over with hugely painful regret. What must be extremely doubtful is whether, now that so much blood had flowed under the bridge, Mowlam could have beaten Livingstone as an emergency draftee at the eleventh hour. This would have reeked of yet more fixing. That Blair pursued this option was a sign of absolute desperation.

Every cylinder of the New Labour machine was backfiring. Livingstone was forced to make an apology to the Commons in April for failing to make a comprehensive declaration of £158,000 earnt from his extra-curricular activities. This might have served to discredit him. Instead it looked like another dirty trick when it emerged that the complaint against him originated with a former campaigner for Trevor Phillips, Dobson's running mate. Stories that Labour was going to question whether Livingstone had exceeded the limit on election expenses further deepened the counter-productive impression that there was no half-cocked device they would not resort to.[42]

Tony Blair did appear to be belatedly absorbing the lesson of his repeated control failures. In a speech to the Scottish Parliament in March, he demonstrated an improving comprehension of the meaning of devolution when he celebrated the dispersal of power for its diversity. 'When people point to differences in devolved policy and ask me: "Isn't this a problem?", my response is: "That is devolution. Not an accident, but the intention."'[43] A month later, he acknowledged that he had fouled-up in Wales. 'I got that judgement wrong,' he confessed. 'Essentially you have to let go of it with devolution.'[44]

This repentance of error was refreshingly attractive in a Prime Minister, but it came far too late for absolution in London. Dobson was a lost cause. At an appearance with him, Blair publicly indicated as much by saying that he would 'work with whoever is elected mayor'.[45] His recommendation of Dobson was riddled with irony. 'Frank is not a media candidate. He is not a showbiz candidate. He has never changed in the twenty years I have known him.'[46] Here was Tony Blair, the man to whom mastery of the media was of such supreme importance and who practised the politics of reinvention to the point where he renamed an entire political party, attacking Ken Livingstone for doing precisely the same. There is nothing more disorientating for a politician than being thrashed at his own game.

Since becoming leader nearly six years earlier, Blair had really only ever known popularity. The butterflies of celebrity had fluttered around his government. Now, they departed him for Livingstone. Chris Evans, erstwhile party guest at Number 10, gave £100,000 to the Livingstone campaign. When Dobson tried to chuckle it off with a galumphing joke – 'My old mum always told me to steer clear of redheads' – Evans doubled the amount.

Having thought of itself as young, hip and thrusting, New Labour was becoming the victim of the fashion it courted. The arbitrators of cool pronounced the government to be middle-aged and dull. Over £100,000 was raised for Livingstone's campaign at an auction of art works donated by Damien Hirst, Tracy Emin and other cutting-edgers. Explaining why, Emin said: 'It's just an incredibly conservative, boring government. Ken's interesting, sexy and dynamic.'[47] Blair was being called old-fashioned in comparison with a fifty-four-year-old man in a raincoat whose hobby was reptiles.

All that stood between Livingstone and victory was himself. After the flying start, he began to display some of his own kamikaze tendencies. Two important constituencies, the Jewish community and the City, were offended by Livingstone's claim that 'each year the international financial system kills more people than World War Two. But at least Hitler was mad, you know?'[48] This provided Blair with the small consolation that at least he did not have to be answerable for such remarks, as he would have been had Livingstone been the Labour candidate. A group of anarchists marked May Day by smashing car windows, trashing the Westminster outlet of McDonald's, painting slogans on the Cenotaph, and defacing Churchill's statue. They daubed him with a swastika and adorned his head with a strip of turf, giving the war leader a green mohican toupee. Livingstone, who had previously made remarks which were open to interpretation as encouraging such nihilism, struggled to disassociate himself from the mob. The *Sun*, at its most brutally effective, put a picture of the rioters on its front page with the headline: 'A Vote For Ken Is A Vote For Them.'

In the last thrashes of the campaign, the press turned. Having clamoured for Livingstone in order to hurt Blair, now there was a venomous assault on Livingstone himself. He had the full-hearted support of only the *Morning Star* and the open-throated opposition of all the tabloids. Pointing to the slide in Livingstone's support, Blair told his aides that had the campaign gone on 'a couple more weeks' Livingstone might have lost.

It was not Dobson who prospered, but the Conservative, Steve Norris, a hardliner on crime, but liberal on race and gays. 'He's the New Labour candidate really,' Blair said to a member of the Cabinet.[49] At rock bottom, Blair was reduced to secretly holding a torch for a Conservative to win London.

The Prime Minister was in Northern Ireland on the day of the elections. Breaking the deadlock over IRA weapons was, commentators noted wryly, easier than decommissioning Livingstone. After the elimination of the also-rans, he beat Norris by 58 per cent to 42 per cent. The blood-caked Frank Dobson came a miserable third. He was spared the even more abject humiliation of coming fourth behind the Liberal Democrat by just 20,000 votes. 'It's a quite wonderful feeling,' declared Mayor Livingstone, returned to power in London after fourteen years in the wilderness. 'I never thought I would be in this position.' Neither did Tony Blair. Livingstone's victory was an assault on the most cherished self-beliefs of the Prime Minister. It had been proved that it was possible to win from the left without being New Labour. More stingingly, Livingstone had won by being specifically not New Labour. The office that Blair had created with a hazy notion that it might suit a friendly entrepreneur or celebrity was occupied by a man who represented everything he detested about his party's past and feared for its future. And nothing was more responsible than the Prime Minister's prolonged procrastination and his apparatchiks' crashing fixing. No one had done more to regenerate Ken Livingstone as mayor of London than Tony Blair, his aides and associates.

Outside London, the Labour May election campaign was a defensive effort employing the lacklustre slogan: 'Lots Done. Lots More To Do.' Designed to strike a note of humility from the government, it instead came over as limp. William Hague, making an aggressively right-wing pitch about asylum-seekers and crime, found a voice which resonated with some voters. Previously disaffected Tories began to return to the Conservatives while the Labour heartlands remained sullen. With the exception of David Blunkett and Jack Straw, Cabinet ministers adopted a grass-cutting profile.

The Conservatives won nearly 600 local council seats, an outcome which the Tory leader could gloss as a 'sensational result' mainly because so little was expected of him that the tariff for success had not been set very high. The Labour candidate in the by-election at Romsey lost his deposit. Ominously for the Conservatives, the Hampshire seat was taken from them by the Liberal Democrats, the first time that the Tories had lost a by-election while in Opposition since 1965. The turn-out everywhere, except Romsey, was poor. The messages were too mixed to justify unambiguous predictions about what they meant for the next general election.

Fear nevertheless rippled the spine of the government. Margaret McDonagh, anticipating that as the party's general secretary she would be made the scapegoat for the defeats, got her retaliation in first. Admitting that Wales and London had been 'very damaging', she complained that 'bloody defensive' ministers were not selling the government's achievements.[50] It was a 'wake-up call', according to John Prescott: 'We have to enthuse our voters. We have to show we are delivering.'[51] Peter Mandelson advised Blair that they would now have to reconsider the plan to work towards a general election in the spring of 2001.[52] When this suggestion filtered into the media it added to the sense that the government was having an anxiety attack.

Tony Blair put on his defiant voice for the world. He would maintain his course 'come fair wind or foul'. It was the batten-the-hatches language used by a Prime Minister when the weather is darkening and the spray is in his face.

# 19. The Only Thing That Can Defeat Us

When he came off stage, the Prime Minister's forehead was creased with perplexity. The jeering and the slow hand-clapping left him not so much furious as flummoxed. 'What on earth was all that about?' Tony Blair complained to Anji Hunter and the other aides who had accompanied him to the Wembley Arena for his bruising encounter with the massed motherlode of the Women's Institute.

He had assumed that this matronly gathering would provide the ideal platform to reimpose himself on the political agenda. The WI had rebranded itself with the slogan 'women in a modern world': verbless verbiage which could have come from the dictionary of New Labour. The largely rural women's organisation liked to present themselves as 'non-political', but were actually highly political: just the patina of non-partisanship which Blair himself often adopted. The 10,000 floral frocks opened their throats and rattled their pearls to sing 'Jerusalem', Blake's anthem to social justice, which the Prime Minister sang with a word-perfect passion entirely missing whenever he was asked to get his lips around the stanzas of 'The Red Flag'.

The first unusual thing about his speech was that he had mostly written it himself while at Chequers during his so-called paternity leave. In a dithersome muddle which was becoming rather too typical, Blair had first said he would ignore Cherie's imprecations to take a vacation from power because the country couldn't do without him. Then, a few weeks later, he had apparently back-tracked by announcing he would take a fortnight off to be with his wife and new-born son. This Prime Minister could never let go just like that. Though he did change some of Leo's nappies, Blair spent big chunks of every day reading government papers, phoning his aides at Number 10, and talking to ministers. Philip Bassett, a Number 10 media aide, had prepared a brief about the WI the better for the Prime Minister to flatter his audience with a knowledge of their campaigns.

On the evening of Sunday 4 June, Blair faxed the speech to his key advisers. In a way that was absolutely characteristic of his synthesising approach, he was attempting to reconcile 'good old British values' with 'the modern world'.

The way we do it is to combine the old and new, traditional British values of responsibility and respect for others; with a new agenda of opportunity for all in a changing world. It's very traditional in one sense . . . but in another way, radical.[1]

Classic synthetic Blair.

When New Labour was fresh to power, this capacity to be everything to everyman and woman was widely regarded as one of his greatest strengths. Three years on, it had become one of his largest liabilities. Philip Gould's focus groups, which he was now conducting weekly as New Labour moved into election campaign mode, were expressing a widening disenchantment which informed the memo sent to Campbell by Gould when he saw a first draft of the WI address. 'This is a speech that looks once again like TB pandering, lacking conviction, unable to hold a position for more than a few weeks, lacking the guts to be able to tough it out.' It was 'condescending' and showed 'a lack of leadership . . . energy, verve, dynamism'.

It reads like TB is reacting to criticism that he has dumped the past, rather than saying what he really believes in, that he was elected to take Britain into the future. The result . . . makes TB look rather sad, a passive observer of events, not a force for change.[2]

The press secretary had also advised against the speech, though he had the grace to admit to Blair afterwards that the more direct approach suggested by Campbell would have bombed even more badly.

Campbell operated the spin cycle for the media at which he had

become so practised that he could virtually do it in his sleep.
The morning of the speech, it was trailed in the *Daily Telegraph*,
presumed to be the archetypal WI member's newspaper of choice,
as 'Blair's back with appeal to tradition'. 'Middle Britain', the paper
reported, would be 'wooed with old values'.[3] But New Labour's
technique of shaping the script to manipulate any given audience
now had a familiarity which bred contempt. The ladies of the WI
subsequently complained that it was the advanced billing that fired
their ire. They felt they were being used.

The occasion was regarded as so safe that Campbell, who would
usually have accompanied Blair to such a big set-piece event, stayed
back at Number 10 to have a meeting with John Prescott. The
television in the press secretary's office was broadcasting the Prime
Minister live on Sky TV, but neither Campbell nor Prescott paid
much attention. Blair seemed to be proving Gould wrong. The
platitudinous patter about community, responsibility and courtesy
went down well. It was as he started to talk about the government's
policies that things fell apart. Only when Campbell's eye caught
the flash of panic crossing Blair's features did he realise that his
master was dying on air. 'Hold on, John,' Campbell interrupted
Prescott and turned up the volume. 'Something's happening.'

The first heckle winded Blair. Recovering his composure, he
went on. Then the protests grew louder. Some of the audience
walked out. He looked, by turns, quizzical, flustered, ratty and
rattled. 'I'm glad we're having a debate,' he feebly answered the
barracking. Grinding to a halt, he turned to the chairwoman, giving
her the beseeching look of a schoolboy begging a teacher to save
him from a gang of bullies. When she asked for quiet, Blair sped
on, cutting bits of the speech as he went, before sitting down to
tepid applause.

The media portrayed it – with ascending degrees of gleeful relish
– as the worst public relations fiasco of his premiership, Blair's
'Black Wednesday', even his 'Ceauşescu moment'. As John Major
was destroyed by sterling's collapse out of the Exchange Rate
Mechanism, and Romania's dictator was ousted by the Bucharest
crowd, so Blair had been booed to oblivion by the WI. This was

overexcited nonsense. What the savagery of the enjoyment of his embarrassment did capture was the violence of the mood swing against New Labour. The Tory press exulted at the handbagging of Blair by their female troopers; the left celebrated the stinging slap from a right-wing constituency he should never have tried to woo.

The fret lines on the face of the Prime Minister mirrored the fractures in his coalition. The barbs from the self-selected matrons of Middle Britain were joined by brickbats from the representatives of Cool Britannia who had once partied with the Prime Minister. Noel Gallagher, one of the gush of pop celebrities invited to Downing Street in the euphoric early phase of the government's life, declared that he would never go back to Number 10 again. More serious constituencies were annoyed. Trade unionists rumbled for a more generous uprating of the minimum wage; businesses grumbled about regulation.

The internal coalition was also becoming ragged. Peter Kilfoyle, once a member of Blair's leadership campaign team who resigned as a defence minister to self-appoint himself as a champion of Labour's heartland voters, declared that the government was coming apart for lack of 'ideological glue'. The former general secretary, Tom Sawyer, one of the architects of party reform, lamented the failing magic of an 'out of touch' Prime Minister. 'I think at the election people kind of did feel this guy, Tony Blair, is "our guy". There's not so much of that around.'⁴ Another impeccably New Labourite figure, Matthew Taylor, the director of the Institute for Public Policy Research, worried that 'new Labour's big tent looks more like an empty Dome'.⁵ The dispossessed joined in. Frank Field and Harriet Harman finally found something to agree on when they attacked the government in similar terms for spinning more than it was delivering. John Prescott could not help sharing with his intimates his amusement: 'It's all his own people who are turning on Tony.'⁶

Some of this was the cyclical blues which afflict governments at mid-term. Natural enemies were becoming more aggressive; fairweather friends were deserting; discarded ministers were releasing their disgruntlement. Some of this was a reaction particular to the manner in which New Labour had alienated several of the constituencies that Blair had assembled to elect him three years earlier. Charter 88, most prominent of the advocates of constitutional radicalism, had rhapsodised over the end of the Conservative era. Now they accused New Labour of creating an 'executive dictatorship' worse than that of Margaret Thatcher.[7] Even allowing for the attention-seeking language of a pressure group, it was a dipstick into a deep disillusion across liberal Britain. The emasculation of the promises of more openness in the Freedom of Information legislation was not just because the Home Secretary had never believed in it. New Labour had a culture of secrecy which had been further ingrained by office. During the Kosovo conflict, Blair was horrified to learn from Bill Clinton that the American President dared not have written advice from his military advisers for fear of public exposure.[8] It was the Prime Minister himself who ruled that the freedom legislation should be manacled, just as his experience of dealing with the coalition governments of Europe had increased his scepticism about electoral reform.

The unresolved contradictions within Blair, the devolving centraliser, the conservative radical, were becoming more painfully obvious. The half-reformed House of Lords was not quite so anachronistic, but it was no less absurd. This was not a legislature you could explain to a foreigner and not expect them to burst out in incredulous laughter. The majority of the Upper House were now appointees of the political parties, while the only element which anyone had voted for were the ninety-two residual hereditaries who had been elected to remain by the rest of their aristocratic ilk. The government's welcome for the Wakeham Commission's proposal that there should be a second chamber in which only a small fraction of members would be elected while the huge majority were placepersons betrayed a general psychology fearful of democracy.

Legislation to curtail the right to trial by jury further repelled liberal Britain. When it was thrown out by the Upper House, Blair's own aides began privately to question the wisdom of a policy which promised relatively small savings for such large amounts of opprobrium. The gratuitous aggravation of sections of opinion that wanted to be supportive of the government was personified in the Home Secretary. A decent man who had trapped himself in a caricature of ersatz working-class populism, Jack Straw scoffed at the 'effete prejudices' of those who tried to guard civil liberties from his depredations. Scorning them as 'woolly-minded', he wore it as a ribbon of honour to be the villain of liberal Britain.

Straw had become the outstanding example of New Labour managing to imprison itself in the worst of both worlds. Assailed by the conservative press for not being harsh enough towards refugees, he responded with measures which were never enough to feed the cravings of the right, but did succeed in churning the stomach of the left. Ministerial rhetoric vilifying asylum-seekers became so inflammatory that it provoked Bill Morris, the loyalist black trade union leader, to accuse the government of being 'degrading' to asylum-seekers and 'playing a hostile tune to black Britons' which had 'given life to racists'.[9] Friends had been alienated by trying to appease unappeasable enemies among the right-wing tabloids.

No previous government had dedicated so much talent and energy to trying to rule through the media. The number of White-hall press officers had expanded to 1,100. The tally of 'special advisers', the college of spin doctors, had more than doubled since May 1997. A basement room at Number 10, previously used to store files relating to the appointment of bishops, had been turned over to the Strategic Communications Unit. This hybrid group of recruits from journalism and the civil service confected articles for the Prime Minister who rarely saw, never mind wrote, what went out in his name. Counting the regional press, they could churn out more than a hundred pieces by 'Tony Blair' in a single week.[10] Campbell even turned his hand to ghost-writing articles in the name of the Prime Minister of Japan and the Presidents of the United States and Argentina.

After three years of this, the currency had become debauched. The spin was spun out. Editors who once fought for articles in the

Prime Minister's name became much less enthusiastic about Tony Blair 'exclusives', and much more interested in excoriating attacks on him.

The same media – often the same journalists – who had once thrown rose petals at Tony Blair for his vision, integrity and strength now scourged him with scorpions as a fantasist, a manipulator and an autocrat. The Prime Minister affected to have developed an armadillo-skinned sanguinity about the media, telling interviewers that he took no interest in the 'passing frenzies' of the press, and confined his reading to a few preferred political columnists. This was not true. He and Campbell had regarded the capture of the *Sun* as their greatest pre-election media coup, and the increasing frazzlement the tabloid caused the government epitomised the reversal of their strategy. On 1 May, a front-page editorial foreshadowed the election reverses under a bellowing 'MAYDAY, MAYDAY' headline. Blair was 'beginning to lose the next election' and William Hague, whom the *Sun* had previously dismissed as a 'dead parrot', they now resuscitated as a man 'maturing into a credible threat'.[11]

So stung was Blair that he spent a Bank Holiday Monday at Chequers handwriting a 975-word reply protesting that this treatment had been 'more than a little unfair'. When the typed-up copy was sent over, the paper's editor, David Yelland, remarked to colleagues that he could tell it was Blair's own work, rather than the hand of Campbell, because 'it isn't as well-written as usual'. When the paper asked for something to authenticate to its readers that this was not a fake Blair, but the real thing, Number 10 sent over some of his handwritten script, complete with crossings-out. Copy that the paper would once have treated reverentially was spat back at the Prime Minister. A rag-out of his hand-crafted apologia appeared with the gloating headline: 'RATTLED'. When Tony Blair and his intimates were really pricked, they did not attempt to intimidate, they sought pity. Both Anji Hunter and Alastair Campbell rang the *Sun*'s editor that morning. 'You shouldn't have done that,' the press secretary moaned to Yelland. 'He is the Prime Minister, you know.'[12]

The lack of a reliable claque of press cheerleaders caused great angst at Number 10. 'Thatcher always had the *Mail*, the *Sun*, the *Telegraph* and *The Times*, day after day, thick and thin, right or wrong,' one of the Prime Minister's closest aides complained. 'There's no one we can rely on.'[13] Blair privately bemoaned that there were 'no New Labour papers' because he was not left-wing enough for the left-wing press and not right-wing enough for the right-wing press.

His pragmatic brand of centrist politics did not suit the lust for circulation-building dramas of the partisan British press. But this also went to his deeper problem. Those who court their natural enemies at the expense of their natural allies are likely to find that, in turbulent times, the foes revert to type while the spurned friends sulk.

The government's loss of touch sparked a recriminatory debate within the New Labour inner circle. Gordon Brown blamed Tony Blair.[14] The Chancellor had never liked the approach fashioned by Peter Mandelson and Philip Gould of projecting New Labour through the prism of the 'presidential' persona of the Prime Minister. Though Brown's view may have been influenced by rivalry and jealousy, he could draw some vindicating satisfaction as Blair's personal approval ratings tumbled into negative territory for the first time. The Chancellor wanted to define the government in more strictly Labour terms as the enemies of privilege. He made a *cause célèbre* of the failure of a teenager from a comprehensive to get a place at Oxford University by launching an offensive on 'élitism' and 'the old school tie' which backfired because Brown did not get his facts right. Campbell, the tribalist, argued with the others that it had nevertheless 'got a controversy up'. He warmed to the idea of waging war on privilege as one of New Labour's big campaign themes. Peter Mandelson, who recoiled at the echoes of 'forces of conservatism', contended that Brown had made a mistake. The public school- and Oxford-educated Blair brought this brief offensive to an end by telling the WI: 'Let's hear no more rubbish about class war.' With typical ambiguity, this was open to meaning either that he disagreed with his Chancellor or that Brown had allowed himself to be misinterpreted.

The great communicators had an image crisis. The spin stylists, these supposed masters of symbolism, had themselves become emblematic of what was most loathsome about the government. Those manipulative skills which had been treated with excessive awe by their opponents and the media were, three years on, used to damn them. The same press which was over-beguiled by the propaganda devices now condemned New Labour as nothing more than a presentational trick.

'This government was elected by spin, and it is dying from spin,' one member of the Cabinet lamented to me.[15] This was an over-harsh assessment from a semi-detached minister, but it reflected an anxiety that seized the heart of New Labour. In his memo to Campbell, Gould had reported: 'TB is not believed to be real. He lacks conviction, he is all spin and presentation, he says things to please people, not because he believes them.'[16] The focus grouper was telling the spinmeister that too many voters saw them as the ventriloquists and Blair as the dummy.

There was a contrary view, that his spin doctors were the tools used by the Prime Minister to do his filthy work for him, which was even more detrimental. It was most vituperatively expressed by Ken Follett, the millionaire novelist, former party fund-raiser and husband of a New Labour MP, who directly accused an 'unmanly' and 'cowardly' Blair of using anonymous briefings to undermine ministers.[17] He hazarded that Blair would be remembered 'as the Prime Minister who made malicious gossip an everyday tool of government . . . the media equivalent of the poison pen letter'.[18]

Alastair Campbell reacted by making threats of legal action. The ferocity of the counter-reaction from Number 10, which lacerated Follett as a man embittered because he had fallen out of New Labour's charmed circles, revealed an extreme sensitivity to the damage this was doing to the Prime Minister. It was a common view within the New Labour high command that as sleaze had eroded the Tories, so spin was corroding public cynicism into the government's general reputation for honesty and the personal standing of the Prime Minister. Having been so successfully marketed three years earlier on trust and sincerity, Tony Blair was now typically portrayed as dishonest and slimy.

He mused aloud about how to shed the reputation for manipulation.

In the last few weeks I've done a lot of reflecting . . . I think we in government – and that means me – have to trust people more. We don't need to fight over every headline. We should put more faith in people's desire to engage in a conversation about the future.[19]

As an apparent token of this, Campbell announced that he would be doing less daily propagandising. Having come to office contemptuous of civil servants and determined to politicise the government communication machine, the spin bowler said he would be semi-retiring to the pavilion and leaving many of the briefings of Westminster correspondents to his deputy, Godric Smith, a straight bat from the civil service. Those wise to the ways of the government wondered whether this was just a new form of top spin. So it proved. Like boozers who can never resist that next drink, it was against New Labour's nature to stop fighting for headlines. Campbell was using his extra time to try to impose an even greater domination of his media agenda on Whitehall. He issued a memo instructing every department that, by the end of June, they should have drawn up a programme to create 'at least two substantial news stories' every week of August and September to put over 'the government's core message'.[20] Hardly had it been written, than the memo was leaked – almost certainly by a civil servant rebelling against the suborning of Whitehall into such blatant partisanship – which sent the media into another frenzy about spin. This was the negative cycle into which New Labour had become locked. The attempts to control had bred a countervailing response from the media which had become as fixated with process at the expense of substance as it accused New Labour of being. Nothing done in the government's name was taken at face value; every ministerial pronouncement was treated with extreme scepticism. It was the perverse achievement of New Labour that the effect of its propagandists was to undermine the public character of the Prime Minister and obscure his government's real successes.

That body of achievement was actually quite considerable. The neophytes to power who arrived in office in May 1997 had passed the basic competency test of governing by not doing anything spectacularly ruinous to the country. They had not perpetrated a Three Day Week, a Winter of Discontent, a Black Wednesday or a Poll Tax. Unlike all their Labour predecessors, this Prime Minister and Chancellor had not been shipwrecked by an economic calamity. The real disposable income of most Britons was rising, and a record number of people were in work. The jobless count, based on claimants, had fallen below 4 per cent, very close to what economists calculate to be full employment. Michael Portillo paid public tribute to the state of the economy: a rare concession by a Shadow Chancellor to the government. He also committed the Conservatives to the goal of full employment, a repudiation of the Thatcherism which he once worshipped. This was another example of New Labour tilting the balance of political argument in favour of progressive values. The underlying rate of inflation, at under 2 per cent, was the lowest in the quarter century that this measure has been taken. The spectre of Labour's historic reputation for economic incompetence, that ghost which had so sweated their nightmares in the early months in office, was exorcised. Gordon Brown would never win personal popularity contests with his Cabinet colleagues, but the combination of sustained growth with low inflation and unemployment raised him to the top of the pantheon of Chancellors.

His decision to stick to the Conservatives' spending plans for the first two years had been the most important strategic choice. It was rewarded with reduction in public debt and credibility in the markets, but there had been a price to pay in public discontent. The effects of the 'stealth taxes' became more immediately obvious than the fruits of the investment in public services they were helping to fund. Brown was sure that his strategy had been right. So was Tony Blair, on most days. Not all of those around him agreed. One close counsellor of the Prime Minister told me: 'The single worst decision we made was not to invest more earlier in education and health.'[21]

The five promises of the pledge card, supposedly easy and early, had proved difficult and slow to deliver. They would not all be fulfilled even by the time of the next election. In the school year beginning September 1999, the number of primary school children in classes over thirty was reduced by two thirds. All four-year-olds and most three-year-olds would have a nursery place. Education, where New Labour had a thought-through strategy and a clear narrative about standards and opportunities, was one of the success stories of the government.

The promised reduction of 100,000 in hospital waiting lists was finally achieved in May 2000. The time taken to get young offenders from arrest to court fell, but not rapidly enough to meet the pledge to halve it by the election. The most obviously broken manifesto commitment was to hold a referendum on electoral reform; a commitment Tony Blair had made out of calculation, not conviction.

In other respects, New Labour was delivering more than it promised.

When he was feeling cheery, Philip Gould was fond of saying to other members of the inner circle:

If I'd have gone to a focus group on April 29th 1997 and said this Labour government is going to run the economy more competently than any other, it's going to invest unprecedented amounts in public services plus it will create a million extra jobs plus it will lift a million people out of poverty, they would have thought I was mad. It was difficult enough getting them to believe our five pledges. They would have called me a Martian![22]

Compared with many governments, this was a well above average record. By the measure of the expectations aroused by the size of the majority, New Labour's transformatory rhetoric and the ambitions that Blair had trumpeted, his government looked less impressive. He implicitly acknowledged that the error of their early period in office was to over-brag too many modest improvements as quantum leaps. He now spoke of government not as a sprint, but as a marathon. He told a private meeting of Labour MPs in June that it was always going to 'take more than one term' to effect substantial change.

Welfare reform was no longer spoken of as the Big Idea. The salami-slicing of entitlements and retargeting of benefits at the more needy was essentially a continuation of the Tory approach with a more redistributive twist. In other areas, the government had downplayed a record that was more radical and redistributive than its rhetoric suggested. New Labour had established the minimum wage, adopted the social chapter, increased taxes on the better-off to give more assistance to the poor, concentrated considerable resources into deprived areas, used the windfall profits from the privatised utilities to create job and training opportunities, and shifted state aid from middle-class students to vocational training favouring the less well-off. None of this would have been done by a Conservative government.

The childless Chancellor had used children as his favoured instrument for directing money towards the poor. On average, the least well-off 10 per cent of families would be about £1,500 a year better off by the end of the parliament. Six and a half billion pounds more than planned by the Conservatives had been spent on pensions, and the largest proportion of it had gone to those most in need. Paradoxically, targeting help on the poorest among the elderly rather than spreading money around all of them, a policy that was one of the government's most obviously socialist, provoked some of the greatest complaints from Labour supporters. Gordon Brown, not a man from whom admissions of error were ever easy to extract, privately confessed that it had been a presentational and political error to increase the general pension by a miserly 75p a week.

Sending Peter Mandelson to Northern Ireland had proved to be a clever piece of casting. Ulster's protagonists talked about him in terms ranging from suspicion to dislike, despite his acquisition of another prop pet, this time not a bulldog, but an image-softening golden retriever called Bobby. Yet Mandelson's ability to read political situations and his feline negotiating skills, along with Blair's continuing engagement with the process, finally achieved implementation of the Good Friday Agreement. Following a meeting between Tony Blair and Gerry Adams at Chequers, in early May the IRA agreed to put its arms verifiably 'beyond use' by opening its arsenal to international inspection. The terrorists came close to an effective declaration that the conflict was over. The Northern Ireland Assembly and Executive, which had earlier collapsed after just seventy-two days, were put back together again in May. When the inspectors, Cyril Ramaphosa, the former secretary-general of the African National Congress, and Martti Ahtisaari, the former President of Finland, were taken to the IRA arms dumps in late June, Blair could claim without much fear of contradiction that peace in Northern Ireland 'has never had a better prospect than it has today'. A durable settlement in Ireland had eluded every Prime Minister since William Gladstone. Set alongside devolution to Scotland and Wales, this had the marks of an epochal achievement.

On the other half of the British Question, relations with Europe, Blair was more sharply impaled than ever on the dilemma which had been left unresolved by the single currency policy adopted in the autumn of 1997. He was no closer to reconciling his aspirations to lead Europe with the hostility to Europe on his own side of the English Channel. The most authoritative survey of attitudes towards the European Union found that, of all member states, the British were at the bottom of the enthusiasm league on every measure. In a majority of other member states people felt somewhat European; in Britain more than two thirds felt exclusively British. Less than a third of Britons thought being a member of the European Union was 'a good thing' or that Britain benefited from membership. By 59 per cent against to 25 per cent in favour, there was a more than two-to-one majority against the European single currency in early 2000, a more antagonistic ratio than when New Labour came to power.[23]

On Europe, above all else, Blair began to pay a steep penalty for his tendency to play for time in the hope that a difficult decision might somehow defuse itself. Paddy Ashdown, once his intimate collaborator, woundingly accused the Prime Minister of replicating the vacillations of John Major. Chris Patten, Blair's personal choice as European Commissioner, lamented that the Prime Minister's failure to give an unequivocal lead had allowed the Eurosceptics to dominate the argument. The favourite uncle, Roy Jenkins, was progressively more soured with Blair's failure to follow his tutorials on electoral reform and Europe. He issued a lordly rebuke to his pupil, telling an interviewer that the equivocating Blair had 'a second-class mind'.[24]

The Cabinet was fraying over the single currency, though it was characteristically New Labour that the ferocity of the divisions was fired less by principle and strategy, and much more by tactics entangled with personalities. Gordon Brown was more adamantine than ever in his conviction that the way to approach the debate about the single currency was to try to smother it. Ranged against the Chancellor were two ancient protagonists, and an enemy Brown had made more recently. Stephen Byers, whose career as Trade and Industry Secretary suffered a near-death experience during the fire sale of the Longbridge car plant by BMW against a general background of complaint from manufacturers and trade unions about the level of the pound, began to make more positive noises about the euro. Robin Cook, whose time at the Foreign Office completed his conversion from Eurosceptic to Euro-enthusiast, saw the cost to British influence the longer the country remained in self-imposed exile from Euroland. Peter Mandelson, the most ardently Euro-enthusiastic member of the Cabinet, believed that a referendum would not be won after the election unless they started to make a vigorous case in advance. Mandelson privately warned Blair that he risked looking timid and evasive without a firmer statement of intent.

Once again, Brown and Mandelson were warring for possession of Blair. Once again, Blair was torn between the two. Brown made sense when he cautioned against allowing the Conservatives to turn the general election into a referendum on Europe. Mandelson was convincing when he warned Blair that the influence in Europe he regarded as so precious was dribbling away. Blair tried to have it both ways by supporting the Chancellor in public while discreetly encouraging the pro-European trio to make more positive noises about joining the single currency.

The predictable result was to inflame the paranoid and possessive streaks of the Chancellor. Brown's increasing irritation with other ministers' incursions into what he regarded as his sovereign territory burst incandescently in mid-May. The *causus belli* was a single line in a speech by Mandelson, who told an audience of trade unionists in Belfast that 'as long as we are outside the euro, there is little we can do to protect industry against destabilising swings in the value of sterling as they affect Europe – the largest market where we have to earn our living'.[25] That night, Byers warned: 'It is vital that we don't by default drift back to a policy of "wait and see". To do so would be to deny a genuine choice to the British people.'[26]

Byers's remark – effectively a repudiation of the Chancellor's strategy – was arguably the more provocative. But it was upon Mandelson that the dark furies of Brown were unleashed. The Chancellor's acolytes briefed journalists that Mandelson had 'the economic intelligence of a pea', to which Mandelson retaliated by counter-briefing that Brown had a 'territorial fetish' and was clumping over the rest of the Cabinet with 'hob-nailed boots'.

Both bitterly complained to Blair that the behaviour of the other was intolerably provocative. The Chancellor privately raged that he would resign if Mandelson made another speech like it.[27] Was this a serious threat? It was more likely to have been a tantrum speaking. What it served to illustrate was that the tormented relationships at the top were as febrile and fratricidal as ever.

Blair was in more despair than ever at the way his two best men brought the worst out in each other. He continued to follow his theory, though it had previously proved disastrous in practice, that by throwing Brown and Mandelson into the joint management of the election campaign, he would force them to work together.

It would be wrong to see Blair as the blameless victim of this infighting. Much of it stemmed from his own habit of hiding behind other ministers as his proxies when he feared himself to confront his powerful Chancellor. In early June, Robin Cook made an appearance before a committee of MPs. The Greeks were going to join the single currency, the Danes were holding a referendum, and the Swedes were conducting a national debate. Though Blair had said that he would 'never allow this country to be isolated or left behind in Europe',[28] Britain could shortly be in a minority of one. Cook quite accurately told the MPs that 'the balance of forces shift further every time someone else joins and we are a smaller minority'.[29] The following day, Byers re-entered the fray by telling an interviewer: 'I think we do have to be putting the case both for Europe and the euro.'[30]

This provoked the inevitable counter-reaction from the Chancellor. He bludgeoned Blair that he, Brown, would be humiliated and his authority undermined – ever his favoured arguments – unless everyone else was made to conform to his policy. On Thursday 15 June, Blair told the Cabinet that they should all fall in line behind the definitive statement on the euro Brown would deliver in a speech to the Mansion House that night. Robin Cook was speaking that afternoon in the Commons. Just before he rose to his feet, he received a note from Number 10 asking him to excise any passages from his speech that might be interpreted as clashing with Brown and feeding further headlines about Cabinet splits. The Foreign Secretary did his duty by government unity, self-censoring on the hoof four references to the euro, including the sentences 'The government will not let Britain lose out by staying out' and 'If our economic conditions are met it would be right in principle to join.' So brittle had things become that Cook was dropping what was actually an unexceptional statement of agreed policy. In his speech in the City, Brown territorially proclaimed the Treasury – in other words, himself – to be 'the guardian of the policy'.[31] Brown's acolytes then infuriated Cook by putting it about that the Foreign Secretary had been forced to submit to the Chancellor.

On Sunday afternoon, Blair, Brown and Cook patched together an agreed line on the euro during the flight to Portugal for the European summit in Feira. A victory over the issue of the withholding tax demonstrated that Britain could get tactical results in Europe.

But the unresolved strategic conundrum was cruelly exposed when France and Germany unveiled a design to create an élite of fast-track European states based on the members of the euro. When Blair protested against this Europe of 'two speeds', Gerhard Schröder and Jacques Chirac slapped him down by correctly pointing out that there were already two speeds: those countries on the eurobahn, and those in the slow lane. In a speech to the Bundestag shortly afterwards, Chirac declared an intention to create 'a pioneer group' of countries, exclusive of Britain. Blair had devoted huge attention to cultivating the President of France and the Chancellor of Germany. Abroad, as at home, the guile and charm with which he had maintained his balancing act were wearing transparently thin. The Cabinet was splintered. The realities of the Paris–Berlin axis were asserting themselves. New Labour's Britain was engaged with Europe. What it was not doing was leading Europe. To do so, the Prime Minister would one day have to demonstrate more determined leadership in Britain.

Office revealed Tony Blair to be an alloy of the bold and the cautious, the decisive and the dithering. He could be as brave as a tiger. In Northern Ireland and Kosovo, breathtaking gambles were rewarded with commensurate successes. 'He is very strong on intuition,' a senior civil servant, who has observed Blair at extremely close quarters, told me. 'He is very like Margaret Thatcher in that respect. He has this instinct for hurling himself at things like Ireland and Kosovo with sheer willpower.'[32] Blair tended to be more impressive in a crisis, when he had no time to allow the nervous side of his nature to prevail over the courageous. His crab-like approach to other challenges and choices was to scuttle sideways. Progress could be made this way, but it substituted the risk of doing bold things now for the equal peril of eventually running out of time and popularity to do them ever.

The personality of the Prime Minister, especially when decision-making was so centrally concentrated, was bound to be reflected in the character of his government. A clear sense of direction and a willingness to take risks have characterised the outstanding Prime

Ministers and governments. Ministers and civil servants need a sure map to guide the myriad decisions they make each day. Without that, governments become the victims of events, at the mercy of the media, and the playthings of the fluctuating passions of public opinion.

New Labour had not yet acquired a reliable compass. Office had been instructive in the limitations of ruling by poll and focus group. Yet it could not give them up. Governing by the fickle gusts of the press was like trying to steer a boat with the sail rather than the tiller. Yet it could not stop itself fighting for every headline. When Blair talked of trying to 'trust people more', he indicated that New Labour did not trust the people because it could not trust itself.

Frequent private panics, teetering into hysteria, had always been there below the surface projection of a masterful Tony Blair driving an assured government. A glimpse of the flailing behind the façade was provided to the public when newspapers got hold of an exchange of confidential memos. Philip Gould, writing around the time of the spring election reverses, hyperventilated to Blair that 'the New Labour brand has been badly contaminated'. He quoted Peter Mandelson: 'Something has gone seriously wrong – but what?'

Most damaging to the public character of the Prime Minister was a memo in his own hand which confirmed that no one was more mesmerised with image than the fevered head of government. Penned at Chequers on 29 April, when the Tories were dominating the law and order agenda, he headlined his angst 'Touchstone Issues'. Blair lamented that on the family 'we are perceived as weak', on asylum-seekers and crime 'we are perceived as soft', and the government was regarded as 'insufficiently assertive' about patriotism. 'All of these things add up to a sense that the government – and this even applies to me – are somehow out of touch with gut British instincts.' The jittery tenor suggested that the Prime Minister overruled Gordon Brown to force an increase in the defence budget simply in order to be seen 'standing up for Britain'. He was casting about for 'two or three eye-catching initiatives'. The eye they were designed to catch was that of headline-writers. 'We should think now of an initiative, e.g. locking up street muggers. Something tough, with immediate bite ... this should be done soon and I, personally, should be associated with it.'

The upshot was a proposal to impose on-the-spot fines on drunken louts which Blair personally associated himself with by dropping it into a speech on global ethics, doubtless to the bafflement of his audience of German scholars. It was precisely this sort of headline-driven, knee-jerk gimmick that had spread the impression of a government – in the words of Gould – 'drifting, growing almost monthly weaker and more diffuse'. The Prime Minister was forced to make an abject démarche when chief constables described the notion of frogmarching drunks to cashpoint machines as unworkable and everyone else lambasted it as fatuous, including the very right-wing tabloids to whom Blair had sought to pander. He floundered at Question Time the following Wednesday. That night, in a denouement that no self-respecting writer of soap opera would dare script, the police found his sixteen-year-old son, Euan, drunk and incapable in the vomitorium of Leicester Square. After a sleepless night spent looking after his chundering eldest son, the following day the Prime Minister sounded like a man groaning under the burden of power. He told an audience of evangelical Christians: 'I know it's only been three years, but sometimes it seems like thirty.' He quoted a gloomy fragment from 'A Village Church', a poem by Henry Longfellow about divine tribulations: 'For thine own purpose thou hast sent strife and discouragement.'

Critics and friends of the government both asked whether the Prime Minister was suffering a crisis of confidence. The truth was that New Labour ever had a palpitating heart.

Just after breakfast on the morning of Thursday 22 June, the blue, premier-class Jaguar – a compensatory perk for being Northern Ireland Secretary – snouted through the gates of Downing Street and cruised up to the door of Number 10. Peter Mandelson joined Tony Blair, Gordon Brown and Alastair Campbell in the intimacy of the Prime Minister's study. The inner quartet of the first election victory were plotting their path to the campaign for the second term. They were so often and so deeply divided, but that burning ambition united all four men. They had gathered to discuss how to recapture the initiative for New Labour. Education was to be the centrepiece when the Chancellor announced the spending plans going forward to the year 2004. A national plan for the health service would also be announced in July along with a ten-year programme for transport. This would not be portrayed as favouring either Middle Britain or the heartlands, but both. All were agreed with Gordon Brown's analysis that making a distinction between the two wings of the coalition was 'a Tory trap'.

The torrents of cash available for release from the Treasury, what Blair referred to as 'Gordon's hoard', placed them in a position of rare power for a government approaching an election. No previous Labour administration had been so well poised. But it was an illustration of their difficulties and their obsessions that a great part of the discussion revolved around how the spending plans should be presented. 'Telephone number' increases did not mean anything to anyone, remarked Blair. The difference between one billion and ten billion was meaningless to most people, agreed Campbell. What impressed voters was real results they could put their hands on. New Labour had learned something from the over-boosting of phoney spending numbers.

There had been much debate between the four about whether they should make a virtue of the fact that they were putting money into public services, rather than tax cuts. Peter Mandelson had taken to wondering aloud whether 'we are still too trapped in the eighties'. Perhaps they should be more relaxed about making the arguments for the virtues of taxation. The voice of Gordon Brown was decisive about this. The Chancellor wanted to be able to argue that he was both spending more and cutting income tax.

They began to plot out a series of statements and events from the spending announcements in July through to the speeches individual ministers would deliver at the autumn party conference and onwards to the election campaign. New Labour loved its 'grids'.

Whatever else had happened to New Labour in government, one thing had remained a constant. The Project was still controlled by less than a handful of men, each one consumed with maintaining his grip on power.

When people called on Tony Blair at Number 10, he was fond of showing them the portraits of previous Prime Ministers which line the staircase up to the first floor. He would point to the empty bit of wall at the top, which would one day be occupied by a picture of himself. He would also note how very few of his most recent predecessors were Labour. The sight refired the ambition to win the unprecedented second full term, 'the most important thing', as he had told me in the garden of Number 10 in the spring of 1997. He should have been more confident than most Prime Ministers of fulfilling that self-cast destiny. The honeymoon might be over, but the electorate was not filing for divorce and showed no desire to re-marry the Conservatives.

The worst of the opinion polls for the government in June still placed Labour on a three-point lead over the Conservatives.[33] The best put the lead over the Tories at 19 per cent.[34] The average lead was 12 per cent. Three years into the life of previous Labour governments, Callaghan was level-pegging with the Tories, Attlee was 9 per cent behind the Conservatives, and Wilson was 19 per cent adrift.[35] With the sole exception of Margaret Thatcher in the middle of the Falklands War against split opponents, no Tory government had led the Opposition at this stage of the parliament. The most level-headed commentators and the shrewder Conservatives believed that New Labour should be more serene about its prospects of re-election than any government since 1945.

Yet Blair was no more inclined to invest faith in the opinion polls or the soothsayers than he had been to believe the exit polls on the night of May Day 1997. In their manic depressive way, some of the New Labour inner circle talked of winning an even fatter parliamentary majority of 200, others of being reduced to the unworkably anorexic margin of 20, and the most pessimistic voices lathered themselves about having no majority at all. Even Campbell, who was probably the most self-confident member of the inner circle, would say: 'There's two people, me and him [Blair], who wake up every day thinking: How can we lose it?'[36]

There was nervousness around the high table. 'The Cabinet is deeply twitchy,' one of its more successful Blairite members told me in the early summer of 2000. Surely, I countered, after three years in power, they had to be more assured of themselves. 'Oh, no,' he shook his head. 'It's worse now. At least then we said to ourselves: "Wow! We're the government." What you have to understand is that every day is a panic. We're so neurotic.'[37]

One of Blair's closest advisers said:

This is a very uncertain time for the duration of the Project. As the election comes closer, will New Labour get a new coherence? We still think more like an Opposition than a government. We're still not confident in government. Have we got an aptitude for government? Wilson said he wanted to make Labour the natural party of government. He failed. We have failed.[38]

This was astonishingly downcast and overly self-damnatory. In many respects, this was not a bad government and, in important ones, it was a good government. What was yet unproven was whether Tony Blair had the courage, capacity and self-confidence to become one of the exceptional Prime Ministers who lead great governments.

One morning that summer, the Prime Minister was taking some of his closest aides on one of those circular tours of his teeming brain that they had become so used to. He was not scared by the Conservatives, he said. 'We are winning the big arguments.' If anything, he wished the Tories were a more plausible threat, the better to galvanise his own party. The Prime Minister was, as usual, querulous and frustrated by the media, but they were not the real menace either. No, Tony Blair concluded: 'The only thing that can defeat us is ourselves.'[39]

The remark sounded outrageously arrogant – until you thought about it for a moment. What it actually spoke to was the enduring and profound insecurity embedded at the heart of New Labour.

They would not be outstanding servants of the people until they had learned to master themselves.

# 20. Twenty-four Hours from Meltdown

Before them in Number 10 lay an early draft of the speech on Europe the Prime Minister would deliver in Warsaw. The senior civil servant from across the road sucked his teeth. 'Isn't it a little Gaullist, Prime Minister?' the official ventured, meaning that it was much too Gaullist for the liking of the Foreign Office. As it happened, Tony Blair had recently read a biography of the French President who was, according to taste, an elective dictator or a visionary titan who restored his country to greatness. Blair looked at the mandarin, stuck up a thumb and grinned: 'Top man, de Gaulle!'[1]

The Prime Minister was enthralled by the idea of the strong leader who masters popular sentiment to change the course of national destiny by his own formidable will. The career of de Gaulle might be an inspiration. The ultimate fall of the General also carried a health warning that unanticipated eruptions of the popular mood can topple even the most apparently impregnable leader.

In the first week of September, Blair's developing taste for the world stage took him to New York to address the United Nations Millennium Summit. Amplifying on the theme he had made his own since the Kosovo war, he told the college of world leaders that they had to equip the UN to take more rapid and robust military action in global trouble spots where human rights were abused. He dwelt most heavily on the developed world's 'dismal record of failure' towards Africa: 'Nowhere are more people dying needlessly from starvation, from disease, from conflict. Deaths caused not by acts of fate, but by acts of man. By bad governance, factional rivalries, state-sponsored theft and corruption.'[2] Back in Britain at the weekend, Blair set an example of what he had preached in New York.

A hundred family and friends were gathered at Chequers on

Saturday night for a belated fiftieth birthday party thrown by Tony for his older brother, Bill. Those who knew him well could tell that a preoccupied Prime Minister was many miles away from the Chilterns. All the guests could see that Blair was rather grotty with jet-lag and anxiety. Only Cherie knew exactly why. That afternoon, her husband had given his personal authorisation to a high-risk operation in Africa to rescue British soldiers and UN personnel who had been taken prisoner in faction-ridden, corrupt, blood-soaked, ungovernable Sierra Leone.

Tired as he was, Blair insisted on being woken as soon as there was news of the outcome of the raid deep in the swamps of west Africa. When the call came through to Chequers, shortly after dawn on Sunday, what he heard was a relief. In a fierce fire fight with the renegade West Side Boys, troops from the 1st Battalion of the Parachute Regiment had killed twenty-five of the rebels for the loss of just one British life. Blair learnt with satisfaction that six British soldiers who had been taken hostage by the rebel gang were now free. He was driven back to Number 10 to make a doorstep statement on Sunday night praising the professionalism of the paratroopers. That weekend, Tony Blair was not much focused on his own country. The Prime Minister's mind wandered other continents: America, Europe and Africa. He was barely aware of a motley band of unarmed rebels at home who were about to bring Britain to the brink of anarchy and his premiership to the cusp of catastrophe.

The swelling complaint about the surging price of petrol had blipped on the government's radar. Private polling and focus group reports from Philip Gould had been warning of deepening public disgruntlement since the beginning of the year. Gordon Brown responded in his March Budget by slamming the brake on the 'fuel duty escalator', the above-inflation increases in the tax on petrol. Though they raised fuel duty in the name of saving the planet from global warming, neither Brown nor Blair had ever made much of the case for high petrol taxes on environmental grounds. Like the Tory predecessors who introduced the escalator, they regarded fuel duty as an extremely lucrative stream of revenue for the government. What relief Brown's Budget palliative offered to drivers was more than negated by the steep rise in the cost of fuel engineered by OPEC, the cartel of oil-producing countries. The price of petrol soared towards £4 a gallon, the highest in Europe, and by far the greatest slice of that was tax. Discontent about fuel prices magnetised together an angry coalition of road hauliers, fighting for their livelihoods in a cut-throat business; fishermen and farmers, under severe financial stress already; and rural drivers who saw high petrol taxes as another assault on the way of life in the countryside by an unsympathetic and alien metropolitan government.

On the night of Thursday 7 September, malcontented truckers and farmers, numbering about 150 in all, gathered at the St Asaph cattle market in north Wales where they spontaneously decided to mimic the protests sweeping the continent by picketing the giant Shell refinery at Stanlow in Cheshire. Few believed him when Brynle Williams, the hillfarmer from Mold who was their chief spokesman, claimed the ability to 'shake this nation to its foundations'. This self-described bunch of nobodies without any obviously organised leadership were not taken terribly seriously, even by themselves. According to a leading light of the Stanlow demonstration, Clive Swan: 'We thought we would stay the night, make our point, go on the morning news and go home.[3] Tom Houghton, an organiser of Farmers For Action, believed the protest 'would go on a few hours. The way it spread across the country astonished us.'[4]

Even as protests did spread, the peaceful good humour displayed at most demonstrations had a lulling effect. A spokeswoman for Esso returned from a picket of one of the company's distribution depots to report: 'It was a very pleasant chance to sunbathe and people were smiling and behaving very nicely. It was all very British.'[5]

John Prescott had sniffed danger. In a memo dashed off to Blair, the Deputy Prime Minister expressed concern that the blockades which had just paralysed France might be repeated in Britain. Prescott was ignored. The general mood of the government was that this was not France, with its ignoble history of weak administrations being beaten into submission by direct action. That sort of thing simply didn't happen in level-headed, law-abiding Britain. That weekend, the Scottish Secretary, John Reid, and the Transport Minister, Gus Macdonald, were the frontmen for the government. That these solid but middle-order ministers were placed in charge was an indicator that the high command of New Labour foresaw no threat. Macdonald reflected the shrugging attitude within the government when he observed that an earlier 'Dump The Pump' boycott had been a damp squib and suggested that the picketing of refineries would also be greeted with a 'very British reaction'.[6] Reid was equally scornful of the protesters, scoffing on Sunday morning: 'The people of this country do not resort to the French way of doing things, which causes massive disruption. We do it the British way – that means listening.'[7]

The threat of disruption did begin to impinge on one member of the Cabinet. The Trade and Industry Secretary was in Hanover on Friday to address an Anglo-German conference about innovation. That morning, Stephen Byers took a call from worried officials in his Private Office back in London. They conveyed to the minister an alert about the protests from Anna Walker, the civil servant who headed his department's energy section. 'Is it really that bad?' asked Byers. Not so long as the protest was confined to Stanlow, the officials told him. Were pickets to block other refineries, then it would be serious. The just-in-time delivery practices of the oil companies meant that supplies of fuel would be rapidly exhausted. His civil servants pointed Byers to his reserve powers under the Energy Act to commandeer supplies and designate filling stations for essential services. Byers delivered his speech in Hanover and flew back across the North Sea. On his way home from Newcastle airport on Friday evening, the Trade and Industry Secretary noted with unease the growing queues at petrol stations. He told his Private Office to draft an Order in Council. This was still regarded as purely precautionary. Even then, virtually no one in government anticipated that they would actually have to resort to taking emergency powers. There was jocularity in Byers's office about having to disturb the Queen's summer sojourn in Scotland to get her rubber-stamp on the document.

By Monday morning, the burgeoning demonstrations were beginning to receive heavy and nationwide media coverage. Blair's attention was finally captured with briefings that there were petrol shortages in the north of England, and hauliers and farmers were planning a campaign of go-slows to seize up major roads. Too late, the government began to wake up.

When Number 10 called for the Home Secretary on Monday morning, Jack Straw was still asleep. And for an entirely natural reason. One of the features of the early stages of the crisis was that the principal ministerial players were exhausted or abroad or both. Straw had just returned by overnight flight from a punishing tour of India and Bangladesh. Desperate for some restorative kip, he had gone to his home in south London and crashed into bed, leaving a note for his daughter asking her to rouse him at eleven. When the Downing Street switchboard rang at eight, Charlotte stalled Number 10 to buy her father enough time to engage his brain for a conversation with the Prime Minister. Once he had unfogged his head with a cup of tea, Straw discussed the protests with Blair.

The Prime Minister and Home Secretary agreed that they should activate Cobra. This viperesque acronym stood for the much less glamorous-sounding Cabinet Office Briefing Room A, a windowless warren of rooms with grey walls and wooden chairs in the basement behind Downing Street next to the old Cabinet war rooms. Connected to Number 10 by tunnels, it is supposed to be the nerve centre from which Britain can be governed in an emergency.

Joining Straw were Byers, Macdonald and the Chief Treasury Secretary, Andrew Smith. At first, Straw's team could not even get into Cobra: the bunker was still being used to wind-up the operation in west Africa. When ministers and some thirty officials finally did begin to move in on Monday afternoon, there were maps of Sierra Leone spread around the place. What there was not was any plan of campaign for coping with the fuel emergency.

The Home Office had large numbers of pre-prepared plans for

dealing with a variety of disasters and emergencies. During the Afghan hijacking at Heathrow earlier in the year, an operation was instantly to hand to deal with it. When Straw asked for a contingency plan to deal with the fuel protests, the alarming reply came back that no such plan existed. No one anywhere in Whitehall had ever anticipated that small groups of protesters could be capable of choking Britain to a standstill by throttling petrol supplies. 'There was no plan at all,' according to one Home Office minister. 'What you have to understand – it was then that I really saw it – is that the civil service is completely useless.'[8] A Cabinet minister from another department concurs: 'You think you've got this Rolls-Royce service and it turns out to be a Robin Reliant.'[9]

Calming public opinion was the paramount concern in Downing Street where their greatest fears revolved around the prospect of panic buying of petrol by motorists. If 26 million drivers tried to fill their tanks at once, the petrol stations would run dry in a day. At the Monday morning briefing at Number 10, the Prime Minister's spokesman told political correspondents that Tony Blair was having no special meetings about the protests. There were 'isolated problems' in parts of the country, but the spokesman laughed in the face of suggestions that this amounted to anything approaching a national crisis. So relaxed was the Prime Minister that he would be carrying on with his scheduled regional tour of the Midlands and the North. Its ironic theme was that New Labour had placed Britain in the vanguard of modernity. At his first venue, a community computer centre in Loughborough, Blair delivered a speech enthusing about the wonders of e-commerce. Into it was hurriedly inserted a clip for the news bulletins. Blair was mindful, and disdainful, of how the French Prime Minister, Lionel Jospin, had capitulated to protests across the Channel, and then seen his public standing collapse.

'We cannot and we will not alter government policy on petrol through blockades and pickets,' declared a no-surrender British Prime Minister. 'That's not the way to make policy in Britain, and as far as I am concerned it never will be.'[10]

The Prime Minister travelled north, taking afternoon tea at a manor house hotel, set in tranquil farmland, near Little Weighton in Humberside. As drowsy shadows lengthened on the croquet lawn, Blair chatted about the sleeping patterns of baby Leo to some of the reporters accompanying his tour. Asked about the fuel protests, he was airily dismissive: 'Very few depots are blocked.'[11]

In fact, by that evening there were demonstrations at six out of nine of Britain's refineries, and the oil firms began to issue warnings that their filling stations were running out of fuel. Organising themselves using mobile phones and the internet — tools of the 'information technology revolution' that Blair had extolled only that morning – the protesters were already beginning to strangle the life of the nation.

The evening had been intended as a celebration. Blair would make a speech at Hull town hall to mark John Prescott's thirty years as an MP and then join him for an anniversary dinner at his deputy's favourite Chinese restaurant, Mr Chu's. Blair and Prescott found themselves besieged at the town hall by demonstrators from the Countryside Alliance who, having originally massed to defend fox-hunting, now embraced the petrol protesters' grievances as their own. The crowd was abusive. When a woman yelled 'fat bastard' at Prescott, an incandescent Deputy Prime Minister charged from his limousine to challenge her to say it to his face. Before the confrontation became any uglier, the woman was bundled away by the police.[12]

They warned the Prime Minister that the protesters were massing to block all escape routes. If Blair persisted with his dinner date with his deputy, then they could not guarantee his safe exit from Mr Chu's. This was a grim prospect: the night spent incarcerated with John Prescott inside a Chinese restaurant in Hull. This brought home the threat. Blair agreed to an alternative plan to smuggle him out of the town hall by a side door. As his chauffeured Jaguar passed the lengthening queues at garages, Blair was now an eyewitness to the gathering crisis. He and his retinue picked up some fish and chips on the way to Sheffield where Blair called Straw and Byers, saying he wanted a nationwide overview of how serious it was getting.

The DTI ministers, Helen Liddell and Richard Caborn, had been dispatched earlier in the day on a clandestine mission to Balmoral. The esoterics of the British constitution required three members of the Privy Council to be present before Her Majesty when she put her seal on the emergency powers to direct fuel deliveries. The Queen's Private Secretary made up the numbers. Blair was anxious that this remain secret, fearing that a leak of the Order in Council would increase public panic. It was Buckingham Palace which blew the government's cover by listing the ministers' unusual attendance on the Queen in the Court Circular which was published by the *Daily Telegraph* and *The Times*. When the circular came into the *Telegraph*, no one there noticed the significance of the Balmoral meeting. It was spotted at *The Times*, which turned the taking of emergency powers into its Tuesday splash. There was no concealing the gravity of the situation any longer.

At six o'clock on Tuesday morning, in the suite of rooms occupied by Blair and his entourage on the fifth floor of the Sheffield Hilton, one of the encrypted fax machines hummed into life. It churned out the latest assessments prepared for the civil contingencies committee chaired by Jack Straw. 'Oil industry reports that the situation is near breaking point,' Blair read from the stark fax. 'There have been no significant breakouts from the oil refineries, forcing the MoD [Ministry of Defence] to look at options for military assistance. Tanker drivers seem to be increasingly reluctant to cross blockades because of safety concerns or picket line sympathy.' The bleak report went on to warn that NHS blood supplies and vaccines would run low, stricken firms would start laying off workers, adding 'food shortages can be expected in the next few days'.

Blair knew there was no longer any denying it either to himself or to the country. This was developing into the worst civil crisis in Britain since the 1970s. Cancelling the remainder of his tour, the Prime Minister made a dash back to London.

He called Gordon Brown, who was flying to Glasgow to address the Trades Union Congress. The Chancellor's aides had been giving Blair's aides the impression that he was reluctant to even mention the fuel protests in his speech. Not for the first time, Number 10 was wary that Brown was putting distance between himself and Blair, leaving the Prime Minister to take the heat. After three phone conversations, Prime Minister and Chancellor agreed that both had no choice but to maintain a united and hard line against the protesters. In his speech to the TUC, Brown echoed Blair's implacable rhetoric, setting his face against 'making tax policy this afternoon because of blockades this morning'.[13] He and Blair also decided that the Chancellor should talk to Bill Morris, the leader of the TGWU, to get the union to persuade its members to resume deliveries.

The tanker drivers' refusal to come out of the refineries was the source of mounting frustration and bafflement to Blair, as was the apparent hesitancy of the police. The instruction had gone out from Cobra to Chief Constables urging them to use the public order laws to ensure safe passage for the tankers. The police responded that there were few grounds on which to arrest what were predominantly well-behaved demonstrators. At a briefing at Number 10, Jack Straw and John Prescott told Blair that, even where there were few pickets outside fuel depots, the drivers were unwilling to drive out because they said they felt threatened. How true this was, the ministers could not be sure. Their intelligence about what was actually going on down on the ground was extraordinarily scant. Though there were sporadic examples of intimidation, this also served as an excuse. Many of the tanker drivers were evidently in sympathy with their fellow hauliers on the other side of the picket line. One driver candidly explained: 'I'm quite in agreement with the principle of the protest. I'm like the next man – I want petrol to be cheap. It's been a weird week. I've been sitting around most days playing cards.'[14]

The oil companies decided on a common front of doing nothing to compel their drivers to make deliveries. The strong popular support for the protesters alarmed oil executives who had won their seats on the board by making profits from drilling and refining, not from handling public order situations. According to one of the ministers who dealt with the oil bosses: 'They were most concerned about their public image.'[15]

Reports now began to flow into Cobra of panic buying of food, and incidents of 'pump rage' as motorists brawled on forecourts. Hospitals started cancelling non-vital surgery. Funeral directors warned that soon they might not be able to bury the dead. The Petrol Retailers Association announced that nine out of ten filling stations would be dry of petrol and diesel by the end of the day. This draining of the national tank was accelerated by the reporting of the crisis. 'Great Petrol Revolt 2000' yelled one tabloid that Tuesday morning. 'Running on Empty' snickered another. 'Showdown at the pumps' shouted a third. 'A nation grinding to a halt' was one broadsheet headline, and all the others were variations on the same ghastly theme.[16] The *Mirror*, usually a Labour cheerleader, targeted the Prime Minister himself. The front-page picture depicted the prime ministerial Daimler purring past a queue at a filling station and ridiculed Blair with the headline: 'I'M ALL RIGHT JAG'.[17] The reporting of panic buying fuelled yet more of it as hysteria fed on itself.

Tony Blair hunkered down in his study that afternoon and began to work the telephone. He put in personal calls to the chairmen and chief executives of the oil companies to try to establish why their tankers weren't making deliveries. He told them he was going to invoke the emergency powers compelling them to deliver to earmarked depots supplying essential services. In return for Blair's promise that there would be a firmer police presence outside the refineries and police escorts for the drivers, the oil chiefs pledged that they could get the tankers moving again.

The Prime Minister clutched at this lifeline – much too hard. After an afternoon discussion in the Cabinet room involving Straw, Byers and Alastair Campbell, Blair decided that the scale of the crisis was now so great he would have to be seen taking personal command. Byers voiced the anxiety of himself and others that Blair would be 'exposed' by calling a news conference on the crisis. Blair, fortified by Campbell's advice to this effect, responded: 'I have to show I am leading.' The news conference was called in the State Dining Room of Number 10 at 6 p.m., live for the evening news bulletins. Blair stood before a portrait of George II, the last king to lead his troops in battle. Even more pertinently, the Hanoverian was an unpopular monarch whose throne was shaken by tax revolts. Blair attempted to reimpose himself as lord of his rebellious realm. Raising the already high stakes by putting his own personal credibility into play, Blair declared: 'We cannot accept as a government or as a nation that policy should be dictated by illegal blockades, pickets or direct action.' He went on: 'Were we to yield to that pressure, it would run counter to every democratic principle that this country believes in.'

This hard talk about the protests came with calming words of reassurance for the public. Blair outlined the bargain he thought he had just brokered:

The oil companies are agreed that they must move supplies. The police are agreed to do all that is necessary to give protection against intimidation. The main union concerned has issued a strong statement urging members to work normally. Everything is now in place to get the tankers moving, refuelling the empty stations as a priority. We hope within the next twenty-four hours to have the situation on the way back to normal.[18]

Within less than twenty-four hours, these words would be ashes in his mouth. Rather than reinvest him with authority, as Blair and Campbell had hoped, it would serve to demonstrate how fast and how far events were slipping beyond the Prime Minister's command.

His chest-beating refired the determination of the protesters: numbers on the picket lines grew. They were thrilling to the exhilaration of having Tony Blair by the throat. For many of the blockaders, this was an opportunity to strike at a government that they loathed for a host of reasons. Margaret Beckett subsequently gave voice to a widespread view within her party that the protesters were 'the industrial wing of the Countryside Alliance':[19] people who could never be reconciled to the idea of a Labour government. This was not disputed by the Countryside Alliance's national gazette. The *Daily Telegraph* editorialised: 'This protest is the Countryside Alliance on wheels. It is the collective expression of those

Forces of Conservatism that, last autumn, Mr Blair pledged himself to eliminate.'[20] They barely concealed their relish that it was now Blair who was facing, if not elimination, then certainly humiliation.

The ministers down in Cobra had a fair idea of how many tankers should be leaving refineries because police escorts had to be assigned to each load. Anxiously they waited for seven o'clock on Tuesday evening, the time set for the beginning of the 'big roll out' of tankers. As the evening lengthened, it became depressingly clear that very few tankers were leaving the refineries. The horror-struck ministers huddled in the Whitehall bunker watched as Blair's pledge was broken before their eyes.

At around eleven that night, Straw, Byers and the Cabinet Secretary went up to Sir Richard Wilson's office to confront the oil industry's representative on Cobra. Neither Straw nor Byers was the type to lose his temper easily, but both Cabinet ministers were at boiling point as they aggressively questioned Malcolm Brinded, the chairman of Shell UK. 'What's your game?' demanded Straw. 'What's happening?' came in Byers. 'You employ these people.' To the consternation of the ministers, Brinded replied that the oil companies didn't actually directly employ most of the drivers. They were on contract, or self-employed. He gave them a tutorial about the chains of command in multinationals. He personally did not have all that much control over Shell refineries. They were the responsibility of executives headquartered in Italy. Byers snapped: 'Well, for God's sake, talk to the guys in Naples then.'[21]

At midnight, the despondent ministers went to report to the Prime Minister that his promise that the tankers would roll was not being fulfilled. 'The break-out hasn't happened,' they told an aghast and angry Blair. 'These people gave assurances. I had a deal,' Blair let rip about the oil company executives. 'For fuck's sake, they gave me assurances.'[22] He hit the phone in the early hours of the morning, again trying to rouse the oil companies and the police to action.

The government was being routed on every conceivable front by the dawn of Wednesday morning. Blair despaired to his press secretary that they had completely lost 'the propaganda battle'. The

*Guardian* headlined its report that the fuel drought was now almost total: 'Down to the last drop'.[23] All the newspapers roared his impotent failure at the Prime Minister. 'EMPTY' shouted a *Mirror* front page with zeroed fuel gauges printed on the foreheads of Blair, Brown and Prescott, along with the caption: 'OUT OF GAS'.[24]

Alastair Campbell drew back from trying to depict the protesters as reckless extremists because every available barometer of opinion showed that the public were overwhelmingly on their side. The mainly rural blockaders enjoyed the sympathy of urban motorists who didn't like paying a lot for petrol either. Of 157,489 listeners to phone Radio Two's Jimmy Young programme over the three worst days of the crisis, 91 per cent supported the protesters' action. A similar massive majority was recorded by a phone poll of 711,000 people for ITV's *Tonight with Trevor McDonald*, which found that 94 per cent thought Blair was handling the situation badly.

None of the arguments for fuel duties deployed by Blair or his ministers was having any traction on either the protesters or the general public. The suggestion that the revenues were needed to fund hospitals and schools lacked credibility when rising oil prices had put more money into the coffers of a Treasury already sitting on a large surplus. More than three quarters of the public rejected that argument; further big majorities blamed the government, not OPEC, for the high cost of petrol; and supported the protests despite their consequences.[25] The environmental argument for higher fuel prices did not melt the ice in the heart of the electorate, not least because the government had never mustered it with any conviction.

At breakfast time on Wednesday, at the first crisis meeting of the day, Blair continued to fume about the oil companies. 'What are they doing?' he demanded. Not much, came the distressing reply from ministers and officials. Suspicion was hardening against the companies. Relations with the pickets, who were often supplied with beverages and food from within the refineries, appeared to be very cordial. A summit with the oil executives was rescheduled from the DTI to Number 10 so that Blair could eyeball them himself. Flanked by the Cabinet Secretary, Prescott, Straw, Byers

and Macdonald, the Prime Minister confronted the chieftains of
Big Oil across the Cabinet table. Blair demanded to know why they
weren't ordering their drivers to move the oil. A finger-thrusting
Prescott angrily remarked that, during the miners' strike in the
1980s, hundreds of tankers thundered through mass picket lines.
The executives responded that it would be derelict of them to force
drivers to take any risks with highly inflammable loads. They
couldn't just bark orders at the drivers. 'We're not running an
army,' replied one of the oilmen. The Prime Minister expressed his
aggravation about the ineptness of the companies' public relations.
'Why did you put up your prices?' Blair rounded on the boss of
one of the smaller companies, TotalFinaElf. 'Because the rest of
them did,' he replied, to embarrassed wriggling among the rest
of the executives. Blair cast a hard look around the table. Byers
theatrically made a note of this exchange. Though it was not made
explicit at this meeting, hanging in the air was the threat that the
government would order an investigation into whether the oil
companies used anti-competitive practices if they were not more
co-operative. Ministers made menacing noises about a new regulator for the oil industry.[26]

The trouble was that the oil executives were not greatly daunted
by the aggression radiating off Blair. These global goliaths regarded
themselves as bigger than any mere Prime Minister. 'We resent
being summoned to Downing Street as though we are just an
outpost of government,' complained one of the oil executives. 'We
are not nationalised industries. We are global companies with, on
the whole, more influence around the world than the British
Government.'[27]

Even more confounding to Blair and those around him was the
national mood. Despite the gravity of the crisis, popular sentiment
was giddy. The petrol shortages might be a pain, but the people
seemed ready to endure them so long as the torture inflicted on the
Prime Minister was greater. TV and newspaper pictures of the
protesters sitting in deck-chairs sipping tea from Thermos flasks
projected them as if they were out on a jolly picnic. Ordinary
motorists – those who still had petrol – would drive by tooting in

solidarity. To his ministers and aides, Blair vented his frustration: 'People have got to understand that this is not a bloody game.'[28]

The original strategy of down-playing the crisis to try to avoid a panic lay in self-evident ruin. The propaganda co-ordinated by Campbell was turned inside-out. Ministers were now ordered to dramatise the drastic consequences of fuel shortages for essential services. The hope was that this would impress the seriousness of the situation on the public and so turn them and the media against the protesters.

The Health Secretary, Alan Milburn, took to the airwaves to declare an 'NHS Red Alert'. An apocalyptic assessment from Cobra was supplied to Andrew Marr, the political editor of the BBC, so that he could wave it live at viewers of the *Nine O'Clock News*. It was that bad: the government was resorting to leaking its own confidential documents to scare viewers of peaktime television.

The smallest things caused a frenzy. Alarmed by the sight of the usual line of official limousines parked outside Number 10, Blair ordered that they be removed to a rear car park for fear that the media would use pictures of the limos to suggest that ministers had privileged reserves of fuel while the country seized up.

Not only was virtually every petrol station in Britain now dry, supermarkets began to introduce the rationing of basic food stuffs for the first time in fifty years. Panic buying was stripping their shelves bare of bread and milk. The only good news came from shops selling bicycles: sales were booming. High street chemists were running short of drugs. Schools were closing. Car manufacturers were half a day away from stopping production. Ever more alarming forecasts were produced in Cobra. The meat diet of most Britons was principally chicken. They also, of course, supplied the nation with eggs. Battery chickens, kept in automated feeding sheds, required constant power. When power to the machinery was cut off, the consequences would be horrid, warned a report prepared for the Home Secretary. 'The chickens will start eating each other,' Jack Straw groaned to his team. 'We are going to have millions of dead chickens on our hands.'[29]

Blair was now warned what would happen if the blockades continued to the end of the working week: the shops would be empty and essential services crippled. It was extremely probable that people would start dying. According to one minister at the centre of the crisis: 'There would be no food. The health service was going to collapse. We were twenty-four hours away from meltdown, at best forty-eight hours away.'[30] The Prime Minister contemplated the abyss.

It was a ragged Blair who stood before his second emergency news conference, late on Wednesday afternoon. Tired before the crisis began, he had slept only briefly and fitfully over the past three nights. He looked palpably aged by the stress; he sounded near desolate. 'This is not on, you know, this is just not right, it's not the way to do it,' he came close to begging the protesters. 'Enough is enough. It's time to stop this.'

He described it as 'an affront' and 'an absurdity' that the pickets were deciding what should be let through as a supply to an essential service. 'Real damage is being done to real people,' implored Blair. 'Lives are at risk.'[31] Under questioning, the Prime Minister refused to rule out mobilising the army to break the blockades.

That night, Blair agonised over activating this last, most desperate resort. The Ministry of Defence had devoted the past forty-eight hours to a frantic search for ways to alleviate the crisis. Geoff Hoon, the Defence Secretary, was initially encouraged to believe that they might be able to move petrol using the Second World War vintage network of underground pipelines connecting army and air bases. A crestfallen Hoon then had to report to Blair that the system was designed only for carrying aviation fuel. It was completely useless for pumping petrol.[32]

So dire had things become that eighty armed forces tankers were dispersed around the country that night carrying the military's own fuel stocks to hospitals. But the army possessed too few of its own tankers to supply even essential services adequately. The question was whether military drivers should now be sent into the refineries to bring out the fuel.

The military were extremely reluctant to be drawn into confrontation with the blockaders. General Sir Charles Guthrie told both Blair and Straw: 'I'd rather do another Sierra Leone.' It was one thing sending British soldiers into action in Africa; it was quite another deploying them against British civilians, a step that had not been taken in modern history.[33]

Blair's own closest advisers were queasy. Campbell was not alone in worrying about the impact of pictures of the army on the streets – and how they would be endlessly replayed against the government by the Tories and the right-wing media.[34] John Prescott heatedly argued against deploying troops. The former shop steward warned Blair that the tanker drivers might react by going on strike. Then where would they be? 'For Christ's sake, Tony, think about this one,' his deputy argued with the Prime Minister. 'It could get a helluva lot worse.'

These darkest hours came just before the dawn. The first glimmer of relief was reported from Scotland. While the corporate bosses whom Blair had courted were failing the government, the trade unions whom he had often snubbed were coming to the rescue. Following persuasion by national officials of the TGWU, at midnight on Wednesday drivers at the Grangemouth refinery near Edinburgh voted to resume deliveries at daybreak.

On the other side of the lines, fresh attempts were being made to break up the blockades. The President of the Association of Chief Police Officers, the Chief Constable of the Devon and Cornwall force, Sir John Evans, was the senior policeman on the Cobra team. He rang round his fellow Chief Constables asking them to use their officers to impress the severity of the situation on the pickets.[35] The protesters were mistrustful of anything coming out of the mouth of the government. Ministerial talk of lives being lost was dismissed as scaremongering spin. The protesters did have good and respectful relations with the police. They were more likely to believe it from officers when they told the blockaders that Britain truly was on the brink of collapse. The Road Haulage Association also appealed to truckers to call the action off.

There was a volte-face by those newspapers which had pumped up the protesters by lionising them as the sturdy champions of

over-taxed motoring Middle Britain. The same papers now
beseeched the protesters to give up in front-page opinion pieces
influenced by warnings to editors that there would soon be no fuel
to deliver their newspapers. On Thursday morning, the *Mirror*
echoed the Prime Minister's message: 'ENOUGH IS ENOUGH'.[36]
The *Daily Mail*, as 'a friend who believes in your cause', urged the
protesters 'to end your blockade today while you still hold the
moral high ground'.[37]

The editors were behind the curve. The blockaders were already
on their way to the conclusion that public opinion would swing
sharply against them when people started dying. Those at Stanlow
seemed genuinely shocked when the chief executive of the NHS's
North-West region, John Ashton, went to the picket line to tell
them that lives were in peril. In the early hours of Thursday
morning, the protesters voted to break up, leaving the refinery
gates with a self-triumphant blaring of their horns. They began to
melt away from blockades elsewhere as quickly as they had first
gathered, claiming a moral victory over the government and threatening to return to action if ministers did not meet a sixty-day
deadline for cuts in fuel duty.

A strained and drained Blair held his third crisis news conference
in as many days on Thursday lunchtime. He conceded that the
blockades had caught his government horribly by surprise. He
displayed anger with Esso for an 'incomprehensible' decision –
swiftly reversed – to raise its pump prices that very morning.
Towards the blockaders Blair adopted more placatory language. 'I
say to the protesters, we understand you have a genuine and
sincerely held grievance.'[38] At the end of the most frightening week
of his premiership, Blair was anxious to send signals that he would
respond to public discontent about fuel prices.

These conciliatory messages from the Prime Minister sparked a
typical flare-up with his Chancellor which illustrated the territorial
and temperamental antagonisms between them. Gordon Brown
authorised his aides to brief against Blair and stamp on the suggestion
that fuel duty might be cut to soothe the seething nation. When he
emerged to give an interview on Saturday, Brown declared that he

would not be making his budgetary decisions on the basis of what he dismissed as 'short-term volatility of oil prices'. The Chancellor refused even to acknowledge that there had been an emergency. Blair had called it a 'national crisis', as had Straw. Brown bluntly refused to agree: 'I don't use these words.'[39]

Blairite ministers endeavoured to spin the message back in the responsive direction desired by the Prime Minister. On Sunday, Geoff Hoon accepted there was discontent 'and we will have to address it'.[40] Stephen Byers weighed in against the Chancellor by saying: 'A government that wants to be re-elected has got to listen.'[41]

Blair and those loyal to him were deeply irritated by what they saw as posturing by Brown now that the crisis was over when the Chancellor had ducked out of the line of fire during the most perilous days. News organisations which sought interviews with the Chancellor and his ministers were told by Treasury spokesmen that it was a public order matter for Number 10 and the Home Office, as if the protests had nothing to do with fuel duty. Those who handled the crisis nurtured bitter memories about Brown's behaviour for many months to come. 'The Chancellor was nowhere to be seen,' one member of the Cabinet complained to me.[42] This was not wholly true. What is fair comment is that Tony Blair led from the front while Gordon Brown was cautious and calibrating about putting his own head above the parapet.

Further suspicion was sowed into their relationship. Privately, among those most intimate with him, Blair made sarcastic reference to 'Gordon's disappearing acts': the Chancellor's habit of never being at the scene of an accident, even when it was his fault. For his part, Brown complained to his familiars that Blair had 'a weakness in his spine': the Prime Minister was too appeasing under pressure.[43]

This tussling between them was hard because both had a serious case. The Chancellor believed it would be disastrous to give the slightest signal that the government could be blackmailed into changing policy. He contended to Blair that to give an inch would diminish the credibility of them both. His repeated private argument with the Prime Minister was that the government could always recover from short-term unpopularity, but once they lost their reputation for strength, they would look forever weak. Once you go down on your knees, Brown fulminated to Blair, you will never get up.

'What we don't do . . . is lurch from one policy to another,' the unbending Chancellor told an interviewer the following week. 'Nor are we going to make policy simply because of the events of one week.' He was sticking to his 'budget process'. To do otherwise would be to wreck the government's standing at home and abroad. He wasn't going to 'be pushed around this week and next week by this group of demonstrators and that'.[44]

While Blair would not disagree with the thrust of that, he was much more sensitive to the risks of further antagonising the majority of voters. Striking a markedly more flexible posture than his Chancellor, the Prime Minister agreed with an interviewer that petrol was 'very expensive' and 'if we possibly can, we should be getting the price down'.[45] This reflected Blair's argument with Brown that neither of them would be strong for very long if they set themselves against nine tenths of public opinion.

The fuel blockade brought Tony Blair to the edge of the sort of reputation-ruining catastrophe from which Prime Ministers never recover. A ragbag of protesters – who even at their strongest never numbered more than 2,500 nationwide – paralysed the country and rendered the government flailingly ineffectual. Philip Gould reported with a post-mortem on the mood of the nation from his focus groups. He told Blair that, damaging though it was, anger about fuel prices was not the worst of it for New Labour. What most profoundly hurt the stature of the government was the spectacle of Blair losing control. Most alienated of all were young women with families who had the most reason to be scared by the spectre of not being able to feed their children.[46]

This was a petrifying week for a government whose pre-eminent obsession was to be competent and in charge – or at least to appear as such. It was a deeply shaking experience for a Prime Minister who set such store by his ability to tune himself to popular sentiment. A chastened and rueful Tony Blair mocked himself: 'I'm the Prime Minister that's supposed to be the great reader of public opinion.'[47]

## 21. Sweating It Out

Waiting staff moved among the guests pouring champagne and serving canapes. Five hundred representatives of the New Establishment and the Old Establishment crowded into a south London art gallery for a celebration of Gordon Brown's summer wedding to Sarah Macaulay. The Archbishop of Canterbury blessed them with his presence. Politicians mingled with newspaper editors, media executives with television celebrities, corporate bosses rubbed suits with trade union leaders. The event was, in the words of one guest, 'the kind of party where you kept looking round to see who wasn't there'.[1] Spouses had not, with a few exceptions, been invited: this was not so much a nuptial festivity as an operation in power networking. The strains between the couple at the pinnacle of government could not be entirely masked. Tony Blair arrived with Cherie through the front door; they slipped away by a rear exit after less than half an hour. The Prime Minister could not help but make a mental note that those quaffing his Chancellor's champagne numbered Ken Follett, the author who had recently savaged the Prime Minister as 'cowardly', and Richard Littlejohn, the tabloid polemicist who routinely ridiculed the Prime Minister as 'the Grinning Jackanapes'.[2]

Gordon Brown was on witty form as he adapted his 'five tests' for entry into the single currency into a metaphor for marriage. He and his bride had agreed on 'convergence' after deciding the conditions were right for 'long-term sustainability' of the union. The Chancellor remarked that the head of one of the security services had invited the couple to join him and his wife for dinner during their honeymoon in Cape Cod. Brown wondered how the spy-master had known where to find them when the groom had stuck to the tradition of keeping the location of the honeymoon secret.

Neither Prime Minister nor Chancellor knew then that a three-year-old affair that they thought they had buried within the New Labour family was about to burst back into life. Newspaper serialisations of *Servants of the People*[3] fed the media's sharp appetite for disclosures about New Labour. As one commentator put it: 'The most damaging bits of Andrew Rawnsley's riveting account of the internal workings of the Government have been splashed all over the papers for weeks.'[4]

I was subsequently told by sources at Number 10 that they anticipated that exposure of the volatility of the relationships within the inner core of New Labour might generate discomforting publicity. What came as a surprise to the government – and also to the author – was the scale of the reaction to the book's revelations about the Bernie Ecclestone donation.[5] The morning after the wedding party, Ecclestone exploded back into the headlines with a ferocity which exceeded the coverage at the actual time of the affair. Three years on, there was a pervasive feeling, among the media, Opposition politicians, the public, even Labour MPs and supporters, that the government had been treated too benignly in its early days in office. During his honeymoon with the electorate, Tony Blair was just about taken on face value when he declared himself to be 'a pretty straight kind of guy'. The revival of interest in the wretched Ecclestone business prompted by the book coincided with a wiser and more jaundiced media and public no longer prepared to take New Labour's word for it that they could be trusted.

When the revelations began to make headlines on Tuesday 19 September, Downing Street and the Treasury at first assumed that the controversy could be simply brushed away as old news that had all been dealt with at the time. As the day wore on, it became evident that there was far too much journalistic interest and Opposition attack to allow them to get away with this approach. The reignited Ecclestone Affair blazed across the newspapers and led the news bulletins. In a double-page spread devoted to the story, the *Sun* pictured Blair and Brown overprinted with the caption: 'The Liars'.[6] From the opposite end of both the newspaper market and the political spectrum, the *Independent* editorialised: 'Downing Street now seems fundamentally dishonest.'[7]

Coming on the heels of the fuel crisis, this compounded the government's sense of itself as totally besieged. This was directly expressed to me in a discussion with someone very senior inside Number 10. Our conversation was at all times civil, if a touch brittle. He complained: 'Now everyone thinks we're a bunch of liars.' When every newspaper and broadcaster, including journalists with sympathy towards the government, were battering them 'it sometimes feels to us as if there is a state media in this country'.

This was slightly self-pitying. In some respects, the government was lucky. With parliament not sitting, Tony Blair managed to avoid questions about the Ecclestone cover-up until the end of the week, which was probably fortunate for the Prime Minister. When he was finally interviewed on the subject, Blair tried to talk his way out of the shadow cast over his integrity by using blanket denials of impropriety. He repeated his misleading claim of three years earlier that he had written to Lord Neill in order to ask the watchdog of ethical standards whether the donation should be returned.[8] Blair, who had hoped to keep the donation secret in the autumn of 1997, had actually been stunned when Neill told him to return the money. The holes in Blair's defence were pounced on by the Tory frontbencher Andrew Lansley: 'The Prime Minister pledged to be purer than pure, but his answers are getting murkier and murkier . . . The man who has described himself as a pretty straight sort of guy is clearly trying to hide something.'[9]

The media caravan moved on, allowing Blair to escape rigorous interrogation. He was further shielded by Number 10's deployment of what one report described as 'the tactic of obfuscation'.[10]

A consequence was that the fiercest heat bore down on Gordon Brown. On the day that the story broke, the chief political correspondent of the *Guardian* reported on the charged atmosphere in the Chancellor's chambers: 'Inside the beleaguered Treasury, the mood darkened as Mr Brown recognised he had to admit he had discussed the Ecclestone donation with the prime minister.'[11]

After a morning of stonewalling, on Tuesday afternoon the

Chancellor authorised his press secretary, Ian Austin, to confirm that Brown had talked about the Ecclestone donation with Blair in the back of the Prime Minister's limousine three days before the Chancellor went on radio and said: 'I've not been told and I certainly don't know what the true position is.' According to one informed interpretation: 'The Chancellor hoped that, by making a clean breast of that detail, he would be believed when he denied deliberately lying.'[12]

The Conservatives seized on Brown's admission to clamour for the Chancellor's resignation. That evening, Michael Portillo, the Shadow Chancellor, said: 'You cannot have a Chancellor of the Exchequer whose word is not his bond. The Prime Minister said that any minister who lied would have to go. It appears that the Chancellor of the Exchequer has lied over a matter of very important public policy. The Chancellor must resign or the Prime Minister must sack him.'[13] This would normally have the effect of providing an embattled minister with a protective shield. When the Opposition is calling for a resignation, colleagues usually rally round. With the exception of Alistair Darling, the fellow Scot who was put up on television and radio as a character witness to the Chancellor's probity, the rest of the Cabinet were conspicuously silent in defence of Gordon Brown. His own habit of vanishing from the scene when Tony Blair or other colleagues were under pressure was now being repaid in the same coin when Brown found himself under the most sustained pummelling of his time as Chancellor.

After sixty hours of pressure about Ecclestone, as well as the continuing fall-out from the fuel protests and a growing row about pensions, on Thursday 21 September, Brown broke cover and offered himself for evening television interviews.

The Chancellor conceded that 'I knew it was a sizeable donation' when he discussed it with Tony Blair during the car journey back from the Anglo-French summit. Under questioning by Jon Snow, Brown denied that his earlier denials had been mendacious. 'I was asked: "Did Bernie Ecclestone give a donation?" I said: "wait and see." Why did I say "wait and see"? Because we had put this to, er, the Neill review. Neill was going to report and I said the true position would become known later.'

Brown contended that he had said 'I don't know what the true position is' because they were still waiting for a reply to the letter sent to Lord Neill. 'On Monday morning we did not know whether the donation would stand or whether the donation would not stand.'

The letter to Neill did not, in fact, disclose the size of the donation to the standards' invigilator, nor did the letter directly ask for instruction about whether or not the donation should be returned.

As the exchanges with Snow became more involved, the interviewer interjected: 'But these are the sort of weasel hair-splittings the Tories used to go in for.'

'No,' responded Brown. 'That is not correct.'

Snow: 'Did you lie?'

'No, I did not lie and I would not lie,' insisted Brown. He also denied the words attributed to him in this book: 'I wouldn't have said that sort of thing. I think people who know me know I wouldn't have said that sort of thing.'[14]

Trevor Kavanagh, the political editor of the *Sun,* called this 'an astonishing display of verbal gymnastics'.[15] Hugo Young, that most distinguished and judicious of political commentators, wrote: 'It is not believable, on the basis of the Treasury's as well as Andrew Rawnsley's evidence, that Gordon Brown was telling the perfect truth about his knowledge of this at the time, or is doing so now in his tortuous explanations.'[16]

What blazed just below the surface of the interview was Brown's fury that he was being asked to answer for the Ecclestone Affair. 'I was angry because, as a point of principle, I don't think the Chancellor should be involved in lists of donations related to political parties. I don't think he should be involved in talking about these things,' he told Snow.

That fury boiled over when a hand-chopping Brown said: 'I've never met Ecclestone, I've never talked to him about donations, I've never talked to anybody about corporate donations to the

Labour Party.' He kept emphasising the point: 'I've not been involved in any dealings or papers or documents relating to this Ecclestone Affair.'[17]

The Chancellor's allies put this even more vehemently in off-the-record briefings. On Brown's behalf, it was claimed that when Blair first told him about the Ecclestone donation, the Chancellor exploded: 'What the fuck are we doing taking money from someone like him?'[18] A journalist well connected with the Brown camp reported: 'Some of those closest to him whisper conspiratorially that in the strange case of Bernie Ecclestone, Mr Brown was fitted up – thrown the £1 million in the back of the prime minister's car so his fingerprints were left all over the cash.'[19]

These recriminations stoked the controversy. There was anger at Number 10 where Blair's aides interpreted Brown's defence as an attempt to dump the Prime Minister back in the mire.[20] The reawakening of the Ecclestone Affair was a caution about the capacity of scandals which the government had assumed were safely neutralised to come back and bite them. Another lesson – still not properly learnt by New Labour – was of the dangers of liaisons with rich men and the even greater perils of trying to hush them up.

The party gathered at Brighton for its annual conference in turbulent and uncharted waters. The large bubble of popularity on which the government had floated for so long was abruptly burst. The poll lead over the Conservatives, in double figures in August, had collapsed under the weight of the shocks of September. The polls put the Conservatives ahead by up to 8 points: the first time Labour was behind in the six years that Tony Blair had been leader, a profoundly alarming turn in opinion for a regime so fixated by polls.[21] The Sunday papers mocked up pictures of William Hague and Ffion waving from the doorstep of Number 10. Jumpy ministers and jittery conference delegates wondered whether the idea was such a joke any more. The polls did not truly indicate that the country desired the return of the Conservatives. What they represented was a grisly referendum on the people's discontent with New Labour.

The grip on public support was broken; the aura of invincibility around both Prime Minister and Chancellor was shattered.

The two camps blamed each other. Brownites suggested that Blair had lost his touch for public opinion; Blairites laid the blame on Brown for his intransigence over fuel duties and pensions. The Chancellor's annual uprating of the pension by a technically correct but insultingly miserable 75p a week threatened the first serious conference revolt since Blair and Brown had taken over the party sworn to consigning Labour splits and party rebellions to the history books. A few months later, I asked the Prime Minister to name his government's greatest mistake. He replied: 'I think the 75p pension, in retrospect. We applied the rules, but it was a mistake. I like to think that we've corrected that with what we've done subsequently.'[22]

Those rules were Brown's rules. The Chancellor was always a great man for his rules. Brown will have noted with displeasure how Blair accepted responsibility for the decision while sliding the blame for it in the direction of the Chancellor.

Labour MPs had returned from their summer holidays to report ever growing complaint about pensions. The eleven million pensioners were not only a third of the electorate, they were a group most likely to use their vote. Philip Gould's research was telling a similar story that the elderly had swung heavily towards the Tories. Aggrieved pensioners displayed their disgust by returning the measly sum to the Treasury. One pensioner who sent a cheque for 75p made out to Gordon Brown discovered, when she looked at her next bank statement, that it had been cashed.[23] He surely did not pocket this small change for himself, but it was taken as emblematic of the insensitivity of the Chancellor. Opponents of the leadership gathered their forces around a conference motion demanding that future increases in pensions matched the rise in earnings. Both the Prime Minister and the Chancellor argued that this was much too expensive a commitment. Moreover, general upratings to the basic pension were not the most effective means of helping the neediest of the elderly. The millionaire Margaret Thatcher would be a beneficiary of a return to the earnings link that her government had sundered. There was a lot of power to these arguments, but they were overwhelmed by the anger that fired the rebellion. On the Sunday night of the conference, the Prime Minister's linkmen with the unions, Jon Cruddas and Pat McFadden, reported to Blair that, unless he found a compromise, he would be defeated. Blair agreed with Sally Morgan, his main adviser on relations with the party, that 'a mega-row' at Brighton was the last thing they needed.

The Cabinet overwhelmingly blamed the Chancellor for not heeding earlier warnings about pensions. Ministers semi-publicly advertised as much. The weekend of the conference, John Prescott told television viewers: 'They [pensioners] don't think they're being helped.' Fingering the Chancellor, he went on: 'Politicians, even if they believe what they are doing is right, have certainly got to convince the electorate that it is right.'[24]

On another channel that Sunday lunchtime, Peter Mandelson remarked that the government was coming over as 'a bit unsympathetic and a little high-handed'. In comments interpreted as a direct attack on Brown over both fuel and pensions, Mandelson went on: 'We got the tone wrong when we eventually did respond by saying, in a highly bureaucratic way, that this all depends on the due process of the Budget-making process. People felt a greater sense of urgency and I understand that.'[25] Brown's allies were furious with this intervention. Blair was also irritated. Not because he disagreed with what Mandelson had said, but because Blair's long experience of managing his Chancellor had taught him that applying public pressure on Brown tended only to make him more obstinate.[26]

The Chancellor used his speech to the conference on the Monday to chide what he saw as the weak-willed colleagues trying to stampede him into surrender. 'However difficult the decisions we have to make, the country will never forgive us if we lurch from one opportunistic tax decision to another and retreat to the old short-termist ways of the past.'[27]

He made some conciliatory noises, promising that within a few weeks he would 'do more' to 'the benefit of all pensioners' after which Ed Balls guided the media to expect the announcement of a generous increase in the pension in the November financial statement. After just twelve hours in Brighton, the Chancellor then swept off, back to a meeting of the International Monetary Fund in Prague. In his absence, Blair and Darling, the Social Security Secretary, searched for a compromise which would avert a defeat for the government.

There was no speech that Blair found more difficult than his own conference oration. 'This speech starts as a small cloud on a summer holiday and it just grows,' he wryly remarked.[28] Both the public polls and Philip Gould's private research found that the voters viewed Blair as both weak and arrogant, unprincipled and out of touch. The speech had to pull off the fiendish trick of answering the charge that Blair was deaf to the nation while reasserting his authority over Britain. So the Prime Minister projected himself as a man who possessed a bedrock of convictions – 'an irreducible core', as he faintly bizarrely put it. At the same time, he presented himself as a leader learning from his recent mistakes. He acknowledged: 'There are things that we have done that made people angry and we should be open enough to admit it.' He came as close as his pride allowed to confessing that 'with hindsight' the Dome had been a mistake. He told his audience that before them – in other words, him – lay 'a fight' to recapture 'the heart and soul of our country'.

The messages of contrition and strength were combined in the litany: 'I am listening. I hear. And I will act.' Listening made more than a dozen appearances in the text. 'So I am listening. But I was also elected to lead.'[29]

The fifty-five-minute speech was grittier in tone than previous conference orations. With less of the candy floss of inanities than before, and sentences which contained vigorous verbs biting on the red meat of argument, this was widely described as among his most impressive conference performances. Even the *Daily Telegraph*, a Conservative paper almost unremittingly hostile to the government, called it 'his best party conference speech as Prime Minister',[30] praise from a right-wing paper all the more striking because Blair had described his ambitions in much more boldly social-democratic language than usual.

The general warmth of this reception came as a great relief to Blair and his intimates who had been even more nervy than usual about how it would go down. By the end of his peroration, a fountain of perspiration was running down the Prime Minister, staining his collar and his shirt front with sweat. An image-neurotic aide sought reassurance from a female journalist: 'Women like that sort of thing, don't they?'[31] Alastair Campbell was thrown into something of a rage when he learnt that the *Sun* was headlining the speech: 'Things Can Only Get Sweatier'. The press secretary cooled off as it became clear that the tabloids were giving an overall cheer for the performance.

Tony Blair had addressed the anger over pensions: 'I tell you now, as Gordon made crystal clear yesterday, we get the message.'[32]

Brown had not really made it that crystal clear. The messages that were reaching him in the Czech Republic from Brighton were disgruntling the Chancellor. His pride in himself as the Iron Chancellor had been wounded by headlines which suggested he was crumbling under pressure. 'In Retreat'[33] and 'Brown bows to pressure over pensions'[34] were typical treatments of his own speech.

At nine o'clock on Tuesday night, a bad-humoured Brown returned to Brighton and his mood darkened further when he was shown the resolution to go before the conference the next day. The motion called for 'further measures to reduce pensioner poverty and boost pensioner income', one of them to be 'linking the basic state pension to, for example, average earnings'. Blair and Darling thought that the insertion of 'for example' was a clever fudge to defuse the row by giving enough latitude to both sides to save the dignity of the unions and the government. Brown furiously told Blair he was having none of this. He wouldn't sign up to this fix. The Chancellor would not accept any phrasing that ran counter to his policy of concentrating help on the poorest pensioners. His resistance to a deal was for the same reason that he had been so utterly opposed to sending any conciliatory signals about fuel taxes. This was a slippery slope, Brown argued with Blair. Compromise would make them look weak.[35]

The Chancellor's exasperated Cabinet colleagues complained that this was another example of Brown's injurious intransigence. This was not quite right. The Chancellor was capable of bending if it suited him. What he was biologically incapable of doing was being seen to do a U-turn. He understood that he would have to salve the anger about pensions, not least because he was taking so much personal flak. What he was insistent on was that he would do it on his own terms in his own good time.

At eleven o'clock that evening, Blair asked John Prescott to join him for a meeting with Rodney Bickerstaffe. The leader of Unison, the largest of the unions, was the chief champion of the pensioners. The talks with the union leader dragged on until past one in the morning. Blair appealed: 'We can't lose this. We can't be defeated on this. Something has to be done.' 'I'm a negotiator,' responded Bickerstaffe. 'All we need is a form of words.' Bickerstaffe told them he did not want to inflict a defeat on the government, but he had to have an honourable way out consistent with his principles. The negotiations with the unions were difficult from the start because their leaders were sore that the original bargain had been unravelled. John Edmonds, the leader of the GMB, complained: 'The Government keeps moving the goalposts.'[36]

When the wrangling in the conference hotel resumed early on Wednesday morning, it soon began to degenerate into macho posturing. At a confrontation with Bickerstaffe and Edmonds, Brown exploded: 'Don't try to dictate to me.' The Chancellor stormed at them: 'You'll lose us the fucking election.'[37] Edmonds, whose own ego was also capaciously prickly, became so enraged that the argument spilled out into a hotel corridor where the GMB leader was witnessed jabbing a finger into Brown's chest.

Blair took a more blandishing approach. One union official claimed that the bargaining involved 'a mixture of an arm up the back and a whiff of ermine',[38] implying that life peerages were being dangled as the reward for backing off. None of which had much leverage on Bickerstaffe, not least because he knew he had the private sympathies of much of the Cabinet, among them John Prescott and David Blunkett. News broadcasts from the Metropole hotel, showing the union leaders scurrying to and from the suites of Brown and Blair, echoed the bad old Labour days.

Hours of grandstanding and haggling got nowhere. At lunchtime on Wednesday, with the conference debate imminent, Brown made a last-gasp attempt to cajole Bickerstaffe to withdraw his motion. When the Chancellor and the union leader met in a room behind the conference platform, Bickerstaffe was surprised to find they had been joined by his friend, Dennis Skinner, totem of the Old Left. 'What are you doing here, Dennis?' wondered Bickerstaffe. Skinner replied that he had been told by Brown's people that it was Bickerstaffe who wanted him along. It then dawned on both of them what was happening. The MP for Bolsover pointed at Brown, himself and Bickerstaffe in sequence: 'He wants me to get you to remit your motion.' Skinner indicated that he would do no such thing – in fact, he would never forgive Bickerstaffe if he withdrew. The Chancellor's odd gambit had failed. As Bickerstaffe rose to leave, Brown pressed him to carry on talking. 'I haven't written my bloody speech yet,' replied the union leader and walked out.[39]

In the debate in the conference hall that afternoon, the two big revolts of that autumn – the fuel protests and the pensioners – became conjoined. 'The pensioners have not blocked the oil refineries; they have not threatened the public services,' shouted Bickerstaffe, moving his motion.[40] Alistair Darling made the counter-case for the government. The conference defeated the leadership by a margin of almost two to one. The union delegations overwhelmingly backed the rebel motion. The important consolation for Blair and Brown was the reaction of party activists. Despite the annual rallying call from Barbara Castle, La Pasionaria of the left, the majority of the constituency delegates, historically the most troublesome element for the leadership, responded to Darling's appeal that help should be concentrated on the poorest pensioners. Such a surprise was this that when one of Blair's aides was shown the 64–36 vote for the leadership among the constituencies, his first reaction was that the figures had to be the wrong way round.

In the wake of the vote, which he dismissed as meaningless, Brown was his usual unbending self: 'I'm not going to give in.'[41]

It was characteristic that Blair should adopt the more placatory approach. On the last day of the conference, when the appearance of Nelson Mandela provided a living symbol of peace and reconciliation for everyone to rally around, Blair sent word to Bickerstaffe to come see him at Number 10 the following Monday. In what was the union leader's first ever one-to-one encounter with the Prime Minister, he heard an emollient Blair express regret that they had become embroiled in this needless bust-up.

This brought to a close the most tumultuous fortnight of the most difficult year of the government's life. Surely, things could only get better.


'What will it look like?' Blair asked his aides. It had long been planned that the Prime Minister would be in Moscow on Guy Fawkes' Night. Now he was having his doubts. 'It'll be "Crisis? What Crisis?"' muttered Blair in dismal memory of the last Labour Prime Minister, James Callaghan, who had gone summiteering abroad during the Winter of Discontent – with fatal effects on his reputation. Blair could visualise how the media would contrast pictures of him sharing toasts in the Kremlin while Britain rotted in the rain.

As October chilled into November, the most severe storms for half a century were putting large areas of the country under water and flooding thousands of homes. A deluge of emergencies drenched the government. In the aftermath of the train crash at Hatfield, the rail network was collapsing with a nervous breakdown.[42]

On top of all that, renewed spasms of panic buying of petrol hit the country as the time ticked down to the deadline the fuel protesters had set the government for a cut in tax. There was an additional factor in the Prime Minister's decision to cancel his trip to Moscow and stay put in Britain. He wanted to be sure that his Chancellor was going to come up with enough money to appease the alienated nation.

There was mounting alarm within Number 10 that the impression was being created of a country coming apart at the seams under a Prime Minister who couldn't get his act together. Counter-intuitively, this concertina of crises combined to the government's advantage in helping to forestall the most worrying menace, a return of the fuel blockades. The volatile weather created a context for greening ministerial rhetoric about the need to respond to global warming. The public reacted to the collapse of the rail network with more sophistication than Blair feared. Polling suggested most voters blamed not him and his government, but incompetence by the train operators and the Conservatives who had privatised them. The paralysis of the rail network made the public less sympathetic to the prospect of petrol supplies being choked again. The government task force under the chairmanship of the Home Secretary had by now prepared much more assured defences against the blockaders.

Fuel was being stockpiled at military depots.[43] The oil companies signed a concordat agreeing to let soldiers drive their tankers, and 1,000 troops were put through crash courses to equip them with the necessary licences. Policing of drive-slows by truckers and farmers was much more aggressive. 'The next time, we were ready for them,' says one of the ministers on the task force.[44]

Alastair Campbell and his propagandists were also being busy. Journalists were encouraged to take an interest in the business background of David Handley, the leader of Farmers For Action. When it was suggested that resumed protests would target food distribution centres, the entire front page of the *Mirror* was devoted to savaging Handley: 'Stop This Silly Fuel'.[45] The media was also encouraged to amplify the splits between the militant and moderate tendencies among the protesters.

The government brandished a big stick in one fist. In the other palm, it held out a plump carrot. As had become something of a practice with the theoretically unbendable Chancellor, Gordon Brown turned his November financial statement into an emergency Budget. Weeks of hardline rhetoric about the protesters laid down cover for the Chancellor to execute a retreat. He announced a freeze in duties until April 2002, and concessions to the hauliers who had humiliated the government worth the equivalent of an 8p a litre cut in diesel duty. Camouflaged as incentives to use greener fuel, the package for motorists was the equivalent of a 4p cut in petrol duty, less than the protesters demanded, but a penny more than had been advocated by the Conservatives. A providential discovery of unspent money from the windfall tax produced extra funding for schools worth up to £30,000 each in the case of the largest secondary schools. To the greatest delight of Labour MPs, the Chancellor used a wedge of his larger than forecast surpluses to announce rises in the pension well above either inflation or earnings over the next two years: £5 a week in the coming year for a single pensioner; £8 for a married couple. An extra £50, bringing it to £200, was added to the winter fuel allowance for pensioners, a ruse to trap the Tories who had stupidly got themselves into the position of saying they would scrap the popular winter warmer. The total cost of assuaging New Labour's autumn of discontents was £4.4 billion next year, rising to £5.7 billion the year after. The *événements* had been costly in every sense.

When things went badly wrong for the Prime Minister, his wife would often offer the homely advice: 'You've just got to dust yourself down and start all over again.'

Two thousand was the year that the roof fell in on New Labour. The government that emerged from the rubble was paradoxically the stronger for the catalogue of alarms and disasters that had befallen it. New Labour was stripped of the last of its innocence and glamour. The shine was all gone. What was left was steelier.

Tony Blair had been anticipating unpopularity throughout his premiership. It was the spook on his shoulder from the day that he stepped over the threshold of Number 10. He was as astonished as his critics that his government had been so airborne in the polls for so long. When the plunge finally happened, it was as if a taboo had been broken. It was even strangely liberating. The hoarder of popularity now had to be a battler for respect.

Blair was compelled to clarify what New Labour was really

about, and delineate the territory on which the government would fight the next election. This process of crisper definition and more solid language had begun with his party conference speech in which he listed the five 'big choices' facing the country and differentiating his government from the Conservatives. He was much more explicit now that one of the biggest of those choices was between cutting taxes and investment in public services.

This shift was encouraged by the dodgy arithmetic of the Conservatives' tax-cutting promises, which invited attack. Feeding into Blair's thinking was all the polling which suggested that the voters were much more interested in improvements to schools and hospitals than they were in tax cuts. It also took place in the context of the defeat of Al Gore, fellow member of the international brotherhood of the Third Way, by the Republican George W. Bush. Philip Gould was closely involved with the Gore campaign, and all the New Labourites watched with horrified fascination as Gore lost the White House. They were shaken by the defeat of their transatlantic soulmate. An incumbent presiding over a sustained period of prosperity had been defeated by a poorly regarded right-winger, an outcome which was as worrying to Tony Blair as it was encouraging for William Hague. The conclusion New Labour drew from this was to be much more vibrant than Gore about explaining to voters how the progressives were rescuing the country from the past failures of the right.

There was a lively debate within New Labour about how to mark the tenth anniversary of the fall of Margaret Thatcher, an occasion which right-wing commentators were using to suggest that Blair was not a patch on their lost leader while some leftish commentators wrote that New Labour had yet to decisively break with her ethos. Blair decided he would prove both wrong by repudiating her.

'I take nothing away from those things that were done in the 1980s that we have kept, but it really is time, in my view, that we moved British politics beyond the time of Margaret Thatcher,' said Blair of the woman whose government he had once praised for 'essential acts of modernisation' and whose good opinion he had courted. 'We are in a new era. Today we have to deal with those problems we inherited from that time – the boom and bust economics, the social division, the chronic under-investment in our public services.'[46]

This renunciation was long overdue for nearly every member of his party, among them the Prime Minister's wife. Cherie and Thatcher found the sight of each other so hard to stomach that whenever they were at the same function they would head for the opposite ends of the room. Baroness Thatcher herself provoked Blair by adding her rasping voice to attacks by the Tories and the Europhobic press on Britain's commitment to the new European rapid reaction force. The Prime Minister made a robust defence of European co-operation. To the surprise of his opponents, he won his case in the court of public opinion. Having faced down the clamour about the so-called European army, later in the year he returned from the Nice summit on enlarging the European Union to deliver a commanding Commons performance in which he crushed William Hague's claims that he had sold out Britain to a European superstate.

The Prime Minister remained an instinctive consensualist, which is why comparisons between him and Thatcher had always been misleading. What Blair now had was a clearer understanding that governing means choosing.

'The biggest single thing that I have learned is that you can't please all the people all the time. In the end, it's less important to be liked than to do the job to the best of your ability, according to the judgements that you make.'[47]

Not that he didn't want to persuade as many people as possible that they should be pleased with his government.

At the end of the year, the Prime Minister appeared on a television programme in a question time format. The audience gave him a rough ride on everything from crime to health to education. One man attacked Blair for holding down spending at the beginning of the parliament. 'I don't intend to become a left-wing Margaret Thatcher,' answered Blair, again reinforcing that break.[48]

At the end of the programme recording, Blair did something that Thatcher would never have thought to do, nor any of his other predecessors as Prime Minister. The programme host, Jonathan Dimbleby, left the studio. The cameras were switched off. Blair stayed on the stage. Sensing the resentment of the many in the audience who had not managed to interrogate him, he carried on taking questions, chairing this impromptu off-camera session himself. Alastair Campbell began to wonder what on earth had happened to Blair. He was supposed to be taking a flight to Belfast for Bill Clinton's valedictory visit to push forward the peace process. Campbell returned to watch Blair carry on taking questions for an hour. At the end, the audience rewarded him with a standing ovation.[49]

To Campbell's regret, hardly anyone had seen his master at his most persuasive and communicative best. The New Year would not be old before everyone saw the government at its very worst – and there was a hint of why that evening.

One man in the audience asked: 'Why does Peter Mandelson seem to have a finger in every pie?' 'Oh, I must tell him that,' responded Blair, smiling.

## 22. Peter's Friends

That Saturday night in late January, like every Saturday night when he was in London, the first editions of the Sunday newspapers were delivered to the Hampstead home of Alastair Campbell. As the Prime Minister's press secretary flicked through the pile, there didn't seem to be anything hugely alarming for the government. He wasn't happy with a page two tale in the *Sunday Times*: 'Mandelson caught in fresh feud with Brown over election planning'.[1] The last thing they needed in the run-up to the election was more headlines about New Labour's eternal, internal, infernal feuding. Campbell also sniffed potential danger in another story on the front page of the *Observer*: 'Mandelson helped Dome backer's passport bid'.[2]

Here was a cocktail of elements that had previously done great damage. The story was about the Millennium Dome, which had turned into New Labour's Tomb of Tutankhamun: everyone who touched it was cursed. The anti-climactic closure at the end of 2000 had not even managed to lance this pustule on the government's reputation when a costly shambles was made of disposing of the Prime Minister's monument.

The story was about New Labour and tycoons, a constantly toxic combination. The phrase 'passports-for-favours' leapt from the page. The New Year began with a rash of nasty headlines following the disclosure of donations to party funds of £2 million apiece from a trio of multimillionaires.[3] The three men were all of unblemished reputation. It was the messy way in which their largesse had been revealed which gave the impression that New Labour was furtive about its relations with the rich.

Finally, the story connected the Dome and passports with Peter Mandelson. In Alastair Campbell's mind, anything with Mandelson in the headline invariably spelt trouble. He rang the press office at

Number 10 to find out if there was much media interest. Told
there was not, Campbell relaxed.

Inquiries did begin to flow into Downing Street during the
course of Sunday. That afternoon, Campbell phoned Mandelson.
The Northern Ireland Secretary appeared to be much more agitated
by the tale in the *Sunday Times*. About the *Observer* story, he was
airy. Number 10 could use the statement he had issued to the
newspaper saying it was an innocent inquiry which had been
handled by officials. Mandelson dismissed it as a 'nothing' story
which was going nowhere.

New Labour's dangerous liaison with the Hinduja brothers dated
back to what might be characterised as its 'Midas period' when rich
men were keen to insinuate themselves into the new order, and
Tony Blair was anxious to plug himself into the wealthy and
well-connected. Of the brothers Hinduja, the oldest, the patriarch,
was Srichand (known as SP). There was also Gopichand (known
as GP) and Prakash (known as PP). With serious problems back
in India, they had long been spreading their tentacles into British
politics.

Even before the 1997 election, according to more than one
report, Blair and Mandelson attended dinner at the Hindujas' home
in Carlton House Terrace, just down the road from Buckingham
Palace.[4] The soon-to-be Prime Minister will have taken note that
the photograph collection on the mantelpiece in the dining room
was a pictorial Who's Who of global leaders and celebrities. The
brothers posed with Margaret Thatcher, the American President
George Bush, the pop singer Michael Jackson, Mother Teresa and
many others from the hall of world fame: a collection to which would
soon be added a snap of the Hindujas with Tony and Cherie Blair.

Three weeks after that bright May Day in 1997, the brothers
threw a party at their London headquarters gazing down on Trafal-
gar Square and the powerhouses of Whitehall. In a short speech,
Peter Mandelson purred to the brothers: 'You are friends of Britain
and friends of New Labour.'[5]

Led by the example of the Prime Minister and his influential vizier, at least a third of the Cabinet had contacts with the Hindujas. The Cabinet Secretary lunched with them, as did Lord Levy, Blair's personal foreign envoy and party fund-raiser, though both men strenuously denied that the subject of passports came up in the conversation.

The great number of New Labour luminaries they sucked into their orbit was the more astonishing because the brothers were the subject of a well-publicised criminal investigation into bribery and corruption concerning the Bofors arms scandal which destroyed the political career of the Indian Prime Minister Rajiv Ghandi. GP and SP Hinduja had earlier applications for British citizenship refused in the early nineties on the grounds that there 'must be some doubt in both cases' whether they would satisfy the requirement to be of 'good character'.[6]

The Hindujas came from a culture in which the borders between politics and business were regarded as blurred, if not non-existent. One person familiar with their methods of operation was quoted saying: 'Their mentality is very much one of the souk, you scratch my back, and I'll scratch yours.'[7] The MP for Leicester East, Keith Vaz, did not deny 'topping and tailing' letters drafted by the Hindujas as well as making what the later inquiry would characterise as 'vigorous' representations in favour of granting them British citizenship.[8] They sent a letter to Blair urging that he should have an Asian minister in his government. Not so long after, Vaz became a minister.

He was small fry in the net of the Hindujas. Peter Mandelson was a much more desirable catch. 'Towards Tony Blair they were sycophantic, fawning, frankly arse-licking,' according to a senior ex-employee. 'To Peter Mandelson they were friendly – but it was a more equal relationship. They saw him as the gatekeeper to Blair – and that was a role he liked to play. Irrespective of whether he was at Northern Ireland, Trade and Industry or a backbencher, the rich and famous were encouraged to queue up at his door to get to Blair.'[9]

The relationship between Number 10 and the brothers was much more involved than anyone realised at this time or even after the

Prime Minister was compelled to order an inquiry into the Hinduja Affair. As with Bernie Ecclestone, the Prime Minister's chief of staff was the main linkman with these wealthy men. There was an exchange of warm correspondence with the brothers – either signed by Jonathan Powell or 'yours ever, Tony'. These letters, mainly on foreign policy topics, made no mention of the brothers' pursuit of passports. The contents were, as Number 10 would insist when they eventually leaked, 'unremarkable'. Their potential capacity to embarrass Tony Blair lay in the fact that they showed a much more intricate relationship with the Hindujas than the Prime Minister wanted disclosed. The letters were never published by the official inquiry, despite the Prime Minister's promise that Sir Anthony Hammond would have Number 10's full co-operation. Either Hammond was not shown this correspondence. Or he left it out of his report.

Powell, like many who dealt with them, found the Hindujas persistent to the point of pushiness in their attentions. But they had wealth, they gave every appearance of being influential figures in the Asian community, and they radiated the impression of power. On a visit to Number 10, the Hindujas came in the company of the Principal Secretary to the Indian Prime Minister.[10] According to Peter Mandelson's allies, it was actually Number 10 that first initiated the involvement of the Hindujas in the sponsorship of the Dome. Supporters of Mandelson say that Powell sent him an official minute suggesting to the then Dome Minister that they were offering money. Written in Powell's typically blunt style, the minute informed Mandelson that SP Hinduja had approached the Prime Minister with an offer to donate to the Dome. Powell told Mandelson that the Prime Minister wanted him to follow this up without delay.[11] Despite the obvious bearing of this memo on the affair, the minute was kept from the Hammond Inquiry, or it was something else that was left out of the published report.

As was invariably the case with New Labour, the root of the affair was the quest for money. The Dome was desperately short of sponsors back in 1997 and 1998. The scramble to secure outside funding had from the beginning programmed a potential minefield of conflicts of interests into the Prime Minister's prestige project.

The reliance on sponsorship left the financing dependent on cheques from rich men who might be looking for favours from the government. The financing of the Spirit Zone – later to transmogrify into the Faith Zone – was especially tricky. It held little attraction to the corporate Mammons looking for opportunities to advertise their companies. Suggestions from the Hindujas that they would write a cheque to pay for the zone were therefore greeted with large relief. The brothers had another interest: they wanted British citizenship. When they had first applied for passports under the Conservatives, the official who recommended refusal noted that they were 'pressing for their applications to be dealt with quickly' because of the criminal investigation in India.[12] On the account of S P Hinduja, his many contacts with Keith Vaz included discussions with Vaz, by then a Foreign Office minister, about 'the protection' that British citizenship might give the brothers against the Indian authorities.[13]

When the brothers revived their previously rejected applications, this time they were indeed dealt with quickly – despite further cautions about them. In November 1996, the civil servant in charge of the Home Office's Nationality Division, Andrew Walmsley, was given a warning in language unusually colourful for officialdom. The head of the Foreign Office's South Asian department wrote: 'At the very least the Hinduja brothers can be said to have sailed close to the wind in the building of their business empire.'[14] The British High Commissioner in India also advised that granting British citizenship to the Hindujas might become an embarrassment to the government.[15] Despite that, in July 1997 Walmsley recommended to the Immigration Minister, Mike O'Brien, that GP be granted citizenship. He got his passport that November, even though GP had not spent the number of days in Britain usually required of successful applicants. Why was he given such a priority and personal service by the senior official? Because the Hindujas had cultivated people with connections. Among those writing letters of support were Sir Edward Heath, the former Conservative Prime Minister. This helped get a result. The more inquiries there were by well-known and influential people, the faster the Home Office processed an application, if only to stop the representations mounting up. That method is open only to the privileged few who are well-connected; not to the many without access to the powerful.

In February 1998, SP wrote to Blair and Mandelson formally offering to contribute to the Dome. By the summer of that year – the period which would be critical to later events – the Hindujas' dealings with the government at various levels were particularly intense. On 4 June, they visited Number 10 in the company of a senior Indian diplomat where they met both the Prime Minister and his chief of staff. GP afterwards wrote to Jonathan Powell thanking him for 'going out of his way' to set things up.[16] On 17 June, the Hinduja Foundation put the Dome offer more firmly. Within the next fortnight, either Mandelson directly – and if not him, certainly his office at his instigation – contacted the Immigration Minister inquiring whether a change to government policy might allow SP Hinduja to revive his previously rejected application for British citizenship. Very shortly afterwards, on 2 July 1998, one of O'Brien's officials e-mailed Walmsley asking whether SP Hinduja might 'benefit' from the 'more positive approach to citizenship' that O'Brien was 'keen to adopt'.[17] The response was affirmative. With delicious irony given what would happen, under the heading 'Handling/Presentational issues', Walmsley wrote: 'None.'[18] On 5 October, O'Brien wrote to Mandelson saying that the Home Office was 'likely to look favourably' on a citizenship application from SP Hinduja.[19] Just nine days later, on 14 October, the Hindujas announced a definite decision to underwrite the Faith Zone to the tune of £3 million. Seven days after that, SP Hinduja reapplied for citizenship.

It was the usual practice of the Millennium Experience Company to check on the status, credit and general reputation of potential sponsors. During the period when the brothers' applications for passports were speeding through the system, the Secret Intelligence Service had – as Sir Anthony Hammond delicately put it in his report – 'accumulated a certain amount of intelligence about the Hindujas' business activities abroad'. In his report, the QC summarised that the material 'raised the possibility that they had been involved in a number of dubious practices, in some cases potentially amounting to illegal activities, but that none of the indications of such involvement was conclusive. The material covered, but was not confined to, the Bofors scandal.' Extraordinarily, according to Hammond, 'none of the material was seen by the Home Office' before it gave a passport to a second Hinduja brother. This was because 'the material had been gathered by SIS in response to a request in a different context'.[20]

What Sir Anthony did not say is that intelligence from MI6 had been gathered to protect the royal family from any taint of sleaze. The Prince of Wales' charitable body, the Prince's Trust, had turned down donations from the Hindujas after being 'warned off' by the security services.[21]

Mandelson started to get the jips about his embroilment with the Hindujas long before it became public knowledge. Having seen the intelligence material, in November 1998 he wrote a minute: 'I agree that they are an above average risk but without firm evidence of wrongdoing how could we bar them from involvement in sponsorship? We are right to reduce our exposure to them. I wonder how this involvement got publicity in the first place.

'Incidentally, if Mr SP Hinduja wishes to pursue his citizenship application he can do so without further involvement or commendation from me!'[22] That last sentence is strikingly dissonant with Mandelson's vehement and repeated assertions when it all started becoming public that he never made more than a 'casual and fleeting' inquiry and never made any representations on behalf of SP Hinduja.

In March 1999, SP Hinduja got his passport, the application having been processed in a quarter of the usual time. The rules about absences had been waived for him: he had spent almost twice as many days abroad as the 450 usually permitted. The Hammond Inquiry would reveal that many of the customary routine checks with the Foreign Office, the police, security services and Inland Revenue were not carried out. Nor were complete records kept.

In June 1999, when the Dome money from the Hindujas was finally confirmed, it turned out to be only £1 million. Once thousands of free tickets to the Dome and a tax bill were deducted, the value of their donation amounted to just £365,000.[23] They got their passports. The Dome received a relatively piffling benefit in proportion to the torrent of grief the Hinduja Affair would inflict on the government.

A shower of confetti and a burst of fireworks were triggered by the arrival on stage of Tony and Cherie. The Prime Minister and his wife were the star attractions when the Hindujas threw a lavish celebration at Alexandra Palace in November 1999. The party was to celebrate Diwali, the Hindu festival of lights representing the victory of wisdom over ignorance, good over evil. What this event more precisely marked was the high point of the Hindujas' successful envelopment of the British political establishment. Sir David Frost was the master of ceremonies. The leaders of all the main parties were invited to dance in attendance. SP and GP escorted Cherie, who was wearing a £1,000 silk churidar kameez. The Prime Minister had the lead role in a lavishly produced souvenir film, distributed on thousands of DVDs by Srichand Hinduja with his Christmas cards. As one of the brothers refers to him as 'Lord Rama', the Hindu god, Tony Blair can be seen smiling a little warily.

There was a lot for the Prime Minister to be nervous about. Margaret Thatcher had been warned off accepting invitations from the Hindujas. Swraj Paul, the rich Indian industrialist and Labour donor, had counselled both Tony Blair and Gordon Brown to steer clear. The Chancellor – to his great later relief – took the advice. The Prime Minister ignored it.

Had Blair not seen any of the serious health warnings from MI6 and the Foreign Office about getting involved with the brothers? If they had been brought to his attention, to continue his entanglement with the Hindujas was reckless. If the Prime Minister was in ignorance, this suggests the most extraordinary lapses. A year or more previously, Peter Mandelson, also in attendance at the party, had definitely seen the warnings from MI6. Had he not shared them with his close friend, the Prime Minister?

Despite his own realisation that they were 'above average risk', Mandelson continued to involve himself with the brothers. In May

2000, he passed a letter to Jack Straw written by GP Hinduja asking whether the government would be positive about a citizenship application from third brother Prakash. The Home Secretary very obligingly sent Mandelson a handwritten acknowledgement saying he was 'following the matter up personally and will be back in touch as soon as I can'.[24]

Straw wrote a note to his private secretary: 'Mara – Mr Mandelson raised this matter with me. Please have a word first and then get some advice.' Underneath, the Home Secretary put: '?Zola Budd', a comment which he circled.[25] There had been a famous furore when the barefoot South African athlete was granted a British passport in a lightning ten days. Straw would tell the inquiry that he 'could not recall' why he scribbled down the athlete's name. His private secretary messaged the civil servant handling the citizenship application urging him to be quick and adding 'the Home Secretary would like the case to be dealt with "helpfully"'.[26] The Hindujas, who were generous with thank you gifts, sent Mandelson some mangoes around this time. He appears to have disposed of the exotic fruits by using them as a substitute for the traditional flowers or chocolates to present to unsuspecting hostesses who had him for dinner.

Alarm bells began to ring at Number 10 in the autumn of 2000. New Labour's intricate enmeshment with the brothers was finally seen for the peril it had always been. In early October, India's Central Bureau of Investigation filed charges of criminal conspiracy and corruption against the Hindujas. From being millionaires with whom the Prime Minister was happy to dine, party, invite to Number 10, exchange warm letters and take money from, the Hindujas were becoming radioactive. Downing Street was suddenly allergic to further dealings with the brothers, and even more fearful of publicity about past contacts. When GP Hinduja wrote to Jonathan Powell assuring him of their innocence, this time he didn't get a reply to his letter from the chief of staff. Number 10 tried to downplay the extent of the Prime Minister's relationship with the brothers to journalists who made inquiries to Downing Street.

The connections had particularly intrigued two men with a record of harrying Mandelson: Anthony Barnett, an investigative reporter with the *Observer*, and the Liberal Democrat MP, Norman Baker, whom Mandelson had long complained was 'stalking' him. In December, Baker tabled a written question to the Home Office, asking what representations had been made about the Hindujas' passport applications by Mandelson and Vaz.

This threw the Home Office into a flap and jangled Mandelson's sensitive nerves. Once disgraced already, he was intensely fearful of any story associating him with further scandal. Geoffrey Robinson's memoirs had been published the previous autumn. Though they proved pretty unexplosive, the brief revival of interest in the home loan affair that caused his first downfall pushed Mandelson to the brink of hysterics. 'It is a piece of terrorism,' he told a journalist particularly close to him. 'They are trying to smear me personally and destroy me politically.'[27] According to one of his closest friends: 'Peter jumped at the least squeak of the door.'[28] He'd jumped again at a story alleging that he'd been thrown a '£5,000 birthday party' by a bidder for the Dome.[29]

Frightened about public exposure of his relationship with the brothers, Mandelson argued with Jack Straw, more than once on the account of the latter, that he, Mandelson, should not be named in connection with the Hindujas. Straw, with his own pressing reasons not to want to associate the Home Office with suggestion of a cover-up, resisted. By 16 January 2001, the parliamentary question was imminently due for an answer. In a phone call that day, Straw contended to Mandelson that any further delay would only arouse suspicions. Straw told the Northern Ireland Secretary that Mandelson had had a conversation with O'Brien, and the answer had to be drafted accordingly. The Home Secretary suggested they play this straight 'for your own protection as well, Peter'.[30] Mandelson eventually agreed so long as the answer was rewritten to stress that he did not make 'representations'.

The production of the written answer provided the *Observer* with its scoop. Had Mandelson left it at that, had he not tried to weave the illusion that Hinduja passports were a matter entirely confined to civil servants, then the fuse might not have been lit on his implosion. The witch doctor of spin could not resist waving his wand over the truth. On Saturday afternoon, as he wandered around a Parisian museum of Asiatic art, he dictated a statement putting the blandest possible construction on his dealings with the Hindujas: 'To the limited extent that I was involved in this matter I was always very sensitive to the proprieties. The matter was dealt with by my private secretary. At no time did I support or endorse this application for citizenship.'[31]

In their conversation on the Sunday, Mandelson suggested that Campbell could use the statement if he was asked any questions about it during his briefing of political correspondents. On Monday, the story ran on some inside pages, but did not feature on the broadcast media. At his briefing that morning, Campbell told the journalists: 'Mr Mandelson had not got involved in the matter – beyond being asked to be involved, which he had refused to do.'[32]

Inadvertently, the direct Campbell had stretched the supple Mandelson's carefully nuanced denial to snapping point. In the Commons that afternoon, the Culture Secretary, Chris Smith, told MPs that Mandelson's 'sole involvement' had been to tell SP Hinduja that his application would be dealt with by civil servants 'in the normal way'.[33]

Warning lights began to flash later that afternoon. Campbell saw 'a line to take' issued by the Home Office. It was proposing to say – contrary to the impression given so far – that Mandelson had made 'verbal enquiries' of O'Brien.

Campbell had Mandelson dragged out of a dinner at Hillsborough Castle with the Chief Constable of the RUC. A conference call was set up involving the Northern Ireland Secretary, the press secretary and O'Brien. Mandelson challenged O'Brien's memory of the phone call about the Hinduja passport. He was sticking to his line that it was dealt with by officials. O'Brien was emphatic that they had spoken in the summer of 1998. Mandelson conceded, claiming afterwards that he did so because he was given the impression by both O'Brien and Campbell that there was a documentary record of this phone call, which it transpired there was not. For their part, in later evidence to the inquiry, Campbell and O'Brien denied ever making any such suggestion.[34]

This phone call would have a pivotal importance in the saga that was now unfolding. Did it actually occur or not? Sir Anthony Hammond concluded it was 'likely' that there was such a phone conversation. Mandelson changed his story, first saying he remembered no call, then accepting there was, before reverting to his original version and claiming to have been briefly and fatally bamboozled into admitting to the call because of the untrue claim there was a record of it. What is beyond dispute is that he was much more involved with Hinduja passports than he had admitted to the *Observer*. Mandelson did not quarrel with evidence from Home Office civil servants that he had talked directly to an official about SP Hinduja. He also told the inquiry that it was conceivable that he had mentioned SP to O'Brien in the Division lobby.[35] The real significance of the phone call was that it became the crucial strand of evidence in the noose by which the Northern Ireland Secretary would be hung.

Mandelson subsequently lamented that his world fell apart because there was no 'agreed sequence of events or "line to take"'.[36] Inadvertently, he put his finger on the nub of his destruction. It had always been part of New Labour's theology of media management – Mandelson and Campbell had together written the bible – that the way to deal with damaging allegations was to answer them with a 'line to take'. So long as everyone involved subscribed to an agreed 'truth' about events – however true or not this 'truth' was – then they could spin their way to safety. The developing problem was that Campbell and Mandelson, the two great storytellers of New Labour, were on their way to a situation where they were in irreconcilable dispute about what was the 'truth'.

The relationship between the mercurial Mandelson and the earthier Campbell was already riddled with some mistrust. Founding figures and close comrades of New Labour they might be, but they were also competitors with abrasive temperaments. The loyalist Campbell had long complained about Mandelson's way of dropping people, how he 'dipped in and out' when it suited him, as Campbell saw it. To others at Number 10, the press secretary had in recent months been calling the Northern Ireland Secretary a 'liability' who was tolerated only because he was 'special', particularly in the eyes of the Prime Minister. For his part, Mandelson had been increasingly critical of aspects of Campbell's behaviour. Mandelson was appalled by a television documentary[37] in which the press secretary took the heroic role in the action and Tony Blair was given a diminishing walk-on part. Mandelson complained to Blair that it made Blair look like 'the hireling' and Campbell look like the Prime Minister.[38]

During the conference call between London and Northern Ireland, Campbell said that he would now have to adjust Downing Street's line about the Hinduja story the next morning. Mandelson ended the call by saying he couldn't leave the Chief Constable any longer.

The thermometer at Number 10 was already rising to panic levels. That same Monday evening, Jonathan Powell asked the Cabinet Secretary to start looking into Mandelson and the Hindujas' passports so that the Prime Minister could be provided with a cast-iron line for Question Time on Wednesday.

At Tuesday morning's lobby briefing, Campbell astonished journalists by telling them that the version he had given them on Monday, based on 'Peter's recollection', was wrong. After 'Mr Mandelson's office had been able to look at the records in full', they 'had discovered that he had had a very brief telephone conversation in June 1998 with Mike O'Brien'. This was simply untrue. Campbell was presumably trying to spin this line to assist Mandelson. What he did next was no help at all.

'Although Mr Mandelson had no recollection of the call, clearly it had taken place.'[39]

The implication that Mandelson had suffered a convenient attack of amnesia about the Hindujas prompted the journalists to the understandable assumption that the serpentine Northern Ireland Secretary had lied about the call to conceal a scandal.

By the afternoon, the Westminster lobby was in full cry about the contradictions in the government's story. They mauled Campbell's deputy, Godric Smith, at the afternoon briefing. A shaken Smith reported to Campbell that he had been through the worst lobby of the government. Blair, now being drawn into this imbroglio, went along with Campbell's advice that Mandelson would have to get on television that evening and make another effort to straighten it out.

After a day devoted to talks about Northern Ireland, and with only a sketchy grasp of the new line spun out from Campbell, Mandelson's first interview was with *Channel 4 News*. He was now directly confronted with the allegation that he was a liar. 'There is no question of my forgetting anything,' he insisted. 'I was not asked until today.' Asked why Number 10 had said he had forgotten the call, Mandelson snapped: 'You will have to ask them that', adding 'Nobody asked me about a phone call on Saturday, Sunday or Monday. Nobody asked me these questions.'[40] When he heard this, the press secretary exploded. He already believed that Mandelson had misled him about the O'Brien call, jeopardising his own credibility with the media, and drawing Chris Smith into misleading the Commons. What Mandelson had now said made him, Campbell, look the liar. In a rage, he went off to find the Prime Minister.

When his pager began to vibrate with the urgent message to call Number 10, Jack Straw was at the Whitbread Book awards. The Home Secretary ducked out of the ceremony to search for somewhere private, eventually ending up in an echoing stairwell. In the words of one aide, Tony Blair was now in his 'barrister-mode', trying to establish for himself what was at the bottom of this morass. Straw told the Prime Minister that Mandelson's claim not to remember the O'Brien call couldn't be right. He, Straw, had reminded Mandelson about the conversation only the previous week. This was fatal for the Northern Ireland Secretary.

'Peter had better have a bloody good defence for this,' Blair said to others at Number 10. The Prime Minister and Mandelson had three telephone conversations that night. The problem, Blair told Mandelson, was the conflict between his statement that it had all been handled by officials and the reminders from Straw that he'd talked to O'Brien. 'In a reasonable world things would be different,' sighed Blair. Now the media would 'whip everything up'.

Early on Wednesday morning, Blair called his closest aides up to his Downing Street flat for a crisis council. Mandelson had no defenders left in the room. Just when the government was trying to get its achievements across in the run-up to the election, the message was being drowned out by another Mandelsonian scandal howling from every media orifice. This was not a first offence. It fitted a pattern of behaviour. No one could forget, least of all Blair and Campbell, how he had concealed his home loan from them. Was there a further calculation about Number 10's own entanglements with the Hindujas in their thinking? Mandelson's allies believe so. In the words of one of them: 'Peter was chopped off at the knees to prevent the scandal touching the Prime Minister. If they left this powderkeg in the Cabinet, sooner or later the Hinduja trail would lead all the way to Blair.'[41] Evidence to support this is that the inquiry announced by the Prime Minister later in the day would be closely restricted to SP Hinduja's passport, and its remit would be extended somewhat only on request of the investigator.

Just after nine, Sir Richard Wilson arrived. As the result of his investigations, the Cabinet Secretary had produced a three-page memo, marked 'RESTRICTED AND PERSONAL'. Wilson wrote that the case fell into a 'slippery area' and warned that 'the Prime Minister and Number 10 should not get too involved in this'. Wilson's suggested 'line' was that 'no one has produced a shred of evidence that anything improper took place'.[42] Blair could have seized on this to put a protective shield around Mandelson. Once he might have done. The view of his aides was that this demonstrated Sir Richard's useless grasp of governing in the media age. Blair had become very defensive about accusations that he presided over a sleaze-ridden and crony-riddled regime. Not because he really accepted the criticism, but because he saw how it corroded his reputation and the potential threat to the government's election ambitions. Even Peter Mandelson, architect of New Labour, was not going to be allowed to stand in the way of Tony Blair's second term.

Next to arrive was Derry Irvine. The Lord Chancellor took up the role of the hanging judge at what Mandelson would later characterise as the 'kangaroo court' that convicted him. The Lord Chancellor pronounced that the evidence appeared incontrovertible.

Mandelson had led Number 10 to believe there was no call to O'Brien when Straw had reminded him that there was such a call. As a result, the lobby had been misled and so had MPs. The Northern Ireland Secretary's fate was being sealed. Even he would subsequently concede: 'If I had been presented with the sort of case against me that was put up to him that Wednesday, I think I would have fired myself.'[43]

Peter Mandelson's friends always knew he was in trouble when they got a call before seven in the morning. Early that Wednesday, he phoned the author Robert Harris. 'I'm in a jam,' said Mandelson. 'It's all a mess.' 'You won't have to resign, will you?' asked Harris. 'No, no,' replied Mandelson, not realising yet that the rope was already tightening around his neck. Harris later recalled: 'He called me at about ten to seven. He was pretty upset, but I didn't get the impression that he thought it was all over.'[44]

Ben Wegg-Prosser, his former aide, also found him 'remarkably upbeat'[45] when they had an early-morning phone conversation. When they talked again, about an hour later, Mandelson's mood had noticeably blackened. He had now read the newspapers. None of the broadsheets and only one, less important tabloid was demanding his head. The tone of the coverage was, however, savage: 'a shrieking media lynch mob, some of them labelling me a liar', Mandelson would later wail.[46] He did not need to guess how this was going down at Number 10.

Clutching two ministerial red boxes, Mandelson emerged from his flat in Notting Hill and sank into his blue armoured Jaguar. At shortly before ten thirty, the limousine delivered him to the car park at the back of Number 10. He slipped in by the rear door to meet the Prime Minister in his study. For the second time, Blair was confronted with the hateful task of sacking his old friend and close ally, fully aware that it would make him look supremely foolish for bringing Mandelson back into the Cabinet. Knowing how queasy the Prime Minister felt about this, his aides hoped that Mandelson might 'do a Captain Oates': leave of his own volition.

'We will have one hell of a fight on our hands', Blair told Mandelson, hoping to lead the other man to his own conclusion that he would have to go. The way Blair said this made it clear that he thought the fight unwinnable – and certainly not worth it. As it became evident that Blair wanted his resignation, Mandelson put up a defence. He couldn't see that he'd done anything wrong. It was all an awful muddle, he protested. When he had made his remarks about 'forgetting' the conversation with O'Brien it was because he thought the allegation was that he had 'deliberately' forgotten. As Mandelson tried to muster a defence, Blair shook his head. This was all 'rubbish', growled Campbell. After a while, the press secretary left the room.

Blair said that the contradictions about the O'Brien call made Mandelson's position 'untenable'. Blair couldn't see an 'alternative' but for him to resign.

Mandelson continued to struggle. Blair was setting up an inquiry. What was the point of that if Number 10 had already convicted and executed him? Why not wait until the inquiry reported? Better resign now, said Blair, rather than go through a prolonged torture at the hands of the media. The Prime Minister had selfish reasons for bringing this to a surgical end. The run-up to the election was not the time he wanted to fight a protracted and probably vain battle with the press over the body of Mandelson.

The clock was ticking against several urgent deadlines. Blair had to answer Prime Minister's Question Time at three that afternoon. Mandelson was due at the dispatch box immediately before him. The most urgent deadline was eleven o'clock. The political correspondents would soon be crowding into the basement of Number 10 for a morning briefing from Alastair Campbell. The press secretary burst back into the Prime Minister's study, interrupting the intense and fraught conversation with Mandelson. More impatient and aggravated than ever, Campbell drummed the table. 'What am

I supposed to tell the fucking lobby? What do I tell them?' he demanded. 'The later I am, the worse it will look.' Campbell shot a look at Blair which said: why the hell haven't you sacked him yet?[47]

Campbell eventually abandoned Blair and Mandelson arguing in the study to go downstairs to face the political correspondents. Though the pack had arrived in lusty anticipation of a good morning's sport, no one expected that Mandelson was about to be sacked. *The Times* had headlined its morning report that Blair would battle to save his Northern Ireland Secretary. Campbell's late arrival was a clue that something big was up; an even more obvious indicator was the press secretary's angry demeanour as he revealed to the journalists that Mandelson had been hauled in to see Blair. Most damningly of all, Campbell refused to say that the Northern Ireland Secretary still enjoyed the confidence of the Prime Minister. Campbell terminated the briefing by telling the journalists that he would be 'more useful upstairs'. From that moment Mandelson was doomed. The television and radio reporters scampered from the room to broadcast it to the world.

Had Blair actually done the deed by this point? More than one witness to this extraordinary morning in the incestuous and volatile melodrama of New Labour thinks not. Was Campbell forcing the knife across Mandelson's throat? It would not be the first time that the press secretary bounced the Prime Minister. Nor would it be the first time that he had been exasperated by Blair havering over an execution. Campbell had been furious with Blair for not disposing of Geoffrey Robinson much more rapidly. Past experience had taught him to worry that the wily Mandelson might sufficiently muddle a hesitant Blair to talk him out of sacking the Northern Ireland Secretary. Campbell had acted to make Mandelson's demise absolutely inevitable.

In the study, the Northern Ireland Secretary was begging the Prime Minister for more time. A second resignation would mean that his political career was 'over', Mandelson pleaded to Blair. 'That's my life, Tony.' Better to go in a way that they might dress up with some dignity, countered the Prime Minister.

Overwhelmed by the forces arrayed against him, in Mandelson's own words 'the fight suddenly went out of me. I felt isolated.'[48]

The first time he was sacked, Campbell ghosted his resignation letter for him. This time, as a broken Mandelson crumpled on the Prime Minister's sofa, Blair wrote out a resignation statement. When he left Blair's study, a tearful Anji Hunter embraced him. Campbell had blubbed and hugged over the first fall. There was no repetition of that lachrymosity on this occasion. The only time he had wept in the past twenty-four hours, Campbell quipped that afternoon, was when he was listening to a radio report of Burnley playing Scunthorpe and his team missed a penalty.

At 1.33 p.m. Mandelson emerged on Downing Street to read out the resignation statement. While continuing to deny that he had acted improperly, he did accept responsibility for giving conflicting accounts of events surrounding the telephone call to O'Brien. He had been sacked by his friends, but the statement depicted him as a man martyred by the media.

I confess in reaching my decision, that there is another factor. As a reading of today's newspapers shows all too graphically, there must be more to politics than the constant media pressure and exposure that has dogged me over the last five or so years. I want to remove myself from the countless stories of controversy, of feuds, of divisions and all the rest, all the other stories that have surrounded me. I want, in other words, to lead a more normal life, both in politics and, in the future, outside.[49]

Normality was never a trait associated with the most vivid member of Blair's Cabinet. His sacking was technicolour in its summary, brutal and ironic justice. He had handed ammunition to the media which he and Campbell had taught Tony Blair to regard with loathing and fear. His folly was to make himself so vulnerable to the very forces he had done so much to conjure into British politics that he was sacked by the Prime Minister he had done so much to create. For the second time. In barely more than two years.

He took a final session of Questions in the Commons that

afternoon, a departing act of some dignity and courage. The rest of the Cabinet gradually filtered on to the frontbench for Prime Minister's Question Time. Jack Straw patted him on the forearm. David Blunkett grasped his hand in a minute-long grip, as if attempting to check whether Mandelson still had a pulse. When Blair arrived by his side, the two men exchanged looks in which affection warred with reproach. While a wan Mandelson hunched on Blair's right, to the Prime Minister's left sat Gordon Brown and John Prescott, sharing a private joke.

Mandelson looked like a ghost; Blair looked as though he had just seen a ghost. A pale and harrowed Prime Minister told MPs: 'I made it clear that if people did something wrong, they would pay the penalty and he has paid the penalty.'

The leader of the Opposition mocked him ferociously. 'Now that the Prime Minister has notched up the historic achievement of being forced to sack the same Minister for the same offence twice in 25 months, does he recognise that his career-long dependency on Mr Mandelson has been a monumental error of judgement?', William Hague taunted him. Blair's voice cracked in reply that the 'tragic' Mandelson was 'a bigger man than many of his critics'.[50]

It is hard to tell which was the more dismal for Mandelson: the joy of his foes – or the condolences of his enemies. As he prepared to leave the Commons, there was a tap on the window of his official car. It was Gordon Brown, just wanting to say that he agreed with Blair that it was a 'tragedy'. They should talk.

Colleagues waved off the funeral barge of Mandelson's career on a river of crocodile tears. Campbell encouraged predictions that the imploded star would quit as an MP by telling journalists: 'I think Peter's making clear from his statement that he is looking to wind down his political activity.'[51]

Geoff Hoon – a man whom Mandelson might once have broken with a jagged whisper – suggested that all that remained of his erstwhile Cabinet colleague's political career was to 'knock on doors and deliver party leaflets'. It was reminiscent of the way in which purged members of Stalin's Politburo were airbrushed out of the picture as if they had never really existed. By teatime, the workmen had arrived in the Cabinet ministers' corridor to pick the letters of his name off the office door.

The first time that he was sacked from the Cabinet, those closest to him feared that Peter Mandelson might take his own life. He had been nursed through the aftermath of that disgrace by no one more than Robert Harris. It was a dejected and shattered Mandelson who spoke to Harris and his remaining friends on Thursday morning. He brooded over the celebratory reaction to his demise. 'Sir, It feels like Christmas again,' read a one-line letter in the *Daily Telegraph*. 'A glittering career in ruins' was the *Guardian* front-page obituary. The *Daily Mail* printed a picture of Blair and Mandelson sitting together with a homoerotic twist in the headline: 'THE END OF THE AFFAIR ... Blair's blackest day'. In the *Daily Express*, Peter Oborne wrote: 'This morning the Labour Party had the bemused and joyful air of a Transylvanian village where news has just come through that Lord Dracula will disturb them no longer.' 'GOODBYE AND GOOD RIDDANCE', cackled the *Sun*, licking vilifying adjectives: 'Mandelson's out on his ear again because he is a lying, manipulative, oily, two-faced, nasty piece of work who should never have been allowed back into the Government.' The tabloid conveniently forgot that it had not only welcomed him back into the government, it had actively campaigned for his return. Even Campbell felt a twinge of sympathy. To others at Number 10, he remarked: 'Even Harold Shipman didn't get as bad a press as Peter.'[52]

Harris said he'd drive up to London from Berkshire the next morning to help plan how Mandelson might retrieve something of his reputation. At a little after ten on Friday, the author arrived at Mandelson's flat to find he was not there. He had gone over to another friend's house in Bayswater where he was told something that seemed to put an entirely new complexion on what had happened. 'Fucking hell,' Mandelson muttered to the others in the room at the end of the phone conversation. Emma Scott, a civil servant who worked in his office at the time of the passport inquiry, was saying that she made the fateful call to O'Brien. And Rupert

Huxter, another of his former officials, was saying that he had tried to communicate this to Number 10 on Wednesday morning only to be rebuffed.

Mandelson went over to his own flat. Falling through the door, he was virtually speechless at first. 'She made the call! She made the call!' he gasped to Harris. Mandelson paced around the flat, chanting the obsessive mantra: 'This changes everything. This changes everything.' It changed little. It certainly could not alter the hard fact that he had been sacked. This would serve only to further muddy very murky waters. Even Harris – and Mandelson had no more dedicated and vociferous champion – accepted that this 'does not, of course, prove in any way that Mr Mandelson did not have a further telephone conversation with Mike O'Brien'. Harris also conceded: 'He should have been more candid earlier with his colleagues.'[53]

What this twist in the tale did offer the desperate Mandelson was a lifeline out of his depression. He was furnished with a reason to believe that perhaps there was a future for him in politics yet. He grasped at this psychological comfort which gave him grounds for arguing, at least to himself, that his fall was not his fault. It had all been 'a ghastly accident'. Dejection gave way to a burning sense of injustice against those whom he thought responsible for his dismissal.

From his flat that morning, Mandelson rang Alastair Campbell. 'I told you, you got it wrong. I told you, you were rushing. I told you,' he ripped into Campbell. 'Don't give me that,' Campbell lost his temper, 'I'm fucking sick of hearing this.' The call became super-charged with emotion. 'You swept me out in the gutter like a piece of old rubbish,' Mandelson shouted down the phone. He got no more satisfaction from calls to the other men he believed to have sat on the hanging bench. 'I think it does change things, Richard,' Mandelson vainly tried to argue with the Cabinet Secretary. To Derry Irvine, Mandelson raged: 'It may be water under the bridge to you! It's not water under the bridge to me!'

Next, it was Mandelson who received a call. Tony Blair had been tipped off by Campbell and Irvine that the former Northern Ireland Secretary was not resting quiet in his grave. Blair was solicitous towards Mandelson. He left the other man with the impression that Blair was already regretful that he had been persuaded to sack him. It would be characteristic of Blair to employ that technique to calm him down. It was too late to go back, the Prime Minister told him. When the call with the Prime Minister was over, Harris remarked: 'You're completely on your own.'

It was originally planned that Mandelson would give his side of the story in an interview for the *Sunday Times* conducted by Harris, an intermittent columnist for the paper. On Saturday morning, Mandelson instead resolved to write his own account. This was a mistake. His plea in self-defence was rambling, contradictory and, in parts, self-damnatory. He may have unconsciously written his own epitaph: 'This relatively trivial error was turned into a huge misjudgement that led to my resignation.'[54] What leapt its way into the headlines was his claim that he had been the victim of a gross travesty of justice by Tony Blair.

While Mandelson spun his line for one newspaper, Campbell was spinning against the fallen minister for all of the Sunday papers. Now alert that the corpse of Mandelson was twitching, the press secretary acted to drive a stake into his heart. There was no group of journalists for whom he professed more contempt than the political correspondents of the Sunday newspapers. Back in May 1997, he memorably opened his first briefing for them: 'Explain to me just why I should waste my time with a load of wankers like you when you're not going to write anything I tell you anyway.'[55]

At half past one on that Friday afternoon, Campbell began to provide such inflammatory copy that the 'wankers' would devour everything he told them for regurgitation on their front pages. Arriving with his usual Burnley FC mug of tea in his fist, Campbell mock-innocently wondered: 'Right, what do you want to talk about?' He knew full well that there was only one topic of interest to the journalists assembled in front of him. He launched into a detailed account of his version of events, including an analysis of Mandelson's mental state. 'Part of the problem, and Peter would accept this, I think, is that there are parts of this that Peter cannot explain and cannot explain to himself,' Campbell told the journalists. 'I think he has been slightly detached.' He also labelled Mandelson 'curiously detached'. Though he would subsequently claim that he had been misinterpreted, Campbell must have known exactly what construction the journalists would put on his words. Simon Walters, the political editor of the *Mail on Sunday*, asked whether he was saying that Mandelson was 'psychologically flawed'. 'Very funny,' sneered Campbell. Joe Murphy, the political editor of the *Sunday Telegraph*, wondered of Campbell whether he was comparing Mandelson's state of mind with that of Ron Davies during his 'moment of madness' on Clapham Common. Campbell did not demur. 'Well, I think it was,' he replied.

So unusually long was this briefing – seventy minutes in all – that Campbell sent out for a second mug of tea. Even when the session was over, he gave supplemental comments to some of the political editors which reinforced the insinuation that Mandelson was a mango short of the full fruit bowl. That Sunday's papers also quoted 'Downing Street sources' – in fact, this was again Campbell speaking – depicting Mandelson as a man who had been 'unfocused' for some time. 'He's been a little bit like that for a while. He's fed up with it. He's kind of had enough.' When Blair grumbled to Campbell that his briefing had served only to further aggravate things, Campbell responded that he was 'trying to be kind'. This was true enough: his observations were actually a censored version of what he really felt about Mandelson.

On Saturday evening, the presses of the Sunday newspapers thundered off headlines screaming that uncivil war had broken out between New Labour's premier propagandists.

Even Robert Harris had been driven to question an aspect of his friend's sanity. 'What are you doing? You're mad,' Harris told Mandelson when he announced that he planned to go to Campbell's house in Hampstead that same Saturday night. The long-standing invitation was to join a birthday party for Audrey Millar, Campbell's partner's mother. The fallen minister cut a forlorn and solitary figure. He stood apart from the other partygoers, positioning himself next to the piano. As the pianist tinkled out a rather maudlin tune, Peter Mandelson began to sing along to it. After an awkward interlude, the other guests slowly joined in.

The first editions of the Sunday papers were delivered to the house, bearing the headlines that the two men had spun against each other. 'Mandelson and Blair go to war over "lies"' was the front page of the *Observer* with the straplines: 'PM aide casts doubt on ex-Minister's state of mind' and 'I should not have quit, says New Labour architect'. The *Sunday Telegraph* also put the story in its biggest type: 'Mandelson and Blair go to war over resignation', 'Disgraced minister says he was forced out', 'Downing Street questions his state of mind'. As they scanned the papers, Campbell told Mandelson that it was nothing 'personal'.

Captured in this surreal scene were the high politics and the low betrayals, the intense comradeship and the internecine rivalries, the fierce love and the fearsome loathing in the turbulent breast of New Labour.

The spin machine that Peter Mandelson had done so much to build was now turned on its creator. At lunchtime on Sunday, Cabinet ministers endeavoured to shovel their erstwhile colleague back under the earth. The Home Secretary told a television audience that 'Peter' had 'to go' because 'there is no doubt by his own admission that he told an untruth'.[56] Jack Straw seemed to talk more in sorrow than anger. Clare Short spoke more in glee than sorrow. 'Peter Mandelson went because he has got problems telling the truth. He wasn't accurate, didn't speak the truth, let himself down and the government.' She clog-danced on his grave. 'Peter Mandelson is over.'[57] One member of the Cabinet was distressed: Tony Blair. A conflicted Prime Minister still felt for Mandelson and, more, this was simply fuelling an inflammation he wanted smothered. Campbell was obliged to issue an extraordinary statement denying all the evidence to the contrary that there was 'war' between Number 10 and the former Northern Ireland Secretary, and protesting that the press secretary had not 'knifed' Mandelson whom he insisted 'was still a friend'.

This did not appease Mandelson and his supporters. Robert Harris deployed his own celebrity on the airwaves and in print to champion the cause of his friend. He described the sacking as 'an extraordinary miscarriage of justice, a kind of contemporary Dreyfus affair'.[58] Even allowing for his distress about the treatment of his friend, this was wildly out of proportion. Harris was not Emile Zola, the great campaigning journalist, but a wealthy penner of accomplished thrillers. Mandelson had not been cast out to Devil's Island; even if, in his own tormented mind, internal exile as backbench MP for Hartlepool might seem an even more diabolical deprivation. Harris, once a great enthusiast for New Labour and friendly with Tony Blair, curdled into a bitter critic of the government. The author lacerated 'Mr Blair and his entourage' for 'their panickiness [sic], their lack of loyalty, their sheer downright nastiness, above all, their astonishing, cack-handed political incompetence'. Harris commented that the sacking of Mandelson to meet the demands of media presentation and news deadlines raised wider questions about 'the whole philosophy which seems to underpin the Blair administration – that government can be conducted as a vast, rolling newsroom in which the press secretary is as powerful as any cabinet minister'.[59]

As a general observation, this had much force. His loyalty to his friend blinded Harris to the towering irony that Peter Mandelson had been instrumental in fashioning the deadline-obsessive, image-driven, headline-fixated philosophy of New Labour. No one more than Mandelson had tutored the Prime Minister to be mesmerised by the media. As Mandelson spun, so he had reaped.

The spinning from beyond the grave was not without some success for Mandelson. Influential opinion formers – such as Hugo Young of the *Guardian* – began to raise doubts about the manner of his dismissal. The editorial writers of the *Daily Telegraph* took up the cause as a stick with which to beat Tony Blair. The unlikely defenders of the Hartlepool One even included Ken Livingstone: 'The second resignation of Peter Mandelson has not been like the first. On the day of the first fall, journalists reported that Labour MPs were popping the champagne corks in the bars of Westminster. This time, however, Peter has become the subject of sympathy as his erstwhile colleagues in spin turn their guns on him.'[60]

Francis Wheen of the *Guardian* satirically wondered why mendacity had become such a capital crime for New Labour. 'A week after his downfall, it is still difficult to see what uniquely vile offence Mandelson committed. If being chummy with the Hindujas is grounds for resignation, the front benches of both major parties would be almost empty. Ah yes, say the tinpot Torquemadas of Westminster, but he told a lie to the *Observer* – or, at the very least, gave a misleading answer . . . If that were the real reason, many other ministers would have preceded him to the gallows.'[61]

Mandelson pursued his own hyperactive campaign of self-vindication, offering interviews and briefings to any newspaper that was interested – as they all were. On Thursday, the news was dominated by briefings he had given to the *Daily Telegraph* and the *Daily Mail* which produced headlines that he was interested in becoming a European Commissioner. Mandelson made himself look foolish by then attempting to dismiss as invention the stories he had himself inspired. Using the two papers most vituperatively opposed to the government, and in such a way that it obliterated a major speech by Tony Blair, drove Downing Street into a frenzy. A 'Downing Street aide' counter-attacked: 'The future for Peter Mandelson now is to shut up, then go off and have a lovely life with Reinaldo. News about the Government has been drowned out by Peter's flaky high drama nonsense. He's shown himself up as someone who is emotionally incontinent.'[62]

This sounded like a dead ringer for Alastair Campbell, though it was not actually the press secretary, but someone of his brutalist school reflecting the fury of the master. For the second Sunday in a row, the newspapers were dominated by the Mandelson Affair. For a fortnight now, the headlines had shouted of little else.

It is often the case that when politicians are claiming to be sweetly united they are actually engaged in the most fratricidal inner struggling. It can also be the case that when the headlines rage with conflict this is just the moment when the protagonists are negotiating behind the scenes to call a truce. Continuation of this internecine poison was mutually destructive to both Blair and Mandelson. The man who had done so much to create the Prime

Minister not only knew where many of the government's bodies
were buried; he possessed a most comprehensively detailed map of
the graveyard. The Prime Minister had many imperatives to shut
him up. It also made sense for Mandelson to go quiet. To antagonise
Blair any further would mean thoroughly alienating the one man
who might help him find some future role in public life. Bizarre as
it may seem, they still both talked of each other as close friends.

The two agreed to a cessation of any further hostilities, and
then co-ordinated a joint response when Sir Anthony Hammond's
inquiry into the Hinduja Affair was published in mid-March. No
member of the government challenged Mandelson's assertion that
he had been completely acquitted. Appearing outside his constituency home in Hartlepool, Mandelson expressed his gratitude to
Hammond 'for clearing my name and restoring my reputation'.
Blair praised Mandelson's integrity, even at the cost of making
himself look exceptionally silly. 'I believed he would be cleared of
any impropriety and I am pleased for his sake that he has been.'
Saying the affair was now 'over and done with' and 'past history',
he praised Mandelson as 'a person of immense ability and indeed
integrity'.[63]

If Mandelson was guiltless, if he was such a rock of integrity,
such a titan of ability, why had the Prime Minister sacked him?

Looking foolish was the least of Tony Blair's worries. On a
superficial reading of the report, it was good for the government.
Sir Anthony Hammond pronounced everyone not guilty. Intentionally or not, the remainder of his 116 pages contained excruciatingly embarrassing details about the government's entanglements
with the Hindujas. Downing Street was braced for extremely
awkward questions about the swift processing of the Hindujas'
passport applications and the Prime Minister's relationship with the
brothers at a time when grave cautions had been issued by the
intelligence services.

Most of the headlines, however, concentrated on Sir Anthony's
one-page conclusion, handily placed near the front of the report,
in which he charitably cleared everyone of everything, and imputed
the best of motives to all concerned, even when their evidence to

him was flatly contradictory. The newspapers noted that Sir Anthony – 'Wally', to his friends – was a government lawyer who conducted his inquiry from quarters in the Home Office whose role was central to his investigations. Sir Wally's generous coating of vinyl silk on this extraordinary episode that had brought down the Prime Minister's closest friend in the Cabinet was lampooned by the media as a 'Whitehall whitewash'. That reaction was greeted with gusts of relief at Number 10. It meant they had escaped searching examination about the questions they feared to answer.

Tiring of the intricacies of the Hinduja Affair, the media sleaze patrol was already moving on to other targets, among them Derry Irvine, so instrumental in removing Mandelson. No one suggested corruption against the Lord Chancellor, but he was widely pronounced guilty of the serious political offence of crass stupidity when he hosted a fund-raiser for lawyers whose future career prospects might be determined by him.

The commons committee which invigilated MPs' behaviour found Keith Vaz guilty of not declaring a financial relationship with a man whom the minister recommended for an honour. Vaz was further rebuked for failing to co-operate with the parliamentary commissioner's investigation into eight other allegations against him. The Mandelson Affair left Blair further disorientated about both what was ethical and what was good for his government. It was universally assumed that Vaz would be dropped from the Foreign Office after the election. Why did not Blair do it immediately? Petulantly defiant about giving another scalp to the media, Blair stubbornly refused to remove this minister who was neither important nor a friend, with the counter-productive consequence that Vaz carried on making damaging headlines all the way until polling day.

The parliamentary commissioner for standards also came to damning conclusions about Geoffrey Robinson, once the sugar-daddy to both Tony Blair and Gordon Brown. She ruled that he had misled MPs about his financial links with Robert Maxwell and that 'on the balance of probability' he had received a £200,000 cheque from a Maxwell company despite his repeated denials to parliament.

Still pleading his innocence, Robinson avoided a near certain suspension from the Commons when he was given three months to prove that he had never banked the money. On that bright dawn on May Day in 1997, Tony Blair surfed to power on a wave of revulsion against Conservative sleaze and with the pledge: 'I want to renew faith in politics.'[64] His own government now enjoyed a reputation no more enviable – and, in some respects, less attractive – than that of the Tories.

Even before the Hinduja Affair, opinion surveys found that most of the public believed there was 'a major problem' with financial sleaze in government, spin doctors manipulating the media, the granting of peerages and honours to party donors, ministers appointing friends to public posts, and putting the interests of business before the people. Ministers 'not telling the truth' was a 'major problem' for two thirds of respondents.[65] In the wake of Peter Mandelson's second fall, 47 per cent told a poll that the government was 'very sleazy and disreputable', a score worse than the Conservatives'.[66]

Spin and sleaze were acid eating into the public's faith in Tony Blair's government. He knew it was doing damage. At his party's spring conference in Glasgow, he reprised a now familiar theme of his speeches by railing against the Tories and elements of the press for promoting the notion that 'all politicians are the same' and accused them of spreading 'cynicism' about the government.[67] There was a touch of the rage of Caliban catching sight of his own reflection in the rock pool. When he asked himself who had given the Opposition and the media the grounds to attack his government, Tony Blair surely saw the answer in the mirror.

## 23. Culling Fields

Whenever the headlines scoured the darker side of his government, the Prime Minister endeavoured to lift the nation's gaze to his promises of a brighter future. The venue chosen for a speech defining his goals for a second term was doubly symbolic. It was a school. And the school was in the outer London suburb of Enfield, the constituency whose rejection of Michael Portillo in 1997 was so emblematic of the landslide with which Tony Blair had begun his first term. The event was an image-maker's double hit.

Preoccupied by the latest twist in the Mandelson imbroglio, the media did not pay either the pictures or the words much attention; the cause of a typical Blair outburst of frustration to his aides about how hard it was to get his message across to the public. The speech actually repaid a lot of attention. Not so much for the outline of the future offered by the Prime Minister as for his remarkably candid self-dissection of the government's past performance.

He put aside his previous hyperbolic claims to have already delivered revolutionary change. Blair now openly acknowledged that the fixation of his first term was to avoid 'the historical mistake of Labour Governments – to try to transform without first getting the fundamentals right'. He confessed to having been driven by the defensive preoccupation of demonstrating to the country that 'Labour could be trusted with power again'. That wasn't enough, said Blair. The second term would be dedicated to building 'on those foundations' to demonstrate that New Labour had a greater ambition than merely being 'a party of competence and modernity'. Yet the most strikingly frank admission was about the self-imposed caution of his first term. 'The first phase of New Labour was essentially one of reassurance.'[1] Allied to which, though this thought he left unvoiced, was the obsession with making absolutely certain that there was a second term.

Confidence that victory was assured was displayed in Gordon Brown's pre-election Budget. He presided over the Commons as the Chancellor who had delivered the lowest inflation and interest rates since the 1960s. The spending corset and tax rises of the early half of the parliament meant that he could boast that he had repaid, in cash terms, more government debt in a single year than all of his predecessors over fifty years. Given the size of his surpluses, Brown could have gone on a much bigger pre-election bonanza. Given the size of the government's advantage over the Conservatives, he did not need to. The country might not be greatly enamoured with all of New Labour's record, and in some quarters the government was deeply disliked, but the great majority of voters were much more repelled by the alternative. The government's lead in the opinion polls made a rapid recovery from the dip of shocking September. It was not so much an election-winning Budget that Brown delivered as the Budget of a Chancellor who believed the election to be as good as won.

Even Blair, usually so neurotic about his popularity, was privately boasting that he would 'win big': the Prime Minister's confidential prediction was that Labour would have a majority in excess of 100.[2] Gordon Brown told a closed meeting of Labour MPs that they might even hope to increase their already huge parliamentary majority.[3]

Brown did not entirely disdain a bit of vote-catching, announcing an increase in maternity pay, a freeze on alcohol duty, the abolition of betting tax, and free entrance to museums. Labour MPs cheered as the Chancellor distributed these lollipops, their common characteristic being that they did not actually come at any great cost to the Exchequer. In a so-called 'families first' Budget which combined caution with populism, Brown contrived to find a modest tax cut for nearly everyone, though there were not as many sweeteners for Middle Britain as Blair might have liked. Most of the money was concentrated on the Chancellor's favourite group: low-earning families with children.

Instead of large tax cuts, the Chancellor produced a further £1 billion each for health and education, on top of the large spending programme already announced for the next three years. This was a demonstration of how dramatically New Labour had changed the terms of political trade. In the run-up to the 1997 election, Blair and Brown had gone to excruciating pains to stress that they would not be a high-spending government. Four years on, they chose to present themselves as the big spenders. Brown repeatedly emphasised that they had chosen to 'invest' – the preferred euphemism for spending – rather than cut taxes. Labour had always before fought elections having to explain how they could increase spending without hiking taxes. This time Blair and Brown wanted to reverse the trap. It would now be for the Conservatives to explain how they could slash taxes without burning essential public services.

The order paper waving congratulations of the Labour backbenches found an echo in the country. Sixty-seven per cent of respondents to one opinion poll said Brown was 'doing a good job', making him the most popular Chancellor since the Second World War.[4]

Rupert Murdoch, following his usual habit of putting his newspapers behind political winners, ordered the *Sun* to switch back into slavish cheer-leading for the government. The following morning, the tabloid's front page displayed Brown holding up his Budget box and captioned the picture: 'It's in the bag!' The *Sun* advised Blair: 'You might as well call the election now.'[5] Calling the election for the first Thursday of May 2001 had been at the back of their minds from the moment they came to office, and the idea had by now hardened into a certainty. Since the beginning of the year, ministerial visits were concentrated in marginal seats. Scheduled for March was a massive government advertising blitz, subliminally reminding voters of all the wonderful things New Labour was doing, which cost twice the spend of Procter & Gamble, the world's biggest commercial advertiser.[6] Increases in the minimum wage and pensions were timed to go into voters' wallets and purses at the end of April.

The New Labourites always needed something to worry about. Their anxiety now was that this was too good to be true, their poll lead was too huge to last. Blair started to fret that he should cash his chips with the electorate. He asked officials at party headquarters to examine accelerating campaign plans to bring the election forward to April.[7]

From the day be became Prime Minister, Tony Blair was haunted by many fears that something would happen to deprive New Labour of the second term. What had never occurred to him, nor to anyone else, was that his best laid plans could be imperilled by a livestock disease which had not been heard of in mainland Britain for more than three decades.

The disease feared by generations of farmers was first detected on 19 February at an abbatoir in Essex. Exports to the European Union and the rest of the world were swiftly banned. It was three days later – which turned out to be three weeks too late – that the Ministry of Agriculture decided on a ban of all livestock movements within Britain. By the time the virus had been traced back to a pig farm at Heddon-on-the-Wall in Northumberland, the government was already way behind the disease. The first warning signal of how far behind came two days later when another outbreak was reported at the other end of England in Devon.

Preoccupied with election planning on top of all the other business of government, Number 10 was initially content to leave it to the Agriculture Minister. Nick Brown sounded confident that his department was containing the contagion. The public seemed to regard this as a weird natural phenomenon which could not be fairly blamed on the government. The Opposition was being careful to sound constructive and supportive in their questioning of ministers. Neither the Prime Minister nor anyone close to him regarded this as a crisis. Not least because they didn't want it to be a crisis.

A crisis it was and it was finally beginning to dawn on them over at Smith Square, the headquarters of the Ministry of Agriculture. In the second week of the outbreak, the government's chief veterinary officer entered Nick Brown's sixth-floor ministerial suite bearing very ill tidings. Jim Scudamore told the minister that the disease had got into sheep. 'That sounds bad news,' said Brown. Scudamore responded: 'It is very bad news.' Brown would subsequently describe this as 'my lowest moment'.[8] The failure to spot the first case earlier had given the disease – in Brown's own words – 'a three week start on the Government'.[9] As the ministry panted to catch up, national parks were closed, horse racing suspended, and rugby championship matches cancelled. The Prime Minister had to abandon any idea of bringing forward the election, reverting to plan A: May. Downing Street still could not believe – the New Labour inner circle were incredulous at the idea – that a livestock virus could jeopardise their election plans. Blair took the department's word for it that they had the measure of the disease. The Prime Minister was breaking Alastair Campbell's first rule of spin: 'Never believe your own propaganda.'[10]

Tony Blair had paid little attention to reforming the civil service, an omission that he privately swore to remedy in his second term as a result of the mishandling of this disease, and the failure of contingency planning during the fuel blockades. He had been especially not interested in Agriculture, the ministry that brought mad cow disease to the nation during the Tory years. His first Agriculture Minister, Jack Cunningham, tried to kick some life into this most backward department in Whitehall. His reward was a series of undermining leaks to the newspapers about 'Junket' Jack's allegedly expensive tastes in office furnishings and foreign travel. For Nick Brown, the posting had been a punishment for his adherence to the Chancellor.

Maff began to slaughter infected animals, the policy for eradicating the virus that had been laid down since the 1920s. This was not because the disease was in any sense deadly. Humans could not catch it, and it gave the animals the equivalent of a dose of flu. Nor was slaughter necessarily the most effective way to contain the outbreak. The policy had been adopted to maintain Britain's disease-free status in order to protect the meat exports of Maff's client group, large farmers. Funeral pyres of carcasses blackened country skies with acrid smoke. These haunting images from the Dark Ages belched across the television screens for day after day, week after week. The public responded all too well to imprecations to avoid spreading the disease by staying out of the countryside. Massive collateral damage was inflicted on tourism, an industry worth twentyfold the value of the meat exports the slaughter policy was designed to protect.

As the number of outbreaks climbed above 100 in the second week of March, ministers and their advisers revealed the confusion within the government by emitting contradictory signals. While Nick Brown continued to moo that he had the disease under control, the Chief Vet admitted that it was still spreading, while the Environment Minister, Michael Meacher, declared that foot and mouth now amounted to 'a national emergency'.[11]

It was becoming painfully clearer that the Ministry of Agriculture had learnt next to nothing from the last big outbreak in 1967–8. It was ignoring the recommendations of an inquiry into that outbreak that the army should be immediately called in to give logistical support. The Ministry of Defence was wary of getting involved; the Ministry of Agriculture didn't ask for assistance, fearing what civil servants characterised as 'military occupation'. This mocked New Labour's promises of 'joined-up government'.

Maff initially underestimated the gravity of the situation. When it finally grasped the scale of the contagion, the bureaucracy was disorientated. According to one scientist involved, the ministry 'just did not think they could do anything about it'. They reacted to warnings that the battle was being lost with a 'defeatist attitude'.[12]

By mid-March, Nick Brown's daily assertions that he had the disease 'under control' were refuted as the number of outbreaks climbed to 200. Half a million sheep now faced slaughter, and an Irish Cabinet minister undiplomatically branded Britain 'the leper of Europe'.[13]

A month on, and the bonfires of the animals continued to blaze across every television bulletin, confounding another of Campbell's dictums that no crisis can last a week before it bores the media. It had grown too big – both as a crisis in itself and as a threat to the government's reputation – for the Prime Minister to ignore any longer.

On Tuesday 19 March, Ben Gill, the President of the National Farmers Union, led a delegation to Number 10 to see the Prime

Minister and his chief of staff. As Tony Blair and Jonathan Powell heard them out, the farmers' leaders gave an exhaustive and detailed critique of the animal culling policy, the salient point of which was that they were failing to control the disease because of the long delays between diagnosis and slaughter of infected beasts. His members were close to revolt, Gill warned Blair. Without a rapid change in government policy, they would lose the support of the NFU. 'Blair knew if they pulled out then the battle was all but lost,' according to one government strategist.[14]

'Give me forty-eight hours,' replied Blair, the direness of the situation at last impressed upon him. The Prime Minister dispatched Powell to investigate why Maff was not getting on top of the contagion. The chief of staff made some shocking discoveries. There were not enough vets. Those vets who were available were often left hanging around for hours between farm visits. Culls were being delayed; carcasses were piling up. Before Thursday's Cabinet, Blair called in Nick Brown to tell him that they had to get the crisis 'by the scruff of the neck'. The Government's credibility was at stake. So were their election plans.

There were mounting demands from the countryside, including the council leaders in the Prime Minister's own county, that an election should not be held whilst so much of rural Britain was distressed and ablaze.

Blair flatly rejected the idea of delaying the May local elections, which everyone understood to be the proxy for a general election. At Prime Minister's Question Time he claimed it would be a further blow to the gasping tourist industry 'if we sent out a message that the democratic process had to go into suspension, that Britain was in a state of quarantine, that we were in some way closed for business.' He ridiculed the idea of delay: 'I simply ask, post-ponement until when? One month, two months, six months?'[15]

He was hoping that anger in the countryside would be relieved by a package of measures to help rural businesses, and that the crisis could be beaten with the belated mobilisation of the army to help with the burial and burning. The Prime Minister felt he had to see – and be seen to be seeing – what was happening on the ground.

His diary was rejigged to fit in a personal tour of severely afflicted Cumbria on Thursday 22 March. This opened his eyes to just how ghastly it was out in the culling fields.

His tour took him to the Auctioneer pub in Carlisle, a farmers' drinking house decorated with watercolours of lambs, adjacent to a usually busy, now deserted cattle market. As he met representatives of local farmers and the tourist industry, protesters ventilated rural wrath, chanting: 'The only good Blair is a dead one.'[16]

He implicity conceded that his government was struggling. 'What we have to do is massively gear up to the scale of the challenge.'[17]

Later that afternoon, his Boeing 146 took off from Carlisle airport, bound for a European summit in Stockholm. From one of his red boxes was pulled a confidential report marked for the Prime Minister's urgent attention. It gave the latest prognosis after meetings between Maff and the Food Standards Agency and drew on computer modelling by epidemiologists from the Institute of Animal Health and the Veterinary Laboratories Agency. Blair read the scientists' chilling predictions: unless much more drastic action was taken, the disease could spread so virulently that by June the number of outbreaks would be running at more than 4,000. There was a heart-murmuring warning from the government's chief scientist, Professor David King. There were far too long delays between diagnosis, slaughter and disposal: 'If we proceed as we are at the moment, the epidemic is out of control.' The worst case scenario forecast that 30 million animals, half the nation's livestock, would have to be slaughtered. Blair muttered to himself: 'This is hellish.'

On his arrival in Stockholm, the Swedish authorities took the humiliating step of insisting that the prime ministerial plane be fumigated lest Blair himself be a carrier of the disease from what the international media were depicting as 'Plague Island'.

The combination of his visit to Cumbria and the apocalyptic warnings from the scientists convinced Blair that he now had no choice but to take personal command of the crisis. Alastair Campbell briefed journalists that the Prime Minister would be leaving the summit early. Cobra, the crisis centre last used during the fuel protests, was to be scrambled into action.

His press secretary continued to maintain the line that election calculations were the last thing on the Prime Minister's mind. Campbell told reporters: 'I can promise you he is not remotely focused on the general election.' Even as the spinmeister was speaking, this was exposed for the fiction it was. Blair was caught on camera discussing election timing with the President of the European Commission, Romano Prodi. 'How long before you must decide? One month?' asked Prodi. A grimacing Blair responded: 'No. Ten days.' A startled Prodi replied: 'You are kidding me – in ten days' time, not later?' Just as he was about to open his mouth again, Blair caught sight of the lurking TV crew, and clunkingly tried to cover himself. 'No, no, it's only the local elections.'[18] No, no, no one was kidded by that.

The virus of panic was now infecting New Labour high command. The smooth progression they had planned from Budget euphoria to election victory was endangered. Staff had been recruited to work at Millbank Tower, expensive poster sites paid for, the campaign gridded out.

Tony Blair spent Monday 26 March trying to get to grips with the details of the disease, and chairing one meeting after another. The more he immersed himself in the crisis, the greater grew his alarm. He told his closest aides that getting a handle on this microscopic invisible foe was more 'nightmarish' than fighting the Kosovo war.[19]

To those who asked him how he was sleeping, Blair replied that he 'counted sheep'. This was a black joke. The Ministry of Agriculture, whose monitoring procedures were exposed as pitifully inadequate, originally estimated that just 2,000 sheep were moved or exported before the disease was detected. Blair made the staggering discovery that actually well over a million sheep, each one a potential carrier of the virus, had criss-crossed Britain in the crucial period. The figure drew gasps from MPs when he revealed it to the Commons. On Wednesday 28 March, the number of detected outbreaks surged to a new record. The government was

still not meeting its target of reducing the lag between identification
of the disease and slaughter to twenty-four hours. By now, more
than 800,000 animals had been slaughtered or earmarked for culling,
almost twice as many as in the whole of the 1967 contagion. As
the Conservatives and the media became ever more aggressive in
their questioning of the government's competence, Blair had to
admit to MPs that 'we cannot be sure' when the disease would be
over.[20]

His decision to take personal command did considerably ratchet
up the government's response. Blair ordered drastic measures. To
create firebreaks, the slaughter was ordered of animals on farms
adjacent to outbreaks of the disease. The Tories had been urging
slaughter-on-suspicion: the killing of animals without waiting for
the results of laboratory tests determining whether they had the
disease. The government now implemented that policy. In this
frantic dash to catch up with the disease, there was little serious
questioning of whether the scorched earth policy was the right
policy. It would subsequently emerge that 30 per cent or more of
the animals slaughtered on suspicion were actually healthy.

The Ministry of Defence had finally been asked for a comprehensive list of what it could do to help, and Maff was instructed by
Number 10 to accept the assistance. General Sir Mike Jackson, the
veteran of Kosovo and commander-in-chief of UK land forces,
was mobilised before the TV cameras to watch the slaughter and
burial of hundreds of thousands of beasts in a mass grave at a disused
airfield near Carlisle.

General Jackson and the Defence Secretary, Geoff Hoon, toured
the Cumbrian countryside in the company of Brigadier Alexander
Birtwistle, the officer in charge of the operation. As they drove
through the fields, the brigadier pointed them towards 'the enemy'
and said: 'Those sheep are dead.'

There was always an alternative to the mass bonfires and burials
which spewed toxic dioxins into the atmosphere and threatened to
poison areas of the water table. Vaccination, which was successfully
used by the Dutch to swiftly eradicate the outbreak in Holland,
had been flatly ruled out by the Ministry of Agriculture from the

beginning. As the epidemic continued to spread into previously uninfected areas, among those lobbying the Prime Minister to have the vaccination option re-examined was Prince Charles who told Blair that mass slaughter was 'mindless'. At the end of March, when the European Commission gave its permission to vaccinate up to 180,000 dairy cattle in Cumbria and Devon, Blair was ready to order vaccination. Left to follow his own instincts, he almost certainly would have done so. The Prime Minister met continuing and fierce resistance from farmers' leaders, worried that the public would not buy milk and meat from vaccinated animals, and as fixated as ever with the consequences for their export trade, whatever the cost to the rest of the rural economy. Meeting heated opposition from Ben Gill and other senior officials from the NFU, Blair vacillated over vaccination. The option was finally abandoned the Thursday after Easter. The Prime Minister did not want this retreat widely advertised. After the meeting with farmers' leaders at Number 10, Alastair Campbell told Gill that the government would stop talking about vaccination so long as the farmers did not present it to the media as a victory for themselves over the Prime Minister.

On the last Tuesday in March, Tony Blair went over to Millbank for a meeting of the party's national executive, a chore he found so tiresome that he had been known to pass notes to his aides asking: 'Can I go yet?' No one around the table wanted to let the Prime Minister go before he had divulged whether the election was going ahead to plan. Blair leant forward over the beechwood table and confided: 'I just haven't made up my mind yet.'[21] Most of those listening assumed he was concealing his intentions. Wrongly. The Prime Minister really didn't know what to do.

Most of his party was champing at the bit. The whips, reporting to Blair on their mass canvass of Labour MPs, told the Prime Minister that the great majority wanted the election to proceed to schedule. Most of his ministers feared the unpredictable hazards of delay. Said one: 'I really hope Tony goes for 3 May. I've run out of time and money.'[22]

The Conservatives had not dared openly demand a cancellation of the election for fear of being accused of running away from a contest every poll said they would lose. That was not a deterrent to their outriders in the press, the *Daily Mail* and *Daily Telegraph*, who accused Blair of being a callous and selfish cynic for even considering the idea of a May election. Some liberal commentators also argued for postponement. Blair would not win the mandate he was looking for if the country went to the polls with the smell of burnt cattle in its nostrils. A poll in May risked being remembered as the Dead Cow election.

This was a minority view. The majority of the press opined that to call off the election would send the worst possible signal to the world and be ruinous for the tourist industry. Like most of his party, they were sure Blair should and would stick to the long-planned schedule. Alastair Campbell was extremely energetic in trying to whip up a climate of opinion which made a May election not only look inevitable, but seem positively desirable. The *Mirror*, *The Times*, the *Financial Times*, the *Independent*, the *Sun* and the *Guardian* all argued, in the words of the latter, that he should 'Call it for May 3rd'.

The press was not always as influential as it liked to think, nor always as potent as tremulous New Labourites tended to believe. The message coming back from polling was that voters, and not just those in rural areas, were becoming sharply negative about a May election. At Millbank, the telephone call centre for conducting mass phone canvassing was now up and running. The cook of the right-wing magazine, the *Spectator*, was one of thousands of voters in marginal seats who were cold-called to ask what she thought of a May election and how it might influence her vote.[23]

As the deadline for a decision tightened around Blair, Philip Gould slipped into Number 10 through the back door. The strategist bore with him for the Prime Minister's personal inspection the results of his focus grouping with swing voters. Gould cautioned that to persist with an election would not make Blair look firm in the eyes of the voters; it would make him seem insensitive. The party's private polling giving New Labour a lead of 16 per cent was in line with published polls.[24] Despite foot and mouth, the voters seemed to have a fairly settled opinion about the relative merits of the government and its opponents. To Gould, this was an argument for delay. They were on course for the second term, but the voters might punish Blair if he went in May. Seats would be lost. If he postponed until June, Gould contended, then he might pull off a double: look the statesman and win large as well. It was precisely the sort of 'Third Way' compromise that appealed to Tony Blair.

Another voice arguing for postponement was Peter Mandelson. It was an illustration of both Blair's continuing reliance on the advice of Mandelson and the Prime Minister's agonies that on one day he phoned him three times to thrash around the arguments between May and delay. Sally Morgan, Charlie Falconer and Anji Hunter were coming down for calling off the election. It would look insensitive and divisive, argued Hunter, adopting her usual role in such internal debates of spokeswoman for Middle Britain.

Alastair Campbell, always the most tribalistic of Blair's closest counsellors, was the longest holdout for May. Campbell had believed that any controversy about election timing would soon blow away after a few days of campaigning. As the week wore on, he began to come round to the argument that Labour's agenda of spending on public services and a strong economy would be obscured by the smoke billowing across the TV screens. The news bulletins were still leading with items ten or more minutes long, subjecting viewers to a nightly diet of sheep being dumped into trenches and charred cattle burning in the culling fields. One senior New Labour apparatchik had been assigned for the duration of the crisis to monitoring the television news. Summarising his view for Campbell, he said: 'The imagery is all wrong.'[25]

After days of internal turmoil, the Prime Minister was hardening on his instinct to delay. That Thursday, the Archbishop of York led a flock of senior bishops preaching to their fellow Anglican at Number 10 that he should demonstrate his compassion for the countryside by calling off the election, which had more impact on Blair than the fact that the Conservatives had finally decided to call openly for a delay as well.

Weighing heavily in the scales of decision was the fact that incidents of foot and mouth were still running at forty a day. In Cumbria, they were way off the twenty-four-hour target from detection to slaughter. Blair had said he was going to 'strain every sinew' to beat the disease. How could he credibly claim to be doing that and launch an election campaign? And worse, the disease might be raging even more fiercely on polling day. The government's chief scientific adviser, Professor David King, plotted various outcomes for the disease. At that morning's Cabinet, Blair showed his ministers a bell graph projecting the latest doomsday scenario from the epidemiologists. The graph showed the contagion peaking at more than 300 outbreaks a day in early May.[26]

Most of his Cabinet were still for steaming ahead regardless. That night, John Prescott was thumping the tub at a warm-up rally for the election, and loudly decrying any suggestion of postponement. 'The date of the next election belongs to the Prime Minister. It does not belong to the Tories. It damn well doesn't belong to the farmers. It belongs to a Labour Prime Minister to make this decision, hopefully this weekend.'[27] Prescott handed out badges and leaflets bearing his mug shot with the words: 'I'm ready. Are you?'

The Prime Minister was not ready. Prescott argued with him that 'the bloody farmers' all voted Tory anyway. Jack Straw, David Blunkett, nearly all of the other senior figures in the government, were for pressing ahead with May.

On Friday, Blair made a final tour of the arguments with his closest advisers and with the Chancellor. Gordon Brown appreciated the risks of pressing ahead. When his own intimates urged him to stick to May, Brown responded: 'But won't we look cynical?'[28] What made Brown nervous of delay during the week of decision was that it coincided with a plunge on Wall Street which took down all world stock markets. This could be the first sneeze of a global economic cold. Brown told Blair that, while a short postponement might be tolerable, delaying into the autumn was freighted with risk. The Prime Minister had better be sure they would be able to call the election in June. In the end, though, the Chancellor did not absolutely press the point. Said Brown: 'It has to be your decision, Tony.' This was a rare, even unique moment when Gordon Brown was happy not to be Prime Minister.

Blair's mind was finally made up against May. This was an illuminating episode about both New Labour and the character of its leader. It was scant surprise that Blair preferred the advice of his unelected inner circle over the views of most of his party and Cabinet, many of whom read about his decision in the press before they heard from the Prime Minister. He had often ignored his ministers. More unusually, he defied the weight of opinion in the press. The polling against a May election obviously featured in his calculations. He had never been moved by the mechanical arguments for delaying the election on the grounds that it would make it difficult to campaign in infected areas of the countryside. For Blair, this was about the mood of the nation and his sense of himself. His acute sensitivity to the accusation that he was arrogant and cynical fed the worry that pressing on with May would reinforce those charges. This was about image, but not in quite such a shallow way as his critics assumed. His anxieties about his image with the voters melded with his self-image as an inclusive leader. One Cabinet minister who tried to argue him out of postponement came away with the conclusion that Blair delayed the election because he conceived of himself as the 'Father of the Nation'.[29] Blair told his closest colleagues and senior officials at Millbank that he was postponing the election. He discussed with Campbell whether he should make the announcement that day.

It was a pity for the Prime Minister that he instead allowed concerns about media management to prevail. There was a problem with the *Sun*. The tabloid had been utterly faithful to Downing Street's previous bidding and loudly clamoured for a May election. Over the headline 'ELECTION DAY: OFFICIAL', the tabloid boasted that it could reveal that 'Blair won't put off poll' proving that '*Sun* was right all along'.[30] This 'exclusive' was a gift from Campbell as a reward for swinging in support of the government. Encouraged by the press secretary to bang away in favour of a May election, the *Sun* devoted another entire front page to a picture of Britain as a padlocked plagued prison; how the country would look, the paper said, if the election were to be postponed. Only that Wednesday, the tabloid declared that any delay 'would be a massive blow to Britain in the eyes of the world'.[31]

Blair's change of heart was going to make the *Sun* look spectacularly stupid, both ill-informed and ignored. The danger was that the paper would displace its fury on to the government. So Blair did not make an announcement that Friday. Instead he allowed the *Sun* to do it for him on Saturday morning. 'ELECTION OFF', the tabloid trumpeted its latest exclusive, with the Blair-friendly spin: 'Now it's June 7 as Blair puts country before party'.[32]

The rest of the media, its jealousy as well as its sense of propriety prickled by the Prime Minister using the *Sun* as his herald, excoriated Blair for announcing the decision through a tabloid newspaper. A typical editorial in the *Guardian* sniffed that it was 'an unfortunate emblem' of the deformations of New Labour that 'Rupert Murdoch's staff learned of Downing Street's change of heart before the Cabinet'.[33] Saying Blair looked 'cowed, muddled and manipulative', the *Independent* complained: 'The *Sun* . . . absurdly now seems to occupy the role allotted to the monarch in our constitution.'[34] Most of the rest of the media commentary was of a similar mocking tone. Not for the first time, the manner in which the decision had been presented managed to obscure the fact that what Blair had done was correct, shrewd and popular with the public. By the time he spoke on the following Monday to explain why 'it would not be appropriate' to have an election in May, it was no longer a secret to anyone that he was now aiming for June. Blair cast himself as the unifier, saying: 'The decision has to be taken in the interests of the whole country, the parts that don't support the government as well as the parts that do. It is time to unify, not divide.'[35]

It is sometimes possible in politics to do something which is both decent and self-serving. The postponement of the election was that rare combination. The general verdict of the media and most of his colleagues was that Blair had displayed a loss of nerve and taken a blundering risk. Ministers muttered that he would be on his own if this proved to be a bad call; the Tories called him 'dithering' and 'weak'. They were all wrong: Blair was proved entirely right. The party most damaged by the delay was the Conservatives. The period of 'phoney war' around Easter was dominated by Tory plots against each other and a controversy over race, both of which made William Hague look like the leader who was weak and dithering. The government's lead in the polls spurted even further ahead. Tony Blair had demonstrated a better feeling for the national mood than either most of the media or the majority of his party. The gamble paid off.

This was in large part because the government at last appeared to be winning its battle with foot and mouth. By the end of April, incidents of the disease were on the downward slope of the bell curve. The earlier hysteria for something, anything to be done was now superseded by a rising public revulsion about the mass slaughter of healthy animals. That found expression in the emotive symbol of a calf with the made-for-headlines name of Phoenix. The slaughtermen arrived to kill her mother and the rest of the cattle on a Devon farm five days after Phoenix was born. The carcasses were left behind closed doors pending disposal, a scene typical across the country. Five days later, the corpses by then putrefying, more men from the ministry arrived to spray the shed with disinfectant. Amidst the stinking carnage, Phoenix rose from her mother's side and walked towards them, mooing.

This cock-up was parleyed into a 'miracle' by the media. As the nation chomped on its steak and tucked into its bacon, the picture of an angelic pure white calf peered sorrowfully out of the front pages and Phoenix gained instant celebrity status on the TV bulletins. The farmer and his wife were portrayed as heroic resistance fighters when they saw off a second attempt to kill the calf. The official for the ministry who insisted that 'Phoenix has to die'[36] was consistent with government policy, but he had no grasp of emotional politics.

Animal rights groups took up the cause, as did MPs and the tabloids. The *Mirror* launched a 'Save Phoenix from the Ashes' campaign. The National Farmers Union made the ludicrously over-the-top claim that slaughtering this calf would 'make King Herod look like a humanitarian'.[37] It was hard to disagree with the spokesman from Maff who expressed himself sickened by this 'hideous sentimentality'. Most farm animals were bred for the dinner plates of the public who were now lowing over one calf.

There were no sentimentalists at Number 10. What they were acutely sensitive to was sentimentality, especially when it was being magnified by the mass market tabloids. Alastair Campbell watched the rising pressure to save Phoenix and feared another public relations disaster just when they hoped to have suppressed media interest in the contagion. On the last Wednesday of April, the fate of Phoenix dominated news bulletins running pictures of ministry officials trying to get access to the farm to slaughter the calf. At five that afternoon, Nick Brown, along with the chief veterinary officer and the chief scientist, met Tony Blair at Number 10 to discuss making the culling policy less draconian.

The formal announcement the next day was not soon enough for Number 10. Campbell was alerted to a plan by his former employer, the *Mirror*, to run a picture of the calf on its front page with the demand: 'Phoenix must be saved'. On Wednesday night – in time for the reprieve to be announced on the ten o'clock news bulletins – Downing Street announced a change in the slaughter policy so that healthy animals in neighbouring farms would no longer be automatically killed. 'Phoenix will be allowed to live,' said a spokeswoman for Number 10.[38] Thus might the Prime Minister who had presided over the mass slaughter of more than two million cattle, pigs, sheep and lambs be projected as the saviour of the calf that had melted the heart of the nation. The ten o'clock nightly news was the first an annoyed Nick Brown heard of this. The following day, the Agriculture Minister swallowed his fury and announced a change to the culling policy dressed up as a 'refinement'. Pigs and sheep near to contagious farms would still be killed. (They should have been more photogenic.) Vets could now pardon cows where they judged them to be minimal risk.

The Phoenix story was the more nauseous when all else was carnage. In the final reckoning, the foot and mouth crisis proved to be ten times worse than the outbreak of the sixties, and worse than any other outbreak anywhere in the world ever. Failing bureaucracy, confused predictions from scientists and self-interested farmers combined with distracted and then panicked politicians to disastrous effect. An emergency was allowed to become a catastrophe as the government began by under-reacting and then lurched into overkill. The more details that emerged, the more the cloven-footed response to the disease seemed monumentally incompetent and incredibly costly. This explains why Michael Meacher's announcement that there would be a full inquiry into the crisis was brutally squashed by Number 10: they wanted the whole subject forgotten.

The relief for the Prime Minister was that his government had come through this ordeal by fire. The number of new incidents of the disease was dropping into single figures by the end of April. On Thursday 3 May, the day originally intended for the election, Tony Blair announced in all but words that the campaign would now begin. Flanked by a victory parade of the government's chief scientist and vet, and the brigadier in battledress, the Prime Minister declared that he had foot and mouth beaten. They were 'on the home straight'.[39] The home straight to the election.

# 24. Masters of the People?

On the following Bank Holiday Monday, the Cabinet were summoned to Number 10 for a choreographed display of unity for the cameras outside and a pep talk from the Prime Minister once they were inside. They gathered in a mood of utter certainty that they had to win the election inflected with a streak of paranoia that somehow victory might slip through their fingers. Once his ministers were settled around the table, Tony Blair delivered one of those lectures against complacency which had become so familiar to them over the past four years. They were to fight the election as if it were on a 'knife-edge', he told them. The party's private surveys agreed with the published polls: Labour would start the campaign with an apparently impregnable lead over the Conservatives. Two things stood out from the reams of research produced for Tony Blair and Gordon Brown, the campaign chieftain. The more affluent segments of the population – the As and the Bs – were swinging even further away from the Tories to New Labour. Blair noted with satisfaction that the suburbanites, the people who decide British elections, supported the government. The worm in the fruit was a widespread disaffection which threatened a historically low turn-out. The party's private pollster, Greg 'Mystic' Cook, was warning that if the Tories were better able to galvanise their supporters, then there was a worst-case scenario in which Labour might even be deprived of a parliamentary majority. It was not just this that fretted the Prime Minister. He did not want to be elected with so few votes that opponents could use it to challenge the legitimacy of his victory. Hinting at the argument between himself and Brown about how the campaign ought to be fought, Blair told the Cabinet that it was not sufficient to rest on the laurels of their economic 'competence'. They had to show that they had 'a vision' and 'a purpose' to transform Britain. Their most potent foes were not the Conservatives. The real enemies were the cynicism of the media, and the indifference of swathes of the electorate.

When the Cabinet broke up, the Health and Education Secretaries were sent out on to Downing Street to repeat the 'knife-edge' message for the cameras. These two ministers were chosen for one very simple reason: all the polling identified hospitals and schools as the uppermost priorities in the minds of the voters.

That the election would be announced the next day and that the date would be 7 June was now the worst-kept secret in the country. In an attempt to invest the announcement with some drama, it was decided that the Prime Minister would not follow the tradition of a statement outside Number 10. After receiving the formal permission of the Queen to fire the starting pistol, he would launch the campaign at a 'beacon' school in south London: a platform on which to boast of the government's success in raising standards.

The advanced guard which preceded him to St Saviour's and St Olave's to organise the media was led by Anji Hunter. Waiting for the Prime Minister, his personal assistant fell into conversation with a senior television correspondent. He wondered of her whether it was entirely wise to launch the campaign at a religious ceremony for schoolchildren. 'What do you mean, a religious ceremony?' Hunter responded sharply, her antennae for trouble beginning to twitch. 'It's not a religious ceremony.' Well look, the journalist pointed out: the Prime Minister would speak before a school assembly at which the children would sing hymns. Hunter's fixed smile of denial turned brittle.

The schoolgirls screamed at Tony Blair as though he were a demi-god of pop when he arrived on stage and shrugged out of his jacket. With a brass crucifix and a stained-glass window as a backdrop, and a glass lectern shipped over from Millbank as his pulpit, the preacher man began: 'I stand before you today with a sense of both humility and hope.' This humble touch was crafted to address the complaint of Philip Gould's focus groups that the government was arrogant. Every vote was 'precious', said Blair. Crosses in ballot boxes weren't sufficient for the televangelist. He wanted 'not just to win your vote, but to win your heart and mind for the change that our country needs'.[1] Had he left it there, then the subsequent backlash might not have been so scornful.

Blair moved into more partisan territory when he described the divide between Labour and Tory as 'more fundamental and more stark than at any time since 1983'. The Prime Minister began to lose the attention of his audience of five hundred schoolgirls when he assaulted Tory 'boom and bust' economics. A passage about 'negative equity' left one girl so unriveted that she pulled her jumper over her head. The TV cameras captured cut-aways of Alastair Campbell looking sinisterly narrow-eyed and hatchet-faced.

'This is the time, and ours is the task, to set your talents free and build a land of hope and opportunity for all,' Blair perorated in campaign cliché. 'Now you, the people, will decide.' None of his immediate audience would decide: they were too young to vote.

There was then a hymn, providing the spectacle of Blair singing: 'I, the Lord of sea and sky, I have heard My people cry.' He had been taken aback when he arrived to find his audience were schoolchildren, and native intuition was beginning to warn him off. He hurried from the stage to the strains of the children singing: 'I, the Lord of snow and rain, I have borne My people's pain.'

Upon the Lord of New Labour descended a hailstorm of derision. The launch was lambasted, even by newspapers sympathetic to the government, as shallow, sickly, twisted: an example of New Labour at its most loathsomely manipulative. 'The whole event stank of spin doctors' sweat,' a journalist from a liberal paper retched to its readers. 'Mr Blair was guilty of child abuse,' pronounced another witness. 'It was breathtakingly, toe-curlingly, hog-whimperingly tasteless,' gagged a third writer.[2] All the press commentary was in the same vein.

The attempt to cut through the crust of media cynicism served only to provoke a pasting about the cynicism of New Labour. The head teacher complained that she and the children had been exploited. Clare Short joined in, saying that choosing an adolescent audience for the campaign launch was 'odd' and 'surprising'.[3] Blair acknowledged that it had played disastrously with the media by making asperic remarks about other events on his itinerary: 'Perhaps I could sing a hymn.'

His aides got ratty. 'It shows our commitment to education,' blustered Campbell. 'It's a way of getting to the issues behind all the headline crap.'[4] Hunter, smarting from internal criticism, told anyone at Millbank who would listen that 'the pictures were wonderful'.

The event did work for the purpose of winning the image battle to grab the front pages and lead the TV bulletins. On the first night of the campaign, as on most nights, selected groups of swing voters were assembled to review the performances of the rival leaders. Alongside pictures of Blair at the school, the focus groups were shown footage of William Hague kicking off the Conservative campaign with an address from a soapbox to an outdoor crowd in Watford. The Tory leader's first campaign appearance, which placed him in a chaotic meleé of heckling opponents and supporters waving 'Save the £' placards, did not project him as the combative straight-talker intended by Tory spin doctors. It looked like a shambles. By a large margin, the verdict of the focus group juries was for Blair.

The negative media reaction nevertheless drilled on New Labour's delicate nerves. When the Conservatives tried to seize the initiative with an early launch of their manifesto, Labour rushed out its pledge card – only to be met with another chorus of disapproval.

It was noted that the five pledges were either so vague ('mortgages as low as possible') that they were meaningless. Or the goals were notably unambitious: 20,000 extra nurses and 10,000 extra doctors over five years was in line with the current recruitment plan; 10,000 more teachers would represent a slower increase than in the first term; 6,000 'extra recruits' for the police did not add up to a promise of 6,000 more police officers. A £4.20 minimum wage was an exceedingly modest increase over five years.

At seven o'clock on Thursday morning, the campaign command met in the first-floor boardroom at Millbank to conduct an autopsy on their shaky first forty-eight hours. Everyone had a voluminous media brief in front of them. Tax – the issue on which Labour was historically most vulnerable – was playing strongly and badly for them. The Tories and the newspapers had seized upon the omission from the pledge card of the 1997 promise not to raise income tax.

The tax pledge was not on the card for the good reason that they thought it would look overly defensive when they needed to be running a campaign which accentuated the positive. The pledge would be in the manifesto to be unveiled the following week. The Prime Minister, ever concerned to cling to the affections of Middle Britain, had been insistent on that.

Tax was running large and hard in the headlines because Blair and Brown were refusing to say in advance of the manifesto launch whether the tax pledge would be repeated. Blair wondered whether they should bring forward the announcement. Brown resisted on the grounds that it would look as though they were panicking. Ever a man for iron rules, the Chancellor was wedded to his grid, the minutely chronicled diary of announcements, speeches and stunts that had been pre-planned weeks beforehand. If they allowed the Tories and the media to knock them off their agenda, argued Brown, they would look 'out of control'. He found an unexpected ally in Philip Gould: tax was not the danger to Labour it once had been, not least because the public did not trust the Tories' arithmetic. Keeping the subject in the headlines might not be such a bad thing, suggested Alastair Campbell. It kept the election argument on the economy where New Labour had a big advantage over the Tories. The formal announcement of the tax pledge was not brought forward; instead it was leaked to a newspaper.

Campaign techniques that once seemed sharp and rapid were beginning to look blunt and clumsy. New Labour had always set great store by parading defectors from the Tories as battle trophies to impress the voters. Geri Halliwell, once a Thatcher-admiring Spice Girl, had a star part in a Labour election broadcast. Celebrity endorsements – especially when it emerged that this princess of pop would not actually be voting – mocked Blair's constant complaint that it was the media who were to blame for obsessing over the 'trimmings and trappings' of the campaign at the expense of issues of substance. The former Tory MP Shaun Woodward was parachuted into a safe Labour seat amidst accusations of a stitch-up. The many mockers wondered whether the millionaire would be showing his butler to the working-class voters of St Helens.

New Labour had forgotten that the first rule of successful theatre is not to let the audience see the stage management. The strings of the puppeteers were much too obvious at a confected event at Leamington Spa's refurbished Royal Pump Rooms. Microphones were attached to the Prime Minister and a carefully selected 'ordinary couple' so that reporters could eavesdrop through headphones on a conversation which could not have gone more smoothly had it been pre-scripted, which it could well have been. The couple were heard lavishing so much praise on his policies that even Blair almost blushed: 'You put it better than I could. Absolutely excellent.' When journalists complained that this was typically contrived and vacuous, the spin doctors responded: 'It will look good on TV.'[5]

More thoughtful members of the campaign team privately confessed that they had been slow to grasp that what looked slick and professional four years before was now coming over as cynical and manipulative.[6]

The atmosphere inside Millbank became fractious. Brown's people blamed Blair's people for the school event; Blair's people blamed Brown's people for the confusion over tax. Backbiting between the camps bubbled up in the newspapers. 'Gordon is trying to run the campaign with himself and a few cronies and is excluding people close to Tony and the full-time officials,' complained one Cabinet minister.[7]

It was widely observed that there was a frost between Blair and Brown. They had a very difficult conversation just before the campaign started about one of the most sensitive edges to their relationship. Blair believed he would have to respond to the inevitable questions about whether he planned to remain Prime Minister for the entirety of the next parliament. Contrary to the line insisted on by the Chancellor's followers, the Prime Minister denied that there was any secret bargain that Blair would retire in favour of Brown. 'As Gordon and I both say whenever we're asked about this, there is no gentleman's agreement.' Was there any agreement at all? 'No,' was Blair's blunt reply.[8]

Whenever Brown was asked about it, this was not at all what he said, and he was deeply aggravated to read Blair putting words into his mouth. The Chancellor was notably sullen whenever the succession issue was raised, and gave blocking answers until his questioners moved on. 'I've never got into the business of talking about these things and I'm not going to get into the business of talking about it now,' he responded stiffly.[9]

The more the press speculated about the state of their marriage, the more it was necessary for the pair to stage displays of togetherness for the cameras. On the second Wednesday of the campaign, a jacketless Blair and a jacketed Brown arrived as a couple to be greeted by a crowd of banner-waving supporters at Euston station. Prime Minister and Chancellor then climbed aboard a special sealed train conveying them, most of the Cabinet and the accompanying media to the manifesto launch in Birmingham. The keynote of Blair's speech was what he described as 'a mission for reform of public services'. Presidentially, he asked the country to award him 'a mandate to get on with the job'.[10]

When Blair was asked why the manifesto contained seven pictures of himself and not one of the Cabinet mutes sat behind him, Brown's features were a study in granite. John Prescott seemed to be having a serious attack of the grumps. He declined to hold up the manifesto for a Cabinet group picture. The Deputy Prime Minister, wearing what his mother called his 'ugly face', looked like a man one provocation away from detonation.

Into the afternoon had been programmed prime ministerial visits to a school and hospital as extended illustrative photo-opportunities to show how much the government was achieving for education and health. Inside Birmingham's Queen Elizabeth hospital, executives, doctors and nurses waited for the Prime Minister to come and admire a handsome new cardiac care unit. The careful script of the day was shredded by an ambush at the entrance to the hospital. Sharon Storrer broke through the *cordon sanitaire* of minders around Tony Blair to puncture the artifice of controlled campaigning. The postmistress exploded into the Prime Minister's face about the cancer care being given to her partner. Blair furrowed his brow and made a prayer formation with his hands, the Vicar of St Albion trying to mollify this incandescent parishioner. 'I'm sorry' were the only words he could get in edgeways as she subjected him to a blistering tirade. 'No, you're not – or you'd do something about it,' she blazed back. Horribly aware that camera crews were greedily devouring his embarrassment, Blair tried to persuade her to come inside for a coffee and private chat. She was having none of that. 'If I can just explain what we're doing . . .' tailed off a despairing Blair as the wrathful Sharon scornfully shouldered him aside.

Alastair Campbell, who had gone inside ahead of Blair, found himself in the role-reversed position of being briefed by the Prime Minister about the scene on the doorstep. As they were driven away from Queen Elizabeth's, Blair and his aides groaned that weeks of meticulous planning for the manifesto launch had been torpedoed by one woman in five minutes.

The Prime Minister felt a further hot blast of voter discontent in the early evening when he recorded a television question time for transmission later that night. The first member of the audience to speak was 'really appalled at the continuing sleaze, lies, hypocrisy and incompetence. You said your government would be different. Why did you say it if you didn't mean it?' The next questioner voted New Labour in 1997 'full of trust and hope'. Four years later, single parents, students and the disabled felt 'betrayed and let down'. The third accused Blair of 'naked ambition' and of being 'dishonest', concluding 'this government lacks trust'. A nurse in this unremittingly hostile audience told him that Sharon Storrer's frustration was a fraction of that felt by staff in the NHS. Other members of the audience lacerated Blair over transport, the Dome, tax and pensioners. The Prime Minister deployed his argument that to do things well took time and money. 'I don't claim in any shape or form that I can make it all better in another term.'[11]

As the Prime Minister endured this battering, his press secretary was reeling from much worse. Just as the recording began, Campbell's mobile rang. It was Joe Irvin, an aide to John Prescott. 'John's been involved in an incident,' Irvin reported. What sort of incident? asked Campbell. During a campaign stop in the Welsh seaside resort of Rhyl, the Deputy Prime Minister had 'whacked' someone. Campbell's immediate anxiety was that the programme-makers would find out about it and spring a question about Prescott on a totally unprepared Prime Minister. To his great relief, Blair was not caught cold.

When the Prime Minister emerged from the studio, Campbell told him that he had bad news. Blair assumed it was about the woman at the hospital. 'No, it isn't that,' grimaced Campbell. 'Prescott thumped someone.' Blair's instant reaction was to laugh. No, this wasn't one of his wind-ups, insisted his press secretary. This was serious.

Blair phoned a distraught Prescott, who had spent the last three hours in the Little Theatre at Rhyl sitting with his head in his hands, plunged in black and self-recriminatory grief that he had wrecked both the campaign and his own political career. Shaken and apologetic, Prescott agreed with Blair that the Deputy Prime Minister would say nothing in public until they had put together a defence for him.

As Blair's Jaguar drove him south back to London, he and Campbell relieved the tension with laughter. Travelling down the motorway, they pointed out lorry drivers who might want to hit the Prime Minister because of the cost of fuel duty.

When initially jumbled reports of Prescott's pugilism reached Millbank the reaction was first shock, hotly followed by panic when a rumour gathered credence that he had clobbered an innocent bystander. There was an agonising wait until eight o'clock when *Sky News* began to run pictures showing a hefty bloke cracking an egg on the deputy leader, Prescott responding with a left jab, and then struggling flat on his back until the protester was dragged off. The 200 staffers and volunteers at party headquarters crowded around the twenty-five TV sets in the campaign war room. A drop-jawed Gordon Brown watched as a video tape of the incident was played and replayed, over and over again. The lawyers of New Labour were scrambled into action. Charlie Falconer was already at Millbank. Derry Irvine watched the pictures at home. Both advised that, because the egg was thrown at such close range, Prescott's best course was to plead self-defence.

Late that night, a statement went out in the name of the Deputy Prime Minister saying that he was intimidated and unprotected, and two female aides were 'knocked to the ground'. The Millbank telephone canvassing operation began calling voters to see how it was playing with the public. The calming response, echoed by Gould's focus groups, was that it wasn't likely to make any difference.

'Right,' sighed Tony Blair at the journalists at the next morning's news conference. 'I know you're all waiting with bated breath to hear about our health and education plans.' He deftly blocked and parried media attempts to give him and his deputy a pummelling. Asked if he would have hit the protester, Blair replied: 'I'm me. John is John. But he's been a wonderful deputy,' like a mother making an excuse for an over-exuberant but much adored son. Adopting a jocular approach to defuse the situation, Blair cracked: 'He's got very, very great strengths – not least in his left arm.'[12]

Public sympathy – admiration even – rallied behind Prescott.[13] His rumble in Rhyl injected into the election the thrill of the unexpected and a touch of humanity which had been missing from a campaign of sterile sound-biting and predictable photo-opportunising. At least now it could be said – even if not in the way that Blair ever intended – that a politician had connected with a voter. The Prescott punch was endlessly replayed on television: freeze-framed, slow-moed, set to the theme of the movie *Rocky*, underlaid with boxing bells and mixed with ringside crowd noises. Boxing experts gave stylistic judgements about Prescott's prowess while loftier commentators dissected what it said about modern politics. The punching power of sixty-two-year-old 'Two Jabs' and 'Raging Bull' commanded acres of space in the mass market tabloids which had not previously taken much front-page interest in the campaign. The *Sun* reckoned: 'Prescott's fracas brought the election alive. It's now a real election for real people on real issues.' For the *Mirror*, 'John Prescott struck a blow for real politics. Let's have more of it.'[14] It was highly debatable whether hitting an egg-throwing protester had anything at all to do with real politics or real issues or real people. Still, the election had briefly come to life in the press most read by those least engaged by the campaign.

'It could have been worse,' Blair privately consoled himself. Thwack Wednesday was good and bad. Prescott's fat left fist flattened coverage of the manifesto launch. On the upside, it did the Prime Minister the favour of deflecting attention from his own wilting experience of voter-rage in Birmingham, and from the barracking of Jack Straw by rank and file police officers. 'It was sort of cathartic,' according to a senior member of the campaign team. 'We got through that strange day and survived. We realised then that incidents like that weren't going to matter. We would still win.'[15]

The opinion polls continued to register unwaveringly high leads for Labour. Yet Tony Blair did not strike most of those who saw him as a man drawing vast enjoyment from his election. When two interviewers from a broadsheet joined him on a train bound for Southampton, they pointed out that he was halfway through the campaign. 'Great!' exclaimed Blair. He was growing increasingly querulous about the media treatment of the election, complaining 'it has revolved to a quite ridiculous degree around process, incidents, personality rather than policy'.[16] While the Prime Minister tore into the media, his press secretary was across the train compartment barking urgent instructions about the arrangements for the next Millbank news conference. 'We must have a woman on the platform even if she's just in the chair,' said Campbell. 'Why can't we have Patricia Hewitt or Tessa Jowell?' The heavy masculinity of the faces fronting the Labour campaign was being criticised. Later in the week, Blair would return to his complaint about 'all the personality nonsense' – in a party election broadcast entirely devoted to himself. He could not see – or did not want to acknowledge – his own part in the creation of a culture that he claimed to detest.

The serious media was actually devoting much effort to scrutinising the policy arguments between the parties, especially in the crucial battleground of taxation and spending. New Labour was put on the back foot about how it could sustain spending increases without tax rises, and got into some further trouble when the Conservatives challenged Gordon Brown to rule out hiking up national insurance contributions, income tax by another name.

The Chancellor was resistant, and with sound reasons, to giving guarantees. As soon as he gave an answer about one tax, he would be pressed on to another, and then another. The downside was several days of pressure about national insurance until Brown was finally forced out on to the airwaves to declare: 'There will be no fifty per cent tax rate and these Tory claims, like their claims about £6 a gallon of petrol, are a typical Tory election smear.'[17] Though not quite a full denial, this just about put the issue to bed.

These Tory stabs drew a little blood, but the Conservatives could not bite more heavily into New Labour because their own promises on taxation and spending were just as suspect, if not more so. With the Conservatives already struggling to convince that they could find £8 billion of tax cuts without slashing public services, their credibility never made a recovery from a story in the *Financial Times* that they would 'shrink state spending dramatically' by finding 'vast savings' worth £20 billion a year by the end of the next parliament.[18]

William Hague had indicated a similar figure some weeks earlier. In the magnifying glass of the campaign, the story caught fire, giving a brief celebrity to Oliver Letwin, the hitherto obscure Tory Treasury spokesman who was unmasked as the paper's source. When Letwin went to ground, Millbank printed 'Wanted' posters bearing his mugshot in such haste that there was a spelling mistake. Lance Price, the Director of Communications, hired bloodhounds to be sent sniffing around Conservative Central Office in search of the elusive Letwin. Into Blair's stump speeches were inserted relentless references to the blood-curdling figure of £20 billion in cuts to schools and hospitals. He mocked 'Hagueonomics'.

Brown mercilessly impaled the Tories on this blunder and made them writhe on the hook for the duration of the campaign. 'Twenty billion pounds of cuts which mean £30 million of cuts in each constituency,' the Chancellor assailed the Conservatives. 'Since he let the cat out of the bag Oliver Letwin has become the invisible man of British politics. You have more chance of finding Lord Lucan. I believe there have been more sightings of Elvis Presley than of Oliver Letwin.' Vaudeville aside, Brown put his finger on why this illustrated how significantly the terms of political trade had shifted: 'A few years ago Thatcherites would have been boasting of their plans to cut public services – now they have to be hidden away.'[19] New Labour might have made a mistake by using the now stale presentational tactics of the last war, but the Conservatives committed the much more grievous strategic error of fighting the war before last. All the evidence was that the majority of voters were much less interested in tax cuts than they were in seeing improvements to public services. That was the basic reason why New Labour was winning the campaign argument allied with its reputation as the party of economic competence. The most important event of the election for most voters had nothing to do with anything said by any politician or journalist. It occurred on the first Thursday: mortgages became the cheapest in forty years when the Bank of England cut interest rates to 5.25 per cent.

The attacks and counter-offensives between the parties, the bombardments of statistics, the attempts to blow 'black holes' in the other side's programmes, all this left most of the country absolutely unmoved. Seventy-seven per cent of respondents to a poll agreed that 'all politicians quote statistics and figures that are meaningless to most people'; 69 per cent thought that 'most of the party leaders are making promises they know they can't fulfil'; 61 per cent believed that 'The Labour Government isn't up to much but the Tories don't offer a real alternative.'[20]

There was a near-universal view that the campaign was developing into one of the most stupefying in electoral history. 'Lifted, lifted, lifted' – the lyric of the New Labour campaign theme – was not the feeling of an underwhelmed Britain. In one sense, this was testimony to the achievement of Blair and Brown. Labour had for years been viewed as too alarming ever to be trusted again with power. The re-election of a centre-left government was now regarded as boringly inevitable.

The tedium was not a compliment to the campaign. Peter Mandelson, confined though he was to internal exile in Hartlepool, was still in regular phone contact with Blair. The twice-fallen Cabinet minister stayed at Chequers the weekend before the campaign began to discuss strategy with Blair. Mandelson made one open contribution to the debate in a signed newspaper article. Staffers at Millbank fell around laughing when they saw the front-page headline: 'Mandelson urges less spin, more vision'.

It was indeed hilariously ironic for the high sorcerer of spin to warn against the old black magic by recommending that New Labour had 'to lift our sights' and 'not simply rely on the well-worn methods of campaigning, message delivery and rebuttal to achieve our ends'.[21] Campbell and Brown both bitterly complained to Blair that this intervention advertised the divisions within New Labour and fuelled media criticism of the campaign.

Blair phoned Mandelson to tell him to silence himself. Not, though, because he thought the thrust of what Mandelson had written was wrong. In fact, it was a fair summation of Blair's own thinking. The Prime Minister agreed with virtually every word of Mandelson's observations, including the lightly coded criticism of Gordon Brown that it was 'not enough' just to fight the campaign on the 'competence and stability' of their economic record. They had to 'explain the vision' to build 'positive support'.

Blair and Brown were effectively fighting parallel – and sometimes divergent – elections. 'There are two campaigns: so what's new?' remarked one senior New Labour politician.[22] For obvious reasons, Brown wanted his large share of the credit both for the government's record and for the reward of election victory. The Chancellor laid the greatest weight on the strength of the economy: an achievement most closely associated with himself. The solid if less than inspirational campaign slogan – 'The Work Goes On' – was imprinted with Brown's midnight toil. He did not see much advantage for the incumbents in taking any gambles with their poll lead.

In contrast to Brown's safety-orientated approach, Blair wanted what he described to me as an 'unremittingly New Labour' campaign. He saw it as an opportunity to equip him with a personal 'mandate' for the most controversial ambitions he had for his second term. He wanted to stress that 'money alone is not enough' to produce 'first-rate' schools and hospitals. In his major speech on the subject, he deliberately emphasised that extra funding had to be accompanied by sweeping reform to what he derogatorily referred to as 'the tradition of monolithic, centrally driven public services'.[23] Blair went out of his way to highlight that this would mean more private sector involvement in the delivery of education and health care. This was certainly a 'real and radical change' to a century of Labour thinking. The Prime Minister contended that 'without reform our public services will be threatened by the alternative – being broken up, torn down, sold off'.[24] Though he pitched the programme in these anti-Tory terms, this was a direct challenge to many working in the public services. 'There should be no barriers, no dogma, no vested interests that stand in the way'[25] semaphored that he expected opposition from the professional bodies and the public sector unions, and was ready to beat it down. They were soon grumbling against what they saw as privatisation: discontent which foreshadowed fierce struggles after the election. Blair gave an insight into why he was putting his ideas in lights: 'Anybody who comes to me after the election from the very traditional old left and says "No you cannot involve the private sector in these things," I want to say "No: I made it clear during the election that we wanted a different partnership between the public and private sector." '[26] This was Blair flying solo. Neither Brown nor many of his other senior colleagues saw a great deal of sense in being this deliberately provocative during the campaign.

The most inflammatory difference between Prime Minister and Chancellor was over the approach they should take to the always vexatious subject of the European single currency. Tony Blair had grown even firmer in his conviction that Britain's destiny had to be as a fully subscribed member of Europe, and it was his historic role to bring this to fruition. He wrote in a memo to his closest aides that the political case for joining the single currency was 'compelling'. Gordon Brown was moving even further in the opposite direction. The Chancellor was even more entrenched in his scepticism about the necessity and the virtues of joining the euro, certainly with any rapidity and especially when it was so burdened with economic and political risks. This was a dispute about power at its most fundamental. Brown feared diminishing his control over the economy as well as his chances of becoming Prime Minister. Blair believed that Britain would not punch at its full weight until it had entered the single currency and he would not fulfil his own destiny as the Prime Minister who settled the relationship with Europe once and for all. He indicated as much in an under-reported, but highly revealing, remark at the very beginning of the campaign. He qualified his pride that Britain was no longer 'marginalised and isolated' in Europe with the observation: 'But we are not yet the leading nation in Europe that our weight, prosperity and history demand.'[27]

The majority of the campaign team were with Brown in questioning the wisdom of giving a high profile to Europe. Most voters put it low on their lists of priority issues, and it was the one subject on which the Conservatives led the government. Brown had long believed that it would be perilous to hand an opportunity to the Tories to turn the election into a referendum about the single currency.

The pact between Prime Minister and Chancellor to keep a lid on their argument during the election was frequently strained as the campaign went on. Though Blair tried to tread around the subject cautiously, he could not always restrain his innate enthusiasm for the euro. In an interview with me in the first week, he was at his most passionately animated describing how Britain had been repeatedly damaged by its history of being late and grudging about joining every great initiative in the development of the European Union. He expressed himself confident that he could turn round public hostility to the single currency in a referendum campaign, even with the voters more than two to one against. 'If you believe the case is right, you've got to make it to the people.' They would be 'open to persuasion' – as clear a signal as there could be that he wanted to call the referendum in his second term. Though 'this is considered somewhat eccentric in certain quarters, I personally believe that Europe will be a winner for us in this election'.[28]

Those quarters that considered the Prime Minister's euro-enthusiasm to be eccentric included his Chancellor. Brown sent out instructions from Millbank that MPs who wanted to make the case for the single currency should shut up. At a news conference he put further obstacles in the way of Britain joining the single currency by deriding aspects of the European Central Bank, criticisms which his aides then amplified in off-the-record briefings to the *Financial Times*. The next day, at very short notice, an interview was fixed with the same paper in which Blair dropped another heavy hint of his desire to enter the euro. He would be 'very active' in making the case for 'a strong Europe', and declared that 'this debate will change' when he fully showed his own hand.[29] A furious Brown complained to Blair that he had breached their campaign rule to talk about Europe, but not the euro. The Prime Minister beat a partial retreat. 'The euro is a subject for another day,' he told his next set of interviewers from a broadsheet. 'It's not the issue of the election.'[30] But Blair again lit up the argument in his major speech on foreign policy. Arguing for Britain to be an 'active, engaged partner', he said 'to regard each pooling of sovereignty as a diminution of national identity is to retreat from modern reality. And for a nation with such a proud history as that of Britain, it is to show a lack of self-confidence wholly at odds with our true potential for leadership.' Ruling out the single currency would be an act of 'isolationism . . . relegating Britain to the sidelines of a Europe in which British jobs and influence are intimately engaged'.[31]

The discerning eye could see the argument between him and the Chancellor blistering back to the surface a few days later. Gordon Brown slapped down Robin Cook for raising the subject by saying it would not be 'fruitful' to talk about what the referendum question might be. Soon afterwards, Blair went on television and did just that. 'Surely there can't be that many complicated ways of putting it to the people: "Do you want to join the euro or not?" [32] All of this pre-figured the massive, probably murderous argument between Prime Minister and Chancellor which would have to happen after the election to resolve this momentous dispute.

The Conservatives did try to turn the election into a referendum on the single currency – to spectacularly self-mutilating effect. With ten days left to polling day, William Hague began campaigning on the slogan 'Ten days to save the pound'. The Tories were thrown into instant disarray when asked whether that meant a Labour victory could be regarded as sanction from the voters to abolish the pound. Though at first worried by the Tory emphasis on the euro, Blair and Brown soon realised that it gave them further opportunity to paint the Conservatives as single issue monomaniacs who banged on about Europe only because they had nothing to say about the public services that really concerned the voters.

The Conservative line was also disintegrated by the eruption into the campaign of Margaret Thatcher declaring, in contradiction to Hague's 'not for five years' policy, that she would 'never' join the single currency. The Baroness announced herself with a speech in Plymouth which she prefaced by saying that she had seen a cinema billboard advertising *The Mummy Returns*. It has to be presumed that this joke was scripted for her. The former Conservative Prime Minister surely had no idea that she was comparing herself to the disinterred monster of a horror movie. Blair's response to the untombing of Thatcher was a striking demonstration of how New Labour had developed over the past four years. In 1997, he courted and won the approval of Thatcher, and promised not to disturb much of her legacy. In 2001, he did something he would never have countenanced then, and some of his advisers still worried was a mistake. He sanctioned an attack ad using the Baroness to ridicule the Conservatives. The Thatcher hairdo was plonked on top of Hague's bald pate accompanied by the slogan: 'Get out and vote. Or they get in.' Planned back in January, the ad was given additional impact by the unexpected prominence she played in the campaign. Blair excoriated the Conservatives for wanting to take

Britain back to the 'selfish opportunism' of her period in power.[33] Opportunism also lay behind his own decision to use Thatcher as a goad to energise Labour supporters to go to the ballot box. Blair had been shown focus group research and polling showing that swing voters wanted a line drawn under her era and she was a net negative for the Tories.

What it also illustrated was how New Labour had moved on. In 1997, Blair led a twitchy campaign on a cautious manifesto loaded with reassurances that he was safe to elect because he would not change too much. He wrote of Euro-dragons to be slain, of love for the pound, and the campaign mascot was a bulldog. He and Gordon Brown promised that they would not spend more than the outgoing Conservative government.

The 2001 campaign displayed a Tony Blair much more liberated from his nerves. He described New Labour as 'a modern, liberal social democratic party'[34] and 'Ambitions For Britain' was a manifesto promising radical change. He enthused about positive engagement with Europe, and hinted at scrapping the pound. He and Gordon Brown bragged endlessly about how much more they were going to spend.

The campaign might not be having great leverage on a weary electorate, but it did have a considerable impact on the Prime Minister. The polling that he studied so closely had warned for a long time that there was great discontent about the state of Britain. What there is no substitute for is hearing it from the voters in the raw. Blair was chastened by his exposure to the deep and wide anger about health, education, transport and crime. He confessed: 'There is a lot of pain out there, a lot of anxiety.'[35] In the last week of the campaign, family doctors threatened to resign en masse over their working conditions, and the leaders of the headteachers' and the nurses' unions said that under-funding had left Britain with 'third world' schools and hospitals. Paradoxically, this worked to New Labour's campaign advantage. Every complaint and challenge from a voter, interest group or union was translated by Blair into an argument for preferring New Labour spending to Tory tax cuts. By the last, gasping days of the election, he was talking about almost nothing but schools and hospitals, demanding that people vote for him as 'an instruction' to spend.

'You must be very pleased,' Nicky Campbell teased the Prime Minister on a Radio Five phone-in. 'Look at the polls, it's in the bag, isn't it? You know, the Deputy Prime Minister could punch every agricultural worker in Wales, you could turn up at your press conferences dressed as a chicken and cluck your way through, you could even call yourself a socialist! You'd still win.' 'Er,' responded Blair, 'I don't take anything for granted at all.'[36]

Everyone else did. The final clutch of opinion polls suggested that Labour had shed about five points of support during the campaign, most of that harmlessly contributing to a rise in support for the Liberal Democrats. With the Conservatives flat-lining on the thirty points where they had begun the campaign, Labour held a sixteen-point lead.[37]

Tony Blair had spent much of the past four weeks and the previous four years expressing bitter frustration about the press, but he had little grounds for dissatisfaction about the voting recommendations the newspapers offered to their readers. With *The Times* declaring for Labour for the first time in that paper's history, the vast majority of the daily press were backing Blair. Only two dailies did not. The *Daily Telegraph* was alone in voting Conservative. The *Daily Mail* had a quiet election. Not wanting to look stupid by recommending William Hague when it knew he would be rejected at the ballot box, even the *Mail* could not bring itself to endorse the Tories. The pattern among the Sundays was similar. In terms of circulation, this gave a crushing and unprecedented press majority to Labour.

The bookies became so certain of the result that the odds at William Hill shortened until a punter had to bet £200 on Labour to win a meagre £1. Ladbrokes closed the book and started paying out on Blair being back in Number 10 before voting had even begun.

The more paranoid element at Millbank saw in this a ruse to help the Tories. It was alien to New Labour's nature not to have something to get neurotic about. These predictions of a landslide now played on their campaign-frayed nerves. The Liberal Democrat leader, Charles Kennedy, astutely marketed his party to lukewarm Labourites and disillusioned Conservatives as a home for their vote so that he could provide 'serious Opposition' to New Labour. In their latest tactical lurch, the Tories soft-pedalled the wildly implausible notion that they could win. William Hague switched to appealing to people to 'lend' him their votes to 'clip Labour's wings'. A Tory attack ad pictured Blair wearing his cheesiest grin with a pin aimed at the inflated smile. The billboard urged: 'Go on, burst his bubble.'

Blair scorned the Tories for 'this last desperate throw of the dice', but the tactic sent a frisson of anxiety around New Labour that it might rouse opponents to the ballot box while inducing lassitude among Labour voters. Blair feared that talk of a landslide could rebound to deprive him of one. On the last campaign day, he made a frenetic 680-mile rush around key constituencies in the East Midlands, North Wales, Derbyshire, the Scottish Borders and the North East, hurling about the country by bus and helicopter as if the election were too close to call. 'Don't let the cynics and pessimists win. Do not let people tell you that this election does not matter. Don't let the pundits and parts of the media and pollsters tell you the election is over,' he told an audience of Labour supporters packed into a pub in the rock-solidly safe seat of Castleford in West Yorkshire. He summoned the ghosts of 'our ancestors, who lived and fought, and sometimes died, for the right to vote'. He delivered a variation on this frantic refrain in the Nottinghamshire marginal of Broxtowe: 'This is your election, this is your moment of maximum power. Tomorrow it is not the media, not the pollsters, not even the politicians who are in power. You are in power. You hold the key to the future. You, the British people, are the boss.'[38] Well, for Thursday, at any rate. 'The vote is a precious thing,' declaimed Blair, ending his campaign on the same note with which it had begun.

Polling day in Sedgefield, as in most parts of Britain, was sunny but blustery. There was a suggestion of dark cloud overhead when the

Blair family – minus a sleeping Leo – walked out of Myrobella on Thursday morning. They strolled across a field of daisies and buttercups to cast two votes for the local candidate, accompanied only by a pack of a hundred reporters, photographers and camera crews, party aides, darting-eyed Special Branch detectives and armed police cradling submachine guns. The rest of the day the Prime Minister spent closeted inside his constituency home with Campbell, Hunter and Powell. They helped plan his next government, a task Blair engaged in with much more confidence than he had done on the eve of the poll in 1997. At just after midnight, the Prime Minister and retinue arrived at his count. He wore an impassive face, a deliberate countenance of restraint, which broke down only once when he emotionally embraced his father. In his speech after being returned as MP for Sedgefield with a personal majority reduced by the low turn-out which would be a feature of the election, Blair drew a contrast with his first victory: 'The judgement is a more sober one and the mood is different, but I believe it is a more reasoned judgement because it is based on a record of office.'

He was not wrong to call it 'an historic moment for the Labour Party'.[39] Where all his predecessors failed, Tony Blair had secured the two full terms that had eluded Labour for 101 years. That ghost of repeated failure which had shadowed him throughout the first term was finally exorcised. With a new parliamentary majority of 167, he had won two successive landslides of enormous magnitude, a feat unmatched by any Prime Minister of modern times. Blair had at last made real Harold Wilson's dream of turning Labour into 'the natural party of government'. The forces of conservatism were utterly crushed; William Hague, who would quit as Tory leader at breakfast time, was obliterated; Thatcherism was buried. The opportunity now lay before Tony Blair to put his name to an era as enduring and as significant.

As the Prime Minister's plane flew him towards another historic dawn in Downing Street and further fresh entries in the record books, the media flock and their shepherdesses partied rowdily. Alastair Campbell made up for the odd gloom that had engulfed

him on the night of the first victory. 'We stuffed 'em,' he cried,
as each incoming result confirmed that the Tories were being
hammered. 'We stuffed 'em.' Surrounded by family, friends and
aides knocking back champagne, Tony Blair toasted his sensational
victory with several stiff drinks – of tea. When he wandered down
the back of the plane to talk to the media, a photographer raised
his camera to take a snap of the double landslide Prime Minister.
'No pictures,' shouted Anji Hunter. When they ought to have
been effervescing they still could not unclench themselves. Blair
was tense and terse with the reporters. 'You must be very excited?'
suggested one journalist. 'I can't say,' Blair responded absently.
'Will you just tell us how you feel?' 'No,' he answered. 'But are
you happy to have won such a landslide again or just relieved?' 'All
of the above,' he replied dully. 'Look, the story of the night is the
Scottish Nationalists . . .' said Blair, most bizarrely.[40]

The message the Prime Minister tried to convey all night and
the following morning was that this was not a time for exuberance.
His focus was on getting back down to work. This humility in
victory was not entirely contrived for the media. The second term
had been obsessively worried over and slaved for. At the successful
climax of the struggle, Blair found himself strangely anti-climactic.
His epic double whammy was tinged with melancholy for another
reason. The nation's verdict was conclusively damning about the
Tories, but about New Labour the country was only conditional.
Blair had secured a 42 per cent share of the vote, a very poor score
for the winning party.[41] No government had achieved office with
the active endorsement of so few voters since 1924. The Tories
were abjectly defeated, but New Labour was a distant second to
the forces of apathy, indifference and cynicism. The most miserable
record set by the election was the turn-out: the lowest since the
introduction of universal suffrage. Though ministers put a brave
public face on this, Blair expressed profound disappointment to his
intimates.[42] The majority might be towering, but 'the mandate' he
had sought was thin. Only a quarter of the potential electorate had
supported him. For every five people who voted for New Labour,
seven voted for someone else, and a further eight voted not at all.

It would be hard for Blair to claim that he had succeeded in his campaign goal of winning the 'hearts and minds' of Britain. The victory was champagne without bubbles.

As attuned as ever to the temper of the nation, Blair issued the strict order that was conveyed by Campbell that there should not be a hint of self-congratulation or glorification. Television cameras were excluded from the victory party at Millbank where the windows were lined with reflective plastic to block prying eyes. The celebratory fizz was handed out in appropriately quarter-sized bottles.

They all agreed that it was not the same as 1997: there was no point pretending otherwise. With few seats changing hands, the attention of the Millbank party was really gripped only by the result from Hartlepool where both the Tories and Jurassic Labour, in the shape of Arthur Scargill, were soundly beaten by Peter Mandelson who made the most extraordinary acceptance speech of the night. 'They underestimated me,' he shouted. Mandelson knew that the spoils of New Labour's epochal victory would not include a senior Cabinet position for himself. The sour-sweet feelings inside Mandelson surged through his normal public mask of cool control. His face began to contort, and his voice grew louder: 'I am a fighter and not a quitter. My political enemies can have their pound of flesh and they do, but they will never cat into the core of my beliefs. That is the inner steel in me,' raged Mandelson. 'I am back on the political map.' There were scattered cheers from some of those watching this on the screens at Millbank. From others, there were cat-calls for one of the founding fathers of the revolution.

At five thirty in the morning, a brief visit to party headquarters by Tony Blair was heralded by the resumed booming of the 'lifted' campaign theme. There were groans.

It was an untriumphant sort of triumph. This time, there were no exulting, flag-waving crowds brought over from Millbank to cheer the Prime Minister into Number 10. In the small speech he made in front of the black door of power, he hedged his smashing win with deflating qualifications. 'It has been a remarkable and historic victory for my party, but I am in no doubt at all as to what it means. It is a mandate for reform and investment in the future and also a very clear instruction to deliver,' said the re-empowered Prime Minister. 'In respect of Europe and the wider world, we need to make changes there, too, so that we are engaged, exerting influence, having the self-belief not to turn our back on the world or retreat into isolationism. These changes will not be easy.' He concluded rather flatly: 'We have laid the foundations, but now is the time to build upon them. Thank you.'[43]

The photographers didn't want to let him go until he had pressed his lips on baby Leo. When Blair hesitated, the snappers yelled: 'Go on, bloody kiss 'im.' So the Prime Minister did. Then, Tony Blair took his family inside Number 10. The door closed with a gentle thud of relief.

The down-beat flavour of that speech was a typically Blairesque reflection back to the nation of its uneuphoric mood. May Day 1997 was hailed as a dazzling new dawn for Britain; this was just another, slightly dreary day in the office. The people had not so much enthused as acquiesced in giving New Labour a second term. The government was on probation to deliver the 'world class public services' that Blair had placed at the centre of his appeal for re-election.

That lack of elation from the nation was mirrored by the atmosphere within the government. Blair and his new ministers burst through the doors of Whitehall in 1997 principally worried whether they were up to the job. Their anxiety this time was sourced in four years of bloodying, grinding, maturing experience of just how difficult it was to deliver.

Outside Number 10, Blair said he hoped he'd 'learnt from the mistakes' of his first four years as Prime Minister. The central theme of the new government that he began to unveil on Friday was an attempt to remedy earlier errors. Alastair Campbell made a complete retreat from daily briefing of the media, putting the task back in the hands of civil servants: a token of Blair's determination that his second term would be much less fixated with chasing headlines and trying to govern through the media. John Prescott's sprawling, ineffectual departmental empire was broken up. He was shunted into a new Office of the Deputy Prime Minister, a shiny doorplate designed to soothe that sensitive ego with the impression that his power was not really being shrunk. The failed Ministry of Agriculture disappeared and Nick Brown was demoted to number two at the new Ministry of Work and Pensions, getting observer status at Cabinet only after a heated intervention by Gordon Brown. In the afternoon, a stunned Robin Cook was told by Blair that he was removing him as Foreign Secretary. Cook spent more than an hour ringing his wife and allies for advice about whether he should take the lesser post of Leader of the House. While an extremely wounded Cook debated whether to resign, other ministers began to crowd into the waiting rooms at Number 10 like jumbos stacking up over Heathrow waiting for the controller to call them in.

The most crucially important move of the reshuffle was the one that the Prime Minister did not make. Some among those aides and ministers he most trusted warned Blair that he would have only one opportunity to finally settle who was the master of the New Labour house. So long as Gordon Brown was at the Treasury, chaining the rest of Whitehall to his purse strings and jealously guarding the economic tests for membership of the euro, the Chancellor wielded a veto over Tony Blair's ambitions. Close counsellors of the Prime Minister urged him to use his moment of maximum personal power to shift Gordon Brown to the Foreign Office.[44] Blair recoiled from this bold act for the usual reasons of admiration and obligation towards the man he had hours earlier hailed as 'an inspiring Chancellor', mixed with his fright of Brown's daunting ability and wrath. Blair left Brown in his mighty place at the Treasury from where the Chancellor would continue to cast his brooding and restless gaze down at Number 10. Second term, like first term, would be defined by the turbulent coupling of Blair and Brown. The rock on which New Labour was built was the rock on which it could one day founder.

Rather than confront his Chancellor, Blair made moves to corral the colossus. A strengthened ministerial team at the Cabinet Office and a plethora of new strategy, policy and delivery units at Number 10 were designed to create a Department of the Prime Minister in

all but name. At last – or so Blair hoped – he would impose his writ
on Whitehall. Jack Straw moved to the Foreign Office for the
counter-intuitively persuasive reason that a man with a past record
as a Eurosceptic would be a more convincing salesman for the
single currency. With David Blunkett at the Home Office, Blair
filled two big offices of state with practical men of stature whom he
trusted: counter-weights to the Chancellor. All the other Cabinet
promotions went to men and women – a record seven of the latter
– whose first loyalty was to the Prime Minister. Hilary Armstrong,
the new Chief Whip, was a long paid-up Blairite. Gordon Brown
was especially resistant to the appointment of Charles Clarke, a
tough character not afraid of the Chancellor, to the newly invented
post of party chairman with a seat at Cabinet. The appointment of
the ardently pro-European Clarke, like the promotion to Trade
and Industry Secretary of Patricia Hewitt, was further evidence of
Blair's desire to try to find a way into the European single currency.
He now believed that he had finally fashioned a government on his
own terms, in his own image, dedicated to delivery of his own
agenda.

New Labour had proved to be a superlative vehicle for the winning
and retaining of power. Tony Blair had demonstrated himself to be
an exceptionally gifted and supremely successful electoral politician.
From the victory sprang the next challenge. The unassailable scale of
his second majority removed all excuse for failing to deliver the more
radical change that he so relentlessly promised.

To be a good servant of the people, New Labour would now
have to consummate Blair's pledges to give Britain 'world-class'
schools and health care. To be a great master of the people, Blair
would now have to overcome their wariness about Europe. History
would not judge him by the size of his majorities but by the scale
of what he achieved with them.

In the back garden of Number 10, four years earlier almost
exactly to the day, he told me that getting re-elected was 'the most
important thing'. Only once that was achieved could Tony Blair
clearly see that winning office was simply the beginning of making
history. The most important thing was changing the future.

# Notes

## Preface to the Penguin Edition

1. *Daily Telegraph*, 11 November 2000
2. *Daily Telegraph*, 21 September 2000
3. *Daily Express*, 23 September 2000
4. Conference speech, Brighton, 26 September 2000

## Introduction: The Few

1. That is what Shawcross is famously remembered as saying. The sense of what he actually said is similar, but expressed less pithily: 'We are the masters at the moment, and not only at the moment, but for a very long time to come.' Hansard, 2 April 1946
2. Hansard, 9 December 1998
3. Labour Manifesto, 1997
4. Hansard, 22 June 1966. Wilson was talking about the seamen's strike in which the young John Prescott played an active part
5. When the first edition was published, some questioned whether Blair and Brown really argued so ferociously and with quite as much swearing. Subsequent public confirmation of this has come from, among others, one of Brown's closest allies. 'They do go at each other and argue with each other. The officials aren't there and they get very frustrated because there's no minute of what is discussed, which is probably just as well, because they do go at each other.' Geoffrey Robinson speaking to Michael Cockerell on *The Rivals*, BBC 2, 25 March 2001

## 1. Dawn

1. Private information
2. Private information
3. Private interview, Blair aide
4. Speech at Royal Festival Hall, 2 May 1997
5. *Daily Mail*, 2 May 1997
6. Private information
7. Remarks at Channel Four

Political Awards, 9 February
2000

8. *Guardian*, 1 May 1997
9. *New Yorker*, 21 April 1997
10. *New York Times*, 23 April
    1997
11. *Observer*, 27 April 1997
12. *New Yorker*, 5 February 1996
13. *Express*, 30 April 1997
14. Roy Hattersley, *Fifty Years
    On*, pp. 378 and 385
15. *Sunday Telegraph*, 27 April
    1997
16. Private information
17. *The Times*, 14 March 1997
18. Speech in City of London, 7
    March 1997
19. Speech at Sedgefield, 2 May
    1997
20. Private information
21. Speech at Royal Festival Hall,
    2 May 1997
22. Ibid.
23. The share of vote is
    alternatively and often put at
    44.3 per cent. That figure
    excludes Northern Ireland
24. Butler and Kavanagh, *The
    British General Election of 1997*,
    Appendix 1
25. Speech in Downing Street, 2
    May 1997
26. Ibid.

## 2. What Do We Do Now?

1. The Derby government lasted
   just five months
2. The Attorney-General, John
   Morris
3. Speech, Labour conference,
   Blackpool, 2 October
   1996
4. Remarks to the author in
   Downing Street garden, 29
   May 1997
5. Hilary Armstrong, Local
   Government Minister
6. Private information
7. Private information
8. *Conference Live*, BBC2, 28
   September 1999
9. *New Statesman*, 8 August
   1996
10. Private interview, civil
    servant
11. Speech to Parliamentary
    Labour Party, Church House,
    7 May 1997
12. Speech to Newspaper
    Society, 10 March 1997
13. Private interview, civil
    servant
14. Peter Oborne, *Alastair
    Campbell*, p. 4
15. The phrase was first reported,
    though the identity of its
    author not revealed, by
    Professor Peter Hennessy
    who organised the seminar

16. Private information

17. Private interview, civil servant

18. Bob Marshall-Andrews, MP for Medway, *Blair's Year*, Brook Lapping for Channel Four, 19 April 1998

19. Remarks to Parliamentary Labour Party, Church House, 7 May 1997


### 3. Bank of Brown

1. Private information

2. Private information

3. Private information

4. Private interview, Cabinet minister

5. Private information

6. Private information

7. Private information

8. Treasury press conference, 6 May 1997

9. *The Times*, 7 May 1997

10. Ibid., 3 May 1999

11. Private information

12. Janet Jones, *Labour of Love*, p. 75

13. Private information

14. *Blair's Year*, Brook Lapping for Channel Four, 19 April 1998

15. Private interview, Cabinet minister's aide

16. Philip Gould, *The Unfinished Revolution*

17. Philip Gould, quoted in Draper, *Blair's 100 Days*, p. 72

18. Private information

19. I am particularly grateful to William Keegan of the *Observer* for sharing his insights into this episode

20. Private information

21. Private interview, Cabinet minister

22. Ironically, after all this, the super-regulator would turn out to be run by staff almost all of whom were transferred from Threadneedle Street

23. Hansard, 20 May 1997

24. BBC Radio, 21 May 1997

25. Private interview, Brown aide

26. *Financial Times*, 22 May 1997

27. Private information

28. The fullest account of 'Operation Autumn' can be found in Hugh Pym and Nick Kochan, *Gordon Brown: The First Year In Power*, Chapter Four

29. Private interview, Treasury civil servant

30. *Confessions of a Spin Doctor*, Channel Four, 26 September 1999

31. *Financial Times*, 15 June 1997

32. Private information

33. Private interview, Blair aide

34. Private information

35. Private interview, civil servant
36. Private interview, civil servant
37. IMF report, 21 July 1997

### 4. Hail to the Chief

1. *Daily Mail*, 1 June 1997
2. Hansard, 24 April 1995
3. Private information
4. BBC Radio 5, 17 November 1997
5. *What Makes Tony Tick?*, BBC2, 30 January 2000
6. Private information
7. Private information
8. Private infromation
9. Margaret Cook, *A Slight and Delicate Creature*, p. 3
10. Private information
11. Remarks at Trimdon church, 31 August 1997
12. Norman Fairclough, *New Labour, New Language?*, p. 103
13. *Daily Telegraph*, 27 November 1997
14. *Sunday Telegraph*, 7 September 1997
15. Quoted in the *Independent*, 1 September 1997
16. As witnessed by Matthew Engel of the *Guardian*, 1 September 1997
17. Private information
18. Private information
19. Private interview, Blair aide
20. Private information
21. Private information
22. Queen's broadcast, 5 September 1997
23. *Observer*, 7 September 1997
24. Speech to 'People's Lunch', 20 November 1997

### 5. Dragons and Lions

1. Private information
2. Conference speech, Blackpool, 4 October 1994
3. Speech at Chatham House, London, 5 April 1995
4. *Sun*, 22 April 1997
5. Ibid., 17 April 1997
6. Private information
7. Speech to the European Socialists Congress, Malmö, 6 June 1997
8. Hugo Young, *This Blessed Plot*, p. 491
9. Private information
10. Private information
11. *Financial Times*, 26 September 1997
12. *We Are The Treasury*, ITV, 30 September 1997
13. To Lucy Ward who reported it after Whelan's fall in the *Guardian*, 5 January 1999
14. *Daily Mail*, 13 October 1997
15. *Independent*, 14 October 1997
16. Private information

17. *The Times*, 18 October 1997
18. According to the well-informed Patrick Wintour, *Observer*, 19 October 1997
19. *Sun*, 18 October 1997
20. Nicholas Jones, *Sultans of Spin*, p. 84
21. Hansard, 27 October 1997
22. Private information
23. Private information
24. Private information
25. Private information
26. Private information
27. *Guardian*, 20 October 1997
28. *Daily Telegraph*, 20 October 1997
29. Private information
30. *Daily Mail*, 22 October 1997
31. Private information
32. Private information
33. Hansard, 27 October 1997
34. Speech at Waterloo station, 5 December 1997

## 6. They'll Get Me for This

1. Private interview, Cabinet minister
2. *Sunday Times*, 19 March 2000
3. *Sunday Telegraph*, 16 November 1997
4. Dobson, speech to RCN, 19 May 1997
5. Ibid.
6. Private information
7. Private information
8. Letter in name of Tom Sawyer, 8 November 1997
9. Ibid.
10. Nicholas Jones, *Sultans of Spin*, p. 125
11. *Today*, BBC Radio Four, 10 November 1997
12. Private information
13. Letter from Sir Patrick Neill QC, 10 November 1997
14. Ibid.
15. *Sun*, 12 November 1997
16. Private information
17. Hansard, 12 November 1997
18. Ibid.
19. *Newsnight*, BBC 2, 14 November 1997
20. Private interview
21. Private information
22. *On the Record*, BBC 1, 16 November 1997
23. *Guardian*, 9 August 1997
24. *On the Record*, BBC 1, 16 November 1997
25. Ibid.
26. Speech to Civil Service College conference, 19 November 1997
27. By Robert Earl of Planet Hollywood

## 7. Department of Social Insecurity

1. Private information
2. Private information
3. Speech to Singapore Business Community, 8 January 1996
4. Private interview, Cabinet minister
5. Hansard, 25 November, 1997
6. Private information
7. Private information
8. Private information
9. Roger Stott, MP for Wigan, quoted in *Sunday Telegraph*, 14 December 1997
10. Private interview, Blair adviser
11. GMTV, 13 December 1997
12. Janet Jones, *Labour of Love*, p. 151
13. *Sunday Telegraph*, 21 December 1997
14. Speech, 20 December 1997
15. *The Times*, 15 January 1998
16. *Observer*, 11 January 1998
17. Campbell memo, 15 January 1998, leaked to the *Express*
18. Ibid., 26 February 1998
19. Private information

## 8. Long Good Friday

1. Private information
2. Speech, Belfast, 16 May 1997
3. When Mowlam left the Northern Ireland Office, she bequeathed *Discipline Over Desire* to her successor, Peter Mandelson – a characteristically mischievous Mowlam joke
4. *The Times*, 5 May 2000
5. *The Westminster Hour*, BBC Radio Four, 12 April 1998
6. George Mitchell, *Making Peace*, p. 126
7. Private information
8. *Independent*, 9 January 1998
9. Ibid.
10. News Letter, 10 January 1998
11. Mitchell, op. cit., p. 137
12. Private information
13. *The Hand of History*, BBC Northern Ireland, quoted by Henry McDonald, *Trimble*, p. 202
14. Mitchell, op. cit., p. 169
15. Private information
16. *Sunday Times*, 12 April 1998
17. Remarks at Hillsborough Castle, 7 April 1998
18. McDonald, op. cit., p. 203
19. Private information
20. *Sunday Telegraph*, 12 April 1998
21. *Independent on Sunday*, 12 April 1998
22. Speech, Blackpool, 29 September 1998
23. Private information

24. Private information
25. Private information
26. *Observer*, 12 April 1998
27. McDonald, op. cit., p. 209
28. Remarks at Castle Buildings, 10 April 1998
29. MRBI/ICM/Harris poll for the *Guardian/Irish Times*, 16 April 1998
30. *Daily Telegraph*, 11 April 1998
31. *Independent*, 11 April 1998
32. *The Westminster Hour*, BBC Radio Four, 12 April 1998
33. *Daily Telegraph*, 16 May 1998
34. Ulster Marketing Services for RTE, 22 May 1998
35. According to a Coopers & Lybrand survey for the *Sunday Times*, 24 May 1998, 55 per cent of Unionists supported the agreement

9. *Psychological Flaws*

1. Private information
2. *Guardian*, 26 September 1998
3. Private information
4. Charlie Falconer quoted by John Rentoul, *Tony Blair*, p. 155
5. Private information
6. Private interview, Cabinet minister
7. Private interview, minister
8. Private interview, Cabinet minister
9. *Harpers & Queen*, August 1992, quoted by Paul Routledge, *Gordon Brown*, p. 255
10. Private information
11. Private interview, minister
12. Private interview, civil servant
13. Private interview, civil servant
14. Private information
15. Private information
16. Peter Oborne, *Alastair Campbell*, p. 164
17. Private information
18. Andrew Rawnsley, 'What Blair Really Thinks Of Brown', *Observer*, 18 January 1998
19. *Six O'Clock News*, BBC Radio Four, 18 January 1998
20. Private information
21. Private information
22. The Book of Genesis, 25: 23–28, Knox translation
23. Private information
24. Private information
25. Private information
26. Private interview
27. Private information
28. Hansard, 17 March 1998
29. Government Statistical Service
30. *Today*, BBC Radio Four, 19 February 1998

31. Private information
32. Private information
33. Private information
34. Private information
35. Hansard, 14 July 1998
36. Speech at Hawley Infant School, 14 July 1998
37. The Labour-dominated Treasury Select Committee detected and criticised the accounting trickery and said spending figures should never be presented in this 'opaque' fashion again
38. Hansard, 14 July 1998
39. Private interview, Blair aide
40. Donald Macintyre, *Mandelson*, p. 409
41. *Mirror*, 28 July 1998
42. Jack Cunningham left the Cabinet in October 1999

## 10. The Ethical Dimension

1. Private information
2. Speech, Foreign Office, 12 May 1997
3. Speech, Human Rights into the New Century, 17 July 1997
4. Private information
5. Written answer, Hansard, 28 July 1997
6. *Observer*, 24 August 1997
7. Written answer, Hansard, 15 March 2000
8. Strategic Export Controls Annual Report, 3 November 1999
9. *How To Be Foreign Secretary*, BBC2, 4 January 1998
10. *Sunday Times*, 10 January 1999
11. Margaret Cook, *A Slight and Delicate Creature*
12. *Guardian*, 27 January 1998
13. *Daily Mail*, 29 January 1998
14. *Independent on Sunday*, 1 February 1998
15. *Sunday Telegraph*, 11 January 1998
16. *Breakfast with Frost*, BBC1, 11 January 1998
17. *Observer*, 26 April 1998
18. Sierra Leone, Report of the Foreign Affairs Committee, 3 February 1999
19. Ibid.
20. Hansard, 12 March 1998
21. Sierra Leone, Report of the Intelligence and Security Committee, 13 May 1999
22. Sierra Leone, Report of the Foreign Affairs Committee, 3 February 1999
23. *Sunday Times*, 3 May 1998
24. Hansard, 6 May 1998
25. *Independent*, 7 May 1998
26. Hansard, 13 May 1998
27. *How To Be Foreign Secretary*, BBC1, 4 January 1998
28. GMTV, 17 May 1998

29. Private information

30. *Today*, BBC Radio Four, 5 March 1999

31. Sierra Leone, Report of the Foreign Affairs Committee, 3 February 1999

32. *Breakfast with Frost*, BBC1, 18 October 1998

33. Private information

34. *Guardian*, 20 October 1998

35. *Observer*, 25 October 1998

36. *Daily Telegraph*, 23 October 1998

37. *Guardian*, 24 July 1998

38. Private interview, minister

39. *The Times*, 25 November 1998

40. *Guardian*, 26 November 1998

41. *Independent*, 30 November 1998

42. *Guardian*, 3 March 2000


11. *Operation Hoover*

1. Private interview, Liberal Democrat

2. Private information

3. *Observer*, 27 July 1997

4. Philip Gould, *The Unfinished Revolution*, p. 27

5. Speech to Labour conference, 30 September 1997

6. Private information

7. Private information

8. David Clark and Gavin Strang

who were sacked in the July 1998 reshuffle

9. *Sunday Telegraph*, 28 November 1999

10. Private interview, Cabinet minister

11. Colin Brown, *Fighting Talk*, p. 318

12. Private information

13. *Sunday Times*, 31 January 1999

14. Private interview, civil servant

15. Speech to Reform Club dinner, reported in *The Times*, 1 December 1997

16. Private information

17. Private information

18. Speech to Liberal Democrat conference, 24 September 1998

19. Ibid.

20. Private information

21. Remarks at press conference at Institute of Directors, 28 October 1998

22. Blair statement, 29 October 1998

23. *Daily Telegraph*, 31 October 1998

24. *Sunday Telegraph*, 24 January 1999

25. Blair and Ashdown joint statement, 11 November 1998

26. *On the Record*, BBC1, 23 November 1998

27. Speech, 7 March 1999

## 12. Black Christmas

1. Speech, Blackpool, 28 September 1998
2. Speech, Blackpool, 29 September 1998
3. Private information
4. *Observer*, 5 July 1998
5. Ibid.
6. I believe it was his apprentice, Draper, appropriately enough, who first made this comparison
7. *Guardian*, 23 November 1998
8. Remarks at conference fringe meeting, Blackpool, 1 October 1998
9. Private interview
10. *Independent on Sunday*, 3 January 1999
11. Private interview
12. Private information
13. See Chapter 13
14. *Newsnight*, BBC2, 27 October 1998
15. Private information
16. Private information
17. Private interview, minister
18. Private information
19. Private information
20. Private information
21. Private interview
22. Private interview
23. Private information
24. Private information
25. Private information
26. Private information
27. Private interview
28. *Newsnight*, BBC2, 21 December 1998
29. *Today*, BBC Radio Four, 22 December 1998
30. Private information
31. Private information
32. In his book *Mandelson*, the thorough and fair-minded Donald Macintyre offers a comprehensive account of Mandelson's version of conversations with the Prime Minister, though Mandelson concealed from his sympathetic biographer the loan, as he also masked Blair's anger and that he was sacked
33. Private information
34. *Guardian*, 24 December 1998
35. Private information
36. *Evening Standard*, 4 January 1999
37. Macintyre, op. cit., p. 447
38. Private information
39. *Guardian*, 9 January 1999
40. Speech to AEEU conference, Jersey, 30 June 1999
41. Private information
42. Gone, but none of them for good. Mandelson returned to the Cabinet in October 1999; Robinson, unaware that Brown had asked Blair to sack

him, continued to do private work for the Chancellor; Whelan, while pursuing a successful new career as a writer and broadcaster, carried on a shadow spin operation for Brown, with the advantage that now Whelan's activities were unofficial they were deniable

43. NOP for the *Express*, 8 January 1999

### 13. New Britain

1. Private information
2. Hansard, 23 February 1999
3. *Sun*, 24 February 1999
4. Speech, Newport, 2 February 1999
5. Speech, *Time* magazine dinner, 30 November 1995
6. Fifth Report of the Committee on Standards in Public Life, 13 October 1998
7. Hansard, 18 December 1998
8. Labour: 39 per cent; SNP: 38 per cent. ICM for *The Scotsman*, 10 March 1998
9. Labour: 36 per cent; SNP: 41 per cent. System Three for *Glasgow Herald*, 6 May 1998
10. Labour: 35 per cent; SNP: 44 per cent. ICM for *The Scotsman*, 5 June 1998
11. Standing up for Scotland.

Labour: 43 per cent; SNP: 77 per cent. ICM for *The Scotsman*, 5 June 1998

12. Private information
13. Private information
14. Private information
15. Private information
16. *BBC News*, 27 October 1998
17. *Sun*, 28 October 1998
18. *Mirror*, 28 October 1998
19. Campbell lobby briefing, 28 October 1998
20. Private information
21. Paul Flynn, *Dragons Led By Poodles*, p. 80
22. Campbell Sunday lobby briefing, 30 October 1998
23. *Guardian*, 5 November 1998
24. *Newsnight*, BBC2, 29 October 1998
25. Private information
26. Private information
27. *Despatches*, Channel Four, 11 February 1999
28. Labour: 44 per cent; SNP: 32 per cent. ICM for *The Scotsman*, 4 February 1999
29. *Guardian*, 12 November 1998
30. *Financial Times*, 7 May 1999
31. Best First Minister. Dewar: 55 per cent, Salmond: 25 per cent. ICM for *The Scotsman*, 12 April 1999
32. *Daily Telegraph*, 6 May 1999
33. Remarks in Downing Street, 7 May 1999

### 14. On a Wing and a Prayer

1. Private information
2. Private information
3. Hansard, 23 March 1999
4. Ibid.
5. *Observer*, 4 April 1999
6. Private interview, Cabinet minister
7. Prime ministerial broadcast, 26 March 1999
8. Private information
9. *War In Europe*, Channel Four, 6 February 2000
10. *Guardian*, 2 April 1999
11. Kenneth Bacon, quoted in the *Observer*, 4 April 1999
12. *Sunday Telegraph*, 4 April 1999
13. *Sky News*, 3 April 1999
14. *Sunday Telegraph*, 4 April 1999
15. Private information
16. *Observer*, 18 July 1999
17. Speech, NATO headquarters, 20 April 1999
18. Hansard, 21 April 1999
19. Ibid., 20 April 1999
20. Private information
21. Private information
22. *Wall Street Journal*, 22 April 1999
23. *Los Angeles Times*, 22 April 1999
24. Speech, 'Doctrine of the International Community', Chicago, 22 April 1999
25. *Sunday Telegraph*, 25 April 1999
26. Private information
27. Private information
28. Private information
29. *The Times*, 4 May 1999
30. *Daily Mail*, 4 May 1999
31. Speech at Stankovich camp, 3 May 1999
32. Private information
33. *Observer*, 28 November 1999
34. Private interview, British officer
35. Private interview, minister
36. Hansard, 10 May 1999
37. Ibid.
38. *Sunday Telegraph*, 9 May 1999
39. Private information
40. Private information
41. *Woman's Hour*, BBC Radio Four, 20 April 1999
42. Private interview, Blair aide
43. Private information
44. Speech in Aachen, Germany, 13 May 1999
45. Speech in Sofia, Bulgaria, 17 May 1999
46. *The Times*, 19 May 1999
47. *Washington Post*, 17 May 1999
48. *Observer*, 18 July 1999
49. *Sunday Telegraph*, 16 May 1999
50. *Independent*, 22 May 1999
51. Guthrie, evidence to Defence Select Committee, 15 March 2000
52. *Observer*, 6 June 1999

53. Remarks in Downing Street, 10 June 1999
54. According to the European Investment Bank
55. Private information
56. Private interview, British officer
57. Private interview, minister

### 15. Scars on My Back

1. Private information
2. *Independent*, 25 June 1999
3. Tony Barker with Iain Byrne and A. Veall, *Ruling by Task Force*
4. *The Westminster Hour*, BBC Radio Four, 4 June 2000
5. *New York Times* magazine, 20 May 2000
6. Private interview, Blair adviser
7. Quoted by Dennis Kavanagh and Anthony Seldon, *The Powers Behind The Prime Minister*, p. 287
8. Private interview, civil servant
9. Private information
10. ITN, 29 September 1999
11. Hansard, 20 July 1998
12. Report by Select Committee on Transport, 27 July 1999
13. ICM for the *Observer*, 20 June 1999
14. Private information
15. *The Times*, 23 June 1999
16. Speech to British Venture Capitalist Association, Intercontinental Hotel, 6 July 1999
17. *New Statesman*, 7 June 1999
18. Speech to Local Government Association, 7 July 1999
19. *The Times*, 8 July 1999
20. Speech to Durham Miners' Gala, 10 July 1999
21. *Question Time*, BBC1, 8 July 1999
22. *Independent*, 30 December 1998
23. Speech, London, 19 June 1999
24. Speech, Birmingham, 22 June 1999
25. Interview with the author, *Observer*, 5 September 1999
26. Ibid.
27. *Independent*, 30 July 1999
28. *Guardian*, 5 July 1999
29. See Chapter 18
30. *Today*, BBC Radio Four, 9 July 1999
31. Remarks in Eddisbury, 19 July 1999
32. Private information
33. Private information
34. Private information
35. See Chapter 18
36. Private information
37. Private information
38. Private information

### 16. Making Enemies

1. *Daily Telegraph*, 23 July 1998
2. Speech to Congress of Socialist Parties, Malmö, 7 June 1997
3. Speech, Confederation of British Industry Annual Dinner, 27 May 1998
4. *The Third Way: New Politics for the New Century*, Fabian Pamphlet 588, September 1998
5. Ibid.
6. Ibid.
7. Speech, Downing Street garden, 30 July 1998
8. *The Third Way*, op. cit.
9. 1998 St Catherine's Lecture, Cumberland Lodge, 24 January 1998
10. David Marquand, *The Progressive Dilemma*
11. *The Third Way*, op cit.
12. 1999 Reith Lecture, quoted in the *Guardian*, 24 November 1999
13. Transcript, Democratic Leadership Council, Washington, 25 April 1999
14. Ibid.
15. *The Westminster Hour*, BBC Radio Four, 21 November 1999
16. *Daily Telegraph*, 23 July 1998

17. *The Times*, 2 September 1999
18. *Observer*, 5 September 1999
19. *Sunday Times*, 26 September 1999
20. *Sunday Telegraph*, 3 October 1999
21. Speech, Bournemouth, 28 September 1999
22. Private information
23. Speech, Bournemouth, 27 September 1999
24. Speech, Bournemouth, 28 September 1999
25. Ibid.
26. *Daily Mail*, 29 September 1999
27. Private information
28. Private information

### 17. Dome's Day

1. Newspaper Conference Annual Lunch, 23 March 1998
2. Private information
3. *Sunday Telegraph*, 2 January 2000
4. Adam Nicolson, *Regeneration*, p. 252
5. *Sunday Times*, 28 May 2000
6. *Guardian*, 5 January 2000
7. *Financial Times*, 25 February 2000
8. *The Times*, 7 February 2000
9. Nicolson, op. cit., p. 137
10. Private information

11. Private information

12. Private information

13. *New Statesman*, 14 January 2000

14. *Today*, BBC Radio Four, 14 January 2000

15. Statement to Press Association, 14 January 2000

16. *Observer*, 16 January 2000

17. Ibid.

18. Private information

19. Private interview, Cabinet minister

20. *Breakfast with Frost*, BBC1, 16 January 2000

21. Private information

22. Campbell lobby briefing, 17 January 2000

23. *Daily Telegraph*, 18 January 2000

24. Hansard, 19 January 2000

25. *Independent*, 26 September 1998

26. Blair–Schröder document, June 1999

27. Private information

28. Hansard, 21 March 2000

29. *Observer*, 26 March 2000

## 18. Control Failure

1. Private information

2. Ken Livingstone, *If Voting Changed Anything They'd Abolish It*

3. *Guardian*, 14 November 1998

4. Private information

5. Private information

6. *New Statesman*, 10 January 2000

7. See Chapter 15

8. Private information

9. See Chapter 15

10. *The Times*, 30 July 1999

11. *Daily Telegraph*, 10 July 1999

12. Private information

13. *On the Record*, BBC2, 10 October 1999

14. Private information

15. Private interview, Cabinet minister

16. Private information

17. *Guardian*, 19 January 2000

18. Ibid.

19. ICM for *Evening Standard*, 15 October 1999

20. Private information

21. Private information

22. *Newsnight*, BBC2, 18 November 1999

23. *Talk* magazine, May 2000

24. *The Times*, 23 December 1999

25. *New Statesman*, 28 January 2000

26. Remarks at Institute of Education, London, 19 January 2000

27. Private information

28. Private information

29. Private information

30. Hansard, 9 February 2000

31. ICM for *Evening Standard*, 21 February 2000

32. Speech, Old Vic, London, 27 February 2000

33. *Guardian*, 20 January 2000

34. *Any Questions*, BBC Radio Four, 28 January 2000

35. Remarks at press conference, BAFTA, London, 6 March 2000

36. *Evening Standard*, 6 March 2000

37. ICM for the *Guardian*, 7 March 2000

38. *Observer*, 12 March 2000

39. Ibid.

40. Private information

41. Private information

42. *Sunday Telegraph*, 30 April 2000

43. Speech, Scottish Parliament, Edinburgh, 9 March 2000

44. *Observer*, 9 April 2000

45. Remarks at Glaziers Hall, London Bridge, 12 April 2000

46. *Guardian*, 21 April 2000

47. Ibid., 5 April 2000

48. *New Musical Express*, 10 April 2000

49. Private information

50. *New Statesman*, 12 May 2000

51. *Independent*, 9 May 2000

52. Private information

### 19. The Only Thing That Can Defeat Us

1. Speech, Wembley Arena, 7 June 2000

2. *Sunday Times*, 11 June 2000

3. *Daily Telegraph*, 7 June 2000

4. *The World This Weekend*, BBC Radio Four, 4 June 2000

5. *The Times*, 15 June 2000

6. Private information

7. *Unlocking Democracy*, Charter 88, 20 June 2000

8. Private information

9. *Independent*, 14 April 2000

10. Peter Oborne, *Alastair Campbell*, p. 143

11. *Sun*, 1 May 2000

12. Private information

13. Private interview, Blair aide

14. Private information

15. Private interview, Cabinet minister

16. *Sunday Times*, 11 June 2000

17. *Breakfast with Frost*, BBC 1, 2 July 2000

18. *Observer*, 2 July 2000

19. Speech, Wembley Arena, 7 June 2000

20. *Guardian*, 28 June 2000

21. Private interview, Blair adviser

22. Private information

23. Eurobarometer, European Commission, April 2000

24. *Spectator*, 24 June 2000
25. Speech, Belfast, 16 May 2000
26. Hansard, 16 May 2000
27. Private information
28. Speech, Blackpool, 4 October 1994
29. Evidence to Foreign Affairs Committee, 7 June 2000
30. *Mirror*, 8 June 2000
31. Speech, Mansion House, 15 June 2000
32. Private interview, civil servant
33. MORI for *Mail on Sunday*, 12 June 2000
34. Gallup for *Daily Telegraph*, 9 June 2000
35. Historic figures from Gallup; prepared by David Cowling
36. *Vanity Fair*, July 2000
37. Private interview, Cabinet minister
38. Private interview, Blair adviser
39. Private information

## 20. Twenty-four Hours from Meltdown

1. Private information
2. Speech to Millennium Summit, New York, 6 September 2000
3. *Guardian*, 16 September 2000
4. *Mail on Sunday*, 17 September 2000
5. *Independent*, 11 September 2000
6. *Daily Express*, 9 September 2000
7. *Sunday*, GMTV, 10 September 2000
8. Private interview, Home Office minister
9. Private interview, Cabinet minister
10. Remarks at community computer centre, Loughborough, 11 September 2000
11. *Mail on Sunday*, 17 September 2000
12. *Sunday Telegraph*, 17 September 2000
13. Speech to TUC, Glasgow, 13 September 2000
14. *Guardian*, 14 September 2000
15. Private interview, Cabinet minister
16. *Sun, Mail, Express, Independent*, 12 September 2000
17. *Mirror*, 12 September 2000
18. News conference at Number 10, 12 September 2000
19. *Guardian*, 16 September 2000
20. *Daily Telegraph*, 14 September 2000
21. Private information
22. Private information
23. *Guardian*, 13 September 2000
24. *Mirror*, 13 September 2000

25. Seventy-seven per cent did not believe Blair's argument that cutting petrol taxes would take money away from schools and hospitals; 78 per cent said they supported the protesters. NOP for *Sunday Times*, 17 September 2000

26. This threat was never made real

27. *Mail on Sunday*, 17 September 2000

28. Private information

29. Private information

30. Private interview, Cabinet minister

31. News conference at Number 10, 13 September 2000

32. Private information

33. Private information

34. Private information

35. Private information

36. *Mirror*, 14 September 2000

37. *Daily Mail*, 14 September 2000

38. News conference at Number 10, 14 September 2000

39. *Today*, BBC Radio Four, 16 September 2000

40. *Sunday*, GMTV, 17 September 2000

41. *Sky News*, 17 September 2000

42. Private interview, Cabinet minister

43. Private information

44. *Channel 4 News*, 21 September 2000

45. *Independent on Sunday*, 24 September 2000

46. Private information

47. Conference speech, Brighton, 26 September 2000

## 21. Sweating It Out

1. As reported by Donald Macintyre, *Independent*, 23 September 2000

2. *Sunday Telegraph*, 24 September 2000

3. Extracts from the first edition of *Servants of the People* were serialised in the *Observer* on 10 and 17 September, and *Daily Mail* on 19–21 September 2000

4. Rachel Sylvester, *Daily Telegraph*, 30 September 2000

5. See Chapter 6

6. *Sun*, 20 September 2000

7. *Independent*, 20 September 2000

8. *Breakfast with Frost*, BBC 1, 24 September 2000

9. *The Times*, 25 September 2000

10. *Sunday Telegraph*, 24 September 2000

11. Patrick Wintour, *Guardian*, 20 September 2000

12. Joe Murphy, *Sunday Telegraph*, 24 September 2000

13. *Daily Telegraph* and *Guardian*, 20 September 2000

14. *Channel 4 News*, 21 September 2000

15. *Sun*, 22 September 2000

16. *Guardian*, 21 September 2000

17. *Channel 4 News*, 21 September 2000

18. *Sunday Telegraph*, 24 September 2000

19. 'Brown's worst week', Kevin Maguire, *Guardian*, 23 September 2000. See also 'Blairites stitched up Brown over £1 million donation, claim Chancellor's allies', *Daily Express*, 21 September 2000

20. For instance: 'Blair allies accuse Brown of shifting blame for F1 row', *Independent*, 23 September 2000

21. A 15 per cent lead for Labour in August became a 2 per cent advantage for the Conservatives, according to Mori, *News of the World*, 17 September. A 10 per cent lead for Labour in August turned into a 4 per cent lead for the Conservatives, according to ICM for the *Guardian*, 18 September. It was worse by the conference. Labour fell to 35 per cent, five points behind the Conservatives, according to Gallup for the *Daily Telegraph*, 21 September. Labour collapsed to 32 per cent, eight points behind the Conservatives on 40 per cent, with the Liberal Democrats on 22 per cent, according to NOP for Channel Four, 23 September 2000

22. Interview with the author and Kamal Ahmed, *Observer*, 13 May 2001

23. *The Times*, 27 September 2000

24. *On the Record*, BBC 1, 24 September 2000

25. *Jonathan Dimbleby*, ITV, 24 September 2000

26. Private information

27. Conference speech, Brighton, 25 September 2000

28. *Independent on Sunday*, 24 September 2000

29. Conference speech, Brighton, 26 September 2000

30. *Daily Telegraph*, 27 September 2000

31. Ann McElvoy, *Independent*, 28 September 2000

32. Conference speech, Brighton, 26 September 2000

33. *Daily Mail*, 26 September 2000

34. *Independent*, 26 September 2000
35. Private information
36. *The Times*, 28 September 2000
37. Private information
38. *Daily Telegraph*, 28 September 2000
39. Private information
40. Conference speech, Brighton, 27 September 2000
41. *The World Tonight*, BBC Radio Four, 27 September 2000
42. I have borrowed the description from Sir Alastair Morton, the head of the Strategic Rail Authority
43. Private information
44. Private interview, Cabinet minister
45. *Mirror*, 2 November 2000
46. News conference, Downing Street, 22 November 2000
47. *Breakfast with Frost*, BBC 1, 7 January 2001
48. *Ask The Prime Minister*, ITV, 12 December 2000
49. I am grateful to Michael Cockerell for this revealing story

## 22. Peter's Friends

1. *Sunday Times*, 21 January 2001
2. *Observer*, 21 January 2001
3. The three men were the Science Minister David Sainsbury; the publisher Paul Hamlyn; and the financier Christopher Ondaatje.
4. *Sunday Telegraph* and *Sunday Times*, 28 January 2001
5. Ibid.
6. Review of the Circumstances Surrounding an Application for Naturalisation by Mr SP Hinduja, Sir Anthony Hammond, KCB, QC, The Stationery Office, March 2001, Annex F, p. 89
7. Chris Blackhurst, *Independent*, 2 March 2001
8. Hammond, p. 67
9. *Independent*, 2 March 2001
10. Ibid., 7 May 2001
11. Private interviews
12. Hammond, Annex F, p. 90
13. *Breakfast with Frost*, BBC 1, 28 January 2001
14. Hammond, Annex H, p. 96
15. Ibid., p. 12
16. *Daily Mail*, 10 May 2001
17. Hammond, Annex I, p. 97
18. Ibid., Annex Q, pp. 108–9
19. Ibid., Annex R, p. 110
20. Ibid., p. 53
21. *Guardian*, 11 May 2001
22. Hammond, p. 70
23. *The Times*, 9 March 2001
24. Hammond, Annex T, p. 113
25. Ibid., pp. 60–61

26. Ibid., p. 62
27. Andrew Grice, *Independent*, 18 October 2000
28. Private interview
29. *The Times*, 4 January 2001
30. Private information
31. *Observer*, 21 January 2001
32. Lobby briefing, 22 January 2001, quoted by Hammond, p. 33
33. Hansard, 22 January 2001
34. About this, as with so many other crucial aspects of the affair, Hammond failed or declined to come to a conclusion about who was telling the truth
35. Hammond, pp. 21–2
36. *Sunday Times*, 28 January 2001
37. *The News From Number 10*, BBC 2, 15 July 2000
38. Private information
39. Lobby briefing, 23 January 2001, quoted by Hammond, p. 36
40. *Channel 4 News*, 23 January 2001
41. Private interview
42. Hammond, Annex P, p. 105
43. *Independent*, 20 March 2001
44. *World Tonight*, BBC Radio Four, 24 January 2001
45. *Guardian*, 25 January 2001
46. *Sunday Times*, 28 January 2001

47. Private information
48. *Sunday Times*, 28 January 2001
49. Statement in Downing Street, 24 January 2001
50. Hansard, 24 January 2001
51. *Guardian*, 25 January 2001
52. Shipman was a serial killer GP who murdered hundreds of elderly women
53. *Independent*, 30 January 2001
54. *Sunday Times*, 28 January 2001
55. Peter Oborne, *Alastair Campbell*, p. 173
56. *Jonathan Dimbleby*, 28 January 2001
57. *The World This Weekend*, 28 January 2001
58. *Independent*, 30 January 2001
59. *Sunday Times*, 4 February 2001
60. *Independent*, 31 January 2001
61. *Guardian*, 31 January 2001
62. *Sunday Times*, 11 February 2001
63. *Independent*, 10 March 2001
64. Labour Manifesto, 1997
65. ICM for State of the Nation poll, Joseph Rowntree Trust, October 2000
66. NOP for *Powerhouse*, Channel 4, 30 January 2001
67. Speech, Labour spring conference, Glasgow, 18 February 2001

### 23. Culling Fields

1. 'The Government's Agenda For The Future', speech at Highlands School, Enfield, London, 8 February 2001
2. Private information
3. *Independent*, 30 April 2001
4. Gallup for *Daily Telegraph*, 10 March 2001
5. *Sun*, 8 March 2001
6. *Evening Standard*, 21 March 2001
7. Private information
8. *Financial Times*, 5 May 2001
9. *Daily Telegraph*, 28 April 2001
10. Private information
11. *The Westminster Hour*, BBC Radio Four, 18 March 2001
12. *Daily Telegraph*, 6 April 2001
13. *Independent*, 13 March 2001
14. *Observer*, 25 March 2001
15. Hansard, 21 March 2001
16. *Guardian*, 23 March 2001
17. *Independent*, 23 March 2001
18. ITN, 23 March 2001
19. Private interviews, Blair aides
20. Hansard, 28 March 2001
21. *Sunday Telegraph*, 1 April 2001
22. *Financial Times*, 30 March 2001
23. *Spectator*, 29 March 2001
24. The Labour lead over the Conservatives was 19 per cent according to Mori for *The Times*, 29 March 2001
25. *Observer*, 1 April 2001
26. Private information
27. Speech to rally at the Institute of Education, London, 29 March 2001, reported by the *Independent*, 31 March 2001
28. Private interview, Brown ally
29. Private interview, Cabinet minister
30. *Sun*, 20 March 2001
31. Ibid., 28 March 2001
32. Ibid., 31 March 2001
33. *Guardian*, 3 April 2001
34. *Independent*, 3 April 2001
35. Remarks in Downing Street, 2 April 2001
36. *Daily Telegraph*, 25 April 2001
37. *Observer*, 29 April 2001
38. Press Association, 25 April 2001
39. News conference at Number 10, 3 May 2001

### 24. Masters of the People?

1. Speech at St Saviour's and St Olave's School, Southwark, London, 8 May 2001
2. Simon Hoggart, *Guardian*; Frank Johnson, *Daily Telegraph*; Matthew Parris, *The Times*, 9 May 2001
3. *Any Questions*, BBC Radio Four, 11 May 2001
4. *Daily Telegraph*, 10 May 2001

5. *Guardian*, 11 May 2001
6. Private interviews
7. *Sunday Telegraph*, 11 May 2001
8. *Evening Standard*, 9 May 2001
9. *Independent on Sunday*, 13 May 2001
10. Speech at the International Convention Centre, Birmingham, 16 May 2001
11. *Ask The Leader*, ITV, 16 May 2001
12. News conference, Millbank, London, 17 May 2001
13. Sixty per cent of 17,000 respondents thought Prescott did 'the right thing', according to a poll for *Sky News Active*. Two thirds believed he was right to 'hit back', according to poll of 6,850 viewers of *The Wright Stuff*, Channel 5.
14. *Sun*, *Mirror*, 18 May 2001
15. Private interview
16. *Independent*, 24 May 2001
17. *BBC News*, 22 May 2001
18. *Financial Times*, 14 May 2001
19. Speech to the GMB conference, Brighton, 3 June 2001
20. Gallup for *Daily Telegraph*, 24 May 2001
21. *Independent*, 14 May 2001
22. Private interview
23. Speech at Woodville Halls, Gravesend, 21 May 2001
24. Speech at the International Convention Centre, Birmingham, 16 May 2001
25. Ibid.
26. *Jimmy Young Programme*, BBC Radio Two, 23 May 2001
27. *Daily Telegraph*, 9 May 2001
28. Interview with the author and Kamal Ahmed, *Observer*, 13 May 2001
29. *Financial Times*, 25 May 2001
30. *Guardian*, 29 May 2001
31. Speech at St Bride's Centre, Edinburgh, 25 May 2001
32. *Question Time Special*, BBC 1, 30 May 2001
33. 'Moving Beyond Thatcherism', speech in Birmingham, 5 June 2001
34. Speech to Sedgefield adoption meeting, Sedgefield, 13 May 2001
35. News conference, Millbank, London, 31 May 2001
36. BBC Radio 5, 21 May 2001
37. Reuters Poll Trend (a moving average of Gallup, ICM and Mori), 7 June 2001
38. *Guardian*, 7 June 2001
39. Acceptance speech at Newton Aycliffe Leisure Centre, Sedgefield, 8 June 2001
40. *Sunday Times*, 10 June 2001
41. Conservatives: 33 per cent;

Liberal Democrats: 19 per cent; other parties: 6 per cent. Turn-out was 59 per cent, the lowest since 1918

42. Private information
43. Speech in Downing Street, 8 June 2001
44. Private information

# Select Bibliography

Barker, Tony with Iain Byrne and A. Veall, *Ruling by Task Force* (Politico's, 1999)

Brown, Colin, *Fighting Talk: The Biography of John Prescott* (Simon & Schuster, 1997)

Butler, David, and Kavanagh, Dennis, *The British General Election of 1997* (Macmillan, 1997)

Cook, Margaret, *A Slight and Delicate Creature* (Weidenfeld & Nicolson, 1999)

Crewe, Ivor, Gosschalk, Brian, and Bartle, John, *Why Labour Won The General Election of 1997* (Frank Cass, 1998)

D'Arcy, Mark, and MacLean, Rory, *Nightmare* (Politico's, 2000)

Draper, Derek, *Blair's 100 Days* (Faber and Faber, 1997)

Fairclough, Norman, *New Labour, New Language?* (Routledge, 2000)

Flynn, Paul, *Dragons Led By Poodles* (Politico's, 1999)

Gould, Philip, *The Unfinished Revolution* (Abacus, 1999)

Hattersley, Roy, *Fifty Years On* (Little, Brown, 1997)

Hughes, Colin, and Wintour, Patrick, *Labour Rebuilt* (Fourth Estate, 1990)

Jones, Janet, *Labour of Love* (Politico's, 1999)

Jones, Nicholas, *Sultans of Spin* (Victor Gollancz, 1999)

Kampfner, John, *Robin Cook* (Phoenix, 1999)

Kavanagh, Dennis, and Seldon, Anthony, *The Powers Behind the Prime Minister* (HarperCollins, 1999)

Livingstone, Ken, *If Voting Changed Anything, They'd Abolish It* (HarperCollins, 1987)

Macintyre, Donald, *Mandelson* (HarperCollins, 1999)

Mandelson, Peter, and Liddle, Roger, *The Blair Revolution* (Faber and Faber, 1996)

Marquand, David, *The Progressive Dilemma* (Phoenix, 1999)

McDonald, Henry, *Trimble* (Bloomsbury, 2000)

Mitchell, Senator George, *Making Peace* (William Heinemann, 1999)

Nicolson, Adam, *Regeneration* (HarperCollins, 1999)

Oborne, Peter, *Alastair Campbell* (Aurum Press, 1999)

Pym, Hugh, and Kochan, Nick, *Gordon Brown: The First Year In Power* (Bloomsbury, 1998)

Rentoul, John, *Tony Blair* (Little, Brown, 1997)

Routledge, Paul, *Gordon Brown* (Simon & Schuster, 1998)

Sopel, Jon, *Tony Blair* (Michael Joseph, 1995)

Stephanopoulos, George, *All Too Human* (Little, Brown, 1999)

Young, Hugo, *This Blessed Plot* (Macmillan, 1998)

# Index

# refresh yourself at penguin.co.uk

Visit penguin.co.uk for exclusive information and interviews with
bestselling authors, fantastic give-aways and the
inside track on all our books, from the Penguin Classics
to the latest bestsellers.

**BE FIRST** ▼

first chapters, first editions, first novels

**EXCLUSIVES** ▼

author chats, video interviews, biographies, special
features

**EVERYONE'S A WINNER** ▼

give-aways, competitions, quizzes, ecards

**READERS GROUPS** ▼

exciting features to support existing groups and
create new ones

**NEWS** ▼

author events, bestsellers, awards, what's new

**EBOOKS** ▼

books that click – download an ePenguin today

**BROWSE AND BUY** ▼

thousands of books to investigate – search, try
and buy the perfect gift online – or treat yourself!

**ABOUT US** ▼

job vacancies, advice for writers and company
history

Get Closer To Penguin ... www.penguin.co.uk